FRED KARNO

Dedication

With love to Deb, Amelia and Charlie
– the three greatest laughter-makers I know.

FRED KARNO

The Legend Behind the Laughter

DAVID B. CRUMP

BREWIN BOOKS

BREWIN BOOKS
19 Enfield Ind. Estate,
Redditch,
Worcestershire,
B97 6BY
www.brewinbooks.com

Published by Brewin Books 2021

Reprinted January 2022

© David B. Crump 2021

The author has asserted his rights in accordance with the Copyright, Designs and Patents Act 1988 to be identified as the author of this work.

All rights reserved. No part of this publication may be reproduced, stored in a retrieval system, or transmitted in any form or by any means, electronic, mechanical, photocopying, recording or otherwise, without the prior permission in writing of the publisher and the copyright owners, or as expressly permitted by law, or under terms agreed with the appropriate reprographics rights organization. Enquiries concerning reproduction outside the terms stated here should be sent to the publishers at the UK address printed on this page.

The author is grateful to all contributors who provided photographs and has endeavoured to credit them accordingly. It has not always been possible to trace copyright. The author and publishers apologise for any inadvertent infringement.

Quotations from other sources are referenced, and are included to elaborate and expand on the material in relation to Karno and his story. This is intended as 'fair use' of such quotations and references, but the publishers apologise should any such use be deemed an infringement of copyright.

All images from Chaplin films made from 1918 onwards, Copyright © Roy Export S.A.S. All rights reserved. Photographs from the Chaplin Archives: Copyright © and/or Property of Roy Export Company Limited. All Rights Reserved. Digitisation of the Chaplin Archives by Cineteca di Bologna. Charlie Chaplin and the Little Tramp are trademarks and/or service marks of Bubbles Inc. S.A., used with permission.

Cover photo of Charles Chaplin from The Kid Copyright © Roy Export S.A.S. Cover photo of Fred Karno courtesy Heritage Collection, Bournemouth Library.

A CIP catalogue record for this book is available from the British Library.

ISBN: 978-1-85858-508-6

Printed and bound in Great Britain
by Dig Print.

Contents

Foreword vii
Introduction and Acknowledgements ix
1. Preface: The Most Famous Man You've Never Heard Of 1
2. Running Away with the Circus 7
3. The Long Road to London 17
4. The Three Karnos. 30
5. How About a Sketch? 43
6. The Show Must Go On 55
7. The Showman. 70
8. Slumming It. 83
9. Saturday to Monday. 96
10. From Here to Paternity 111
11. Princes and Principals 126
12. Thieves and Tricksters 138
13. I Want to be in America 151
14. Stabbed in the Back 165
15. Strikers 182
16. Bodies and Bailiffs 198
17. The Little Fellow 214
18. Postmen, Pugilists, Politicians and Pratfalls 229
19. All at Sea 245
20. Mr Fearless 261
21. Astoria. 276
22. Karsino's Curse 294
23. Cheerio Charlie! 310

24. Fred Karno's Army 326

25. The Millionaire Tramp .344

26. All Women 360

27. Making Hay. 375

28. Money to Burn 389

29. Prodigal Sons 402

30. Stormy Weather 417

31. Riches to Rags. 431

32. Hooray for Hollywood 444

33. Crashing Out 458

34. We're All Crazy Now .475

35. Reel to Real 492

36. Finale 506

37. Encore. 522

Endnotes 534

Karnography 564

Bibliography 573

Index 576

Foreword

IN 1983 I had embarked on a formidable task: to explore the Chaplin archives for the purposes of an authoritative and documented biography of the greatest comic actor. But "archives" was a grave misnomer for this cellar stacked with a hundred or so large removal boxes of unsorted documents, scattered pages of scripts, correspondence, manuscript scribbles, photographs, newspaper cuttings, and any old bits and pieces – probably just as they were hurled into boxes when Chaplin's Hollywood studio was hastily stripped after he was exiled from the United States in 1952. The work was further obstructed by a massive ancient red cabin trunk which stood immoveable in the middle of the floor. Oona Chaplin came down one day and said, "This was brother Sydney's – his widow Gypsy gave it to us. Maybe we should take a look."

It was entirely filled with papers: documents, posters, photographs – every kind of document which Sydney had secreted, knowing that Charlie would have cheerfully junked it all. A great deal of it was from Sydney's years with Fred Karno, and the very first things we found were all the brothers' successive contracts with Karno and with Mack Sennett's Keystone Studio. If we had not known before, it was clear how great an influence Karno's genius for comedy had upon the Chaplins – as on so many others. I had to know more…

Chance played a big role in the 'Quest for Karno'. I haunted ephemera fairs in search of evidence. One regular stall-holder stood out. I never knew his name, but he was a familiar figure as an extra in television crime series, reliably type-cast as a very nasty-looking low-life gangster. But with ephemera he knew his stuff, and one day proudly told me about a great new haul. By astonishing chance, his East End house was next door to the widow of someone connected to Karno or one of his heirs. She died, and the house-clearance people lit a big bonfire in the garden. The gangster-look-alike hopped over the fence and found a stack of files and boxes which seemed to be Fred Karno's business papers and accounts. "They go back to the beginning: there are even the shipping bookings when the companies were sent to the United States, Chaplin among them." My excitement was short-lived: "I'm not letting you or anyone else see them. I'll be the one to publish them…"

I felt that when the first excitement wore off, he might be more forthcoming, maybe for a price. So a month or two later I went back, and again and again – but he was never there. Finally I asked the fair organizer: "Didn't you know? He had a heart attack and dropped down dead. And he wasn't all that old…"

I guess there was another garden fire in that same back street.

It sounds like a very tall story, but this is exactly as it was. And ever since I have suffered from the memory of all that history that went up, presumably, in smoke. Karno in his prime was so active and so famous, yet so little has been known about him except hundreds of show titles and theatre programmes. Karno has been the victim of two earlier biographies, in 1931 and 1979, whose particular biases and omissions are explained in the present book.

Because now, four decades after that disaster, comes Dave Crump, obsessively determined to put things right. More than a decade ago he embarked on his relentless search for every fragment of evidence of Karno: every press mention, every traceable document, every person, dead or alive, with any memory or evidence. Even more astounding is his search and rediscovery of the humble places of Karno's birth, childhood, and first steps as a plumber's apprentice and then trainee acrobat, in the poor streets and shabby show-places of 19th century Nottingham.

The research and retelling makes for an unsparingly detailed narrative, but it is never arduous reading. Dave Crump has an easy, familiar, literate and often cheerfully jokey way of writing. It is a lesson that scholarship has no need to be forbidding and exclusive. Karno is a singular story of rags to riches and back again. He enriched the world with comedy, enjoyed enormous success and riches, but died in poverty. This amazing book makes him some posthumous amends.

David Robinson
Film Critic and
Chaplin Biographer

Introduction and Acknowledgements

ONCE UPON a time somewhere in Lichfield, my secretary, Sandra Goldsmith, tripped over a discarded box of files and cursed the disorganised mess of a room she had to work in: "It's like Fred Karno's Army in here," she grumbled. "What does that mean?" I said, helping her to clear a pathway through mountains of office debris. She shrugged: "It's just something you say – you know, it means everything's chaotic."

I didn't know – but I was intrigued. It turned out that Karno was a real person; a colourful music hall impresario, whose life-story was the kind of 'rags to riches' epic that every storyteller dreams about. He also happened to be a long-forgotten comedy genius who had discovered Charlie Chaplin and Stan Laurel.

I managed to find a dog-eared biography of Karno, published half a century ago, and although it painted a dark picture of a deeply flawed character, I was soon fascinated by this extraordinary man's life. My first Karno project was based on that book, a stage musical entitled *Khaotic!* – it turned out to be just the beginning.

In the process of that project I unearthed a mountain of new information which cast doubt on much of the previous biography. So I set out to tell the true story of Fred Karno and, now it is complete, I hope it will put him back where he belongs – amongst the world's greatest comics.

This book would not have been possible without the many people who have given me help, guidance, encouragement, and support. Biographers, archivists, researchers and enthusiasts in their own fields: Kate Guyonvarch, David Robinson, Tony Staveacre, Frank Scheide, Richard Bann, the late Chuck McCann, Ian Smith, Ralph Nicholson, the late Roy Hudd, Tess Nowell, Barry Anthony, Bryan Clough, Andy Nicholson, John Ullah, Tony Barker and Graham

Rinaldi. Particular thanks to A.J. Marriot for being a fount of all knowledge, a mentor and friend throughout the whole process, and to the peerless David Robinson for writing a wonderful foreword – both have also been extraordinarily generous in providing images. Relatives of Karno comics: the late Lois Laurel, Louisa Sewell, Debbie Pillai, June Russell, Norman Bush, Jeremy Hoare, Joanne Golding, Vivienne Drewitt, Keith Ripley, Bill Asher, Heather Walker, Neil Wholey, Donna Tobitt, Marianne Morgan, and Frederick Simon Kitchen-Dunn. A cast of thousands has also helped along the way: Peter Smith, the man who put music to my words and helped me bring Stiffy the Goalkeeper, Sergeant Lightning and all the other Karno characters to life; Jodie Cockeram and the late Steve Birch for help with research; Langley Iddins and David Gilmore for access to the Astoria; Noel Perkins and Conor Masterson for access to the Fun Factory; Roger Robinson and Carole Mulroney for information on Edith Karno's life in Southend on Sea; Ned Comstock and Sandra Garcia-Myers of the Cinematic Arts Library and Archives at the University of Southern California; Patricia Moloney of Richmond and Wandsworth local studies team; Adrian Barry of the Music Hall Guild of America and Great Britain; Adam Borzone, David Reed, and Brian O'Gorman of the British Music Hall Society; Peter Hinton of the Royal Variety Charity; 'From The Top Theatre Company' for their support of the project from the outset; staff of the British Library; the Sons of the Desert; Matthew Lloyd for his extraordinary website www.arthurlloyd.co.uk; Lucinda Gosling of the Mary Evans Picture Library; Ken Joy of the Grand Order of Water Rats; Nick Whitehouse, Peter Glanville, Graham Robinson, Melanie Carr, Rowan Gibbs, Trevor Buckingham, Roy Kneath, James Walker, Victor Wellan, Phil Rowbotham, June Fisher, David Tomlinson, and Philip Heath.

Thanks also to Alan and Alistair Brewin and the team at Brewin Books for their support and patience! I owe a significant debt to the extraordinary online British Newspaper Archive (BNA) which has been the backbone of my research. Arnold Lazano of the Chaplin archive, Eddie Bundy of the BNA and Lucinda Gosling of the Mary Evans Picture Library were all incredibly helpful in sourcing photographs, and I'm grateful to the many individuals and organisations who have provided additional images.

Most of all I would like to thank the Karno family, especially Louise Karno Murchison (Leslie Karno's granddaughter) and Jo Sexton (Fred Karno Junior's stepdaughter) – without them this book would not exist. I was fortunate to meet Karno's grandsons, now sadly no longer with us, Kenneth and Fred Westcott, both then living in California, and also great-nephew Warren Karno Atkins in New Zealand. They all shared with me their memories and a huge family archive of documents, letters, scripts, photographs, and legal papers which have fully revealed Karno's story for the first time.

It is certain that I've missed some people or organisations from this very long list so, suffice to say, I owe you all a debt and thank you for your contribution to what I hope is the definitive biography of Karno.

Final thanks go to my family for their support: my parents Bob and Sue; my brother Vincent for editing, advice, and guidance; my children Amelia and Charlie who have grown up in a house full of Karnoesque chaos; and most of all my wife Debbie without whom none of this would have been possible.

It is ten years since Sandra tripped over that box and started a glorious obsession that has taken me half-way around the world and introduced me to some wonderful friends. I wish I could thank her personally. She would have loved this book.

David B Crump
Lichfield, England, 2021
www.fredkarno.com

Fred Karno – the most famous man you've never heard of (courtesy Louise Murchison).

1.
Preface: The Most Famous Man You've Never Heard Of

It's a wise joke that knows its own father.
(The Merry Book of the Moore & Burgess Minstrels, 1898)

Fred Karno didn't teach Charlie and me all we know about comedy … he just taught us most of it. If I had to pick an adjective to fit Karno, it would be supple. That's what Karno was mentally and physically, even when he was an old man. He was flexible in just about everything, and above all he taught us to be supple … he taught us to be precise. Out of all that endless rehearsal and performance came Charlie, the most supple and precise comedian of our time.[1]

SO WROTE Stan Laurel, who, like Charlie Chaplin, was a graduate of the 'Fun Factory'; a nursery of nonsense where Fred Karno trained generations of performers whose stock-in-trade was visual comedy. His influence on the greatest comics of the twentieth century should have secured his place in history, yet he is at best misunderstood or worse, forgotten.

'It's like Fred Karno's Army' (or 'Fred Karno's Circus'), a once common simile for any chaotic situation, now endures mostly as a favourite of political speechwriters. Future Prime Minister Theresa May, in a debate about rail services in 2002, said: 'And so the entertainment continues – as Fred Karno's army parade one by one this afternoon.'[2] Lord Kingsland in 2005 noted: 'There is no more damaging emotion for the electorate to experience about the Government than that of ridicule. Their conduct seemed to be orchestrated by a choreographer employed by the legendary Fred Karno.'[3]

Fred Karno did not have an army (he didn't even serve in the military) and although he began his career in the circus, he never had one to call his own. He was a mere music hall acrobat who became the undisputed king of slapstick comedy. His anarchic, physical shows made him famous around the world, but the empire he painstakingly built came crashing down and his pivotal role in the history of comedy is now a mere footnote on the careers of others.

During a working life that spanned from the age of Jack the Ripper to the Second World War, he pushed the boundaries of comedy, helped establish copyright law and broke down barriers between 'legitimate' theatre and music hall. A small man with a big personality, he was described by Charlie Chaplin as 'a thick-set, bronzed little man, with keen sparkling eyes that were always appraising.'[4] The self-appointed king of the Thames Riviera, he had a personal life every bit as colourful as his professional one. Always looking for new worlds to conquer, this insatiably ambitious Napoleon of the music hall left a trail of devastation behind him and a family wrecked on the rocks of hubris. He was reportedly mean yet generous; shy yet flamboyant; ruthless yet benevolent; charismatic yet vicious. In private he was rough, with few social graces, but amongst high society he could be charming – the life and soul of the party. He took pride in his ability to mix with anyone, saying 'I'm at home with dukes and dustmen,' but had few real friends amongst either. Karno was full of contradictions, as Laurel's biographer John McCabe put it: 'a jovial Jekyll and Hyde.'

There have been two previous biographies of Karno: J.P. Gallagher's *Fred Karno – Master of Mirth and Tears* (1971) and Edwin Adeler and Con West's *Remember Fred Karno? – The Life of a Great Showman* (1939). Historian Andrew Horrall described the latter as 'illiterate Fred Karno's autobiography';[5] and he isn't the only one to have suggested Karno was illiterate. He was no such thing; the family archive is full of his letters and notes. Horrall was right to suggest that the book was Karno's own account though; Adeler and West described it as his memoirs (and I shall do the same).

Con West was a writer who worked extensively with Karno in later life, whereas Adeler was a veteran performer and impresario (best known for his numerous seaside Pierrot troupes)[6] who had known Karno since the early days. Adeler, the original driving force behind the biography, commenced writing in

1. THE MOST FAMOUS MAN YOU'VE NEVER HEARD OF

1931; Karno invited West to edit the draft manuscript three years later. They agreed to split the profits equally but after West rewrote much of the text, Karno suggested an alternative arrangement: 'Perhaps I could arrange with Adeler to offer him a few quid for his bit, and then you and I go fifty-fifty.'[7]

West was a man of firmer principles and honoured the arrangement (perhaps because he had once been a performer in Adeler's troupe himself). They recounted an illustrious career but said nothing about Karno's personal life. It was thirty years before tabloid journalist Joe Gallagher revisited the story. *Master of Mirth and Tears* remains the last word on Karno (until now) and is a key source for every subsequent biography of Chaplin and Laurel, despite being largely fiction. It is a dramatised account, full of colourful scenes Gallagher admits to imagining, which amounts to a comprehensive character assassination. It begins with a graphic account of alleged domestic violence towards Edith, Karno's first wife, and goes downhill from there. This negative portrayal may have come about because the author relied heavily on the testimony of Edith's friends. A few years into their marriage Karno ran off with a chorus girl, abandoning Edith with a young family – she never got over it. She lived a lonely life, sustained by alcohol, before dying at fifty-six – it seems those closest to her exacted a posthumous revenge.

So, let's consider the reliability of those friends. Marguerite (Madge) Proctor was Edith's closest companion; they lived together for the final eleven years of Edith's life. Madge was twenty-three years Edith's junior and just a child when Edith and Karno separated. They met ten years later, so Madge had no first-hand knowledge of the man or the events leading up to the separation. Novelist and actress Naomi Jacob, Gallagher's other major source, was a famously eccentric raconteur, who never let the facts get in the way of a bawdy anecdote – the more salacious the better. Her biographer Paul Bailey notes that Jacob's many volumes of autobiography are notoriously inaccurate, contradictory and vague on anything resembling a date or a fact.[8] Jacob befriended Edith at the end of her marriage to Karno, when she was no doubt at her lowest ebb, and I think we can safely take Jacob's stories with a large pinch of salt. Gallagher wrote: 'Miss Jacob wrote thousands of words from her own recollections of Edith Karno, including her famous interview with Fred.'[9] Jacob was a prolific writer; her dozen or so volumes of autobiography go into infinite detail about her everyday life, but I have yet to come across these 'thousands of words' or any interview with Karno. What I have found is brief and included in this book.

Gallagher made only one connection to the Karno family in the course of his research – Olive Karno, the second wife of Karno's late son Fred Jr. Olive and Fred Jr. met in 1948 and he died in 1961 (before Gallagher began his biography).

Olive never met Karno (who died in 1941) and only met his other son Leslie twice, so her material was at best third-hand. It is easy to imagine how stories of Karno's colourful life might have been exaggerated in the telling by born entertainer Fred Jr. In the preface to his book Gallagher says: 'I have taken a limited degree of freedom to present probable conversations, but the great majority of these were remembered by the various people I have mentioned, and especially by Fred Karno Junior, who, shortly before his death, made very full notes and vividly recorded many of the scenes reported here.'[10] Thanks to Olive's daughter, Jo, I have Fred Jr.'s notes: they amount to seven and a half sheets of paper and do not include Gallagher's stories of Karno's darker side, or family troubles.

Gallagher also quoted Stan Laurel and Christopher Clayton Hutton as his most important sources, both of whom only knew Karno professionally and years after he split with Edith – it seems unlikely that the lurid personal stories came from them. Hutton initially worked with Gallagher on the book, writing to *The Stage* in 1962: '[Karno] was a friend of mine for many years and I was the only one to make any of his famous sketches into films … Mrs Olive Karno has entrusted me with writing a life of this remarkable man – whose life … was a huge comedy in itself.'[11] Hutton's involvement ceased soon afterward. Perhaps as a friend (and fan) of Karno, he did not want to be associated with the lurid stories Gallagher majored on.

Gallagher's last major contributor was burlesque dancer Phyllis Dixey, who appears to have been the most unreliable of all – as we shall see. Remarkably Gallagher made an initial contact with Karno's youngest son Leslie, but never followed this up with further correspondence or an interview; nor did he contact Karno's grandsons Kenneth and Fred. I know they could have provided him with a wealth of information because they did so for me: Kenneth and Fred in person (I met them both in 2010, aged 89 and 91 respectively), and Leslie via his extensive archive and the stories he passed on to his granddaughter Louise. Prior to publication Leslie was sent a draft copy of Gallagher's book by the publishers, who asked him to confirm a handful of points – he refused and, in response, expressed dismay at Gallagher's account:

1. THE MOST FAMOUS MAN YOU'VE NEVER HEARD OF

> It would be a relatively simple matter to comply with your request but to do so would imply my approval of the remainder of the book ... there are so many inaccuracies throughout ... that ... to attempt to correct this, would almost mean re-writing whole sections of the book. Much of this need not have happened had the author followed up his intention to discuss this with me ... Most of the information I fear, is gathered from people who never even met him ... I would like to also point out that Mrs Olive Karno ... did not meet my brother until a number of years after my father's death ... she knows nothing of the family at all and most certainly should not be looked upon as a source of information in this respect.[12]

No reply appears to have been received. Leslie literally wept when the book was published and did his utmost to have it withdrawn. Newspaper reviews included one in *The People*, which ran the headline: 'Fred Karno's Circus Included Sex Gymnastics!' Quite where that came from is unclear since the book provides no information on Karno's sex life other than to suggest that it was 'perverted' – what that means we are left to guess. If further evidence were needed that Gallagher was more interested in a salacious story than finding the truth, he wrote an article for the pornographic magazine *Mayfair*, which ran under the title 'Fun-Sex and Ruin.'[13] Despite the headline, the article didn't detail any sexual antics at all.

Gallagher may have lacked objectivity in writing Karno's story as a bodice-ripper, but there was undoubtedly a darker side to Karno, and the stories of infidelity and bad behaviour can't be completely discounted. I hope that I've painted a more balanced picture of this complex character, without suggesting, as Adeler and West did, that Karno was a saint.

So, despite two biographies we are left to fill in many blanks and correct significant mistakes. In doing so I have endeavoured to go back to contemporary sources wherever possible, and where these are vague or inconsistent, I have said so.

Those interested in finding out more about Karno should beware that Fred Karno (Frederick John Westcott) (1866-1941) begat Frederick Arthur Westcott (Fred Jr.) (1891-1961), who begat Fred Karno Westcott the third (1920-2011). Karno also had a nephew named Frederick John Westcott (1896-1965) and all these Fred Westcotts ended up as professional performers. This has inevitably led to confusion and many individual accounts of 'working with Fred Karno' were actually with his son or nephew.

To make life simple I have generally referred to Fred Karno Sr. as simply Karno (even before he changed his name from Fred Westcott), his son as Fred Jr. and his nephew as Freddie Westcott. Similarly, I have generally referred to Charlie Chaplin simply as Chaplin to distinguish him from his father Charles Chaplin Sr., and his brother Syd Chaplin. Stan Laurel worked with Karno under his real name of Jefferson, but I have generally used Laurel for clarity except where there is specific reference to Stanley Jefferson in a review or report. Karno sketches played under different titles in the U.S., and I have referred to them by these alternative titles where appropriate.

No doubt I have fallen into the odd trap or two, and should any errors be discovered (or if you dear reader have any Karno stories or information you'd like to share with me) please contact me via my website. I should be delighted to hear from you and will endeavour to make appropriate corrections in any subsequent edition.

A final thought before we begin: Will Hay's biographers, Seaton and Martin, wrote: 'Karno's influence on English humour has been profound and greatly undervalued, possibly because of an excessive emphasis by writers on his personal follies.'[14] I hope I have avoided repeating that mistake.

2.
Running Away with the Circus

*I've got a sure-footed horse. He kicked me
three times in exactly the same place.*

(The Merry Book of the Moore & Burgess Minstrels, 1898)

DAN LENO, the greatest comedian of the music hall era, had some advice for those embarking on an autobiography: 'The first thing is to get yourself born. That's most important, in fact it's the most important thing that can happen to anyone.'[1]

In January 2018, a rare celestial event took place: a 'blue' moon and a lunar eclipse combined, a phenomenon known as a super blue blood moon. The last time this had happened was in late March 1866. Great comics come along once in a blue moon, and sure enough Frederick John Westcott (better known as Fred Karno) was born on 26 March 1866. He was the eldest of John and Emily Westcott's seven children (six boys and a girl) and with only John's income as a cabinet maker[2] to support them, theirs was a life of Victorian working-class hardship. Home was Paul Street, Exeter, a Dickensian thoroughfare full of side alleys and 'courts' which has since given way to a faceless tunnel of a street, squeezed between the blank brick facades of two shopping centres.

2.1 Paul Street, Exeter, 1911 (reproduced by kind permission of Devon Archives & Local Studies).

7

Before Karno's fifth birthday they had moved to Castle Street, Salisbury; then, around 1875, they settled permanently at 1 Carey's Place, Nottingham.[3] The motive for leaving Exeter is unclear; whilst there was mass migration from rural areas to the burgeoning industrial towns at the time, the Westcotts moved from one city to another (and John continued in the same trade) so presumably didn't relocate to find work. Salisbury was perhaps a stop on a planned move to London, but why they then elected to turn north to the Midlands remains a mystery. To get to Nottingham they would have bypassed other towns, not least Birmingham (where Karno said they lived for a while),[4] so it seems likely that there was a family connection to Nottingham which remains unclear.

2.2 Coalpit Lane, Nottingham, 1915 (© picturenottingham.co.uk).

Housing in Nottingham had failed to keep pace with rapid population growth and by the mid-1800s the city had become one of the worst slums in the country. A lack of basic sanitation was only addressed after the appointment (in 1859) of the marvellously named Marriott Ogle Tarbotton as borough surveyor – a name to inspire a Karno character if ever there was one. It took Tarbotton eight years to persuade the corporation to begin the work of improving the town's infrastructure. Meanwhile Nottingham's poverty and degradation inspired William Booth to begin his work with the poor and later establish the Salvation Army. Karno recalled as a boy seeing Booth's New Army on the march in the town and considered him to be as much a showman as a Samaritan. Thirty years later Karno would do his own good deed when, as a wealthy impresario, he provided one of his theatres free of charge to the Salvation Army for a benefit concert – perhaps he remembered the deprivation of his Nottingham childhood and the succour Booth's disciples had offered.

Carey's Place was one of a series of small back-to-back yards which ran off Coalpit Lane (now Cranbrook Street) so the family's accommodation was basic; but his father had employment and, at a time when school was neither compulsory nor free, the children received a form of education. By the time he was thirteen Karno was a 'half-timer', attending school in the morning and working at a lace factory in the afternoon. Lace making was a booming industry

2. RUNNING AWAY WITH THE CIRCUS

in Nottingham, reliant on a labour force of women and children, with hundreds of small factories operating from four in the morning until midnight. Karno's job was 'jacking off', stripping the ends of yarn from the bobbins for reuse (a skilled job but hard on the fingers), for which he earnt the princely sum of two shillings a week. Karno's father was a strict Victorian disciplinarian who ensured that his children earnt their place at the supper table, so Karno's wages went straight into the family coffers and, after school and work, he still had to do his share of the chores. This upbringing instilled in him a tireless work ethic which led to his eventual success, but with his father's edict "no work – no supper" constantly ringing in his ears, Karno felt his upbringing had been hard. He detested housework but failure to complete his chores meant going hungry (or a beating) so, despite occasional defiance, he had little choice but to comply.

Apart from these early recollections, Karno's family is notably absent from his memoirs; we only know what can be gleaned from historical records. Emily seems to have stayed at home raising the family but spent her later years separated from John, who suffered from dementia and was cared for by Karno in London. Emily remained in Nottingham where she died, aged fifty-seven, in 1903.

While life was tough, there were opportunities for enterprising young teenagers and Karno was always on the lookout for ways to earn a few shillings. One day his father dispatched him to get his razor sharpened but, rather than simply waiting as the barber attended to the task, he took it upon himself to sweep the floor. The barber was delighted and rewarded him by sharpening the razor for free. Karno pocketed the ninepence and for once didn't have to donate his secret earnings to the family pot. He had earnt more in ten minutes than in an hour at the laceworks, so was delighted when the barber offered him a job at five shillings a week; he was three shillings a week better off and his parents didn't have to know a thing about it.

The entrepreneurial seed had been sown and, as he stashed away his additional earnings, he was already planning his next venture. He rented a lock-up shop where, at night, he and a pal would clean milkmen's carts for a shilling a week. Although Karno couldn't recall his friend's name, he did remember that he had only one arm – Karno probably made him work twice as hard for his share. Pretty soon he was making ten shillings a week, whereupon the landlord of the lock-up promptly ejected them and took over the enterprise for himself. Waving goodbye to his lucrative little earner, Karno learnt a valuable lesson – always get a contract. His subsequent legal wrangling with artists and managers was the stuff of legend.

He tried his hand at all manner of jobs from barrow-boy to bricklayer's labourer, before securing a position as a shop-boy for a chemist called Shepherd. Shepherd's competition was 'M. & J. Boot – Herbalists', in Goosegate, and Karno's duties included enticing customers away from this rival. History has shown that he lost the battle – Boots achieved slightly more success.

Throughout his life Karno proved unable to stick to one thing for very long and constantly sought new challenges; it was a trait which led to regular bursts of creativity, innovation and business expansion, but for now it meant that Mr Shepherd was soon searching for a new shop-boy. As Karno approached his fifteenth birthday, he became indentured to a plumber and began a seven-year apprenticeship. Such indentures were legally binding; the penalty for breaking them was three months in jail. His plumbing job soon felt like a straightjacket – a whole new career was in the pipeline.

He may not have been destined for a life in drainage, but two plumbing jobs were to have a lasting impact. Tackling a job at a local prison (probably the Nottingham House of Correction),[5] he found himself assisted by two convicts who regaled him with hilarious tales of their hapless adventures in crime. He later used their comical escapades as the basis for an early sketch, *Jail Birds*, and convicts subsequently became a repeating theme (along with associated policemen, warders and accomplices). Thanks to Karno and his comics these ideas gravitated into early film – ever wonder why there are so many cops and robbers in silent comedies? More significantly Karno later found himself working at a gymnasium where he saw acrobats in action for the first time and signed up for lessons; it was quickly evident that he had a natural flair for acrobatics.

Where Karno trained is unknown, but it was probably the Nottingham Gymnasium, just half a mile from his front door. It was part of an entertainment complex in Talbot Street called the Alexandra which contained a roller-skating rink, two small halls and a 2500 capacity main auditorium; today it is a music venue called Rock City.

Karno had finally found something that he was interested in and enjoyed;

2.3 Possibly Karno's gym: Rock City Nottingham, formerly the Alexandra (author's photograph).

2. RUNNING AWAY WITH THE CIRCUS

he worked hard and was soon winning competitions at fetes and galas. The prizes at these events were usually donated by local farmers, so he often brought home joints of meat and sacks of vegetables – reason enough for his father to tolerate this new diversion. Eventually Karno felt confident enough to enter an amateur competition at 'the old Alhambra Theatre' (presumably the Royal Alhambra Music Hall in St Mary's Gate).[6] The Alhambra had been the city's original Theatre Royal and the grandeur of the venue tore his nerves to shreds. Stepping onto a stage for the very first time he was overwhelmed with panic and froze on the spot, but encouraged by the audience's applause, he mustered his courage, chalked his hands and grasped the horizontal bars. Instinct and muscle memory took over and he was soon twisting and spinning through his repertoire of elaborate set pieces. The crowd went wild and first prize was in the bag. Karno knew at that moment that this was the life for him, there would be no going back.

2.4 *The Royal Alhambra Music Hall, Nottingham (courtesy Andrew Nicholson).*

We don't know the exact date of that stage debut but Karno is listed on the April 1881 census as a plumber, and it seems likely that it was sometime later that year, in which case he was just fifteen. With new-found confidence, he practised tirelessly and took every opportunity to watch and learn from other gymnasts. One such act was a wire-walker and juggler who went by the wonderful title of 'Monsieur Olvene, Equilibrist.'[7] After seeing his act, Karno ambushed Olvene at the stage door and brazenly requested a position as his assistant, pointing out that he could do every trick in Olvene's routine. Olvene took this with a pinch of salt but, impressed by the youngster's pluck, he invited the lad to audition for him at the theatre at ten o'clock the following morning. Karno literally jumped at the chance, but sneaking off work for a day would mean breaking his indentures. He did it anyway – prison was evidently a risk worth taking. He duly turned up and found Olvene sitting alone in the middle of an empty auditorium; a far more daunting audience than a packed house could ever be – there would be no applause to encourage him. Karno dug deep, performed his prize-winning routine and, to his surprise and delight, Olvene agreed 'to try him out' in some local engagements.

So, who was the man who gave Karno his first big break? Olvene is difficult to track down but appears to have been a man named Tom Hillery, then twenty-nine, married to Laura, and living at 2 Theakers Street, Nottingham.[8] Tom had just become a father to Charles who, seventy years later, wrote to *The Stage* to share his memories of performing with his father from the age of eight. Charles also claimed to have befriended Chaplin during his time with Karno, which suggests that Karno and Olvene remained in touch for many years.[9] In his memoirs Karno described Olvene as pompous: 'a real old timer, rather of the early actor type'; which does not sound like Tom Hillery, a twenty-nine-year-old Nottingham lad with a young family – perhaps Karno embellished the character for dramatic licence. The real Olvene appears to have been a low-ranking performer playing circuses and small halls (he barely appears in contemporary reviews); he was not even a full-time acrobat – the 1881 census lists him as a 'rotary hose hand'.

A photograph in Karno's memoirs captioned 'The Two Olvenes – Karno's first stage appearance' claims to record their first performance together – but I'm not so sure. A small boy sits proudly on a vaulting horse next to Olvene who looks to be in his late thirties – the ages don't tie up at all (Olvene was 29 and Karno 15 when they performed together). What's more Olvene and Karno never appeared as 'The Two Olvenes' (Olvene didn't use this billing until fifteen years later); however, Olvene was in another double act (from 1888) with 'Nestal' which is almost certainly his son Charles. I am sure that the picture is of them around that time – Olvene would have been thirty-six and Charles eight. So, disappointingly, this photograph shows Olvene but does not record Karno's first stage appearance.

Back to our story; Karno began training with Olvene in the evening, while continuing his apprenticeship during the day. They developed a two-man routine performing at local events, until Olvene decided Karno was ready for his first professional engagement. They had been rehearsing at the Crown and Cushion,[10] at Weekday Cross, which was run by a Mrs Metheringham who evidently liked what she saw and booked their new act. Karno received

2.5 Karno's mentor – Olvene (seen here with 'Nestal', his son Charles).

2. RUNNING AWAY WITH THE CIRCUS

no payment for this first performance but was now officially Olvene's partner and that was reward enough – for now.

The only thing holding Karno back was the small matter of his indentures, but fate stepped in and at that very moment his employer died. Suddenly free to pursue a career on the stage, he packed a bag and ran away to join the circus. They headed off to Hutchinson and Tayleur's Circus in Cardiff and set their minds to finding an exotic sounding name; Fred Westcott would never do. By the time they arrived, they had become 'Olvene and Leonaro'.

The circus as we know it today was pioneered by Philip Astley in the 1770s. Astley had been a cavalry officer and his exceptional horsemanship was the basis of his first shows. He instigated the circus ring to enable horses to be presented galloping in front of an audience and gradually these equestrian demonstrations were supplemented with acrobatics,

2.6 The Crown and Cushion, Nottingham, 1911 (© picturenottingham.co.uk).

balancing and juggling. By the late nineteenth century exotic animal acts, clowns and freak show exhibits had been added; 'Elephant Man' Joseph Merrick was exhibited as a circus attraction around the same time Karno made his debut.

Hutchinson and Tayleur's was an established touring company with a permanent venue in Cardiff, where they overwintered.[11] 'Hutchinson & Tayleur's Circus and Grand Palace of Variety' (otherwise known as 'The Wooden Circus Theatre') stood on the junction of Westgate Street, St Mary Street and Wood Street. Karno knew it simply as 'The Octagon'.

Hutchinson's medicine men were not beyond a bit of back-street dentistry, and it was also a venue for bare-knuckle boxing bouts. Despite these colourful activities, Hutchinson and Tayleur endeavoured to present a respectable front: their shows included grand tableaus of beautiful maidens; re-enactments of fables such as *George and the Dragon* and spectacular displays from acrobats and horsemen. They also did their bit for charity, holding benefit nights for good causes, which encouraged polite society to attend. An article advertising the grand opening of the Octagon in 1870 extolled the virtues of the place:

> This new and magnificent building erected ... at a cost of £1,000 will open for the season on Monday evening ... the handsomest Circus ever erected in Cardiff ... replete with every comfort, and capable of accommodating 2,000 visitors, presenting a perfect model of classical ornamentation of taste. The finest equestrian troupe ... that has ever appeared here. The stud of trained Arabian Blood Horses ... animals of the most rare and beautiful symmetry ... The Entertainments will be varied nightly, and include ... daring Gymnastic Exploits, grand Entrees and Cavalcades, brilliant Spectacles, Historical Pageants, and a host of Novel Scenes ... the most sparkling entertainment ever introduced to a Cardiff audience.[12]

In contrast, Karno described it as being in the midst of a slum. His new environment was spectacular, dramatic, vibrant and intoxicating yet brutal, chaotic and dangerous – it was a long way from plumbing, and he loved it.

Olvene and Leonaro quickly developed an excellent partnership and Karno benefitted greatly from the older man's tutelage. Olvene advised that he should never make his act look too easy; the audience would respond much better to an acrobat who seemingly came close to missing a difficult move than to one who executed it with ease. They clearly did enough to excite the crowd in Cardiff, as their engagement was extended and they subsequently stayed with the company on a tented tour of Welsh mining towns through spring and summer 1882.

Touring circus performers endured a basic existence; they had no accommodation of their own and would either find their own digs or sleep in the hay of the animal tents. Working with animals (exotic ones at that) was another new experience which Karno relished; he became extremely competent with horses and soon found himself driving the circus wagons from town to town. On one occasion he was nearly killed when he lost control on a steep hill and smashed the cart into a railway bridge (jumping clear in the nick of time). Assuming the company made it to a town in one piece, the first order of business was to stage a spectacular parade led by Karno driving the 'bandwagon' which, as the name suggests, was an elaborately decorated cart carrying a band of musicians, literally drumming up trade. The townsfolk would fall in behind the procession and follow it to the showground, where the artistes would create a shop window for the delights awaiting them inside the big top. This procedure was known as the 'Comic Hop' and, with the ringmaster's cries of "walk up, walk up" ringing in their ears, the performers would stage mini versions of their acts on a platform outside the tent until enough people had bought a ticket to warrant starting the show inside. The success of such aggressive promotion was not lost on Karno and he later employed parades to create a stir in any town where his touring companies performed.

Olvene and Leonaro performed twice a day, and Karno no doubt looked resplendent in his leotard, spangled neckpiece, trunks and rubber galoshes. Pink tights were standard acrobat's attire but were expensive, so to stretch his twelve shillings a week wages, Karno bought cheaper white ones and dyed them with a bottle of red ink. His ability with horses enabled him to graduate to the 'Riding Machine' stunt which was part of the grand finale. A child, apparently plucked from the audience but almost certainly a stooge, would ride around the ring on a pony, whilst Karno performed acrobatics on, over and under the moving steed – a routine requiring extraordinary strength, skill and dexterity.

When the show was over the work continued. Every member of the company pulled together to pitch the tents, rig the trapeze and look after the animals. This involvement in every aspect of the show instilled in Karno a need to understand and control his future productions from top to bottom. The circus also reinforced his childhood work ethic: he was incredibly hardworking, tireless in fact, and he expected the same effort from everyone he later employed. He was to become a control freak, a perfectionist with meticulous attention to detail, which often caused friction with his artistes but ensured consistently high-quality productions. His most successful protégés were to share this approach (as we shall see). Karno found his new life challenging but loved every minute of it, describing himself as being ridiculously happy during those days. He said that on that first circus tour, 'more experiences, humorous, pathetic and sometimes tragic, were crowded into a few short months than are to be found in the average man's lifetime.'[13]

The circus clearly had a huge effect on Karno's formative years, but the most important influence was the comedy of the clowns. Astley had borrowed the clown character from Georgian theatre to fill the pauses between acts with burlesques of juggling, tumbling, rope-dancing and trick-riding. They were often drawn from the highly skilled acrobats and Karno was expected to don his comedy boots with the rest of them; as Adeler and West noted: 'He would make up ... with whitened face, painted red lips and big flap shoes. He had a tiny carriage and pony to match and would sit with his great boots upended, trying to do comic stunts.'[14]

This was an experience he did not enjoy, recalling that the clowns were considered fair game for rough audience participation and the crowd would throw everything from coins to manure. Nevertheless, he learnt more valuable lessons: how to warm up a crowd, how to generate laughter purely from visual material and how to use props to add to the effect. He also saw that whilst the clowns appeared chaotic, they worked carefully rehearsed routines. One audience member recounted a visit to Hutchinson's Octagon as follows: 'A Cardiff clown called Joey Haynes would climb to the top of the building and pretend to lose his hold and fall to the ground. It was really a dummy that fell, but the scene was so realistic that it had the ladies reaching for their smelling salts.'[15]

Karno would soon bring these slapstick skills to the music hall and he has been credited with inventing the custard pie in the face gag. Adeler and West more accurately said: 'Grimaldi and others may have thrown custard pies long before. But it was Karno who brought this form of entertainment to a fine art.'[16] He went on to introduce broad physical humour to a mass audience, developing what he had learnt in the circus ring. Twenty-five years later one critic wrote: 'Originally a gymnast – a daring one too – Fred Karno served his apprenticeship with some of the old-time travelling circuses, and much of his powers as a pantomimist, and a teacher of same, are due to his association with the circus ballets which in bygone days converted the ring into a sky of vivid colour … Mr Karno today realises how much he learned from that association.'[17]

Whether it was an inability to stick at anything or a burning ambition to improve, Karno never rested on his laurels and, as he gained in ability and experience, he began looking for his next opportunity. He owed his career to Olvene but when the touring season finished in September 1882, their partnership ended with it. Perhaps Olvene wanted to return home to his young family or Karno felt he had outgrown his mentor; either way, they parted amicably. Karno left the stability of Hutchinson's and the protective care of Olvene, supremely confident that he was going on to greater things. He was wrong – things were about to get very tough indeed.

3.

The Long Road to London

He was fond of high living. He slept on the roof.
(The Merry Book of the Moore & Burgess Minstrels, 1898)

THE ATTRACTION for Karno of striking out on his own was obvious: he took a job as a single-handed gymnast with Proctor's circus on a wage of twenty-five shillings a week (with a penny for extra shows), and overnight doubled his earnings.[1] Whilst the pay was better, the company performed at smaller fairgrounds and he certainly earned his money; on New Year's Day 1883, in Sheffield, he recalled playing twenty-two shows in a day. As well as performing his own routine on the double trapeze and horizontal bars, he acted as ringmaster for the 'Fortune Telling Pony', joined in the clowns' slapstick and played multiple parts in a dramatic pantomime sketch called *Dick Turpin*. Such sketches were true pantomimes: dramatic presentations of well-known stories, told entirely in mime. Some re-enacted famous cavalry battles (enabling the horsemen to display their riding skills); others were based on folk tales and legends. All were carefully choreographed sketches, combining acrobatics and slapstick, which formed the grand finale to the show.

After a few months of touring northern England, Proctor's found itself unable to attract a large enough audience to cover the performers' wages and they were forced to accept a co-operative arrangement. Essentials came first: feed for the animals and ground rent; if there was anything left, the manager took fifty percent and the remainder was shared between the artistes. This quickly dwindled to nothing. Karno and his colleagues took to busking, begging and even scaring local schoolchildren into giving up their bread and jam, to stay alive.

In desperation they would slip a villager a free ticket, or plug a local business during the show, in return for a square meal. After weeks of no pay and little food, Karno added injury to insult.

They were performing at the Flat Iron Market, in Salford, when disaster struck. Flying high on the trapeze, Karno launched himself into his big finish, the 'Leap for Life', but the excited gasps from the audience turned to screams of terror when the king pole of the tent shattered, sending Karno crashing to the ground and into the burning naphtha lamps. Miraculously his injuries weren't too serious, but it was the final straw – he decided to seek pastures new. Karno (or Fred Leonaro as he was then), still only seventeen, joined his third company, Harry Manley's Chinese Circus. Manley's was renowned for 'subtle and graceful' sketches and a new one would appear each week: *The Bear and Sentinel*, *Love in a Tub*, *The Prince and The Tinker* and *The Copper Ballet* were typical routines. Here Karno learnt a subtler approach to visual performance, and he credited Manley's with completing his education in the fine art of pantomime. After twelve months with them, Karno's regular employment in circuses, and the first phase of his career, came to an end. The character traits which would serve him well throughout his life were now well and truly ingrained. He was technically skilled and physically strong; he had learnt to be adaptive and opportunistic; he was able to turn his hand to a variety of tasks and work hard; he understood how to drum up a crowd and the importance of engaging with an audience. Most of all he had learnt the true currency of comedy – a visual gag is far more potent than a spoken one.

He also had the confidence of youth, and his next move was to team up with another acrobat, 'Rudolph', and head for the music halls. With no mentor or circus troupe to help him, he was truly self-reliant for the first time in his life. He would have to live by his wits and trust his own judgement – it was to be the final stage in the formation of his character and the toughest yet.

Records of this new double act are non-existent except for a notable week in March 1884 when Karno recalled them being engaged by Hyram Travers, a highly successful 'coster' comedian and proprietor of the Prince of Wales Theatre of Varieties, Northampton. *The Stage* captured their appearance for posterity: 'Rudolph and Leonaro – clever trapeze artistes'.[2] This seems to be the only appearance of 'Leonaro' in a listing and it happened to be the week of his eighteenth birthday. Karno remembered this engagement for another reason: it was the week he met the champion jockey, Fred Archer. Karno recalled being

3. THE LONG ROAD TO LONDON

thrilled to meet him,[3] and this may have sparked an interest in horse racing which stayed with Karno throughout his life. Perhaps he had celebrated his birthday by watching Archer ride a winner that week.

After Northampton, work dried up and he returned to Nottingham with his tail between his legs. Whether he received a warm embrace from his mother, or a clip around the ear from his father, is unrecorded, but either way he found there was no work to be had in his home town either. There was only one thing for it – he would head for the bright lights of London, where the streets were paved with gold and a music hall adorned every street corner. With a pal called Mike (who may have been Rudolph), he set off on a 130-mile walk to the capital. Such a journey seems incredible to us today, but it was not uncommon at the time. Comedian Bud Flanagan recorded walking most of the way from London to Glasgow in search of work as late as 1923.[4] Karno and Mike made it even harder for themselves back in 1884 by tackling the trek at the onset of winter.

To earn a crust Karno decided that he would revisit his plumbing career and do odd jobs on the way. Plumbers undertook any kind of leadwork, including re-glazing leaded lights, so Karno carried a glazier's kit on his back and, with a cry of "windows to mend," they made a few shillings along the road. Gallagher wrote that our hero created a ready supply of customers by breaking windows at night then offering to repair them the following morning. That bit of business went on to become one of the most famous sequences in film comedy history. In *The Kid* (1921) Charlie Chaplin resorts to this nefarious activity, with a young Jackie Coogan as his accomplice, right under the nose of a watching flatfoot. It is one of the funniest and most memorable scenes in one of the greatest films of all time – but was it inspired by Karno's real-life experience? Most Chaplin biographers repeat Gallagher's story, but I am not convinced. He claimed that the anecdote came from Fred Karno Jr., yet it is not included in Junior's 1961 version of his father's life story. What's more there is no mention of the tale in Karno's own memoirs – and he would not have missed the opportunity to claim the credit for Chaplin's gag. The reality is that Karno did draw on his own history when he included a jobbing glazier character in a sketch, *Early Birds* (1899), but I've yet to find a review of the show which suggests that he used this joke. So while Chaplin may have been inspired by the glazier in *Early Birds*, the idea of breaking windows to then repair them seems to have been his own idea, which later found its way into Karno family legend. Chaplin biographer Simon Louvish shares my incredulity, writing that the story 'may reflect the fanciful invention of Fred Junior.'[5]

3.1 Chaplin as a glazier in The Kid *(1921) (courtesy Roy Export/Chaplin Archive).*

Back to our teenage hero. Karno recalled that it took them three weeks to reach Leicester, a leisurely nine miles a week but still too strenuous for Mike who abandoned the attempt, leaving Karno to fend for himself. Cold, alone and with his resources exhausted, Karno pressed on, relying on bread thrown out for the birds for sustenance. He made it another sixteen miles (to Market Harborough) before turning back. As night fell, he was caught in a snowstorm and, in desperation, knocked at the door of a large house to ask for help. Despite being almost turned away as a tramp he persuaded the owner that he was a bona-fide glazier in need of work and the man took pity on him. He was given two shillings for bed and board and told to report to the man's factory the following morning. Karno was given a day's work and some much-needed income from his benefactor. He never forgot this act of kindness, recalling in his memoirs that he returned many years later to thank the man in person. Arriving at the house in his expensive car, Karno was disappointed to find that he had retired and moved away. Strangely Fred Jr. records this differently in his own recollections, saying that he and his father travelled to Market Harborough whilst on their way to the Palace Theatre, Leicester, and found the gentleman still in residence. According to Fred Jr., Karno repaid his debt by treating the old man to dinner and tickets to his show. Whichever version is correct, Karno never forgot the kindness he'd been shown by a stranger.

Back in 1884, Karno abandoned his expedition to London and once again returned to Nottingham. He soon partnered up with a lad called Tommy Whittaker and together they toured the fairgrounds, performing in a small tent known as a 'ponging booth'. Carting their equipment on their backs, they worked the small towns and villages of the East Midlands; first Castle Donington then on to Melbourne, where they set up their horizontal bars in the market square and made six shillings each for the week (barely ten percent of his earnings with Hyram Travers a year earlier). They may not have made their fortune but two single nineteen-year-old lads, physically fit and with the added allure that all performers generate, found themselves extremely popular with a group of young ladies from one of Melbourne's many boot factories. They were found lodgings in a secluded barn and supplied with food, water and as much feminine company as they could stand. After a week of this adulation, Karno decided to quit while he was ahead and suggested they seek a position with George Ginnett's Circus, which was at Derby. Whittaker was keen to stay in their cosy hayloft, but Karno insisted that an audience should always be left wanting more. There were sobs and sighs as they were waved off at the station by the heartbroken girls – a send-off Karno recalled as the most memorable of his entire career.

Karno and Whittaker were to be disappointed at Derby as Ginnett had no vacancies,[6] so they spent the summer of 1885 as jobbing acrobats taking any work they could get. In October an advert appeared in *The Era*: 'The Marvellous Leonaro Brothers, Gymnasts & co, will shortly be at liberty to accept engagements for their four distinct acts, for terms – permanent address 4 Plattoff Street, Nottingham.'[7] There is no record of their subsequent engagements but we know that they stuck together until the following summer, when Karno saw a notice seeking an acrobat to join an act called 'The Four Aubreys' on a European tour. It was just the opportunity he had been waiting for: 'Wanted – lad who has knowledge of trapeze and rings or would join partner. Tour made up – care of "The Era" office.'[8] Karno was quick to apply and his reply came two weeks later: 'Wanted – Fred Leonaro to send his address to James Malcolm, Scotia Glasgow, business of importance and to his advantage.'[9]

The Four Aubreys were a high-quality act with a good reputation, but they had disbanded as a quartet the previous spring and American Bob Aubrey had developed a new two-way act with 'Mademoiselle Zulia'. During an extended run at the Liverpool Zoological Gardens in 1885 they had elicited 'a wonderful display of gymnastic skill in their entertainment entitled "Aerostation" … an elaborate silver-plated apparatus fixed at a dizzy height is watched with breathless interest by the spectators below.'[10] Previous accounts suggest that Zulia was Aubrey's Liverpudlian wife Sarah, but this is problematic. Sarah was just sixteen and was mother to their new baby son Charles (born sometime between April 1885 and April 1886) so quite how she performed in the act is something of a mystery. Either way, at some point the double act became a trio with the addition of an acrobat they christened 'Alto', and they toured in this form until July 1886. Then, just as they were about to embark on a European tour, Alto was forced to leave due to illness. Aubrey must have been desperate to find a replacement, hence the *Era* advertisement and his willingness to take on a relatively inexperienced recruit.

Karno recalled that he joined them for rehearsals at MacDonald's Music Hall, Glasgow,[11] before opening at the Scotia, one of the biggest halls in Scotland; but Karno's memory let him down.[12] The Aubreys were not about to risk their reputation on an unknown quantity and instead tried out the new recruit for a week at small venues: Cooke's Circus in Greenock and Frame's Royal Concert Hall.

Even if they didn't play the enormous Scotia, joining the Aubreys must have been a daunting experience. Bob Aubrey was a year younger than Karno (just nineteen) but was already a headliner and often commanded top billing. Much to Karno's relief, he made the grade and was taken on at twenty-five shillings a week – a salary he'd not enjoyed since leaving Olvene three years earlier. The new trio (with baby Charles in tow) set off for the continent in the second week of September 1886. It was Karno's first experience of foreign travel and one he was unlikely to forget – they started in style at Oscar Carré's Circus in Cologne. Carré's was at its zenith and Karno described its circus theatre as a grand building of 'vast size'; Aubrey was taking a considerable risk with his new protégé and it went horribly wrong.

The finale to their trapeze act was Karno's flying double somersault but, overawed by the scale of the venue, he mistimed his leap, slipped through the outstretched arms of Zulia and landed in the net. The trio was dismissed from Carré forthwith. They moved on to Belgium, but things went from bad to worse as Karno suffered a bout of blood poisoning (which he put down to rubbing resin into his hands), leading to a nasty abscess under his arm. Karno's misery was confirmed by comic Fred Kitchen (who later worked extensively with him); Kitchen told how his elder brother Dick was in Brussels and witnessed Karno slip while practising and burst into tears:

> Dick went to him and saw that his hands were raw and bleeding. They had made the poor little chap work without hand pads and the resin had got into the broken blisters and must have been giving him hell. That was enough for kind-hearted Dick. And Dick was already a big man – as important and influential a performer as he was physically fine and fit. He went to Bob Aubrey and told him that if he dared work the child again before his hands were properly healed – well he'd be seeing him … and Fred Karno was always grateful.[13]

3. THE LONG ROAD TO LONDON

Karno had managed to get them sacked from their first engagement and was now unable to work through injury; Aubrey must have rued the day he employed him. Karno was no doubt anxious to put things right and appears to have tried to find someone to cover for him, placing the following notice in *The Era*: 'Wanted James Alexander address, late with Proctor's Circus, Fred Leonaro, La Scala Theatre, Antwerp, Belgium.'[14]

Karno remembered their next engagement as the Eden Theatre in Brussels (rather than La Scala) but wherever it was, James Alexander did not appear, Karno's abscess was lanced and he soldiered on. Despite being the oldest of the trio, Karno was very much the junior partner and the Aubreys ensured he earned his keep in more ways than one. When not on stage Karno was required, much to his indignation, to help look after young Charles. He got his revenge by using the baby's sweet money to buy tobacco and covered his tracks by sprinkling a little sugar around the baby's mouth. David Robinson notes that this story may have been the inspiration for a scene in Chaplin's *The Circus* (1928), where he steals a hot dog from a child then wipes its face when its father turns around.

The Aubreys' tour seems to have been doomed, with each venue being smaller than the last. From the Eden, to Flagen's Circus, Rotterdam, and finally the Vereeniging Theatre, Amsterdam, where the stage was so small that the safety net had to be stretched out over the orchestra pit. Falling into the net one night, Karno landed on the conductor's stand and was seriously injured – he was lucky to avoid breaking his back. They could find no more work in theatres and resorted to a tour of Dutch fairs or 'kermesses' (quite a comedown for the headline acrobats from Carré's circus) before admitting defeat and returning to Britain.

In his memoirs Karno claimed that there was no work to be had back in England, but listings show that they toured the provinces as 'Zulia, Aubrey and Alto' for several weeks before their final appearance as a trio at Culeen's Circus, Accrington, in mid-March 1887. Karno's memoirs also suggest that he left them around this time, but I'm not so sure. They certainly refreshed the act, and after a six week break reappeared as a quartet, billed (with significant artistic licence) as: 'The American Wonders – Their first appearance in England after an absence of nearly three years.'[15]

At this point our story is complicated by the fact that in his memoirs Karno fails to record the events of the subsequent twelve months (spring 1887-1888), and Gallagher only adds confusion (as we shall see). We will clear this up in the next chapter, but let's stick with Karno's account for now, which states that he returned from Europe, left Aubrey, and finally found himself in London.

Before we move on, among many listings in the theatrical press, one example of the Aubreys' bill matter stands out: 'Twenty laughs in twenty minutes.'[16] So, whilst Karno does not mention it in his memoirs, the Aubreys were a comedy acrobatic troupe – literally a laugh a minute. Comedy and acrobatics were never mutually exclusive – later in Karno's career he didn't give up one to take up the other, it was simply a natural progression from an acrobatic act with some laughs into a comedy act with some acrobatics.

No matter how exciting, technically complex or elaborate the performance, an audience will always welcome some light relief – magicians and jugglers know this well. Such humour can be even more effective when combined with another heady ingredient – danger. Convince the audience that there is a real risk to the performer (the lady cut in half, the knife juggler, or high wire walker) then, when the tension becomes almost unbearable, hit them with a gag and the release guarantees the laugh (exhibit A: Joey Haynes, the clown who plunged to his death three times a night in the Cardiff circus). The same is true of an audience presented with a sad or tragic story: when you have them reaching for the hankies hit them with a gag and the emotional relief secures a bigger laugh than the joke would have done in isolation. Pathos, that hard to define combination of humour and drama, would later be at the heart of Karno's greatest successes.

So, Karno's account jumps forward from March 1887 to early 1888, where we find him looking for work in London. His timing couldn't have been better: the 1880s marked the zenith of the music hall era. According to a parliamentary report, in 1888 there were fifty theatres in London, thirty-five concert halls and 473 music halls.[17] The music hall world was a vibrant one full of interesting characters and performers, but it was not for the faint hearted. A major port and the gateway to the continent, London was teeming with millions of people of all races, creeds and colours and with every possible vice.

It is easy to picture the London of that year since at the same time two characters appeared who have remained in the public consciousness ever since: Sherlock Holmes, Conan Doyle's great fictional detective, and Jack the Ripper, Britain's most infamous serial killer. London was a place of gas-lit,

3.2 Fred Westcott, circa 1888.

smog-filled streets, opium dens, slum housing and rudimentary policing, where music hall artistes exhibited their abilities twice-nightly, plus matinees. Daniel Farson, in his biography of music hall superstar Marie Lloyd, wrote:

> Writers referred to 'the people of the abyss', 'the destitute' … Overcrowding was so bad that ten to fifteen thousand men, women and children roamed the streets at night and slept out. Others shared a 4d bed, sleeping in shifts. Houses containing twenty-four people were built on dust heaps and the smell from the refuse below combined with the stink from the gutters to poison an air already stale from over-use … Prostitution was inevitable. Three thousand brothels were listed officially and there were at least 80,000 prostitutes or 'lost women' in London … they flocked to the music halls in search of trade.[18]

One wonders how young female performers must have felt walking home from the halls after midnight – or, for that matter, young Karno: carrying his horizontal bars on his back, with a serial killer lurking in the shadows. Londoners were completely terrorized by the Ripper that summer, which must have added a high sense of drama to Karno's first few months in the capital. He came closest to the murders whilst playing the Oxford Music Hall (on the corner of Tottenham Court Road) in the first two weeks of November. On the 9th, a mile away in Dorset Street, the Ripper claimed his last victim, Mary Kelly – it must have felt a little too close for comfort.

Notwithstanding the danger around every corner, music hall had been born to an age of relative prosperity and peace: Queen Victoria's empire had made Britain the greatest superpower in the world. The developing cities were full to bursting with migrants who'd gravitated from rural areas during the Industrial Revolution; London's population increased from one million in 1800 to six and a half million by 1900 (over twenty percent of the entire population of England). The music hall was somewhere for the downtrodden masses to escape to and, for many, the entertainment was secondary: the halls were warm, inviting, sumptuous palaces of luxury – a world away from home. They could also be a catalyst for urban improvement, as this report reveals:

> Surely a music hall was never more advantageously placed than the Euston, which lights up what was at one time one of the frowsiest [sic]

> neighbourhoods in the north-western district. Squalor and something worse have been replaced by brightness and beauty … and the passer-by is cheered by the brilliant incandescence of electric burners, which throw their beams on a handsome façade … The promoters of the Euston … are public benefactors; for we think there is far more practical philanthropy in bringing a cheap and wholesome entertainment to the doors of a teeming population than in reams of tracts.[19]

Halls had sprung up all over the country, beginning as 'song and supper rooms' on the back of pubs, with no fixed seating and audiences coming and going as they pleased. The entertainment was provided solely to encourage people to stay and continue to spend money on beer and food. The artistes had to work above the noise and faced a raucous barrage from the audience which ranged from joining in the singing to throwing whatever came to hand if the act didn't come up to scratch. Near the markets of London's East End this might be rotten cabbages, in Glasgow it was more likely to be iron rivets – the dockers, in the oft-repeated quote, keen to 'leave no turn un-stoned'. Controlling this rabble was the chairman – who would announce the next act and do his best to contain the excesses of the crowd. Music hall chairmen were always great characters, and they commanded considerable authority.

The poorly ventilated, hot, sweaty rooms were generally thick with smoke, and fire was a significant danger. Some halls banned smoking, not because of any health risk but because the smoke was so thick the audience couldn't see the performers. Prompted in part by several devastating fires, the design of halls changed rapidly in the second half of the nineteenth century as the introduction of fixed seating and u-shaped auditoriums totally transformed the physical space. Halls gradually developed into more sophisticated venues focusing on the entertainment rather than the drinking. Some had promenades or balconies where you might find a young 'man about town', with cane and monocle, indicating his openness to an approach by a prostitute by wearing his hat at a jaunty angle. These 'swells', or 'mashers', were the 'Champagne Charlies' immortalised by George Leybourne in the famous music hall song. As standards in the halls improved and the clientele moved upmarket, the swells were usurped by the 'costers': comedians and singers who represented London's barrow boys and market traders. In both cases the audience were amused by familiar characters they could either look up to or down upon.

3. THE LONG ROAD TO LONDON

Hall owners gradually sought to widen their appeal and some offered museums, art galleries and other diversions considered acceptable to the middle classes. Halls began to rival 'legitimate' theatres in their design and facilities, and the chairman became a dying breed. Inevitably London was at the forefront of these changes: in the provinces old-style halls survived for much longer – every town had at least one and usually half a dozen. Today only a handful of such early halls survive: Hoxton and Wilton's music halls (both in London), Leeds City Varieties and Britannia Panopticon in Glasgow (where Stan Laurel made his stage debut). All evoke the atmosphere of the halls, but one must work hard to imagine the chaotic, smoky, noisy, alcohol-fuelled evenings of the mid-Victorian age.

Whatever the type of hall, all presented an extraordinary mix of entertainment. Comics, dog acts, black-faced minstrels, strongmen, jugglers, mind readers, magicians, champion whistlers, boxing kangaroos, elephants and lions, fire eaters, sporting exhibitions, opera, ballet, scientific demonstrations, one-legged tap dancers, living statues, men dressed as women and, much more shocking, women dressed as men, and of course those magnificent men on the flying trapeze – the acrobats.

3.3 The interior of The Oxford, circa 1875.

Whilst audience facilities gradually improved, the artistes' conditions remained primitive. Backstage was always crowded with performers, crew, props, scenery and costumes; not to mention the exotic animals that added sounds, smells and a genuine risk of injury to their fellow performers. Dressing rooms were often makeshift and always cramped and cold. In small halls artistes might have to enter and leave via the auditorium – particularly humiliating if they had 'died' on stage. Acts would usually give multiple performances in different halls on the same night; with a crack of the driver's whip, they would rush from one stage-door to another in a fast hansom cab or (if they could afford it) a brougham carriage.

It wasn't an easy life, but it offered an opportunity to escape from poverty – all you needed was some talent. In that respect it was a great leveller, performers were judged on their abilities, not on their age, wealth, social class or gender. Years before equality was even a twinkle in Emmeline Pankhurst's eye, the music hall was one of the few places where women had any significant public presence. Female performers were vibrant, vivacious, daring and as tough as they come. The uncrowned queen of them all was Marie Lloyd, best remembered for the song *Don't Dilly Dally on the Way*. She was charismatic, risqué, funny, and had power and authority over her adoring audience – Karno knew her well, as we shall see.

Performers who achieved any degree of popularity demanded extremely high salaries and even mediocre artistes were comparatively well paid. This encouraged many to try their luck in the halls but few carved long-term careers. For every star there were hundreds of acts lower down the bill, starting or ending the programme to half-filled auditoriums. They would have to endure the apathy of a cold crowd or the abusive drunken stragglers. These artistes scraped by on three or four pounds per week 'amongst the wines and spirits' (meaning at the bottom of the bill where the drink prices were noted). From these meagre wages they would have to find rail fares, pay their agent's ten percent, buy the manager a drink and the conductor a cigar, and tip the stage manager and crew. What was left had to cover accommodation and food, so life on tour often meant living three to a room in grubby digs. Success had its problems too – sudden and enormous wealth could be hard to handle. Spectacular falls from grace through drink, drugs, infidelity or exhaustion were commonplace. Personal tragedy often played out in public on the pages of the newspapers, or worse still on the stage itself. Fortunately for him, Karno's dramas remained largely behind closed doors.

The names of the halls were sometimes derived from the pubs they had once been, or the names of their proprietors. Others aimed to evoke the exotic or the spectacular: the Britannia, the Coliseum, the Aquarium, the Empire and so on. Some became immortalised in songs and stories, or in the case of the Eagle Tavern on London's City Road, in a nursery rhyme: 'Up and down the city road, in and out the Eagle, that's the way the money goes, pop goes the weasel.' The Eagle stood halfway between a lunatic asylum and the workhouse and its stars were highly likely to end up in either. Unsurprisingly, given their lifestyle, music hall performers had a poor chance of making fifty.

The development of the railway network in the 1840s was both a blessing and a curse for performers. It became much easier to travel to engagements in far-flung parts of the country and so they were more likely to be kept in work, but there was the added pressure of travelling long distances carting equipment, props and costumes. The best went further and performed in all corners of the Empire and

3. THE LONG ROAD TO LONDON

Europe; North America, Australia and South Africa were particularly welcoming to British artistes. At home, the music hall fed the population's jingoistic urges and the common man could easily be roused to patriotic fervour; the halls were the perfect platform for orators to spread their message and many songs of the era were written specifically to encourage support of military campaigns or political ideas. The unsung heroes of the halls (or should that be sung heroes?) were the writers who could churn out a topical or satirical ditty at the drop of a hat. The morning news was often that evening's comic song, and a good one, probably bought for a few pence at the stage door, could be the basis of an artiste's entire career.

Amongst all this were the acrobats. Some halls were designed specifically for circus-style performance; others could accommodate high-wire equipment or trapezes, which were often hung over the audience to make the displays even more thrilling. Such displays were curtailed by the introduction of horseshoe-shaped auditoriums, forcing acrobats to restrict their displays to the stage, but skilled performers could still evoke the excitement of the big top.

3.4 Music hall gymnasts in action, The Graphic, *2 September 1893 (courtesy Mary Evans Picture Library).*

Karno must have found London exciting and terrifying in equal measure. After several false starts only exhaustive hard work, perseverance, personal ambition and pure bloody-mindedness had got him there and they would keep him there. The die was cast – Karno's character was now beyond redemption.

4.

The Three Karnos

Are you secretly married?
No – she knows about it.
(Fred Karno personal joke archive, 15 August 1932)

ARTISTES TRAVELLED to provincial bookings by train, so Waterloo (then London's central railway terminal) became a focal point for performers. Agents established themselves nearby, and the York Hotel was a favourite haunt for the entire profession. Each morning artistes in search of work would congregate where York Road met Stamford Street,[1] enabling agents to simply step out of their offices and announce to the expectant crowd that they needed a dog act, conjuror or 'serio comic', and then choose from the hopefuls who came forward. The winner of this lottery would disappear on a train to some far-flung provincial town whilst those left behind loitered, hoping they would be next. The spot earnt its name – Poverty Corner.

Karno joined this crowd hoping for a chance of his own, and one can only imagine the sights and sounds of the place. Amongst the destitute artistes long past their prime – the sick, the mad, the drunk and the untalented – it was not uncommon to find successful performers, decked out in their furs and jewels, perhaps hoping to meet with an agent or just to catch up on the gossip. Karno soon got to know fellow speciality acts such as the Selbini trick cyclists, the Bale Troupe and Ella Zuila (known as 'the Female Blondin'), who could walk a high-wire blindfolded with her feet in baskets. He struck up a friendship with two older acrobats: twenty-six-year-old Londoner Bob Sewell and twenty-five-year-old Brummie Edwin (Ted) Tysall.[2]

4. THE THREE KARNOS

4.1 Walter Lambert's famous painting 'Popularity', depicting music hall artistes on Poverty Corner (courtesy of the Museum of London).

According to Karno, one fateful day (after Tysall and Sewell had abandoned all hope and headed home) he knocked on the door of Richard Warner's agency (at 11 York Road) to ask if he had anything available. He was in luck; one of Warner's managers, Maurice de Frece,[3] offered Karno the opportunity that changed his life: "There's been a disappointment at the Met tonight. It's the Three Carnos, and the salary is six pounds. Can you deputise?"[4] Karno made the most impetuous and far-reaching decision of his life – signing a contract on the spot. He left the office with something of a problem: he had just committed himself, Sewell and Tysall to appear in one of London's most popular music halls later that same night, having never performed or rehearsed together. They had no act, no equipment, no music and it was four o'clock in the afternoon – he must have really needed the work.

His first task was to convince the others it was possible; then he pawned his watch so that they could hire a cart to carry the necessary equipment. They borrowed a few props from Tom Bassett's theatrical supply shop and appropriated horizontal bars from Bob Aubrey's stores in Lambeth Walk (they worried about asking Aubrey after the event). Fully equipped they made their way to the Metropolitan Music Hall in Edgware Road, arriving at six o'clock.

Dramatic though Karno's story sounds, it seems unlikely that three acrobats, independently searching for work, would have no props, equipment or transport of their own. How would they have taken any engagement if they were not availed of the basic tools of their trade? Not letting this inconsistency get in the way of a good story, we rejoin our boys, who found (to their relief) that they were not due on stage until eleven o'clock. This was a poor position on the bill, but it suited them perfectly.

This momentous date was Whit Monday, 21 May 1888, so their first engagement was also an important bank holiday show, which would have put the young acrobats under even more pressure. The halls always pushed the boat out on public holidays and the bill for that week was impressive, including stars such as Jenny Hill, Charles Coborn and Vesta Tilley. This makes it even more surprising that the Metropolitan's manager, William Bailey, was not told that they were deputising: Fred Westcott, Bob Sewell and Ted Tysall presented themselves as the real Three Carnos – it was quite a risk! The imposters used the time to work out an act as best they could and went on completely cold, persuading the conductor that they had lost their music on the train. To the strains of whatever music the band had to hand, they put on a very basic, if enthusiastic, routine which included 'a series of "shoulder rolls" round the stage while endeavouring to kill a butterfly which was suspended from [Karno's] forehead by a wire.'[5]

Imagine their relief and surprise when they were so well received that Bailey gave them a month's contract.[6] They were now in a tricky position – at what point should they come clean and reveal that they were not the Three Carnos at all?

At this point our story becomes complicated by confusion between the genuine article and the imposters, so to follow the trail of Karno's fledgling trio we also need to touch on the story of the original Carnos, who were advertised thus: 'The Three Carnos – Fred, Hugh and Harry, greatest breakneck negro comedians and burlesque sketch artistes extant, introducing our unequalled acrobatic and Arab tumbling act.'[7] They had appeared in pantomime in London at Christmas 1886, and then toured throughout 1887; including a notable appearance at the Eldorado Theatre, Paris, where they performed 'a new white act'. They began touring with Hamilton's Diorama in early February 1888,[8] and Karno recorded that it was being 'stuck up north' with Hamilton's that prevented them fulfilling the Met engagement.

Although not mentioned in earlier Karno biographies, you will have noticed that the Three Carnos were a 'negro' act, performing like thousands of others in 'blackface'. Why acrobats would black-up is not clear except that black-faced performers were so popular that many artistes decided it was a sure-fire route to

4.2 The scene of the Three Karnos' debut – the Metropolitan Music Hall, Edgware Road.

4. THE THREE KARNOS

success. So, let's just accept that's how it was 130 years ago and move on – there is plenty of period sexism and racism to come. Although Karno claims not to have seen the originals perform, he would have seen their bill matter at the Met and, since William Bailey was unaware that they were imposters, Karno, Bob and Ted must also have blacked-up. According to Karno there was no problem with them impersonating the real Carnos because he claimed that they broke up around this time; but it is not that simple. Trying to work out what really happened to the original Carnos is a minefield. They were certainly still around in August (in Scotland) as this press listing confirms: 'Special engagement at great expense previous to their departure for America, 3 Carnos … the funniest acrobats in Europe … having just finished a two-year continental tour.'[9]

So did the Carnos go to America in autumn 1888 rather than break up as Karno thought? 'A two-year continental tour' is also confusing: we know that they had been appearing mostly in the UK, so this must be advertising licence (prompted by their engagement at the Eldorado in Paris the previous year). A few months later the Three Carnos' advertising noted that they would be at the Folies Bergère, Paris, the following March. To complicate things even further, two years earlier the original Three Carnos had themselves had a split; one of their members set up a rival group using the same name. The original line-up was Fred, Hugh and Harry; but, in autumn 1886, Harry was replaced by John and their advertisement in *The Era* included the following: 'THE THREE CARNOS, the originals (Hugh, Fred and John). Wonderful acrobats … our name can be copied but our business is beyond the reach of ambitious Imitators … take no notice they faded away.' Meanwhile Harry placed his own notice in the same edition: 'THE FOUR CARNOS. The original is Henri Carno, one of the above quartet. Advertise the truth or leave it alone.'[10] Vicious rivalry indeed.

So, we had two rival Carno troupes even before our imposters created a third, making it impossible to be certain which troupe is being referred to in many of the listings during this early period. 'Fred Carno' also turns up as a solo acrobat in some listings (this being the Fred from the original Carnos). Karno even said that later one of the original Carnos joined him (a fact I have not been able to confirm) which simply muddies the waters further. It must have been very confusing for managers; particularly since both the originals and Karno's new Carnos were represented by Dick Warner.

Karno noted that there was some ill feeling between the two troupes and in August they attempted an alternative name: 'The Brothers Carno', before eventually (at De Frece's suggestion) simply switching the 'C' for a 'K' – appearing as 'The Three Karnos' in September. All three adopted the surname Karno and never looked back.

Can we breathe a sigh of relief that they are now easy to trace? Not a chance: they were occasionally spelt 'Carno' in listings forever more, and there is another breakaway yet to come! So, is that the whole story of how the Three Karnos got their name? Not quite. The president of France at the time was Marie François Sadi Carnot, and Karno's son, Leslie, later said that his father took the name as he thought it sounded grand. However, since Karno doesn't mention this in his memoirs and his own account is supported by the contemporary records, this seems to be a family story without foundation.

Karno's memoirs suggest that, having found their own identity, they were immediately engaged at the famous Westminster Aquarium, but their next engagement was actually the Aquarium, Brighton – not quite as grand. This was followed by appearances at various halls before securing their first significant engagement – a residency with the Moore and Burgess Minstrels at St James's Hall, in the heart of London's West End.

George Washington 'Pony' Moore and Frederick Burgess produced the Christmas show at St James's every year for thirty-five years (from 1865) and to be invited to join the company was a real accolade. Minstrel shows were considered to be more respectable than music hall, so attracted the middle classes. Moore and Burgess's star turn was the great Eugene Stratton (he was with them for eleven years),[11] but they were a nursery for many lesser lights and writers such as Leslie Stuart (who wrote the smash-hit musical *Floradora*[12] and a number of Stratton hits including *Lily of Laguna*) and Joseph Tabrar (a prolific songsmith whose efforts included *Daddy Wouldn't Buy*

4.3 Advertisement for the Moore and Burgess Minstrels.

4. THE THREE KARNOS

Me a Bow-Wow). An advertisement on 17 December proclaimed: 'Moore and Burgess Minstrels ... an entirely new and gigantic entertainment replete with the most brilliant and attractive novelties. New and most important additions will be made to the magnificent company. Five thousand luxurious seats in the most beautiful hall in Europe.'[13] This was followed on 22 December by: 'First appearance of The Three Karnos the wonderful grotesque artistes, who will appear in a novel and screamingly funny pantomime sketch called Summer Borders [sic].'[14] The show opened on Boxing Day, 26 December, 1888.

So, the Karnos were originally a 'blackface' act who, just six months after forming, were engaged for a West End Christmas show in which they performed a comedy sketch – three facts which are totally contrary to previous biographies, including his own memoirs.

Minstrel troupes like Moore and Burgess combined songs, sketches, acrobatics and dramatic pieces – all, of course, in 'blackface'. It is difficult to see past the racism, but whilst the performers used stereotypes which we now find abhorrent, their intention was to bring these musical and comedy styles to a wider audience, not to ridicule them, but to celebrate them – their mistake was thinking they had to look like the performers they were inspired by. Even African American performers felt the need to play these stereotypes and, bizarrely, many used blackface make-up on their naturally dark skin. D. Travis Stewart notes that the influence of the minstrels on popular culture is hard to overstate: one can draw a direct line from them through ragtime, jazz and blues, to rock and roll. In his book on the history of vaudeville, he describes the minstrels songs and routines as a wonderful product now tarnished by association, like Hitler's Volkswagen.[15]

Minstrel comedy routines followed a standard format, with a trio of performers: Mr Interlocutor known as the 'middle man', and his two 'end men' Mr Tambo and Mr Bones, named after the instruments they played (tambourine and bone castanets). Interlocutor was the straight-man to the pair of idiot comedians and this leads to a common assertion that the black characters were the butt of the comedy. Whilst there is certainly truth in this, it is an over-simplification; all the protagonists were in blackface (including the smart straight-man). This comedy format was as influential as the music: it was the origin of cross-talk 'patter' and arguably the first comedy which involved a team – Mr Interlocutor, Tambo and Bones are the very heart of sketch comedy, and would have been a key influence on Karno.

I have a Moore and Burgess joke book from 1898 which includes many corny gags you will still find in Christmas pantomimes today, but these early sketch comedians were capable of surreal ideas too – here's a lovely example: 'I've seen it so cold that the words would freeze in your mouth. I've seen the footpath covered with conversation, and we had to take the conversation into the house and put it in the frying pan … to know what we were talking about.'[16] Still think surreal comedy was invented by the Goons?

Despite the way we look upon blackface today, the music hall world was far more inclusive than society at large. On stage, people of colour, women and gay performers (all of whom were treated like second-class citizens in everyday life) became heroes. Their antics were restricted only by the public's degree of tolerance at a time when surprising things were capable of causing offence, as these reviews reveal: 'The gymnastic performances of the Three Karnos were very clever. Though it was quite unnecessary to put one of them into (exceedingly brief) petticoats.'[17] And: 'With fun and skill combined and displayed on the horizontal bars. The cleverest of the part however … adopts the objectionable practice of putting on petticoats. Without them he would be just as much admired.'[18] Karno's memoirs include a photograph which suggests he was the one in drag and it's worth noting that he was already being singled out as the best of the trio.

By the time those memoirs were published in the late 1930s, blackface was out of fashion and a growing number of groups (at least in America) were fighting against the racial stereotype. This may be why Karno wiped Moore and Burgess from his personal history – or perhaps it was because one of their chorus girls would later cause the destruction of his family.

4.4 Fred Karno 'in skirts'.

This omission is so significant that we need to be sure that Moore and Burgess really did engage Karno's new trio and not the original Three Carnos – so, what evidence do we have? First, the most obvious – Karno with a K not a C. As an established act the originals would not have made that mistake in their billing, and a typing error would not have been repeated week after week in several newspapers. Second, Dick Warner advertised future engagements for the original Carnos in November 1888 and Moore and Burgess was not one of them. Interestingly, Gallagher noted that Karno once had a solo engagement

4. THE THREE KARNOS

as 'Sambo the Slave' in a John M. East production of *Uncle Tom's Cabin*, at the South London Palace, and whilst I have been unable to find any corroborating evidence for this strange diversion, a Karno sketch did appear there in January 1895.[19] Moore and Burgess sometimes included a version of *Uncle Tom's Cabin* in their show, so Karno's ability to take on the part adds to the evidence that he had played with the Minstrels.

The Three Karnos worked hard. Whilst playing a matinee and one evening performance at St James's, they also performed later slots at two other halls in the same evening. Their last Moore and Burgess performance was 19 January 1889 after which they toured the provinces with *Summer Boarders* – which means that we can justifiably record it as the first Karno sketch.

So much for Karno the performer – what about Karno the man? Karno said nothing about his personal life in his memoirs whereas Gallagher focused on Karno's tempestuous relationship with his first wife; which brings us to how (and when) Karno met Edith Cuthbert.

Gallagher thought that rather than Christmas with Moore and Burgess, the Three Karnos broke up and took separate engagements in Christmas pantomimes around the country. Karno supposedly appeared at the Theatre Royal, Stockport; where he met and fell in love with the demure girl in the box office. He describes the briefest of romances: Karno, unpopular with Edith's parents, supposedly dragged her away to London to get married six weeks later. We now know that Karno was nowhere near Stockport that Christmas but, to remove all doubt, the Stockport pantomime that year was *Sinbad The Sailor* and Karno is not listed in the cast.

One thing is certain: Edith Cuthbert and Fred Karno were married at Lambeth Register Office on 15 January 1889 (the same week they finished with Moore and Burgess) – so something doesn't add up. Is the year wrong? Did Karno appear in pantomime at Stockport in December 1887 rather than 1888? Plausible but impossible: the Stockport Opera House (as it was then known) burnt down at midnight on 25 August 1887 and wasn't rebuilt until June 1888 (when it was renamed the Theatre Royal). So, when did Karno meet Edith? The answer to this puzzle is in that missing year of Karno's story, between March 1887 (when he apparently left the Aubreys) and May 1888 (when he appears on Poverty Corner), but it isn't easy to straighten out.

We need to trace the Four Aubreys through that same period to find the answer. They had returned from their European disaster and reformed as a quartet in spring 1888: I believe this was Bob Aubrey, Zulia, Karno and a new recruit named William Morganti. Although Karno claimed that he left them when they came back to England, I believe he was with them that summer, not least because on 27 June they performed at the Opera House, Stockport,[20] which must have been when Karno met Edith.

Edith Blanche Cuthbert was born at 3 Green Lane, Heaton Norris, Stockport, on 19 January 1871; the daughter of John (a rope maker) and Ellen (a washerwoman), she was hardly from theatrical stock.[21] She met plenty of performers though, because the family let their spare rooms as theatrical digs – no doubt this led to her job in the Opera House box office.

So, let's assume Karno played the Opera House with the Aubreys in late June; even if he'd lodged at Edith's house, a week later he'd have been off to their next engagement – hardly time for love to blossom. However, another man's misfortune gave Karno the chance he needed. Bob Aubrey's luck with assistants was not improving and at the People's Hall, Manchester, on 20 July, Morganti badly broke his leg. They lost the next three weeks' work (presumably while they found a replacement) and, with nothing better to do, I believe Karno took the opportunity to return to nearby Stockport and court Edith.

The Aubreys resumed their northern tour at the Princess Theatre, Leeds, on 22 August; by then Edith and Karno must have been in love, but Edith could hardly give up her job at the Opera House and run off with a travelling acrobat. Now it was her turn to benefit from others' misfortune: three days after Karno went back on the road, the Opera House burnt to the ground and Edith was out of a job. It seems entirely plausible in those circumstances that her new boyfriend persuaded her to run away with him and his acrobat friends. At least that's my theory – if I'm right, then it was a whirlwind romance, and she did leave home just a few weeks after meeting Karno. She was just sixteen,[22] five years his junior, so it's probably also true that her parents didn't think much of their future son-in-law or his career choice.

After a week in Huddersfield the Aubreys headed for the bright lights of London, and a two-week engagement at the Middlesex Music Hall; and that, ladies and gentlemen, is how Karno finally arrived in London in early September 1887 – still with the Aubreys and with Edith by his side. By this time, reviews reveal that the Aubreys are now comedic sketch artistes: 'Four Aubreys … will perform their original, comical, and classical speciality: – the Hotel – The Stranger – The Unwelcome Visitor – Imagination – The Denouement – The

4. THE THREE KARNOS

extraordinary finale being their unparalleled performance upon the double horizontal bars.'[23] Karno was evidently an experienced sketch performer by the time he left Aubrey.

So, what happened next? The only thing we know for certain is that nine months later Karno persuaded Bob Sewell and Ted Tysall to play the Met masquerading as the Three Carnos. We can't trace Karno through this period, but the Aubreys played in London until the end of September then returned to Europe (apart from a two-week appearance as a speciality act in pantomime, in Leeds in January). On their return to London in April 1888, they advertised: 'Just concluded most successful Continental Engagements at Somossy's Orpheum, Budapest; Danzer's Orpheum, Vienna; Folies Bergère, Paris ... La Scala, Antwerp.'[24] On 23 April they appeared at none other than the Metropolitan Music Hall, where they played every night for the next three weeks — which means that they were at the Met. the week before the Three Karnos' debut.

What does this mean for our story? Well, it seems certain that Karno was still with the Aubreys through the summer and autumn of 1887, during which time he met Edith and came to London. So far so good. There are two possibilities as to what happened next: first, when the Aubreys returned to Europe, in September 1887, Karno could have stayed in London with Edith and scratched around for eight months before meeting Ted Tysall and Bob Sewell on Poverty Corner, the following May, which seems unlikely: how did they survive as strangers in a big city? There is no evidence of him appearing as a solo act and his memoirs suggest he teamed up with the others straight after leaving Aubrey. The more likely possibility is that he (and Edith) stayed with Aubrey for this second European tour, returning in April 1888 and playing the Met.[25] with them. If so, the European tour Karno wrote about in his memoirs was in fact two tours (it may even have been during the second one that things went horribly wrong).

Now let's think again about Maurice de Frece asking Karno to step in for the Three Carnos at the Met. Is it likely that Dick Warner and De Frece would entrust this important bank holiday booking, amongst a bill of top-class performers, to an unknown young stranger with no troupe and no equipment? Or that Warner would run the risk of trying to pull one over William Bailey? Isn't it much more likely that when the Three Carnos couldn't get to the Met, Dick Warner (or even Bailey the manager) would have turned to the acrobatic troupe that had just played a three-week engagement there and ask them to do another week? But the Aubreys must have been committed to another continental tour (they disappear from the listings for the next eight weeks); so, what does Bob Aubrey do? He recommends our hero. This would also explain why Karno 'borrowed' Aubrey's equipment. With Bob Aubrey's recommendation, Warner would have been likely to give them a chance, and Bailey had seen Karno perform there with the Aubreys during the previous month. In those circumstances the only plausible explanation for them to appear as the Three Carnos would have been to save Bailey having to reprint all his programmes and posters. So, a week after performing with the Aubreys at the Met, Karno is back with his two recruits as the Carno imposters. That's what I think really happened – but it's just a theory.

Edith had been travelling with Karno (initially with the Aubreys and then with the Three Karnos) since August 1887; it was perhaps inevitable that she would end up on the stage. Both previous Karno biographies make no mention of Edith's career but, with the stage name Winnie Warren, she became a capable performer in her own right. She first appeared, aged seventeen, as a 'serio comic' at Vento's Varieties, Portsmouth, in late June 1888 (the week after the Karnos debut run at the Met). She then disappears from the listings for over a year, no doubt helping behind the scenes with the Karnos while working on her own act. In the meantime, after an eighteen-month engagement, Karno and Edith were married, in Lambeth (in January 1889). A few months later, a mile or so away in East Street, Hannah Chaplin gave birth to a boy who was to become Karno's greatest protégé and the most famous comic the world has ever seen.

On their marriage certificate Edith put her age as twenty-one and Karno claimed to be twenty-three; in fact Edith was just a few days shy of eighteen and Karno wouldn't be twenty-three for another two months. Ted Tysall and his wife Mary acted as their witnesses. History, or Gallagher's version of it, has recorded Edith as a gentle soul, attractive, petite and sweet natured; in truth, the new Mrs Karno was every bit as tough as her husband.

4.5 Edith Karno (courtesy Louise Murchison).

4. THE THREE KARNOS

There was no time or money for a honeymoon, it was straight off to provincial engagements, beginning with a week at the Pavilion, Swansea. Life on the road was tough: moving from town to town, staying in damp, flea-ridden digs and scraping by on meagre wages. Like all artistes, the Karnos travelled on Sundays and rehearsed the next day – Naomi Jacob described her own experience of those Monday mornings:

> They are uninspiring affairs. The curtain is up, and the "house" is swathed in dust-sheets. Here and there cleaners move about, going through mechanical movements with brushes and dust-pans. I don't think they ever actually clean anything. The band is ready, they all look slightly depressed and very untidy … The performers trickle down … it is a matter of "first come first serve" … all except the wretched acrobats who, if they want to rehearse with their apparatus, must wait until the rest have all finished and the stage is clear.[26]

In Bud Flanagan's autobiography he recalled a story told to him by comedian Billy Bennett (two great comedians with Karno connections we will come to later): 'When he [Bennett] was a small boy, the great Eugene Stratton took him on his knee and asked him what he wanted to be. "An acrobat," said young Bill without hesitation. Stratton shook his head. "No son, don't be an acrobat; they're the labourers of our profession."'[27] One wonders if Stratton had in mind the tireless work of the Karnos in the Moore and Burgess Christmas show.

The Three Karnos spent the next five years together in this form and, as they toured the music halls of Britain, one of their members began to stand out, as this review reveals: 'A very lively turn is that of the Three Karnos, whose energetic, skilful, and agile horizontal bar show is continually enlivened by the doings of a capital clown who knows how to keep an audience amused.'[28] I think we can say with some certainty that it is Karno leading the comedy element of the performance, with his experience of circus clowning and the Aubreys' sketches.

The trio were usually in work but there are occasional gaps in the listings, so they were always on the lookout to supplement their income. Both Tysall and Karno played the mandolin and Sewell apparently had a good singing voice so, with their extensive repertoire of one song (*Funiculi Funicula*) they decided to try their hand at busking. Karno claimed the trio could earn forty shillings a week playing the streets of the West End, and on Sundays they would go further afield, to the locks on the Thames – Richmond, Teddington and sometimes as far as Molesey (fifteen miles up-river). Molesey was just thirty-five minutes from Waterloo and a popular place to escape the city and mess about on boats. The area had plenty of other attractions: a picturesque weir; the wooded tranquillity of Tagg's Island; the Tudor magnificence of Hampton Court Palace; Hurst Park racecourse; East Molesey Cricket Club; and Kempton Park. David Garrick, the famous Georgian actor, once had a grand house there, establishing the area as a playground for the theatrical set, including J.M. Barrie and T.S. Eliot, who both found it an idyllic place to work.

4.6 A rainbow heap – boaters at Molesey Lock (author's collection).

The sheer number of visitors in summer was extraordinary and Molesey regatta was considered second only to Henley. During the 1895 event 4000 boats passed through Molesey lock.[29] In *Three Men in a Boat* (1889) Jerome K. Jerome described the scene:

> The busiest lock on the river. I have stood and watched it sometimes, when you could not see any water at all, but only a brilliant tangle of bright blazers, and gay caps, and saucy hats and many-coloured parasols … and streaming ribbons … when looking down into the lock … you might fancy it was a huge box into which flowers of every hue and shade had been thrown pell-mell and lay piled up in a rainbow heap.[30]

It was rich pickings for our intrepid buskers, who would invite the boaters to pop their offering into a fishing net thrust at them from the bank. One evening the trio were told to clear off by some local busybody and, as they made a hasty retreat, Karno declared that one day he'd buy Tagg's Island: "That would show 'em!" It was an idea which grew in his mind and would one day be his undoing.

5.
How About a Sketch?

"I am an officer and a gentleman."
"You are not an officer!"
"Certainly I am. I'm captain of the bicycle club."
(The Yap Yaps, 1908)

KARNO'S MEMOIRS recount how the trio went on to secure a tour of southern Europe, and although he is not clear on the date or the year, he recalls that they returned to Britain on Derby Day. Their first engagement back on home soil was supposedly at Dave Barnard's Amphitheatre, Portsmouth. This is a key moment in Karno's story as, while they were there, a boxing exhibition between the 'Mace brothers' had to be cancelled and Karno came to the rescue, suggesting to Barnard that they stage an improvised version of an old circus routine called *Love in a Tub*.

The Amphitheatre was an old-style music hall, still boasting a chairman, which had developed on the back of the Old Blue Bell Tavern on St Mary's Street. It was a raucous hall with an eclectic clientele of sailors and merchants from all corners of the Empire. Barnard must have been panicking when the Maces pulled out and the rabble were denied a punch-up, so he jumped at Karno's offer. The trio roped in another comic on the bill, Tom Leamore, and, with very little rehearsal, staged the sketch to rapturous applause – much to Barnard's delight. Karno singled out Leamore for his contribution to its success, recalling how at one point he brought on a live goat with candles tied to its horns, to much amusement. Inexplicably, Karno recorded this as his first sketch experience, claiming that at that moment he had an epiphany and realised his future lay in comedy.

Love in a Tub was a staple of the clowns' repertoire (Karno had performed it with Manley's) and it appears regularly in listings of the period. The week before Karno staged it, it was being performed by a company in Dover (where *The Era* described it as a 'laughable ballet') and in September it had appeared at the Dalston Coliseum (billed as a 'ballet d'action'); yet we know very little about it. As far back as 1664, *Love in a Tub* was the title of a Restoration comedy by Sir George Etherege (also known as *The Comical Revenge*) which, according to one review, 'did much to elevate comedy from mere buffoonery'[1] and this may have been the basis of the subsequent circus routine. Charles Lauri, a well-respected Drury Lane pantomimist, recorded suffering an accident whilst performing *Love in a Tub*, which gives us a glimpse of what it was all about and a sense of Karno's physical comedy:

> I was enacting the part of an old man in a pantomime called 'Love in a Tub'. In a certain scene a number of soldiers fire a volley at my feet, the effect of which is supposed to blow me out of sight, my shattered remains falling from the 'flies' immediately after. On this particular night … I was pulled up to the flies by means of an invisible wire … worked by India rubber springs … up I went quick as lightning. The men in the flies failed to catch me, and … I fell, like a monkey on all fours, rebounded from the boards, something like 10ft, to the back of the stage, but managed to pick myself up and make my accustomed bow … I did not recover from the effect of that jump for four months.[2]

Karno was clearly not breaking new ground with this 'improvised' sketch, but did probably save Barnard's Amphitheatre from being ripped to shreds by an angry mob – all those involved received an extra ten shillings as a reward. According to Karno, a few weeks later they appeared at the Gaiety, Birmingham, which was run by Dave Barnard's brother Charles, who supposedly asked them to repeat their sketch performance. The Gaiety (in Coleshill Street) was another old-fashioned hall, with a legendary chairman called Harry Hendricks. Karno recalled how with a Brummie cry of: "Now then, yo' lads," Hendricks could bring the most boisterous audience to order. Karno was initially reluctant to re-stage *Love in a Tub* as he thought it was rough and ready, but Barnard's offer of an extra ten pounds quickly changed his mind. Tom Leamore's place was taken,

5. HOW ABOUT A SKETCH?

with equal success, by a skilled visual comic called Rick Klaie, who had a 'leg-mania' act.[3] Klaie and the Karnos then toured on the same circuit in Scotland where they worked up an original sketch, *Hilarity*. They returned to the Gaiety to premiere their new creation and Karno never looked back. Unfortunately, as usual, the real story is not as neat as Karno's account.

We have already established that the Karnos' first sketch was actually *Summer Boarders*, which they continued to perform throughout 1889. In September, a year after her debut, Edith reappeared in the listings – billed as 'Premiere Tyrolean Vocalist and Serio' – and her advertisements reveal that the Karnos were now living at 83 Page Street, Westminster. So, what of the *Love in a Tub* story and the subsequent first original sketch, *Hilarity*? Let's attempt to piece together an accurate course of events.

There are two gaps in the Karnos' listings during 1889: the whole of June and four weeks from late September into October, suggesting that one of these periods must have been the European tour Karno recalled (although neither ends around Derby Day). October seems the most likely since this was immediately followed by a three-week run on the south coast.

Karno recalled the tour as starting inauspiciously: a week across country to Naples by train, cooking their meals on a camping stove, and sleeping in a third-class compartment which Karno described as 'a pig sty on wheels.' The journey may have been rough but it wasn't all bad; accompanied by their wives, they enjoyed discovering the food and wine, and taking in the sights of Pompeii and Capri. From the dressing room window of their Neapolitan music hall they watched Vesuvius, five miles to the east, rumble and glow (its lava flows were bright enough to put on their make-up by). Then it was over the Alps to Lyon, after which Edith, Elizabeth Sewell and Ted and Mary Tysall all headed home by train,[4] whilst Karno and Bob elected to cycle back to England. Karno had bought himself some new cycling breeches in London for the occasion, so they must have planned this final leg of their adventure from the outset. After 337 miles, Sewell and Karno arrived in Dieppe, extremely saddle sore, covered in mud, and with their cycling breeches in tatters – they spent the boat journey as embarrassed as they were uncomfortable. Despite this undignified arrival, he described returning full of energy and extremely positive about the future: 'The summer breezes blew gently round the hole in the seat of his pants. But he didn't care. He had life, youth, health, and engagements ahead, a moderate success behind him, and the firm belief that much greater success would be his for the taking in the near future.'[5]

They then appeared for a week at the Royal York Pavilion, Southampton, followed by the two weeks at Barnard's Amphitheatre (meanwhile Edith performed at the Portsmouth Gaiety).

Tom Leamore was on the Amphitheatre bill for their second week and the Mace brothers appeared there a few weeks later[6] (probably fulfilling the engagement they were forced to cancel), both of which suggest that we have the right date. The night in question was therefore 4 November 1889,[7] but importantly, the Karnos are listed as performing *Summer Boarders* so, whilst *Love in a Tub* may have been an unrehearsed filler, they were already billed as a sketch company.

So, did Karno then go on to repeat his success at Charles Barnard's Gaiety Concert Hall in Birmingham a few weeks later and then write *Hilarity*, with Rick Klaie, whilst touring Scotland? Well, Karno did appear at the Birmingham Gaiety in late December, but

5.1 Miss Winnie Warren, Tyrolean Vocalist – Edith Karno in costume, 1901 (courtesy Louise Murchison).

his account immediately unravels: Rick Klaie was not on the bill, there is no mention of a sketch in the listings, and the Karnos did not go on to Scotland. They toured all over Britain through the winter, and the following spring were back on the continent, advertising themselves as 'the greatest and funniest bar performers extant and Champion Mandolinists now appearing with terrific success Folies Bergère Paris, fifth week and re-engaged until further notice. Warner & Co.'[8] and: 'The pets of Paris ... the Comicalists of Comicalists ... a new sketch in preparation ... Every afternoon Eiffel Tower.'[9]

Karno makes no mention of this Paris engagement in his memoirs, which is surprising since the Folies Bergère was a significant venue and Paris was at the centre of La Belle Époque, a golden age for the arts. Karno's appearance at the Eiffel Tower would have been memorable too – it had only been open a year. Surprisingly, 'another sketch in preparation' was not, as you might have expected, *Hilarity*. When they returned to England (in April) they had a new routine called *The American Boxing Ball*,[10] which must go down as the second Karno comedy routine of note:

5. HOW ABOUT A SKETCH?

> The three Karnos … introduced … their "lively ball," challenging any two of the audience to come onto the stage and try and hit it. Two young fellows responded; one got on fairly well … but the other youth didn't know his antagonist's strength, and so had to pay for his experience. All confidence, he squared up to the ball and hit straight out from the shoulder with his left, and then … he followed up, got it full in the face, and was on the floor immediately. When the young man arose … he looked a bit crestfallen and went for the lively ball in much more wary fashion. Improving upon acquaintance, and, being cheered by those in front, he forgot his lesson, and once more hit hard a good slogging blow, but it was all the worse for him, for back to him came the ball, and the face and floor proceeding was repeated. This ball caused, perhaps, more genuine amusement to the audience than any item in the bill.[11]

Karno credited this routine with teaching him that an audience would always laugh at someone else's misfortune, although it's a wonder he wasn't on the receiving end of a left hook from the embarrassed bruiser.

In August 1890 the Karnos appeared again at the Gaiety, Birmingham,[12] and this time Rick Klaie was on the same bill, so this must have been the week they restaged *Love in a Tub* (although they are again billed with *Summer Boarders*). The Karnos then continued to tour with *Summer Boarders* and *The American Boxing Ball* and listings increasingly referred to them as 'musical eccentrics', 'musical grotesques' and even 'grotesque marvels'. They finally arrived in Scotland the following spring.[13] In March 1891 they were at the Britannia Music Hall, Glasgow, where the musical element is mentioned in reviews: 'A clever and amusing sketch, in which they introduce a comical double bar act, and some pleasing playing upon guitars.'[14] They then played towns in both England and Scotland,[15] before we find them back at the Birmingham Gaiety on 27 June. This is the most likely debut for *Hilarity* because Klaie is also on the bill. The sketch was not quite fully formed though, and it began life under a different title: 'He Knocked Them – performed by Messrs Klaie and Karno's company.'[16]

The Three Karnos don't appear in the listings throughout the whole of the following month apart from popping up at that year's 'Musical Hall Sports' competition at Stamford Bridge. His backside-punishing trip back from Europe now a mere memory, Karno won the two-mile bicycle handicap and the 'Eccentric Bicycle Race' – by coming last. So he appears to have taken a break to develop *He Knocked Them* into its final form, *Hilarity*, but he had another reason to down tools: on 27 July 1891 Edith gave birth to their first child, Frederick Arthur Westcott.

Gallagher claimed that during these early years Edith worked tirelessly behind the scenes, with Karno forcing her to clean the stage after each performance and pander to his every whim. The truth was rather different; Edith was her own woman and made of stern stuff. 'Winnie Warren' was often not even performing in the same city as Karno, never mind the same theatre waiting on him hand and foot; besides, cleaning the stage would have been the responsibility of the stagehands not the artistes. Edith was billed as: 'Charming Serio Queen of all Tyrolean Vocalists' and her solo reviews noted her as 'an accomplished comedienne'.

Gallagher claimed that Karno refused to let Edith rest, forcing her to work throughout her pregnancy, but once again the listings exonerate our man. Edith's last engagement was four months before the birth and she did not work again until December. At a time when no work meant no pay, this must have put pressure on their finances, but they were rewarded with a healthy baby and their happiness was complete. Fred Junior came into the world at 1 Napoleon Terrace, Bell Street, Nottingham, the home of Edith's sister Mary (known as Polly) Mosley. It was here that Fred Jr. spent much of his early life whilst his parents were away on tour, although the Karnos did make a home of their own in London, at 115 Page Street, which the 1891 census reveals to be a tenement they shared with five other families.

So, Karno became father to two new babies that summer – Fred Jr. and *Hilarity* – and his good luck continued when he secured a large London hall in which to stage the finished sketch for the first time, the Westminster Aquarium. When it was built in 1876, the Aquarium was envisaged as one the grandest and most ambitious pleasure palaces of its day, with lofty ambitions as an entertainment centre for polite society and, at its heart, the Victorian fascination with the natural world. A 150,000-gallon water tank, for swimming and diving exhibitions, was surrounded by a 'winter garden' where visitors could promenade amongst

5.2 Fred Karno Jr., 1910 (courtesy Jane Koszuta, www.theroyalzanettos.com).

huge tanks full of crocodiles, whales and walruses. In the evening, music hall acts performed on the main stage, but there were also art galleries, billiard and reading rooms, classical music recitals, flower shows and trade exhibitions.

Despite good intentions, a few years after opening the Aquarium faced financial disaster and turned to more populist entertainment. Under the management of a Mr Farini the 'scientific' exhibits morphed into the sort of circus side-shows P.T. Barnum would have been proud of: manatees exhibited as mermaids, 'friendly Zulus', human cannonballs, and gymnastic displays. As the entertainment went downmarket so did the clientele and it gained a reputation as a beacon for prostitutes and ne'er-do-wells. Enter our heroes, who found themselves in an environment much more akin to a circus than a music hall. With multiple performance areas, they were put to work at varying times, doing their own act as well as helping with other sketches and circus routines. No doubt the artistes working in this melting pot of variety formed the same sort of bonds as the old circus troupes. If one was injured or ill they didn't get paid, and Karno recalled spending two weeks standing in for a sick Italian acrobat undetected, thanks to make-up and a false moustache. It was during this month-long run at the Aquarium that Karno first met future comedy collaborator Fred Kitchen, who later confirmed Karno's story in his autobiography – adding that the Italian was one of a troupe called the Four Polos. *Hilarity* premiered on 31 August 1891, meriting a single line in the *London Evening Standard*: 'The Karnos pantomimists in their laughable sketch Hilarity.'[17]

5.3 The Royal Aquarium, Westminster.

It was twenty minutes of true silent pantomime and for good reason: the law did not allow dialogue in the music hall (more on this later), so Karno used every physical and visual trick in the book to create a comic story in mime. Wordless it may have been but he made sure it had strong characters and a plot, recalling that it was 'crammed with laughs from start to finish … destined to be the vanguard of the afterwards world famous Karno brand of humour.'[18] Karno played an old father figure, Rick Klaie played a girl and Bob Sewell her lover. Karno recalled that it was an immediate sensation and, importantly, he felt he'd discovered a completely fresh approach to this kind of physical comedy, describing it as 'a great deal of rough and tumble acrobatic fun that would have made the older school of pantomimists turn in their graves.'[19]

Audiences were used to seeing at most two comics with a cross-talk routine and a couple of comedy songs (although American duo the Two Macs are credited with introducing a heavy slapstick element to this in the 1870s and another famous American duo, Weber and Fields, had a similar slapstick approach). Karno raised the stakes by delivering a quartet of comics (the Karnos and Klaie) knocking each other about and including a storyline, as this review reveals: 'Much amusement is to be derived from the doings of The Karnos who play fantastic tricks in the pantomimic farce Hilarity. A property donkey, a practicable cabinet and a collapsible balcony are all pressed into the service of fun, which runs fast and furious.'[20]

The Karnos were certainly not the only knockabout comedy company on the circuit. We know the Aubreys were doing acrobatic comedy, and Karno noted other peers: Charles Lauri, Paul Martinetti, the Boisset Family and the Leopolds (who had a very similar sounding sketch, *Frivolity*). One group, the Hanlon Brothers (sometimes known as Hanlon-Lees), combined acrobatics and clowning in the halls as early as 1847. As David Robinson notes, a description of their show from 1880 suggests they were a prototype for Karno's sketches: 'It included a bus smash, a chaotic scene on board a ship in a storm, an exploding Pullman car, a banquet transformed into a wholesale juggling party after one of the Hanlons had crashed through the ceiling on to the table, and one of the cleverest drunk scenes ever presented on the stage.'[21]

Karno believed his material was a cut above these competitors and predecessors, claiming it to be faster, slicker and more elaborate – and critics agreed. At a time when most acts played in front of whatever backcloth the music hall decided to hang, Karno, like the Hanlons, used elaborate props and scenery. Later his shows would be famed as some of the most technically elaborate of their era. These reviews are typical:

> A truly hilarious pantomime sketch appropriately entitled 'Hilarity' evokes much merriment. The members of Fred Karno and Co. are graceful and artistic tumblers, and nothing in that line appears too formidable for them. Surrounded by rustic scenery, they fall from a balcony outside a dainty cottage, go through doors, disappear with alarming alacrity, and dodge one another with marvellous dexterity.[22]

5. HOW ABOUT A SKETCH?

And:

> The trick scenery aids the effective finale, but it is the conspicuous ability of the principal members of the company that compels the admiration of the critic surfeited with melodramatic and dull pantomimes. Hilarity is to be seen not to be described.[23]

Karno's memoirs detail a bit of business where a soda siphon spout is connected wrongly, spraying the comic in the face – a classic piece of slapstick. That soda siphon was to cost him dear as we shall see.

> Who can help laughing at the pranks played by the mischievous page who delights in worrying elderly gentlemen and young lovers, and upsets everybody in turn? The tiresome boy is chased by the irate victims … but the punishment intended for him generally falls upon an innocent person. A good deal of fun is also caused by the eccentric behaviour of the animal attached to the little cart which conveys some of the party on to the stage.[24]

Hilarity was Karno's first home-grown sketch. *Summer Boarders* was born of Moore and Burgess, and the comedy punchbag routine was far from original (it appeared for instance in Fox and Fox's *Fun in a Gymnasium* around that time) – perhaps this is why Karno cited *Hilarity* as the beginning of his sketch career.

The troupe spent the next year touring and improving the act. As they did so, their bill matter varied significantly and Fred Karno became firmly established as the leader of the company: 'The Karno Combination', 'The Karno Company', 'The Hilarity Pantomimic and Burlesque Company', and my favourite: 'Mirth making merchants, Fred Karno and his sorrow shifters'. Edith's billing varied too: she reappeared at the New Star, Liverpool, in December 1891, billed as a 'characteristic singer' and performing her own comic songs. Her appearances are notably less frequent during this period though – probably taking time between engagements to visit Fred Jr. in Nottingham. In June 1892 Karno made a triumphant return to the Aquarium, with *Hilarity* now a well-established barnstormer on the provincial circuit: 'The star of the week … a pantomimic absurdity, entitled, "Hilarity," which is brim-full of humour. It sets the audience into fits of laughter … it was splendidly performed by the Karnos … In answer to repeated calls the four artistes came twice before the curtain, but this was not enough for their admirers, who were not satisfied until two of the troupe gave an extra turn, consisting of an acrobatic dance.'[25]

That same summer, Olvene placed a notice in *The Era* seeking work – potential employers were requested to contact him via Fred Karno (who was at the Grand Varieties, Sheffield). Karno was evidently trying to help his old partner find work, which suggests a degree of loyalty to those who had been good to him on the way up. Another advertisement later that year is for a dresser looking for a position, who notes: 'recommended by Fred Karno.' The Karno name was beginning to have a currency of its own.

Meanwhile new elements continued to be introduced into the act: 'The Three Karnos do a capital turn, which includes acrobating, dancing and playing musical instruments; they met with a hearty reception. We liked their gag of "Hey presto changeo to Beero," but we took good care they didn't get our pennies to do their tricks with.'[26] The format of the act may have been dependent on the availability of Rick Klaie since he was not a consistent member of the company and maintained his own troupe at the same time. (It is worth noting here that Klaie had once been in a double act called 'Klaie and Karnes' but, contrary to some accounts, this was not Fred Karno – the similar names are mere coincidence.)[27]

Often the Karnos and the Klaies would appear as separate troupes on the same bill and then perform a sketch together. At Glasgow's Scotia, in December, they were billed as 'The Karno Combination' and performed *Hilarity* as a troupe of seven. Karno soon began to realise the need to establish a consistent larger company.

At Christmas, the Karnos performed both *Hilarity* and the traditional Harlequinade in the pantomime *Bluebeard* at the Shakespeare Theatre, Liverpool. Surprisingly, this was their first (and last) appearance in a Christmas pantomime, and Karno made no mention of it in his memoirs despite it being reported as 'the most novel Harlequinade ever produced.' (The Harlequinade will be explained later, in a thrilling chapter on the history of Georgian theatre.) Despite advertising, earlier in the year, that she was available for pantomime Edith was not part of the *Bluebeard* cast – by then she was expecting baby number two.

The new year brought another chance for the Karnos to show off their athleticism. In February 1893 they took part in the Liverpool Pantomime Artistes' Gala, where Karno came second in the hundred yards dash and Ted Tysall third, Karno won the quarter mile and Tysall was fourth. This may have been a friendly competition, but Ted was getting tired of coming in behind his

5. HOW ABOUT A SKETCH?

old pal. Karno's advancement to self-proclaimed leader of the trio had led to rising tension in the group and Tysall decided to make a break for it.

On New Year's Eve Ted had placed an advertisement in *The Era* proclaiming that he would soon be appearing with singer Cora Carnot and 'a new instrument in hand'[28] – the wonderfully named 'banjomando' (which for the uninitiated is a banjo mandolin). But Karno may initially have persuaded him to stay, for it was some weeks before he followed through with his plan. In February he placed another notice: 'Wanted known. Ted Karno, the clown, comedian, and musical expert, joins Cora Carnot, instrumentalist, shortly. Keep your eyes on them.'[29] Any attempt at reconciliation had clearly failed, as in the same edition Cora placed her own advertisement: 'Cora Carnot the Musical Belle … will shortly take into partnership Mr Ted Karno, A famous comedian and Musical Expert, and will produce a Screaming Musical Absurdity, one you can laugh at.'[30]

Ouch. Cora Carnot had first appeared in listings in December 1891, as a singer who could also knock out a tune on twenty instruments (including the sleigh bells). In July 1892 she was on the bill when the Karnos made their triumphant return to the Aquarium, and she then continued to tour with them around the Moss and Thornton circuit[31] – so who was she? Karno's memoirs reveal all: 'He [Karno] was accepted as the head of the combination everywhere, and this did not meet with the approval of his partner, Tysall, who began to plan a breakaway. One day Fred was passing Tysall's open window and heard him rehearsing a sketch with his wife. Thus it came as no surprise when, a week or two later, Ted gave him two weeks' notice.'[32] Like Edith, Mary Tysall had been forging a solo career under a stage name.

How the Three Karnos managed to complete their final few weeks of engagements without coming to blows is hard to imagine. The last performance by the original trio was at the Swansea Empire on 18 March 1893. Ted and Mary had recruited a third comic, someone they announced as James Karno Della, and immediately advertised themselves as 'The Three Karnos', with a familiar sounding routine: *The Comical Boxing Ball*. However, Tysall must have realised the practical problems this would cause and, after just one week, they became 'The Karno Trio'. They soon came up with some original material (a sketch called *Blunders* appeared a month later) and sought other ways to differentiate themselves – music was a significant component of their act and they were billed as 'musical eccentrics'.

Confusion amongst reviewers, managers and agents was inevitable, and Karno was forced to write to *The Era*: 'Hilarity … Managers should take particular notice that we are not a Trio, but the old established Karno Troupe.'³³ Despite the split the Karnos' engagements continued unabated, suggesting that Karno and Klaie were pooling resources, and their advertising confirms that the two men were sharing management responsibilities. Edith,

5.4 The breakaway – Ted Tysall's Karno Trio perform their boxing ball routine (from the 'A.J.' Marriot archive).

meanwhile, had dropped out of the listings the previous October – she had more important things than yodelling to think about. The day before Ted Tysall left the company she gave birth to another son – they called him Horace: 'March 17th at Nottingham, the wife of Fred Karno, Winnie Warren, of a son, both doing well.'³⁴ New babies and new partners – it was the end of an era.

So, what became of Karno's original two partners? The 1901 census lists Bob Sewell as a gymnast living with his wife Elizabeth and seven children at Peabody Buildings; the same address he'd had when they first met on Poverty Corner. Ten years later the family had moved to Vaughan Road, Camberwell, next door to what was by then Karno's headquarters. Sewell was then fifty and working as a theatre dresser – presumably one of Karno's backroom staff, as was his seventeen-year-old son Alfred (a painter). Karno gave Bob Sewell a job for life.

Tysall's Karno Trio toured for many years and Mary was replaced by a lad who took the name William Karno. They produced several sketches over the next twenty years including: *A Quick Supper, Dinner Hour, The Merry Carpenters* and *A Weekend at Hotel De Quick*.³⁵ They had some success and, in 1897, toured America. By 1911 Ted and Mary were combining performing with running a boarding house in Camberwell but the First World War seems to have brought Ted's company to an end. Tysall died in 1922, aged sixty, in the Constance Road Institution, after being admitted suffering from 'General Paralysis of the Insane' – perhaps his old partner's success was ultimately too much to bear.

6.

The Show Must Go On

"I'm going to be as busy as a one-armed paper hanger with an itch."
(The Football Match, 1906)

SPRING 1893 had been eventful. The original Karnos broke up, Horace was born and Karno was achieving increasing success as the lead comedian in a growing troupe of acrobatic comics. In April they played two weeks at the Middlesex Music Hall, Drury Lane. The first week they performed *Hilarity* but in the second they played a Klaie company sketch called *Over the Garden Wall*. They christened this combined troupe 'Karno and Klaie's Company of Stars', and soon secured an engagement at the Theatre De Vereeniging, Amsterdam. They looked well placed to build on this success but for some unknown reason Klaie suddenly disappeared into thin air. He is never again listed as part of the company or as a solo artiste. In fact, apart from the 1891 census, Klaie is notably absent from any other contemporary records. What became of him, and their partnership, is a mystery.

Edith had returned to work three months after having Horace, but her return was short-lived. Perhaps unable to leave the new baby, she disappeared from the listings again – her break from the stage would turn out to be longer than she expected. With two young mouths to feed, and without Klaie to help run things, Karno worked harder than ever and the troupe was rarely out of work. In August they performed in Hammersmith on the same bill as Charles Chaplin Senior (singing *As the Church Bell Chimes*). In the same month they appeared at the opening night of Farini's new London music hall, the Olympic: 'Karnos, a comic pantomime, was a wild knockabout orgy, marred, however, by one instance of gross vulgarity. This Mr Farini will, no doubt, take care not to have repeated.'[1] I suspect some dropped trousers were involved, probably much to the delight of the packed Olympic gallery if not to the *Evening Standard* critic. Such a poor review was unusual and prompted a response from a rival critic at *The London and Provincial Entr'acte*: 'By-the-way, what was the "gross vulgarity" attributed by "The Standard" to The Karnos? I have seen these performers many a time but have never considered that their doings were marred by grossness.'[2]

Despite the increasing emphasis on comedy, acrobatics remained an important part of their act: 'The feats performed by The Karnos on the horizontal bars are really astonishing, and the house is not backward in showing its appreciation. They also introduce some very clever eccentric acrobatic performances, in which instrumental music plays an important part.'[3] Karno had begun to use a surprisingly highbrow musical accompaniment for his sketches, and experimented to see how music and sound effects could be used to enhance the performance – this comedy soundtrack would become another Karno trademark.

In early September, they performed *Hilarity* at The Star, Dublin, under an alternative title which never appeared again: *The Lover's Serenade*. The following week Ted Tysall followed them into the same theatre. The Karno name, propagated by both Karno's troupe and Ted Karno's Trio, was becoming well known amongst music hall patrons and he even endorsed a brand of 'gymnastic suspenders'. They all pulled their socks up and were literally flying high, with glowing reviews and continuous work, when Karno was suddenly brought down to earth with a bump. Whilst appearing in Brighton, tragedy struck: 'On Sept 27th at Stockport, Horace, the beloved son of Mr and Mrs Fred Karno, aged six months. Deeply regretted.'[4]

Horace had died while in the care of Edith's cousin, John Kay, in Stockport. Edith immediately stopped performing but no work meant no pay, so Karno had little choice but to continue. He was soon back on the continent, appearing in Cologne, Berlin and finally Hanover in early December. The Karnos then appear to have taken a break for two months, perhaps a chance to mourn their lost child and to spend Christmas at home with Fred Jr. They soon had some good news: Edith quickly fell pregnant again, and in the spring their European success was repeated. Their tour began in February 1894 in Copenhagen (where they were billed as 'The Continental Rage'), then it was on to Berlin and Vienna. Touring Europe with a large troupe was not an easy undertaking, and they were delayed for three days en route to Amsterdam (their final engagement) when

6. THE SHOW MUST GO ON

the railway line was washed away by severe weather. They had to continue the journey, through deep floodwater, by horse-drawn wagon. They returned to England ten weeks before the new baby arrived: 'On Sept. 17th at Nottingham, the wife of Fred Karno (Karno's "Hilarity" Troupe of comedians), of a daughter. Both doing fine.'[5] They named her Nellie. It must have been a week of mixed emotions – she was born almost a year to the day that Horace died.

Edith took another two months off while the Karnos continued to tour at a frantic pace through the autumn: Plymouth, Bristol, South Wales and then on to Ireland, before returning to London for Christmas. Edith rejoined *Hilarity* at the end of November but her solo yodelling appearances were now infrequent. Perhaps mindful of the loss of Horace, she wanted to ensure Nellie was well cared for.

Karno now began advertising for artistes to join 'The Karno Combination' – but he remained the principal comedian, risking life and limb for the sake of a gag. In November he suffered a nasty accident in Cardiff:

> A rather serious accident happened … during the interval … two members of the Karno Troupe … were engaged in pumping air into a syphon … the syphon burst and the glass flying about, several pieces struck Mr Fred Karno, the principal member of the company, in the face. The cuts inflicted were somewhat severe and Dr Wallace who was called in, dressed the injuries. The accident, however, did not interfere with the company giving their sketch in the second house.[6]

During the show Karno (the old man) slept in a chair as two lovers canoodled; every time the lovers reached an interesting moment, a mischievous page boy would wake up the old man by dangling a butterfly from a fishing line from a balcony above. On the night of the accident the doctor had enacted a quick repair by sewing up Karno with steel wire, and the fishing hook now managed to get entangled in his face. This caused great amusement among the audience, who thought his scream-ridden attempts to disentangle the butterfly were all part of the fun.

The new year found the Karnos residing at 86 Kennington Road, overlooking Bethlem Hospital (better known as Bedlam) in a neighbourhood popular with music hall artistes. His career continued to go from strength to strength, and he now decided to offer managers an entire evening's entertainment by working with other artistes to put together the bill. Listings suggest that this first attempt at becoming an impresario was short-lived, but it broadened his connections with fellow performers. Such friendships were often strong: most had shared experiences of hardship, and given the anti-social hours and demands of touring, relationships with those outside the industry could be difficult. This camaraderie meant that performers were always quick to support a good cause, and Karno was no exception. In February, the Karnos were back at the Gaiety in Birmingham, and while in the city appeared in a fundraiser at the Prince of Wales Theatre and at a charity sports day in Aston, which included a friendly soccer match against Aston Villa (ending in a ten-all draw). Three Karno artistes, including Karno himself, won honours in various events – and interestingly all called themselves Karno (the other two winners were B. Karno and M. Karno). The name was becoming a valuable asset in comedy circles, and some kept it when they went on to carve out their own careers, such as double acts 'Dale and Karno' and 'Karno and Lester'. According to an advertisement in *The Era*, one John Karno evidently felt he'd been instrumental in devising *Hilarity*: 'Wanted, August Harold [an acrobat], late of the Karno Troupe, to send address to John Karno, late director and sole Inventor of Karno's Hilarity Pantomime.'[7] John Karno's identity is not clear but he may have been Rick Klaie – that would explain both the advertisement and Klaie's disappearance. Perhaps a lack of recognition for their contributions encouraged these comics to strike out on their own. Karno would face similar battles with disgruntled employees throughout his career.

Nellie was six months old before Edith returned to the stage (in March at the Dewsbury Empire), resuming her appearances as both a solo Tyrolean vocalist and in *Hilarity*. It must have been difficult to leave the baby with Polly, as Edith would be far from home. They toured northern England and Scotland throughout the first half of the year, followed by a return to Naples, where their advertising began to include (perhaps not unreasonably) the epithet 'world famous'. They headed north over the next few weeks, via Munich to the Victoria Saloon in Dresden, when tragedy struck again: 'Nellie, the dear little daughter of Mr and Mrs Fred Karno, aged twelve months, Deeply regretted.'[8] Nellie was just ten days past her first birthday when she succumbed to a stomach virus. In a cruel twist of fate, she died on the same day as Horace had two years earlier – the Karnos must have dreaded 27 September for evermore.

Gallagher claimed that on hearing the news of Nellie's death,[9] Edith collapsed and miscarried another baby. He writes that despite this double tragedy, Karno forced her to perform that night – but this seems unlikely to me. Could a woman collapse with a miscarriage then perform an acrobatic comedy act within a few hours? Gallagher added that Karno then left Edith to her own devices and cycled back to England with Sewell. We know this to be untrue: the return from Europe by bike was five years earlier, so accounts have clearly got confused here and we must take the whole story with a pinch of salt.

Edith does not appear in listings from then on, so she may have returned to England to make funeral arrangements, but Karno had no choice but to continue. He had a troupe of people to support as well as himself; he was the leading comic and could not afford to break his contract. It was an age when there would have been little sympathy from management: infant mortality was a harsh fact of life (in some cities the death rate was as high as twenty percent), and the Karnos' experience was commonplace.

So, Karno pressed on with the tour: Darmstadt, Prague, Hanover, Rotterdam. Along the way he almost gave Edith cause to organise a second funeral:

> An accident which might have been serious happened to Fred Karno … appearing at the Mellini's Theatre, Hanover. At the conclusion of the pantomime the hook which supports F. Karno while hanging upside down above the balcony of the house-piece snapped in two, and Fred Karno came to the ground, but his presence of mind in turning in the fall saved him from what might have been a fatal accident.[10]

He laboured on, and returned to London in the first week of December 1895. Karno coped with the loss of two children by becoming a workaholic. He threw all his energies into creating ever more complex, imaginative and dynamic material. His sketches were original, slick, fast, daring and most of all hilariously funny. However, there was one constraint on his imagination – his comedy was silent. Perhaps this is as good a time as any to consider the origins of this slapstick approach and discover what made our hero stand out.

Karno's physical style, sometimes called broad or low comedy, can be traced back to the Ancient Greeks, on through the Italian tradition of Commedia Dell'arte, and from there to the Georgian circus. Pioneers such as John Rich, and Thomas and Charles Dibdin, took Astley's circus pantomimes and introduced them into serious theatrical programmes at Drury Lane, Sadler's Wells and Covent Garden – even David Garrick included them in his productions as afterpieces. Garrick had a love-hate relationship with pantomime – he considered it vulgar and populist but a commercial necessity, lamenting: "If you won't come to Lear or Hamlet, I must give you Harlequin."[11] It's a sentiment that would not be lost on many an artistic director today.

These free-flowing comedy dramas in mime developed a consistent format: the four main characters would first appear wearing oversized heads, before a transformation scene where they would become Harlequin and Columbine (two lovers), Pantaloon (a lecherous old miser) and Clown (Pantaloon's manservant). They would then enact the 'Harlequinade' in which Harlequin and Columbine would be harangued by Pantaloon and Clown. Harlequin had a magical sword that could transform objects at will (a challenge of scenic ingenuity for the theatre carpenters), whilst Clown carried the bulk of the comedy business and acrobatic tricks, with a tendency for ever-increasing larceny. One can immediately see the outlines of *Hilarity,* with its scenic tricks and the same characters: Karno as the old man (Pantaloon) pestered by the page boy (Clown) whilst interrupting the lovers (Harlequin and Columbine).

Georgian pantomimes were bawdy adult affairs and performed all year round – far removed from the children's Christmas shows of today. And the man credited with much of the development of the Harlequinade is Joseph Grimaldi, the greatest clown of the Georgian theatre and still considered one of the most influential comedians of all time (he's the reason clowns are called Joey). Although an extraordinary gymnast, Grimaldi developed a subtler comedy of movement which got laughs without a word being spoken. One reviewer said that his facial expressions were 'an encyclopaedia of wit'. Over the course of his forty years at Drury Lane, Sadler's Wells and Covent Garden, he gradually transformed what had been a pantomime element of a wider programme into a stand-alone show. In 1800 Drury Lane introduced several innovations including a colourful clown costume (Clown had previously worn rags) and a multicoloured symmetrical patterned costume and Venetian mask for Harlequin. The evolution of the clown was completed when Jean Baptiste Laurent donned large flappy shoes, and at Sadler's Wells Grimaldi added the full-face make-up which clowns have worn ever since.

In 1806 Thomas Dibdin, a prolific writer of Harlequinades, was doing his best to move on to more serious work when, late in the day, Covent Garden roped him in for another season. The lack of time meant Dibdin had to place more emphasis on the story and less on the technical trickery. The large heads had to go, songs were introduced to fill the time, and the comic abilities of the actors had to carry the show. The resulting *Mother Goose* became the basis of modern pantomime. It was a huge success, running for ninety-two performances, and made its star, Grimaldi, the first 'celebrity'.[12] Biographer Andrew McConnell Stott noted that Grimaldi's greatest legacy was to develop pantomime into a subtle and complex form: 'Joey had been the first great experiment in comic persona, and by shifting the emphasis of clowning from tricks and pratfalls to characterization, satire and a full sense of personhood, he had established himself as the spiritual father of all those later comedians whose humour stems first and foremost from a strong sense of identity – Charlie Chaplin, for example, Laurel and Hardy, or Tommy Cooper.'[13]

Karno took Grimaldi's acrobatic comedy style out of the legitimate theatre and into the music hall, but why was this an innovation? The answer is also the reason that Karno's comics performed without dialogue – the law of the land had, until then, effectively prevented sketch comedy from being staged on the halls.

Following the restoration of the monarchy in 1660, theatres (previously banned by the Puritans) reappeared in Britain. Initially the King granted patents to just two London playhouses, but gradually more were issued in other towns (these being named 'Theatre Royals'), and various statutes, notably the Theatrical Licensing Act of 1737, established a rigid legal framework incorporating draconian censorship controls. Only these 'legitimate' theatres could stage plays; other venues were able to present pantomime, melodrama, ballet and opera, but only where these relied largely on music and mime to tell the story (such productions did not fall under the licensing act). Any transgression brought serious penalties (a clown called Delpini was once imprisoned for uttering "roast beef" on a minor stage); hence Grimaldi and his peers were forced to rely on physical comedy and visual effects.

The Theatres Act of 1843 removed the patent monopoly, allowing local authorities to issue licences for performance to a wider variety of venues, but with a catch – smoking and the consumption of alcohol were banned. Paradoxically, the same legislation allowed public houses to be licensed for performance, legalising 'saloon theatres' and 'song and supper rooms'. Victorian efforts to clean up the legitimate theatre therefore created its bawdy little brother – the grit in the oyster that became music hall.

Censorship remained: any play with dialogue had to be submitted to the Lord Chamberlain seven days before performance, along with details of the venue, time, location and nature of the production. This was impractical for itinerant performers playing multiple venues with constantly changing bills, so music hall was effectively restricted to singers, variety acts and comics (cross-talking double acts seem to have been the limit of what was acceptable as dialogue). This didn't stop flouting of the law though, and some halls (especially in the provinces) presented sketches, short dramas or parodies of plays, leading to inevitable prosecutions and friction between theatre proprietors and hall owners.

So, sketch companies were barely a feature of music halls until Karno came along with his troupe of madcap knockabouts, bringing acrobatic clowning to a new audience and avoiding the censorship problem by presenting his comedy entirely in mime.

While the Lord Chamberlain policed the theatre, the halls had an unofficial censorship authority who took it upon themselves to bring any morally questionable material to the attention of the magistrates. These Orwellian-sounding 'Vigilance Committees' fought a cat-and-mouse game with performers, who delighted in finding ways to introduce innuendo into their material – much to the delight of their audiences. Perhaps the greatest exponent of this was Marie Lloyd, who could make the most innocent lyric saucy with a mere wink and a knowing smile. In early December 1895 Lloyd appeared alongside *Hilarity* at the Middlesex, on a star-studded bill celebrating the twenty-fifth anniversary of its ownership by J.L. Graydon, and this may be where she struck up what was to become a close friendship with Edith. By then Karno's sketch had been touring for well over four years – it was time for something new.

6.1 Jail Birds – *Top of the bill, 1903 (author's collection).*

Karno set about creating a new routine as the Christmas attraction for George Adney Payne's Paragon Theatre of Varieties, in London's Mile End

Road. For inspiration he turned to the two comical inmates of Nottingham Gaol who had entertained him so many years before, and called his new sketch *Jail Birds*. It opened on 23 December 1895 and was such a success that it ran for eight weeks – unheard of at a hall which usually changed its bill weekly. The Paragon's programme labelled the company 'Karno's Speechless Comedians', and described the sketch as: 'The most original pantomime ever placed before the public.' Everything about *Jail Birds* was on a bigger scale, with elaborate mechanical effects and a cast of twenty, including a chorus of background performers or 'supers' (short for supernumeraries):

> The first scene represents the quarry at Portland. Blasting operations are in progress. The convicts shoulder their pickaxes and begin work, but most of their time is spent in 'larking' and playing practical jokes on the warders and visitors. A gentleman escorting a young lady … loses his watch and chain, and a red faced official is ignominiously hoisted aloft by a crane employed for lifting the blocks of stone, which are also freely used for pelting inquisitive visitors. The scene closes with a tremendous explosion of dynamite, which shatters a wooden bridge … Dinner time comes and the inmates … have their basins filled with an unsavoury looking liquid labelled "paste." Batches of loaves arrive but are so hard that it necessitates the use of a carpenter's saw to divide them … In the final scene, the exterior of the cells, the warder's office, and the carpenters' and barbers' shops are shown. The shaving and hairdressing of the convicts is represented by means of clever pantomime … one of the most agile of the prisoners manages to creep down a chimney and steal from a sleeping warder the keys of the jail. Armed with these he liberates his comrades; the warder awakes and sounds an alarm; and then follows an exciting chase … Walls and floors open as if by magic, to make way for pursuers and the pursued, and finally the curtain falls on an effective tableau. Mr Fred Karno and his company are excellent pantomimists … deserving of the warmest praise.[14]

This sounds like an extraordinarily complex set of scenery, props and effects; one has to wonder how a wooden bridge can be shattered to smithereens twice nightly.[15] It is easy to see why film historian Simon Louvish described Karno's sketches as the missing link between Grimaldi and the future silent-movie comedians.[16]

Sketch companies had begun to pop up all over the halls, but the scale and complexity of *Jail Birds* differentiated Karno from his peers. Reviewers noted that his was a much more sophisticated form of slapstick: one called *Jail Birds* 'an ambitious experiment'. Sidney Theodore Felstead, an early historian of the halls, wrote of the sketch producers: 'Fred Karno … Lew Lake, Joe Elvin, Joe Boganny … and the Six Brothers Luck … are the most memorable of this brigade – Karno easily the best of them all.'[17]

Karno credited George Adney Payne with being an instrumental part of the sketch's success; it was the beginning of a long association and the Paragon became a testbed for many later sketches.

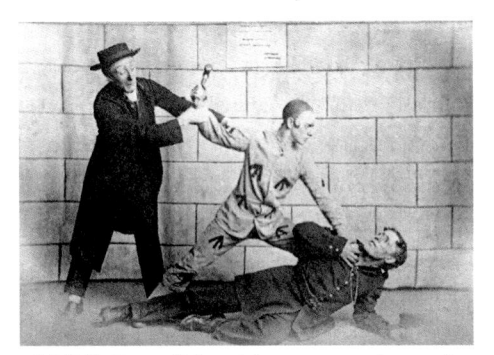

6.2 Billy Reeves fights with a parson and a warden in Jail Birds *(courtesy David Robinson).*

Despite *Jail Birds'* initial success, the Karnos went back to playing *Hilarity* in the new year as a company of six – one suspects that touring such a complex sketch was beyond the fledgling Karno machine. At Easter, the troupe were in illustrious company at the Tivoli, where Dan Leno, George Robey and Eugene Stratton were on the same bill. In the same week they also played at the Met alongside Marie Lloyd. They could now hold their own with the greatest stars of the era and their advertising claimed they had no free dates until 1899. Most artistes would have been content to play this repertoire of sketches until they retired, but Karno was never one to rest on his laurels – he had an insatiable appetite for new projects.

Victorian Britain was the ideas capital of the world, and demonstrations of new inventions were as popular on the music hall stage as any singer or comic. Whilst on a tour of halls managed by the Livermore Brothers, at Bristol, Karno bumped into a sea captain who persuaded him to invest in a new American novelty called a phonograph.[18] He parted with fifteen hard-earned pounds[19] and set about incorporating it into an act. When he first tried it out at the theatre he recalled: 'Artistes who were rehearsing, cleaners, stagehands, all stood in amazement, and presently the manager … came out of his office to join the curious crowd.'[20] In an ill-fitting evening suit, Karno would begin his presentation with an introductory lecture before inviting members of the audience, or other artistes on the bill, to come up and speak into the tube and have their voice recorded onto a wax cylinder – it was an immediate sensation. Although the machine mesmerised audiences (some were too scared to speak into it, believing it to be 'magic'), Karno felt it lacked something. He was first and foremost a showman, and the role of passive phonograph expert was not enough. So he fixed bicycle pumps and fake cables to the machine, which he then operated as though playing a musical instrument. With a final creative flourish, and scant regard for Edison's sensitivities, he christened this contraption 'the Karnophone'[21] (or the Karnograph) and it was well received by critics and audiences alike: 'The specially interesting feature of the evening was the introduction of the 'Karnograph' by Fred Karno, which reproduced military bands, minstrels, and comic vocalists … evoking hearty applause.'[22]

The date of Karno's first phonograph display is unclear: the erratic chronology of his memoirs suggests that it might have been as early as 1892 (Edison invented the machine as a piece of office equipment in 1877). But apart from one or two scientific exhibitions,[23] the first record of a phonograph being presented in any music hall appears to be at the Brighton Aquarium in July 1895, and Karno's first listing with his own machine comes in September 1896 (at the Portsmouth Empire). Over the course of the next few months Karno recalled capturing recordings of many stars, including the greatest comic of his generation, Dan Leno.[24]

Karno had met Dan Leno before (the press reported that he had 'entertained' Leno at a supper party in Edinburgh in October 1892), and like every other comic of that era he was undoubtedly influenced by Leno's style. The greatest comic of his generation, Leno epitomized the sad clown and was the undisputed master of pathos, pioneering the combination of tragedy and comedy which later became Karno's stock in trade. The diminutive comic (he was just five feet three inches tall) had a rubber-like, melancholic face and piercing eyes. Marie Lloyd said: 'Ever looked at his eyes? They're the saddest eyes in the world. If we didn't all kill ourselves laughing at Dan, we'd cry our hearts out.'[25]

In late October 1896 Karno went on record to thank various artistes (including T.E. Dunville, Lizzie Howard and May Evans) for kindly recording their songs on his Karnophone. A month later, he appeared at a benefit concert (along with Eugene Stratton and George Robey) with another incarnation of his toy – 'Professor Karno's Gramophone'. As this new technology became more widespread, the novelty began to wear off and he eventually dropped it completely,[26] but not before appearing alongside the first incarnation of another new scientific wonder in December: 'Special attractions were the phonograph exhibited by Mr Fred Karno and the interesting series of pictures of everyday life shown by the vitamotograph.'[27]

In the days before mass media, a performer could play the same act for their entire career; Karno took the opposite approach – electing to launch a new show when the last one was at the peak of its popularity. It worked. Whilst others toured the same old routine until they struggled to get half a dozen people through the door, Karno packed them to the rafters week after week, year after year. So within a few months of launching *Jail Birds*, he turned his attention to another new show and, in August 1896, *The New Woman's Club* appeared in his advertising. It was then just a work in progress: Karno was merely trying to tempt proprietors and gauge their enthusiasm for the title. There were no takers at first, so he focused on adapting *Jail Birds* for touring. It was relaunched at another George Adney Payne hall, the South London, in October, and Payne went all out to advertise the sketch: 'The funniest thing on earth … continuous yells of laughter. Three specially constructed mechanical scenes. The inside of Portland Prison. Most realistic representation possible. Specially photographed and designed for this establishment.'[28]

That greatest of all showmen, P.T. Barnum, is quoted as saying: "Without promotion, something terrible happens – nothing!"[29] Music hall owners were generally responsible for publicising their shows, rather than the artistes, and some were more creative than others. Albert Gilmer, of the Prince's Theatre, once engaged a hundred men to loiter along the length of Regent Street and discuss loudly how Queen Victoria would shortly pass by, until huge numbers of people lined the pavements in anticipation – just in time for a procession of artistes waving banners proclaiming Gilmer's latest show. Another master of the publicity stunt was Arthur 'AJ' Jefferson, Stan Laurel's father, who was a playwright, actor, light comedian and the lessee of various theatres in the North East. He promoted one of his plays, *The Bootblack*, with a parade by the 'Bootblack Brigade Band', with advertising banners hanging from balloons. He once had a cage driven through the streets containing a lion ripping a man to shreds (a dummy of course), while on another occasion a bloody 'corpse' with a knife in its chest dangled precariously from a hansom cab as it clattered through the cobbled streets, leading the inevitable crowd to the box office.

Not all managers were so proactive, so Karno took the unusual step of self-publicising his sketches. His first wheeze was to spend ten pounds on an old Black Maria he found discarded at Wandsworth Gaol – it was worth every penny, as the press coverage reveals: 'Fred Karno ... has struck a brilliant idea as an advertisement to work with his sketch, "The Jail Bird [sic]." It consists of a real live police van ... driven by a properly dressed policeman with an attendant copper hanging on behind. Quite a big sensation is caused by its standing outside the Washington and Collins' halls this week.'[30]

Karno hired a well-known London cab driver, one J. 'Mouldy' Smith, to drive the Black Maria. Years later Mouldy recalled:

> Fred Karno ... engaged me to drive them to the theatre in a prison van ... There was nothing on the outside to indicate that it was an advertisement, as I was got up in a policeman's uniform. All went well until we reached the Albert Hall, when suddenly, for no reason at all, one of the horses fell down. In a flash the other was on top of him, the van turned over ... a policeman had seen the accident, and he whistled for help, thinking, no doubt, that prisoners were inside, and would try to escape. It was a good joke when the law turned up in full force. It took us some time to convince them that Fred Karno was not a convict.[31]

Karno tells it slightly differently, saying that not only did he adorn the prison van with 'Fred Karno's Jail Birds' banners, he had one of his comics as the driver, with others as policemen or warders, and the rest of the cast as convicts in the wagon. The Black Maria would arrive at the stage door, let the convicts out, and then patiently wait to collect them at the end, as if they were genuine villains. So convincing was this idea that, in rougher areas, Karno's policemen were pelted with rotten fruit and vegetables. This wasn't the only stunt: when the Karnos played a new town, four of the company would dress as convicts handcuffed to prison warders and arrive separately by train. At the station, the convicts would make a break for it, pursued by the warders and (with luck) half the town. The chase would end at the theatre, where banners would unfurl proclaiming 'Karno's Jail Birds'.

In December 1896 Karno felt secure enough to invest in a new base for his growing empire, renting Park House (28 Vaughan Road) in Camberwell from a man called Douglas Young. The house served as both the family home and his administrative headquarters. A few years later (around 1905) he was able to purchase the house and two adjacent properties (26 and 28a), combining them all into one huge complex. He called it 'Karno's Theatrical Factory', but it was known in the profession by many other names: 'Karno's Fun Foundry', 'Hilarity Villas' and the one which has endured – 'The Fun Factory'. It was a name later given to both Mack Sennett's Keystone Studios and Oliver Hardy's private theatre in the grounds of his Los Angeles home, but Karno's Fun Factory was the granddaddy of them all.

6.3 The Fun Factory, Vaughan Road (courtesy David Robinson).

As he established his new headquarters he continued as lead comic in *Hilarity*, supported by Edith – literally:

> Mr Fred Karno the famous pantomimist, during … his sketch Hilarity at the Washington Theatre … narrowly escaped a serious accident. During the rally he is suspended in an inverted position high up on the house piece. The house piece was just about to fall on the stage, the braces having given way, when Mr Marshall Rhodes … rushed to the help of Mrs Karno, who had discovered that the scene was falling. Seizing the braces, she managed to hang on to them till further assistance arrived. Mrs Karno slightly sprained her wrist, and Mr Marshall Rhodes escaped with a contusion. Mr Karno was however, safely released from his dangerous position.[32]

Slapstick chaos off-stage as well as on. When Karno wasn't hanging upside-down he was planning his next sketch, and in spring and summer 1897 a handful of listings appear for *A Day Out*. No detailed review seems to exist but in March, at the Barnard Palace of Varieties, Chatham,[33] it received: 'Fred Karno and Company, in their comic ballet, entitled "A Day Out" are making a score, and their doings are rewarded by cheers so enthusiastic as to leave no doubt of their sincere genuineness.'[34] Despite being well received, this sketch disappeared again, which suggests it may have been a try-out version of *New Woman's Club*.

6. THE SHOW MUST GO ON

Fortunately, he had finally developed *Jail Birds* for a provincial tour which commenced in July:

> The very appearance of Mr Karno's string of convicts invokes a smile, while the antics of the gang as they proceed to work in the quarry convulse the house. Naturally the warders come in for a deal of their mischievous attentions, but they escape very lightly in comparison to the proselytizing curate or the young gentleman who, while visiting the prison, is stripped of his clothes and made to change places with one of the gang. His unavailing explanations to the sceptical warders increase the merriment … cleverly conceived and brilliantly carried out.[35]

There is no mention of spectacular effects in this detailed review, confirming that it was a simplified version of the sketch and therefore more reliant on the individual performances of the comics. They were up to the challenge and by October record houses were being reported. At Thornton's Varieties, in South Shields, their engagement was extended 'at enormous expense'. Whilst there, Karno wrote to *The Era*: 'Rumour has lately been spread that one of my troupe is really a discharged convict … I am asked to give publicity to the fact that none of them has ever been in 'chokey' excepting myself. I visited Portland to gather material for my sketch.'[36] *Jail Birds* had settled in for a long stretch, now he was ready to put all the resources of the Fun Factory into a follow-up.

6.4 Karno at the Fun Factory (courtesy David Robinson).

7.
The Showman

He does business on a large scale – he's a coal dealer.
(The Merry Book of the Moore & Burgess Minstrels, 1898)

JAIL BIRDS was now being listed as: 'Under the direction of the celebrated Fred Karno'. Karno was not just the star comedian but the undisputed director and producer of the show, and as his power and authority increased, so did his resources. The Fun Factory was divided into offices, rehearsal rooms and workshops; behind the house were stables for his growing fleet of carriages and a menagerie of animals. Karno began supplying other people's productions, in both music hall and legitimate theatre, and quickly gained a reputation for quality scenery and effects. Theatre manager Percy Court recalled how he started out in this workshop making scenery for *Jail Birds* – he found Karno a tough taskmaster but added: 'Fred Karno, it is a magical name and, as long as music hall is counted as a form of English entertainment – so will the name of Fred Karno.'[1]

7.1 Karno the comedian – in character for Jail Birds, *drawn by Frank O'Neill, 1897 (courtesy David Robinson).*

In August 1897 Karno had his first, but certainly not his last, appearance in court:

7. THE SHOWMAN

> Fred Karno a music-hall artiste, was summoned by the Excise for keeping a carriage without a licence ... an officer of the Inland Revenue ... saw Mr Karno using a small two wheeled carriage drawn by a small pony. The Defendant then said he was not aware he had to have a licence ... Mr Armstrong: Did he tell you that this was a "trick" carriage used in his sketch "Hilarity" ... that it would take to pieces and pack in a box? – Witness: No. Mr Armstrong: Did he point out painted on the trap "Fred Karno's Hilarity Co."? – Witness: Yes. Mr Armstrong remarked that ... on pulling a string it all fell to pieces ... it was only used by the Defendant for professional purposes.[2]

Karno was fined twenty-five shillings. Notwithstanding minor brushes with the authorities, business was booming – it was only a matter of time before he took the opportunity to double his income. This is how it was reported in *The Era*: 'Mr Karno ... was playing at Dublin, and ... heard ... that Belfast wanted a "top of the bill" ... for that night, as the "star" attraction had suddenly fallen ill. Someone said jokingly to Mr Karno, "why not split our company for tonight, or until they get another turn; half of us can go to Belfast, and it will save the situation" ... the Belfast manager ... jumped at the offer. Since then Mr Karno's companies have been numerous.'[3] This may have happened during their run in Belfast in summer 1896, but the existence of a second company is not confirmed until January 1898, when he advertised for new recruits: 'First class pantomimists, must be good knockabouts, for Fred Karno's No 2 "Hilarity" company.'[4]

Riding high in 1898, Karno decided with characteristic flair to take the whole cast of *Jail Birds* to Epsom on Derby Day. The race was one of the highlights of the Victorian social calendar and he didn't miss the opportunity for some publicity, as *The Stage* reported: 'With some of the comedians dressed as drivers and warders, the remainder of the company as criminals; [Karno] drove to the Derby, creating nothing short of a sensation all along the route.'[5] Karno was not an extravagant gambler, putting just ten shillings on rank outsider Jeddah, but he also generously put on half-a-crown for every member of his troupe. In one of the most extraordinary Derby victories ever, Jeddah won at odds of 100 to 1. The racegoers returned to London in high spirits, singing their way along the Clapham Road in a procession which Karno recalled was worthy of his old circus days: the Black Maria, banners, minstrels and carriages full of merry gentlemen, garnished with the underwear of their wives.

This story is not the only evidence of Karno's generosity: he supported good causes throughout his career. As early as 1896, he is listed contributing ten shillings to the 'Folly Fund' for a paralysed performer. Contributors to such appeals were listed individually in the press – a public display of largesse and an opportunity for publicity worth more than any donation.

Spring saw the second *Hilarity* company head off to play the Casino, in Paris, while number one company finally tackled the sketch that had been on the drawing board for nearly two years. *New Woman's Club* opened at London's prestigious Oxford Music Hall on 30 May 1898, as part of an illustrious bank holiday bill which included Dan Leno, G.H. Chirgwin, Alec Hurley and Eugene Stratton.

The show was written by Karno and comic singer Fred Redfern (the first of many collaborators)[6] and they took their inspiration from contemporary events. 'New Women'[7] were members of the rapidly developing feminist movement, which was proving to be an easy target for comedians. An 1894 song entitled *New Women*, by Herbert Campbell, had mocked the National Vigilance Association's leader Laura Ormiston Chant and her fight against the prostitutes who promenaded in the halls. Campbell sang: 'Oh! A woman is an artful card, if she mayn't promenade, if Mrs Ormiston has to chant, let her chant in her own back yard.'[8] He performed wearing a tweed skirt, jacket, collar and tie, and the implication was clear – these were women who really wanted to be men – but no amount of mockery could stop the rise of the New Women. The Women's Union of Suffrage Societies was founded in 1897, and in an increasingly charged political climate, Karno's sketch was soon the talk of London.

> Fred Karno and his company … are appearing in a new and original pantomime absurdity entitled 'The New Woman's Club' … it is a skit on the ladies … who emulate the opposite sex in every department of life. The New Woman must, of course, have a club of her own … the walls of which are inscribed with various strange legends, and the lady members are … a rollicking set … A stout middle-aged female … is the central figure in the fun … a member of the club returns from a bicycle trip in a muddled condition and tries the sobering effects of a bath … the fun becomes fast and furious when the stout lady mounts the machine and … careers around … She clings to an overhanding chandelier … and … to the horror of her companions, is precipitated through the wall … Comical incidents keep the audience in roars of laughter … In the

7. THE SHOWMAN

course of the entertainment one of the performers, dressed as a woman, enters a bathroom from which he emerges apparently tipsy and partly clothed, an accident happening to his bloomers, which slip downwards, the effect being startling.[9]

The business with the bicycle was itself satirical: American suffragette Susan B. Anthony considered that the bicycle did more to emancipate women than anything else in the world.[10] Karno was inspired by the new breed of female cyclists who ditched their many layers of petticoats and dared to ride bicycles in bloomers (which were known as 'the Rational', espoused by the 'Rational Dress Society') – women were literally wearing the trousers for the first time.

> The new women have engaged a waiter of the most impudent and aggressive type. The fantastic tricks which he plays upon the members of the club are very droll ... An elderly member ... gets into a quarrel with another new woman over a game at cards. They result to physical force to decide their dispute, slapping and kicking each other ferociously. The elderly lady's husband, a thin, timid creature, calls with the baby which he hands to the mother to be attended to; but she gives the infant back to him and beats him angrily out of the establishment ... A comely young man comes to the club, and the elderly lady "goes through" his pockets, afterwards exhibiting her spoils. The young man ... fetches the police. When the latter arrive, they find the interior of the club altered ... to a serious aspect; the ladies clad in black robes, and one of their number playing a hymn.[11]

7.2 New Woman's Club advertisement (from the 'A.J.' Marriot archive).

The Morning Post added: 'their institution becomes the object of a police raid, which is met by such an astonishing mechanical change that the officers are led to think that they have inadvertently strayed on a mothers' meeting, and depart with apologies.'[12] This transformation from the riotous women's club into a staid and sober room was the kind of effect that had been the mainstay of the Harlequinade, as Karno built on the technical wizardry he'd employed in *Jail Birds*.

Although Karno's bill matter at the time was the rather unexciting 'funnier than the funniest', *The New Woman's Club* was imaginative, and in his own words had 'more breadth of treatment'. One of the sketch's henpecked husbands was a young comic called Billy Reeves, who would go on to be Karno's first star. Reeves claimed to have come from a circus family – his mother was a trick rider and his father a lion tamer – so he was no stranger to knockabout clowning. The large elderly lady who rode around the stage standing on the saddle, before swinging off a chandelier and through an oil painting, was Karno – as close as he ever came to playing pantomime dame.

Such an elaborate sketch caused some problems. Since Grimaldi's time, pantomimists had relied on the goodwill of the stage carpenters and crew – they ensured the trapdoors were working and made for soft landings (or otherwise). There are numerous examples of clowns being seriously injured or killed at the hands of stage crew they'd in some way angered. Karno's sets and effects had to be rigged quickly (while a solo artiste played on a front-cloth) and then removed again, twice a night. At a time when most acts turned up with no more than a suitcase full of props and some sheet music, it is easy to see why Karno's troupe might be unpopular with stagehands. Letters in his archive reveal that one way the crew would get their own back was to mix up the 'paste' for the custard pies with urine instead of water – nice. One evening Karno was on the receiving end of a particularly nasty stagehand's revenge: when he swung from the chandelier and through the wall, he found his soft landing (a well-placed rostrum) had disappeared – he crashed to the floor and was knocked out. He managed to recover and complete the sketch, but one can imagine his conversation with the crew!

In August 1898 *New Woman's Club* appeared at the Forester's Music Hall, London; the following week it moved to the New London, whilst another Karno company presented *A Day Out* (which hadn't been seen for eighteen months) at the Forester's. I suggested earlier that *A Day Out* may have been an early try-out version of *New Woman's Club*, but it seems unlikely that he would perform two different versions of the same sketch at the same venue one week after another – whatever it was, it was never seen again. As the sketches toured throughout the summer, Karno's company continued to grow. In addition to the comics on his payroll, he would rope in some locals from each town to make up the crowd scenes.

7. THE SHOWMAN

It was common practice for theatre companies to advertise for such 'supers' the week before a show hit town, and this approach enabled Karno to create impressive ensemble scenes without having to engage too many full-time artistes. He soon began to advertise his troupe as 'Fred Karno's Mammoth Company of Comedians'.

7.3 The nerve centre – The Fun Factory administration office (courtesy David Robinson).

Imagine the logistics of being a music hall artiste at the time: there were bookings to be sought, agents and contracts to deal with, trains to book, music to obtain, accommodation to find, billing to argue over, scenery, props and costumes to source and transport, and all that on top of writing, directing and performing. With a growing number of artistes in his employ, two companies running concurrently, and an expanding theatrical supplies business, it is no surprise that Karno engaged his first business manager, George Hall, in September 1898. This enabled him to focus on new material as well as developing the existing sketches. New ideas and bits of business always suggested themselves during performance, and the shows were also adapted for differing sizes of troupe or venue, which significantly improved their longevity. Karno began extending his sketches into a longer format, and in early 1899 he engaged Chris Davies (who had cut his teeth writing for 'The Brothers Luck') to rewrite *Jail Birds*, which subsequently opened in Manchester in March. The sketch now began with a society dinner party then the burglary, before returning to the convicts' incarceration.

7.4 Rehearsals at the Fun Factory, 1904 (courtesy David Robinson).

Karno continued to look for novel ways to promote his shows and soon had another weapon in his arsenal, as this advertisement from spring 1899 reveals: 'For Sale – Fred Karno's miniature pony trap complete. Reason for selling – have purchased a motor car.'[13] Only the very wealthy could afford a car (there were only seven or eight hundred on Britain's roads at the time), so his purchase was a measure of his success – it was also the beginning of a lifelong love affair with the motor-car. He wasn't the only music hall performer to see the benefits of being able to travel independently from hall to hall, and one fellow enthusiast was another rising star – the comedian Harry Tate. The pair became close friends, although somehow Tate beat Karno to the idea of using the car on stage (*Motoring* became his most successful sketch). Like Mr Toad in *The Wind in the Willows*, Karno would tear around the highways and byways of England sending pedestrians diving into the hedgerows in his wake. His car was more than capable of drawing a crowd on its own, especially in provincial towns, but to maximise the effect he had it painted red and yellow and emblazoned his name on the side – he later christened it 'the Early Bird'.

When the troupe arrived in a new town, he would pull up outside a pub and buy everyone in the place a drink, or give away a few free tickets. Having made plenty of friends he would wave farewell, at which point the car would mysteriously fail to start or get stuck between the tramlines. As his hapless chauffeur (one of his comics) made frantic and comical attempts to start the engine, his comrades would hand out flyers. He developed many similar ruses. One of the company lodged with a Grenadier Guards' trombonist called Victor Smallcalder, who taught the comics to play musical instruments. Wearing elaborate uniforms, Karno's incompetent bandsmen would parade through the town blowing their horns for all they were worth. This cacophony was followed by the rest of the company in wagons (including the Black Maria), and bringing up the rear Karno himself in his colourful car – the 'Convict Brass Band Parade' became a favourite crowd-puller. He had huge balloons emblazoned with 'Fred Karno's Speechless Comedians' float over the parade to drop flyers on the crowd. Often these caused chaos by getting tangled in the overhead tramwires, causing sparks to fly and putting the trams out of action (for which he occasionally received a fine). It was a small price to pay for such publicity.

This showmanship endeared him to both the public and managers – a Karno show almost guaranteed a full house. Before long they were breaking box office records. What he needed now was more material and, in June 1899, at the Royal Albert music hall, he staged a try-out of a new sketch entitled *The Dossers*,[14] which quietly disappeared again. Instead Karno turned his attention to developing a completely different style of show – and on such a grand scale that it wasn't

7. THE SHOWMAN

7.5 Karno's Convict Band (courtesy David Robinson).

ready until the following Easter. Called *Her Majesty's Guests*, it was written and composed by comedian Herbert Darnley, who came with a fine pedigree: he had worked as Dan Leno's musical director. Darnley and his brother Albert had appeared as a double act on the same bill as the Karnos several times that year and had obviously impressed – uncharacteristically, Karno gave Darnley total responsibility for the new show.

Karno prepared the ground carefully: advertising invited proprietors to pre-book and reminded them that his sketches were record-breakers: 'Proof of the pudding – receipts!'[15] He also staged a series of try-outs: the Christmas bill at the London, for instance, included 'Fred Karno's The Burglary',[16] which was actually a revised first scene from *Jail Birds*, being tested for the new show.

While he was developing ideas for *Her Majesty's Guests*, he had also been busy at home. On 27 December 1899, a late Christmas present arrived: 'The wife of Fred Karno ... of a fine son – both doing splendid.'[17] Karno got on extremely well with his new partner (later appointing Darnley business manager for the entire empire), which probably explains why they chose to name the new baby Herbert.

A few months later Karno's other baby arrived: *Her Majesty's Guests* opened on 26 March 1900 at the Princess of Wales Theatre, Kennington. This was no thirty-minute rough-and-tumble music hall sketch, it was a two-hour song-and-dance extravaganza, with a story and plenty of dialogue. Critics were taken by surprise and struggled to define it: some saw it as a sketch, some a farce, others a musical comedy – one described it as 'a pantomime play' – Karno billed it a 'musical pantomimical comedy'.

Walter Groves took the leading comic role (the first time Karno had not fronted a new show himself). Groves was no stranger to the music hall but also had a good track record as a comedy actor on the legitimate stage and in pantomime. His co-stars included Dolly Harmer (who went on to have a long and distinguished comedy partnership with 'Wee' Georgie Wood) and Fred Whittaker (a famously acrobatic Cat in many productions of *Dick Whittington*).[18] Music was provided by the Camille Quartet, and John Donald (a very experienced Christmas pantomime producer) was brought in as production manager. The inclusion of singers and experienced theatre actors was a significant diversion from the previous sketches, but listings demonstrate that, amongst the dialogue, the Karno silent knockabouts were still there: 'Words and Music by Herbert Darnley, Pantomimical Business and Situations Arranged and Invented by Mr Fred Karno.'[19] The slapstick was in the hands of experienced pantomimists including Harry Oxberry (who had been with Karno for three years), Amy Minister and Billie Ritchie.

Theatre actors and audiences believed themselves a million miles away from their music hall counterparts, so Karno's decision to stage the show at the Princess of Wales Theatre wasn't well received by some self-important critics. *The London Evening Standard* could hardly contain its disgust: 'Mr Robert Arthur's playhouse at Kennington is far too fine a theatre to be turned into a music-hall, as it practically is this week by the performance of a piece entitled "Her Majesty's Guests" … a polite reception was accorded the first production last night, but unquestionably the right place for such a harlequinade is upon the music hall stage.'[20] Fortunately the snobbery of the legitimate theatre was not evident in *The Era* critic's review:

> A rather ingenious blending of … The New Woman's Club and Jail Birds … The sketches have been elaborated and expanded by the introduction of new songs, dances, and pantomime business … Leading characters are an adventurer … Lord Hoodo and an adventuress … Lady Maud, who claim to be brother and sister. They contrive to get an invitation to the house of Mr Miffin, an elderly gentleman with a prim wife and a pretty daughter. Lord Hoodo is … the leader of a gang of thieves…His supposed lordship however, falls a victim to the

7. THE SHOWMAN

charms of Dolly Miffin, who is dazzled at the prospect of becoming a titled lady and throws over her humble but devoted admirer Sam Potts. The … first act is the gardens of Winklemere House, the residence of Mr Miffin, and much fun arises from the sayings and doings of P.C. Lightning … with a catch phrase "I'm a watching yer." He has a nimble co-operator in Bunker, a footman, and in this scene the Fred Karno Troupe appear as … burglars, who in chorus sing a parody on "the ten little niggers," which was encored on Monday night … the second act … represents the interior of the New Woman's Club … Dolly is made a member … A game of cards for high stakes is played and Lord Hoodo is detected cheating, which leads to a fistic encounter between him and Sam Potts. Then the alarm is given that the police are raiding the premises, but by the time the representatives of the law reach the club-room the members … are found singing a hymn … the third act is … where Mr Miffin holds a grand reception … Lord Hoodo and Dolly appear. She is about to elope with him, but his lordship's plan is quite upset by the appearance of Lady Maud and Dolly is compelled to return to her bedroom. Then occurs the breaking in … by the comic burglars, who go about their work in such a noisy fashion that the sleeping inmates are aroused, and a fight … brings the scene to an exciting conclusion. Sam Potts, the page Bunker, and the foolish policeman, Lightning, are however, the only ones that are captured, and, being found guilty of burglary, are eventually sent to Portland … Mr Walter Groves gives an amusingly stolid portrayal of P.C. Lightning, and … by rapid changes of dress represents in succession a black man, a Jew pedlar, a pugilist, and an Irishwoman. Later he … cleverly impersonates a West End fashionable physician as contrasted with an East-End doctor, a travelling quack. Miss Dolly Harmer puts much life and spirit into her embodiment of Lady Maud … John Henderson is … Lord Hoodo … Lew Maskell … as Sam Potts, and Mr Fred Whittaker is … amusing as Bunker. Mr Harry Oxberry is an appropriately meek and mild young parson, and Mr George Craig renders energetic … service as Mr Miffin. Mr W. Ritchie is an active Warder Lockem … and Miss Winifred Wilmer deserves commendation for her portrayal of the deaf Mrs Miffin.[21]

The show introduced Karno's first great comic character, P.C. Lightning, a bumbling idiot who would make a name for many great comics yet to come. While the characters were strong, Darnley's story left the critics unimpressed: 'Herbert Darnley ... does not shine as a purveyor of fare for the regular theatres in the present production ... he has endeavoured to string the two sketches together on some sort of story, but we cannot congratulate him on his efforts as a plot contriver.'[22] Fortunately Karno was the greatest visualiser of comedic situations of his generation, and his slapstick contribution carried the show as it set off on tour.

Meanwhile, Britain was in the midst of the Boer War. In May there was an extraordinary collective outpouring of emotion as the country riotously celebrated 'Mafeking Night', when news reached home that the town, besieged for 217 days, had been relieved by British troops. The response to *Her Majesty's Guests* wasn't quite as hysterical – the tour ended on 9 June.

Since this was Karno's first experiment in this kind of show, it's not surprising that it took a while to find the right balance between the various elements. He spent the next few weeks polishing it, and advertised for fresh talent in typical brusque style: 'Must be young and experienced – otherwise useless.'[23] When the show reappeared, in August, two of his new recruits were comics who would go on to rank among Karno's greatest finds: Charles Baldwin, who took on Lord Hoodo (renamed Lord Easem); and Fred Kitchen, who played Fritz and later Warder Keys (replacing Billie Ritchie's Warder Lockem). Reviews rapidly improved when Karno asked Baldwin and fellow cast member John Henderson to beef up the gags, and Alfred Tonne, the musical director, was set to work on the musical elements. Baldwin became a longstanding collaborator and friend: he was a comic and a writer but also acted as stage manager for the tour – and his 'leg-mania' routine was incorporated into the show. His Lord Easem quickly overshadowed Groves' P.C. Lightning (although promotion to comedy sergeant may have softened the blow), and young Fred Kitchen was also starting to get noticed: 'Mr Fred Kitchen's broken English as Fritz was responsible for much of the prevailing merriment.'[24] Perhaps Groves tired of being upstaged by the two new boys – by the end of the year Lightning was being played by Bernard Mervyn.

The show's subsequent success cemented Karno's reputation; he was described by *The Blackburn Standard* (and they should know) as 'a very big star in the music hall firmament'. Unfortunately such plaudits led to a bout of over-confidence. Feeling that he had elevated himself above mere music hall, he

7. THE SHOWMAN

began to seek recognition and respect from the wider theatrical fraternity. The king of slapstick now decided to turn his hand to straight drama – what could possibly go wrong?

An American actor called Nick Hughes persuaded Karno to stage a melodrama called *Marked for Life*. Hughes, billed as 'America's greatest imitator of the Negro characters,' played the lead, alongside George France (who was the author and oversaw the production).[25] After opening on 29 October 1900 at the Victoria Theatre, Walthamstow, it toured northern England, where its exciting story of bank robbers, gamblers, shoot-outs, murder and mistaken identity impressed the critics: 'Nick Hughes as … Skid Stubbes, gives an excellent impersonation of a true-hearted black … Geo. France as Jack Tatters, a hard up poet, author and actor is amusing with his "heavy" tragic business … The great railroad scene, with an express passing through a burning forest is most thrilling.'[26]

An express train in a burning forest? Wow! As one review put it: 'The most wonderful and thrilling railroad scene ever presented on any stage.'[27] Not for the first time, one wonders how Karno's effects were achieved. Despite critical acclaim, *Marked for Life* played to half-empty houses and closed after a few weeks.[28] Karno had made a fundamental error: his name above the door was enough to sell a show, but his audience didn't bother to read the advertising. They knew what to expect – riotous comedy – and when he served up drama they were left disappointed. He candidly admitted his mistake: 'Paradoxically … the name of Karno killed an otherwise excellent play.'[29] We might forgive him this error, since until then everything he touched had turned to gold but there was a silver lining: Karno's sojourn into straight theatre prompted him to include more light and shade in his subsequent comedies – he was about to invent the comedy-drama.

A few weeks before launching *Marked for Life*, Karno had blown the dust off *The Dossers* and staged it under a new title, *Early Birds*. It was a tale of life in the dark recesses of Whitechapel, the haunt of Jack the Ripper and an area with a large immigrant population (including a community of Jewish refugees who had fled the Russian pogroms). It wasn't an easy place to live, as Jerome K. Jerome described: 'There is a menace, a haunting terror, that is to be found nowhere else … The awful silence of its weary streets. The ashen faces, with their lifeless eye that rise out of the shadows and are lost.'[30] The East End was perceived to be a crime-riddled, vice-stricken ghetto, but Karno was no Dickensian moral crusader – he was just looking for gags, and colourful characters to deliver them.

The sketch was in two parts: 'Lively scenes in Whitechapel' and 'The birds go to roost'. *The Era* tells us more:

> The first scene discloses a coffee stall … a flower girl, paper boy, blind man, swell, and eccentric-looking tipsy female … all indulge in much fun of the rough-and-tumble order … Eventually they are joined by an itinerant cornet player … a policeman also engages in the melee, and the curtain falls amidst much confusion. The second half of the sketch takes place inside a common lodging house. Many disreputable-looking loafers turn in for the night, including an old Jew and a young man who is evidently wanted by the police. A member of the force comes in search of him, but he is saved from arrest by the ingenuity of a fellow lodger. Finally, the old Jew is "touched" for his money, after having carefully counted it out and placed it under his pillow. The robbery is at first fixed on the wrong man, but … the "dosser" who has stolen the shekels is stabbed by the Hebrew – a very dramatic finish to a most interesting and smartly performed little sketch … this speechless playlet is really clever, the facial expression, ingenuity, and real humour frequently displayed being admirable.[31]

Dramatic indeed – not many comedy sketches end with a fatal stabbing. Karno was playing with new ideas and working out how best to introduce pathos into his comedy. He realised that the biggest laughs came from situations where the audience could see the mishap about to befall the comic, but the victim could not. He would gradually build on this idea, ensuring that before the comic got the inevitable pie in the face or kick up the backside, he had gained the audience's sympathy and affection. You will have noticed that the sketch included a blind man and a flower girl – and if that isn't a good starting point for pathos, nothing is. Chaplin later squeezed every drop out of a blind flower-seller in his 1931 masterpiece *City Lights* – and as we've already noted, some claim that the old Jewish glazier played by Karno in *Early Birds* may have provided inspiration for *The Kid*.

It was the inclusion of death and drama, played for laughs, that marks *Early Birds* as an important step in Karno's career development. But it still wasn't up to his exacting standards, and for now went back on the shelf while he tried to work out the right balance between pantomime and poignancy. In the meantime, he had genuine death and drama to deal with.

8.
Slumming It

When I married my wife, she was twenty-four
– she would have been twenty-eight,
but she was in jail for four years.
(The Merry Book of the Moore & Burgess Minstrels, 1898)

KARNO MUST have reflected on 1900 as an eventful year both professionally and privately. The Fun Factory had become a fantastically creative environment where he could work on new ideas with his troupe. For Edith it was home, an anchor to their nomadic lifestyle, somewhere safe and secure to bring up young Fred and grow their family. After years of living in shabby digs, she must finally have felt able to enjoy the fruits of their labours. She was to be disappointed – the Fun Factory would prove to be anything but fun for her.

The new year started badly and got worse. On the evening of 22 January 1901, Queen Victoria died; as *The Stage* reported, *Her Majesty's Guests* was playing Shrewsbury: 'The news of the death of Her Majesty did not reach Shrewsbury until close upon eight o'clock … the performance … was abruptly stopped … the manager … announced the death of the Queen, intimating that the theatre would at once be closed.'[1] The show took a week's break then it was business as usual, although the press speculated that an obvious change was needed: 'Her Majesty's Guests, the title of which in light of recent events is rather unfortunate, but will doubtless be amended in due course … a musical comedy … developing as the plot unravels into uproariously funny pantomime.'[2]

Meanwhile Edith and Karno were touring with the *Jail Birds* company. Having lost their last two babies whilst away on tour, they had elected to take

Herbert with them – it made no difference. On 3 February,[3] the day after Queen Victoria's funeral, he died in their arms whilst they were staying in digs in Birmingham. The cause was bronchopneumonia – a winter tour of cold, damp theatrical digs was evidently death's accomplice.[4] The loss of three children in seven years inevitably cast a shadow over the Karnos' marriage: he threw himself into work, she reached for the bottle – and cracks soon began to show.

We have already disproved previous claims that Karno pushed Edith to work while heavily pregnant (and straight after giving birth), and that he was unmoved by the loss of his children. Now we must take a moment to correct a significant miscarriage of justice against our hero. Gallagher documented another son, Albert (Bertie), born in 1894, who supposedly died on the same day as Queen Victoria. He writes a dramatic account of how, on hearing the news of their six-year-old boy's death, Karno insisted that Edith still perform that night. Moments later, news of the Queen's demise gave Edith a reprieve as the show was cancelled – much to Karno's annoyance. A dramatic story, but a complete fiction. Albert did not exist. There is no record of him anywhere in the archives. What's more, if Albert had been six at the time of the Queen's death he would have been born in the same year as Herbert and Nellie, which is impossible unless he was a twin (in which case he would have also been in their birth announcements).

We know that Herbert perished twelve days after Queen Victoria, so if the mysterious Albert did die on the same day as Victoria, Karno lost two sons within a fortnight – highly unlikely. So where does the story come from? Horace and Herbert are not mentioned at all in Gallagher's biography, and this is where I think the confusion lies. Somehow he connected Horace's birth (1893) with Herbert's death (1901) and thought that this was the same person – 'Bertie' (my guess is that he assumed Bertie was short for the more common Albert, rather than Herbert). The Karnos provide the final evidence themselves: the 1911 census records three children lost in infancy, Horace, Nellie and Herbert. There never was a six-year-old Albert and he didn't die on the same day as Queen Victoria: it was baby Herbert that the Karnos had to mourn that spring.

The Queen's death prompted national mourning, with the public directed to wear mourning clothes until 6 March – the Karnos must have felt like the whole country was sharing their grief.

Apart from *Her Majesty's Guests*, Karno's shows ran as normal in the two weeks after the Queen's death but none appeared in the first week of February

8. SLUMMING IT

(coinciding with Victoria's funeral). The following Monday, the day after Herbert died, a retitled *His Majesty's Guests* opened at the Liverpool Grand.

On the 31 March 1901 the national census was taken; Karno and Edith were listed at digs in Kingston upon Hull (*His Majesty's Guests* was at Gateshead). Fred Jr., now nearly ten, was cared for by relatives in Stockport – in this case Sarah Kay, Edith's eighty-year-old great-aunt, who ran a grocery store in Green Lane. Karno's mother Emily and his siblings were still living in Nottingham (at 3 West Street) but Karno's father John was living at the Fun Factory (along with a housemaid) and is incorrectly listed as a widower. The error perhaps supports Gallagher's suggestion that John suffered from dementia in later life and was taken in by Karno. One wonders why Karno didn't take his mother in too. John Westcott died in Nottingham seven years later – how he got back there is lost to history.

Karno was now a wealthy man: he and Edith could have hung up their boots and lived as a family at the Fun Factory, but he continued to lead his troupes from the front. There was no reason for Karno to force Edith into harness – he had fifty other artistes to choose from – but, perhaps not relishing lonely nights in London, she kept working too.

A listing from around this time provides us with the names of Karno's 'number one company': Fred Karno, Edith Karno, Charlie Bell, Billy Reeves, Harry Oxberry, Tom Manardo, Fred Evans, Billie Ritchie and 'Little' Joey Hindle.[5] This group continued to tour the North of England, and in April Edith was reported as kicking off an Empire Day charity football match in South Shields. They supported many similar charity events during the year – in September, for example, Karno's Convict Band led the parade at a charity cricket match at the Oval. Dan Leno was master of ceremonies and captained a music hall side against a team fielded by the whisky magnate Thomas Dewar. Herbert Campbell was umpire and refused to declare his comedy partner out: Leno eventually announced he'd scored 999 and was carried off the pitch. That summer Karno also sat on the Grand Order of Water Rats' subcommittee tasked with opening the 'Vaudeville Club' at 98 Charing Cross Road. The Water Rats was (and still is) a charity which supports those from the entertainment industry in need of

8.1 Early Karno recruit, Charlie Bell (courtesy Donna Tobin).

help – and since the order appears frequently in our story, we should take a moment to relate its illustrious history.

It all began in 1889, when a small racing syndicate led by the music hall performer Joe Elvin procured a pony named Magpie and began staging short Sunday morning street races. One day, when Magpie was returning to stables in torrential rain, a passing bus driver suggested to Elvin that his sodden 'trotter' looked more like a water rat than a horse. Magpie was renamed and became the stuff of legend. After one successful Sunday's racing, Elvin suggested the formation of a charitable fellowship – the 'Pals of the Water Rat' – and the pony's winnings were the basis of their charitable funds. The initial membership of twelve was soon extended to twenty and then forty.

In May 1890 a rival organisation known as the 'Terriers' (which was actually a subscription 'friendly society') was formed. Races between the Water Rat and Boneyard, the Terriers' pony, were fiercely contested but good-humoured. Karno was an active member of the Rats (he joined in 1898 as member 107) but never held formal office – perhaps he was just too busy running his growing empire.

His Majesty's Guests continued to tour throughout 1901, with Fred Kitchen taking on the lead role of Sergeant Lightning. *The Era* noted: 'Premier honours fall to Mr Fred Kitchen, whose comedy policeman is one of the most laughable creations imaginable.'[6] Despite Kitchen's efforts the show was finally running out of steam and, as late as October, Karno was advertising that it had not yet been booked for Christmas and New Year. The same month, he was at Peter Watson's Palace Theatre in Manchester with *Jail Birds* and evidently asked Watson if he would take *His Majesty's Guests*' vacant weeks at Christmas. Watson agreed but must have demanded a fresh version of the show, and Karno spent November on a major rewrite.

8.2 Fred Kitchen as Sergeant Lightning (author's collection).

Although the show had been touring for two years, it was presented as being a new production:

> Mr Fred Karno … has been specially commissioned by the directorate of The Palace Theatre, Manchester, to produce a new big spectacular sketch at that house on Dec 23rd. The attraction will take the form of

a musical and pantomimical extravaganza in novel lines and produced on the most elaborate and finished scale. ... The sketch will form the chief Christmas attraction at Manchester for some weeks.[7]

Despite the major overhaul, Karno did not change the title. He engaged Dudley Powell (the musical director of the biggest musical of the day, *Floradora*) to rewrite the music (although Darnley's *Ten Little Burglars* remained the hit of the show), and revamped the story to include a scene in a department store (Miffin's Emporium), which Karno based on Swan & Edgar in Piccadilly. The Camille Quartet was replaced by the St James Quintet, which was a remnant of the Moore and Burgess Minstrels (which had broken up by then), while a final flourish came with the inclusion of a leggy female chorus, enticingly called the Amazonian Beauties.

Karno knew exactly who he wanted to spearhead this new production. Fred Kitchen had excelled in the previous show, and when Karno asked if he could take on the lead, he replied: "You bet I can Guv'nor." It was to be Kitchen's big break, although he was no beginner.

In 1891 (at the age of eighteen) Kitchen had played his first Drury Lane pantomime as part of a famous cast led by Dan Leno, Marie Lloyd, Herbert Campbell and Little Tich (Kitchen's various roles included the back legs of an enormous pantomime cat). Subsequent appearances included playing Harlequin there in 1896, the year that saw the death of Drury Lane's greatest impresario, Sir Augustus Harris. However, his career had not been plain sailing: he had been frequently out of work or barely scraping by, including a long period of illness with typhoid. When he accepted his first minor role with Karno it was a backward step, so it is easy to see how he quickly came to the fore, and Karno's profile made Kitchen a household name. In his autobiography he wrote: 'It was during this period, when I came to know Fred Karno, not only as ... the producer of world-famous sketches, but as an artist and a friend, that I really created for myself whatever little reputation I have enjoyed in the profession. I had some great opportunities and I made the most of them.'[8]

Kitchen's Sergeant Lightning wore oversized shoes and had a characteristic gait which was enough for him to garner laughs simply by walking on to the stage. He said he based this half-hopping shamble on his father, whose own clown performance had been physically affected by severe gout and rheumatism (although Karno said Walter Groves, the original Lightning, established the walk and Kitchen retained it as part of the character). Costume, mannerisms and style were collectively termed the 'make-up' of a character, and Lightning's was a tour de force – a 'make-up' and a walk that would inspire one or two later Karno clowns too, as we shall see.

The new improved *His Majesty's Guests* opened on 23 December 1901 and played for four weeks,[9] to rave reviews like this: 'The bulk of the humour was sustained by Mr Fred Kitchen, who served it up hot and strong and well-cooked for nearly three hours as the absurd and ridiculous policeman, Sergeant Lightning.'[10]

The Amazonians – tall, fashionable ladies who paraded through Miffin's carrying their lap dogs – made a big impression on critics and audiences alike. Their charms weren't lost on Karno either. Edith was packed off on a tour of the North West with *Jail Birds* whilst he worked closely with the new company – perhaps more closely than was strictly necessary.

One of those leggy Amazonians was a twenty-year-old chorus girl called Marie Moore. Marie was the daughter of Tom Moore, a veteran vaudeville performer from Boston, Massachusetts, who had come to Britain and married an Englishwoman (Eliza). Although Tom worked with Moore and Burgess Minstrels, there appears to be no family connection to George 'Pony' Moore.[11] He came to England in 1877 in a double act with a comic called Monty Collins. They joined Moore and Burgess later that year, and Pony Moore named them 'The Boston Boys'. Tom adopted the stage-name Tom Birchmore and continued with the Minstrels for many years. On the 1901 census he is listed as a comedian, Eliza as a wardrobe mistress, and Marie (who was born in Liverpool in 1881) as a wardrobe assistant. I have found no evidence that Marie was a performer before joining Karno's chorus, so how she came to tread the boards is unclear,[12] but the circumstances suggest that she may have been part of the St James Quintet. However it came about, she was now in Karno's life and, despite a fifteen-year age gap, the old acrobat fell head over heels in love with her.

After a triumphant Christmas in Manchester, the company set off on tour with an hour-long take on the show entitled *The Dandy Thieves*.[13]

While Kitchen was creating mayhem as an inept member of the constabulary, Edith was helping the police with their enquiries in real life. In late January 1902, in Sunderland, miles away from Karno, she got her name into the newspapers for all the wrong reasons: 'At the Borough Police Court today … a Mrs Karno was summoned for assaulting Winifred Stewart. Mr Edward Bell, solicitor,

8. SLUMMING IT

stated that the defendant had apologised, and had agreed to pay the costs … he was instructed to ask the magistrate to allow the case to be withdrawn. The magistrate agreed. The parties are understood to be associated with the stage.'[14] The Sunderland hack didn't appear to realise that the lady in the dock was Fred Karno's wife, which might have made for bigger headlines.

Edith was no shrinking violet; she was a New Woman, and not one to be messed with. Contemporary photographs show her to be a stocky woman, perfectly capable of throwing a good left hook (as Karno would later find out), and she was obviously not averse to a public brawl. One wonders what caused the punch-up. Karno's troupe were playing *New Woman's Club* at the People's Palace and Edith's co-combatant, Winifred Stewart, was appearing in *Robinson Crusoe* at the nearby Avenue Theatre, but some digging reveals that Stewart was also a Karno artiste. She had appeared in *His Majesty's Guests* earlier that year, so she may have been a Karno conquest Edith got to hear about, or perhaps she was gossiping about Karno's flirtation with Marie Moore. There is, however, another possible explanation – it may have been Edith, not Karno, who was the subject of backstage gossip. The Principal Boy playing opposite Stewart in *Robinson Crusoe* was Marguerite Broadfoote, a close friend of Edith's – possibly too close. Edith's relationships may have been just as intriguing as Karno's, as we shall see.

After *His Majesty's Guests* Karno returned to smaller knockabout sketches, perhaps intending to develop them as the raw material for subsequent larger shows. So, *Early Birds* was next to receive a Chris Davies rewrite and reappeared, with Karno in the lead, as *The Dossers*, on the important Easter Monday bill at the Canterbury. The title reverted to *Early Birds* when it subsequently began a provincial tour (in a double bill with *Hilarity*), and it was well received by the critics: 'Early Birds for over half-an-hour keeps the house in a roar.'[15] Karno's Jewish pedlar (now called 'Ikey Cofenstein') was elevated from a wandering glazier to the proprietor of the Kerbstone Café, but he was still down on his luck, as this review makes clear:

8.3 George Craig as the Jew in Early Birds *(courtesy Heather Walker).*

> It is a rather curious form of enjoyment to witness a burlesque of the life of the very poor and wretched … The coffee stall man is beset on every side by thieves from the moment of opening to the time when the policeman is locked in the stall, which is pulled away with the representative of the law inside. The subsequent scene in the doss-house, where the old Jew robs his sleeping companions in distress and is robbed in turn, is a very lively representation, and sleep and safety seem to be the last things attainable in this stage doss-house.[16]

Still doesn't sound like a bundle of laughs does it? The pedlar has now turned villain as well as victim, but at least no-one got stabbed to death at the end. Musical director Joe Cleve[17] provided a score which Karno felt gave the show a unique atmosphere – some might say it was instrumental to its success. Adeler and West noted: 'Cleeve [sic] had the knack of explaining the situation by the aid of the orchestra, and it may well be realised what a valuable addition such music could be to the pantomime sketches.'[18] Using the music to help tell the story was a revelation, and something Karno used consistently thereafter. John McCabe credits him with being the first to synchronize pantomime with music in this way, but the credit should really go to Joe Cleve. We now take this for granted – imagine any film (particularly a silent) without a corresponding musical accompaniment. Cleve's choice of music was in a relatively sophisticated, classical style, and assisted the storytelling without competing with the action or trying to be funny. Charlie Chaplin would later compose music for his own films and acknowledged his mentor, saying:

> It's very important, music … I use it as a counterpoint, and I learnt that from the Fred Karno company; they had splendid music. For instance, if they had a squalor surroundings with a lot of comedy tramps working in it, then you see they would have very beautiful boudoir music, something of the eighteenth century, very lush and very grandiose … I copied a great deal from Mr Fred Karno in that direction.[19]

Music wasn't the only *Early Birds* innovation: Karno effected a complex change from a dank alleyway to a handsome interior by what he claimed to be the first use of a stage revolve in Britain. If this is true, it is remarkable. The mighty London Coliseum, jewel in the crown of the impresario Oswald Stoll, is officially credited with this innovation, two years later. Karno's revolve must have been small-scale – capable of moving from hall to hall – and seems to have gone largely unrecognized at the time, although neither he nor Stoll invented the idea. The revolving stage originated in Japan before being introduced to western audiences at the Residenztheater, in Munich, in 1896, so it's possible that Karno picked up the idea whilst touring Germany around that time. Similarly, *Early Birds* played several Stoll theatres, so it is conceivable that Stoll took his inspiration from Karno's sketch. As Karno put it in his memoirs: 'Very little is really new in the world of the theatre stage. Every "startling novelty" had been done before … every trick had been exploited years ago. The only real novelty is in the method of exploitation and that is where the real showman shines.'[20]

Perhaps it was the revolve, the pathos, the music, or all three, that made Karno consider *Early Birds* one of the best shows he ever produced. It toured for the next ten years to rave reviews: 'Fred Karno's Troupe … in their realistic scenes … 30 performers … an exact reproduction of the Actual Life that at the present day Exists in London – its Pathos, Poverty, Crime … A LESSON TO HUMANITY!'[21]

Humanity was in short supply at home. Coping with the loss of the children whilst nursing an ailing father, Karno found his relationship with Edith hanging by a thread – no wonder pathos found its way into *Early Birds*.

In October 1902 Karno headlined a Stoll benefit night to raise funds for the Leicester Infirmary. Stoll expected the artistes working on his circuit to give freely of their time for such fundraisers, but this occasion must have caused some annoyance to Karno since it meant appearing on the same bill as Ted Tysall's Karno Trio – one imagines the dressing rooms were even frostier than usual. The following month *His Majesty's Guests* appeared at Arthur Jefferson's Borough Theatre, North Shields.[22] Had Karno glanced offstage, he might have spotted Jefferson's son Stanley, not yet a teenager but already watching from the wings and dreaming of the day he might join the biggest comedy company on the halls.

The Karnos moved on to Bradford, where a notable review records Karno himself playing Sergeant Lightning at the Prince's Theatre: 'Fred Karno is eliciting hearty laughter for his very funny acting in the part of the heroic Sgt. Lightning'[23] – a rare example of Karno taking a comic part with dialogue. It seems likely that he had to step in for Fred Kitchen for some reason, since Kitchen was back in the part the following week. Later that month, Karno provided the scenery and took part in the annual Water Rats' charity matinee at the London Pavilion, under the chairmanship of King Rat Wal Pink.[24] *The Era* noted: 'Much diversion was caused by Fred Karno and company as six little burglars.'[25] The matinee also included a sketch entitled *Showing for the Shah*, which 'evoked roars of laughter' and would later inspire Karno's most famous sketch, as we shall see. He repeated his comedy singing efforts the following week, when the *Six Little Burglars* appeared at a Music Hall Benevolent Fund gala show at the Oxford. Top of a bill numbering nearly two hundred artistes was Marie Lloyd, who by then was forming a close friendship with Edith.

Karno was busy: he now had four sketches as well as *His Majesty's Guests* and *The Dandy Thieves* all touring. This required a fleet of vehicles to ferry comics, scenery and props to the halls and a stable full of horses to pull them. Karno would usually buy ex-artillery nags (which he called his 'Old Soldiers'), and enjoyed literal horse-trading with dealers. His companies playing in London would congregate each day at the Fun Factory to catch a crimson red Karno omnibus, emblazoned in gold with 'Karno's Speechless Comedians'. According to Charlie Chaplin, this extraordinary photograph (fig 8.4) shows five companies heading off to the halls[26] – and if a picture says a thousand words, this one

8.4 Karno omnibuses outside the Fun Factory, ferrying artistes to the halls, circa 1907.

speaks volumes about the scale of the Karno empire by the middle of the first decade of the twentieth century. This fleet of buses would whisk the comics to their first performance, then rush them to another hall for a second or perhaps third in the same evening. Speeding from hall to hall could be a risky business: Karno's drivers didn't spare the horses. In 1910 one was arrested for running over a pedestrian while en route from the Euston to the Paragon: witnesses reported that the horse-drawn bus was travelling at 'fire engine speed' – six miles an hour! A few months later a bus overturned, throwing the entire company into the road, but there were advantages to being an acrobat when hazardous transport was the norm (or when the driver was a practical joker), as this later report reveals:

> Their turn was one calling for acrobatic skill … the bus driver tried a practical joke on them. Down a sharpish hill … the speed of the bus increased ominously, and … the driver gave his passengers to understand that the vehicle was out of control … as the bus got nearer and nearer to a nasty turn at the bottom of the hill. Here of course the driver began to slow down, and, looking round, he was surprised to find his bus empty. As soon as the speed had become apparently dangerous, the whole company had merely got out and walked.[27]

When they weren't running over pedestrians or jumping from speeding omnibuses, Karno's comics ploughed on around the country. *His Majesty's Guests* (or rather 'an up to date second edition') returned to the Palace, Manchester, for a second Christmas – which says a lot about its appeal – and sharing the festive programme was a young American juggler by the name of W.C. Fields.[28] The twentieth century was well underway, and future Hollywood stars were beginning to appear in music hall's incubator of comedy.

Up to now, none of the sketches had relied on a big-name performer (other than Karno himself), and his mantra "There's my name on the show" was enough to dispel any manager's concern. However, Karno could always gauge the mood of his audiences, so when they began to latch on to Fred Kitchen Karno added his name to the advertising. The nursery of comedy had delivered its first star comic.

Meanwhile, Karno was still adding to his personal kindergarten. On 10 February 1903, almost exactly two years after losing Herbert, the Fun Factory echoed to the cries of another baby boy, Leslie Karno Westcott. According to Leslie's granddaughter, Edith gave birth to twins but one was a stillbirth – if true, this twin went unrecorded. The surviving twin was a sickly baby and, determined not to lose another child, Edith gave up performing forever.

According to Naomi Jacob the baby was named after his godfather, Leslie Stuart,[29] a close family friend from Moore and Burgess days. Surprisingly Stuart is not mentioned in Karno's memoirs (a mystery we will return to), not even when Karno records that he once found himself playing next-door to Stuart's *Floradora* in Bolton. He shared a hotel with the musical's business manager and, as they walked to the theatre, the manager commiserated with Karno for having to compete with the biggest theatrical smash of the day. The queues for the box office were down the street and he gave a knowing smile – it was quickly wiped off his face when he realised they were for Karno's show.

If Edith thought another baby would maintain Karno's interest in her, she was mistaken – their marriage was all but over. Artistic temperaments, long periods apart and the pressure and insecurity of fame and fortune make a toxic cocktail for wedded bliss. Add the loss of at least three children in infancy, and their break-up was perhaps inevitable. Gallagher's version of what happened next is one of the most extraordinary claims in his biography. Three weeks after the birth of Leslie (whilst her husband was away on tour), Edith supposedly received a package containing sexually explicit photographs of Karno and his mistress, including pictures of them posing naked sitting on a gate, and having sex in a field. The arrival of these photographs was apparently witnessed by Fred Jr., then aged eleven, and Edith showed them to the boy as evidence of the monster his father had become. You might assume that Karno had been caught 'in flagrante delicto' and someone had sent Edith the evidence, but Gallagher claims this someone was Karno himself – which if true, would make him the stupidest man in Christendom.

Gallagher's reasoning is that Karno sent the photos as a form of cruel and unusual punishment, prompting Edith to grab their two children and hightail it out of the Fun Factory. Karno supposedly then moved Marie Moore in, and hung enlarged canvases of the photographs about the place for all to see. The epilogue to this story is that when they subsequently met in the divorce court, and the case was going against her, Edith (against her judgement and fearing scandal) was persuaded to submit the photographs as evidence, forcing Karno to acquiesce to her request for a separation.

Phew! This tale needs a reality check, so let's unpick Gallagher's account. First, he has his dates in a mess: Leslie was born in February 1903 (Gallagher says it was

1902), and subsequent divorce proceedings prove that Edith did not become aware of Karno's affair until August 1903 and walked out at Christmas. What about the photographs themselves? Is it plausible that Karno, a high-profile impresario with a reputation he fought hard to protect, would send pornographic photographs of himself to his own wife? Think about the technology of the time: whilst small 'box' cameras were commercially available, the film would have required development in a processing lab. Even if the images did exist, is it likely that he had them mounted on the walls of the Fun Factory for the servants and staff to see? Finally, Fred Jr., whose autobiographical notes include some great stories, does not mention this most extraordinary set of circumstances, despite him supposedly witnessing it.

If there remains any doubt as to this fiction, when Karno and Edith eventually got to court, details such as when she became aware of the affair, when she left, the date of a brief reconciliation and the eventual explosive break-up, were all meticulously set out in the court record. They threw everything at each other, literally, and Karno fought the case very hard indeed – yet examination of the court papers shows the alleged photographs are not mentioned.

Ironically, Gallagher expressed his own shock and disgust at the story in an article he wrote for pornographic magazine *Mayfair* (I really did buy it for the articles).[30] So, this extraordinary story appears to be a tall tale, but that doesn't mean the Karnos' break-up was not dramatic – there are plenty of fireworks to come.

8.5 His Majesty's Guests *poster (Mary Evans Picture Library)*.

9.

Saturday to Monday

*"I'm afraid, my dear husband, that absence
will conquer your love,"
said a fond wife on the eve of her husband's departure.
"Never fear," he said, "the longer you are away
from me the better I will like you."*
(The Merry Book of the Moore & Burgess Minstrels, 1898)

BACK TO reality. In the summer of 1903, Edith bounced Leslie on her knee, blissfully unaware of Karno's affair. The baby grew in strength but there was still a dose of family tragedy when Karno's mother, Emily, died in April. We know nothing about their relationship, but one wonders whether the death of his mother, at a time when he was also nursing his senile father, added to the strains on the marriage. We also know that Edith was drinking, but whether this helped to cause Karno's infidelity or was a direct result of it, we can only speculate. What really happened a few weeks after Leslie arrived is that Karno took on another new theatrical challenge:

> Mr Fred Karno has purchased the Sole and Exclusive Rights and Entire Production of the Song Sketch known as "My Japanese Cherry Blossom," which created such a great success at the Tivoli and Oxford recently … a Brilliant Company … has been Engaged for this Delightful Little Operetta. The Daintiest, Prettiest, and Most Ear-Haunting Songs Scena ever put on the Variety Stage.[1]

Dainty? Pretty? Ear-Haunting? Hardly standard Karno material. The operetta was taken from a show called *Hoity Toity*, by Edgar Smith and John Stromberg, and had already done good business at the Oxford, where it was described as 'A big coon novelty' (presumably referring to the style of the music, rather than suggesting blacked-up geishas). When the show was made available to other producers, Karno snapped it up. Previous experiments with new genres had not gone well, but he'd learnt some lessons and this time he put his ten dainty lady singers on the same bill as his sketches. In this way the operetta was just another act on the programme, and those who came to see knockabout Karno comedy were not disappointed. *My Japanese Cherry Blossom* first appeared in late February 1903 at the Circus of Varieties in Rochdale, where it was described as: 'A pretty combination of dances and singing, most gracefully and tastefully executed.'[2] The early twentieth century saw an explosion of interest in all things Japanese, influencing fashion, architecture, horticulture and furniture, so Karno's show was in tune with public taste. He went all out to create an authentic-looking Japanese garden, with garlands of silk flowers and lanterns set against a backdrop of Japanese houses.

On 6 March, a benefit was held for Fred Kitchen at the Empire Palace, South Shields. At such performances the takings went to the guest of honour; sometimes because they needed financial support, or (as in Kitchen's case) simply as a thank you for services rendered. They often included appearances by artistes from nearby theatres or friends of the recipient, and the guest star at Kitchen's benefit was George Formby (the father of the ukulele-playing film star). The Karnos staged *Love in a Tub*, in what appears to have been its one and only public performance since the days of the Three Karnos. Perhaps the sketch had been retained as a training routine for new comics – it would certainly have been a good initiation into Karno comedy and a nod to his small beginnings.

Karno's world wasn't small anymore: there were now seventy comics tumbling from venue to venue. They called themselves 'Karno plonks' and one critic dubbed them 'the best masters of finesse to visit the varieties.'[3] The plonks were always at the heart of the comedy but usually remained anonymous in the listings, just occasionally a review or advertisement might reveal an identity or two. So around that time we are able to establish that Billy Reeves was playing the villain (described as the Bill Sykes character) in *Early Birds*, alongside Charlie Bell and Arthur Gallimore; whilst *Jail Birds* employed Billie Ritchie, his wife Winnie, Fred Evans and Harry Royston. Karno was constantly scouting for more like these, aiming to discover young talent rather than use established performers. Adeler and West noted: 'Fred would say "Any fool can engage an established comedian at three hundred pounds a week. I prefer to back my own judgement by selecting a man … who has not yet had the chance to show his talent. If I don't have to pay one man three hundred pounds out of the week's takings, there is all the more for the supporting artistes."'[4] This approach generated a whole army of young comics eager to grab their opportunity, and Karno's most significant legacy is the host of stars who served their apprenticeship in his school of slapstick.

With business booming, Karno's car was invaluable. It allowed him to keep an eye on his troupes in every corner of Britain, but his typically energetic approach to motoring soon got him into trouble (and into the press): 'Fred Karno … was fined £5 … for furiously driving a motor car in Church [a village near Blackburn]. It was alleged that Mr Karno was driving … at 17 miles an hour and knocked down a boy, breaking his leg in two places.'[5] Cue red-nosed comic: 'Well your honour, the lad shouldn't have been in those two places.'

In the days of unmade roads and horse-drawn carts, cars could be a menace. Many new motorists were wealthy young men, prone to reckless speeding and showing off. They frequently found themselves in trouble with the law, earning themselves the nickname 'scorchers'. Karno fitted the description, and two months after the incident in Blackburn he was at it again: 'Fred Karno … was charged with furiously driving his motor car … through Todmorden at the rate of 25 to 30 miles per hour … chairman of the Bench said that scorchers brought discredit upon other motorists, and great danger followed. The magistrates were determined to suppress scorching, and as a warning, imposed upon the defendant the full penalty of £10.'[6] The press went on to report that when the arresting officer had asked for his name, Karno suggested that he read the side of the car!

Such fines were a regular occurrence over the years: just a few weeks after the Todmorden case he was caught again, this time doing an eye-watering twenty-three miles an hour before being dramatically stopped by police: 'Delinquents Before the Magistrates – Karno … refused to stop when signalled to do so, and Police constable Brett, who clung onto the back of the car, was dragged past the Golden Cross before Karno stopped.'[7] One can only imagine poor PC Brett hanging on for dear life, shouting for Karno to stop as he was dragged along the street – a one man prequel to the Keystone Cops.

9. SATURDAY TO MONDAY

Meanwhile, Karno's favourite policeman was going from strength to strength and Fred Kitchen's star continued to rise as he made Sergeant Lightning his signature part. In August 1903 his brother Dick (who was fourteen years older than Fred) made his first appearance in a Karno listing when he briefly took over the role. How things had changed since he saved a young Karno from the harsh treatment of Bob Aubrey back in 1886.

Karno was doing his own bit for those in need, with his charitable efforts continuing through the autumn. In November Harry Tate, Little Tich and Eugene Stratton, were just three of the famous names who performed in a version of *Dandy Thieves* in a Water Rats' matinee at the London Pavilion. The same stars had already appeared with Karno at another charity show at the Brighton Alhambra, in September. That same month Karno was well represented at the third and final 'Comic Cricket Carnival' at the Oval. The usual master of ceremonies, Dan Leno, was notable by his absence – by then he had been committed to a mental asylum.

9.1 Billy Reeves in the comedy cricket match at the Oval, 1903 (© Illustrated London News Ltd/ Mary Evans Picture Library).

9.2 Billy Reeves caught out (© Illustrated London News Ltd/ Mary Evans Picture Library).

Although both of these photographs (from *The Tatler*) show Billy Reeves, they were captioned 'Fred Karno caught out', and that is exactly what had happened behind closed doors – Edith had finally become aware of his affair. Although she found out in August, she didn't leave the Fun Factory until Christmas, so those final months of 1903 must have been turbulent. Karno's listings reduced significantly during this period, and while this may have been due to personal distractions, he was also working hard on a new show. Having been invited to stage another Christmas spectacular at Manchester's Palace Theatre, he commissioned Fred Kitchen, Charles Baldwin and Dudley Powell to write his next large-scale musical comedy – *Saturday to Monday*.

As usual, Karno staged a try-out performance (a process Fred Kitchen called 'trying it on the dog') at the Prince of Wales in Grimsby, where Kitchen and Cossie Noel led the cast of forty performers. Meanwhile Harry Roxbury got his big break, stepping into Kitchen's shoes to keep *His Majesty's Guests* on the road – a decision that Karno later had cause to regret.

Kitchen played Jaggs, a reluctant bridegroom, in what was a family affair: the cast also included both his brother Dick and son Fred Jr. (playing Jaggs Jr.). Baldwin played the best man and the Camille Quartet reappeared to take on Dudley Powell's songs with the support of a full military band. The show was in three scenes: 'The Wedding' (a room at Mr Blake's), 'The Departure' (a railway station) and 'The Honeymoon' (the pier at Saltsea):

9.3 Saturday to Monday *advertisement (author's collection).*

> John Willie Jaggs ... is seen ... in his bedroom. He has been forcibly confined there by his prospective father-in-law, Mr Blake, so that he shall not escape marrying Clorinda Blake, an elder daughter. Jaggs had had a night of it, and after emptying the water jug is roused by his best man ... "you've got to be married in twenty minutes – wake up!" ... Plenty of fun is dispensed in the second scene – a railway station ... In the final scene near the Casino of a Continental town, the fun is fast and furious, and the curtain falls to vociferous applause.[8]

Whilst some critics suggested that the plot was thin, all agreed that Kitchen was 'excruciatingly funny': 'Kitchen ... whether as the bridegroom at the wedding breakfast, the improvised porter at the railway station, or as the butt of the children at the seaside, kept the house in roars of laughter.'[9] Some critics were even more gushing: 'We have never seen anything to equal ... Karno's musical extravaganza "Saturday to Monday" ... Beyond question it is Mr Karno's masterpiece.'[10] A later review gives us a tantalizing glimpse of some Kitchen business: 'No-one seems to know what he will do next ... when he is in the midst of his fun making those in the vicinity have to mind the things flying around ... [Kitchen] plays comic billiards with a French roll and loaves of bread.'[11]

9. SATURDAY TO MONDAY

Like the critics, Karno had no doubt what a brilliant comic Kitchen was, telling Adeler and West: 'There is the comedian born, and the comedian who is manufactured. The latter's technique may be sheer perfection; he may have rehearsed every gesture ... he may try his voice inflections in a thousand different ways ... and by sheer study and hard work he may get right to the top ... but comedy was and is inherent in Fred Kitchen; it is bone of his bone and flesh of his flesh.'[12]

9.4 Fred Kitchen (left) in Saturday to Monday *(courtesy Simon Kitchen Dunn).*

Karno comics were beginning to make the transition from being purely physical, visual performers to actors delivering verbal gags – silent movie comics would face the same challenge twenty or so years later. Kitchen excelled at both. His turn of phrase, slight lisp and vaguely Lancastrian accent (he was actually a Londoner) were immensely comical, and he affected a whistle in his speech by leaving out his five false front teeth. Combining this with magnificent timing and a natural comedic physicality, he could make people laugh just by walking onto the stage, and a resigned shrug of his burly shoulders was enough to have the audience in hysterics. Kitchen inevitably influenced those Karno comics who followed him, not least Charlie Chaplin, who Kitchen believed had copied his style so closely that he subsequently felt unable to accept offers of work in America, or on film, for fear he would labelled a Chaplin impersonator. Karno considered that the Little Tramp's famous walk was copied from Fred Kitchen, and Chaplin acknowledged he had been one of many inspirations for the character.

Kitchen and Karno shared a sense of humour, a work ethic and a love of horse racing, and they soon became close friends. Karno described his star comedian as 'the gentlest, kindest, most unselfish and most unassuming of men – and generous to a fault. No one has ever heard a fellow artiste speak ill of him, and there could be no higher testimonial to an actor's character.'[13] Despite later nurturing superstars like Chaplin and Laurel, Karno said that of all his artistes no one ever did him more credit than Fred Kitchen.

So, 1903 was busy at work and stressful at home; Karno needed somewhere to escape to. He found his retreat at Molesey Lock, where he'd busked with his mandolin years before. He purchased a houseboat, the Highland Lassie,[14] and moored it at Tagg's Island, where he fell in love with life on the Thames whilst bedding his mistress to his heart's content. Karno's nautical neighbours included Henry Lytton, later to be knighted for his achievements with the Savoy Opera, and theatrical agent Lionel Wallace. The three men joined forces to organise countless social events, fetes and charity galas. It was easy for them to persuade famous artistes to appear at these gatherings, including Evie Greene (star of *Floradora*) and Courtice Pounds (principal tenor of the Savoy). Karno recalled that one event was opened by the Duchess of Albany, who took great pleasure in joining in one of his sketches as a boisterous member of the audience. Here is a typical press report of one of their efforts: 'Tagg's island will be the scene of a novel function … A Fete de Theatres will be held at the upper end of the island under the auspices of The Molesey Invitation Regatta Committee. It will include a concert under the direction of Mr H.A. Lytton, introducing many people well known in the theatrical world. A special variety entertainment will be given by Mr Fred Karno's troupe including a performance of walking on water.'[15]

With his new-found wealth, Karno was keen to elevate himself into the upper echelons of Edwardian society, and Molesey proved the perfect setting for a social climbing expedition – although to paraphrase Alan Bennett, he remained on the lower slopes. As a working-class lad who'd literally crawled off the floor of the elephant house, he was never going to be among equals – no amount of money could buy class.

What must have seemed like a million miles away, in Vaughan Road, Karno's family was unravelling as Edith left the Fun Factory and Marie Moore moved in. Edith and the children were given sanctuary by Karno comic Charlie Bell and his wife Clara,[16] which no doubt caused some friction at rehearsals! Edith subsequently rented a flat next door to the Bells'[17] whilst her separation from Karno played out in the courts. Initially work seemed unaffected: after a triumphant Christmas in Manchester, *Saturday to Monday* secured a regional tour, but before the troupe set off they played an extra week at the Palace, staging *Early Birds* with Karno in the lead – it was one of his last performances. Chaplin recalled that the story of Karno's last stand went on to be a favourite anecdote amongst the plonks:

> He [Karno] himself was an excellent comedian and originated many comedy roles. He continued playing even when he had five other companies on the road … One night in Manchester … the troupe complained that Karno's timing was off and that he had ruined the laughs. Karno, who had then accumulated £50,000 from his five shows, said: "Well, boys, if that's the way you feel, I'll quit!" then, taking off his wig, he dropped it on the dressing-table and grinned. "You can accept that as my resignation."[18]

Karno hung up his boots and concentrated on producing new shows, and his next sketch would go on to be the Speechless Comedians' finest hour – *Mumming Birds*.

According to his memoirs, Karno had the idea after seeing a show called *Entertaining the Shah*, but (as we've already seen) it was actually *Showing for the Shah*, a sketch in the Water Rats' charity matinee of 1902. That year Britain had hosted a visit from Mozaffar ad-Din Shah Qajar, the Shah of Persia, and as he toured the country, the newspapers were full of reports of events and attractions he witnessed, often under the headline 'Entertaining The Shah'. Provincial dignitaries the length and breadth of the land had to come up with whatever entertainment they could, and often found themselves calling on some decidedly amateur local talent, with embarrassing results – it was an obvious subject for the Water Rats to satirise. In *Showing for the Shah* they presented a performance by apparent amateurs, while 'the Shah' became so frustrated at their terrible performances that he felt compelled to join in:

> Mr Tom McNaughton played the part of the gentleman seeking for talent; and when such 'novices' as Frank Haytor and others took the floor to burlesque acrobatism the Shah and his suite … seated in the boxes, would have none of it, and came on to the stage to do a show on their own. They were the Craig Troupe. It was all very merry fooling, and the heartiness of the applause was quite one of the pleasantest features of a most enjoyable interlude…

So far so good, but this review goes on describe another sketch in the same show, which also made an impression on Karno:

Carkeek, the American champion wrestler, entered the arena to wrestle an 'unknown', who turned out to be none other than Frank Haytor … and that comedian, with a figure as attenuated as a lamp-post, appeared in a grotesque make up. His brother wheeling onto the stage a bag, upon which was inscribed £50, his stake money. Time was immediately called, and the men embraced … The marvellous prowess of Haytor and his contortions provoked great amusement … Carkeek … left Haytor doubled up like a trussed fowl … was handed the £50 and, seizing the bag … with the right hand, he raised Haytor with the left, and carried both triumphantly from the stage, amid roars of laughter.[19]

9.5 One of many 'boys in the box' – George Hoare (courtesy Jeremy Hoare).

Karno had provided the scenery for this Water Rats' matinee and was not one to let it go to waste, so over the next eighteen months he mulled over these ideas before combining them into a sketch he initially called *Twice Nightly*. The title would later change to *Mumming Birds,* and it deserves special attention for two reasons: it would become the longest running music hall sketch of all time, and it would make Charlie Chaplin's name.

The premise was a show within a show, with comics taking the part of both the music hall performers and the 'audience'. Every turn was heralded with a number being displayed on an easel, and each was more terrible than the last. The focus of the comedy, however, was not on the acts but on the reaction of the audience members in the stage boxes. On one side sat a drunken masher; on the other a boy dressed in an Eton suit,[20] accompanied by his elderly uncle. The drunk encourages, heckles or joins in – making a fool of both himself and the performers in the process. Meanwhile the boy, a dab hand with a pea shooter, works his way through a picnic, most of which gets thrown at the artistes.[21] Here is an opening night review from *The Stage*:

> The curtain rises on the interior of a music-hall … with the programme in full swing … The droll antics of the occupants of the boxes are as

> equally diverting as … the artistes … The "turns" comprise a "ballad" vocalist, a serio and dancer, a mesmerist, conjuror and general charlatan, and the inevitable champion wrestler, who trades under the pseudonym "Turkey." … Deserving of special mention is the bibulous gentleman occupying the prompt stage box; he … succeeds in keeping his audience in an uninterrupted roar of laughter by his eccentricities and well-assumed expression of inanity.[22]

Although these antics were largely in mime (with musical accompaniment), every fall of the drunk, every round from the pea shooter and every punch on the nose had a perfectly timed comic sound effect.[23]

The artiste line-up changed regularly over the years, but a 1907 listing gives us as good a playlist as any: 1. The Topical Vocalist, 2. The Swiss Nightingale, 3. The Rustic Glee Party, 4. The Prestidigitator, 5. The Saucy Serio, and 6. The Terrible Turkey. In other words: a male singer, a female singer, a male quartet, a magician (playing it for laughs many years before Tommy Cooper donned his fez), a soubrette and a wrestling bout. Fred Karno Jr.'s version of the sketch, performed many years later, included a double act called Duff and Dire and included the songs *Let's All Go to the Music Hall, Come Birdie Come and Live with Me* and *You Naughty Naughty Man*.

Another script, kindly shared with me by David Robinson, reveals more of the comedy business: the Eton boy and his uncle sit in the box stage right as the drunk is escorted to his box stage left; an usher offers him a programme, he grabs her hand and tries to kiss her – she pushes him away (the first of many comedy falls). Duff and Dire enter and are heckled by the boy and the drunk, who decides he will remove them from the stage but cannot get out of his box without falling over again, whilst the boy in the opposite box resorts to throwing oranges. The comedians do a dance, fall over each other and crawl off; they are replaced by a tuneless opera singer who is dragged off by the drunk. The conjuror enters and the boy volunteers as his assistant; the drunk interferes and gives away the tricks. The conjuror exits in disgust to be replaced by a discordant singing quartet. The drunk beats them off with a cushion, leaving one remaining 'glee' singer screeching to himself. The drunk is passed a custard pie by the boy, which is delivered (with a flourish) as the singer misses the final top note. The saucy soubrette enters, arousing lustful interest from the boy and the drunk, who try in vain to tempt her with flowers and fruit. The drunk follows her into the wings but is dragged back to his box by the attendant. Described in the script as 'business with drunk', this no doubt took ten minutes and brought the house down. (Robert Downey Jr. gives us a brief flavour of this routine in Richard Attenborough's 1992 biopic *Chaplin*.)

John McCabe provides yet more detail about the drunk's routine: on finding his seat he peels off a glove, and then attempts to do so again with the same, now bare, hand; he tries to light a cigarette from the electric lightbulb on his box, realises his mistake and leans toward the box on the opposite side, tumbling over onto the stage.[24]

9.6 A later Mumming Birds *finale – a Cossack dance (from the 'A.J.' Marriot archive).*

In Robinson's script the finale was a Cossack dance with all the protagonists joining in, leading to an exhausted climactic collapse; but originally the finale was the second piece of business Karno purloined from the Water Rats' show – a wrestling bout between a professional and a 'volunteer' planted in the audience. Karno was satirising another contemporary event: on 30 January 1904, at Olympia, Charles B. Cochran promoted a much anticipated Greco-Roman wrestling match between two strongmen – Hackenschmidt (The Russian Lion) and Ahmed Madrali (The Terrible Turk). In advance of the match the press were full of tales of the Terrible Turk, who apparently ate a whole sheep every day and occasionally killed his sparring partners. Cochran wrote: 'All England had gone wrestling mad. Wherever one went, wrestling was talked; in bars, clubs, and at family parties the mysteries of the "half-nelson" were discussed, coats were taken off and demonstrations … were given.'[25] Karno named his comedy protagonist Marconi Ali – 'The Terrible Turkey'.

On one occasion Bill Fern (as the Turkey) threw down the challenge and a burly sailor lurched onto the stage before the plant had time to respond. Fern abandoned the play-acting and had to fight for his life – the victor is unrecorded. Later versions more closely reflected the Water Rats' original, with the master of ceremonies giving the Turkey a huge and terrifying build-up, only for a wimpish character to enter – thin as a rake and wearing long johns, a fez and a large moustache. The malnourished Turkey would leap on a bun thrown by the Eton Boy, devouring it as if he'd not eaten for weeks, while the master of ceremonies cried: "Back, back!" Whichever version of the Turkey appeared, the drunk eventually ended up as his opponent and his inevitable victory was achieved by various means, including tickling and custard pies. There were limitless opportunities for the piece to spiral out of control, as the lunatics increasingly took over the asylum – *Mumming Birds* was joyful, unadulterated comedy chaos.

Although the sketch was a return to Karno's silent slapstick, it was a sophisticated show with a complex set. The four theatre boxes on the stage itself (two either side, one above the other) required complex logistics, technical planning and a competent crew to put them all together. Karno recounted that the boxes were prone to damage if the cast got carried away, and on one occasion they came crashing to the ground – landing half his troupe in hospital.

In developing the sketch, Karno came to recognise a fundamental truth – the essential cruelty of an audience. He had been inspired, in part, by the 'hook' used to drag failing acts off the stage (he believed this was originated around this time in Paris)[26] and realised that the more officious and important the victim, the funnier the fall from grace proved to be. Karno acknowledged that this idea was as old as the hills, but the concept of a show within a show, intentionally bad performances being played for laughs, and interaction between acts and an audience (even a fake one), were all *Mumming Birds* innovations – innovations which the cast, and some audiences, initially struggled to understand. Billy Reeves (the first drunk in the box) said: "Surely Guv'nor you don't seriously intend to do this rubbish! They'll never stand for it."

9.7 Mumming Birds *advertisement from 1917.*

So, the cast took some convincing as Karno took personal charge of rehearsals, working with them to develop the individual pieces of physical business and sight gags. Alongside Reeves as the drunk, the original Terrible Turkey was Arthur Gallimore, the bungling magician (named as Professor Bunco) was Billie Ritchie, the saucy soubrette was Amy Minister, the Eton boy was Charlie Bell and the uncle was George Craig. Winnie Ritchie was also in the original cast – probably as the Swiss Nightingale. No doubt they all stepped onto the stage for the sketch's first performance (in mid-April 1904) with some trepidation, but it was well received in London. This was not always the case in the provinces – some audiences missed the joke and thought they'd simply witnessed a poor-quality variety bill. Moss Empires' director Frank Allen didn't like it either, rejecting it as too rough for his circuit. A few years later Allen was eating his words and scrambling to book the sketch as it swept the country.

Some accounts suggest that *Mumming Birds* was written quickly as a gap-filler and that Reeves was a Karno baggage man, supposedly the only person available at the time to play the part. This tall tale originates from Henry Chance Newton's 1928 memoir, in which he recalled giving the sketch a favourable review and singling out the drunk in the box, whilst noting that he could not give the actor due credit as he was not named in the programme. He subsequently received this letter from Billy Reeves: 'I am the nameless "pro." who played the drunk in Mumming Birds … up to the time when I went on in the part at short notice, I was Fred Karno's two-pound-a-week baggage man. Since your notice, I can get more than that.'[27] This is nonsense: Karno planned and rehearsed the sketch meticulously and Reeves was an experienced comic with several sketches under his belt – one can only assume he wrote in jest and Chance Newton fell for it. One thing is certain: if Fred Kitchen was the star of Karno's musical comedies, Billy Reeves was now the undisputed star of the knockabout plonks.

Convincing the cast and audience of the show's merits wasn't Karno's only challenge – he struggled to decide on a title. It appeared as both *Twice Nightly* and *A Stage Upon A Stage* before arriving at the Canterbury, on 6 June, where the proprietor Fred Miller felt *Twice Nightly* would confuse his punters. The Canterbury only ran one performance of the programme each evening, and *Twice Nightly* once nightly was bound to cause problems. Karno recalled Miller suggested that since

9.8 The original drunk in the box – Billy Reeves (author's collection).

he'd already had *Jail Birds* and *Early Birds*, why not *Mumming Birds*? Listings confirm that it first appeared under this title at Miller's Canterbury, but a later report suggests the evolution of the name wasn't quite so straightforward:

> Fred Karno's troupe … supply the principal sketch. This was produced some weeks ago, under the title of "Twice Nightly." That … was found to be a confusing line upon the bill of a "one-house-a-night" establishment: so, the title was altered to "A Stage Upon A Stage." Quite recently, again, the sketch figured as "The Mumming Birds." Now … all three titles are introduced upon the programme … "Twice Nightly, or The Mumming Birds; a Stage upon a Stage." One may reflect, however, that a funny sketch, under any name, still remains a funny sketch; so, the confusion may be pardoned in view of the roars of laughter with which this thrice-named production is received.[28]

The new title stemmed back to a folk tradition of short, often comic, plays performed by nomadic pantomime troupes throughout the nineteenth century. Naomi Jacob recalled the mummers of her youth: 'At Christmas time we … had … Mummers, who go around the larger houses and enact a sort of Miracle Play … spoken in rough-rhymed couplets. There are several characters: Saint George, The Dragon, The Doctor, and a lady – she is always a man, wearing rather draggled skirts, known as Mince Pie.'[29] So, mummers were the ancestors of the speechless comedians and Karno was to keep their memory alive half a century after the real mummers had disappeared.

Karno claimed authorship of the sketch but no doubt other comics in his company provided some ideas – Charles Baldwin claimed to have done more than that:

> I wrote Mumming Birds for Fred Karno … for five pounds all at. But mark my doom! On the day I touched for the fiver, I went into Romano's. There I met a man who had lent me two quid, so I paid him … and stood him a drink. Shortly after, I met a cove, who was bloomin' broke, so I gave him a quid. Then in the pride of my heart, at my great success … I stood drinks all round … I came out of the bar, and accidentally dropped the last quid down a hole in the gutter. And that's all I got out of Mumming Birds.[30]

Karno and Baldwin's creation headed off on a tour that never really stopped. Fred Karno Jr. was still performing a version of it in 1948 – an almost unbroken forty-four-year run. There are a variety of reasons for this longevity: the concept was timeless, the 'acts' could be updated and developed to reflect passing fashions and topical events, or to parody other artistes. It also achieved huge international success – with no language barrier, it was just as popular in Naples as New York. In later years it was helped significantly by its association with Chaplin, but above all it was a brilliantly funny show which Stan Laurel described as 'one of the most fantastically funny acts ever known – probably the greatest ensemble of the century.'[31]

Chaplin's association with the sketch we will return to later, but it's worth noting one of the many Karno references he later peppered his films with: the *Mumming Birds* magician was called Professor Bunco and Chaplin subsequently used the name Professor Bosco for both his magician in *The Circus* (1928) and for the flea circus owner in an earlier (unreleased) film, *The Professor* (1919).[32]

Mumming Birds would ultimately break Karno in America, where *Billboard* called it 'Perhaps the funniest act ever to hit vaudeville'[33] – but that success was yet to come. For some reason Karno was reluctant to tackle international tours. Instead, in July 1904, *The Era* reported that he had licensed his sketches to another producer: 'Mr Reed Pinaud has acquired the sole rights of performance of all Mr Fred Karno's sketches in the United States, the Continent of Europe, Australia, New Zealand, and South Africa. He will organise a company of twelve principals and is now busily engaged in making his selections.'[34]

This was destined to cause all sorts of trouble – he and Theodore Reed Pinaud would soon come to blows. In the meantime, Mr and Mrs Karno were coming to blows at home.

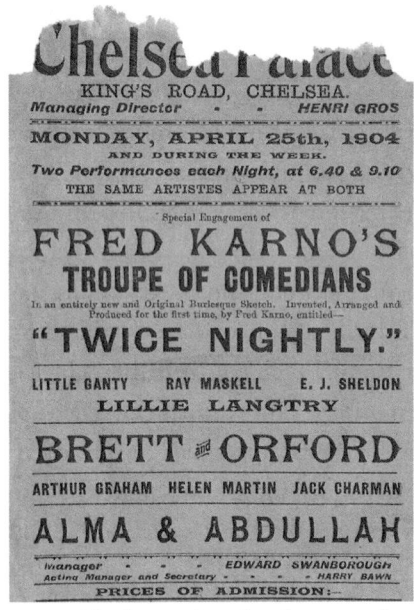

9.9 *The first confirmed performance of Karno's greatest show (author's collection).*

10.

From Here to Paternity

Love is blind, and marriage is an eye opener.
(The Merry Book of the Moore & Burgess Minstrels, 1898)

IN MARCH 1904, three months after walking out, Edith returned to live at the Fun Factory. This may have been a genuine attempt at reconciliation, but it seems more likely that Karno had an ulterior motive for tempting her back, which will shortly become clear. Gallagher claimed that Karno tried to persuade Edith to live with him and Marie Moore in a ménage-à-trois – Edith gave the idea short shrift and Marie was instead secreted at a nearby address. Gallagher's narrative paints Moore and Karno as sexual deviants, while Edith is depicted as their innocent victim. His description of the two women is startling in its bias: 'Edith was blonde, petite, gentle in nature and with an almost virginal mind. Marie was a raven haired brunette, a statuesque girl whose bust was rivalled only by her hips, a sexual extrovert, a voluptuary with a shrewd, hard, business mind and above all a girl who knew when she was on to a good thing.'[1] I had to look up voluptuary (a person devoted to luxury and sensual pleasure). So much for the tabloid version, let's see if we can get to the facts.

As Karno launched *Mumming Birds* he was trying to play happy families with Edith, but it was hopeless. She was a woman scorned – understandably hurt, resentful and turning to drink. After two months, tensions boiled over into a vicious fight. In their subsequent court battle, Edith claimed Karno hit her and, while she was on the ground, trod on her face leaving a heel-shaped scar. Karno counter-claimed, stating that she was violently drunk and he was forced to defend himself when she attacked him with a glass soda siphon. Despite this

10.1 Edith, Fred Jr. (left) and Leslie, circa 1903 (courtesy Louise Murchison).

fight they continued to live under the same roof for a few more weeks, presumably with the office staff downstairs trying to ignore the sound of breaking ornaments.

What really happened between them is impossible to establish with certainty, but (since we must start somewhere) let's start with Gallagher's version. It paints a one-sided picture, noting Edith's claim that Karno hit her but not Karno's counter-claim that Edith was a violent drunk. He further alleged that Edith had suffered repeated attacks in punishment for refusing Karno's sexual advances, or for failing to properly clean the stage before a performance. However Gallagher did not have access to the court papers (they were released in 2006), and although these record the fight I describe above, they also fail to mention any previous physical abuse, nor any animosity between Edith and Karno before his affair with Marie Moore. The fact that there is no other testimony from friends, colleagues or acquaintances to suggest Karno was a violent man, and the fact that his subsequent forty-year relationship with Marie appears to have been a very happy one, suggests there is at least room to doubt Edith's allegations. We also know that Edith could be violent (remember the punch-up in Sunderland?) and that Leslie, the son she idolised, corroborated Karno's claim that Edith was a drinker – he said she often had a Black Velvet (Guinness with Champagne) for breakfast.

The legal records show that Edith walked out for the second and final time on 10 June, the very day that the renamed *Mumming Birds* first appeared at the Canterbury. According to Karno's testimony, she returned two days later in a drunken rage, threatened him with a knife, smashed furniture and set fire to the house, sending the servants fleeing in terror. Edith told it very differently, simply stating that she returned to the house, they fought, and Karno slapped her face – a second alleged assault (which will be relevant later). Edith subsequently filed for legal separation on 27 June.

Divorce in Edwardian England was rare – around one thousand cases each year. It was socially frowned-upon, legally difficult and the outcome was heavily weighted in the husband's favour. Women not only suffered a damaged reputation

10. FROM HERE TO PATERNITY

(at a time when that meant something), but the husband was likely to keep any money his wife had brought into the marriage and usually got custody of the children. An alternative to divorce was 'judicial separation', which severed a couple's legal ties but wasn't a complete break since neither party was free to re-marry. Edith supposedly made it clear to her lawyer that she had no intention of ever marrying again and, since it was also easier to achieve, opted for judicial separation. She may also have wanted to prevent Karno from marrying his mistress.

At that time there was a serious imbalance between the parties in respect of the grounds for divorce or separation. All a husband needed was for his wife to be unfaithful, but in contrast, a woman could not divorce because of her husband's adultery alone – he had to give her a second cause. What's more, a husband could sue his wife's lover for damages but a wife had no such recourse against her husband's mistress. These inequities reflected the fact that adultery by men was commonplace and considered unremarkable.

So, consider Edith's position: she could not end her marriage to Karno because of his adultery alone – the law required a second cause. You might think domestic violence would count, but this was not necessarily the case. The extent, and tacit acceptance, of domestic abuse during the Victorian era is well documented, so the additional grounds women had to endure were more extreme than a husband raising his hand in anger: incest, bigamy, rape, sodomy, bestiality, adultery coupled with cruelty, or adultery coupled with at least two years' desertion. Edith was therefore reliant on 'adultery coupled with cruelty' and cruelty was hard to define, especially given that the courts had a high degree of tolerance for such matters – bodily hurt or injury to health was considered a minimum requirement. Finally and significantly, at least two acts of such cruelty had to be evidenced.

In her petition, Edith accused Karno of adultery (he was undoubtedly guilty of this) and of the two violent assaults we've already noted. Is it a coincidence that there are two acts of physical abuse cited by Edith, one sufficiently strong to meet the court's definition of bodily harm, thereby satisfying the minimum requirement exactly? Her lawyer noted: 'Frederick John Westcott violently assaulted your Petitioner by knocking her down and putting his heel on her face giving her a black eye and causing her to bleed very much and bruising her severely on the limbs.'[2]

I am not seeking to trivialise the attack, but as Simon Louvish noted (when commenting on Oliver Hardy's bitter divorce): 'We should bear in mind, the legal struggle ... to avoid liabilities and alimony payments by painting the opponent in devil's hues. It is the lawyers, after all, writing the scripts.'[3]

Edith's claim, writ large on page one of Gallagher's biography, destroyed Karno's reputation thirty years after his death, so we must consider whether it is plausible. If Karno had trodden on his wife's face sufficiently violently to leave a permanent scar, would it not have required some medical attention? The legal papers don't mention Edith needing to see a doctor. Naomi Jacob said she carried a scar on her cheek from the attack, but despite being her friend for twenty-five years, admitted she had never seen it as Edith 'always covered it with make-up.'[4] No scar is visible on any photograph of Edith that I have seen.

So where did Karno stand in the face of these accusations? He had a mistress but, given the law at the time, would probably have come out of a divorce unscathed apart from a minor public scandal. He was thick-skinned and wealthy enough to ride out that storm, so why didn't he just accept Edith's claim and let her go? Instead he chose to go into battle and defend himself.

There were three circumstances under which the judge might throw out Edith's petition. First 'condonation' (if Edith had forgiven the behaviour); second 'connivance' (if the adultery had been with Edith's consent); and finally 'collusion', where both parties engineered the circumstances to enable them to achieve a mutually desirable divorce (this was common at a time when achieving divorce was difficult). Karno asking Edith to come back now makes sense: he was able to claim that by returning to the family home, she had condoned the adultery. Sure enough, the record states: 'That the adultery alleged ... has been condoned by the Petitioner by co-habitation with the Respondent as her husband ... from March to the 10th of June 1904.' In respect of their fight, he claimed self-defence: 'If on any occasion he has been guilty of violence to Petitioner, such violence was provoked by the drunken and violent conduct of Petitioner to himself.'[5]

Having decided to contest the case, Karno filed a counter-petition which turned the tables. Edith now faced far more severe consequences should the judge find in Karno's favour – she stood to lose everything. Karno's petition stated:

> (3) Edith Westcott is a woman of violent and intemperate habits, that she has been for many years and constantly is under the influence of drink. That she has frequently threatened your Petitioners life and the life of the aforesaid child Leslie Karno Westcott. (4) That on the occasion in the

10. FROM HERE TO PATERNITY

> month of May 1904 the said Edith Westcott was very drunk and violent and threw a glass syphon of soda water at your Petitioner. (5) That on the 12th day of June 1904 the said Edith Westcott was very violent and took up a knife and threatened to kill the Petitioner saying she would "rip his b__ guts out" She also broke up the furniture in the house and set it on fire and was so violent that the servants would not stay in the house with her alone. (6) … Edith Westcott is unfit by reason of her intemperate habits to have the custody of the children.[6]

Leslie was sixteen months old, Fred Jr. was thirteen (and therefore of working age), and Edith only filed for custody of Leslie whereas Karno asked for custody of both boys. Did he genuinely feel they were at risk from Edith's drunken behaviour, or was this just a way of punishing her?[7] If the latter, he kept it up a long time – he was still trying to get custody of Leslie eight years later.

Both parties signed sworn affidavits that their accounts were true and having taken testimony from both parties[8] (and an unnamed witness who spoke on Edith's behalf)[9] the judge consolidated the two petitions into one case and went away to deliberate.

Edith was subsequently granted judicial separation on 25 May 1905. The judge cited Karno's adultery but made no reference to the alleged cruelty or violence. He gave custody of Leslie to Edith but Fred Jr. to Karno; both were granted free access to both children. Karno was ordered to pay Edith an alimony allowance of ten pounds per week for the rest of their joint lives.[10] This doesn't sound a huge amount in comparison to Karno's wealth,[11] but it was still ten times the national average wage at the time – Karno paid it until the day Edith died.

And that was that: claim, counterclaim, and more questions than answers. If Karno was a serial adulterer, as Gallagher suggested, why was Marie Moore any different from his other conquests? Why did Edith decide to leave this time? Why did he fight the case? Why not go further and divorce, so that he could marry Marie? Why did Edith recall her days with Karno as being the happiest of her life?

In trying to answer these questions, I consulted with retired solicitor Nick Whitehouse who, by his own admission, is old enough to remember practising when some elements of Edwardian divorce law were still relevant. Having studied the legal documents, he believes that Karno and Edith probably colluded in the separation and fabricated or exaggerated the claims they made against one another for the benefit of the court. What is the basis for Whitehouse's conclusion? First, they were effectively granted joint custody of the children, suggesting some mutual agreement. Second, the only logical explanation for Karno incriminating himself by sending the photographs (if you believe that story) would be a set-up planned by Karno and Edith. Third, Edith's claim against Karno fitted exactly the minimum requirement for acceptable grounds – no more, no less. The collusion theory would also explain why there is no evidence of Karno being adulterous or violent to Edith, or anyone else, before or afterwards.

There are other less tangible clues: extraordinarily, the case went completely unreported in the press at a time when all divorce cases were newsworthy. Karno's fame, with the addition of the lurid sex and violence, would have been meat and drink to the press, yet they were silent on this salacious split. By contrast a report from July 1908 recounts how the wife of Karno comic John Doyle was granted a legal separation because he beat her – the journalist could not resist the headline 'Knockabout Comic'. Imagine the field day they would have had with Karno. Did Karno and Edith agree somehow to keep it out of the public eye as part of a deal? More compelling is that Karno's family archive contains letters proving that Karno and Edith remained in contact and on good terms after they separated. Leslie Karno, abandoned as a toddler by Karno and brought up by his mother, also maintained a good relationship with his father. He fought hard against the Gallagher biography, defending Karno's honour years after his death – why? Whitehouse's conclusion would provide an explanation. Had Edith confided in Leslie that their break-up was more amicable than it appeared?

It seems convincing, but there are flaws in Whitehouse's collusion theory: Karno's spirited defence appears genuine; what did his counter-petition achieve? And (for me the strongest counter argument) if they were working together, why not go for a full divorce which would allow Karno to remarry?

Whatever the circumstances, when you consider their relative positions financially, socially and legally, Edith was brave to go into battle with Karno. Perhaps she was encouraged by her friend Marie Lloyd, who by then had been estranged from her first husband Percy Courtenay for ten years. Their violent marriage had been widely reported in the newspapers, Lloyd claiming she once had to fight off Courtenay with a horse whip. She later married genial Alec Hurley, only to abandon him for another abuser, the jockey Bernard Dillon.

10. FROM HERE TO PATERNITY

Reports of their subsequent separation in 1920 included excruciating details of his physical violence towards her. Edith's situation would have been enough to rouse Marie Lloyd's fervour – she loved to stand up for the underdog. Naomi Jacob recalled: 'The moment anyone was attacked, Marie automatically became their champion ... up in arms defending them.'[12]

Extraordinarily, Marie Lloyd's divorce from Percy Courtenay was made absolute on 22 May 1905, so Edith and Lloyd got their freedom in the same week – one imagines there was a party that weekend. Gallagher suggested that after Edith's separation Lloyd was hostile to Karno, but this isn't borne out by the archives. She regularly appeared on the same bill as Karno troupes over the years and even worked directly for him (in March 1910 and August 1912); on the latter occasion she said she was performing due to Karno showing great care and perseverance in endeavouring to get her to appear.[13]

We will never know the full story, but we can say that previous accounts don't fit the evidence of the court record, and it is possible that Edith's accusation of assault may have been exaggerated to meet the minimum requirements of the law. Based on the documents alone, there is no clarity as to who attacked whom, and they point to the incident being a one-off fight which may have had as much to do with Edith's drunkenness as Karno's anger.

However, that's not the end of the saga. There is reason to suspect that the Karnos' relationship breakdown was caused by more than his adultery; reasons which might explain how Edith knew she would never remarry and why Karno's behaviour deteriorated so badly – let's dig a little into Edith's social life.

Gallagher relied heavily on the recollections of Naomi Jacob, who was an extraordinary woman. Known to her friends as Mickie, Jacob was a prolific writer and actress, and a true English eccentric. She was involved in the embryonic Labour Party and the suffrage movement, and she was gay. She began her working life as a teacher, before becoming secretary to music hall singer Marguerite Broadfoote. Although Broadfoote was married and had a young son, she and Jacob became lovers, until her husband put an end to their relationship – Broadfoote died soon afterwards.[14] Jacob formed strong friendships with both Edith Karno and Marie Lloyd and went on to write a sycophantic biography of Lloyd in 1936. After the First World War Jacob embarked on her own stage career, which saw her typecast as manly harridans throughout the 1920s. Ill-health eventually led her to settle in Italy, where she lived a bohemian existence, carving out a new career as a novelist whilst force-feeding her Italian friends

Yorkshire pudding. Unable to take on the Germans single-handed, she returned to London during the Second World War and remained a frequent visitor afterwards. Overtly masculine, wearing tweed suits, smoking cigars and sporting the lesbian secret sign (the monocle), Jacob became an institution at Soho's gay clubs in the 1950s and, to quote *The Evening Standard*, 'died a queer legend in 1964, a gloriously absurd monstre-sacre.'[15]

Jacob's numerous volumes of autobiography give an insight into many aspects of our story and, having read them all, I can't help liking her – not least because having won the prestigious Eichelberger International Humane Award in 1935, she rejected it on the basis that her co-recipient was Adolf Hitler. She was a straight-talking Yorkshirewoman: opinionated, loyal, funny, modest and formidable.

10.2 Naomi Jacob – 'Mickie' (courtesy Louise Murchison).

Music hall artistes were particularly susceptible to the perils of alcohol and Jacob, Edith and Marie Lloyd were part of the same hard-drinking circle of friends. On tour a local hostelry was far more sociable, warm and comfortable than theatrical digs, and artistes were also expected to mingle with the punters in the bar after their turn. Some proprietors even paid artistes part cash and the balance in drink – recouping much of their outlay behind the bar. Lloyd was certainly more than fond of a tipple and her preference, like Edith's, was 'Black Velvet' – but she was also known to drink beer at breakfast as if it were tea. Jacob wrote:

> Friends become a real danger. When some kindly soul says: ... "You want something to pull you together." And it is said in all kindness. "Have a little brandy and soda ... put you right in no time." And it does – the first time ... Sends you on, feeling ... that you can face the chilly stalls and a noisy gallery ... Only one drawback ... the small one becomes a large one, because the effect wears off, and ... that's the beginning of the end.[16]

Biographer Daniel Farson noted that it was Lloyd's friends who encouraged her to drink. Was Edith part of the problem or a victim of the same peer pressure? Jacob adds:

10. FROM HERE TO PATERNITY

> So often when I ask; "What's happened to so-and-so?" then people look down their noses and say coldly, "My dear, she never works now – she's quite impossible, drinks terribly." I long to ask them: "Well, did you ever try to do anything about it?" … Drink, drugs, immorality – reprehensible, terrible, disgusting, but also pitiful, desperately sad, and tragic … I can recall three who were all friends of mine. They were loyal, brilliant, kind, open-hearted – "the loveliest and the best." In each case the love and devotion which they gave so lavishly to the man they trusted was betrayed – and that is why today not one of those three women is with us. Believe me, the world is the poorer lacking their presence.[17]

I suspect the three women she was referring to were Marie Lloyd, Edith Karno and Marguerite Broadfoote, but Jacob was no innocent, as her friend and biographer James Norbury made clear: 'Let me be quite honest about this, Mickie had always been a heavy drinker but never an alcoholic.'[18] Norbury suggested that a lifetime of drinking made her memory hazy at best, and noted that she loved salacious stories, the taller the better.

You will have to forgive me for now trying to untangle something of Jacob's life – and how and when she met Edith – but it is relevant to our story. Jacob's autobiographies are famously vague on dates, but according to the website dedicated to her life, she began working as Broadfoote's secretary around 1902 (when Jacob was eighteen). In September 1903, *Early Birds* appeared on the same bill as Marguerite Broadfoote at the Hammersmith Palace of Varieties, which may have been where Edith met Broadfoote and Jacob – if so, it exactly coincided with her becoming aware of her husband's affair, which might explain why Jacob took an immediate and intense dislike to Karno. However biographer Paul Bailey, piecing together hundreds of stories from various sources, believes Jacob joined Broadfoote later – around 1905. Either way, we can be certain that her friendship with Edith must have started well before 1908, since by then Edith had moved away from London.

So, the evidence indicates that Jacob started working for Marguerite Broadfoote sometime between 1902 and 1905. So far so good – except that this date contradicts Jacob's own account of how she met Marguerite Broadfoote. So, let's take a look at that story.

Jacob said that she was introduced to Broadfoote by a young man named Wilkinson, with whom she had a brief romantic liaison whilst working as a student teacher in Middlesbrough: 'I indulged in a small sentimental interlude.'[19] Wilkinson performed on the halls as Wilkie Warren and took Jacob backstage one night to introduce her to Broadfoote. Later that year they met again when Broadfoote returned to Middlesbrough, starring as principal boy in pantomime (alongside Ernest Rees as Dame), and this led to her becoming Broadfoote's secretary. That's Jacob's story, but it doesn't stack up.

Listings show that Wilkie Warren did not appear on the halls until 1908, and Broadfoote's appearance in the pantomime with Rees was at Christmas 1909, so if the Wilkie Warren story is true, then Jacob didn't start working for Broadfoote until 1909, which we know to be impossible. Jacob met Broadfoote sometime around 1903, so it can't have stemmed from a fling with Wilkie Warren – not only was he not on the halls, he was five years younger than Jacob and would have been just fourteen. So Jacob's Wilkie Warren story appears to be a complete fiction – why?

Well, I have a possible explanation, but it's just a theory. Jacob told Gallagher that Edith was especially close to both her and Marguerite Broadfoote, so two of Edith's best friends were in a lesbian relationship. Jacob wrote of Edith: 'She was a beautiful woman, with lovely "real" golden hair. Her nature was as good as her looks; she was witty and a wonderful mimic.'[20] In later letters to Leslie, Jacob refers to Edith as 'our dear angel'. Was it more than friendship? Had Karno's *New Woman's Club* been a reaction to Edith's circle of friends? Gay women certainly embraced the New Woman movement, finding the close-knit groups a perfect cover to engage in clandestine relationships.[21] Unlike gay men, lesbians were not criminalised, but they remained a group living in a hidden world of half-truths, deceit and pretence, and many, like Broadfoote, were married (as, briefly, was Jacob – a mistake hastily rectified).

Edith had met Karno at an early age and they'd married quickly, whilst she was no doubt still innocent in the ways of the world. According to Gallagher, Edith confided to her friend Madge Proctor that Karno had been very demanding sexually and wanted all sorts of 'perversions'. The fact she found sex with her husband objectionable, never remarried and formed very close relationships with gay women, all suggests that Edith may have been gay or bisexual. Years later, Edith's granddaughter Patsy certainly thought so. When she and Karno separated, Edith made it very clear to her lawyer that she had absolutely no intention of ever remarrying. Gallagher interprets this as a woman spending the rest of her life pining for her one true love, but the reality is that her closest friends were gay

10. FROM HERE TO PATERNITY

and she had a constant stream of live-in female companions – by the time she separated from Karno, perhaps she knew that she would never want another man.

Once free from her marriage Edith threw herself into good causes, and at several functions arrived with a mysterious 'Miss Karno' in tow. This may have been a relative but there is no obvious candidate in the family tree (and Karno was just a stage name); was this mystery woman actually Edith's partner, being passed off as a relative? There are numerous examples: Miss Alice Karno is listed with her at one Christmas event,[22] and around the same time Miss Ethel Karno appears on a bill at the Alexandra Palace. No trace of either Alice or Ethel can be found elsewhere.

Leslie recalled that his childhood home with Edith was an open house. His nanny was a companion of his mother's, a female wrestler he called Aunt Selina. This may have been Selina Seaforth, who as part of a sketch trio called Seaforth, Daltry and Higgins, made a name for herself as a singer, sketch comedienne and champion lady boxer. Seaforth occasionally appeared on the same bill as Karno troupes and the 1901 census places her in Camberwell, so she could have been a friend of Edith's. She also disappears from the stage around 1908, at the same time as Edith leaves London. In later years Edith had a much younger live-in companion, Gallagher's key source Madge Proctor. When Edith died her will revealed that among her prized possessions were many pictures of one woman – Marguerite Broadfoote.[23]

If Edith was gay or bisexual, it may explain something else. We have concluded that Wilkie Warren could not have introduced Jacob to Broadfoote, so why did Jacob create this elaborate charade? Was it deliberate misdirection? In Jacob's many autobiographies, written in sexually repressive times, she does not talk about her love life, marriage or true sexuality – except for this one liaison with Wilkie Warren. What if the brief romantic interlude she had was not with Wilkie Warren, but with Winnie Warren – aka Edith Karno? The co-incidence of the names is striking to say the least. Was the brief romantic relationship which introduced Jacob to the music halls (and perhaps even to her own sexuality in 1902 at the age of eighteen) with Edith? It seems just too much of a co-incidence that Jacob claimed a relationship with a man called Wilkie Warren (which was impossible given the dates), when it appears that the real object of her affections was a woman who went by the name of Winnie Warren. The story could have been Jacob's way of recording her relationship with Edith for posterity without anyone knowing the truth.[24]

Jacob contributed this about Edith to Gallagher's biography:

> I believe that a more saintly woman never lived … her life was good. She spoke ill of no one and the man who had wronged her, spoken evil of her, tried to blacken her character in every possible way, and marked her for life with his beatings and violence, she never ceased to love, and I never heard her speak against him. She was very fair, with natural golden hair, a beautiful skin and very wide laughing blue eyes. Her figure was very trim with small, fine-shaped hands and feet. She had a great sense of humour – had she not had that she could never have got through all that she had to face. There was also considerable wit and a great ease of manner. Yet such a woman was regularly subjected to incredible degradations by her husband, indignities which even in these days of frank writing could not be publicly described.[25]

You will note the inconsistency that Edith apparently never spoke ill of Karno and yet Jacob claimed to be aware of his behaviour in their most intimate moments. Remember also that this saintly woman was the same heavy-drinking street brawler who Karno swore on oath threatened him with a knife and set fire to the furniture. Years later Jacob wrote to Leslie: 'Edie … and dear, dear Margeret [sic] Broadfoote were, perhaps, more to me than any other women will ever be.'[26] These two women, Broadfoote and Edith Karno, were perhaps the loves of Jacob's life.

There is a lot of conjecture on my part here, but if Edith was gay the failure of the Karnos' marriage is thrown into a whole new light and other pieces of the puzzle start to fall into place. First, it was while Broadfoote was playing Robinson Crusoe in Sunderland in 1902 that Edith got into that punch-up with Broadfoote's co-star, Winifred Stewart. What would it take to make two actresses get into a brawl? Did Stewart say something out of turn about Jacob or Broadfoote, or insinuate something about their friendship with Edith? Second, what about Gallagher's claim that Karno suggested he, Edith and Marie Moore might live in a ménage-à-trois? Does this suggest he suspected Edith's true sexuality?

I have now speculated that Edith may have strayed with one or more of her female companions, was a heavy drinker and prone to violence, so having

10. FROM HERE TO PATERNITY

established that she had demons of her own, let's add one more – for some reason Karno suspected that Leslie was not his child.

By the time Leslie was conceived, Karno was almost certainly having an affair with Marie Moore and Edith may have been in clandestine relationships with women – might Edith also have had an affair with another man? My case for this is admittedly thin, and reliant on Gallagher, so I should stress that there is no tangible evidence for Karno's suspicions. It is only worthy of consideration because the suggestion came from Karno himself, albeit some years after the event. He certainly had no such suspicions at the time Leslie was born, because he expressed no doubts about Edith's fidelity during their legal separation – even the suggestion of Edith being adulterous would have destroyed her case.

So how do we know that he later had his doubts? Naomi Jacob told Gallagher that sometime around 1913 she was looking after Leslie (along with Broadfoote's son Bobbie) at Marguerite's house, when Karno came knocking on their door. He was apparently in a rage, having been told by an acquaintance that Edith was not looking after their son properly, and more interestingly he 'made certain allegations against Mrs Karno's chastity, adding; "You must know something!".' Jacob said she sent him packing, adding: 'That was the last time I saw him, thank God!'[27] Gallagher then recounted a second incident some years later: Karno and Edith apparently got into a dispute about the amount of her alimony, and Karno refused to pay up on the basis that he believed Leslie was not his. Leslie supposedly confronted his father and demanded an explanation, prompting Karno to back down and confess that it had all been just a pretence aimed at reducing Edith's allowance.[28] Whether the detail of these stories is correct, something must have put the seed of doubt in Karno's mind – is there anything to suggest he might have been right?

We are into the realms of pure speculation now, but there are perhaps some genetic clues. Karno and Fred Jr. were short, dark, stocky men; Edith was blonde but similarly short and stocky. In contrast Leslie had matinee idol looks: tall and handsome, with fair hair and a chiselled jaw. The two sons' personalities were somewhat different too: Leslie supposedly took after his mother, gentle and sympathetic in nature, whereas Fred Jr. was impetuous and temperamental – a definite chip off the old block. However the brothers had plenty in common too, not least their undeniable talents as comic performers.

For completeness, I dug deep into the archives to see if I could find anything to support Karno's claim, and found nothing of substance. However, circumstantial evidence suggests that if Edith did have an affair, the number one suspect may have been a close family friend – Leslie Stuart. Stuart and Karno had many connections as we've already seen. Stuart was also part of a social circle which included his agent Reginald Golding Bright and his wife Mary Chavelita Dunne Bright, both significant players in the New Woman movement.[29] But the most notable clue is that Edith named her son after Stuart and made him the boy's godfather.

I wonder whether Karno had the same suspicion: it would certainly explain a few things. Stuart was a close friend and extremely famous, with a major hit (*Floradora*) in the bag just as Karno was producing his first musical comedy – so why did they never work together? Why was Stuart not mentioned in Karno's memoirs and vice versa? Is it pertinent that Karno first became suspicious about Edith's fidelity in 1913 (when he confronted Naomi Jacob about it), around the same time that Leslie Stuart's marriage failed? Did this skeleton somehow fall out of Stuart's closet during the course of his own break-up?[30]

10.3 The Godfather – Leslie Stuart, composer of Floradora.

Tellingly, Jacob wrote this of Edith: 'Life didn't treat her too well ... she carried on her cheek the mark which resembled a small horseshoe ... it was the memento of a boot heel which was implanted on her face! Her second son was called Leslie after his godfather, Leslie Stuart.'[31] Her comment about Stuart bears no relation whatsoever to the rest of the passage. Could this be Jacob sending a posthumous message to Karno, the man she believed branded her friend? Read between the lines: you hurt my friend and she had her revenge – Leslie was not your son.

It's an idea, but the family are certain that Leslie didn't doubt he was Karno's child, and father and son had a strong relationship in later life, so there is no family anecdote or rumour to support the theory. What's more, the notion of Edith bearing a child by another man is at odds with my proposition that she was gay. Perhaps the whole idea was nothing more than Karno's paranoia.

So, what should we conclude about Karno and Edith's break-up, other than that it would make for a great mini-series? You might contend that Edith was the victim of an abusive, adulterous husband who flaunted it in her face and tried

10. FROM HERE TO PATERNITY

10.4 A teenage Leslie Karno (courtesy Louise Murchison).

to compromise her into condoning it. If she fought back it was in self-defence, and if she drank he drove her to it. Alternatively, you might decide that Karno was forced to defend himself from a violent alcoholic who was having affairs with other men and women while being an unwilling partner in his own bed, driving him into the arms of another. When Edith took him to court, he fought in vain to prevent the separation and afterwards sought custody of his children to protect them from her.

These poorly educated working-class people had become wealthy and famous while coping with the loss of several children and the pressures of life on the road. Moral degradation followed: drink, infidelity, violence. I suspect Karno was a bully and an adulterer, Edith was a drinker with a temper. Perhaps she was gay, perhaps she was just an innocent married to a sexual adventurer – not a good match in the bedroom either way, and both sought solace in the arms of others. From this distance we'll never know which of them drove the other to their bad behaviour, but we can say that Edith's life was every bit as colourful as her husband's, and that Gallagher's portrayal of Karno as a wife-beating monster was a wildly one-sided interpretation. As for the rest? You be the judge.

11.
Princes and Principals

*All that is required in the enjoyment
of love and sausages is confidence.*
(The Merry Book of the Moore & Burgess Minstrels, 1898)

WHATEVER THE truth of the split, Edith had to find a new furrow to plough and she did so in a surprising way. In the final days of their separation battle she felt the court case was going against her and, terrified of being left penniless, she set about writing a sketch of her own.

Her libretto, a musical comedy called *The Prince of Monte Carlo*, was supposedly completed in the space of two nights (thanks to gallons of strong coffee). Gallagher recorded that on the very day Edith was granted her separation, Harry Roxbury bought the rights to her show and agreed to pay her fifty pounds every week it was staged (for up to a year).

This begs the question: had Edith written anything before? Naomi Jacob certainly thought so:

> He [Karno] had the cleverest mime artiste I have seen in the person of his wife. How many of those successful sketches – His Majesty's Guests, Mumming Birds, to name the two most successful – were devised, planned and arranged by Edie Karno the public never knew. She played in Karno's earlier and less successful days, when he had with him the two Chaplins – Syd and Charles, Charlie Austin, and many more comedians who have since become famous.[1]

11. PRINCES AND PRINCIPALS

We've already noted how inaccurate Jacob's recollections could be (for instance Edith left Karno four years before Charlie Chaplin joined him and Charlie Austin never worked for Karno), so it's perhaps no surprise that in a previous autobiography Jacob had written: 'Edie Karno herself often appeared in [Karno's sketches], and – although I never actually saw her work – I have been told that, without speaking a word, she could keep an audience rocking with laughter for three or four minutes. (That is a long time on stage remember).'[2]

It certainly is a long time, and if Edith had been capable of keeping a crowd in hysterics her name would have been mentioned in Karno's reviews, but it never was. We also know that the earliest date Jacob could have met Edith was 1902, by which time she had retired from performing. Although we know she appeared in the early sketches, the suggestion that she was instrumental in the creation of *His Majesty's Guests* and *Mumming Birds* seems unlikely. Given his relationship with chorus girl Marie Moore, Karno kept Edith well away from *His Majesty's Guests*, and *Mumming Birds* was created at a time when their marriage was breaking up.

Although Edith had been a performer there is no evidence that she had any writing experience, so this new-found ability is remarkable – but the listings bear out the story. In early September 1905, *The Era* lists *The Prince of Monte Carlo* by Harry Roxbury and Co. at the Middlesex Theatre (Edith is uncredited). Roxbury was one of many comics who repaid Karno's patronage by kicking him in the teeth. Karno had given Roxbury his big break: stepping into Fred Kitchen's shoes as Sergeant Lightning, along with a significant pay rise[3] and the rare honour of being billed by name. Karno must have been furious when, eighteen months later, Roxbury set up his own company to produce Edith's sketch.

Edith borrowed heavily from Karno's style and characters: Lady Carr, the owner of a villa in Monte Carlo, suspects two men of being card sharps and hires a detective (PC Longfellow) to investigate. He pretends to be the Prince of Monte Carlo and comedy chaos ensues when the real prince turns up.[4] Roxbury led from the front as PC Longfellow, channelling his Sergeant Lightning to great effect (a similarity not lost on the critics). He also capitalised on his career with Karno in his advertising: 'Famous as Sergeant Lightning.' How galling it must have been for Karno to see his most popular character used to advertise an ex-Karno comic's production of his ex-wife's sketch.

The show was still running a year later, so Edith netted two thousand six hundred pounds (over forty times the average annual wage) – not a bad pay day – although she might have held on for more. Roxbury made his name with the sketch and it toured for the next nine years. The sketch gave Edith financial independence and she was able to move into a large flat at 69 Primrose Mansions in London's Prince of Wales Road. Gallagher claimed that Karno, accompanied by Marie Moore, would drive past this flat every day to jeer at Edith as she tended her garden in tears, a story Leslie angrily refuted when Gallagher's book was published.

As an epilogue to this story, a 1924 report about Roxbury included the following intriguing snippet: 'Beginning his stage career at the age of 16, Harry Roxbury … has practically toured the world in the famous musical play "The Prince of Monte Carlo," the piece in which Charlie Chaplin first appeared.'[5] How ironic it would be if Chaplin had made his debut in an Edith Karno sketch! However, there is no evidence to support this: like many ex-Karno comics, Roxbury was presumably bolstering his career by implying a connection with the world's most famous comedian – the newspapers of the twenties were full of such claims.

Roxbury and other Karno contemporaries were pantomimists in the literal sense of performing in mime – not to be confused with the quintessentially British phenomenon of festive pantomime, which brings delight to children at Christmas and to theatre managers' bank balances all year around. Tempted by high salaries and secure employment, music hall artistes like Marie Lloyd and Dan Leno had crossed over into legitimate theatre by taking leading roles in pantomime – much to the dismay of those who felt the trend was an affront to theatrical decency. It was only a matter of time before Karno saw the potential of producing pantomimes of his own. He may also have been motivated by the fact that in 1904 the Palace, Manchester, decided to ditch him after three years of Christmas productions and stage a traditional panto instead.

With his experience of musical comedy and slapstick, Christmas pantomime was a natural progression, but for his first attempt Karno elected to stage one with a proven track record. He collaborated with Walter Summers, an established writer and producer (Karno called him 'a genius') who had produced a spectacular *Cinderella* at the Grand Theatre in Birmingham the previous season. Karno paid him five hundred pounds for the rights, secured the Alexandra Theatre in Stoke Newington, and began engaging artistes, including the Scottish comic Neil Kenyon to star as 'Baron McTavish'.[6] Summers was the producer but Karno's fingerprints were all over it, and *The Stage* remarked: 'Mr Fred Karno deserves praise for his share in the work of direction.'[7]

At thirty-eight Summers already had a distinguished career behind him, but he was suffering from poor health and found rehearsals so stressful that Karno

11. PRINCES AND PRINCIPALS

thought the show might finish him off. While struggling with a troublesome chorus line, Summers retorted: "I hope I shan't have as much trouble with the angels where I'm going, as I'm having with you girls."[8] Summers may have found it challenging but from its opening night on 29 December 1904 *Cinderella* was a smash hit, as this report on its final performance testifies: 'After a last week which broke all records, Mr Fred Karno's perfect pantomime Cinderella, finished its triumphant run … amid a scene of wild enthusiasm … the principals were recalled again and again, and the packed house seemed loath to part with those special favourites.'[9]

In those days a pantomime would sometimes be staged at one venue then transfer to another for the second half of the season, playing on until Easter. So in March Karno moved the show from London to the Theatre Royal, Sheffield. In the meantime he staged a benefit for Summers, who had remained ill throughout the run. The *Cinderella* company appeared, and he also persuaded Harry Tate and Bransby Williams to perform, raising enough money to send Summers on holiday to recuperate – but it was not enough. He was choreographing the angels by the time the pantomime season was over.

Summers' swansong was just the beginning for Karno. The following season he restaged *Cinderella* in Dublin and then Manchester, but decided against engaging a known comic in the lead and instead relied on his stock company, including Amy and Ada Minister, Jack Melville and Muriel and Fred Palmer – reviews were disappointing. For Christmas 1906 he was engaged to produce a pantomime for the Grand Theatre in Glasgow and, keen to avoid the same mistake, he put his faith in the biggest name in his team, casting Fred Kitchen as dame. He felt confident enough to produce an original show this time, and engaged Leonard Durrell to write the libretto. (Durrell's previous credits included a fantastic sounding 'aquatic pantomime' called *The Walrus Hunt* – who could resist that?) The music was in the capable hands of Dudley Powell and between them they created *The House That Jack Built*, a story combining several classic nursery rhymes.

The Glasgow Grand was an important venue, and Karno threw everything at the production. It had become common for American impresarios to come to London looking for talent and vice-versa, and Karno had made his first trans-Atlantic trip that September, booking an African American marching band called the Fourteen Black Hussars. They were the brainchild of a young cornet player turned agent called Jesse Lasky,[10] who shared many qualities with Karno.

In his self-effacing autobiography Lasky wrote: 'My own two most negotiable abilities – a Geiger-counter instinct for spotting potential star material when it is just talent in the raw, and a knack for making other people believe me when I only half believe in myself.'[11]

Karno assembled a further cast of 150 performers, including an act called Kirby's Flying Ballet, and continued to look for weird and wonderful ways to squeeze every ounce of comedy out of the show. Fred Whittaker played the pantomime cat, and Kitchen persuaded Karno to have Whittaker accompanied on stage by several real cats. Karno avoided the cost of an animal trainer and came to the theatre one night having purchased a sackful of alley cats. These street fighters had no intention of following direction, and Whittaker had a miserable time, being scratched and spat at as he literally tried to herd cats through the scenes – the feline chorus was quickly abandoned. With ideas like that it is no surprise that nothing seemed to go right at rehearsals and tempers became frayed. Kitchen had never played dame and was uncharacteristically nervous: he knew it had been the undoing of many otherwise excellent comics and convinced himself that the show would be a disaster. Karno was equally concerned and oversaw final rehearsals personally. Much to their amazement, opening night was such a triumph that Kitchen subsequently recalled it as one of the greatest successes of his career. As one local newspaper put it: 'A continual roar of laughter. An unparalleled company of fun makers, includes ... Fred Kitchen, the heart and soul of pantomime, his Dame Trot is a masterpiece.'[12]

At the end of that opening night the audience demanded Karno say a few words, and he was reluctantly persuaded to express his thanks to all concerned. He had spent a fortune, staked his reputation on the show and put his star comic in the lead – it paid off. The reviews were gushing about everything – even the

11.1 Karno's The House That Jack Built *– this image from a 1909 production at the Broadway Theatre, New Cross (© The Michael Diamond Collection/Mary Evans Picture Library).*

11. PRINCES AND PRINCIPALS

11.2 Neil Kenyon as pantomime Dame (author's collection).

scenery, which included a ballroom to rival Versailles and a village green with a working mill wheel (and real ducks). The show was so successful that Karno created a reduced version, *Dame Trot*, which opened at the Ardwick Empire in March before beginning a long provincial tour.

With three successful seasons under his belt, Karno was now confident in his ability to deliver pantomimes and so was the Glasgow Grand, which engaged him again the following year. *Humpty Dumpty* opened on 4 December 1907, but it nearly never happened – the show was staged by arrangement with the theatre's liquidators as the Grand had gone bust a week earlier. Moss Empires subsequently bought the theatre and Karno was out on his ear, so for the 1908 season he staged *The House That Jack Built* at the Marlborough, Islington. Moss Empires must have seen a dip in box office receipts and regretted their decision – Karno was back at the Glasgow Grand in 1909 with Neil Kenyon taking the title role in *Mother Goose*.

Karno had always included strong female comics in his sketches and these spectacular Christmas pantomimes enabled him to work with some fine performers, many of whom were at the start of illustrious careers. In 1907 Karno also staged *The House That Jack Built* in Sunderland, featuring a thirteen-year-old Mona Vivian – she went on to be one of the most prolific pantomime stars of the era. Alongside her was an actress called Muriel Harding, later talent-spotted and taken to America by Jesse Lasky to appear at his Folies Bergère Theatre on Broadway, where he renamed her Olga Petrova. Harding kept up the pretence of being a Russian starlet for the rest of her career (on stage and off) and became a major silent film star.

11.3 Muriel Harding, aka Olga Petrova, with Charlie and Syd Chaplin (courtesy Roy Export/Chaplin Archive).

While Vivian and Harding were slapping their thighs in Sunderland, Karno was having all sorts of trouble with another future star in Glasgow. Clarice Mayne had begun her career in the summer of 1906 as a singer and impersonator, quickly becoming a favourite with music hall audiences, so Karno was no doubt delighted to engage her as *Humpty Dumpty's* principal boy. It was her first pantomime role, and when rehearsals began, he discovered a problem. At a time when ladies' skirts reached the floor (and even their undergarments were below the knee), a principal boy's shorts and tights provided a rare treat for male theatregoers – but Mayne found the thought of exposing her legs horribly distressing and was in constant floods of tears. When she insisted on wearing a dressing gown during dress rehearsals, Karno realised he had to find a solution. He hit upon the idea of dressing her in very high-legged boots, coupled with a long jacket, to protect her modesty – even then he had to push her on stage on opening night. Mayne went on to become a celebrated pantomime performer, and the convention of principal boys wearing thigh-length boots endures to this day.

11.4 Mabel Green (right), Clarice Mayne and the thighs in question, Humpty Dumpty, *1907 (author's collection).*

Karno's musical director for that 1907 *Humpty Dumpty* was James W. Tate,[13] who had previously contributed material to *Saturday to Monday* with great success. Tate was married to music hall singer Lottie Collins, who found fame with *Ta-ra-ra Boom-de-ay!*, but when Collins died three years later, Tate married Mayne. They went on to have great success as a double act, 'Clarice Mayne and That' – perhaps we have Karno to thank for introducing them.

Tate was no doubt impressed by those legs, and one wonders whether they had come under close scrutiny when she was cast, since according to Gallagher, Karno was not only a serial adulterer but a keen exponent of the casting couch. Once again, we must go in search of the evidence.

Gallagher's key source for the claim was Phyllis Dixey, whom he interviewed shortly before her death. Dixey told him that in 1932, when she was eighteen, she auditioned for the Karno production *Laffs* at the London Palladium, and that he groped her before offering her the part. She apparently signed her contract but stabbed Karno's hand with the pen for his trouble.

Dixey went on to be the 'Queen of Striptease' and made a career as a burlesque dancer in the 1930s and '40s under the guidance of impresario Wallace Parnell. By modern standards, her act was classy. Surrounded by ballet dancers and nude chorus girls (painted white to look like statues), she would pose with feathered fans and sing risqué songs. She pioneered the kind of show that marked the beginning of the end for variety as it descended into seediness, with strip shows hosted by blue comedians and catering for audiences of wartime servicemen. Unsurprisingly, Dixey became a forces' sweetheart.

Parnell made her both a sex symbol and his mistress. Dixey's biographers Philip Purser and Jenny Wilkes describe him as a sexual adventurer whose parties were apparently opportunities to indulge in group sex. Not surprisingly his shows gained a seedy reputation, and some landladies refused to put up the girls – one retorted: 'I'm not having any more lazenbies in my digs.' Off stage Dixey was the very essence of a prim and proper lady, with the saddest of stories. As her star faded she worked increasingly grubby venues, before being declared bankrupt and dying of cancer, aged fifty, in 1964. As Purser and Wilkes put it: 'She had been employed for her looks rather than her talent and had learned to rely on her looks – and her sex – in order to stay in the business. The girls all did the same … In the gipsy life of a touring company morals were what you made them.'[14]

Dixey's shows had a consistent theme – how best to use her feminine charms to her advantage. Gallagher quoted a song of hers which included the line: 'I failed my first audition … I couldn't sing in a horizontal position.'[15] A wry observation on the ubiquitous casting couch, but there is no such song among those recorded by Purser and Wilkes, nor have I been able to find any trace of it elsewhere. Perhaps Gallagher misquoted her *Confessions of a Fan Dancer*, which included the line: 'Some stars rise from the ranks of the chorus, some from the beds of producers.' The casting couch was nothing new – as far back as 1885 an article by the moral campaigner W.T. Stead noted: 'Some theatrical managers are rightly or wrongly accused of insisting upon a claim to ruin actresses whom they allow to appear on their boards.'[16] While Stead's *Pall Mall Gazette* was strongly anti-music hall and pro-temperance, it is fair to assume that the casting couch had been standard equipment for impresarios, agents and producers since time immemorial – Karno was probably no exception.

When the chance to work in the music halls meant a route out of poverty, sexual exploitation was all too easy. In his autobiography *Clips From A Life*, the humorist Denis Norden recalled that when he put out a general casting call for a revue in the late 1930s, many of the applicants included the letters MPR under their signature, standing for 'management's privileges respected'.[17] Many women expected to have to prostitute themselves for a role.

Notwithstanding the danger of exploitation, a dancer's appearance and figure were paramount and theatrical newspapers of the day are littered with advertisements stating that good looks were essential. Louisa Millar, who joined Karno as a dancer in the early twenties, recalled her audition: having just arrived from Liverpool, she turned up at his office in an old fur coat and with precious little else to her name. Karno asked her to strip to her underwear and she didn't hesitate (despite wearing a bra she'd made herself from black handkerchiefs). He stared for a moment then simply announced: "Bloody marvellous – you're in." She got dressed and that was that – although Karno later decided that Louisa's legs were too thin and had his costume department make special tights with padding to give them more shape. Louisa insisted that Karno never tried it on with her, which was fortunate since she went on to marry his son, Leslie.

Back to our accuser. I'm increasingly feeling like Karno's defence lawyer, but Dixey's account of auditioning for *Laffs* at the Palladium in 1932 is full of holes. By then Karno was at the very end of his career, with very few productions, and Dixey does not appear in the listings for *Laffs* or any other Karno show. Purser and Wilkes do not record Dixey ever working with Karno, and as they point out she was neither a competent singer or dancer and would have been unlikely to get past the stage door. Their account also shows that Dixey was actually appearing in Parnell's *Spice of Paris* at the time.[18] What's more, *Laffs* never played the London Palladium, a fact we'll come back to shortly.

So where does this story come from? The Purser and Wilkes biography of Dixey reveals that her mother Selena (who contributed to their book) worked for Karno as a waitress at his ill-fated hotel, Karsino, just after the First World War. Selena recalled that she had to take her children (including Phyllis, then aged five) to work with her because her husband was frequently away at sea. While there, the infant Phyllis would apparently dance the hornpipe for the staff – her first taste of applause. Selena paints a picture of Karno as a kindly gent, doting on Phyllis and her brother Ernie, and obviously accommodating enough to let her bring them to work at Karsino. Is it likely that Karno would have then sexually assaulted an eighteen-year-old Phyllis in 1932? And wouldn't Phyllis have mentioned this to her mother, who was clearly an admirer of his? Purser and Wilkes seemed to think it lacked credibility: they don't repeat Gallagher's account and simply state: 'According to Karno's biographer J.P. Gallagher he made an improper advance which she repelled.'[19] That's it. No mention of her working for Karno and no outrage at a man behaving this way to a girl he'd known since childhood. I'm sure if they'd believed the story, Purser and Wilkes would not have let Karno off so lightly. They underlined this by putting Selena's glowing endorsement of Karno's character on the first page of their book: 'Mr Karno had no children of his own. He loved my kids. He was kindness itself, the nicest man that God put breath in.'[20]

Purser and Wilkes go on to explain why they had little confidence in Dixey's account – by the early sixties she was in failing physical and mental health. Near bankruptcy and with the loss of her youth and figure taking their toll, she suffered a severe nervous breakdown. At the same time, who should appear in her life but tabloid journalist J.P. Gallagher, who began work on a biography, assuring her 'he was confident of selling it to a Sunday paper.' Purser and Wilkes add: 'The memoirs which she had composed with Joe Gallagher were full of self-justification, stories of attackers and peeping Toms, extravagant denunciations of everything that in her eyes was immoral … as a warning to girls who might be tempted to follow her.'[21]

As Purser and Wilkes make clear, Dixey was anything but the victim of this kind of behaviour. She had the protection of being in a relationship with the man in charge: first a long affair with Wallace Parnell (who later came to a sticky end in America, where he murdered his secretary then shot himself) and then marrying Jack Tracey, a comic with whom she established and ran her shows. Purser and Wilkes provide no stories of producers making improper advances to her directly and conclude that Gallagher was taking testimony from a sick and dying woman whose stories were the ramblings of a fantasist: a woman who had lived her life being leered at on the stage and now saw sexual predators around every corner. Perhaps Dixey had remembered Karno as a child and confused this with recollections of some other lecherous producer. It is worth noting that while *Laffs* never played the London Palladium, Karno did license the show to George Black, who used it as the basis of a subsequent Palladium show starring the 'Crazy Gang' in 1932 (much more on this later). Karno had no direct involvement in the show – the man responsible for putting it together was Black's deputy Val Parnell, the brother of Dixey's lover Wallace.

Gallagher's biography of Dixey came to nothing. In March 1963 he wrote to tell her that his publishers weren't interested in her story. By then Gallagher had switched his attentions to Karno – and a year later Dixey was dead.

Dixey's mother's story throws up another puzzle. You will have noticed that while employed at Karsino around 1919, Selena evidently thought Karno had no children of his own, which is strange since Fred Jr. and Leslie were by then working with their father. Perhaps her recollections of Karsino were from a year earlier, when Leslie was still living away from London with Edith, and Fred Jr. was serving in the First World War. Either way he must have kept his personal life very private for his own staff not to know of his children's existence.

With Dixey's claim questionable, is there any other evidence to suggest Karno preyed on young wannabes? Well, we've established that the casting couch culture was endemic, and Fred Jr. certainly believed that his father had numerous girlfriends over the years (as a child he would supposedly be given a few shillings to keep quiet about them). Junior's wife Olive recounted to Gallagher some family stories which support the idea of Karno as a philanderer.[22] For instance, one night when Fred Jr. was staying with his father on his houseboat, he apparently became aware that Karno had secreted one of his female companions in his cabin. The following morning, ever the dutiful son, he knocked quietly on his father's bedroom door with two cups of tea. He found Karno sitting up in bed with not one but two women. With a grin as wide as a Cheshire cat, his father merely said: "Don't just stand there son – get another cup!"[23]

11.5 "Don't just stand there son – get another cup." Fred Karno entertains on his houseboat (courtesy Roy Export/Chaplin Archive).

On another occasion, Karno had cause to discipline a waiter at Karsino and the disgruntled employee took revenge by untying his houseboat, allowing it to drift quietly into the middle of the Thames. This came to the attention of the staff and guests because a young lady, who had been waiting in Karno's cabin, was now in the full glare of Karsino's lights, running around the deck in her underwear and screaming to be rescued. The ferrymen frantically scrambled to retrieve the boat as Karno sprinted across the croquet lawn bellowing: "Get below you silly bitch!"

11. PRINCES AND PRINCIPALS

The most scandalous of these stories involves a chorus girl who apparently turned up at Karsino, confronted Karno in the crowded ballroom, and announced that she was six months pregnant with his child. With a word in the ear of the maître d she was quickly despatched. Shaggy dog stories like these fitted Gallagher's narrative perfectly, but there is only one piece of contemporary evidence to support the idea that Karno saw sex as a tool of the trade. One of the greatest stand-up comics of his generation, Max Miller, worked with Karno in a revue in 1927, and recalled the following story to his biographer John East. The show was going badly and Karno confronted Miller in his dressing room – he proposed an unusual solution:

> "A few double acts, that's what's needed to liven it up a bit," said Karno.
> "But I'm a solo turn. I work alone," replied Miller.
> "I don't mean that sort of double act, you twerp. I mean f**k a few of the chorus girls, Miller. That'll make 'em happy and that's good for the production. It'll show, it'll show."[24]

Karno was a man of few words but the ones he used could be colourful – Adeler and West said his language could turn taxi drivers 'pink with envy'. If Karno was rough, Miller was rougher, so the language here may have been Miller's (every direct quote in East's biography uses similar expletives), but you get the idea – and the story is one of the few that really gives us a flavour of Karno's coarseness. He was as common as muck, no matter how hard he tried to hide it, and it was writ large in his language, accent and his aggressive approach to managing his artistes. Nonetheless he could certainly turn on the charm – both of his wives adored him. Edith eventually walked out, but Marie must have either been blissfully unaware of, or accepted, Karno's dalliances as a price worth paying to be Mrs Fred Karno – their relationship lasted thirty-nine years.

We have digressed from our story, so let's return to summer 1904, where we left Karno launching *Mumming Birds* while trading blows with Edith. As his empire continued to expand, the once happy family of comics at the Fun Factory was becoming more difficult to control. Karno's artistes and staff saw the extraordinary wealth he was accruing and many began to feel hard done by; others may have turned against him as his marriage broke down – after all, Edith had been one of them. Whatever the reasons, personal and professional tensions were about to boil over.

12.

Thieves and Tricksters

When is a theatrical manager like an astronomer?
When he discovers a new star.
(The Merry Book of the Moore & Burgess Minstrels, 1898)

WE HAVE taken a lengthy detour. Before we examined Karno's love life and family break-up, we had followed his career up to 1904, the year of his first Christmas pantomime. *Mumming Birds* was his latest sketch, and he'd struck an agreement with Reed Pinaud to license his shows in America. As well as these new initiatives, the old sketches and musical comedies were doing steady business. Oswald Stoll was sufficiently impressed by *Saturday to Monday* to have it top the bill on opening night of his new Ardwick Empire in July, and its female star, Aggie Morris, was making a name for herself, becoming the first Karno comedienne to be named in the billing. Karno created a second *Saturday to Monday* company for a provincial tour, which opened in September at the Theatre Royal, Sheffield. For some reason Karno decided to stage the show under a different name, *The New Mama*, but this only lasted a week before reverting to the usual title. You may remember Jaggs, the reluctant bridegroom? Reviews now reveal that he had three children from previous liaisons (hence the new title) and the kids caused him no end of trouble, particularly in the closing scene on the coast at Saltsea.

Karno gave his comedians the opportunity to learn their craft in a creative, if chaotic, environment which engendered loyalty and team spirit. This camaraderie led to many lively japes and Karno wasn't averse to a practical joke of his own. Fred Jr. recorded that his father was good natured if eccentric, with a sarcastic

12. THIEVES AND TRICKSTERS

but playful sense of humour. He recalled that Karno once woke him at two in the morning and told him to get up and join him in the Fun Factory kitchen. Junior was surprised not only at the hour, but because Karno was supposed to be in Birmingham. Downstairs he found that his father had prepared a tray of tea with bread and cheese, plus a pillow, hot water bottle and travelling rug. Karno raised his finger to his lips with a "shh" and beckoned Fred to help him carry the things into the yard. Fred thought Karno was going mad until they entered the scenery store, where the night-watchman was discovered, sleeping soundly at his post. Karno gave a little cough and the watchman awoke. Startled and embarrassed, he attempted to jump to his feet but Karno insisted he stay settled, asked whether he took sugar, fluffed the pillow and tucked him in with the blanket. Fred Jr. recorded that Karno bore the man no ill-will and they remained on good terms, but his little performance ensured that the night-watchman never fell asleep on duty again. The fact Karno didn't sack him on the spot supports Junior's view that: 'Whatever his faults, he did not bear malice.'[1] Adeler and West added:

> In presenting the life of FK there is no desire to reveal him as a sort of little tin angel. He had his faults and foibles as have other men and, like most of us, he has been guilty of many follies. But vindictiveness is not one of his sins. He can tell stories of his past dealings with certain people, events that would make many men red in the neck with indignation, placidly evenly and without acrimonious comment … in viewing his past associates he is "to their faults a little blind, and to their virtues very kind."[2]

After the death of the Duke of Cambridge in March 1904, his estate and effects were sold at auction[3] and Karno bought two state carriages with full livery. What better way to promote his extravagant shows than with a procession of royal coaches through London? The press found it highly amusing:

> A State coach … heavily gilt enrichments, massive furniture upholstered in yellow-figured satin, panels handsomely painted with Royal Coat of Arms … and another State Coach, were bought for Mr Fred Karno at 38 and 20 guineas respectively. Thus, the coaches that ornamented many State processions will hence forward carry a music hall troupe to and from the halls. Let us hope that the old Duke will rest quietly in his grave.[4]

Karno's gag soon gathered momentum as he recruited some of the plonks to obtain costumes for footmen and 'swells' from Morris Angel's costume hire and, with their occupants suitably attired, despatched the coaches to collect Fred Kitchen from his flat in Balham. Kitchen, already in his make-up for that evening's performance of *Saturday to Monday*, walked serenely down his front steps and into the coach, to the bewilderment of neighbours and assembled street urchins. After stopping off in Coldharbour Lane to pick up leading lady Cossie Noel, the coaches processed through the capital, generating waving crowds as they went. On London Bridge the police stopped the traffic for them, soldiers saluted, and shopkeepers and passers-by cheered, all believing that the coaches contained some royal personage. When they arrived at the Paragon Theatre, such a large crowd had assembled that they could hardly reach the stage door.

Karno had intended to include the coaches in *Cinderella*, but they were too big to fit on the stage. Instead he had 'Karno's Speechless Comedians' emblazoned on their sides and used them on tour as an advertising gimmick – they always caused a sensation. Once the novelty had worn off he sold them,[5] supposedly to a Chinese mandarin who continued to use them for civic occasions in China (complete with Karno advertising).

12.1 Causing a stir – the Duke of Cambridge's carriage (© Illustrated London News Ltd/Mary Evans Picture Library).

He wasn't above playing a joke on his own children, too. Family history has it that both Fred Jr. and Leslie were privately educated (Fred Jr. at Acton College[6] and Leslie at Margate College), and Junior recalled feeling out of place among the children of the wealthy. This was brought home to him whenever a letter arrived, as it was always in an ostentatious company envelope – bright red with 'Karno' in gold lettering. When he asked his father to use plain stationery, Karno (and co-conspirator Harry Tate) decided to deliver Junior's next letter personally, in a large van with 'Fred Karno's Komics' on the side. Leslie felt similarly embarrassed when his father turned up at Margate in his bright purple Rolls Royce.

Some tricks were more than just fun, they could be an effective way to keep his troupes in line. Comedians could be difficult people to manage, as Adeler and West put it:

12. THIEVES AND TRICKSTERS

> Of all the quaint birds in the human aviary the comedian ... is by far the oddest. [Karno] knew all the little tricks and idiosyncrasies common to the species, including the indisputable fact that even when the bird was caught and caged by a contract it wasn't always possible to make him sing. Too little bird-seed made him sulky; too much gave him a bad attack of megalomania.[7]

Karno's answer was to rule with a rod of iron, which resulted in a reputation for harshness – although he considered himself firm but fair. Karno comic Freddie Forbes recalled the Guv'nor's approach in an interview in 1925: 'Karno ... took a lot of trouble with his boys ... rehearsed them daily, and while he was ready to encourage a promising lad, he did not encourage self-complacency. "I'll have to put you back in the oven, my lad," he would say to any boy who developed signs of a swelled head: "You're only half baked".'[8]

While he didn't pay the best wages, Karno's artistes had consistent employment all year round, giving them far greater security than their peers. While some found him hard to work for, others clearly appreciated this, and the trade press is full of notices from people thanking Karno for paying them between shows or over holiday periods. Remunerating artistes who were not performing was unprecedented at that time. However, his early years had taught him the value of money, and he was a tough negotiator when faced with pay demands. One can imagine him saying: "When I was your age, I was sleeping on the floor of the elephant house and nicking sweets off babies to survive."

Karno felt particularly aggrieved by comedians who, having tasted success with his shows, decided they were now worthy of immediate fame and fortune. His solution was to have two oversized hats made (a boater for summer and a bowler for winter), which hung on his office wall. When a comic demanded more cash, Karno would pass him a hat and explain that it was all he had for big-heads. A repeat offender was a comedian called Albert Bruno who, at the end of yet another discussion about money, saw Karno reach for the cupboard and cried: "Guv'nor, for God's sake don't give me the hat!"

It wasn't just financial demands that were problematic: an inflated ego could seriously diminish a comedian's performance. Karno recalled how comics would sometimes get complacent and 'walk through' their part, or would complain about the length of rehearsals. His answer was to suggest the offender deserved a rest and give the understudy a chance (they would often take the show by storm). Unsurprisingly, the star would quickly fall back into line. Other comics caused problems by arguing with Karno or insisting on doing things a different way – he had a solution for that too:

> Fred would say: "Well I'll tell you what we'll do. You play it your way in the first house and try it my way in the second. We'll let the people who pay at the doors decide." The comic ... would do his damnedest in the first house and ... underplay when carrying out the boss's ideas yet, in nine cases out of ten, the laughter and applause of the second house would prove ... Karno was right.[9]

Karno was no fool – the first house was always harder to please than the second.

For every temperamental star there were twenty lesser lights for whom secure, continuous employment was enough – it certainly beat the more typical hand-to-mouth existence on the halls. A number stayed with Karno for many years. He may have been a tough taskmaster, but Adeler and West described him as a generous director: 'He never turns a deaf ear to any suggestion, even from the humblest member of his staff. By receiving it first with encouragement and analysing its possibilities later, he creates a reputation for human understanding, at the same time gaining many valuable discoveries.'[10]

This was an approach that rubbed off on his disciples – not least Charlie Chaplin, one of whose co-stars later said: 'Chaplin listened to everybody's ideas and evaluated them with an unerring instinct for those that were good.'[11] Karno was unapologetic in driving his comics to achieve their best, and this gained him their respect. John McCabe wrote: 'He was the ultimate professional, aware precisely of effects needed, and if he was unrelenting and sometimes harsh in his work methods, he was considerate and kindly to his performers. His two most distinguished proteges, Charlie Chaplin and Stan Laurel, retained grateful memories of him all their days.'[12]

Karno discipline helped to develop a consistent comic style in his artistes. Witnessing Stan's impersonation of Chaplin, John McCabe saw first-hand what he described as the superb litheness, mimetic grace and gentle sadness that both men shared. Other biographers have been in no doubt as to Karno's importance. Simon Louvish wrote of his influence on Laurel and Chaplin: 'Outside the intellectual middle classes, it was comedy that was king. And the king of comedy

12. THIEVES AND TRICKSTERS

was Fred Karno ... the significance of Karno in both these actors' inheritance goes deeper than merely that of a mentor.'[13]

With a growing empire, handling comics wasn't Karno's only challenge: he also had to deal with managers, musicians, agents, hangers-on and con artists. After falling for one sob story, Karno lent a theatre manager £2000, a huge sum at the time, which he never saw again. Such experiences further tightened his grip on his wallet, and he began to gain a reputation for meanness which belies the evidence of his charitable efforts.

Karno relished the creative and commercial challenges of running a large business, but found constant pilfering of his material (and his artistes) by his rivals enormously frustrating. He described himself as being hard to beat, and took 'a certain almost puckish delight in outwitting those who clashed swords with him,'[14] which led to numerous courtroom battles. Karno hated liars, injustice, misrepresentation and poor service, but like everything else in his life, this was taken to extremes – he took pleasure in catching people out, and doing so in public to maximise their embarrassment. He once had a gas fire installed at the Fun Factory which the manufacturer proclaimed as revolutionary in that it could be installed 'with no visible pipes'. When the fitter had finished, Karno rounded up his entire staff to see the wonderful new fire, then, with an inscrutable smile, pointed out an inch of copper pipe that could be seen where the gas connection was made: "No pipes you said." The gas fitter, suitably embarrassed, was instructed to remove the lot and never darken Karno's door again. Another family story has it that Karno and Leslie were driving up the Strand when he spotted a tailor selling 'off the peg shirts, guaranteed to fit' – a challenge Karno couldn't resist. He was short but broad and muscular (a lifetime of acrobatics had seen to that) – so unsurprisingly, the sleeves were far too long. "See? See? See?" he cried with glee: "This man's a bloody liar. Thieves and robbers they are; thieves and robbers."

Some might say Karno was irritated by those not meeting his own exacting standards, others that he enjoyed making people feel uncomfortable. Either way, since that childhood experience of being cheated out of his milk-cart cleaning business, he hated what he called 'thieves and tricksters'. Adeler and West noted that he saved his most intense dislike for those who cheated him in business: 'Fred Karno's brains have been shamelessly exploited many times ... but he had often been able to protect himself against thieves and tricksters.'[15]

In July 1904 Karno had granted Theodore Reed Pinaud the international rights to *Mumming Birds* and *Early Birds*. Reed Pinaud was American, and had made a name for himself in a troupe famous for their comedic high-kicking. Since settling in Britain, he had become a committee member of the Water Rats, which may be how he came to meet Karno. With a background in physical comedy and American vaudeville connections, he seemed a good choice to introduce Karno's material to a global audience. His advertising indicates that he took a company to America in autumn 1904, and while I have been unable to find any evidence of this, he certainly had European engagements in 1905. By that summer he had also secured an agreement with producer Charles Frohman for a subsequent U.S. tour. In the meantime, he and Karno had become embroiled in an acrimonious legal battle.

12.2 See you in court – Theodore Reed Pinaud.

In August 1905 Karno sued Reed Pinaud, alleging that having paid one hundred pounds to license the sketches, he had reneged on the second part of the agreement, which was to pay an additional royalty for each performance. Reed Pinaud counterclaimed that Karno had failed to provide the scripts, music and scenery plans which were essential for him to produce the sketches. Initially the American seemed to have the upper hand, writing to *The Era*: 'I, T. Reed Pinaud on the 10th day of August, 1905, succeeded in quashing an injunction which had been obtained against me in my absence abroad by Mr Fred Karno, in which he sought to restrain me from producing … "The Early Bird" and "The Mumming Bird" … which I acquired by payment to him of a large sum. I accordingly open with my company on Saturday next … at the Scala Theatre Copenhagen.'[16]

Although Reed Pinaud describes his initial payment to Karno as a large sum, one hundred pounds seems relatively paltry – the royalty component must therefore have been a significant part of the deal. Karno fought

12.3 Fred Evans as the glazier Jew in Reed Pinaud's Early Birds *– Amsterdam, January 1905 (courtesy Marianne Morgan).*

12. THIEVES AND TRICKSTERS

back in the following week's edition: 'I ... beg to inform Proprietors, Managers, Agents, and all others ... that, notwithstanding the statement made by T. Reed Pinaud ... the agreement ... is null and void ... the action instituted by me for an injunction and damages, is still pending, and has yet to be decided by the High Courts.'[17]

12.4 Reed Pinaud's Early Birds *company, January 1905 – left to right: Fred Evans, W. Le Fre, William Moran, James Le Fre – all ex-Karno plonks. (courtesy Marianne Morgan).*

The battle raged on for months. Karno recalled despatching Herbert Darnley, by then his general manager, to the continent to put a stop to a copycat version of *Mumming Birds* touring Germany – presumably Reed Pinaud's troupe. Injunctions flew back and forward until, in March 1906, Karno received an early fortieth birthday present: 'The supreme court of the State of New York on the 8th March 1906 ... in the case of Pinaud against Karno, judgement [sic] was given in favour of Fred Karno.'[18] The battle in Europe continued, however, and in September Karno lost a similar action in the French courts and Pinaud retained the right to stage the show in Paris. In October *The Era* records an eight-week run of *An Evening in an English Music Hall* at the Theatre Marigny, with a comic called Gus Le Clerq playing the drunk in the box. Reed Pinaud's *Mumming Birds* played Paris again a year later, and although his company disappears from the British press after this, his 1925 obituary stated that his last appearance on the stage was in *Mumming Birds* in Hamburg in 1908, so the tour evidently continued for at least another six months.

The Reed Pinaud dispute was one of many such battles, and Karno gained a reputation for being litigious – but the cases were not all at his instigation.[19] He claimed never to have won a case but this is far from the truth, so let's take a detour and look at a few examples – one of which was extremely important. The press records over a dozen cases involving Karno in the period from 1904 to 1930 and he also occasionally appeared as a witness in other disputes. It is worth setting this in context: Karno's career spanned well over forty years, and at its peak he had up to ten troupes touring concurrently – he must have entered into thousands of contracts with theatres, syndicates, suppliers, artistes and agents.

So to have found himself in legal dispute a dozen times doesn't seem overly litigious in the scale of things.

Some of the cases were fought over 'barring clauses', which aimed to prevent an artiste from performing their act within a certain distance of a hall where they had recently appeared. This caused particular problems for those with multiple troupes, as some managers interpreted the clause as applying not just to the sketch they had booked, but to any Karno production. For instance, in September 1904, Walter Gibbons (the son-in-law of George Adney Payne and a powerful syndicate owner himself) engaged a Karno sketch and then successfully sued him for putting another into a nearby hall. Karno lost similar battles with both the Empress, Camberwell,[20] and the Euston Theatre – the judge in the latter case ruled that his shows were similar enough to compete with one another. With multiple touring companies and hundreds of artistes to keep busy, being prevented from playing not just the same sketch but any sketch was unmanageable – Karno was almost bound to fall foul of it. The use of barring clauses by larger syndicates was intended to stamp out competition from smaller independent halls, but the artistes got caught in the crossfire. As we shall see, these restrictive practices eventually led to an all-out strike by performers.

12.5 No holds barred – Walter Gibbons.

Most of Karno's other cases were minor squabbles over agents' commissions or artistes' terms, and Karno was more often the defendant than the plaintiff. In Graydon vs. Karno (1905), an agent successfully sued him over disputed commission terms – then two weeks later, Graydon asked Karno to act as a defence witness for him in another similar case! Interestingly, Graydon noted that Karno was the only client who paid five instead of ten per cent commission: 'Mr Karno would not pay more as he is well up in the profession and his engagements were so easy to get.'[21] In Brookes vs. Kirby (1908), Karno was a witness in an important test case between an agent and Kirby's Aerial Ballet, an acrobatic troupe he had engaged for *The House That Jack Built*. Kirby had been introduced to Karno by an agent (Brookes), but they failed to make a deal. Subsequently Karno and Kirby came to a private arrangement and, when he found out, Brookes sued Kirby for his commission. The judge considered that Brookes had been cut out, and found in his favour. This set a precedent that when an

12. THIEVES AND TRICKSTERS

agent had instigated an introduction, an implied contract existed between him and the artiste.

In Kendall vs. Karno (1906), Karno was sued for damages by a musician. During a production of *Early Birds*, the plonks managed to send the pedlar's coffee-stall crashing into the orchestra pit, breaking the unfortunate chap's shoulder blade. All parties agreed it was an accident, not negligence, but the musician was still awarded sixty pounds plus costs. In Hilliard vs. Karno (1907), Harold Hilliard sued Karno over the work deemed to be included in his basic salary. Hilliard had been engaged to produce *The House That Jack Built* in 1906, and subsequently paid for his contribution as a writer to various sketches. Karno then appointed him general manager on a salary of five pounds per week, which he deemed to include any writing work. Hilliard, however, was under the impression that he would receive an extra ten pounds each time he wrote a sketch. The disagreement ended up in court, where the judge found against Karno and awarded Hilliard thirty-five pounds (plus costs).

In Cave vs. Karno (1907), Karno was sued by Joseph Cave, an eighty-four-year-old veteran clown, for failing to pay for material he contributed to a production at Olympia (which we'll come to later). Cave was old enough to have seen Joe Grimaldi himself perform – a generational bridge between the Georgian Harlequinade and Karno's plonks. He had blown the dust off his old routines having been told that Karno would 'make it worth his while.' It turned out that this amounted to ten shillings. The court deemed this insufficient and forced Karno to cough up twenty-five pounds – he put up no defence.

Things didn't always go against Karno. In 1909 he successfully defended a case for wrongful dismissal brought against him by comic Tom Mackney and his wife, whom he had sacked for drunkenness. Another time Karno was sued by Francis Cox for allegedly stealing a script Cox had submitted called *Timothy MP* (or *The Suffragettes at St. Stephens*), only for his accuser to drop the case. Perhaps Karno had settled out of court to avoid negative publicity. Such an amicable resolution was not uncommon. For example, Karno once contracted Seymour Hicks to appear in a show with a woman called Zena Dare. When Dare subsequently declined to appear, Karno sued Hicks for damages. It transpired that Zena was in poor health and the sketch (in which she played a Greek model) required some energetic dancing. Karno's counsel asked Hicks: "Greek statues don't kick high do they?" to which Hicks replied: "Well it depends what music hall they're in!" (much to the amusement of the court). Karno and Hicks eventually settled amicably and the judge commended Karno for behaving 'with great courtesy'. In one case Karno was sued by a proprietor when an effect in one of his revues failed to work – a projected bubble was supposed to expand in size during a song entitled *Bubbles*. The judge offered the two sides the chance to reach their own agreement and, having consulted in a side room, they announced that they'd tossed a coin to settle the matter.

Among these run-of-the-mill legal actions, one case had far reaching effects. Karno vs. Pathé Frères Limited (1908) was a landmark case – almost certainly the first legal action brought for copyright infringement in the new medium of film. Copyright law then existed in the form of a variety of statutes, notably the Dramatic Copyright Act 1833, which provided a degree of protection for plays from plagiarism. But film was obviously not anticipated by the legislation, so there was no clear basis for establishing whether a filmed version of someone else's material breached their copyright.

The French film company Pathé Frères had made a version of *Mumming Birds* called *Au Music Hall*, which starred Max Linder[22] as the drunk. By now films were beginning to be shown as novelty items on music hall bills, so Karno found his troupe turning up at theatres to find punters had seen the show the week before – he took to the courts.

The film was re-discovered in 2014, and it condenses the entire sketch into four minutes – to the modern eye there is barely a gag in sight. Linder falls in and out of the box repeatedly but in no way acrobatically, and his physical comedy is unimpressive. A magician enters, a table is placed centre stage and the Eton boy volunteers to be the assistant. The magician holds up a sheet in front of the boy and he disappears. The drunk jumps onto the stage and tips over the table, revealing the boy underneath. The Terrible Turkey enters but Linder instead fights a dummy which is placed on a chair for no apparent reason. He then takes on the Turkey, a bout which amounts to them hitting each other with balloons.

12.6 Max Linder with Charlie Chaplin (courtesy Roy Export/Chaplin Archive).

12. THIEVES AND TRICKSTERS

Au Music Hall is such a pale reflection of the energy, humour and physical acrobatics of the original that it is hard to imagine it seriously threatening Karno's real-life performers, but clearly it did – such was the novelty of film at the time. French companies were at the forefront of film development and Pathé was an early pioneer of screen comedy. King of silent movie slapstick (and Chaplin's first studio boss) Mack Sennett once said: 'It was those Frenchmen who invented slapstick and I imitated them … I stole my first ideas from the Pathés.'[23] Clearly Pathé's directors were stealing their first ideas from Karno!

The detail of the legal case (which filled pages and pages of the theatrical press at the time) is beyond the scope of this book, but the key principles are worth noting. Pathé did not deny that the film was Karno's material, rather they relied on the fact that copyright law covered only 'representation' of a 'dramatic piece'. They argued that a film was not a 'representation' (as defined in the act) and, even if it was, they weren't responsible for the actual showing of it, so couldn't be deemed to be 'representing' it. Their third main argument was that 'dramatic pieces' required dialogue and a published script[24] – a show in mime was therefore not protected.

As a test case for the new medium, Karno's battle was watched with keen interest by the entire profession and it had its moments of excitement. Judge Justice Jelf watched a private staging of *Mumming Birds* at the Oxford to understand the piece, and according to *The Stage* he not only thoroughly enjoyed himself but was left in no doubt that Pathé's film was a direct copy. He also held that Pathé was deliberately anticipating the arrival of Karno's touring troupe and using his advance publicity to trail their film. So far so good. However, despite Jelf's personal view, he found in favour of Pathé based on legal technicalities and gaps in the law. First, and most importantly, he was forced to agree that *Mumming Birds* could not be considered a 'dramatic work' since there was no scripted dialogue. Jelf also agreed that manufacturing and distributing the film did not constitute 'representing it' – he concluded that 'representation' was instead the act of the individual showing the film. Karno's only legal redress would therefore have been against the theatre's projectionist!

It was cold comfort that Jelf noted that the law prevented him from reaching what appeared to be an obvious decision in Karno's favour. Clearly the new medium of film required new and appropriately worded legislation, but Jelf also observed that the existing law failed to take into consideration the type of show *Mumming Birds* was. He said these issues needed to be addressed in future legislation, as this was not just a problem for 'low comedy' like Karno's slapstick, there were highbrow pieces which relied on mime to tell their story: Debussy's cantata *L'Enfant Prodigue* was cited as an example.

Karno appealed, but with the same outcome. His loss was felt by the industry at large: *The Stage* described it as 'unexpected and disconcerting', adding: 'Everyone will sympathize with Mr Fred Karno in the loss of this case. He took action over a grievance of growing dimensions, and it was not because his cause was not just, but because the law … was defective, that he failed in his public-spirited attempt.'[25]

Karno may have taken some consolation from the fact that his case made a significant contribution to the subsequent development of copyright law, culminating in the Copyright Act of 1911 which cleared up two issues that had gone against him: productions in 'dumb show' were now protected, and making or exhibiting films (not just projecting them) fell under its auspice.

Given how hard Karno fought Pathé, it is surprising to discover that their version of *Mumming Birds* may not have been his first sketch to be filmed. According to the British Film Institute, an early film called *A Raid On A Club* (made in 1905 by Walturdaw) was also based on a Karno piece. The title suggests this was *New Woman's Club,* although the film is now lost so we can't be sure. There is no mention of this in Karno's memoirs or the press at the time, so perhaps he was simply unaware of it.

So, what do these legal cases tell us about Karno's relationship with the judiciary? What emerges is a picture of a man who was not a habitual contract-breaker, but rather someone with a strong sense of fairness who was prepared to have his day in court. His inherent belligerence was compounded by a belief that his success brought a constant stream of people trying to rip him off. Karno sometimes acted on matters of principle, but more often was simply unwilling to give in to those who, in his view, were trying to take advantage of him. Whether he was in the right or the wrong, his biggest battles were yet to come.

13.

I Want to be in America

*"We have to make this post-office into a paying concern
– in future we'll send the 8am mail out at 7am."*
"Whatever for?"
"To get there before the other post-offices you fool!"
(The G.P.O., 1908)

IN SEPTEMBER 1904 Arthur Jefferson won a long-standing legal dispute of his own, and regained control of the Theatre Royal in North Shields. It was an important moment in his career, and Jefferson chose to celebrate by hosting Karno's *His Majesty's Guests* the week after he took over. It was another chance for young Stan, now fourteen, to watch Karno's boys at work. His father's victory was short-lived: his fortunes in the North East soon declined and within a year the family had decided to make a fresh start in Glasgow, where Stan would later make his professional debut. Meanwhile, Karno finally turned his attention to new material, staging a try-out of a sketch entitled *The Thirsty First*, which was reported as doing good business but ran for just one week at the Paragon in mid-November – it would be a year before it reappeared. Later that month Karno performed in another Water Rats' charity matinee, as one of a group of stars who staged a sketch entitled *The Wife with a Smile*.[1] This comedy supergroup comprised Little Tich, the McNaughtons, Paul Martinetti, Harry Tate, Alice Lloyd (Marie's sister) and our hero – he was clearly still able to hold his own as a comic. The Paragon played host to another charity show early in the new year (for the St George's and Wapping Relief Fund), to which Karno contributed a skit entitled *Pot Pourri*. This never appeared again, and the name suggests it was probably an amalgamation of business from existing sketches.

While he may have been struggling to get new material off the ground, the older sketches continued to tour and were often at the top of the bill. His 'Gigantic Vaudeville Company of Star Artistes' now utilised 'ten tons of magnificent scenery' as they combined *Jail Birds*, *Early Birds* and *Mumming Birds* into a triple bill. Karno was a busy man and as he rushed around the country, tearing up the highways and byways, his car troubles continued. Perhaps to minimise his risk of speeding fines (or to enable canoodling with Marie Moore in the back seat) he employed a driver, John Hallas, who turned out to be a liability. Having been fined ten pounds for drink-driving the previous summer, Hallas found himself before the magistrates again in March 1905:

> He drove his car into the Fulham road and crashed into a coffee stall, which was overturned and partially wrecked. He was brought to a standstill 200 yards further on by two policemen ... seeing that he was the worse for drink, one of them told him he would be taken into custody. He immediately dashed off, but the policemen sprang on the car and blew whistles, and the driver of a water cart ... turned his vehicle broadside on the road and the prisoner had to pull up.[2]

Hallas was given a month's hard-labour – they knew how to deal with drink-driving in those days. Karno had repeated problems with drivers over the years: in 1909 he sacked another chauffeur and then took him to court to secure the return of his uniform! The most serious incident was during the blackout of December 1917, when the latest in a long line of chauffeurs, Charles Kelly, ran over and killed Henry Russell, an elderly inmate of the Westminster workhouse (although Kelly was exonerated of any blame).

Karno and Edith's separation was finalised in May 1905 and this seems to have been a catalyst for new material. A few weeks later he advertised a try-out of the fantastical-sounding *Diving Birds*: 'The New and Original Burlesque Aquatic Pantomime Sketch ... by Fred Karno, Chas. Baldwin and Herbert Darnley ... produced for copyright purposes on Friday 15th June 1905 at The Metropole Camberwell.'[3] The writing team of Baldwin and Darnley should have been a powerful combination, but instead of an aquatic triumph, it was a damp squib. Although it remained in Karno's advertising for some time,

13. I WANT TO BE IN AMERICA

there is no listing or review for the sketch that week or ever again – *Diving Birds* sank without trace. With both this and *The Thirsty First* failing to get out of the starting gate, he had not had a successful new sketch in over a year, yet his relentless business expansion continued. By the end of the summer he had completed an extension to the Fun Factory and *The Era* ran the following advertisement:

> Karno's Colossal Combine. Productions from start to finish ... Mr Karno has just completed what are perhaps the finest theatrical premises in Great Britain ... and the finest rehearsal room in London ... the general management is in the hands of that well-known author and producer Mr Herbert Darnley, the whole under the personal supervision of Mr Fred Karno, who will be pleased to arrange for the stage management and rehearsal of plays, construction and painting of scenery, designing and execution of costumes, making of properties, engaging of artistes, booking of dates, and, in fact, the full, or part, production of any kind of sketch or stage play.[4]

Karno began placing large-scale weekly advertisements in the theatrical press and *The Era* ran a major editorial on his new venture:

> Mr Fred Karno ... is now prepared to undertake the full and entire production of any play for the legitimate stage ... he will ... find suitable plays for anyone who desires them. Mr Karno has a few words to say in explanation of his project: "If a man wants to produce a comic opera, he has to go all around the agents to book his company. Then he has to find a man who will paint his scenery ... make his dresses ... book the dates ... lend his stage for the purpose of rehearsals, and ... make his props. Now ... we are in a position to do the whole of the work ourselves."
>
> "Do I understand that you lay yourselves out to find the ... cast?"
>
> "Even that ... we should save a manager a considerable amount of money ... At least thirty percent ... I guarantee that everything will be done in first-class style."
>
> ... The "place" ... comprises three residences ... and rumour goes forth in the neighbourhood that every house in the street will soon form part of the Karno Combine. From the general office on the ground floor,

where the rapid clicking of typewriter keys, and the rushing sound of scribbling pens seems to indicate a very busy staff ... to Mr Darnley's office, a really beautiful room, furnished in the cosiest style ... past the wardrobe room ... the scene-painters' apartments ... The carpenters' workshops ... the property master is giving the finishing touches with his paintbrush to a trick piano ... A glimpse into the stables ... seven or eight well-groomed horses, and in the coach-house ... three motor cars, two "Royal" coaches ... omnibuses, broughams, lorries, and traps. Upstairs again, the rehearsal room ... the sun shines through the glass roof ... the whole establishment could not have been better planned and appointed ... The frontage of the building ... is very handsome, and an electrically lighted figure of Mercury in the centre of the roof tells the visitor that Mr Karno is at home ... He is shortly sending out a troupe to Paris, and ... another troupe will find their way to America ... Mr Karno employs some two hundred persons.[5]

This paints a wonderful picture of the Fun Factory at full blast, and as for that statue of Mercury on the roof – it's a wonder Karno wasn't flying the Royal Standard. The Fun Factory now offered not just theatrical supplies but a one-stop shop for producers, yet Karno was still seeking yet more opportunities to diversify his business. He aimed to control the whole supply chain, even down to

13.1 Fun Factory prop and model making room (courtesy David Robinson).

13. I WANT TO BE IN AMERICA

the company that printed his posters, becoming a director and major shareholder in John Waddington Ltd.[6]

That long *Era* editorial went on to say that Karno was still working on *Diving Birds* and *The Thirsty First*, and also had a new show lined up for Christmas called *Moses and Son*. With space in the Fun Factory at a premium, Karno and Marie moved out of Vaughan Road and took up residence on the Highland Lassie, at Tagg's Island. No longer living over the shop, he could escape from work and relax. It was also a darn sight easier to pass off Marie as 'Mrs Karno' among a new circle of friends in East Molesey than in London. This was the absolute zenith of his career: he had well-established sketches and musical productions touring at home and abroad, a diversified business with a huge staff, new premises to house it all in, and freedom from an unhappy marriage – it doesn't get any better for Karno.

13.2 Fun Factory scenery workshop (courtesy David Robinson).

13.3 Fun Factory paint frame (courtesy David Robinson).

You will have noticed that he now harboured ambitions to take his own companies abroad, and it is no coincidence that *The Era* editorial appeared in the same edition as Reed Pinaud's notice confirming Karno's injunction and the beginning of their lengthy legal battle. We will never know if Karno decided to tackle America after the deal with Reed Pinaud fell apart, or whether he realised he had missed an opportunity by selling the rights and engineered the whole dispute in order to pave the way for his own tours. If the latter, Karno wasn't the only one being devious – Reed Pinaud also had a few cards up his sleeve.

As the drunk in *Mumming Birds*, Billy Reeves was important enough to have his name ahead of the sketch in the listings, so it must have been a blow when, in September, Reeves turned traitor and joined Reed Pinaud's company at the Folies Bergère.[7] Reeves was one of a number of Karno comics who had defected to the rival company, but there was worse to come. A more vicious viper than Reed Pinaud was nestling in Karno's bosom, waiting to strike.

Despite the outward signs of success, cracks were beginning to show across the business. Reviews suggest that *Saturday to Monday* was running out of steam, and artistes – some of whom had been with Karno for many years – were beginning to jump ship. As well as Billy Reeves, Harry Roxbury left to form his *Prince of Monte Carlo* company that autumn, and George Craig and Harry Royston broke away to form a double act. It wasn't always the end of the story: many found life on the outside more challenging than they anticipated. Karno consistently welcomed them back with open arms (Craig and Royston were back within a year) and these signs of discord were, for now, mere ripples on Karno's pond. Meanwhile, in his weekly advertisement for 'The Karno Combine' (which now filled an entire *Era* column) he couldn't resist the opportunity to have a dig at Reed Pinaud:

> Mr Fred Karno's companies: His Majesty's Guests, Saturday to Monday, Dandy Thieves, Mumming Birds, Jail Birds, Early Birds, Diving Birds, Thirsty First, Hilarity. Christmas 1905-06 Cinderella pantomime Gaiety Theatre Dublin. Grand new production 'Moses and Son', Empire, Liverpool. American troupe in repertoire, Paris troupe in repertoire. At the Olympia, Paris. The greatest success ever made by any English company, and this even after others have made a DISMAL FAILURE in their vain efforts to produce Karno comedies.[8]

13.4 Members of the first Karno American company, thought to be taken on board ship, October 1905. Arthur Gallimore (far left), Billie Ritchie (second from left, obscured), Alf Reeves (far right) (courtesy Marianne Morgan).

Although Billy Reeves had defected, his brother Alf was working as a Karno manager and was put in charge of the first American company. The pioneers, who set sail on the SS Philadelphia on 7 October 1905, were: William Anstell, Charles Cardon, Maisie Cook, Arthur Gallimore, Charles Griffiths, Joe Huda, Dick McAllister, Billie Ritchie and his wife Winnie.

London and Paris were the twin centres of the entertainment universe and, since only the best crossed the pond, Americans knew that a British act was worth seeing. Given that his troupes' performances were silent,

13. I WANT TO BE IN AMERICA

Karno needed to make it clear they were British, so they were billed as 'Karno's English Comedians' and *Mumming Birds* was renamed *A Night in an English Music Hall* – although ironically, some reports suggest that this title may first have been coined by Reed Pinaud.

Karno had initially secured only an eight-week tour, beginning at Hammerstein's Victoria Theatre in New York on 16 October 1905, and it was up to Alf Reeves to negotiate any further engagements. Reeves did more than that – he proved to be a superb manager and was largely responsible for Karno maintaining an almost constant presence in the U.S. for the next nine years. One reporter later wrote of him:

> Alf Reeves … will hand himself souvenirs … this coming week when he plays his fiftieth week in New York City … for twenty-nine months the company has continued without a break … Mr Reeves has had entire management of the act since its arrival in this country, and the adroitness with which he has met the altered conditions of business, so different from the methods obtained in England, has won him the respect and friendship of the managers.[9]

Karno's memoirs suggest that he quickly sent out a second troupe, but A.J. Marriot's research indicates that apart from one or two comics coming home and being replaced, it was a year before a second company was dispatched – in August 1906.[10] America posed a new challenge for the Karno organisation: controlling a troupe thousands of miles away was a tall order, and once his comics had their first taste of the Big Apple, the Bradford Alhambra lost some of its appeal.

Retaining artistes began to become a problem and Karno relied heavily on Alf Reeves to keep the ship afloat, but initially all was well and his advertisements soon included glowing reviews for the American company: 'It brought forth uproarious mirth … A performance that was unequalled for dainty wit … Mr Karno's company scored a hit and will prove a drawing attraction.'[11] After their pre-booked engagements, Alf Reeves secured a tour on the Poli circuit, a cluster of small theatres in New England with a reputation for hosting acts that couldn't get bookings elsewhere. But this was a mere stopgap – they were back at Hammerstein's in New York by Christmas.

Back home, Karno had a huge empire to feed: applause-hungry artistes, success-seeking proprietors and the Great British public all wanted more. Karno's advertising now extended to two columns and, for the first time, listed the members of each company by name. While not wholly reliable (for instance comics might be listed in different countries at the same time), they remain a good guide to Karno's stable – here is a partial example from autumn 1905:

Hammerstein's Theatre New York: "Mumming Birds" – Billie Ritchie, Arthur Gallimore, Ping Pong, Chas Griffiths, Chas Cardon, H. Walton, Geo. Lee, F. Birrell, Winnie Ritchie, Alice Kyre, Agnes Bonson, Cissie Fremton …

Winter Gardens Berlin: "Early Birds" – Chas. Bell, Dick Kitchen … A Darnley … Clara Bell …

Palace, Southampton: "Early Birds" – Albert Weston, Geo. Welch … J. Huda …

Olympia Paris: "Mumming Birds" – Fred Whittaker … W. Fern … Bert Williams … Ada Minister … Rose D'Alberg

Grand Theatre, Hanley: "Early Birds" – J. Doyle … Arthur Dandoe … Alf Reeves …

Theatre Royal Preston: "His Majesty's Guests" – George Hestor … Fred Whittaker … Chas. Cardon … Ada Minister …

Opera House, Bury: "Saturday to Monday" – Fred Kitchen … Jack Melville … Amy Minister … Muriel Palmer.[12]

13.5 The end of a shift at the Fun Factory (courtesy David Robinson).

Karno's column reveals that he had engaged one of the most important booking agencies in America to represent his international interests: H.B. Marinelli, which claimed to represent 'all the first-class houses in the Universe.'[13] Such listings also show that there were many members of the same family in some companies, which could be a cause of tension. In 1910 the following appeared in the press: 'Fred Karno has issued a new edict. From now on the producer will engage only single people. The married folks are too prone to air their family troubles, thinks the manager (who ought to know) and it causes internal eruptions in his companies.'[14] One wonders what they meant by 'he ought to know'!

Whatever Karno's feelings on the matter, he wasn't practicing what he preached – he employed plenty of members of his own brood. In October the *Saturday to Monday* company included 'Mr Westcott', which could be Karno's brother Albert but is more likely to be the professional debut of fourteen-year-old Fred Jr. Marie Moore put in an appearance in *Early Birds* and *Mumming Birds* too, although she only lasted a few weeks before giving up the stage for good. Albert Darnley (Herbert's brother) was in one of the three *Early Birds* companies which included three married couples.

In mid-October, Karno began advertising some future titles: *Moses and Son*, *Thumbs Down* and *The Gladiators* (although the last two sound like they had the same subject matter). As well as new shows there were new comics appearing: names that will feature prominently later in our story, such as Frank O'Neill and Albert Austin. Meanwhile, older hands needed new challenges. Fred Kitchen had been playing the lead in *Saturday to Monday* for two years, carrying the comedy and singing a number entitled *That's the time to go* – now it was. He was given star billing in the first of Karno's new sketches, *Moses and Son*, and with it a new character to get his teeth into.

Before radio and television, a comic could forge an entire career with one act – or at most, a consistent character used in a handful of short routines. New material had a better chance of success when played in the guise of a comedy persona audiences were already familiar with. It is a concept evident in early film comedy: Chaplin, Buster Keaton, Laurel and Hardy, and Harold Lloyd all portrayed essentially the same characters in a wide range of scenarios. Later British comics like Robb Wilton, Sandy Powell and Will Hay (who all worked with Karno) followed this same approach. American movie heroes tended to play everyman characters: the down and out, the all-American boy, the hapless employee of a big corporation; whereas British comics preferred to parody authority figures – teacher, fireman, politician, magistrate or policeman. The greatest British exponent of this on film was Will Hay, who said: 'I've always found something funny in the idea of a hopelessly inefficient man blundering through a job he knows nothing about.'[15] Long before any of these superstar comics there was Fred Kitchen, whose new Karno character embodied the idea of a man promoted way beyond his level of competence – Mr Perkins.

Moses and Son was set in a moneylender's office, which could have caused problems with the Jewish community (Charlie Chaplin learnt this the hard way with a short-lived Jewish stand-up act in his youth). Karno sought to avoid offence by engaging only Jewish comedians for the sketch, apart from Kitchen and Aggie Morris (who was billed as 'Leah Morris' to ensure she blended in). While to modern eyes the set-up is a racial stereotype, at the time it simply reflected the reality that many moneylenders were Jewish, and Karno did not portray Mr Moses as a comic or a villain, but as a respectable businessman. He had no prejudice against Jewish performers, and engaged fine actors for whom he had great respect[16] – including Herbert Landeck, who went on to appear in many Karno shows and act as a production manager.

Fred Kitchen recalled: 'It was popular with the Jewish race … When we came to the Holborn Empire … on the first night the theatre was packed to overflowing with Jews, who, I honestly believe, had come with the full expectation that they were going to see a show burlesquing their … race … they went away delighted, for the sketch had been written in anything but a hostile spirit.'[17]

The show was written by Karno, Kitchen and Harold Gatty with music by Dudley Powell, although it included some J.P. Harrington and J.W. Tate songs, such as *I Love Rebecca*, *Nothing To Do With Me* and *The Multi-millionaire*. However it was very much Kitchen's show, and he had a shaky start. Karno noted that Kitchen (like many comics) believed he was a dramatic actor fighting to get out of a comedian's body, and on this occasion he decided to adopt a 'method' approach. Seeking to elevate his performance beyond the bumbling idiot (which he played brilliantly), he immersed himself in London's Jewish community. Jack the Ripper may have been a mere memory to the oldest inhabitants of Whitechapel, but the East End still had plenty of dark and dangerous corners and it was here that Kitchen sought inspiration. He subsequently decided to ditch his familiar comic get-up: the ruddy nose, shambling walk and big boots were all abandoned, replaced by a cleaner make-up and a large walrus moustache. Karno was worried.

13. I WANT TO BE IN AMERICA

Moses and Son was set to open on Boxing Day as the big Christmas show at the Empire, Liverpool, but first Karno staged a try-out at the Bordesley Palace, Birmingham. Unconvinced by Kitchen's approach, he took the unusual step of staging a full dress-rehearsal on the Sunday night – and with some help from the theatre manager, filled the stalls with regulars, friends and performers from nearby theatres.

It was a catastrophe. Kitchen failed to raise a titter and the invited audience gradually made their excuses and sneaked out. Karno claimed to have calmly requested the cast reassemble at ten thirty the following morning to sort out the problem, but it's highly unlikely he was the slightest bit calm. Karno was scathing and extremely straight-talking at such times, and the cast probably returned to their digs with their tails between their legs. For Kitchen, the author and star of the show, it must have been humiliating and terrifying – I doubt he got much sleep that night.

Neither did Karno. Returning to his room at the Stork Hotel, on Corporation Street, he totally rewrote the show (claiming to have left barely a line unchanged). He beefed up the plot, incorporated significant amounts of fresh comedy 'business' and, most notably, introduced 'a quiet note of pathos.'[18] Monday was spent rehearsing and as the curtain went up that night, Karno watched nervously from the back of the auditorium – with one eye on *The Era* critic in the front row:

> Moses and Son ... is not intended as a burlesque on Judaism, and ... is rather flattering, to the ancient race. The house of Moses and Son is ... as wealthy as a dozen Rothschilds, and the head of the firm is a highly cultured gentleman whose dealings are ... on a colossal scale ... Mr Moses receives inquiries from the German Government ... the Norwegian Government ... and even from the little principality of Servia ... the King offering as security his crown. This security is deemed unsafe, and the King is advised to keep his crown 'while he can'. The good heart of the Jew is shown when he assists a friend of former days ... the domestic side ... is displayed with the sudden arrival of his wife on an urgent matter concerning "the twins." All this time the stage is crowded with lady typists at work, clerks, partners, brokers and ... Perkins ... general cleaner, is summoned forth to open the windows ... whereupon the fun takes a lively turn. All save Perkins disperse for luncheon, when a commotion is heard from outside, and the eldest son of

> Mr Moses, Barney, enters, bearing on his arm his sister who has fainted in a carriage accident ... being habited in racing garb, and fearing his father's displeasure thereat, [he] retires to a room to change his dress, during which time his sister "comes to," and seeing Perkins before her instantly claims him as her preserver ... An altercation with the office-boy, a "deal" with a sham broker, and a scene with a "pore" woman ... all afford fine opportunities for the "heroic" Perkins ... The avowal of Barney's love for Leah, one of his father's typists, leads to him being disowned by Mr Moses, his father, who, however, promises to receive him again when he shall find a millionaire husband for his sister Rebecca. This he does eventually, and the eligible partner is none other than ... Perkins, who in some mysterious way has become a "multi-multi-multi-millionaire." Perkins is a fraud, and is unmasked ... Nevertheless, the daughter, Rebecca, clings to him, and the curtain falls on the lovers' happiness. The sketch is ... a spectacular and sartorial triumph. The ballroom at the Moses mansion, Park-Lane, is a positive blaze of light and colour, and on the opening night elicited a burst of applause ... Fred Kitchen puts in some of his best work, never allowing the fun to flag for one moment, and the audience roared its appreciation.[19]

Karno recalled that a standing ovation and several curtain calls were demanded by the cheering crowd, Kitchen stepped forward and told the audience of the overnight rewrite, and the Guv'nor was dragged onto the stage to make 'one of the few speeches of his career' (although since *The Era* correspondent doesn't mention any of this we must take the account with a pinch of salt). Karno had snatched victory from the jaws of defeat and Perkins, the hapless caretaker, was to overtake Sergeant Lightning in the public's affections.

The sketch was notable for a little piece of business originated by Kitchen that always brought the house down. A messenger arrives with a telegram, which Perkins opens. Screwing the envelope up into a ball, he flips it over his right shoulder with his right hand and kicks it up with the heel of his left foot. It was a gag that later found its way into Chaplin's repertoire (sometimes with a cigarette) – one of many Karno influences in the Little Fellow's comedy.

After pulling *Moses and Son* out of the bag,[20] Karno turned his attention back to the knockabout silent comedians and relaunched *The Thirsty First*, with Albert Darnley in the lead (Emily Darnley was also in the cast):

13. I WANT TO BE IN AMERICA

Hilarity is the watchword of all Mr Karno's productions, and in his latest venture, which is brim-full of bustle and excitement, there is no departure from so welcome a rule … the opening reveals the interior of 'The Rifleman', a beer-house … some very lively incidents are caused by an enthusiastic demand for drinks. A fillip to the fun is given by the arrival of a match-boy and a tramp, who cause many diversions by their comic antics … Ben, a Bully, who engages in a game of dominoes with an old pensioner, and … wins all his money. The old veteran discovers the cheat … whereupon the bully strikes him a brutal blow but is himself floored by a colour-sergeant who comes to enrol recruits. All the male occupants of the bar enlist; and in the second scene, the Exterior of the Barracks, the match-boy is found doing "sentry-go." The home-call is sounded, and men in uniform come rushing in from all directions, until the gate is closed, and a quartet of revellers are shut out. Their efforts to climb over the wall are made very funny, and … the sentry sinks promptly to sleep. The Encampment, with its long array of tents, is revealed in scene three … Ben the Bully has a dispute with his superior officer and is placed under arrest. Night comes on, and the officer enters his tent, through which, by an ingenious lighting arrangement, he is seen preparing to retire. The contents of his portmanteau excite … Ben … and with the help of the tramp he purloins the valuables. The theft is discovered … but while the officer and the bully are engaged in a terrific fight, a storm breaks … and the tents are whirled into the air by the force of the gale, revealing the occupants in various stages of undress. A fearful thunderbolt completes the devastation … It was … remarkable that the fun, all performed in dumb show, should be kept going so briskly … Mr Albert Darnley, who appears as the colour-sergeant … looks the parts to the life, and though he has no word to speak, his movements and facial play are full of meaning … Ben the Bully … played with well-marked intensity by Mr Albert Weston, has a most expressive countenance, and is able to work up a scowl of which no burglar need be ashamed … the encampment, with its military impedimenta and long array of tents, forms a most inspiring scene … the sketch was received with uproarious laughter.[21]

It is very apparent how good Karno's comics were at creating humour without uttering a word: movement, expression and reaction had to tell the story (and get the laughs). Within a decade many of the *Thirsty First* platoon would be doing it for real on the Western Front, but those dangers were yet to come – and there were plenty of real and present ones in the here and now. One comic, James (Jem) Sipple,[22] required a minor operation after being hit in the eye by a flying piece of bread during a performance of *Early Birds* – and died under the anaesthetic. A few years later, props boy Robert Adams lost an eye when a stage pistol exploded – being a Karno plonk could be a risky business.

The Thirsty First was the beginning of another significant expansion plan, with *The Era* noting that 'this will form the first of the series of Fred Karno's new repertoire.'[23] Subsequent listings claimed there were eighteen new sketches in preparation, but such rapid growth was increasingly difficult to control. 'Karno's Theatrical Factory' needed the steady hand of its general manager, Herbert Darnley, more than ever.

Just a few months earlier Karno's *Era* editorial had ignored the growing exodus of comics and concluded with: 'Mr Darnley tells us that the majority of people remain with him in spite of tempting offers from other quarters. This in itself is an excellent testimonial.'[24] But by the time *The Thirsty First* was launched, Darnley's claim was revealed to be extraordinarily disingenuous – he and Karno were at war.

13.6 A viper in the nest – Karno's general manager, Herbert Darnley (courtesy David Robinson).

14.

Stabbed in the Back

*"It gives me great pleasure to present you
with this handsome alarm clock
and I hope it will be always like you
– keep good time and never go on strike."*

(The Smoking Concert, 1906)

DARNLEY WALKED out in late November 1905 and proceeded to set up his own sketch company. To add insult to injury he immediately began signing as many Karno comics as he could persuade to turn traitor. One of the first was Charlie Bell, who had been with Karno for ten years. Bell was a close friend of Edith's, so perhaps his departure was only a matter of time, but Joe Cleve, the musical director credited with creating the Karno soundtrack, was a more surprising defector. Darnley's new troupe soon staged its first production, *Moving In*, a sketch about incompetent removal men which ended with a gas explosion destroying the set.

Karno maintained good relationships with rivals like Wal Pink (who had run his own comedy sketch company since 1894), and he did not usually hold a grudge. But in this case he made an exception – Darnley seemed intent on causing Karno as much trouble as possible. A war of words was soon writ large across the theatrical press, with Darnley advertising his sketch right next to Karno's *Era* column. Karno immediately threw the kitchen sink at his advertising, listing a completely new repertoire of sketches:

'The Gladiators', 'London Suburbia', 'The Yap-Yaps', 'The Yellow Birds', 'The Fire Brigade', 'Sea-view Hotel', 'English Sports', 'The Cab Rank', 'The Washerwoman', 'The Baby Farm', 'The Nursery', 'The Wedding Party', 'The Explorers', 'Daisy's Downfall', 'Spring Cleaning', 'The Village Fair', 'The Colliers', 'The Book Worms', 'Willie's Birthday', 'Flanagan's Restaurant', 'The Painter and Decorators', 'Our Neighbours', 'Skylarks', 'The Cow Boys', 'The Chimney Sweeps', 'The Marines', 'The Football Match', 'Thumbs Down', 'Diving Birds'.[1]

Over the next few weeks Karno added *The Dentists, The Hop-pickers, The Three Brass Balls, The Auction Mart, The Waxworks, The Crooked House* and *The Haymakers* to the list. Sadly most of these titles never made it to the stage, which is a shame as we'll never know what caused Daisy's downfall or what *The Baby Farm* was all about. Karno was clearly seeking to intimidate Darnley by sheer weight of material (as well as securing his own copyright for these ideas). He also reinforced his claim to ownership of the existing sketches by publishing the date they had been prepared and citing himself as their sole author. Darnley responded by listing the Karno material he claimed to have been responsible for, and took the chance to praise his new recruits: 'Herbert Darnley acknowledges the splendid work of his loyal little company.' You can imagine the great impresario exploding in his office as his traitorous partner listed Karno sketches as his own. Darnley seemed intent on twisting the knife as much as possible: in an undisguised dig at Karno's very beginnings, he went on to claim *Moving In* to be 'The greatest hit of any dumb show since the days of "Love in a Tub".'[2] Apart from increasing his advertising Karno did not rise to the bait publicly, but on 10 March 1906 Darnley's advertisement ended with 'Verbum sat sapienti' – a word is enough to a wise man – which is a polite way of telling Karno to back off. Perhaps pressure was somehow being applied in private.

14.1 May all get their due – Herbert Darnley.

Darnley continued to vent his frustration in subsequent weeks. One advertisement stated 'The reward of refinement is success'; another was headed 'Suum cuique' (may all get their due), followed by 'Herbert Darnley speaks –

Listen!' He then went on to list every contribution he'd ever made to a Karno show: writer of *Her Majesty's Guests;* inventor of Sergeant Lightning; composer of *Six Little Burglars;* part-author of *Moses and Son, Saturday to Monday, Thumbs Down, Diving Birds,* and 'a clean (but unfortunately not produced) *Thirsty First.*'[3] It doesn't take a rocket scientist to detect that the latter was behind their dispute – Darnley evidently believed Karno's version vulgar and rude.[4] To emphasise the point, he announced that his next sketch would be *The Thirsty First* by another name – *The Raw Recruits* (later *The Skirmishers*), 'a wordless comedy without a tinge of vulgarity.'[5] So what was so offensive? This review reveals all:

> Realism on stage – A woman's fight of an extraordinary character ... The scene is the interior of a public house, and two girls who are escorted by soldier lovers, quarrel ... the women rush at one another like viragos. The hair, of course, is the first object of attack ... Then comes a whirl of female attire which is rapidly stripped from the person of each combatant. Bodices are clutched and literally torn away and flung aside. Corsets, skirts, and other articles are ripped off, and an elderly woman who ... comes between them, is disrobed at one fell swoop. At the psychological moment darkness falls on the scene and the curtain comes down. It might be added that the performance inspired the deepest disgust among a portion of the audience.[6]

The women's fight was considered so scandalous in 1906 that this report made the newspapers in Los Angeles. But Karno, unlike Darnley, wasn't worried about sensibilities and good taste. He was in the business of big laughs and bums on seats, and there's nothing like a bit of titillation and a good fight to bring in the crowds – *The Thirsty First* toured to overflowing houses.

The feud continued week after week until Darnley delivered what appeared to be a killer blow. Karno must have choked on his porridge the morning he opened the paper to read: 'Who has engaged FRED KITCHEN for a period of six years? Why Herbert Darnley.'[7] So there.

Could this be true? Could Karno's star turn and closest friend in the business have betrayed him with his fiercest rival? The gloves came off and Karno finally bit back publicly: two weeks later his advertisement was headed 'Nemo me impune lacessit' – no one attacks me with impunity. One can imagine Karno, literally behind the scenes, calling in favours and pressuring managers and agents not to engage Darnley. Negotiations, double-crossing and bullying must have been rife on both sides. The poor old plonks were caught in the middle, and Albert and Emily Darnley unsurprisingly got the boot. Calling on every ounce of his experience, and probably resorting to emotional blackmail, Karno somehow persuaded Kitchen to stay. Darnley must have been crushed: he had been so excited to snare the great comic that he had made his announcement before signing contracts; now he faced public humiliation. Sounding like a broken man, the header of his next column read: 'In spite of everything'.

Darnley had not quite surrendered, though. Two weeks later he secured the next best thing: the original star of the Karno plonks, the speechless comedian to beat all others, Billy Reeves. Reeves was looking for pastures new since Reed Pinaud had lost his own battle with Karno a few weeks previously. Reeves was to star in a new Darnley sketch called *The Panorama,* a skit on the dioramas of early music hall, followed by the wonderfully titled *Bailum and Barmey's – The Thickest Show on Earth.* What comic could resist that? In reuniting the two original stars of *Mumming Birds,* Reeves and Bell, Darnley could claim a small victory. He headed his subsequent column 'Vincit omnia veritas' (truth conquers all), and laid down the gauntlet by stating that he would soon produce his own versions of shows he'd written for Karno, including *Saturday to Monday* and *Diving Birds.*

It was a hollow victory. Perhaps the Kitchen debacle damaged Darnley's confidence or his reputation with managers, maybe Karno threatened legal action – either way his column in *The Era* soon disappeared, and while his troupe continued to stage *Moving In, Skirmishers* and a further sketch called *Muscles,* his currency fell into steady decline. By the end of the year the three sketches were only occasionally playing small halls, and Darnley was forced to take a job managing the Mansfield Hippodrome. Karno must have felt very pleased with himself: he had vanquished Darnley and won his legal battle with Reed Pinaud. His *Era* column was headed: 'He who laughs last, laughs last'.[8]

Billy Reeves asked for his old job back and got it. Karno was delighted, listing Reeves second only to Kitchen in his roll call of artistes in the press. Darnley went away to lick his wounds and plan his revenge. All this was the incentive Karno needed to push on with new projects, and at just the right time – theatre managers were complaining of a dearth of fresh sketch material. One reviewer noted: 'Good farcical sketches ... are rare things nowadays and consequently the managers of theatres have too often to adhere to the old ones which have once proved attractive.'[9] None of Karno's contemporaries produced anything like the

14. STABBED IN THE BACK

volume of sketches he did – he was a godsend to the managers and in a class of his own when it came to original ideas.

The Darnley defections put added pressure on Karno to recruit and nurture fresh talent, and in April 1906 he engaged Albert Bruno, a stout man with a face like a bulldog, who had made a name for himself as a comedian in *Floradora*. Bruno quickly formed a memorable partnership with Fred Kitchen and became Karno's number two musical comedy comedian.[10]

In the same month, Karno finally came good on his promise to release a new sketch. Easter weekend was a rare holiday for working people and they flocked to the halls. Managers responded by pulling out all the stops, presenting new shows and the biggest names. So when Karno launched *The Smoking Concert* at the Oxford, it shared a bill with an all-star line-up, including George Robey, Gus Elen and Harry Tate. Written by Karno, Harold Gatty and Frank Dix, the sketch took one of Karno's favourite pastimes as its theme: set in 'the Semolina Cycling Club',[11] it was advertised as 'founded on observation'.

> Mr Fred Karno always shows so much ingenuity in his farcical concoctions that one always looks forward in any new production … for a feast of fun … The Smoking Concert should pan out into one of the most successful of the Karno farces. Its main idea is to burlesque the amateur vocalist … The scene is the club-room of the Semolina Cycling Club … the merry wheelers give themselves up to the delights of listening to the untutored efforts of their chums … There is the sentimental vocalist who gets underway and finds the key too high. This is changed, and then it is too low. When it is properly adjusted … he forgets his words … A couple of jolly old dogs sing an old-fashioned duet, garnished with angular gestures that degenerate into wild gesticulations and ultimate collapse. The assembly … chant the chorus, "Sit down." A surprising piece of impromptu conjuring is introduced by a young gentleman … who, on removing his overcoat, displays a broad arrowed uniform. He borrows watches, money, and other articles of value … The harmonic meeting is broken up by the entry of a couple of policemen in search of the convict, and in the midst of an amusing melee the curtain falls … a laugh from start to finish … "Karnomania" at its very best.[12]

Later versions of the sketch ditched the convict and policemen but added a rheumatic old man who staggered up only to be revealed as the winner of the 100-yard dash. A key protagonist was a heckling drunk, Archibald Binks (a repeating Karno character), who delights in knocking the prizes out of people's hands or challenging other players to a fight. A young girl presents a recitation of *The Collier's Dying Child* which brings all the members to tears, except for Binks who sits eating crackers and sprays the crumbs about the place. After her recital the girl is given a cash prize, which Binks steals – another fight ensues. The chairman regains order and they all join in a song as the curtain falls.

14.2 The Smoking Concert. *This photograph is actually from the American tour version,* A Night in a London Club *– with Charlie Chaplin as the drunk (courtesy Jane Koszuta, www.theroyalzanettos.com).*

The sketch was clearly a variation on *Mumming Birds*, but a notable difference is that here the interfering drunk is a wholly unpleasant character. He is no longer the audience's hero, lampooning bad professionals who might have been fair game; now he is ridiculing, robbing and fighting fellow club members and an innocent child. Binks could come over as obnoxious rather than funny – the fact that he doesn't is testament to the quality of the comedy, which is so strong that the audience forgive his unpleasantness. We see the same in Chaplin's early films: his character is often unpleasant – smoking, stealing, fighting (including hitting women), drinking and philandering, all behaviour which was genuinely scandalous to polite society at the time. Yet we laugh because of his wit, originality, skill and the twinkle in his eye.

The Smoking Concert was a simple pantomime sketch which used ideas from elsewhere, so one senses it was thrown together quickly to make good on Karno's promise of an avalanche of new material – Darnley had pushed him to deliver quantity rather than quality. In the rush he appears to have dispensed with his usual try-out before launching in London – a risky strategy, especially at a significant hall like the Oxford. However, in the same week at the Palace Theatre, Glasgow, a strange listing appeared: 'Fred Karno's absurdity, Our Annual Social, presented by Lee Simpson's company.'[13] Despite Karno's keenness to announce every show he could think of, *Our Annual Social* doesn't appear in his advertising, so what was it? One explanation might be that he had intended to stage a try-out version of *Smoking Concert* in Glasgow but, feeling the pressure from Darnley, brought forward the London production, leaving another company to fulfil the Glasgow engagement under licence and with a changed title (although this doesn't explain why there seems to be no record of Lee Simpson before or since). Demand for Karno material was so high that around this time he had begun to license sketches to other producers. For instance, in October a revised version of *Mumming Birds* was produced with Karno's permission by W.B. Crabtree, and played by a group called the Crantons.[14]

Karno's attention was not solely on new material. Back in 1900 he had bought some shares in the New Palace Theatre, Blackburn – simply a financial investment, but it gave him a taste for theatre ownership. Now, in March 1906, while in a maelstrom of new material, vicious rivalries, American tours and defecting comics, Karno decided to join a consortium (with J.B. Mullholland, Fred Fredericks, E. Stevens, and R.C. Buchanan) which took on the lease of the Marlborough Theatre in Holloway Road, Islington. In the same month (along with Buchanan) he joined another group building the New King's Theatre in Sunderland.[15] A year later he became licensee of the New Hippodrome, Cambridge. His involvement in these legitimate theatres must have seemed a shrewd move: his Fun Factory was soon supplying their productions with scenery, costumes and props, prompting more expansion at Vaughan Road. That summer he secured the adjacent property and built a four storey extension, advertising in *The Era*: 'The magnificent new wing ... comprising a paint room, rehearsal room and storage dock ... the new rehearsal room is 72 feet long, 21 feet wide,

14.3 The Fun Factory's four storey extension.

and owing to its exceptional height (26 feet, 6 inches) can be used as a practice room for any Gymnastic or Aerial acts. The huge storage dock ... covers an area of 316 square yards.'[16]

There was no end to Karno's ambition, but the expansion into theatre ownership proved misguided and he chose his partners badly. Buchanan and his pals had varied business interests, most notably Scotland's Provincial Theatre Group, but they spent much of their time lurching from one financial challenge to another. More worryingly, the theatre development bubble was about to burst. Fred Miller, the manager who had christened *Mumming Birds,* wrote:

> Our programmes are getting more and more expensive, the salaries paid to artistes having reached exceedingly high proportions. This ... combined with the ever-increasing rivalry of newly erected halls, renders the managing directors' task a herculean one, to engage that public drawing talent which is yearly getting so difficult to obtain ... and the fact of our having so many music halls nowadays ... that the populations of the various districts are hardly numerous enough to fill every hall nightly, nor rich enough to support them, act as influences against the making of huge dividends by variety concerns.[17]

The music hall was suffering from over-supply even before cinema came along to kill it stone dead. Tight margins would soon turn into huge losses, and managers were increasingly searching for ways to protect their profits. There was strength in numbers, and large syndicates became the dominant force in the industry, squeezing small independent halls out of existence and deploying tactics which would soon lead to all-out war with the artistes. All of this was to come. In the summer of 1906 Karno seemed unstoppable, and now had eight companies: three in London (two *Mumming Birds*, one *Early Birds*); *Moses and Son, Saturday to Monday* and *His Majesty's Guests* touring the provinces; *A Night in an English Music Hall* in New York and *Jail Birds* in Paris. A tour of Australia and South Africa was apparently imminent[18] and *Moses and Son* was advertised as the next sketch intended to tour America (although it never did). Karno's *Era* column lists 130 comics, five managers and three musical directors. It even names the technical staff making scenery, props and costumes – they include some of the comics such as Fred Jr., who were obviously required to turn their hand to other work. Nowhere else could a young performer receive such an apprenticeship in the art of comedy.

Karno's weekly advertisements now enable us to spot more characters who will play a part in our story later. For instance, in December a *Dandy Thieves* company included J. Hylton, which may be the future band leader and impresario

14. STABBED IN THE BACK

Jack Hylton (then just fourteen). Although Hylton's biographer Peter Faint has no record of him working with Karno's troupes,[19] he certainly appeared in the halls as a boy soprano (billed as 'the Singing Mill Boy'), and the following year he performed with our old friend Edwin Adeler's troupe, where he met fellow juvenile Con West. Hylton and West went on to form a prolific songwriting partnership.

Charlie Chaplin joined Karno's company soon after this, and he later recalled his experiences as part of this rapidly expanding business. It took weeks to fully rehearse a sketch, Chaplin remembered, and each comic had to know all the parts thoroughly – if someone left it was like taking a pin out of a very delicate piece of machinery. However, that description is belied by the theatre listings, which suggest new comics were added to the troupes with relatively little rehearsal time, and frequently moved from company to company. Reviews also demonstrate that Karno's sketches continually changed and developed as a show toured – they were more fluid than Chaplin implied. In reality there was a huge turnover of people: each sketch had new cast members every week, which would be hard to manage in any business but is hard to believe possible in acrobatic sketch companies.

Karno was largely an uneducated man so it's not surprising that he increasingly relied on accountants, secretaries, lawyers and administrators – but after the Darnley debacle he found it hard to trust these advisers, and perhaps with good reason. Long-time company secretary William Chippendale was arrested for allegedly forging a Karno bank order (he was acquitted), and everywhere he turned it seemed there were drunken chauffeurs, defectors, pirates, thieves and maladministrators. A report that summer in *The Edinburgh Evening News* shows that, even in adversity, his comics didn't lose their sense of humour: 'A young man who was charged at Marlborough Police Court … with drunkenness and disorder said he had been in Fred Karno's "Jail Birds", and now felt that he was going to realise it.'[20]

1906 was already the busiest year of Karno's career but there was yet one more diversion to occupy him – a return to his roots. Before the advent of the song and supper rooms, Londoners had been entertained at sprawling outdoor pleasure gardens and fairs. One of the most famous was Bartholomew's, based on the site of what later became Smithfield market, and once memorably described as 'that annual festival of mud, dung and riot.'[21] Now, at Olympia in Kensington, impresario Charles B. Cochran recreated a traditional fair on a grand scale and called it *Fun City*. He travelled around Europe collecting the world's finest circus acts, exhibits and sideshows, as *The Era* reported: 'In the central hippodrome the … equestrian show. Sedgewick's incomparable menagerie … various ferocious and untameable beasts … Forrest's Military Band … feats of strength … galloping horses and motor cars … Wingate's bicycle circus … the distorting mirror show … White's Indian menagerie … and all the fun of the fair.'[22] One review notes: 'A spectacular reproduction of a train robbery … a miniature city populated by 100 midgets.'[23] Another records: 'The great ostrich farm of 200 birds reaches England this week-end.'[24]

Fun City opened on Christmas Eve and ran for eight weeks. Karno was invited to take part and recreated an act whose name epitomised the traditional fairground attraction: *The Old Time Richardson's Show*, which *The Era* described as 'a faithful revival of all the old glamour and glory of one of the most amusing and best loved features of old English fair life.'[25] Richardson's show had been a fixture at Bartholomew's, and in the 1830s Charles Dickens also recorded it as the main attraction at Greenwich Fair: 'In the very centre and heart of the fair this immense booth, with the large stage in front, so brightly illuminated with variegated lamps, and pots of burning fat, is 'Richardson's', where you have a melodrama (with three murders and a ghost), a pantomime, a comic song, an overture, and some incidental music, all done in five-and-twenty minutes.'[26]

Karno advertised for 'old mummers', stating that only those used to 'portables', 'fair business' and 'parading' need apply. The press reported that octogenarian Joe Cave stepped up: 'The old time Richardson's show by Fred Karno is already assured of great success … Karno has had the valuable aid of Mr J.A. Cave the oldest living actor.'[27] Cochran later recounted Karno's contribution:

> I was anxious that my Fun City should include a … Mumming Booth … Karno found an old mummer whose father had been with the original Richardson … Karno's troupe played "The murder of Maria Martin in the Red Barn," … and other blood-curdlers. He made the band appear in old-fashioned toppers, and gathered together an excellent lot of "paraders," including the veteran clown Harry Paulo … Karno had known the mumming booths, although he was, of course, too young to remember Richardson. But he worked the fairs doing what is known as a "perch act" for many years before the mumming booths and the "ghost" shows … were wiped out when every village got its stationary picture theatre.[28]

14. STABBED IN THE BACK

The Era provides more detail:

> Fred Karno ... will endeavour to restore the glories of the palmy days of the British drama. This is a show that we shall delight to see, and if the mummers of today can inspire us with one half the admiration and the pleasure that the mummers ... of forty years ago gave us, we shall arise and bless the name of Karno. We understand that the chief character on the outside, Richardson himself, will be taken by one of the most celebrated of the real showmen of today, Mr B. T. Burnett having been retained for the leading part ... Richardson, the doorsman of his own show.[29]

This was not an original idea: exactly ten years earlier Augustus Harris had also recreated Richardson's at Olympia, engaging the famous Drury Lane clown Tom 'Whimsical' Walker (who will make an appearance later in our story) to find a cast and play Hamlet in the spoof *Hamlet in a Hurry*. Walker had also called on the talents of Joe Cave, whom he described as: 'One of the most cantankerous men I ever came across and ... very unpopular.'[30] Cave didn't mellow with age – you may remember that he later sued Karno for more money. Karno's 1906 version was a continuous series of thirty-minute performances worthy of Grimaldi himself, including one called *Harlequin Statue or the Bogie and the Fairy*. Cochran forged a firm friendship with Karno, later writing:

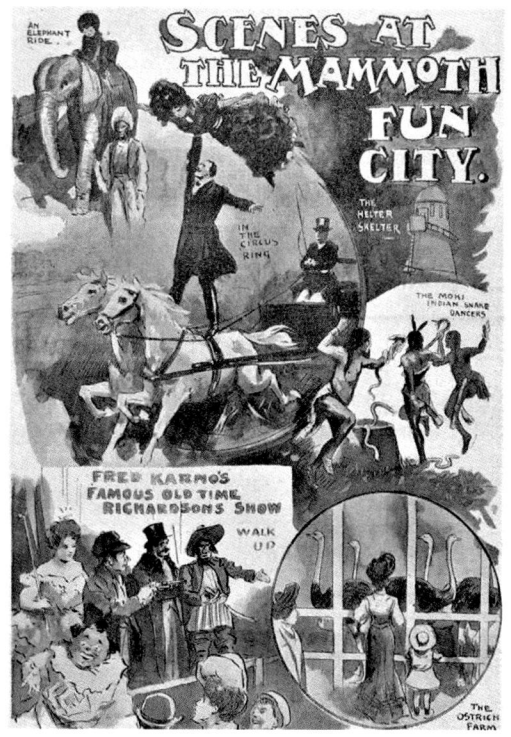

14.4 Advertisement for Olympia's Fun City
(© The British Library Board. All rights reserved. With thanks to the British Newspaper Archive www.britishnewspaperarchive.co.uk).

> Karno was the genius who created the funny business which was put over by Chaplin, Billy Reeves … and all the other fantastic creatures in Mumming Birds and many other Karno sketches which then had an enormous vogue in London, throughout Great Britain and on the Continent. The only name known in connection with these brilliant pantomime sketches which kept audiences convulsed in all countries … was … their creator, Fred Karno.[31]

It is ironic that Karno, always keen to produce something new, was now seen as the greatest exponent of nostalgic entertainments and a grandee of the industry. In July he had sponsored the Karno Challenge Cup (a one-mile race) at the Music Hall Benevolent Fund's annual sports day; the same month he was in the Water Rats' chorus singing on the platform of Waterloo Station to wish Joe O'Gorman bon voyage as he set off for a South African tour. His adverts were now headed 'The Old Firm' – he could not have been more establishment if he tried. Darnley hadn't stood a chance, but across the Atlantic Karno's status held no such fear for rivals, who merrily helped themselves to his material and his performers.[32] His first American company had worked its way around the U.S., playing venues as far afield as New York and San Francisco, but by the spring of 1906 Alf Reeves was finding it difficult to hold 'vaudeville's largest comedy troupe'[33] together. By July, the trickle of defectors had become a torrent and lead comedian Billie Ritchie joined the exodus. Fresh comics were sent over throughout the summer, including Harry Royston, George Welch and a recent recruit called Syd Chaplin.

14.5 A young Syd Chaplin (courtesy Roy Export/ Chaplin Archive).

As we noted earlier, Karno established a second U.S. company that autumn, managed by Arthur Forrest, which included Bill Fern, Amy Minister, Arthur Dandoe and Jimmy Aubrey (the seventeen-year-old son of Karno's old boss Bob Aubrey). Royston was given the lead in this new company and Billy Reeves replaced Billie Ritchie in his brother Alf's original U.S. troupe. Royston's troupe (including Syd Chaplin as the magician) played *A Night in an English Music Hall* around New York, while Reeves' troupe staged *A Night in the Slums of London* (*Early Birds*) and *Jail Birds* (which for some reason was not given a new title). Reeves' company initially received muted reviews, so *Jail Birds* was dropped in favour of *A Night in a London Club* (*The Smoking Concert*). At the Orpheum in New York the press noted: 'it was a little too English,' but reviews soon improved. American audiences did not take so well to *A Night in the Slums of London*, with some critics finding the Jewish character offensive – Karno was finding America far from plain sailing.

Most of the defecting comics were being poached by copycat companies who were blatantly ripping off Karno's material and undercutting his prices, encouraged by the syndicates. The Keith circuit openly advertised for acts similar to Karno's who were willing to work for less money. One of these 'vaude-villains' was Jean Bedini, who stole away Arthur Gallimore and presented *A Night in English Vaudeville*. King of the music hall monologue Bransby Williams was astounded at such piracy, writing that in New York he found Karno's *A Night in an English Music Hall* and Bedini's identical show both playing in the same district. Alf Reeves threatened legal action via the pages of *Variety*, prompting Bedini to respond claiming all innocence,[34] and the press took up the story:

> The talk last week was of the reproduction of the Karno's "Night in an English Music Hall" … at Henderson's at Coney Island. The sketch is so exactly like Karno's act that Bedini's defence, which is that Karno was not the first to have an act of this sort, does not hold water … There are about eight reproductions of this act now being given … [Alf] Reeves has already brought suit against F. Proctor for a cancellation of Newark last week … He sent his baggage to the theatre and reported for rehearsal, expecting to play, when the stage manager notified him that he was not on the bill, and put his baggage out on the street. Reeves asserts that the act was cancelled because the Bedini act might be had more cheaply.[35]

There were others too: producer Gus Hill expanded *Mumming Birds* into a musical called *Around the Clock*, with a cast almost entirely made up of former Karno comics, including Billie and Winnie Ritchie. In September, the press reported that Karno had taken matters into his own hands: 'Unscrupulous managers in America bodily appropriated the "Mumming Birds" sketch … Mr Karno at once paid a flying visit to America, and has now instructed his attorney William Grossman, to have all the Karno productions … fully protected by copyright.'[36] *Music Hall and Theatre Review* added: 'Karno arrived in New York on Monday … He says he had no idea New York was such a large place.'[37]

He wasted no time in tracking down Gus Hill's show in Philadelphia where, instead of taking the matter up with the theatre manager, he planted himself in the audience and watched the comics he'd recruited, trained and introduced to American vaudeville shamelessly perform his material. Eventually he could stand it no longer, and when the Terrible Turkey invited someone to take him on, Karno leapt to his feet and stormed the stage. Real-life chaos ensued as Ritchie and his turncoats bolted in all directions with cries of "My god, it's the Guv'nor!",[38] while Karno shouted of their betrayal to the audience until the stage manager brought the curtain crashing down.

Legal action followed and Gus Hill eventually paid Karno $3000 in damages, albeit with an agreement to produce the show for another season.[39] Hill's production, now officially licensed, was billed as 'the Ritchie London Comedy Company'. In January 1907 Karno also won his fight against Bedini, who was ostracised by the industry for his plagiarism. Karno's legal battles helped to establish copyright protection for stage material in America, as one report put it: 'The question of a producer's and an artist's rights in America has been finally determined upon the application of an Englishman.'[40] Years later Karno was still being cited as a key player in the fight for artistes' rights at home and abroad:

14.6 Karno proclaims victory against the copyists.

> Mumming Birds is a sketch of note in that it has created history. It had not been long produced, when it was seized upon by Americans … This glaring piracy … cost Mr Karno considerable time and money before he could assert his rights. The question was raised before the American courts, with the result that "Mumming Birds" paved the way for more equitable recognition of the rights of English acts.[41]

14. STABBED IN THE BACK

Karno stayed in New York for only two weeks, booking Jesse Lasky's Fourteen Black Hussars for *The House That Jack Built* while he was there. He returned on 8 October, leaving his lawyers to deal with the arguments and both of his companies to continue their tour of the Eastern Seaboard. While he would eventually win his battles, the damage was done: Harry Royston's company was scrapped and returned home in early December, whereupon Royston sued Karno for breach of contract:

> [Royston] said that in July 1906, he received a letter from Mr Karno … he wanted him to go to America to play in his sketch called 'The Mumming Birds'… The defendant said that he could engage the plaintiff for twelve months … On July the 25, 1906, the plaintiff sailed for America and played with the company there … Mr Reeves, the defendant's manager in America, dismissed him on November 24, 1906 … The agreement, he [Karno] said fixed no date but was for the tour, which ended at the Doric Theatre, Yonkers, on November 26, 1906, when the company … disbanded. The mischief arose … through a system prevailing in America whereby a company could steal a sketch and produce it in a town before the owner of the sketch arrived with it … several of his "boys" had left his company and joined opposition companies. It was a very strong opposition especially when some of the company worked for half price.[42]

This wasn't the whole story. Royston was convinced that Alf Reeves had an ulterior motive for sending him home. He believed that as soon as Billy Reeves returned to the Karno fold, his brother used the troubles with imposters as an excuse to push Royston out. Royston wired Karno at the time: 'Shady business with Reeves here … I am willing to stay, don't be misled.' Despite his paranoia, listings show that both Royston's and Reeves' companies toured concurrently for some weeks suggesting that Karno had every intention of running both troupes. Whatever the reason for the failure of the second company, the judge ordered Karno to pay Royston seventy-five pounds in damages.

Among the rollcall of comics crossing the Atlantic in the summer of 1906, one name stands out – Syd Chaplin.[43] Born illegitimately on 16 March 1885, Syd took the Chaplin name when his mother, Hannah, married the singer Charles Chaplin later that year. It was a tempestuous union, doomed to failure and marred by drunkenness and infidelity on both sides, but its product was Syd's half-brother, Charles Spencer Chaplin – born on 16 April 1889.[44] The brothers' poverty-stricken childhood and Hannah's decline from music hall singer to mentally ill asylum inmate is well documented. They lived hand to mouth, in and out of the workhouse, and often had to fend for themselves among the waifs and strays of London. From time to time they were reunited with their mother, depending on her state of financial security and mental health, or found themselves under the care of their estranged father, who would go on to drink himself into an early grave in 1901.

Syd's escape route was going to sea at the age of eleven; Charlie elected to follow in his parents' footsteps and aspired to become an actor. Charles Chaplin Senior apparently secured his younger son's first professional engagement in spring 1899, when he persuaded John Willie Jackson to accept the boy into his juvenile clog-dancing troupe, the Eight Lancashire Lads. Almost immediately they shared a bill with a Karno company at the Nottingham Empire, in July 1899, and ten-year-old Chaplin was no doubt transfixed by the madcap antics of the bill-topping speechless comedians. Chaplin cut his teeth as a clog dancer, touring the country for the next two years before winning a small part in a Christmas pantomime and later a role in a H.A. Saintsbury play, *Jim: A Romance of Cockayne*. He was then cast as Billy, a page boy, in Saintsbury's next production, *Sherlock Holmes* (a play which had been a great success for William Gillette), and began to be noticed by the critics.

Meanwhile, Syd had developed a taste for performing while doing his duty as ship's bugler and appearing in concert parties. Many hours spent in the exercise yard – both in the workhouse and during naval training – also gave him a flair for gymnastics. When Syd returned to London, he joined his brother in Saintsbury's company. Chaplin made the part of Billy his own in several touring companies over the next few years, before being invited to join Gillette himself, initially in a new piece called *The Painful*

14.7 Wal Pink's Repairs *– Charlie Chaplin centre, Syd left, at top of ladder (courtesy Roy Export/Chaplin Archive).*

14. STABBED IN THE BACK

Predicament of Sherlock Holmes (a ten-minute curtain-raising parody) and then in Gillette's *Sherlock Holmes* revival in London. A subsequent provincial tour with Harry Yorke's company (Syd was also in the cast) ran until February 1906, at which point legitimate acting opportunities dried up. The brothers' next move was significant: they obtained their first experience of comedy, joining a company playing a Wal Pink sketch called *Repairs*.[45] It featured lunatic builders and decorators creating Karno-esque slapstick chaos, with Syd as a foreman and Charlie a plumber's assistant. Both Karno and Chaplin would return to similar themes later, and one wonders whether this sketch was the progenitor of the now classic pantomime decorators' routine.

The Chaplins' double act was short lived. Charlie left after just a few weeks (in early May) to join Will Murray's company touring with *Casey's Circus*; a sequel to Murray's more famous *Casey's Court* (both involved juveniles enacting a spoof variety show, in a circus ring or their back yard respectively). Chaplin was a natural mimic and impersonated stars such as Bransby Williams (whose monologues introduced Chaplin to the delights of Dickens) and quack physician Dr Walford Bodie. He soon became a featured artist, yet in his autobiography Chaplin makes only a very brief mention of his time with the show, acknowledging that it gave him a taste for comedy but describing it as 'awful'. He toured with Murray for most of the next two years. Meanwhile, Syd stayed with *Repairs* a little longer, until the fateful day that opportunity knocked.[46]

How he came to join Karno is uncertain, but according to John McCabe, the impresario saw Syd in *Repairs* and immediately offered him a contract – he signed on 9 July 1906. Signing with Karno was a momentous occasion for any young comic and Syd was no exception – twenty years later he wrote to his younger brother: 'When I am feeling sort of worried ... I always think of the great joy, happiness and elated feeling I had when I signed on the dotted line for Fred Karno ... I ran all the way to Kennington Road to send you the glad news.'[47]

Despite his relative inexperience, Syd must have impressed Karno immediately: three weeks later he was off to New York. By then he had already appeared in both *Mumming Birds* and *Jail Birds* – so much for months of rehearsals in a finely tuned machine! He proved to be a reliable and capable comic, and a year later signed a further two-year contract at four pounds per week, with an option for another year.[48] Syd Chaplin was set to become one of Karno's biggest assets.

15.

Strikers

Trainer: Stiffy – can you run?
Stiffy: Run? I could run a mile a minute,
if it wasn't for one thing.
Trainer: What's that?
Stiffy: The distance – it's too much for the time.

(The Football Match, 1906)

AFTER SEPARATING from her husband, Edith Karno stepped out of the limelight and immersed herself in charity work. On 25 September 1906, the Music Hall Ladies' Guild (MHLG) was founded to support female artistes fallen on hard times. Edith was the guild's first treasurer and her friend Marie Lloyd its president.

A month after the guild was founded, Lloyd married coster comedian Alec Hurley and Edith was among the guests.[1] This was a surprisingly rare appearance of Edith's name in the press; others were exclusively in relation to her work for the guild and always as Mrs Fred Karno. One wonders why Edith didn't revert to her real name, Westcott? Or her maiden name, Cuthbert? Or even her stage name, Warren? Perhaps this affection for the Karno name is another clue that they remained on good terms.

Edith kept a low profile and never performed again, even when given the opportunity. The Guild's first major fundraiser was a charity matinee at the Canterbury Theatre in November 1906. It was staged entirely by women (including the crew, stage manager and orchestra) – which led to much comment

15. STRIKERS

in the press – and even though committee members formed a singing chorus, Edith was not tempted to give her Tyrolean vocal cords an airing, and instead acted as a steward. She seemed comfortable in the background, supporting her more famous friends. In her biography of Marie Lloyd, Naomi Jacob gave us a glimpse of this friendship:

> Edith Karno, herself a great "mime" artiste, used to say that once, when Marie was appearing at the Lane [Drury Lane], she went round to her dressing-room and prepared to say all the right things. Marie turned from where she was removing grease paint and said:
> "Hello Edie, what was I like?"
> "Very good, Marie – that dance you do is –"
> "Yes, well, cut out the dance. What about the rest?"
> "I thought that song about the –"
> "Yes, yes! … never mind about the songs and the dances and all the rest of it – what was I like?"
> Edith Karno, the kindest soul in the world, and one of Marie's most devoted friends, hummed and hawed.
> "Well, to tell you the truth, I don't think perhaps – what I mean is – you see, Marie, dear, one's so used to – you know, it's difficult to –"
> Marie grinned her adorable 'street-urchin' grin.
> "That's all right. I was b— awful, eh? That's just what I think!"[2]

Lloyd was a proactive guild president but Edith went above and beyond, as *The Era* reported: 'The Music Hall Ladies' Guild is progressing apace. Mrs Karno, an enthusiastic member, has placed her flat in Primrose Mansions at the guild's service for a year.'[3]

While Fred Karno Jr. was learning slapstick from his father, Leslie was being educated in generosity by his mother. His first mention in the press came aged four: 'In answer to her appeal … for the children this Christmastide, Miss Anna Grey [The MHLG secretary] is pleased to acknowledge the following contributions … Mrs Fred Karno, children's clothing, and a gift of butter; Master Leslie Karno, toys, money-boxes (each containing a three penny piece), and a large box of biscuits.'[4] Another Christmas had rolled around and Karno was invited to return to the Palace, Manchester, with another new show, *The Football Match*, which kicked off on Christmas Eve 1906. His co-writer Fred Kitchen was otherwise engaged as Dame Trot in Glasgow and Albert Bruno was leading *Moses and Son*, so Karno engaged an up-and-coming young comic who had abandoned a career as a florist to try his luck on the halls. Harry Weldon would be cultivated in Karno's nursery and bloom into another major star.[5]

Weldon had a unique drawling delivery which Karno described as a whistling gurgle, and with this whistle on the letter s, his catchphrase 'It's no use' always brought the house down. Although Weldon was a Liverpudlian and Kitchen a Londoner, they both affected a vaguely Lancastrian lilt. This was no accident of accents: Karno liked northern comics and found they were welcomed in any town, whereas southern comics rarely did well in the North. Years later, when music hall was in its death throes, Karno remained convinced that the northern comic would endure:

15.1 "It's no use" – Harry Weldon (author's collection).

> Karno believed that the best music-hall talent was still to be found in Lancashire and Yorkshire. Asked what he would do if he were given a roving commission … to produce a new crop of comedians, he replied: "I'd go to Manchester, to Birmingham, to Wigan and Rochdale and … spend my nights sitting through the cheap touring revues. In the summer I'd go to the seaside towns and have a good look at the Pierrots. And then – then I'd come back with the talent."[6]

He was proved right. In the 1960s and 70s, when music hall was a mere memory, northern working men's clubs remained the most fertile breeding ground for comics.

The Football Match brought together Weldon with the remnants of Royston's returning American company (including Syd Chaplin and Jimmy Russell) and another new face, Will Poluski Jr. (who later married Marie Lloyd's sister Rosie). Having assembled a strong cast of both verbal comics and knockabouts, Karno pulled off a stroke of genius by engaging famous footballers to take part in the show. The two principal parts were 'Stiffy' the goalkeeper (Weldon) and 'Ratty', a centre forward (Poluski); their arena was 'The Cup Tie Final – a struggle for supremacy between Midnight Wanderers and Middleton Pie Cans.' A villain called Bottlewit unsuccessfully attempts to fix the match by bribing Stiffy with liquor. Rebuffed, he has more success with Ratty, who is found out, sacked by Hobson the trainer and promptly joins the opposing side for what is then a grudge match. Karno was unable to resist cops and robbers, even in a sketch about football, and Bottlewit is pursued by a detective named Rabbit. Charlie Chaplin would later appear as the villain, and he recalled slapstick entanglement in the training equipment and a punch-ball which rebounded into his face (a straight lift from Karno's *American Boxing Ball*) – gags which are easy to find in his subsequent films. *The Era* provides us with a comprehensive review:

> The expectation of a mirth provoker ... attracted one of the biggest audiences that have ever been seen in this popular music hall ... the action opens in the training quarters of the Middleton Pie-cans, at "The Bull," where members of this wonderful combination of players are getting fit for the coming struggle ... Athletic exercises are, of course, less in evidence than eccentric acrobatics ... the general physique of the club is hardly on the side of fitness and symmetry. An attempt to bribe certain members to lose the match is afoot, and the attempt is watched by a detective ... The chief person to be bribed is Stiffy, the goalkeeper, whose integrity ... is proof against temptation. What his prowess may be on the field does not really matter ... the extent of his fitness for the stage is demonstrated with ample effect by Mr Harry Weldon ... accompanied by uproarious laughter, which continued through the second scene – the exterior of the football ground – where a most realistic effect was produced by the turnstiles, and a crowd of a hundred auxiliaries ... The third scene, the Dressing room, gave a ... peep into the immediate preliminaries of a match; and the fourth ... proved a spacious and lifelike picture of a football field ... Some one-time famous players ... J. W. Crabtree and W. C. Athersmith (late of Aston Villa), and Fred Spiksley (late of Sheffield Wednesday) ... added a touch of realism ... Goals were scored ... but the chances against the Pie-cans ... are nullified by an arrangement ... that no matter how many goals may be scored on either side the result shall be announced as a draw, no score. The match ... was brought to a conclusion by a heavy fall of rain, which on Monday looked as though the actual wet afternoon outside had suddenly broken furiously through the roof ... The piece plays close upon two hours and is likely to prove an enormous attraction for the holiday season.[7]

A lifelike football pitch and indoor rain? Karno's Fun Factory had excelled itself, and nearly four thousand people crammed into the Palace every night to prove it. There were plenty of people on stage too, and Karno had some tricks to make this crowd of one hundred supers appear even bigger. They would march off stage-right, dash around the back, then re-enter stage-left – creating an unending parade of spectators. Upstage Karno placed a grandstand with taller supers at the bottom and shorter ones at the back, creating a forced perspective to increase the sense of scale. Behind this he had a scenic backcloth painted with more spectators and incorporated false arms clutching handkerchiefs and hats, which (thanks to large fans) waved merrily whenever a goal was scored. Hey presto, one hundred supers had become a thousand. It may even have been the first ever football played on astro-turf – although this caused some problems, as the comedian Sandy Powell recalled:

> Billy Poluski told me that ... the fire people used to come round to make sure that the scenery was fireproof. Well the fire chief came on the stage and said to Fred "Mr Karno, what about all this scenery – is it fireproof?" Fred Karno said, "Oh yes." ... they had the whole stage covered with artificial grass – a wonderful effect ... Fred Karno said, "Have you got a match?" The Fire Chief said "Yes." ... Karno lit the match, threw it on the floor and woosh! The whole lot went up.[8]

For all the spectacle, Weldon's lugubrious, lisping, inept goalkeeper stole the show. In an old brown hat perched on top of a ginger wig, and puffing on a clay pipe, Stiffy cut a remarkable figure as the supreme athlete of the team. When the striker approached goal, Stiffy pulled down a sign saying 'early closing'. He congratulated those who put one past him, suggested a penalty should be re-taken when he saved it, and took corners against himself. It was wonderfully surreal comedy in the hands of a master, and the critics loved it: 'Stiffy, the goalkeeper, is represented by Harry Weldon, whose sole companion is a whiskey jar, which he terms his training oil ... Stiffy is photographed by the wet plate process, which proved to consist of a syphon concealed in a camera, which was squirted at Stiffy, causing screams of laughter.'[9]

Weldon held the audience in the palm of his hand as he read a newspaper during the match to establish whether his team had any chance of winning. His repertoire of visual gags would be instantly recognisable to any Stan Laurel fan, and Sandy Powell recalled a great example: 'He would lean dolefully against the goalpost … trying to fold his arms which kept slipping through each other.[10] Then there would be a flurry of excitement caused by an impending attack and this would be followed by another period of tedium when he tried to put his hands into his pockets only to find that his shorts had no pockets. It was … superbly timed mime.'[11]

Spiksley, Athersmith and Crabtree were all ex-England internationals, but Karno found engaging them was far from straightforward. The Football Association, then a fledgling organisation keen to stamp its authority on the game, tried to outlaw any match (including exhibitions) which did not fall under its control; anyone playing in such events could be banned from the official game for life. Karno solved this problem by engaging stars whose careers had been cut short by injury (Spiksley's career was ended by a dislocated knee in 1903) or who had already fallen foul of the F.A. in some way.[12] According to Spiksley's descendants he was already friends with Karno through a shared a love of horse racing, and it was his idea to include real footballers on stage (he also helped recruit the others).[13]

15.2 *Hark who they're shouting – Stiffy the Goalkeeper.*

Christmas in Manchester was followed by a tour of the Moss and Stoll circuit, for which the show was reduced to forty-five minutes and given some new elements, not least 'the Canadian Lady Football Players'. In the provinces Karno ensured an even more enthusiastic welcome by recruiting heroes from local clubs: he described their reception each night as 'deafening'. Some fans could barely contain their excitement: at the Glasgow Coliseum (during a later tour) a man called Alexander Russell got carried away and laughed himself over the side of a box. Russell was unhurt, but the unfortunate man he landed on, William Forsyth, died instantly from a broken neck.

The Football Match

Cast:
Stiffy – The goalkeeper – and what a goalkeeper!
Ratty – the centre forward.
Percy Bottlewit – a villain of the deepest dolly dye.
Hobson – the trainer.
Beresford – a player who favours Woodbines.
Jones – a half back.
Robinson – a weak back.
Gatekeeper – Ils ne passeront pas.
Bill – a hard hearted tough.
Agnes – his downtrodden wife.
Susie – Oh if you knew Susie!

In the first scene, Ratty and Stiffy are vying for the affection of the barmaid at the Bull's Head:

Stiffy: I say Susie, you know I have a lovely motor car, will you come for a ride?
Susie: If you don't go too far.
Stiffy: We'll go to Blackpool and see the girls bathing.
Susie: Do you like bathing girls?
Stiffy: I haven't tried it yet.

And later:

Stiffy: Susie, you mustn't kiss me while I'm in training, I'll lose all my strength.
Susie: Then Ratty must be as weak as a kitten.
Stiffy: Have you been letting Ratty kiss you?
Susie: Yes, but I know how to keep a man's strength up.
Stiffy: How?
Susie: With this (passing him a bottle).
Stiffy: What malted milk?
Susie: Yes, but I have put a kick in it – taste it.

15. STRIKERS

He does, it has a shot of whiskey in it. Stiffy smiles, takes a bigger swig then kisses Susie passionately. She comes up for air with a huge grin on her face, swaying gently.

Stiffy: When I kiss them, they stay kissed.
Susie: Do it again, I'm still conscious (he does, and she staggers out).
Stiffy: (To Ratty) You know, she swears she's never been kissed.
Ratty: Perhaps that's why she swears.

Meanwhile, Hobson continues to instil the merits of training:

Hobson: Do you drink?
Stiffy: No.
Hobson: Do you smoke?
Stiffy: No.
Hobson: Do you run after girls?
Stiffy: No.
Hobson: What do you do?
Stiffy: I tell lies.

Having failed to bribe Stiffy ("Mr Bottlewit, you'll get no chance with me"), the villain turns his attention to Ratty:

Bottlewit: Suppose I was to offer you a thousand pounds to do a job, would you do it?
Ratty: Is it honest?
Bottlewit: No.
Ratty: Then I'll do it!
Bottlewit: Good.
Ratty: Now, who do you want murdered?
Bottlewit: All in good time, at the moment I merely want you to do your utmost to let the other team win.

The final scene is the chaotic football match, which climaxes with Stiffy saving a penalty (in slow motion), winning his team the match.

Harry Weldon used Stiffy in his later solo career, recordings of which survive – when he would open with a song (to the tune of the hymn 'Thine be the Glory'):

> Hark, who they're shouting, Stiffy is the man they're cheering.
> Stiffy is the best goalkeeper, that ever let a ball go through.
> They said this morning, that by a hundred goals they'd beat me,
> But they didn't know the man they had to deal with, 'cause we only lost by forty-two.

It ended with:

> As Vivian Woodward [a great England captain] says, when I start me moves and tricks,
>   What's the good of me trying to score, when Stiffy's between the sticks!

Then Stiffy leans against the goalpost and begins his monologue:

Stiffy: You talk about your Hardys and your Ruddies, and your other 'internatural' goalkeepers, not in the same street with Stiffy, I've had more goals scored against me than all the lot of them put together.

Boy: Paper, paper! Result of the big match.

Stiffy: Let's have a paper son, I want to see how we've gone on … Here it is, the match of the season. (*Reading*) Stiffy the goalkeeper in wonderful form. Three hundred and fifty thousand spectators. (*To the boy*) I thought there were more than that. (*Reading*) From the time the match was started all eyes were on the impossible Stiffy. The first shot sent in was one that would have brained any human goalkeeper but not the marvellous Stiffy. He calmly got the ball, carefully placed it at the opposing centre forward's foot, who immediately banged it into the net. (*To the boy*) Wants a bit of doing that you know. (*Reading*) Half-time was called and Stiffy was still alive. No sooner was the ball kicked off in the second half … Stiffy rushed at the half back and when he'd

15. STRIKERS

> done … the half back couldn't get his jaw back … Everyone shouted penalty, Stiffy louder than anybody … The centre forward … sent in a wonderful shot and Stiffy brought off a marvellous save. But it is doubtful if he will ever get the front of his face round from the back of his neck.

Delivering a comedy monologue like this required immaculate timing. Comic Will Hay recalled Karno telling him that even the funniest gag could be ruined by a line mistimed by a split second: "Get your timing right and the rest will follow."[14]

Despite the success of *The Football Match*, Weldon did not appear in any other Karno production. Perhaps he was considered too unreliable thanks to the drink problem which ultimately led to his death at the age of 49 (in 1930). Karno wrote: 'Weldon was undoubtedly one of the greatest music hall comedians of all time. He had that curious indefinable method of getting laughs that, for want of a better word, we call unction. He was no teetotaller … his death was probably hastened by his convivial habits. But … if he had had one or even more "over the eight" he was funnier than ever.'[15] Karno was not a boozer – Gallagher noted that the most he would drink was an occasional weak whiskey and water – but heavy drinking was so endemic in the trade that he was supposedly compelled to cross the street from the Fun Factory and deal with some artistes around a table at the Enterprise pub.[16]

The Football Match was another sketch to be inspired by contemporary events. In spring 1905, a bad-tempered match between Manchester City and Aston Villa had culminated in a major brawl. The F.A. launched an enquiry, which inadvertently uncovered a much bigger story: City's star player, Billy Meredith, had allegedly offered the Aston Villa captain, Alex Leake, ten pounds to throw the match. Meredith was the finest winger of his generation and achieved stardom with Manchester City, Manchester United and Wales – he was still playing well into his forties, and always with his signature toothpick in his mouth. The subsequent enquiry uncovered other irregularities, including illegal payments in City's accounts, and developed into a major scandal which nearly destroyed the club.

After a year's suspension, Meredith joined Manchester United in January 1907, and his return to the game was a huge news story. As he trotted onto the pitch at Old Trafford, the crowd went wild with support. Could it be a coincidence that his return just happened to come in the week *The Football Match* had its premiere in (where else?) Manchester.

Match fixing wasn't the only issue rocking football at the time: the clubs were in open revolt against the F.A.'s maximum wage (four pounds per week). A Mr Tagg[17] attempted to form a rival league, set himself up as an agent (which was against F.A. rules) and recruited several players to his scheme. Tagg's 'National Football Agency' formed a side which toured Germany in 1905, resulting in the F.A. banning his players for eighteen months. These miscreants included Athersmith and Crabtree, whose ban meant they were free to appear in Karno's show – where ironically, they earnt an F.A. busting £7 10 shillings per week.

Meredith himself would have been a natural for *The Football Match*, but despite his biographer John Harding noting he appeared in it[18] I've found no evidence of this in the press. Meredith did however associate himself with the show: a newspaper advertisement for the sketch (at the London Coliseum in 1908) included 'Stiffy thanks the following well known footballers for wires of congratulations – Wm Meredith …'[19]

There are other clues to suggest that Karno was inspired by the Manchester City case. Meredith was a friend of several football-mad music hall stars, including Weldon; when *The Football Match* toured in 1908, Weldon organised a charity football match in nearly every town they played and in recognition of these efforts, he was presented with a commemorative football by – you guessed it – Billy Meredith. Karno maximised the publicity potential from such charity events, and under Weldon's captaincy (and benefitting from

15.3 The Welsh Wizard – Billy Meredith.

15.4 The Karno first XI (© The British Library Board. All rights reserved. With thanks to the British Newspaper Archive – www.britishnewspaperarchive.co.uk).

several ex-internationals in the squad), his football team became a formidable side. This report is typical: 'A football match ... between Karno XI and Deptford ... a £10 profit on the gate, which amount was handed over to the Mayor of Greenwich's fund for boots for bootless children.'[20] Whether Deptford had boots or not, the Karno XI beat them 3-2. Other games were played against rival theatre companies: in Manchester in January 1907, they overcame the cast of *Puss in Boots* 6-2, in conditions so atrocious that comedian Sam Mayo wore his overcoat throughout the match 'to prevent his blood congealing'.[21] Weldon's footballers were not the only Karno sportsmen, and newspapers of the time are full of Karno teams: Kitchen captained another football eleven and the *Moses and Son* company fielded a cricket side. For both players and spectators, such recreations were a diversion from the harsh realities of daily life.

In those early years of the twentieth century, poverty and social inequality began to breed political upheaval. Trade unions increased in size and strength and the 1906 general election saw significant gains for the Labour movement. The entertainment industry was not unaffected and an actors' union was formed in 1907, but it struggled to decide who could join. Music hall artistes were initially excluded, although at a meeting in May it was noted that sketch performers might be admitted. Karno artistes were cited as an example, reflecting the fact that producers like him had developed material with large casts, dialogue and increasingly sophisticated plots – the line between legitimate theatre and music hall was blurring. The union was clear about one thing though – they did not want ladies on their committee and, as *The Era* reported, some didn't seem to mind: 'Miss Gladys Ffolliott[22] gave it as her view that ladies should not be allowed on the committee, because they frequently permitted their judgement to be warped by sentiment where the hard reasoning of a man was required.'[23]

The most significant industry organisation was the Music Hall Artistes' Railway Association (MHARA). Originally established in 1897 with the aim of negotiating cheap rail fares, it later became a champion for performers' rights. As the music hall began to suffer from over-capacity, the syndicates imposed increasingly draconian conditions on artistes: they were forced to play more performances for the same money (including extra matinees) and were required to sign contracts with restrictive barring clauses (as we have seen).

Artistes' groups began to organise, and in 1906 the MHARA (along with several smaller organisations) requested talks with the owners. Only Oswald Stoll (who, along with Edward Moss and Richard Thornton, ran a circuit of around forty theatres) bothered to respond – and he steadfastly refused to consider amending terms. Such intransigence encouraged the various organisations to join forces and establish the Variety Artistes' Federation (VAF). Members were quickly recruited and the first hundred were given founder status: these pioneers of the new trade union included Harry Weldon (number 29) and Fred Karno (number 31). Within a year the VAF had four thousand members, its own periodical (*The Performer*) and the support of the fledgling Labour Party.

The VAF first flexed its muscles in an argument with Walter Gibbons, when he attempted to move artistes between his two Brixton theatres with no notice. The VAF picketed both venues for two weeks and Gibbons capitulated. It was a mere chink in the managers' armour, but the VAF smelt blood. It formed an alliance with groups representing stagehands and musicians, and issued Gibbons with a series of demands for better working practices. When Gibbons failed to respond by the VAF's deadline (21 January 1907), it picketed his Holborn Empire. The action quickly escalated as artistes and technicians walked out and began picketing theatres across London. What became known as the Music Hall War had begun.

Many stars supported the strike and the associated fundraising effort:[24] Marie Lloyd relished shouting the odds on the picket line draped in her finest furs, proclaiming: "We (the stars) can dictate our own terms. We are fighting ... for the poorer members of the profession, earning thirty shillings to £3 a week. For this they have to do double turns, and now matinées ... These poor things have been compelled to submit to unfair terms of employment, and I mean to back up the federation in whatever steps are taken."[25]

Comedian Bud Flanagan was a ten-year-old call boy at the time, and had vivid memories of the strike:

> There were blacklegs ... some couldn't afford to lay off ... others cashed in while the stars were picketing the halls ... I wasn't worried by the strikers ... They weren't really rough, only to the extent of grabbing a bottle of stout or some fish and chips out of my hand and asking whom they were for ... the lot would finish in the gutter. With tears in my eyes I would run ... to the stage manager ... and let him know what had happened, but mostly I was left alone.[26]

Those blacklegs included Lockhart's Elephants; when asked why they continued to perform during the strike, their trainer replied that he had been unable to ascertain how the elephants felt about the matter. Much to the annoyance of their peers, some proprietors conceded to the VAF's demands, such as W. Grimes of the Empress, Brixton. The Empress was therefore deemed a 'fair house', and at the height of the strike Marie Lloyd appeared there, alongside Karno who performed a new sketch. This one-off performance was recorded by *Music Hall and Theatre Review*: '"What Uncle Lost," is the title of the newest production from Fred Karno … It chiefly concerns the adventures of one Joe, a performer on the Margate Beech [sic], who has fallen in love with the mayor's niece. While the mayor is taking a morning dip Joe steals his trousers and only consents to give them up in exchange for permission to marry the girl … the fun is brisk.'[27] It was written by Syd O'Malley, not a known Karno writer, and since it bears no resemblance to any other subsequent sketch it wasn't a try out; I suspect it was thrown together in the heat of the dispute as a one-off.[28]

The strike ended in mid-February after an arbitrator, George Askwith, was appointed by the Board of Trade and persuaded both sides to end hostilities while he brokered a settlement. Negotiations took some months, but most of the artistes' demands (including a minimum wage and maximum working week) were eventually met. The war was not without casualties: Karno's friend George Adney Payne died of a heart attack after a car accident in May, and his widow blamed his demise on the stress of the strike. It had been a turbulent time, but it enhanced the artistes' bonds of fellowship. Later that year Joe Elvin founded the Variety Artistes' Benevolent Fund which two years later established Brinsworth

15.5 Campaign flyer issued during the Music Hall War.

House, a retirement home for performers. Six hundred artistes each contributed two pounds ten shillings to fund the project: 'the Noble 600' were recorded on a memorial board which still hangs at Brinsworth today – Karno's name is among them.[29]

Karno, a veteran of numerous battles with the managers, a Water Rat and one of the first members of the VAF, was squarely with the artistes, yet his troupes continued to work during the strike – how was this possible? Karno was not a solo artiste with no-one to worry about except himself, he had multiple troupes to consider. Downing tools would have left well over a hundred comics without any income and spelt commercial suicide for the Fun Factory. Fortunately the Alliance allowed members in his position to continue working as long as they paid a five per cent levy to the fighting fund. By this mechanism Karno was a major financial supporter of the VAF, coughing up fifty guineas just two weeks into the strike.[30] Despite all this, his role in the dispute has been misrepresented by other biographers, who have suggested he was one of the managers fighting the artistes. The source of this confusion appears to be an interview given late in life by Karno comic Jack Melville, which appeared in a book about the history of industrial relations:

> Agents would go round the … clubs, get hold of budding comics and sign them up for £5 or £6 a week, then trade them like cattle to proprietors … for £15 or £16 … It was called 'farming.' So, there was a lot of discontent. Music hall was in its heyday … we would be taken from one theatre to another, People would shout "There goes Karnos." They'd laugh at us even before we got in the theatre. There were 200 of us going to all the halls in London. I was appearing … in The Hydro and … The Slavey. Sometimes they were both in the same bill and with two houses a night it was hard work … We thought we were being badly paid. But Karno was doing very nicely. He might take a lump sum for a sketch, say £300. With 30 people, the highest he would pay would be £4, and many of us were getting between £1 and 30s … There was such enormous business being done, the Guv'nors driving about in huge cars, we felt we should have some share in it. And we could see that other people all around were going on strike. So, we went on strike.
>
> A lot of the top-notchers, people like R.G. Knowles and George Robey, came out with us, because they disagreed with the whole business

15. STRIKERS

of farming. Marie Lloyd joined in. She didn't have much to complain about, but she supported us. We met outside the Empress Music Hall in Brixton and marched to Fred Karno's office in Camberwell, where our leader spoke to him. Marie Lloyd sang to the tune of 'Oh! Mr Porter': 'Oh Mr Karno, what are you trying to do, Make more money from the sketches, if what they say is true, All your lads are winners, not one's an also-ran, Oh, Mr Karno, don't be a silly man.' The upshot of it was Karno gave us all another five bob a week.[31]

Interviewed for a 1971 television documentary Melville had also said:

Marie Lloyd, who was always a great friend of the underdog, stuck with us ... made a speech on our behalf, and sang our little song "Karno, Karno, open your eyes and wake. You're keeping your people's salaries down soon they'll have nothing to take. While you're on your houseboat your manager'll sell you a pup. If you don't want to lose the best boys you've got – Karno wake up."[32]

We must ignore the fact that Melville's lyric doesn't fit the tune of *Oh! Mr Porter* and unpick the rest of his story: contrary to Melville's account of the scenes at the Empress, we know that Karno and Lloyd performed together there during the Music Hall War in aid of the Alliance. What's more the story of Lloyd singing her support for Karno's plonks does not appear in any Lloyd biography prior to Melville's interview, nor in any contemporary press report (and such a high-profile attack from Lloyd would not have gone unreported). Something is wrong here. Careful inspection of Melville's account reveals how the confusion has come about: his story actually recounted events five years after the Music Hall War: *The Hydro* did not premiere until in 1912 and *The New Slavey* 1910. It becomes clear that Melville's strike had nothing to do with the Music Hall War and was just an isolated row between Karno and the plonks (no doubt encouraged by the general environment of industrial unrest at that time).[33]

In conclusion, we can safely say that in the Music Hall War at least, Karno was firmly with the artistes.

16.
Bodies and Bailiffs

"Rumour tells me you drink."
"Then he's a liar!"
(The Bailiff, 1907)

FOR SOME the Music Hall War was a genuine fight for survival in a punishing industry, and organisations like the Music Hall Ladies' Guild were a literal lifesaver. In October 1907 it held its first annual meeting and reflected on a year in which it had supported fifty-eight families (including paying for the funerals of three children). The guild's annual report noted: 'Music hall artists ... are noted for their charity ... well aware of the misery that often lurks behind the "stage smile." To these the committee confidently appeal to make the second year as full of happy memories of good deeds done as the twelve months of which this report is a compendious record.'[1]

Edith's large flat in Battersea was expensive to heat and considered too far out of town, so the guild had decided to move to Covent Garden, but she was thanked for her generosity: 'By the great kindness of Mrs Fred Karno, we have had use of her flat at Battersea ... not only did she pay our rent for last year, but she contributed most handsomely to our Christmas fund.'[2] By then Edith had resigned as treasurer as she began to cut her ties with her old life; a year later she would leave London for Leigh-on-Sea,[3] never to return.

Edith was replaced by Belle Elmore,[4] a bottom-of-the-bill singer with limited talent and even less taste. The brash New Yorker had been a blackleg during the strike, which did not ingratiate her to Marie Lloyd, who also accused Elmore of stealing her material. One night she was seen elbowing her way through the

16. BODIES AND BAILIFFS

16.1 The ill-fated Belle Elmore.

pickets, prompting Lloyd to shout: "Let her in, she'll empty the theatre."[5] Her involvement with the guild may have prompted Marie Lloyd to step down as president around the same time, but Elmore proved to be an enthusiastic and popular treasurer,[6] and her success as a tenacious fundraiser was recognised when her fellow guild members presented her with a gold bangle inscribed 'The Hustler'. Elmore's husband, Hawley, was far less generous and universally unpopular in music hall circles – he was dubbed the Half Crown King due to his tendency to forget his wallet rather than buy a drink. Nonetheless, by 1909 the guild had moved its headquarters again, into the same building as Hawley's office – Albion House, New Oxford Street. Then, at the beginning of February 1910, Belle Elmore disappeared.

Her husband's secretary, Ethel Le Neve, appeared at a guild meeting to deliver a letter from Elmore, explaining that she had gone to America to visit a sick relative. Weeks passed without a word from Elmore, then on 20 February Hawley brought Le Neve to a charity ball, where Marie Lloyd supposedly spotted that she was wearing Elmore's jewellery. Edwin Adeler was also at the ball, and later told Naomi Jacob: 'Tongues began to wag, questions to be asked.'[7] A month later the guild received a telegram from Hawley telling them that Elmore had died in America. It soon became clear that Hawley and Le Neve were in a relationship, and suspicions grew when friends of Elmore visited America and found no trace of her. The guild re-examined Elmore's letter and realised that it was not in her handwriting and her name had been misspelt – it called in Scotland Yard.

Guild members were right to be suspicious of Elmore's husband. Failing to buy a round of drinks was the least of Dr Hawley Crippen's crimes – Belle Elmore was discovered buried in his cellar. The guild's members were key witnesses in one of the most notorious murder cases in British legal history. If Edith had not resigned, elevating Elmore to treasurer, the disappearance of an unpopular American music hall singer might have gone unnoticed and Crippen may have evaded justice – in the event he went to the gallows on 23 November 1910.

While Elmore was being butchered by Crippen, Karno was inadvertently providing the murder weapon for another grisly crime. Tom Jesshope, a fireman at the Camberwell Empire, had been sacked for drunkenness and now had revenge on his mind. At midnight on the 28 March, he slipped back in and hid himself in the pit. In his pocket, he clutched a knife which the Karno company had left in the theatre. When stagehand John Healey (whom he incorrectly blamed for his dismissal) began to lock up, Jesshope leapt from his hiding place and stabbed the innocent man through the heart. He was hanged for his crime two months later.

We have leapt forward; back in spring 1907, the Music Hall War came to an end and so did *The Football Match*. Weldon went back to his solo career, clutching a contract for a re-match the following winter, and the rest of the company (which included Syd Chaplin) returned to the older sketches under the leadership of Jimmy Russell. After Russell's company staged *Early Birds* at the Dundee Empire (where it broke box office records), the local newspaper reported that one audience member laughed so much they needed medical attention. He wasn't the only one: while Fred Kitchen had been doing his stuff as Dame Trot over Christmas, his older brother Dick was touring Scotland in *His Majesty's Guests* and receiving notices like this: 'The farcical comedy was presented with a verve and go that secured pronounced success ... Sergeant Lightning (Mr Dick Kitchen) was the life and soul of the piece.'[8] Two days after that review, Dick Kitchen stepped off the stage and collapsed. He died of double pneumonia a few days later, aged just forty-six, leaving a widow and two children.

Fred Kitchen was devastated. Dick had been more than a brother, he'd been a friend who had taught him his craft and supported him when work was short. It has been a repeated theme of this story that 'the show must go on', but Kitchen sat in front of the dressing room mirror that evening unable to make up and, for one night, he allowed his understudy to step in. Karno must have felt the loss too: Dick had rescued him from Bob Aubrey twenty years before and had since become the Fun Factory's Mr Reliable, willing and able to step into any role at a moment's notice. Legal battles and strikes were short-lived but deaths and defections were harder to manage.

That year, Karno had cause to place this in *The Era*: 'Chorus and show ladies having signed contracts with me are expected to fulfil them. The names of those failing to do so will be published and proceedings will be taken to restrain them from appearing elsewhere.'[9] With so many performers on his payroll, it was perhaps inevitable that Karno began to see all but his star comics as mere

16. BODIES AND BAILIFFS

numbers in a ledger. On one occasion he was summoned before the magistrates for operating his omnibuses without a licence, and his defence was that they were used for transporting 'goods or burden', so should be considered commercial vehicles (which were exempt).[10] The Judge was aghast that Karno considered the ladies of his company 'goods'; his solicitor quipped that while they might not be goods, they certainly might be a burden. Karno paid up.

He had as much trouble with his menagerie of animals as his comics: he decided to use real deer in that year's pantomime and, rather than go to an animal trainer, captured two wild ones in Bushy Park and attempted to bring them home in the back of his car. *The Stage* takes up the story:

> Mr Fred Karno ... had an extraordinary "hunt" on Sunday ... Mr Karno had set out by motor ... to secure two young deer, that are to play important parts in ... Humpty Dumpty. His young novices behaved with the utmost decorum ensconced inside the car until ... they suddenly, with malice prepense ... leapt from the car, and set off in the opposite direction ... the automobilist hunters, soon gained upon them, not, however, before the whole neighbourhood was aroused and a hue and cry raised. They are now safe in Mr Karno's tutorial hands and will doubtless ... add additional lustre to the pantomime.[11]

The deer ripped the scenery to pieces on the opening night. Karno swiftly returned them to the park and purchased some tame ones. After the pantomime season he advertised them for sale: 'Used to the stage!' We don't know if they sold, and one wonders whether they were too dear. Another report reveals that they weren't the only animals causing problems:

> Mrs Katherine Galois brought an action to recover damages from Mr Fred Karno ... having been bitten by one of his dogs ... two of Mr Karno's dogs ran into her garden ... sprang up and bit her on the cheek ... The wound was a severe one ... As she was too ill to go herself, her husband went to the defendant ... Answered Mr Karno ... "Send her to the doctor at once and I will pay the bill." Mr Karno did not offer any compensation ... [Karno] said he did not intend to pay ... as his dog was allowed a first bite ... A coachman in the defendant's service, asked what sort of a dog the animal complained of was, said it was a

thoroughbred mongrel (laughter) … We got it in July, and … had to keep it on the chain for two months and could not get near it. That's the sort of dog it was (laughter) … Have you known it to bite anyone? I should think I have. It flew at me in a public house one day, and bit me on the thumb – I fainted … The night watchman said the dog was very quiet, but he caused some laughter by adding that … on one occasion it bit through the toe of his boot.[12]

Karno considered Mrs Galois to be just another opportunist looking for a chance to sue him, complaining: 'I have so many people who are after me for something for nothing.'[13] The trials and tribulations of a millionaire could be as entertaining as any sketch. This story had everything: chaos, danger, live animals, slapstick, pathos, and (thanks to the hapless witnesses) plenty of laughs too. The pain and humiliation of the neighbour was perfectly offset by the idiot night-watchman, gamely insisting that the dog was a gentle soul even as he hopped about with its teeth buried deep in his boot.

Among all the mad dogs, deaths, desertions and strikes, Karno still found time to launch new projects, and Easter saw him stage a *Grand Mammoth Easter Fete and Gala* in Belfast. This one-off event seems to have involved him acting as an agent for a collection of circus acts, probably those he'd gathered for the Olympia show – so while it might be the closest he ever got to 'Fred Karno's Circus', it was not something he pursued. He was much more interested in his next theatrical production.

With Leonard Durrell and Fred Kitchen, Karno had been working on another sketch for his popular character Perkins, and it turned out to be a barnstormer – *The Bailiff*. It was a sequel to *Moses and Son* and both Herbert Landeck and Aggie Morris reprised their roles. Perkins was promoted to broker's man, aided and abetted in his debt-collecting duties by an incompetent sidekick played by Albert Bruno. Karno was probably still making the most of the publicity swirling around football's scandals when he christened the idiot sidekick Meredith (although Fred Kitchen claimed, less interestingly, that the name was inspired by a tin of Meredith and Drew biscuits).

The Bailiff first appeared on 15 April 1907, in a double bill with *Dame Trot* at the Wigan Hippodrome (the following week Karno tried an alternative title, *The Hire System*, but this never appeared again). The public immediately took to Kitchen as part of a double act, and it is easy to see why. Perkins, the tall, broad,

16. BODIES AND BAILIFFS

senior partner, believed himself to be more intelligent than short, fat Meredith, but in reality was simply the more deluded of two bumbling fools – a winning formula that would serve Laurel and Hardy well in years to come. As Oliver Hardy once said of his own comedy persona: "There is no one as dumb as a dumb guy who thinks he's smart."

Debt collection doesn't sound like a natural source of comedy, until you understand the strange rules that bailiffs operated by at the time. First, they had to obtain a warrant to seize property or possessions, then they had to serve the warrant in person – before sunset. If they managed this, they were able to enter the property (known as 'taking possession') and then simply sit it out alongside the debtors – sometimes for days – until the debt was settled. Hence the sketch's strapline: 'Perkins in Possession'.

16.2 "Meredith, we're in!" – Albert Bruno (author's collection).

In the first scene, Mr Moses struggles to explain to the idiot bailiffs that they are to repossess the house of Mr Pendlebury, who has failed to repay a debt on account of being on his deathbed. Meanwhile, Jacobs (the chief clerk) departs on honeymoon, blissfully unaware that Perkins is about to wreak havoc by mistaking his house for Pendlebury's. The second scene depicts the bailiffs' attempts to get past Jacob's servant who answers the door and finally, having gained entry, they proceed to hold a grand auction of the contents.

> Mr Fred Kitchen is funnier than ever in the role. Accompanied by a very beery looking individual named Meredith, he seeks to serve a distress warrant … and the various shifts and disguises he resorts to in order to gain admission "before sunset" cause laughter of the heartiest kind. At last after all their trouble, they gain an easy entrance into the house simply by stating their real mission; and it is only after the two men have … commenced a vigorous auction of the various goods and chattels, that it is discovered that they are really in the wrong house.[14]

The sketch had a great set-up and a superbly chaotic finale, but it was the second scene that really made a mark: each time Perkins thought of a new ruse for gaining entry to the house, he explained it to Meredith and concluded with "then – Meredith, we're in!" Repeated throughout the sketch as the ideas became increasingly absurd, the phrase stuck – one of the earliest examples of catchphrase comedy, it was soon heard the length and breadth of the country whenever anyone successfully secured an objective. Chaplin, for example, wrote of his early career: 'You may be surprised but my boyhood finished at the age of seven, for a little after that time I was busily working on the music halls, not for much, it must be admitted, but like Meredith, I was in!'[15]

Whether or not Billy Meredith was the inspiration for the character, cries of "Meredith we're in!" echoed from the terraces for the rest of his career. What better advert for Karno than thousands of football fans chanting his material every Saturday afternoon?

The Bailiff

Perkins and Meredith are considering ways to gain entry to the house:

Perkins: Meredith, we've got to be wonderfully careful, mind you. We've got to use a little strathology.

Meredith: No, no. Strategy.

Perkins: Yes, that's it. We've got to use some of that (*pulls out the warrant and tears it in two, giving one half to Meredith*). You'd better have a bit of it in case you're in first.

Meredith: Oh yes, but what's the number of the house?

Perkins: It's on the warrant you fool. (*They look for the house*) Now Meredith we have got to be very careful, very careful … I'll disguise myself as a something or t'other, you be on the alert, over there as it were. Now then, all you have to do is stand by, you find all the brains, I do all the laborious work … I knock at the door, they open the door, no sooner they open the door, I get my foot in. No sooner you see me get my foot in, you come off the alert, you follow me up the steps, you give a slight push – and Meredith, we're in!

Meredith: Very good idea.

Perkins: What do you think we had better start with?

Meredith: I suggest a drink (*they leave their bag and head off towards the pub. A policeman picks up their bag and they return*).

Meredith: Do you mind putting those things down?

16. BODIES AND BAILIFFS

Perkins:	Yes, do you mind putting those things down please?
Cop:	Does this old rubbish belong to you?
Perkins:	Rubbish? What do you mean rubbish?
Meredith:	My dear boy, you cannot expect a mere emissary of the law to be able to designate articles of such intrinsic value by their correct cognomen.
Perkins:	(*To policeman*) There you are, that knocks you. That's geography. Don't you understand a word he said? I didn't.
Cop:	Move on, I cannot have you about like this, move on.
Perkins:	Meredith, fetch a policeman.
Cop:	I shall very likely take the pair of you in for loitering.
Meredith:	Indeed! And where's your warrant?
Perkins:	Yes, where's your warrant. (*To Meredith*) I'm very glad you thought of that. Where's your warrant? (*To Meredith*) Say some more big words to him.

The policeman inspects their warrant then leaves, allowing them to set about their scheme to gain entry. First, Perkins impersonates a gas inspector come to read the meter (thwarted by "We're all electric"). Next, he disguises himself as a charwoman:

Perkins:	I'll ask them if they want the steps cleaning, if they say yes, they must give me a pail of water. No sooner they open the door to give me the water, I get my foot in, you follow me up. Meredith – we're in! (*He starts putting on the disguise*) What's this?
Meredith:	That's the blouse.
Perkins:	Who am I supposed to be riding for? (*Puts on the skirt*) Where's the other leg?
Meredith:	It's a skirt. You've got it on the wrong way.
Perkins:	What do you mean the wrong way? You silly fool. Show's what you know about it (*he puts on a bonnet, then knocks on door*).

Although they manage to persuade the maid to pass them a pail of water, she does so through the window and the door remains firmly shut. After they've cleaned the step, getting most of the water on themselves, the maid retrieves the pail and they make a rush for it, managing to trap Perkins' fingers in the door. We pick it back up on their final attempt:

Perkins: Let's try the fainting man …. you faint outside the house, I knock the door, ask for brandy, they bring out the brandy, you get hold of the brandy.

Meredith: Good.

Perkins: No, I'll get hold of the brandy. You can't get hold of the brandy, you are in a fit. You might spill it. I give you what's left, you come to. I take back the empty glass … you follow me up the stairs, I get my foot in – we're in!

Meredith: Good (*Meredith falls on his back and pretends to be in a fit. Perkins looks on and shakes his head*).

Perkins: No. Nothing like it … You don't seem to have any idea. You are about the worst fitter I've ever seen. You are supposed to be in a fit, not a shipwreck. You want to faint naturally like … here faint on the doorstep – about two up. (*Meredith has a fit, Perkins rushes up steps and knocks at knocker. The maid comes to the window*).

Maid: What's the matter now?

Perkins: A poor man in a fit. Quick please a little drop of brandy.

Maid: There isn't any brandy.

Perkins: A little drop of whiskey, anything, m'am.

Maid: We haven't any whiskey.

Perkins: Well two mild beers.[16]

Maid: (*In a rage*) There's a public house just round the corner, it won't take you two minutes to get there.

Perkins: But he won't live a minute. A drop of water, anything, anything m'am.

Maid: There's plenty of water in the pail, use that (*slams window as Perkins throws the bucket of water over Meredith*).

In desperation, Meredith pushes Perkins to get out of the way and knocks the door himself:

16. BODIES AND BAILIFFS

Meredith: Good morning miss.
Maid: Good morning.
Meredith: We are from Moses and Son, we want to take possession, we are in for debt.
Maid: Oh, I've been wondering who you were – come in.

Once inside, they make the most of the opulent surroundings, helping themselves to the drinks trolley while Perkins unsuccessfully attempts to seduce an elderly spinster. Eventually they launch into a chaotic auction, which is brought to a halt when Moses bursts in, reveals that they are in the wrong house and fires them on the spot. The bailiffs face destitution until the spinster announces that she will marry Perkins and Meredith can live with them – curtain.

Fred Kitchen had a long and illustrious career, but it was Perkins the Bailiff who cemented his place in the affections of the British public. His enduring catchphrase became his epitaph – his tombstone in London's West Norwood Cemetery is simply inscribed: Meredith we're in!

16.3 Karno's first superstar – Fred Kitchen (courtesy British Music Hall Society).

With sketches like this Karno was openly flouting the law restricting dialogue in the halls, and he was not alone. As theatre managers, music hall proprietors and the licensing authorities battled one another, it was obvious that the industry was unable to find a solution to 'the sketch problem'. An attempt at compromise tried restricting sketches to no more than thirty minutes, but this was routinely ignored – the Theatrical Managers' Association had to threaten Karno with legal action before he agreed to cut down *Moses and Son*. This contemporary article sums up the scale of the problem:

In the absence of any censorship the music-hall has gradually expanded and grown until ... it has certainly outrivalled the theatre ... In the course of its extraordinary development it has been discovered that the music-hall public like to see performed in music-halls short amusing or sensational plays. These are illegal … whether they are long or whether they are short … It is perfectly obvious that their performance has got to be either entirely prevented or entirely legalized … Fred Karno, George Gray, Arthur Roberts, and so on … are very highly paid … £625,000 per year is earned by sketches … and some 5000 people are employed in earning it. Can such an industry be stopped … abolished in a stroke? Clearly it cannot. The sketch that we all know is illegal, has become so important that it must be made legal.[17]

Later that year the requirement for theatres to obtain a licence for each production became voluntary. As long as his material was clean enough not to trouble the vigilance committees, Karno could now include as much dialogue as he liked. Modern sketch comedy was born, and Karno had been instrumental in its conception.

Extra dialogue wasn't the only important development in Karno's style. He had gradually ratcheted up the pathos in his comedy, from the poverty-stricken dossers of *Early Birds* to the customers in *Moses and Son,* and continued this trend with *The Bailiff,* as this review noted: 'Mrs Pendlebury, the wife of the debtor, is pathetically portrayed by Miss Madge Rockingham.'[18] Karno recalled that you could hear a pin drop in the auditorium as the desperate woman begged for more time to repay her debts, and by subsequently breaking this tension with a gag the audience were caught off-guard: 'Comedy stood out in bold relief, like a burst of sunshine after a dark cloud has passed over.'[19]

The combination of comedy and pathos was nothing new: Fred Kitchen and Charlie Chaplin both claimed to have been inspired by Dickens, and perhaps Karno was too – one American critic pointed out the similarity between *A Night in a London Club* and the Pickwick Club. Stan Laurel said: 'I don't remember if he [Karno] was the one who originated the idea of putting a bit of sentiment right in the midst of a funny music hall turn, but I know he did it all the time.' Stan added that Karno's favourite piece of advice during rehearsal was: "Keep it wistful, gentlemen … That's hard to do but we want sympathy with the laughter."[20]

Fred Kitchen had no difficulty keeping it wistful. Theatre critic James Agate wrote: '[Kitchen] is an actor … possessed … with an extraordinary gift of pathos; and it should be written over every comedian's door that "only the player who … can make an audience cry, can make an audience laugh".'[21] Chaplin would later be hailed as a genius of originality for his use of pathos in comedy. Agate later wrote: 'I do not laugh at Charlie till I cry. I laugh lest I cry, which is a very different matter.'[22]

The suggestion that comedians are privately depressive has become an intrinsic part of our culture, and owes much to those who recognised the power of combining comedy with pathos. The idea is inextricably linked to the fate of Grimaldi, whose wife died in childbirth at the very moment of his greatest success, as the star of the 1800 Drury Lane pantomime. He was never truly happy again and died aged forty-eight, crippled with arthritis from a lifetime of tumbling. These circumstances led to a much-repeated apocryphal story: a man goes to see the doctor suffering from depression; the doctor prescribes an evening of laughter. "Go along to the theatre and see Grimaldi, he'll cheer you up." "I can't do that," replies the man, "I *am* Grimaldi." Chaplin included this story in an article he wrote early in his career, and he certainly fits the same profile. He said: "To truly laugh, you must be able to take your pain and play with it."[23] His mother, Hannah, added this: "I can't see why people laugh at him … for he does not seem to me to be amusing. He is always sad at his work, and depressed because he cannot do as well as he wants to."[24]

Depression certainly appears to be a common affliction among the most inventive and surreal comics of each generation, and this has been the subject of much research: Dan Leno, Spike Milligan and Peter Sellers are well known examples. Some were overwhelmed by it and paid the ultimate price: Tony Hancock, Kenneth Williams, Mark Sheridan, Robin Williams and Max Linder. Kenneth Williams once said: "All the comedians I've ever known have been deeply depressive people, manic depressive. They keep it at bay with this façade."[25] In his autobiography Chaplin even noted the frequency of suicide among music hall comics. He struck up an unlikely friendship with Winston Churchill, which some have suggested stemmed from a shared experience of depression (Churchill called it his 'Black Dog'). After seeing Chaplin's *Limelight*, Churchill wrote him a congratulatory letter in which he quoted Socrates: 'The genius of tragedy and comedy is essentially the same and they should be written by the same author.'[26]

Before Chaplin, Karno was that author: combining subtle pathos with the broadest comedy imaginable satisfied not only his audience but his own artistic temperament. We don't know whether Karno was a depressive but he certainly had some character traits which suggest it, and having employed pathos to such good effect, it is interesting that he next decided to stage a comedy about suicide. *The Stage* reported: 'Mr Arthur Williams and Mr Fred Emney will be chief merrymakers in a new rollicking farcical sketch, to be produced by Mr Fred Karno ... The piece deals with the vagaries of a would be felo-de-se ... Williams will play the part of the hesitant suicide.'[27]

Williams later declined the part, the lead instead being played by John Bradbourne – he proved to be a poor choice. Written by Karno and Durrell, with music by returning Darnley defector Joe Cleve, the sketch opened at the Manchester Hippodrome in early July 1907 under the title *A Tragedy of Errors*:

> The idea is essentially humorous, though grimly so ... Harry Righton ... has risked his well-being by indulgence in horse racing and ... stocks and shares ... bills are coming in from his creditors in shoals; and, to make matters worse, his fiancée, on a misunderstanding, returns his ring, with a declaration that all is at an end between them. Harry is ... plunged into despair ... he will shoot himself ... But he finds the idea easier to conceive than to carry out ... a friend bursts in and ... The upshot is an arrangement that the friend (who really intends to repair the situation) shall bring death upon Harry unexpectedly ... and be exonerated by a written statement of the victim ... In the second scene, the salon of the Hotel du Louvre, Paris, Harry's terror of death is worked up to a high pitch. Knowing that his friend will be disguised, he suspects first one unlikely person and then another ... being taken for a madman by everyone ... having disguised himself in a mock armour suit of culinary utensils from the kitchen, he steals out of the hotel ... for he has received a telegram that some of his shares ... made him a rich man; so that death is now by no means to be desired. The friend and Lucy follow him to the gardens of the Pera Palace Hotel, Constantinople ... On Harry's appearance here he is equipped with a life belt, a bullet proof screen, and a bomb ... he ... terrifies the whole assemblage ... and is finally pacified and reconciled to the lady ... the production was an immediate success.[28]

Despite excellent reviews, trouble was brewing. Bradbourne, a theatre actor, was outraged when he realised he was expected to play two performances each night. Matters got worse when Karno changed the title to *Up the Pole* (considered a coarse expression for madness), which Bradbourne thought too vulgar. Eventually, at the Holborn Empire, he refused to go on stage for the

16. BODIES AND BAILIFFS

second show and left the theatre. Karno had little choice but to move everyone up into the next largest part and persuaded one of the stage crew to fill in. Unsurprisingly the show descended into real, rather than imaginary, chaos. The booking manager recalled: 'They were all at sea … it was a terrible show.'[29] Karno sued Bradbourne for breach of contract, but lost because his contract was deemed to be unclear on the twice-nightly requirement. The sketch subsequently toured the north of England and Scotland, with an array of actors taking the lead, before returning to London for a final few weeks in the autumn. At the West London Palace of Varieties Karno even stepped in to play the part himself, 'with great success'.[30]

This rare return to performing confirms that the great showman could deliver a credible acting performance despite being a nervous public speaker. Karno hated making speeches. Adeler and West wrote: 'He possesses an inferiority complex in this respect, and the mere thought of it terrifies him.' Grimaldi apparently shared this fear, which may have stemmed from their accents. Both had a strange mixture of dialects: in Grimaldi's case Cockney and Italian; in Karno's, Nottingham and Exeter. Gallagher variously described Karno's accent as appalling, ghastly, ugly and horrible, which is a pretty strong condemnation of a voice he'd never heard, although Karno certainly lacked the clipped vowels of his Edwardian contemporaries, and plenty of people remarked on his lack of eloquence. Sidney Theodore Felstead said: 'To the end of his days he could never properly speak the King's English.'[31] Adeler and West described him as: 'The genteel, immaculately dressed, dapper little man … His manner of speaking is exceedingly quiet, and his apologetic little cough is probably an unconscious request to give attention to his modest and unassuming voice.'[32] Jack Melville described Karno's speaking voice as little more than a mumble. Even his sons waded in: Leslie said he was inarticulate and Fred Jr. described him as poorly educated. Cockney comic Max Miller, proving his point eloquently (or rather ineloquently), said of Karno: "Rough he was too, blimey, I spoke better grammar than he did."[33]

Karno clearly struggled with words, once giving a comic the following direction: "Collaboration, that's what you need, plenty of collaboration."[34] On another occasion his general manager, Tommy Dawe, presented him with a letter to sign which included the word 'adamant'. Karno said: "Tommy, we can't have that. It's the stuff they use to make lavatories."[35]

For all his wealth, Karno remained a common man in an uncommon environment. Among his comics he was comfortable, but before a large crowd or in high society he knew that his voice would betray his humble origins. He had a peculiar affectation too, which Adeler and West described as 'a faint staccato cough that resembles a postman's knock in tempo ... Fred Karno's personal trade-mark ... known throughout the entertainment world.' Leslie Karno described it as more of a 'tut', and Fred Jr. noted: 'His peculiar little cough was well known throughout the profession as a prelude to some sarcastic remark.'[36] This may have been the involuntary consequence of a lifetime of pipe-smoking, but Karno used it to his advantage – that little cough was capable of reducing a performer to jelly.

16.4 Browned off – Freddie Forbes (author's collection).

Andrew McConnell Stott suggested that Grimaldi's aversion to public speaking may have stemmed from dyslexia – another trait seemingly more prevalent among successful artistes (including comics) – and this may have been Karno's problem too. There is significant scientific evidence of a link between dyslexia and visual spatial ability, so perhaps it explains his need to work in pictures not words. Jack Melville recalled that Karno always finished a direction with 'See? See?', and went on to say: 'What you saw was all that mattered to him.' Unable to articulate his visual comedy any other way, he directed by acting out the moves for his comics to copy (Chaplin took the same approach). An interview with Freddie Forbes, who joined Karno around 1910, reveals how far he took this principle: 'Karno ... never asked any comedian to do anything he could not do himself. On one occasion he asked Freddie to fall downstairs, but the youthful comedian's attempt was somewhat amateurish. Karno immediately took off his coat and did the stunt himself, with the offhand remark to Freddie, "You should go in the oven and be browned a bit."'[37]

Karno's willingness to fall down the stairs as an example to his lads must have earnt their respect, even if they didn't like him. Some called him cruel, even vicious; others said he was charming, funny and a delight. He seems to have been capable of huge mood swings, from quiet and introverted to sarcastic and rude – even tyrannical. These moods were interspersed with creative periods of overconfident elation, where his ambition knew no bounds and all his life's dreams were realisable. I'm no expert, but the contradictions in his character suggest to me that Karno may have suffered with some form of bipolar disorder.

16. BODIES AND BAILIFFS

One thing's for sure, Adeler and West were being somewhat disingenuous when they described him thus: 'A man of even temper. He is not irascible, irritable, or easily put out.'[38]

Perhaps he just had the same rare combination of personality traits that John McCabe identified in Chaplin: 'To be both deeply shy and heartily outgoing is a rare form of temperament, and in possessing it Chaplin inevitably suffered at those moments when duty or circumstances forced him in one of the moods to display the other.'[39] Actors who worked with Chaplin had their own views: 'Charlie was no tyrant … A hard worker, he expected hard work, damned hard work. And the cast loved him … He had that curious mixture of a hot temper and very great patience.'[40] That could easily have been written about Karno, as could this: 'Charlie has a sadistic streak in him. Even if he's very fond of you he'll try and lick you mentally, to cow you, to get your goat. He can't help it. You'll be surprised how many friends he's alienated through that one trait.'[41]

Karno was a demanding boss but that didn't matter to those aspiring to join the greatest comedy company in Britain. A successful auditioning comic or dancer would simply be given: "You're in!" – two words which amounted to the chance of a lifetime. Freddie Forbes recalled how he got his break:

> I went along to Fred Karno's office in Brixton … The place was crowded with applicants, and my heart sank … I had not been in many minutes when a lady came in … I rose and offered her my chair. She thanked me, but … passed straight into the sanctum. Immediately after, the office page came out and said Mr Karno would like to see me. I stood in the great man's office fumbling with my hat. "I am going to give you a job because you were very courteous to Mrs Karno," he said. I nearly collapsed![42]

The constant stream of wannabes knocking on Karno's door didn't stop him dashing around the country to look for talent on the recommendation of an agent. Many turned out to be duff, and when the agent chased Karno for feedback he would retort: "If it were my show, I should have him at the door taking the tickets." He found plenty of wheat among the chaff though, as Adeler and West noted: 'Throughout his long career, Karno was never wrong in his judgement of an artiste. His list of discoveries is almost limitless.'

It wouldn't be long before Karno would make the greatest discovery of them all – Charlie Chaplin's audition was just around the corner.

17.

The Little Fellow

"I've got a splitting headache."
"What have you taken for it?"
"Twelve pints last night."
(The Football Match, 1906)

WHILE WE'RE waiting for Chaplin to turn up, Karno had some other things to attend to through the summer of 1907. When the run of *Dame Trot* ended, he kept the cast under contract and they toured as a variety company, performing *The Bailiff*, their own solo acts and even other writers' sketches such as Matt Wilkinson's *The Registry*. He soon expanded this to two troupes, which travelled the country as 'Karno's Vaudeville Road Show'. He took pains to advertise that his production was staged at a cost of three hundred pounds per week and that his company would be 'travelling by motor'.[1] Despite this pomp, it was a small-scale troupe playing provincial venues (such as town halls). Why Karno ran these companies is unclear: perhaps his interest in various theatres meant he saw value in being able to fill an entire programme from his own resources; perhaps it was a way of trying out artistes for future pantomimes.[2]

It was a particularly busy year for charity events: in June, Karno took part in a Federation Day show at Crystal Palace to mark the founding of the VAF, and with Henry Lytton he organised a water carnival at Molesey he called *The Grand Fete des Theatres*. Most notably, he collaborated with Wal Pink to write a sketch for the annual Water Rats' fundraising matinee entitled *The Popular Workhouse*, which *The Era* described as: 'A little matter of Rats and Taxes. To

17. THE LITTLE FELLOW

the concoction of which Wal Pink pleads guilty but indicts Fred Karno as an accessory before the fact.'[3] The sketch starred Harry Tate as a Dickensian-sounding workhouse guardian:

> Mr Harry Tate ... as Cackleton Smiggs, who from his motor-car addressed a mass meeting of voters, with a view to his being elected to the board of guardians ... became the butt of an overwhelming dose of questions from the mob regarding "Home Rule". The suffragettes represented by Mr Tom McNaughton as Mrs Wranter ... tried to elucidate some insurance complications. Cackleton ... hastily decided to depart. In the next scene ... the ratepayers were busy delivering vast quantities of wealth to the inmates. Laughter was uncontrollable when Mr George French as Mr Hevvy [sic], a very miserable individual, appealed to the board on behalf of his starving child ... The youngster's mischievous antics easily persuade the board to satisfy his parents' requirements ... Then came a visit from the Board of Guardians, who were greeted with bumper glasses of champagne, which lead to a hilarious display of dancing, and on which the curtain fell.[4]

The sketch parodied a topical story: a new workhouse called the Poplar Training School had recently been built in Essex, and its elaborate design and excessive cost had become a cause célèbre. The public were outraged at the idea of workhouse inmates living in luxury, and the scandal was raised in parliament, where one honourable member remarked: "The beams in the dining hall would do credit to an English Cathedral"[5] – rich pickings for our comedic Water Rats.

Other Karno fundraising efforts included charity matinees, football matches and personal donations to various good causes. If such good deeds were intended to boost his standing in the industry, it paid off when he was appointed chairman of the Music Hall Sick Fund,[6] a subscription fund providing support to artistes suffering ill-health. Such charitable endeavours were only possible because of the continued success of the sketches, so new ones had to keep coming. Jimmy Russell's troupe, which included Syd Chaplin, George Craig and a new face, Stanley Crump (who by name alone must have been a comedy genius), were entrusted with Karno's third sketch in as many months. *London Suburbia* opened with a two-week try-out in mid-June 1907 at the Canterbury and the Paragon. *The Stage* recorded its opening week:

> A fantastic production of life in rural London ... with characters descriptive of The Irritable Author, The Homely Landlady, The Mischievous Boy, The Faithless Wife, The Forgiving Husband, The Noisy Lodgers, and The Calling Costers ... The scene is a very realistic picture of the front view of three suburban villas. Servants are cleaning the doorsteps, and are ... stumbled over by various callers, including an author in search of quiet for his work, who is persuaded to take the front parlour of one of the houses. Then follows a perfect pandemonium of street noises ... An interlude takes place in the affectionate departure of the husband ... and the speedy arrival of a lover, followed by the return of the husband and the expulsion of the wife and lover. The second scene reveals the backs of the same three houses ... A similar confusion ... takes place, including a reconciliation scene between the injured husband and his wife ... The inhabitants ... go to bed, affording an opportunity for shadow displays on the various blinds, after which a fire breaks out, and they all make their exits from the windows with acrobatic agility.[7]

Karno may have written this from personal experience – trying to find some peace and quiet to work on his scripts while his wife takes a lover before setting fire to the furniture.

Karno's sketches mirrored the change in his circumstances: *Early Birds* had shone a spotlight on the slums of the East End, now he was parodying life among the lower middle classes ('villa-dom' as one critic called it). Two weeks after the try-out it reappeared in a double bill

17.1 The cast of London Suburbia, *Syd Chaplin second from left, back row (courtesy Roy Export/Chaplin Archive).*

with *The Smoking Concert*; the most significant change (as far as I am concerned) was that Stanley Crump was no longer in the cast (evidently not a comic genius after all). By September, *London Suburbia* had been taken on by another Karno troupe led by Albert Weston, which included sixteen-year-old Fred Jr.

17. THE LITTLE FELLOW

In early December Karno advertised for artistes and finalised arrangements for his Christmas pantomimes (this was the first year he had staged two concurrently): 'Wanted immediately – twelve cornet players able to play trumpet. Wire lowest terms. Fred Karno.'[8] One wonders why he didn't ask for twelve trumpet players. Meanwhile, the Glasgow Coliseum welcomed *The Football Match* for a second season under the captaincy of Harry Weldon. After Glasgow, Weldon's company headed off on a whirlwind tour of theatres and charity matches, arriving in London in late January, where we finally reach the moment you've all been waiting for. At the New Cross Empire, 10 February 1908, Mr Charles Chaplin Jr. makes his first recorded appearance on a Karno cast list.[9]

We left Chaplin touring as the lead juvenile in Will Murray's company. When he later became a superstar, anyone and everyone who had ever worked with him claimed to be instrumental in discovering his talent, and Murray was no exception. In *Casey's Circus* Chaplin had some freedom to improvise, created his own characters and began to develop his comedic abilities. Murray subsequently claimed credit for teaching Chaplin everything he knew (including his signature 'turning corners' move),[10] saying: 'Charlie made such a tremendous success … he was spoken of as a coming "star". So much so that Fred Karno came after him and offered more money … if "Casey's Court Circus" has done nothing else, it can take the credit for having produced so great a genius.'[11] Contrast that account of Chaplin's discovery with Karno's memoirs:

> FK does not claim … to have 'made' Charlie Chaplin. Managers don't make artistes – though through sheer crass stupidity, they often unmake them by robbing them of opportunity, or by putting square pegs into round holes. What Fred Karno did was to set the boy on the right road to fan the faint glow of his genius till it flamed up, to give him the parts that suited him and the chances to make good. To do him justice Charlie Chaplin has always gladly acknowledged this fact. Hence the close friendship that exists to-day between the world's greatest comic genius and his old guv'nor.[12]

Murray claimed that he and Karno got into a bidding war for Chaplin's talents, but this seems unlikely. A.J. Marriot showed that Chaplin left *Casey's Circus* in July 1907 then spent six months looking for work before joining Karno.

A place in Karno's company was the holy grail for every young comedian, but it was more than that for Chaplin, thanks to a precious childhood memory. While working in a timber yard as a young lad, he and a pal had been treated by their boss to gallery seats for *Early Birds* at the South London Music Hall. His companion was so excited he suffered an epileptic fit; Chaplin saw the show anyway, and it made a lasting impression.

Karno's coming together with Chaplin has been much written about; it was, after all, a meeting of two geniuses which would shape the direction of comedy in the twentieth century. As John McCabe put it, Karno was 'the most intriguing of [Chaplin's] mentors, the man who would bring him unerringly into the highest rank of comedy.'[13]

In his memoirs Karno noted that his meeting with Charlie Chaplin had, even then, been written about in countless books, biographies and newspapers. Karno said he felt it necessary to set the record straight, and claimed his memoirs were the unequivocal true version of events. Helpfully, he then fails to include an account of that first meeting! We must instead rely on snippets pieced together from several sources. In a 1929 article Karno explained how Syd Chaplin persuaded him to give Charlie a chance:

17.2 Charlie Chaplin in Karno days (courtesy Roy Export/Chaplin Archive).

> "Guv'nor," [Syd] said "I've been wondering if you could make an opening for a young brother of mine. His name's Charlie … he's much cleverer than I am, though he's only a kid." … "Bring the young brother along" I said. "I'll have a look at him." So, one day along with Syd came this pale sad looking boy … I must say that at first sight, he looked to me far too shy to do any good on the stage, especially in the kind of knock-about work in which I specialized. He had almost a shrinking air. I asked him briefly what he had been doing and he told me. "I feel I've been wasting my time," he said. "I'd like to get into something with more scope." "All right. Your brother has made good with me, and on that account, I'll give you a trial."[14]

17. THE LITTLE FELLOW

McCabe added: 'Karno described the scene: a young – extraordinarily young – boy, standing in the doorway. "He looked under-nourished and frightened," Karno said, "as though he expected me to raise my hand to hit him."'[15] In 1935 Karno wrote:

> If anyone had offered then and there to lay you one and ninepence to a mansion in Park Lane against that boy ever becoming a millionaire, you'd have cheerfully risked your mansion. He was half-grown and ill-nourished, but he had something – a kind of pathetic stout-heartedness, a take-it-and-come-up-for-more attitude to life that somehow seized my imagination. I hired him at £3 per week – more for Syd's sake than because I felt he was worth the money just then. Syd was getting £4. I believed in paying them high salaries.[16]

A Karno family story has it that Syd enlisted the help of Fred Jr. to persuade the old man to see his brother. If this is true, Charlie owed a great debt to Fred Jr. which he failed to repay in later life. Whoever instigated it, Karno took the lad on, against his better judgement.

In 1931 Karno wrote: 'For a time the best I could offer him was what is called … "supering" on the stage.'[17] As an anonymous 'super', Chaplin's first engagement is impossible to date, however it seems likely that he began making up the numbers in crowd scenes in autumn 1907.[18] Fred Jr. recounted that this was initially with the *London Suburbia* company, where Chaplin supposedly appeared as a rag-and-bone man – a background character which, as he grew in confidence, became a scene stealer. I have yet to find any review that mentions a rag-and-bone man, so if he did steal the show there was no critic to record it. Karno later said that Chaplin was initially 'one of the least important cogs in the Karno fun making machine.'[19]

So, how influential was Karno on this unimportant cog? At the Fun Factory the Chaplin brothers were immersed in wall-to-wall comedy, but they also gained two fundamental career building blocks. First, Karno provided a degree of stability and financial security in their lives; second, Syd and Charlie had no acrobatic or circus background,[20] so it was Karno who introduced them to physical slapstick – the comedy style which came to define them. Syd's biographer Lisa Stein noted: 'Karno can be thanked, really, for saving the Chaplin brothers and encouraging talents and abilities that would last a lifetime.'[21]

Chaplin may have begun his Karno journey as a super in *London Suburbia* but Karno himself recalled: 'Charlie first played for me as one of the football crowd.'[22] In his autobiography, Chaplin recalled it as rather more than that:

> Mr Karno's home was in Coldharbour Lane ... When I arrived, he received me kindly. "Sydney's been telling me how good you are," he said. "Do you think you could play opposite Harry Weldon in The Football Match?" ... "All I need is the opportunity," I said confidently. He smiled. "Seventeen's very young, and you look even younger." I shrugged off-handedly. "That's a question of make-up." Karno laughed. That shrug, he told Sydney later, got me the job.[23]

Let's start by pointing out that Chaplin was actually nearly nineteen when this meeting occurred, then consider what he claimed happened next. According to Chaplin, a few days after joining the largest, most prestigious, and most meticulously rehearsed slapstick comedy company in Britain, and after just two rehearsals, this young lad (who Karno thought looked completely incapable of physical comedy) stepped into a leading part opposite Harry Weldon in one of Karno's greatest sketches, at the biggest music hall in the country, the London Coliseum, and stole the show. This is obviously hogwash. As A.J. Marriot points out, Karno was much too sensible to risk an unknown comic in a lead role.

It was only a matter of time though, and Karno eventually spotted Chaplin's potential shining through from the back row of the ensemble:

> I watched him closely ... and, as soon as an opportunity occurred, I put him into my "Football Match" sketch ... Charlie had the part of a sort of burlesque villain, who was always trying to tempt "Stiffy" ... to sell the match. I kept an eye on him in this part, and came to the conclusion that, good as he was, there was a lot more in him than appeared on the surface.[24]

He still wasn't the lead though: Marriot notes that Weldon and Poluski (as Stiffy and Ratty) were the stars of the sketch – the villain ranked at best equal-third lead, with the detective. Bob Lewis, who had been playing the villain, remained in the company for a few weeks, alternating the role with Chaplin as he was eased in, and enabling Karno to judge his abilities.

17. THE LITTLE FELLOW

Dressed in an Inverness coat with a slouch hat, Chaplin's debut was more Victorian gentleman than Little Tramp,[25] but Karno was impressed. On 21 February 1908, he gave him a formal contract at three pounds, ten shillings per week.

So we now have a more realistic picture of Chaplin's beginnings with Karno, but we haven't finished with his dramatised version quite yet. Chaplin described how he delivered a comic tour-de-force on his opening night, with ad-libs and new business which got laughs where there had previously been none. He recalled how this caused problems with Weldon, and for good measure added that Weldon's style did not go down well in the south of England. Let's consider the second part of this claim first. Once again, A.J. Marriot's meticulous research shows that Weldon was equally well received in reviews all over the country. He was a superb performer who carried the sketch through several tours, a fact that Chaplin acknowledges (thereby contradicting himself) by saying: 'Although *The Football Match* was a burlesque slapstick affair, there was not a laugh in it until Weldon appeared. Everything led up to his entrance, and of course Weldon, excellent comedian that he was, kept the audience in continuous laughter from the moment he came on.'[26]

Chaplin claimed that Weldon became jealous of his abilities and took it out on him with overly physical knockabout on stage, once leaving him with a bloody nose. Fellow Karno comic George Carney corroborated this, recalling that Weldon and Chaplin had a particularly physical section in the turnstile scene and Chaplin was often hurt. One night, Chaplin was suffering with a headache and Carney apparently told Weldon to go easy on the lad. Weldon didn't, and Carney claimed that the two comics subsequently came to blows. Perhaps Weldon, a great solo comic, did not relish sketches where the laughs were shared – that may also explain why Karno didn't use him in anything else. However Chaplin barely scrapes a mention in the press, while Weldon and Poluski took the honours throughout the subsequent tour, so there is no evidence that Chaplin did upstage Weldon. What's more, Chaplin and Weldon worked together for three tours of the sketch, suggesting that if they did clash, they got over it.

One final source of confusion about Chaplin's debut stems from an article in a 1952 edition of *The Picturegoer* which said that his first part with Karno was in another sketch, *G.P.O.*, which starred Fred Kitchen. It goes on to claim that Kitchen's penchant for quick-witted ad-libs prompted Chaplin to respond with yet funnier lines, and that this caused so much trouble between them that Karno moved Chaplin to *The Football Match* instead. Several biographers repeat this story, but it doesn't stack up: Chaplin appeared in *The Football Match* in early February 1908, eight months before *G.P.O.* was first staged.

While no listing puts Chaplin in the same cast as Kitchen, then or later, Marriot points out that there is a missing chunk of Chaplin's career around late 1909, not recorded in his autobiography. This may have included a run in *G.P.O.* Certainly Kitchen recounted working with Chaplin and said that he liked the young comic, taking him under his wing and schooling him in how to avoid 'over-playing' the comedy. Kitchen taught him subtlety and a few tricks along the way, and Chaplin later credited Kitchen with being an influence on him – unlikely if they'd clashed.

Whatever the truth of Chaplin's relationship with these more established stars, Karno did note that the young comic found it difficult to fit in with the group. Jack Melville (who was also in the *Football Match* cast) recalled that as he grew in confidence, Chaplin became aloof and distant, noting that Weldon would say: "Here comes our little genius."[27] As we've already noted, what his co-stars took to be arrogance appears to have been a peculiar mix of self-confidence with an audience and shyness with his peers. This was Karno's view:

> People who were with Chaplin in the old Karno days tell all sorts of stories of his self-absorption … On long train journeys when the other boys in the company were playing ha'penny nap or reading the Sunday papers, or discussing football, or racing, or girls, Charlie would sit in a corner by himself gazing not at the scenery but into space. They thought he was moonstruck, but he was dreaming – dreaming of a possible future, a future of greatness, wealth and power. Certain it is that in his wildest moments he never dreamed that he would reach the pinnacle of fame that was to be his in a few short years.[28]

Chaplin was so focused on his performance that he paid scant attention to anything else. Jack Melville said: "He was untidy. He used to sit in his pyjamas all day playing his violin … all he concentrated on was his work, no thought about his appearance."[29] In contrast Karno was always immaculately dressed, and the following press report suggests that he expected (and rewarded) the same standards in his comics:

17. THE LITTLE FELLOW

> Once [Charlie's] brother Sid [sic] said to Fred Kitchen … "if you lend me 7s 6d., I'll buy Charlie a new pair of boots. Then Karno might give him another half a crown a week." Sid … found Charlie and said, "How are your socks?" … "One's all right," replied Charlie. So, Sid and Fred took him along to a boot shop where Charlie, taking off the wrong boot, laughed, and exposed half a sock! They left him there, in disgust.[30]

When touring, Chaplin was always late. He'd eventually appear, collar half-buttoned and still in his slippers, running to catch the train. However, Chaplin excelled at his presentation when he applied his mind to it, as Karno recalled:

> For weeks on end he would go about … looking like an out and out tramp. His face would be dirty and unshaven, while his boots were never polished, and had no laces in them. I have known him wear a collar for a fortnight … But Charlie could transform himself when he liked … Immaculate new wash leather gloves, the colour of rich butter, snowy white spats, spotless collar and cuffs, and a spick and span soft felt hat on his head at a jaunty angle, made him a different person.[31]

17.3 Chaplin in his Sunday best (courtesy Roy Export/Chaplin Archive).

Jack Melville added that having spent all his money on such fancy clothes, they'd be ruined within a week. Chaplin acknowledged this tendency to slovenliness, blaming it on the pressures of touring, but it is clear that he simply had more interesting things to think about. He spent his spare time on self-improvement (a habit he never lost), burying himself deep in books on a huge variety of subjects. He taught himself to play piano and violin and would later compose music for his films (although he could not read a note). It is easy to see why he seemed unorthodox among a group of happy-go-lucky knockabout comics. Karno said:

> There is, I think little doubt that some of the stuff of which his dreams were made concerned music … had he had the necessary technical training in early youth a great musician might have been gained to the world and a great comedian lost … in those early days … Charlie purchased a second hand cello, which he carted about from town to town and … tried his best to play.[32]

In 1908 London hosted the Olympics, and as one great sporting event began, another came to an end. In May *The Football Match* completed its second tour in style at the London Coliseum, and Chaplin joined his brother's company playing *Mumming Birds*, *The Smoking Concert* and a new sketch called *The Casuals* – Syd now had top billing over Jimmy Russell. It was a happy time for Chaplin. He and Syd settled into a newly rented flat in Brixton Road, a short walk from the Fun Factory, and his comedy education really got underway. As one new comic was being nurtured, an old one was welcomed back to the fold. Albert Darnley joined Syd's company, Karno's feud with his brother presumably put behind them – for now. *The Casuals* appeared in late March, after a try-out week as *The Outcasts*. It was the first of a number of sketches Karno listed as being 'in preparation' that spring. Written by Karno and Tom Tindall, it was probably based on *The Popular Workhouse* ('casuals' were workhouse residents accommodated for a single night rather than permanently):

> The fun begins as soon as the curtain rises, revealing the casuals awaiting the opening of the door. One gentleman appears who has transferred a valuable ring from its previous owner to his own pocket. This he passes to his female accomplice … the company indulge in jest, music and dancing until they are received inside the house. In the second scene plenty of fun is got out of the inspection and search and the serving of supper. The cleansing of a particularly dirty looking gentleman, who is subjected to very rigorous treatment, affords the greatest amusement … the arrest of the genius of the ring (betrayed by his fellow guests) brought the merry trifle to an end.[33]

Later reviews mention accidental 'casuals' taking up residence in the belief that the workhouse was a country club, and its chairman siphoning off coal from the boiler room for his own fireplace. Amid the comedy, Karno again shone a light on the harsh realities of life, and this was not lost on one reviewer:

17. THE LITTLE FELLOW

> The slyness and impudence of the professional loafer and tramp are laughably satirised ... at the same time the casual ward is sometimes the scene of veritable tragedy. The sketch recognizes this, too, and perhaps it may help to bring about some improvements in the methods of management ... This was strongly recommended by a recent committee of enquiry, but, as it would involve some real benefit to the poor, it is naturally neglected by a Government of friends of the people.[34]

The Government was hardly likely to set policy on the basis of Karno's sketches, but they would have been familiar with his name. As Adeler and West noted, his anarchic chaos was becoming a byword for disorder and mismanagement: 'It became a national joke – anything that was comically bad was Fred Karno's – train, bus and tram services ... Fred didn't mind ... no showman objects to a free ad.'[35]

Karno's name was all over the newspapers that spring as he began his battle with Pathé over Max Linder's film version of *Mumming Birds*. When he staged a private performance of the sketch for Justice Jelf, it was Syd Chaplin playing the drunk in the box – one wonders what Syd and his brother made of it all. Years later Chaplin would make his own film version of the sketch; and count Linder amongst his friends.

17.4 Syd Chaplin as the drunk in the box (courtesy Roy Export/Chaplin Archive).

Karno's attention was now on the legal case, and although he found time to increase his interests in theatre ownership (which we'll come to shortly), it would be some months before he successfully launched another sketch. In the meantime, his listings included an oddity: he advertised that in the first week of June he intended to stage a sketch called *A Trip to Whitby*. This was written by Syd O'Malley and Will Letters, so may have been a revised version of *What Uncle Lost* (the O'Malley sketch Karno staged during the Music Hall War), but there is no sign of it ever being performed. Perhaps Karno was giving a couple of his young comics a chance to write something but got cold feet at the last minute.[36]

225

Such false starts weren't the only signs that Karno had taken his eye off the ball. His advertising column disappeared from the press, and although reviews for his touring troupes remained positive, Karno was beginning to be perceived as a veteran. This was reinforced by numerous articles reminiscing on his early career:

> From plumber's apprentice to music hall manager is a big jump ... "I was originally," he writes, "one of the submerged. And that I am not today one of the 'won't-works' I attribute to the fact that good old Dame Nature gave me an energetic disposition and a taste for athletics. I may say I was a born gymnast and was engaged to give exhibitions at fetes and galas, till finally I came under the notice of Mons. Alvene [sic], a well-known equilibrist ... At last jumping over many ups-and-downs, mostly the latter, I came to my first sketch in a London Music Hall."[37]

Reviewers still described Karno's sketches in warm terms: 'as good as ever' or 'funny as always', but they were now old friends that audiences were pleased to see again rather than exciting new spectacles not to be missed. Things were rather different in America where the Karno company was still a relatively new phenomenon, as *The Era* noted: 'One of the best drawing cards in vaudeville, for while they occupy the stage the audience laughs continuously.'[38]

Billy Reeves' company had now been touring the same two sketches (*A Night in an English Music Hall* and *A Night in the Slums of London*)[39] for over eighteen months, with a pretty stable cast including George Welch, Bill Fern, Amy Minister, Jimmy Aubrey and Will Crackles. Interestingly, at that time a new element of vaudeville was reported to be all the rage: 'Amateur Night', where all-comers could perform. A key element of this was 'the hook', wielded by the stage manager when an act had more ambition than ability. *A Night in an English Music Hall* audiences must have spent their evenings trying to work out whether they were watching Karno's professionals pretending to be bad amateurs, or bad amateurs trying to be professionals.

This wasn't the only point of confusion: in May, *The Stage* records *Fred Karno's London Fire Brigade* in New York, but this was not a Karno show. It was our old friend Billie Ritchie's company[40] and it prompted another battle, with Alf Reeves and Ritchie fighting it out on the letters page of *Variety*. Reeves claimed

17. THE LITTLE FELLOW

Ritchie (who had teamed up with ex-Karno plonk Joey Hindle) had strung together old Karno sketches; Ritchie unsurprisingly claimed the work to be his own. Ritchie had form of course, and he certainly stole the idea: *The Fire Brigade* was one of the 'sketches in preparation' Karno had advertised back in 1906.

The American tour finally came to an end in June 1908, but Billy Reeves did not head home. Instead he abandoned Karno to join *The Ziegfeld Follies*, a new style of musical comedy revue recently established by Florenz Ziegfeld on Broadway. Reeves (who went on to make a career of playing versions of the drunk in the box) contributed a 'drunken prize fight' to the *Follies* which bore an uncanny resemblance to the Terrible Turkey routine. Karno continued to battle such poaching by other vaudeville producers, but had not yet appreciated the real threat – the new kid on the block, cinema.

17.5 Early defector – Billie Ritchie.

Even then, one reporter foresaw that the new medium might spell disaster for vaudeville, although he felt the danger was in its potential damage to an artiste's appeal, rather than seeing cinema as direct competition: 'Vaudeville artists are falling easy victims to the offers of large sums to pose for films, not recognizing that these same moving pictures will prove their ultimate destruction, since no manager will care to book an attraction, the bloom of which has been worn off in the five cent places.'[41]

Despite losing Billy Reeves, Karno quickly secured a return to the States for the autumn, and such was the demand for *A Night in an English Music Hall* that Alf Reeves and his company sailed slightly earlier than planned. This later caused a problem as their scenery did not arrive in time, and for the first week (at Hammerstein's in New York) they had to improvise a set. Interestingly, advertising in *Variety* stated that 'Charlie Chapman' would be leading the company[42] – a listing which has had biographers guessing ever since. Did they mean Chaplin? Had Karno intended to send Chaplin just six months after he'd joined his company? If so, something happened – Chaplin was not on that tour, and it was Bert Weston who had the unenviable task of stepping into Reeves' shoes as the new drunk in the box. A.J. Marriot speculates that Chaplin was intended to lead the tour but elected to stay at home as he had fallen head over heels in love with a girl named Hetty Kelly. Anything's possible, but Chaplin was not a lead player in Karno's companies at that stage, and none of the well-documented accounts of how he was chosen for his first U.S. tour, two years later, suggest that Karno considered him for this 1908 trip. Perhaps the *Variety* advertisement was another case of mistaken identity. Either confusion between the two Chaplin brothers, or an error in an agent's office, since Dick Warner's agency had a well-known agent called Charlie Chapman. Whatever the answer to that mystery, Chaplin certainly did meet and fall in love with Hetty Kelly, adding an even brighter shine to an already very happy summer for the young comic.

Since Chaplin's meeting with Kelly has been the subject of intense scrutiny by historians, we might take a moment to note a Karno connection to their first tryst. Felstead records that Karno was leasing the Montpelier Palace[43] in Walworth as rehearsal space, and that this is where Chaplin met Kelly, who was in a dance troupe. So far so good, except that Felstead's account (which is generally unreliable) appears to be the only source for Karno's use of the Montpelier – it is not corroborated by any contemporary records. Chaplin's autobiography is no help: he says that they met while on the same bill at the Streatham Empire, which A.J. Marriot debunks.[44]

The where and when would not have mattered to Chaplin, it was the who that counted. Hetty Kelly was his first love and left a lasting impression, even though (or perhaps because) she quickly broke his heart. And Chaplin wasn't the only one left feeling dejected at the end of that summer – one senses a general malaise falling over the Karno operation. The year had begun badly: Karno's father passed away on 10 January, aged sixty-six, and in July, one of his female comics, Amy Rogerson (who had played leading roles in *His Majesty's Guests* and *Saturday to Monday*), died at the age of forty, leaving three children. Later in the year one of Karno's longstanding managers, Arthur Forrest, passed away, aged fifty. It seemed there was no good news – that summer he also lost his legal case against Pathé. Something was needed to bring the Karno company out of the doldrums.

18.
Postmen, Pugilists, Politicians and Pratfalls

A lady went to the post-office to buy a postage stamp.
When she had purchased the stamp, she asked the man at
the window if she should put the stamp on herself.
"No – put it on the envelope."
(The Merry Book of the Moore & Burgess Minstrels, 1898)

THOMAS MONTAGUE Sylvester was a former circus bareback rider who had graduated to theatre impresario via a career chequered with bankruptcy and dodgy dealing. By 1908 he was the proud owner of the Palace, Maidstone, and the New Hippodrome, Peterborough. Karno had provided scenery at both theatres and Sylvester, unable to pay the bill, persuaded him to accept shares in his company instead. A few weeks later Sylvester went bust, leaving Karno down £650. Instead of cutting his losses, Karno and business partner Alfred H. Edwards purchased the leases to both theatres from the liquidator at auction – they must have been determined to win, as within two hours posters were distributed showing their bill for the following week. Karno and Edwards also acquired the lease on another Sylvester failure, the Royal Public Rooms, Exeter. *The Era* noted: 'The fact that Mr Karno is a native of Exeter should add not a little to the popularity of the project … Exeter therefore forms the third link in a circuit which it is intended to eventually run through the provinces.'[1] It was actually his fourth theatre (he also had the Marlborough), and while Karno may have fancied himself as the next Oswald Stoll, he had purchased low-quality venues which would prove hard to make pay.

The Peterborough Hippodrome was less than two years old but poorly designed: it was not unusual for the show to be stopped because of noise from hailstones hitting the corrugated tin roof (some reports suggest this happened on Karno's opening night – surely an ill omen). The Public Rooms in Exeter was even less salubrious, and Karno's original intention was to demolish the building. Grand plans were drawn up by noted theatre architect Bertie Crewe, but these were abandoned in favour of a quick refurbishment and a small extension to the rear. Keen to retain Gilbert's Circus for the summer season, which Sylvester had already booked, Karno gave the builders just two weeks to complete the works – and progress was hampered by a Salvation Army event booked by General Bramwell Booth, which had to be staged amid the chaos. Booth was far from happy, and let everyone know what he thought of Karno in less than Christian language. Karno placated the General, recounting how he had met and listened to his father back in his youth in Nottingham. Perhaps in recompense, he allowed Booth to use the theatre for a fundraiser the following year.

Karno's 'New Exeter Hippodrome' opened on 2 November, but the works were far from complete and the back wall (removed for the extension but not yet rebuilt) had to be hastily sealed up with tarpaulins. Despite these challenges, he later recalled that the opening night was a triumph.

Karno evidently saw Sylvester's failure as an opportunity to acquire venues cheaply, rather than a symptom of a struggling industry – Fred Miller's warning of a theatre development bubble went unheeded. What's more, he increased his risk by investing not in music halls but in legitimate theatres,[2] which he knew less about. Given his ongoing battle with Pathé, he also seemed surprisingly oblivious to the impact the fledgling film industry might have on his new business. This advertisement for *Dandy Thieves,* at the Kilburn Empire that October, shows that film was beginning to have an impact: 'Special engagement, at enormous expense, of Fred Karno's Co. in The Dandy Thieves – Note … NOT an animated picture.'[3]

The week that work started on his building project in Exeter, Karno launched *G.P.O.* in Sheffield. Fred Kitchen was the creative force behind the new sketch (although Karno and Frank Calvert were credited as co-writers), and led from the front as Perkins, supported by Albert Bruno as the fantastically named villain Herbert Realstiff.

The Era tells us more:

18. POSTMEN, PUGILISTS, POLITICIANS AND PRATFALLS

Mr Fred Kitchen, who in the part of Perkins is supplied with unlimited scope and endless opportunities for the display of the eccentricities and quaint mannerisms which have made him so popular … G.P.O. … is not all comedy, for there is now and then … a touch of real pathos which lends a bit of interest to the sketch. The first scene is the exterior of the G.P.O. where Mary Wilson, in a vain attempt to beg assistance from her vile betrayer Realstiff, is seen bemoaning her sad fate. Perkins enters; and there are "hands" wanted at the G.P.O. … We see him duly appointed as a postman in a busy scene of the interior of the G.P.O., and he indulges in a song with a chorus by postmen and telegraph girls. The postmaster enters, and takes quite a fancy to Perkins, to whom he hands the key of the safe, £20 for temporary expenses, gives him entire charge of the office and then goes on a holiday.[4]

In the first scene, Perkins arrives outside the post office and spots the notice advertising for staff. Karno recalled that Kitchen kept the audience in hysterics for two minutes without saying a word, just by the way he examined the sign (a feat he described as incredible). Once inside, Perkins inevitably caused chaos, as this script from Fred Junior's archive makes clear:

The G.P.O.

Perkins has been put in charge, the postmaster hands him the keys and exits:

Perkins: (*Looking at safe keys*) Now we can back some winners. (*Jolly enters*) Ah Jolly, I've just been made postmaster. That's what you want to do, climb the ladder of fame. And when you get to the top, we may let you clean the windows. Now … first of all we've got to make this place into a paying concern. For instance, in future, we'll send the 8 a.m. mail out at seven.

Jolly: Whatever for?

Perkins: To get there before the other post offices you fool! (*A toff enters.*)

Toff: Do you sell stamps here?

Perkins: Can't say for certain. I'll go and see. (*To girl behind counter*) Do we sell stamps here?

Girl: Of course we do!

Perkins:	(*Returns to toff*) Of course we do!
Toff:	Well what prices do you have?
Perkins:	(*To girl*) What prices do we have?
Girl:	Halfpenny, thee 'appence, tuppence and so on.
Perkins:	(*To toff*) Halfpenny, thee 'appence, tuppence and so on.
Toff:	Show me some nice halfpenny ones.
Perkins:	(*To girl*) Show me some nice halfpenny ones (*she hands him a large sheet of stamps and he returns to the toff*). Here we are; we are selling quite a lot of these. They all have sticky backs and are perforated in every hole.
Toff:	(*Pointing to stamp in centre of the sheet*) I'll have that one.

Perkins chases the toff off with a mallet. A doctor enters carrying a letter, buys a stamp then begins to examine Perkins. He checks his pulse, then shakes his head and gestures for Perkins to stick out his tongue. Perkins does so, enabling the doctor to wet his stamp and stick it on his letter. An old lady enters, clearly in need of some money. She is told that her pension will not be paid until tomorrow and she bursts into tears. Perkins, overcome with emotion, gets a large bundle of cash from the safe and gives it to the old lady:

Old Lady:	Oh, how can I ever thank you?
Perkins:	No trouble mother, if you run short this afternoon pop in again.

A Frenchman arrives and persuades Perkins to help him write a love letter, a tramp appeals unsuccessfully for funds, and finally Realstiff appears and blackmails Perkins into being his accomplice later that night. Perkins exits and a tearful woman enters carrying a young child, which she abandons, leaving a note: 'Whoever finds this little girl, be good to her. God help me I can keep her no longer.' Perkins returns for his hat and discovers the girl:

Girl:	Are you my daddy?
Perkins:	I can't say for certain – I've travelled a lot.

Reading the note and realising the child is freezing, he creates a makeshift bed for her under the counter and she settles down for the night. Realstiff knocks at

18. POSTMEN, PUGILISTS, POLITICIANS AND PRATFALLS

the window, Perkins breaks the window with a mallet and throws out the keys ("Well they can't say I let him in!"). The villain enters and opens the safe – quick as a flash, Perkins pushes him inside. At that moment the postmaster and staff return, Perkins is accused of stealing and dismissed. Suddenly he remembers the little girl, picks her up and carries her to the door. The postmaster, his resolve softened by the sight of the child, asks Perkins what possessed him to take something from the safe: "I wasn't taking something out, sir, I was putting something in!" The safe is opened and Realstiff is apprehended – Perkins is proclaimed a hero.

Some of those gags may be familiar to fans of film comedy: Chaplin gets someone to stick out his tongue to lick a stamp in *The Bank* (1915), and W.C. Fields used the customer requesting a stamp from the middle of the sheet in *The Pharmacist* (1933).

Just six weeks after *G.P.O.* opened Karno launched another new sketch, *The Yap Yaps*, which had a try-out in Margate before transferring to the Paragon. It was the first of many collaborations between Karno and J. Hickory Wood, who wrote Drury Lane pantomimes for Dan Leno and had worked with Leslie Stuart. *The Yap Yaps* took another sporting theme, boxing, which had been growing in popularity since the founding of the National Sporting Club in Covent Garden in 1891. Interest was particularly high in 1908, as the black American boxer Jack Johnson arrived in London seeking challengers. His promotional engagements included a series of exhibition events at the Oxford Music Hall, as Britain searched for a 'Great White Hope' to take him on. Karno avoided any racist undertones in his sketch and instead included an exhibition bout between Johnny Summers and Young Joseph, two well-known welterweights who battled each other for supremacy throughout the first decade of the twentieth century. It seems extraordinary to imagine two professional boxers working in a comedy sketch while still competing at the highest level, but the halls offered a chance for boxers to promote themselves and earn extra income. Some even commissioned their own melodramas, starring as the heroic pugilist who saves the heroine from the villain in a finale that was literally a knockout.

The Yap Yaps opened with a seafront scene at Brighton, where Karno employed his huge fans (last seen waving arms around in *The Football Match*) to play havoc with the hats and hair of promenading ladies – and more besides, as he himself recalled: 'What a delicious naughty display of lingeries [sic] … it was said that cloakroom attendants did a roaring trade getting bald-headed old gentlemen's eyes back into their sockets ... the audiences of those days shrieked with unholy joy as the girls' skirts blew over their heads.'[5] Scene two was in a bar, where some young dandies, all members of a club calling themselves the Yap Yaps, get into an altercation with a group of boxers. A Yap Yap called Charlie Chinn challenges Big Ben Burley to a match at the National Sporting Club, setting up the next scene: Covent Garden. Karno recalled that this was a particularly fine backcloth, and his chorus of eighty supers attired as market traders, newspaper vendors and elegant spectators made for an extremely realistic street scene. Enter Charlie's sister, who tries everything to talk Big Ben out of beating her brother to a pulp. Ben agrees not to hurt him, promising instead to 'put him to sleep'. The scene transforms into the grand finale, which impressed the critic from *The Stage*: 'The Interior of the Club, with its elevated, roped in ring, its well-dressed sporting crowd ... and the act-drop of the stage in the background is probably as faithful a reproduction of a Monday night at "The National" as can be achieved by scenic art.'[6]

Before the big fight came a series of amateur bouts, with prizes for any locals foolish enough to take part. There was never a shortage of volunteers, and in Karno's words "they always put up a good scrap." Next came the exhibition bout between Summers and Joseph, which certainly interested the press: 'The contest... is an exceedingly clever exhibition. It should also help keep Summers in good trim for his forthcoming contest with Jimmy Britt.'[7] This forthcoming bout with Britt, an American, was a much-anticipated rematch. He had recently beaten Summers and they were to meet again the following February at the real-life National Sporting Club. When the fight came around, Summers won on points – three days afterwards he was back in *The Yap Yaps* and his vanquished opponent was the guest of honour watching the show!

Back to the sketch, and it was time for the main event – Chinn versus Burley. Chinn was played by Gus Le Clerq, who according to Karno was a good amateur boxer, and despite being much smaller than his opponent (played by Jimmy Prior) put up a genuinely challenging fight before reverting to the script and taking a fall. (You may recall that Le Clerq had been part of Reed Pinaud's company before joining Karno, which might explain why he was cast in a part where he had to fight for his life twice nightly.)[8] All is not over for our hero: a second rushes into the ring with an oxygen bottle, puts a tube in Chinn's mouth and re-inflates him with such vigour that he jumps to his feet and knocks out Burley with a single punch (along with his own second and the referee) before

18. POSTMEN, PUGILISTS, POLITICIANS AND PRATFALLS

claiming his prize. A series of amateur boxing matches, a professional exhibition bout and what Karno recalled as one of his funniest sketches – not bad for sixpence.

Stan Laurel later recalled an example of Karno's 'wistful' ideas, which may well have been from *The Yap Yaps*:

> I forget the Karno sketch but there was one in which a chap got all beat up – deservedly. He was the villain … and the audience was happy to see him get his. Then Karno added this little bit after the man was knocked down. He had the hero … walk over to the villain and make him feel easier. Put a pig's bladder under his head … it got a laugh, and at the same time it was a bit touching … I seem to recall you would have to look sorry, really sorry, for a few seconds after hitting someone on the head. Karno would say, "wistful, please, wistful!" It was only a bit of a look, but somehow it made the whole thing funnier … Karno really knew how to sharpen comedy in that way.[9]

It is not difficult to see that these ideas were a huge influence on the future work of Karno comics, and this kind of reversal (hitting a man then kissing it better) was certainly a consistent Chaplin device. In 1918's *Triple Trouble*,[10] for example, he knocks out a noisy drunk then tucks him up in bed with a pillow. There are boxing routines in several Chaplin films, including *The Knockout* (1914), where he plays referee to Fatty Arbuckle's pugilist, and *The Champion* (1915) – both may have included some *Yap Yap* ideas. Gags from *The Football Match* are certainly evident in the latter, as Chaplin lifts both weights and beer bottles in a gymnasium before being offered a bribe to throw the fight. He gets hit in the face by a punchball too, and that idea also crops up in *Mabel's Married Life* (1914), where he has a protracted battle with a dummy he believes to be a real person.

With so much to occupy him at home, and his international ambitions focused on America, Karno decided he had no appetite to manage other far-flung international tours. He sold those rights to a producer named Bert Bernard, who quickly began producing the sketches to critical acclaim – including a year-long tour of South America which saw *Early Birds*, *London Suburbia* and *Mumming Birds* play in Brazil, Argentina and Uruguay.[11] Bernard followed this with two months in Russia – Karno was now a truly global brand.

Back home, a busy Christmas saw another season of *The Football Match* (with Weldon back as Stiffy), accompanied by the usual charity games. Meanwhile, Karno supported a Water Rats show at the London Coliseum in aid of 'Sir William Treloar's Christmas Fund for the Little Cripples of London,' where *Mumming Birds* was part of an enormous bill which also included Marie Lloyd, Eugene Stratton, Joe Elvin, Harry Tate, Gus Elen and Chirgwin. There were plenty of other demands on his fundraising resources, too. On 28 December, 100,000 people were killed by Europe's worst ever earthquake, which destroyed the Italian cities of Messina and Reggio Calabria: Karno raised funds for an earthquake appeal by staging special matinees in both Exeter and Bristol.

Christmas also meant pantomime of course, and he produced *The House That Jack Built* at his own Marlborough Theatre, with a new libretto by J. Hickory Wood, music by Dudley Powell and the formidable comic Fred Emney as Mother Hubbard.[12] It ran until February and was an extraordinary hit, as this review makes clear:

18.1 Nothing like a Dame – Fred Emney (author's collection).

> If volume of sound could lift a roof, then the pretty, well appointed, playhouse ... would today be without a covering ... the audience voiced their appreciation with all the breath they could raise, in addition to beating their hands together until they were nearly reduced to a pulp. The remarkable enthusiasm ... lasted half an hour ... When Mr Fred Karno stepped out from the side of the stage a great cheer went up; and when he, with his usual modesty, made for the exit, he was stopped by a tumultuous cry for a speech ... Mr Karno thanked the audience on behalf of the company ... and somebody started 'For he's a jolly good fellow!' ... still the audience were not satisfied [all the leading cast members then made speeches and were showered with flowers] ... This was the climax of one of the biggest pantomime successes in the suburbs ... it is our very pleasing privilege to record ... the receipt by Mr J. Murray Herriot, a prince among managers, of a charmingly

18. POSTMEN, PUGILISTS, POLITICIANS AND PRATFALLS

characteristic letter from Mr Fred Karno ... thanking Mr Herriot for his untiring efforts to make the pantomime a success and expressing his appreciation of "what you have done and the way you have done it".[13]

This critic filled half a page with the details of the flowers, the speeches and everyone singing Auld Lang Syne. Not only does his report confirm Karno's reluctance to make a speech, but also that he was clearly well-liked by the cast and crew and appreciative of their efforts.

Karno's latest sketches joined all the others on the circuit: even *Hilarity* (now twenty years old), *Early Birds* and *His Majesty's Guests* were still doing the rounds. In Europe and around the Empire, Bert Bernard was flying the Karno flag and Alf Reeves' company continued to tour the States. The new productions were also proving a big box-office draw: at the New Cross Empire, hundreds were disappointed when they were unable to get tickets for *G.P.O.*, and theatres put out the 'standing room only' signs throughout its tour. Unfortunately, Karno had little time to bask in these glories – he was too busy trying to sort out trouble in Devon.

The Exeter Hippodrome had been a challenge from the day it opened. Almost immediately he had found himself in a dispute over completion of the lease, and then became embroiled in a legal battle with neighbours who claimed the extension had blocked their natural light. Karno and Edwards were forced to pay the hefty sum of £225 in compensation. This seems to have driven a wedge between the men, and Karno commenced legal proceedings against Edwards, which led to the dissolution of their partnership on 24 April 1909.

Despite this, a few weeks later they filed a joint action for slander against another neighbour, James Spratt, whose curio shop was directly linked to the theatre. Spratt had made it publicly known that, in his view, the new theatre wasn't safe. He claimed a fire in his property had originated in the Hippodrome (it was later proved not to have done so), and complained that people queuing for tickets would loiter outside his shop and lean on his windows. Karno and Edwards accused Spratt of publicly decrying their reputation, but lost the case when the judge held that he was not seeking to maliciously damage the men's standing. Karno appealed but was judged 'out of time', having submitted the case to the wrong court – he just couldn't get a break.[14]

He may have come off worst in these legal tussles, but at least he had become the Hippodrome's sole proprietor. He quickly employed a new manager, Fred Sandy, to run the day to day operations in Exeter and put some effort back into his business in London, including resuming advertising his 'Theatrical Factory' in the press. Most importantly he set to work on a new production: here he was on safer ground, if not a steadier footing – his next sketch would be on wheels.

There was a new craze sweeping Britain: roller skating. Rinks began springing up all over the country, but the American Roller Rink at Olympia set the trend, and became a magnet for theatricals and the fashionable set. *The Era* ran a regular 'Rinking Gossip' page, with all the latest skating news and roller-hockey match reports. Always keen to seize an opportunity, Karno threw himself wholeheartedly at the new pastime, quickly becoming an accomplished skater, and in April 1909 he started a new venture – Karno's Rinks.[15] He established rinks in several towns and engaged expert skaters from Earls Court to manage them. It will come as no surprise that he soon had a new challenge for the plonks.

The imaginatively titled *Skating* debuted in the first week of May 1909, at the Queen's Palace of Varieties, Poplar. It came from the pen of J. Hickory Wood, who had now become Karno's number one writer, ably assisted by the star of the sketch, Syd Chaplin[16] (receiving his first writing credit). Syd turned out to be as good a writer as he was a skater. *The Era* reported:

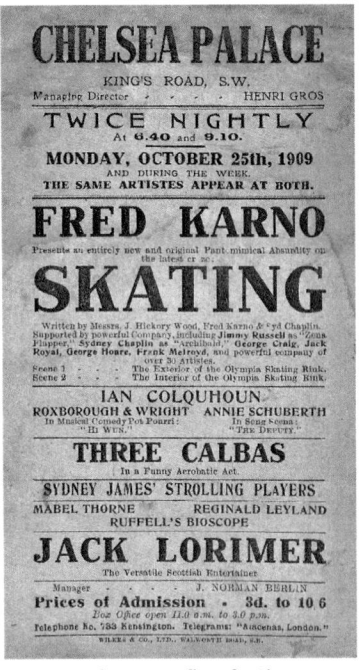

18.2 Advertising flyer for Skating, *with Syd Chaplin and Jimmy Russell (author's collection).*

> Whatever may be the particular craze … it is sure to receive humorous attention at the hands of that prince of mirth-providers Mr Fred Karno … there are two scenes, the first representing the outside of an entrance to Olympia, with all the details of payboxes and turnstiles, while the second scene represents the interior of the vast hall. As a background there is a magnificent scene-cloth depicting the snowy range of the Alps, with the Matterhorn in the distance … Of plot or story there is of course nothing, the fun in the opening scene consisting of the side-splitting eccentricities of a volunteer door-keeper … To him in turn there

18. POSTMEN, PUGILISTS, POLITICIANS AND PRATFALLS

appeal for admission the distressed maiden who has lost her purse, the Dundreary dandy, the old lady in crinoline, and her nephew, who desires to break her neck on the rink. The great skating professor fails to turn up, and the volunteer door-keeper undertakes to save the situation ... From the start to the fall of the curtain there is not one dull moment, and seldom an interval when the house is not convulsed with laughter.[17]

Syd led from the front as the volunteer doorkeeper, Archibald.[18] Jimmy Russell and Harry Oxberry appeared in drag as Miss Zena Flapper and Auntie respectively, and Frank Melroyd played Dundreary; but Syd's most important co-star was a minor player, Minnie Gilbert – the future Mrs Syd Chaplin.

18.3 Syd and Minnie Chaplin in Skating *(courtesy Roy Export/Chaplin Archive).*

18.4 George Hoare, a later Zena Flapper, in Skating *(courtesy Jeremy Hoare).*

The sketch required special flooring to be laid on the stage and theatre managers made the most of it, engaging other freewheeling artistes to complete the bill, such as the Olympian Ladies Troupe of trick skaters. One wonders why Karno didn't think to incorporate such exhibition displays into the sketch himself. The acrobatic plonks were clearly accomplished skaters – it is not easy to do something badly on purpose, and a quadrille dance in the second scene must have been particularly tricky. Unsurprisingly, the cast also formed a roller-hockey team and competed in charity matches. Not all were naturals on wheels, though. Writing to Fred Karno Jr. in 1959, Stan Laurel recalled fellow comic George Farnley struggling to keep upright: 'Old George Farnley – what characters they were! We don't see those type of personalities any more, what funny comics … Farnley could never skate, before we went on he used to say "Now not too boisterous boys, I can't walk with these bloody wheels on me plates, if you knock me down you'll bloody well 'ave to drag me orf – so 'elp me I'll never be able to get up again!"'[19]

Syd was beginning to get noticed by the critics, but his brother was still working his apprenticeship and gradually developing as a comic, sketch by sketch. Even if Charlie Chaplin had stood out to reviewers, they wouldn't have been able to identify him, as Karno deliberately avoided naming the knockabout plonks in the programme. This anonymity helped to maintain a team ethos in what needed to be a closely knit group.[20] The plonks were much more akin to an acrobatic troupe than a company of comedians, so singling them out might have caused issues with the others – and when you are relying on your co-star to catch you from a great height, that can be a problem. Nonetheless, Chaplin had shown talent – it was time for Karno to give him a chance in the spotlight.

As *Skating* opened, *The Football Match* tour was coming to a close. Chaplin had been reprising his role as the villain, but at the end of the run Karno gave him the opportunity to play Stiffy the goalkeeper for one night. Weldon watched from the stalls, unimpressed – later recalling that he and his fellow comics couldn't see what Karno thought so promising in the young comic. While Chaplin had a flair for pantomime, Weldon thought his delivery of verbal gags was weak and he lacked the physique to play Stiffy.[21] Chaplin received favourable press reviews however, which was lucky as Weldon inexplicably left the company, perhaps prompted by Karno's decision to let the young pretender try his part.

So Chaplin was left to play the lead for the last week of the tour, and Weldon never again

18.5 Weldon turns his back on The Football Match *(author's collection).*

18. POSTMEN, PUGILISTS, POLITICIANS AND PRATFALLS

appeared in a Karno sketch. The archives suggest there were other potential Weldon sketches, at least on paper,[22] and he later traded on his status as a Karno comic – his billing usually noted he was 'Stiffy in *The Football Match*'. So was it an argument over Chaplin, Weldon's drinking, or just a lack of team spirit which consigned their association to history?

Even more perplexing is that Karno also dumped the immensely popular character of Stiffy, even though he could have used it in future sketches, as he had with Perkins and would again with Archibald Binks. What's more he allowed Weldon to portray Stiffy in various guises throughout his subsequent solo career: as 'Stiffy the Great White Hope', 'Stiffy the prison warder' and many more. It seems likely therefore that the character was a Weldon creation. Here's a taste of Stiffy the prison warder: '[Stiffy is seen] knitting a pair of socks for a convict to go to a fancy-dress parade, brushing the convicts' hair and telling them (when they hurry back out of the rain) "Oh well, you can't mess the prison about. Either you stay in or you go out, one thing or the other. There's other people wanting to come in besides you."'[23] Weldon's style is easily recognisable to anyone who has seen the film comedies of Robb Wilton or Will Hay[24] – both would be future students in the Karno school.

Meanwhile Charlie Chaplin was impressing his mentor, not only as a performer but with his ability to grasp an idea, stepping in when Karno's lack of verbal dexterity let him down. Karno recalled:

> He was extremely useful to me outside of his own part … when I held a rehearsal for the purpose of showing the company any new business I had invented, I found myself very often at my wit's end to get them to grasp what I wanted, for I tried to convey my ideas by word of mouth … Then, when I had made a score of abortive attempts, Charlie would speak up. "I say, sir, would you allow me to show them. I think I know what you want." Then he would step out of the crowd and go through a few movements, a walk, a turn, or an exit or entrance, and the very thing I wanted was there to the life. There was no sign of show or swank about this. He would do it quietly and as earnestly as if he was rehearsing a funeral.[25]

Which sketches Chaplin appeared in over the following months is unknown, since he fell back into the company of anonymous plonks, but if he was in *The*

Smoking Concert at the Empire Palace, Dublin, in June (as indicated by Marriot's research), he shared the stage with another future film star, 29-year-old juggler W.C. Fields.[26] This would support the idea that the pair once performed on the same bill in their early days, although legend has it this was at the Folies Bergère – a story Simon Louvish debunks by establishing that Fields was not in Paris at the same time as Chaplin.[27] However, now that we know Chaplin and Fields were almost certainly together in Dublin a few months earlier, this is perhaps the origin of a story which remains of great interest to film historians as Fields famously hated Chaplin in later life. One wonders who upstaged whom.

So, Syd had become the star of the knockabouts and his brother was on the way up, but Fred Kitchen remained the undisputed lead comic of the Karno empire. Looking back on his career, Kitchen noted that he'd always received support from the public and the press, and that Karno had a lot to do with it: 'I credit Fred Karno for this happy fact as much as I do my own work … for if I was able to interpret my parts happily it was made easy for me by the fact that Fred Karno produced his shows so wonderfully. A new Karno sketch … was a … source of delight.'[28] After he'd toured with *G.P.O.* for nine months, one of those new sketches now appeared: Perkins embarked on the ultimate career for an incompetent buffoon, with the launch of *Perkins MP*.[29]

In 1909 Britain was gripped by a political and constitutional crisis. The Chancellor of the Exchequer, David Lloyd George, had put forward what became known as the People's Budget, significantly increasing taxes to fund social welfare and reform. The budget was rejected by the House of Lords and the country was forced into a general election, resulting in a hung parliament in January 1910. Although an amended budget passed in April, a further election followed. Meanwhile the Labour Party was beginning to make its presence felt and the suffragette movement was building momentum with regular, sometimes violent protests – all rich pickings for comedy.

Perkins was cast as a Labour Party candidate and 'suffragette's pet'. He strongly supported votes for women, mostly because he fancied their leader, the appropriately named Miss Hotposh. From this distance it is difficult to establish whether Karno sympathised with the suffragettes' cause or made them the butt of the joke – either way, he certainly gave them a new platform, even if they had to suffer the ignominy of their advocate being the bumbling Perkins. Idiot or not, at the climax of the sketch the new MP for Mudlark succeeds in persuading parliament to give women the vote.

18. POSTMEN, PUGILISTS, POLITICIANS AND PRATFALLS

After a try-out at the Leicester Palace in mid-July, the sketch transferred to the Kilburn Empire, where *The Stage* provides us with a review:

> Perkins ... is found throwing up his job at the local factory ... to devote his energies to Parliamentary work. He addresses meetings, obtains assistance of the women suffragists, and does his own canvassing gorgeously arrayed in motor costume. The last scene shows the interior of the House of Commons ... Perkins plays havoc with all rules of procedure, points of order and matters of the House's ancient privileges and laws ... on the questions of 'Votes for Women' ... succeeds in carrying his motion, with the result that the House is stormed by women wearing the familiar purple, white and green ... a worthy companion to Mr Karno's other successes.[30]

The scenery was elaborate and the House of Commons was reported to be particularly impressive: it must have given many people their first sense of what parliament looked like. The sketch also gave the press a golden opportunity to play off Karno's chaos against the real debating chamber. A typical article, in *The Woolwich Gazette*, compared left-wing orator (and recently unseated MP) Victor Grayson's speeches as being every bit as funny as anything Perkins could come up with.[31]

With Fred Kitchen ensconced on the back benches, Karno launched his second new show of the summer: *Spring Cleaning*. The sketch was based around a chaotic decorating routine, and probably borrowed ideas from Wal Pink's *Repairs*. Chaplin would later create his own paint and paper chaos in his film *Work* (1915), although his story bears no resemblance to either sketch. Chaplin had a soft spot for decorator comedy, revisiting it in both *The Circus* (1928) and *A King in New York* (1957).

Spring Cleaning was written by Karno and Tom Nelson, a Yorkshire comic who Karno described as being 'a natural gump' – Nelson also played the lead, Amos Snicker. Albert Darnley took a leading role as Timothy Stubbs, his repatriation to the Karno fold complete:

> The scene opens with a drawing-room ... where Mr and Mrs Stubbs ... are choosing the wallpaper. Selina announces the arrival of the workmen, and from then the fun is fast and furious. The transformation from the

peaceful to the much-upset villa … is exceedingly funny; but the climax is reached when the much-worried Mr Stubbs offers the workmen extra money for the completion … in a specified time … The scene is changed from a hopeless muddle to cleanliness and order. The City Surveyor now calls upon Mr Stubbs, informing him that, owing to the Underground Railway improvements, the house has been condemned as unsafe for habitation … the curtain falls upon one of the brightest and cleverest sketches we have witnessed for some time.[32]

Although this was a small-scale sketch with one setting, Karno used some ingenious tricks to effect the transformation from chaos to a newly decorated room – for instance overlayered paper was torn off to reveal the finished walls. Modest it may have been, but *Spring Cleaning* received the lion's share of Karno's attention and advertising budget, while *Perkins MP* went relatively unnoticed by the press. It was the first sign of problems between Karno and Kitchen, which would soon come to a head.

18.6 Unsigned sketch sent to Karno, September 1910, appearing to depict Lloyd George and other members of the cabinet. Perhaps a satire on the political chaos of the day as the late William Gladstone, Grand Old Man of the Liberal party, doffs his hat to the king of chaos (courtesy David Robinson).

19.

All at Sea

*Trainer: You should drink water;
you can't get drunk on water.
Stiffy: You can get just as drunk
on water as you can on land.*

(The Football Match, 1906)

KARNO'S NEW sketches toured throughout 1909, but *Hilarity* and *Early Birds* were finally put out to grass. While we don't know which sketches Chaplin appeared in through most of this period, certainly he was in a *Mumming Birds* company at the Folies Bergère in Paris in November. The city was a cosmopolitan adventure playground for a young comic, and after sampling its delights Chaplin was sorry to come home. Many biographers have assumed he played the drunk in the box in Paris,[1] but Chaplin doesn't say this in his autobiography and evidence suggests he was not elevated to that part until the new year. He didn't have to wait long to be a lead comic though, as Christmas heralded another tour of *The Football Match*, which kicked off at London's Oxford Music Hall. Most of the cast reprised their previous roles, including Chaplin as the villain, but Weldon did not. Stiffy was played by Will Poluski until Gilbert Childs (who had previously played Meredith in *The Bailiff* and Sergeant Lightning in *Dandy Thieves*) was able to join the company, enabling Poluski to return to his usual part of Ratty. Karno couldn't seem to decide who should replace his lost star, so as well as Poluski and Childs, he gave Chaplin another chance. This is how Chaplin remembered it:

News came from the London office that made life more exciting ... I was to take the place of Harry Weldon in the second season [sic – it was the fourth] of The Football Match ... this was my chance. Although I had made a success in Mumming Birds and other sketches in our repertoire, those were minor achievements compared to playing the lead ... we were to open at The Oxford ... and I was to have my name featured for the first time at the top of the bill. This was a considerable step up.[2]

Having claimed that he was in the lead from the outset at the Oxford, Chaplin recorded that a bout of laryngitis forced him to give up the role and return to the silent *Mumming Birds*. However A.J. Marriot's research shows that in the week commencing 13 December 1909, it was Poluski who took the lead at the Oxford (Chaplin was the villain) and Charlie was given his chance as Stiffy for their second performance at the Willesden Hippodrome. He may then have taken ill with laryngitis for a week or two but was advertised in the lead for Christmas week at the Chelsea Palace,[3] and garnered good reviews when he reappeared as Stiffy in the first week of January at the Metropolitan.[4] With or without laryngitis, he had done enough to secure his place as a lead comic and was immediately dispatched to Liverpool to finally take on the drunk in *Mumming Birds* – it would become his signature part.

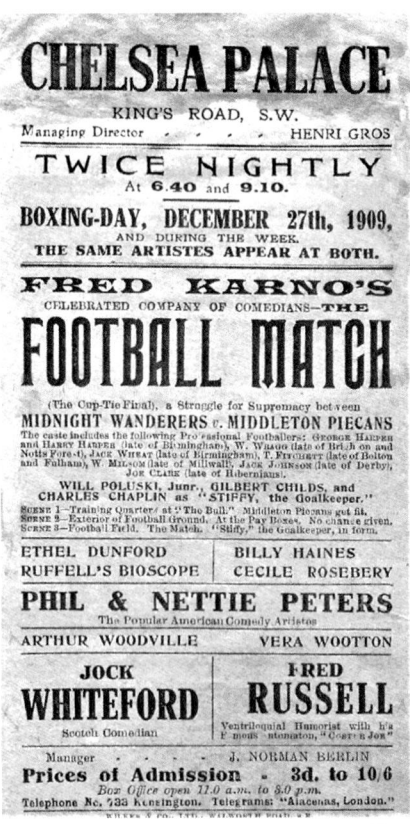

19.1 Advertising flyer for The Football Match *with Charlie Chaplin as Stiffy (author's collection).*

Meanwhile Karno was busy staging two pantomimes. First, he directed *The House That Jack Built* at the Broadway Theatre in New Cross, where it broke box office records,[5] with Fred Emney as dame and up-and-coming Karno comic Syd Walker as the squire. Second, he produced a spectacular *Mother Goose* at

19. ALL AT SEA

the Glasgow Grand, with a script by J. Hickory Wood and a strong cast led by Neil Kenyon as dame and Lily Morris (who later found fame with the song *Why am I Always the Bridesmaid?*) as principal boy. The lord mayor was played by a legitimate theatre actor called Charles A. East, who weighed in at twenty stone and had an extraordinary appetite. Before appearing on stage he habitually consumed a leg of bacon with pease pudding, swilled down with a pint of ox blood purchased from the nearest slaughterhouse, which he insisted was delivered 'warm from the animal'.[6] This cast of colourful characters was a great success, and on opening night Karno had to wade through the bouquets of flowers to say a few words to his appreciative audience. *Mother Goose* marks another milestone in our story, for it was during rehearsals in Glasgow that Karno first met Arthur Stanley Jefferson.

Like Chaplin's, Stan Laurel's life story has been written many times over, so we need only mention briefly how he came to find himself at Karno's door. Stan was born in June 1890 in Ulverston, Lancashire, to theatrical parents, Arthur and Margaret (Madge) Jefferson. Stan was fascinated by the stage, and from an early age was as interested in directing, writing and producing as he was in performing. He was soon organising his own little productions with friends, in a makeshift theatre his father created for him in the attic. Most of all, he hankered to be a comic like his hero Dan Leno.

19.2 Stanley Jefferson around the time he joined Karno (from the 'A.J.' Marriot archive).

As we've noted, his father's career took the family from Ulverston to Tyneside, and then to Glasgow. Arthur managed the Metropole Theatre (formerly the Scotia), and as the popularity of Victorian melodrama waned he turned to writing comedy sketches,[7] often taking the lead role himself. Sometime in the spring or early summer of 1907,[8] Stan secretly obtained his first engagement at the nearby Britannia Music Hall (otherwise known as the Panopticon), run by the eccentric showman Albert E. Pickard. Arthur happened to walk past the theatre and, bumping into Pickard, was invited (much to his surprise) to see his son's debut. He subsequently encouraged Stan's fledgling career, helping him secure a role as a golliwog in a pantomime, *Sleeping Beauty*. Minor acting roles followed, including PC Stoney Broke in a play called *Alone in the World,* where his comedic abilities were first noted by the critics: 'Mr Stanley Jefferson … is a first-rate comedian and dancer, and his eccentricities create roars of laughter.'[9]

In a 1957 radio interview, Stan said his father had asked Karno to give him an opportunity and he subsequently went along to the Grand, where Karno was overseeing rehearsals:

> I presented my card with a request for an interview and was promptly ushered onto the stage where a gentle-voiced little man came forward to meet me. "Well, Mr Jefferson Junior," he said, "What can I do for you?" I told him I wanted to see Mr Karno. "You're seeing him now," he replied quietly. It was quite a shock and such a relief to find him such a pleasant, friendly man. Briefly I explained that I wanted a job as a comedian. "Are you funny?" he asked. I told him of my youthful experience. He nodded. "Very well," he said, "I'll try you out at two pounds a week. Report to Frank O'Neill, who is running my Mumming Birds company in Manchester. Push yourself forward, and I'll see you in London in a few weeks' time. Bewildered at the suddenness of it all, I blurted out my thanks and staggered into the street in a daze. I had achieved the height of every budding comedian's ambition – I was one of Fred Karno's Comedians.[10]

This account tells us a great deal: first, Karno received Stan with good grace and friendliness; second, he took a chance on a complete unknown (perhaps because he knew and respected Stan's father); and third, Stan was encouraged from this first conversation to 'push himself forward', suggesting that Karno wanted his comics to have ambition. In a letter to Fred Jr. written in 1959, Stan added more detail – and a slightly different version of events:

> I remember very well … first meeting your dad … at the Theatre Royal in Glasgow … he was producing a Panto, featuring two comics 'Burley & Burley', Harry Morgan was stage manager … I first met Morgan (the rehearsal was in full swing). He read my letter, [presumably a letter of introduction from his father] then took me over to meet your dad – after

19. ALL AT SEA

he read the letter he got up and took me by the hand and tip-toed with me behind some flats [large pieces of scenery] leaning against the wall … before he asked me, he looked out again from back of the scenery to be sure no one was listening – it scared the hell out of me, he was so mysterious. He finally said: "How much do you want?" I blurted out loud £2 a week. He put his finger to his lips and said "Ssh! Don't let anybody know," then he said; "Can you take the nap?" and made a pass at me [threw a fake punch]. I didn't know what he was talking about and stood there confused. He took me by the hand again and tip-toed me … over to Morgan and whispered in his ear. Everybody was wondering what had happened and were all staring at me, trying to figure out who this stupid looking guy was! Morgan … said "you leave for Manchester tonight to join the troupe at the Hippodrome Hulme. I'll notify the Manager right away" (Frank O'Neill). Needless to tell you how happy I was.[11]

19.3 Sketch of Frank O'Neill as the drunk in Mumming Birds *(author's collection).*

Stan got the right panto but the wrong venue; he was also mistaken about Burley and Burley being in the show – they appeared in Karno's Glasgow panto the following season. Stan later recalled that his first appearance was at 'Manchester Hippodrome', but there were three Hippodromes in the city: Oxford Street, Hulme and Salford. Stan certainly joined the *Mumming Birds* company in Hulme, so this was probably his Karno debut – 6 December 1909, thrust straight in among the supers. Alternatively he may have joined the company merely as an observer, rehearsed for two weeks (Hulme and then Warrington), before making his debut on the 20th when the company appeared at the Royal Hippodrome, Salford.

In the second week of January, we have our first contemporary evidence of Stan's whereabouts[12] – a small advertisement in *The Stage*: 'Jefferson, Stan.,

Comedian and Dancer, Fred Karno's Co. This Pav. Liverpool, Next H. [Hippodrome] Bury.'[13] It was also the moment that our two stars collide. 10 January 1910, at the Pavilion in Liverpool, was when Charlie Chaplin took over from Frank O'Neill as lead comedian in *Mumming Birds*. Stan recalled being summoned by the wardrobe mistress and told:

> "There's a new comedian just joined us from one of the other companies. He's taking over Mr O'Neill's part as 'the drunken swell'. I haven't a suit to fit him, except the one you are wearing, so I'm afraid you will have to take that off and hand it over." Reluctantly I removed the suit and took it along to the new comedian's dressing room. I found him to be a pleasant little fellow with dark, curly hair, blue eyes, very white teeth, and a friendly smile. I took to him right away, and in the course of time we became close friends, sharing rooms together on tour ... his name was Charlie Chaplin.[14]

19.4 Karno's roller hockey team, Stan (back row, left), Chaplin (front row, second from left) (from the 'A.J.' Marriot archive).

McCabe suggests that *Mumming Birds* was a run-of-the-mill show until Chaplin took on the lead, but this belies the sketch's previous success and does his predecessors a disservice. That said, Chaplin was superb in the role, and his ability to play a drunk spectacularly well is later evidenced in many of his films. Stan Laurel recalled that Chaplin had the ability to make his fellow comics laugh even after they'd played the show hundreds of times. Stan put this down not to his physicality, but to his facial expressions – he could hold an audience or spark a reaction with a mere glance. This same expressive quality later made Chaplin dazzle on the silver screen.

Stan's whirlwind apprenticeship was underway, and in Bury the company switched to playing *The Casuals* and *Skating* (with Chaplin leading as Archibald). Within a month Stan had played three different sketches, and was having the time of his life on the road with a lively group of young comics.

19. ALL AT SEA

While Karno's future superstars were beginning their ascent to greatness, his current star was about to fall to earth. There had been signs of trouble the previous summer, when Karno's advertisements for *The Bailiff* noted it as 'Planned, invented and produced by its sole owner and proprietor, Mr Fred Karno'[15] – despite its having been co-written with Fred Kitchen. Such advertising was a familiar tactic when Karno sensed someone was about to steal his material. He had also announced that Kitchen and Neil Kenyon would both appear in the Glasgow pantomime, but when Christmas rolled around the former remained with *Perkins M.P.* There was clearly something wrong. Karno's enemies were circling and they had old scores to settle.

On 13 January 1910, the same issue of *The Stage* which recorded Stan's arrival also announced a shock departure: 'The long association of Fred Kitchen ... with Fred Karno's sketches terminates in the course of a week or so, and he then comes under the banner of Herbert Darnley.'[16]

Darnley had struggled ever since he failed to sign Kitchen four years earlier; in January 1909 he'd been declared bankrupt and forced to sell the rights to all his songs for a few pounds. (Evidently it was a difficult time to be a theatrical manager: Arthur Jefferson was declared bankrupt in the same month.) Through 1909 Darnley had slowly rebuilt his reputation (and his troupe) with sketches such as *The Brigands of Tarragona* and *John Jay, Junior*. Evidently he and Kitchen had been in cahoots for some time, since back in October Darnley had staged *The Barnstormers* (starring himself, Charlie Bell and comic Arthur Lloyd), which was reportedly 'full of Kitchenisms'[17] – it later transpired that Kitchen had co-written the sketch. Fred did not join the *Barnstormers* company though: instead, he went on to star in another sketch which combined the incompetent persona of Perkins with the premise of *The Thirsty First – Private Potts*.

The new partnership catapulted Darnley back into direct competition with Karno – they soon recommenced hostilities in earnest. Delighting in twisting the knife, Darnley placed a notice in the press:

> Herbert Darnley presents ... a new roaring military extravaganza ... entitled Private Potts, introducing the King of Comedians Fred Kitchen ... and a full powerful company of over 50 performers ... ONE TOUCH OF KITCHEN MAKES THE WHOLE WORLD GRIN ... produced under the supervision of Herbert Darnley, author of "Moses and Son", "His Majesty's Guests", &c.[18]

Darnley's revenge had been served very cold indeed. Karno was understandably furious and no doubt hurt: his old enemy had not only stolen his greatest comic and finest writer, he'd also deprived him of a close friendship. *The Music Hall and Theatre Review* didn't help his temper when they erroneously announced that it was Fred Karno who had begun working under Darnley's management, rather than Fred Kitchen. The retraction that followed conjures images of the telephone conversation Karno must have had with the editor:

> In our issue of last week ... we were in the position of making the grotesque announcement that Mr Karno, the multitude and magnitude of whose managerial engagements is of world-knowledge, was appearing under another management. The mistake was obvious, we suppose, to every reader of the paragraph. Its occurrence we greatly regret; but, as Mr Karno demands that we should unreservedly retract and apologise for this ... mishap of typography – why, we do so unreservedly retract and apologise, having never had the thought of distressing or discrediting a worthy and estimable man.[19]

Darnley rubbed more salt into Karno's wound by also stealing one of Kitchen's sidekicks: the diminutive comic Harry Lappo, who had been a superb stooge in *Moses and Son* and *The Bailiff*. Lappo was so small that he had played one of the children in *Saturday to Monday*.

After Kitchen's final performance in *Perkins M.P.*, his co-stars held a dinner in his honour which *The Era* managed to make sound like a wake: 'Fred Kitchen was a type of man who seemed to make everybody with whom he came into contact happy ... it was good to see how an artiste could endear himself to and gain the love and affection of his fellow workers.'[20] Karno did not attend, probably brooding somewhere, and plotting his retaliation. He wasn't the only one sulking: with Kitchen and Lappo now on board, Darnley's loyal lieutenant Charlie Bell must have felt overlooked. The following year Bell launched his own company with a sketch called *The Photographers*, which involved an inept passer-by (with the great name of Bobby Bacon) being left in charge of a photographer's shop – sound familiar? No wonder reviewers continued to refer to him as 'ex-Karno comedian' for the rest of his career.

For Karno, more losses followed: a few months later George Hestor left to join Robert Courtneidge's *The Arcadians,* one of the most successful musical comedies

19. ALL AT SEA

of the era, having carried a seemingly endless run of *His Majesty's Guests*. Karno instigated an immediate reshuffle: Albert Bruno stepped into Kitchen's shoes in *Perkins M.P.,* and Harold Wellesley took over from Bruno in *The Bailiff.* Bruno must have relished his promotion to number-one comic, and Karno was lucky to have such a strong substitute, as this review (from the week after Kitchen left) demonstrates: 'Karno's production of Perkins M.P. is a scream of laughter throughout, thanks to the antics of Albert Bruno and his colleagues.'[21]

Karno needed more new material to compete with a reinvigorated Darnley – and fortunately he had two writers of equal calibre to Kitchen: J. Hickory Wood and Charles Baldwin. Baldwin had been instrumental in some of Karno's greatest successes over the previous decade, despite not being on the permanent payroll: he had written for other artistes and staged his own sketch, *Baldwin's Bank Clerks.* Like Kitchen, he was a firm friend and Karno respected him greatly, recalling that he was a natural comic and a great raconteur. Karno commissioned Baldwin and Wood to write something that would blow Darnley out of the water – literally.

While they went off to sharpen their pencils, Karno had to keep day to day operations going – including his little theatre circuit. Despite management headaches, his favourite venue was the Exeter Hippodrome. It was also the first to host his own sketches, and in spring 1910 he installed his longtime collaborator Dudley Powell as its musical director. At the same time the Peterborough Hippodrome caused him some trouble when one of his advertising hoardings caught in the wind and caused a collision between two carts: several people were injured and Karno was successfully sued for damages. One wonders whether his hoardings were promoting his latest innovation – in February his Peterborough billing had included: 'The Karnoscope shows some new pictures.'[22] There is no evidence of Karno going into film production, so it appears he was putting his name to the projection equipment in the same way he had with the phonograph. A search of the archives reveals that this was not the first time: as far back as August 1906, a listing for *The Dandy Thieves* also includes 'the Karno Bioscope' on the bill. Film technology had been around since the mid-1890s, and short films had soon appeared as a novelty item on music hall bills. Cinemas as stand-alone venues began to appear around 1906 (although before then Bioscope presentations were common side-shows at fairgrounds), and by the end of 1910 there were 375 dedicated cinemas in London, compared to 51 theatres and 49 music halls. Two years later there were 500 – and the biggest boom, created by the advent of 'talkies', was still fifteen years away.

Many of that new industry's future stars were for now toiling away in Karno companies, and just beginning to be noticed by critics. This review of *Skating* is from February 1910: 'The efforts of [Karno's] company in burlesquing this latest craze sent the house into screams of laughter, and especially humorous were Charlie Chaplin and Johnny Doyle. The merriment is present from start to finish, and some clever exhibitions of roller skating are also given when the scene is laid inside the rink.'[23] As we have seen the knockabout comics were usually anonymous, but this was gradually changing: another review from this time notes that Chaplin and Doyle were supported by Arthur Dandoe, J. Beresford, B.A. Daniels, W. Williams and 'thirty auxiliaries'[24] (who presumably included Stan Laurel).

Chaplin's skating skills are preserved for posterity in *The Rink* (1916), a film often said to have been based on *Skating*. However, apart from its setting in a public rink, Chaplin's film bears little resemblance to Karno's sketch. *Skating* has almost no plot and is little more than an exhibition of as many ways to fall over as possible (thanks to the doorkeeper pretending to be an instructor), whereas *The Rink* is predominantly set in a restaurant, and tells the story of a waiter saving a girl from the unwanted attentions of 'Mr Stout'. Nonetheless *Skating* certainly introduced Chaplin to the potential for comedy on wheels, and no doubt some of the falls and tricks found their way into his film. He returned to skates in *Modern Times* (1936), where he wheels perilously close to an unguarded stairwell in a department store – one of the film's most memorable sequences.

19.5 Charlie Chaplin in Skating *(courtesy Roy Export/Chaplin Archive).*

19.6 The Rink *Chaplin in a tangle with ex-Karno comics Eric Campbell and Albert Austin (courtesy Roy Export/ Chaplin Archive).*

19. ALL AT SEA

Chaplin's original two-year contract expired on 21 February 1910 (although Karno had an option for a further year), and with his confidence growing he took the opportunity to ask for a rise. This would be no easy task: 'Karno could be cynical and cruel to anyone he disliked. Because he liked me I had never seen that side of him, but he could indeed be most crushing in a vulgar way … if he did not like a comedian, he would stand in the wings and hold his nose and give an audible raspberry … now I stood confronting him about a new contract.'[25]

Karno's response was to suggest that Chaplin's company hadn't been performing well – and to prove it he telephoned the manager at the Star in Bermondsey, who was quick to tell Chaplin his performance in *Mumming Birds* stank. David Robinson concludes that there was a plant on the end of the line, but A.J. Marriot thinks otherwise: the Star was a hall where almost everybody got the bird, and Karno probably knew his call would elicit the desired response. Marriot speculates that he may have deliberately placed the company there just so they would bomb, keeping his young genius in check, although this idea seems overly Machiavellian – even for Karno.

Karno may have played hardball, but Chaplin unknowingly had the upper hand. With Darnley waiting in the wings, ready to pounce on any comic who felt undervalued, the Guv'nor was vulnerable. Karno exercised the option to extend Chaplin's contract by a further year – and gave him the rise.

Another future Hollywood star made his first Karno appearance that spring. Weighing in at twenty stone, 6ft 5in Eric Campbell was ideally cast as Big Ben Burley in *The Yap Yaps*. Campbell had made a name for himself as a legitimate theatre actor and pantomime baddie (Karno had spotted him in *Dick Whittington* in Liverpool), and he would go on to play memorable villains in Chaplin's early films. However Campbell and Chaplin didn't cross paths while with Karno: they never appeared in the same sketches and didn't meet until years later – in rather different circumstances.

Hollywood would come calling for Chaplin and Campbell later, but Karno's American company was already there – and nearing the end of another season. Alf Reeves seems to have been looking for ways to reinvigorate the tour, and for the last few weeks they staged *Dandy Thieves* in New York, garnering this review: 'Albert Weston has made an excellent impression in America in Fred Kitchen's original part in The Dandy Thieves … The act had a splendid reception at The Plaza, New York.'[26] A subsequent review reveals that this American version was played in dumb show, but apart from the lack of dialogue it had the same storyline as the original and retained the song and dance numbers – the plonks evidently had hidden talents.

As they sailed back home a few weeks later, Reeves no doubt wondered what the following season would bring – he could never have imagined that his next troupe would change the face of comedy forever.

At that time there was only one way to reach America – by ship. Several companies plied this transatlantic trade, most notably Cunard and White Star, and they competed on luxury, size and speed, with the Blue Riband for the fastest crossing considered the ultimate accolade. Since the launch of Oceanic in 1870, White Star had traditionally named its ships with the suffix 'ic' – Celtic, Adriatic, Olympic, Majestic, Britannic and most famous of all, the ill-fated Titanic. Cunard used the suffix 'ia' – Carpathia (which went to the aid of Titanic), Aquitania, Mauretania and its own tragedy-in-waiting, Lusitania, whose 1915 sinking by a German submarine was instrumental in bringing America into the First World War.[27] Inspired by these queens of the ocean, Karno, Baldwin and Hickory Wood created a new sketch set on a liner, and referenced both Cunard and White Star by calling her 'Wontdetania', sailing under the flag of 'the Star Line'.

The Wontdetania was launched at the Paragon on 11 April 1910 and like the ships which inspired it, the show was a truly magnificent spectacle on a mindboggling scale.[28] The set took forty men twenty-four hours to rig, and consisted of a realistic representation of a liner sitting at the quayside, on a flooded stage. The Paragon's stage was thirty-four feet wide and sixty-four feet deep – RMS Wontdetania filled it to the brim. She was one hundred and twenty feet long, built in five demountable steel sections set on three water-pressured hydraulic rams (one at the back and one either side) – the hydraulics alone cost Karno over £2,000. This mechanical trickery enabled the ship to bob about in the swell to such an extent that the cast were often seasick. Some halls were too small to take the

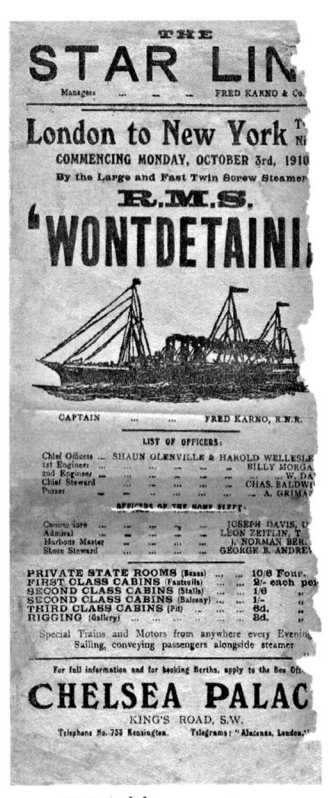

19.7 A delicate survivor – Advertising flyer for The Wontdetania *(author's collection).*

19. ALL AT SEA

show, and the mechanics were so complex that Karno had to get local authority confirmation that the installation was safe before the curtain could go up.

Today we are used to seeing complex technical effects in West End productions: Chitty Chitty Bang Bang flying over the audience, a helicopter landing on stage in *Miss Saigon*, or the Phantom punting through the Paris Opera's catacombs, but the complexity of *Wontdetania* was really extraordinary for its time. Aquatic shows were not uncommon and many halls could flood their stage to present acrobatic swimmers or diving displays. As early as 1803, Charles Dibdin had built a 65,000-gallon tank under the stage of Sadler's Wells and re-enacted Nelson's sea battles. Jump forward one hundred years to January 1904, and the London Hippodrome presented 'Busch's Plunging Elephants', which plummeted down a 40ft slide into the stage pool. It seems quite likely that Karno had been thinking about some form of water-based sketch since the abortive *Diving Birds* five years earlier, and now he had the chance to push the boundaries of technical knowhow and create something that would make Darnley's *Private Potts* look very tame indeed.

Inevitably the show had its teething troubles: Karno's daughter-in-law Louisa recounted how the hydraulics regularly malfunctioned and the ship tilted at such a precarious angle that the cast had to cling on to the railings for dear life. Initially it appeared there might be no tilting at all on opening night: Charles Baldwin recalled that having completed the set-up, the crew discovered that the Paragon had insufficient water pressure to work the hydraulics. Baldwin and the rest of the company trudged to the pub disconsolate, certain that the show was a wash-out. Staggering back to the theatre a few hours (and drinks) later they were amazed to find the good ship Wontdetania bobbing about beautifully. In their absence Karno had sent out to Merryweather's, a famous manufacturer of fire appliances, which had dispatched an engine to top up the pressure. Keeping Wontdetania afloat would prove to be a major challenge, as stage carpenter Percy Court recalled:

> There must have been five tons of steel in its construction … At each side and on the back of the stage were three hydraulic rams which rocked the ship … in the large scene dock there also was a huge tank … to which hose pipes from the fire hydrants, added to the success (or failure) of this weird contraption … on Thursday evening second performance, the man in charge of the fire engine, had a little too much and fell into the tank of water … the fire hoses … all burst, flooding the stage [and] two dressing

rooms … occupied by … The Four Janowskys … the water rose over two feet in height … Its major wave was a wash over the footlights into the Stalls, chaos everywhere. The head Janowsky said a lot in German … He yelled – raved and shouted, his moustache going up and down his little nose, like a flue brush: "se going Mr Karno – Nu Karno … Mr Karno's waters everywhere, ze waters over me dressing room – mein geback – kaput!"[29]

This story appears in several music hall histories, often recounted as an opening night disaster with those seated in the stalls fleeing for the exits lest they drown, but boringly there is no press report of any such accident ever happening, and opening night was plain sailing: 'The launching of the "R.M.S. Wontdetania" was carried out with complete success on Monday at the Paragon … No gayer company ever assisted such a vessel on her maiden trip.'[30]

The show opened with the huge liner moored at the dock and passengers and crew wishing each other "bon voyage". We are then introduced to Patsy O'Flynn the purser, played by Shaun Glenville, an Irish comedian who would go on to have a prolific career on stage and screen. He arrives slightly the worse for drink and in the company of a bevy of girls. Captain Nelson is less than impressed and fires him on the spot. O'Flynn exits as the last of the passengers embark – and then, amazingly, the ship 'sails' off stage. The steel hull was made in large sections fitted on railway lines, and as each section came off into the wings it was wheeled around backstage and reconnected to the other end, entering again and giving the effect of a continuous hull sailing by. *The Era* recorded the liner as one hundred and twenty feet long, which suggests the entire contraption must have gone full circle three times. As this unfolded, both decks (yes, there were two) were crammed with passengers waving frantically at the crowd on the quayside, amid the tumultuous sound of farewells, sirens, whistles and bells, all overseen by the captain, played by the gigantic Charles East. At the last minute, Patsy the purser sprints on stage and clambers aboard by acrobatically scaling a rope, while another man, Percy Dart – a 'dude' of dubious character played by Deane Tribune – dives onto the ship through an open porthole. It must have been epic.

The next scene showed the deck of the liner at night. Karno described this as a uniquely realistic effect, achieved by painting on velvet, which gave the ship intense definition against the starry sky. This cloth was then flown out to reveal the most elaborate scene of all: a multi-level section through the entire ship, showing

19. ALL AT SEA

both dining hall and upper decks, with people dancing and eating in sumptuous surroundings below, and the crew on watch above. Critics were overwhelmed:

> R.M.S. Wontdetania is the greatest ... also the most ambitious, of any production yet attempted by Mr Fred Karno ... the whole breadth of the stage is taken up with a realistic representation of a big liner ... the smokestacks are emitting steam, the officers and seamen are at their posts, cargo and luggage is being taken aboard, fond farewells are being spoken, and we are introduced to the two comedians, Patsy O'Flynn ... and Percy Dart ... The illusion of the liner backing out into midstream ... was deservedly appreciated by a packed audience. But if this item was good, how much more so were the two succeeding scenes! The second was a superb picture of the huge craft in mid-ocean and moonlight. There on the main deck we find ... two naughty characters plotting to get possession of [a] diamond necklet ... One cannot do justice to the last scene, in which we get a sectional view of the grand dining saloon ... The picture is a triumph ... and the most realistic scene of the kind undoubtedly ever seen in a theatre. The beautiful dining-room is an art study in cream and gold. Sixty diners ... in evening dress are seated at the many tables ... Above we get a picture of the officer on the watch and the star lit sky and ocean. The whole scene is a moving one as the ship rolls and plunges through the Atlantic ... There is no finer setting on the variety stage today.[31]

All the reviews were equally gushing:

> This scene should be Mr Karno's triumph for all time. The spectator is held literally spellbound at the completeness and perfection of the apartment, laid out for dinner with dozens and dozens of smartly dressed people seated. The eye wanders from the spotless napery over the cutlery, the glass, and the table decorations to the beautifully designed panels in the walls and thence to the ceiling, a truly magnificent example of plaster work, from which is suspended innumerable glittering bowls electrically illuminated.[32]

This review goes on to recount how the stewards clear the tables for dancing, the four main protagonists share a hand of cards and, when the necklace is eventually stolen, Patsy the purser reveals himself to be from Scotland Yard and arrests the villains. Even on board a liner, Karno couldn't resist a heist.

According to a story recounted by Felstead, Karno asked a real naval officer to review rehearsals and advise whether the dialogue between captain and crew was realistic. The seaman was not impressed: "Damn it! … who ever heard of a British officer saying to his crew, 'What are you a-doin'?' And look at the men themselves! Standing around just like a lot of confounded automatons." Karno was quick to act on his advice: "'Right,' said Fred. "Much obliged to you. I'll soon cure 'em." Next morning he paraded the entire company … he shouted to them, "What do you mean loafing around like a lot of ottomans! Put some life into it or you're fired." Poor Charles East didn't escape Karno's attention either: "Don't you know better as a British officer than to say to your men 'What are you a-doin'?' What you've got to say, my lad, is 'What are you a doin' of?'"[33]

While Karno may have been wide of the mark when it came to clipped vowels and military bearing, his ship was a majestic triumph. The show smashed box-office records at the Paragon, no doubt assisted by the fact that topping the bill that week was Harry Lauder, the hugely popular Scottish comedian. One wonders how Lauder responded when he discovered he would be working only the 'front cloth' – the stage having been given over entirely to Karno's set.

After its opening week *Wontdetania* transferred to the New Cross Empire, then Liverpool, then Glasgow, steaming around the Moss Empires circuit as fast as any Blue Riband challenger. She'd made her maiden voyage in the dying embers of the Edwardian era: in early May 1910 King Edward VII passed away. His death marked the end of a prolonged period of relative peace and stability at home and abroad; the crowned heads of Europe (most of whom had direct lineage to Victoria) would soon be challenging each other for supremacy, sowing the seeds of the greatest conflict the world had known. Karno, like everyone else, was oblivious to the impending disaster just four years away, a war which would immortalise his name forever. In the meantime, there was more comedy to think about.

Perhaps keen to ensure his acrobatic plonks were not left out, he chose to launch a small-scale knockabout sketch at the same time as *Wontdetania*. Charles Baldwin and Frank O'Neill created *Jimmy the Fearless*, which was set to open at the Holloway Empire on the same night *Wontdetania* premiered at the Paragon. From one extreme to the other – *Jimmy the Fearless* was a short and simple pantomime. It would have been unremarkable if not for its cast and the impact it had on their lives.

20.

Mr Fearless

"Tell Brown I can't come to his place for dinner tonight."
"But you're not invited!"
"I know, that's why I can't come."
(The Wow Wows, 1910)

AFTER PROVING himself a capable lead, Chaplin was offered the title role in *Jimmy the Fearless*. It would be the first time he had led a sketch from the outset, and a significant step up. A.J. Marriot speculates that Karno may have gifted him the opportunity to mark his twenty-first birthday, which was just days away; if so, Chaplin threw it back in his face. Karno later recalled:

> I was producing another show … a … story of a lad who, imbued with ideas he had picked up from reading the "penny dreadfuls" … dreamed of marvellous deeds … of valour incredible that brought him the heart and hand of the heroine, the paternal blessing and the wealth of a millionaire. I offered the part to Charlie, expecting that he would jump at the opportunity, but, to my surprise, he didn't seem at all keen. I don't mind confessing that I was a little bit "huffed." An offer of such a chance from Fred Karno was, in those days, a somewhat rare opportunity.'[1]

For a young comic to decline the opportunity to star in a Karno sketch was astonishing, and biographers have been arguing about Chaplin's motives ever since. So, can we shed any new light on what happened?

Everyone had an opinion. Karno thought that either Chaplin didn't like the sound of the part, or was suffering an attack of nerves; Fred Jr. recalled that he simply decided the role was unsuitable for him; Jack Melville believed Chaplin thought the part 'too vocal' and his voice wouldn't carry over the footlights.[2] Stan Laurel provided two versions of events – and in both, Chaplin initially accepted the part. In one interview, Stan recalled that Karno came to see rehearsals and was critical of Chaplin's performance – the young comic responded by politely telling him where to stick it.[3] In another, Stan said Chaplin simply decided on the Friday of rehearsal week that he didn't like the part, and refused to do it.[4] Whatever the reason, walking out of rehearsals a few days before opening night did not go down well with the boss.

With his lead gone, and encouraged by Frank O'Neill, Karno made an extraordinary decision. He offered the part to Stan – a young lad who had only been with him for a few months, and who was in the back row of the cowboy chorus line. The only logical explanation for this is that Karno was furious and gave the part to the lowliest member of the troupe to teach Chaplin a lesson. It was an adaptation of his old trick of offering a complacent comic's part to his understudy 'to give him a rest', which was guaranteed to give the comic a new lease of life. I think he expected Chaplin to immediately change his mind – but he didn't and Stan jumped at his chance in the spotlight. Against the odds, Karno recounted that Stan was a big success – remarkable given that he only had two days of rehearsal.[5] Stan recalled: 'The show was a terrific hit. I had to take five curtain calls. You can imagine how I felt. I was a "star" comedian, at last, and a Karno one at that!'[6]

We don't need to imagine how Chaplin felt: sitting in the stalls, he watched the audience response to Stan's performance and had a change of heart. Stan later said: 'I never quite understood why Charlie didn't take the part ... I jumped at the chance to play Jimmy ... Charlie was out front the opening night and right after the show he told Karno he had made a mistake. He wanted to play Jimmy.'[7] Stan suffered what must have been a cruel blow – playing his first lead to rapturous applause, only to see it whipped off him faster than a Yap Yap's uppercut. Karno had taken the lead off a young comic who'd made a success of it, and given it back to an upstart who believed he was too good for it. He must have really rated Chaplin to give him this second chance.

In Karno's memoirs, Adeler and West noted: 'Charlie expressed his sorrow that he hadn't taken the offer. So Fred, who had other plans for Laurel, moved

20. MR FEARLESS

him elsewhere, and gave Charlie the part.'[8] By the time that was written Stan was a major star, and Karno was no doubt keen to defend his decision – but his explanation is unconvincing. If he had been serious about replacing Chaplin he would have cast an experienced comic from another company. And he had no plan for Stan: he was given the lead to make a point, and once it was made Karno sent him straight back to his lowly place in the ensemble.

In a 1957 radio interview Stan suggested another possible reason for Karno's decision. Chaplin was under contract, so he was being paid whether he performed or not, whereas Stan was merely a jobbing actor paid by the week – it simply made commercial sense to use a contracted comic. This theory is not convincing either: Chaplin could have been moved into a different sketch and Karno would have gained a new star in Stan, probably at a lower price. Remember Karno's advice when he signed Stan? 'Push yourself forward' – he had done so with great success. There is no way Karno would have dropped him unless he only gave him the part to teach Chaplin he could be replaced by anyone, even a raw recruit. It was a message: "You may be good, but there are lots more where you came from."

A.J. Marriot has a compelling theory about why Chaplin didn't take the part initially. First, the material was thin – there is barely a gag in it. Second, in his career to date he had always followed someone else into an established part. Chaplin's greatest skill was as a mimic: he had only once attempted to create a part from scratch – a stand-up routine as a Jewish character he called Sam Cohen, which had been a one-night-only disaster. So he may have struggled to interpret a part, or lacked the confidence to try, without first seeing someone else perform it.[9] If so Stan did more than just give up his part to Chaplin, he showed him how it should be played. Chaplin himself recalled that at the time his confidence was low, having (as he saw it) failed as Stiffy due to his laryngitis: 'As I had not fully retrieved my confidence, every new sketch in which I played the leading comedy part was a trial of fear.'[10]

Chaplin's autobiography does not give us his side of the *Jimmy the Fearless* story – perhaps keen to ignore the only time he was ever overshadowed by Stan Laurel. Ironically that silence has made his biographers write about it all the more.

Stan's loss was Karno's gain: he got the lead he wanted and put a defiant Chaplin firmly back in his place. Stan was collateral damage in a battle of egos, and must have been devastated – but he was magnanimous, at least in public: 'I didn't feel bitter about it. For me, Charlie was, is, and will be always the greatest comedian in the world. I thought he should have played it to begin with. But after that I used to kid him – always very proudly – that for once in my life Charlie Chaplin was my replacement.'[11]

One might expect there to have been ill-feeling between Chaplin and Laurel, but they appear to have maintained a reasonable friendship as we shall see. In typically self-effacing style, Stan always described himself as Chaplin's understudy. He was never again given the chance to star in a Karno sketch and it undoubtedly affected his confidence – his journey to fame and fortune would be a long one.

Back to the sketch: its first performance is difficult to pin down, as Stan's triumph appears to have been overlooked by the critics. As already noted, it was advertised to open at the Holloway Empire on 11 April 1910 but did not appear there that week. Perhaps Karno thought better of opening on the same night as *Wontdetania*, or delayed to give Laurel a week's rehearsal (although Stan recalled he only had two days). If the latter, then Chaplin's walk-out cost him a week's income too. Stan later said that the sketch opened at Ealing,[12] and that he played it for a week before Chaplin took over, but the first listing with Charlie in the lead (at the Stratford Empire on 25 April) notes: 'Presented here after a preliminary run at Willesden.'[13] As A.J. Marriot concludes, it seems likely that Stan first performed the sketch at both Ealing and Willesden in the week commencing 18 April.

So, what was it all about? After a night on the town, Jimmy, a working-class lad, returns home to a scolding from his father. His parents go to bed and he settles down to eat his supper and read a penny dreadful. Getting lost in this pulp fiction, he falls asleep by the fire and dreams of being the hero of the adventure.[14] *The Era* picks up the story:

> The scene is transferred to the saloon of a settlers' camp in the Wild West; bushrangers and Indians abound; pistols are fired galore; a lonely maiden is kidnapped and … rescued single-handed by the valiant Jimmy, who subsequently, with the aid of friendly Redskins, vanquishes the robbers, in addition to defeating their chief in a duel with swords … the scene is changed to Jimmy's home, ten years later, which sees his parents being turned out penniless. Enter the now prosperous Jimmy, and the homestead is saved … The end sees Jimmy awakened from his slumbers by a wrathful father, who puts the would-be hero across his knee and soundly trounces him.[15]

20. MR FEARLESS

Each generation of teenagers has its own slice of popular culture to mystify and terrify parents in equal measure – in 1910 it was the penny dreadful. Sensational stories of detectives, highwaymen, murderers and supernatural entities were seen as a bad influence on young people, which explains why Jimmy receives a good thrashing at the end of the sketch. Jimmy's father was played by Arthur Dandoe, who disliked Chaplin (as we shall see) and no doubt took some pleasure in dishing out his punishment. The other principals were Emily Seaman as the mother, Bert Williams as 'Alkali Ike', Mike Asher as 'Mike' and Albert Austin as 'Washti Wampa'.

Critics were far from enthusiastic at first. *The Era* said: 'Mr Karno's latest sketch ... is ... probably intended as a skit against the pernicious "penny dreadful" habit, which the present-day youngster is wisely forsaking for the Boy Scout movement. Thus, it would be unfair to make a comparison between it and the highly popular sketches with which Mr Karno's name is associated.'

The Stage went further: 'The name of Fred Karno has so long been a household word ... and the popularity of his entertainments so indisputable, that ... it is therefore surprising that Jimmy the Fearless ... should prove such a feeble affair ... humorous situations and individual cleverness ... are strangely absent ... Jimmy the Fearless is hardly likely to emulate the success of its predecessors.'[16]

20.1 Jimmy The Fearless *drawing by Arthur Dandoe (author's collection)*.

Perhaps this lacklustre initial reception reflects Chaplin struggling to create a character for himself, as A.J. Marriot suggested. Contrastingly Stan seems to have knocked it out of the park straight away – Chaplin's initial reviews must have added to Stan's frustration. Karno recalled it slightly differently, to say the least:

[Chaplin's] opening night was the Alhambra Theatre Bradford, [sic – it was the Stratford Empire] and he fulfilled all my hopes. He was more than good. He was great! He was colossal! He foreshadowed that night the greatness he was afterwards to achieve. Feeling very pleased with myself I invited all the managers I could get to come to see his performance on the second night. They all turned up – and he was just as bad as he was brilliant at the initial show. You see, all geniuses are temperamental, and even in those early days Charlie had all the earmarks of genius. What occurred I never knew. Whether something happened in the day to upset him, whether he was frightened of his own success, whether it was second-night over-confidence (a common complaint with actors), or whether it was just pure cussedness, will forever remain a mystery. I don't suppose Charlie himself knows![17]

Fortunately for all concerned, Chaplin grew into the part, gradually developing ideas and gaining in confidence. Karno recalled great laughs coming from some antics with a loaf of bread, when in one smooth movement Chaplin carved it into a concertina – although in an article unearthed by A.J. Marriot, Stan claimed to have invented this bit of business during his brief stint in the role. Either way, it may well have been inspired by Fred Kitchen's routine with a French loaf in *Saturday to Monday*. The origin of Chaplin's bread-based humour is of interest since he includes the concertina gag in *Jitney Elopement* (1915), and his bread-roll dance in *The Gold Rush* (1925) is lauded as a classic piece of silent comedy.[18] Sadly, the potential of this staple foodstuff has been lost to today's comedians – even material of this quality can get stale.

While *Jimmy the Fearless* may have failed to enthuse London audiences, it went down much better in the provinces – and Chaplin certainly had a soft spot for it. As Karno put it: 'In this simple and homely little play, we get the germ and genesis of a dozen Chaplin films that have made the whole world laugh, with just a little sob in the midst of the laughter … Charlie used this theme in his earlier pictures, together with many other ideas inspired during his apprenticeship in Fred Karno's school.'[19] Stan Laurel agreed: 'You can see Jimmy the Fearless all over some of his pictures – dream sequences for instance. He was fond of them, especially in his early pictures.'[20]

Chaplin was certainly one of the first to use the concept of filming a man's inner thoughts. In *Cruel Cruel Love* (1914) we see him imagining himself in hell, while the same year *His Prehistoric Past* (1914) is entirely a dream in which he becomes king of the cavemen. In *The Bank* (1915) he dreams of foiling a robbery, and there are similar ideas in *The Kid* (1921), *The Gold Rush* (1925) and *Modern Times* (1936). Most ambitious of all is the magnificent *Shoulder*

Arms (1918), where the little fellow wins the war single-handedly – in a dream sequence. Buster Keaton's classic *Sherlock Junior* (1924), the story of a movie projectionist who falls asleep and dreams he is the hero of the film, surely comes from the same lineage.

John McCabe believed *Jimmy the Fearless* was more than just an early inspiration, suggesting the character reflected Chaplin's own personality, upbringing and future hopes and dreams. The theme of a little guy who becomes a hero then falls back to earth recurs in Chaplin's work. Stan Laurel said: 'Charlie as a performer and as a person ... was a shy, timid man who kept getting up courage to do the most wonderful, adventurous things. Jimmy the Fearless. He can mix with anybody in the world when he wants to, then he retires to shyness again.'[21] McCabe concludes his biography of Chaplin by noting that he *was* Jimmy the Fearless: a shy, slight, poor man who made his dreams come to life. We'll give the last word to Stan: 'Charlie loved to play Jimmy, and the memory of that role ... stayed with him all his life ... when it comes right down to it, I've always thought that poor, brave, dreamy Jimmy one day grew up to be Charlie the Tramp.'[22]

So much for Chaplin's big moment. While countless biographers have focused on the circumstances in which he landed the part, they neglect to ask why Karno, the master talent-spotter, failed to recognise how well Stan had done and give him another opportunity. While Karno talks extensively about Chaplin in his memoirs, Stan's success is barely acknowledged, even though he did more to help his old boss in later life than perhaps any other comic, as we shall see. This is even more surprising given that when Adeler and West wrote Karno's memoirs in 1939, Stan was a global superstar with a higher profile than any other ex-Karno comic, maybe even Chaplin. Would acknowledging Stan's success have meant admitting that he'd failed to spot his talent? Or did guilt over the *Jimmy the Fearless* episode prevent Karno from taking credit for his discovery?

Today Chaplin is regarded as the master of pathos, while Stan's abilities in that regard are underrated. Chaplin's success gave him complete creative control and the freedom to introduce more pathos to his comedy, whereas Stan (although instrumental in writing and directing his movies) worked in a two-man team and under the control of studio producers – he had less opportunity to develop such ideas. Stan once shared his philosophy on pathos in slapstick: 'The sympathy for the little fellow who is knocked about and kicked around is as strong as ever. In my opinion it will always be one of the best-liked things in comedy, simply because in the heart of so many of us, there is something of the little fellow himself.'[23] It is no coincidence that Chaplin always called his iconic character the Little Fellow rather than the Little Tramp.

Stan's ability to deliver pathos was at least appreciated by Karno, who paid him a rare compliment by comparing his style to the great Dan Leno.[24] Stan's talents weren't entirely lost on the critics either: years later, during his early days as a solo film comedian, one reporter recognised that he had the same rare talent as Chaplin – the pathos Karno had instilled in both of them: 'Every now and then there comes to the screen a young man … who appears … a mere clowning fool, but who, more thoughtfully considered, shows himself that rarest of artists … gifted with the power of bringing laughter which is strangely close to tears. Such a man is Charlie Chaplin; and such a man Stan Laurel is… becoming fast.'[25] Stan's father knew he had a broader range than his films demonstrated, too. In 1932 Arthur Jefferson said: 'I would tell you that there is much more in him than the films have brought out as yet. He has the humour that makes you cry … but that form of humour … very near to pathos – has never been brought out fully in his films.'[26] Perhaps the fact Stan never got the chance to shine with Karno, a chance he clearly deserved, is the most poignant note of pathos of all.

With Darnley nipping at his heels, Karno continued to roll out new material. Just a month after *Wontdetania* and *Jimmy the Fearless*, he launched *The Annual Sports* by Charles Baldwin and Syd Walker. A wicked squire hosts a sports competition on the village green, and with the aid of two bookmaker accomplices intends to fleece the villagers of their hard-earned cash. Inevitably his bumbling accomplices make a mess of it, and the squire loses the lot. Despite a promising premise however, the sketch suffered for the lack of an established comic (the cast are unnamed in reviews) and quickly fizzled out.

It was still a busy time to be a plonk: Harold Wellesley (billed as 'Karno's Little Comedian') was proving himself as Perkins in *The Bailiff* and *G.P.O.*, while this report demonstrates that Albert Bruno was certainly earning his money in *Perkins MP*: 'Albert Bruno, Mr Karno's principal comedian, had a particularly busy time last week … giving six performances of leading parts in sketches on Monday and Tuesday evenings, and four each evening during the remainder of the week.'[27]

Bruno's regular demands for more money meant he never developed a friendship with the Guv'nor, but his talent and work ethic were undeniable, so it was only a matter of time before Karno invited him to write a sketch. The result was *Mr Justice Perkins*, which saw our now familiar idiot taking his place

20. MR FEARLESS

on the magistrates' bench.[28] Bruno took the lead, supported by Herbert Sidney (who co-wrote the sketch) and Aggie Morris.

> The action opens in a scene outside a country inn ... Perkins, who is being tormented by the attentions of a lady of questionable age, is elected ... to be a magistrate ... The quality of the justice he deals out may be readily imagined. A husband and wife, in a case of assault, are drastically treated, while an offending bookmaker, who happens to be an old friend of his, is ... invited to join him in a "pint." Finally, the lady ... with whose affections he has been tampering, puts in an appearance, upon breach of promise bent, but gets only a farthing damages for her trouble, a verdict which is the result of Mr Justice Perkins having "intimidated" the jury with a revolver.[29]

After a week's try-out in Bristol, *Mr Justice Perkins* transferred to London and played at both the Canterbury and the Metropolitan, before heading off on tour. This was swiftly followed by yet another new sketch (the sixth in twelve months), which opened at the Tottenham Palace in early August. This time Karno returned to the setting of a private club, but whereas in *New Woman's Club*, *The Smoking Concert* and *The Yap Yaps* it was merely a backdrop for the chaos, now the club itself was the subject of the comedy, as the plonks revealed the inner workings and secret rituals of a fraternal society – *The Wow Wows*.[30]

The protagonist was once again nice but dim Archibald Binks, initially played by a new recruit called J.C. Piddock Jr. Piddock was supported by Jimmy Russell (Bottles) and Albert Darnley (Blazer). The three scenes were 'the Nook up the river', 'Preparing room, corridor in Brown's club house', and 'The initiation'. In later versions 'Brown's Club House' became the 'Secret Society's Chamber of Horrors'[31] – the password to enter being: "Kiss me good night nurse." The sketch was a return to the style of *Tragedy of Errors* (a comedy play with a small cast) and this review from *The Stage* tells us more:

> The Wow Wows promises to be one of the best of the Karno sketches, and the ... quieter form of humour ... will come as a welcome change after the knockabout business of many of the other sketches ... The scene opens up the river. ... There is a large party of young fellows all, with one exception, being on exceptionally good terms ... The dissentient

one, however, is Mr Archibald Binks, who has a conscientious objection to work in all its forms, and … borrows all round, from a stud to the last five shillings of one member of the party … it is resolved that some means must be tried to cure Archibald of his bad habits. And so, the Wow-Wows come into existence … – the friends of Archibald – who have formed themselves into a secret society, and the recital of the items on their programme make Archibald long to become a member … Archibald is received into the company of the Wow-Wows, who have arrayed themselves in fearful and wonderful costumes, only after prolonged tests of an exasperating character to the subject, but very amusing to the spectators, and he is obliged to promise never to borrow again.[32]

The Stage goes on to say that the sketch needed some further 'working up', but that it was sure to be a success and Piddock would fit in well alongside Karno's other lead comics. The man himself didn't agree; the following week the part was given to Syd Chaplin and Piddock evaporated into obscurity.

The Wow Wows

Archibald Binks, Charlie Blazer, Jimmy Bottles, Freddy Brunton and Billie Brindle are enjoying a holiday. They are accompanied by Lydia Flopp (Archie's sweetheart) and other 'up-river girls'.

Archie:	I say Jimmy, what have you for breakfast?
Jimmy:	There's two eggs, but they're both rotten.
Archie:	Oh, that's too bad.

And they get worse:

Archie:	I've had my usual river plunge.
Lydia:	Was the water up to your expectations?
Archie:	No, only up to my knees.

The jolly chaps then form the Wow Wows. Archie is blindfolded for his inauguration and his pals appear, dressed in grotesque robes. Amid plenty of chanting ("Wow, wow, wow"), Archie is forced to kiss a casket containing a haddock and dance on an 'electric' carpet:

Brunton:	Are you prepared to take the oath of allegiance?
Archie:	I am prepared to swear.
Blazer:	Then swear.
Archie:	Damn, damn, damn, damn.

Oh dear. Eventually Archie is let in on the joke and gets his revenge by herding his tormentors onto the electric carpet and throwing the switch – curtain.

It is hard to see the laughs in these lines, but what's missing of course is the talent of the comic. The gesture, the look, the raised eyebrow or the inflection on a word, all of which create comedy where on the printed page there is none. Imagine the same lines delivered by a great comic (Eric Morecambe, Peter Cook or Tommy Cooper) and you start to get an understanding of how these sketches were a success.

In September, *The Football Match* opened at the Edinburgh Empire for yet another winter season, with Will Poluski as Stiffy. While Harry Weldon was just a distant memory, it must still have stung when press reports announced he was joining Herbert Darnley to take the principal part in 'the biggest thing Mr Darnley has yet attempted.'[33] Whatever it was, it didn't happen – Weldon never starred in a Darnley sketch. This would have been cold comfort to Karno, since by then Darnley was the least of his worries – he faced a much bigger threat.

He had suffered from artistes and ideas being pilfered by rival theatrical producers almost from the first American

20.2 – Syd Chaplin in The Wow Wows *(courtesy Roy Export/Chaplin Archive).*

tour, and now there were new, more significant poachers: the fledgling movie studios had a voracious appetite for talent. He recalled: 'Having discovered that the actors trained in the Karno school were ideal for their purposes they came along and made a noise like an awful lot of dollars luring them into the primrose path of the pictures.'[34] Karno's highly trained, experienced, acrobatic comedians were manna from heaven for the studio bosses, who didn't hesitate to steal them away. As Karno put it: "One cannot altogether blame them."[35]

Establishing who jumped ship and when is difficult, as some left for rival vaudeville companies before making their way into movies,[36] but one way or another Hollywood was soon full of Karno comics. The early comedies churned out by the studios (one every few days) had little plot or substance: the comics would be put into a situation – perhaps in a park or by a lake – and simply run around, knock each other about and try to be funny. There were similarities with Karno's approach: he also relied heavily on the inventiveness of his performers. Karno comic Bert Murray once said: 'My part consisted of whatever Fred could write for me on the back of an envelope – I had to be able to create business.'[37] Similarly, Adeler and West wrote: 'Content with devising the situation, he has sat back, and allowed others to take the kudos attached to the delivery of the goods.'[38]

But it wasn't just the plonks' improvisational skills that were valuable. The issue for early movie studios was that most actors were making the transition from the theatre to a medium that was entirely silent – the reverse of the problem they subsequently faced when talkies came along. If stage actors with experience in mime were like gold dust, Karno's comedians were a truck full of bullion. They were incredibly good at falling on their backsides with seemingly little or no associated ill effects, and could somersault, spin on their heads and fall out of tall buildings too – no stunt doubles required. Karno had a battle on his hands, as Adeler and West noted: 'The drain was terrible. Cables for fresh people were continually flashing across the Atlantic. It was putting him in a most awkward position in the States and was also visibly affecting his home market.'[39]

With these pressures at the forefront of his mind, Karno had to plan the 1910 autumn U.S. tour. He decided he would stage *The Wow Wows* and tasked Alf Reeves with assembling the company. The obvious candidate for lead comic was Syd Chaplin, but Karno felt he couldn't afford to risk losing Syd to the studios,[40] so Reeves turned to some up-and-coming talent – the *Jimmy the Fearless* cast. This prompted Karno to advise American syndicates that his company would play *Jimmy the Fearless* in the States,[41] but for some reason he had a change of heart and reverted to *The Wow Wows*.

Reeves had seen Charlie Chaplin in *Jimmy the Fearless* and – supposedly encouraged by Chaplin's friend Amy Minister – decided he was capable of leading the U.S. company. Marriot records that Chaplin's troupe returned to London to see Syd's company in *The Wow Wows*,[42] and then played in the sketch for two weeks to get the hang of it. Strangely, in a 1959 interview Stan Laurel recalled that they had no rehearsal time and had never seen the show before sailing to America.[43] Either

20. MR FEARLESS

way, they didn't like it. Both Chaplin and Alf Reeves tried to persuade Karno that it would not go well stateside, but to no avail – Karno believed that Americans were fascinated with secret societies. He had a point: there was no shortage of members for college fraternity houses and masonic lodges, although his comics' costumes suggest Karno may have been thinking of a rather different organisation.

Karno always sought to put in place a new artiste's contract months before the old one expired, enabling him to arrange tours well in advance. (He had, for instance, signed Syd up to a new three-year contract in April, which didn't come into effect until August.) As we've seen, Karno had already extended Charlie's contract until February 1911, and this was likely to expire while he was in America, with the obvious risk that he would then defect. So Karno gave Chaplin a new three-year contract, which he signed on 19 September 1910, the day before he sailed. This was dated to come into force on 6 March 1911, and he increased Chaplin's salary to ten, then twelve and finally fifteen pounds (for years one, two and three respectively).

Having secured his man, Karno prepared him for the trip with a stern talking to. He reminded Chaplin what a great opportunity he was giving him, and how he had always looked after the young lad. Now he expected loyalty in return: 'I said to Charlie: "I'm going to send you over to the States. But I'm going to have a cast iron contract with you. You know how many of my men over there have cut adrift … I don't want to provide you with a free passage and then find you quitting me in the same way." Charlie grinned … "There's no fear of that, Sir," he said, "I could never see myself being funny in front of a camera."'[44]

20.3 The Wow Wows *advertisement (from the 'A.J.' Marriot archive).*

Karno was reassured, telling his friend Charles Cochran that Chaplin was not interested in making films because he didn't think he could be funny without a live audience – or as Chaplin put it: "with the Wood family in front" (an empty house).[45]

On 20 September, with the ink on his new contract barely dry, Chaplin and the rest of the *Jimmy the Fearless* cast headed for Southampton and stepped aboard the Cairnrona bound for Montreal (via Quebec).[46] The members of that company would go on to weave a golden thread of Karno through twentieth century comedy and play major parts in our story, so it's worth recording them: Chaplin's cohorts were Alf Reeves, Albert Austin, Arthur Dandoe, Stan Laurel (back then Stan Jefferson of course), George and Emily Seaman, Bert Williams, Charlie Griffiths, Fred and Muriel Palmer, Amy Minister, Frank Melroyd, Mike Asher and, making a comeback in our story, Fred Karno Jr. (listed as Fred Westcott).

It was appropriate that they were the 'fearless' company – they needed to be. Although described as 'one of the most modern and best-found ships of the emigrant trade',[47] Cairnrona was a converted cattle transport, refitted to convey large numbers of immigrants cheaply. When built as 'Consuelo' by Swan and Hunter in 1900, she was designed to carry just thirteen first-class passengers. In 1909 the Thompson line bought her, renamed her and converted her to carry fifty first-class and eight hundred third-class passengers – a human cargo of emigrants to the New World. A few months before Chaplin's troupe sailed, the ship had been severely damaged in a coal bunker explosion – a baby and a steward died, and several others were severely injured. And although she was swiftly repaired, many of her passengers (mostly Russian immigrants who had been waiting in England) refused to set foot on her again. So for this crossing there were just one hundred

20.4 Aboard Cairnrona. Left to right: Front row: Muriel Palmer, Mike Asher, Amy Minister, Cairnrona officer (probably captain C.J. Stooke); Middle row: Stan Laurel, Fred Karno Jr., Charlie Chaplin, Arthur Dandoe; Back row: Albert Austin, Fred Palmer, Bert Williams, George Seaman, Frank Melroyd (courtesy Roy Export/Chaplin Archive).

20. MR FEARLESS

and seventeen passengers, all third-class. This did not improve the comfort of the trip: Chaplin recalled having to throw his shoes at the rats to keep them off his bunk. To make matters worse, the company had planned to rehearse *The Wow Wows* on board, but rough seas and seasickness put paid to that. They arrived in Quebec on 1 October – ten days after leaving Southampton.[48] The torturous journey wasn't all in vain: seasickness became a repeating gag in a number of Chaplin films, notably *Shanghaied* (1915) and *The Immigrant* (1917); and in Stan Laurel's *Half A Man* (1925) and *Get 'Em Young* (1926).

Karno did not usually send his troupes halfway around the world in such rough conditions – most crossings were on much more salubrious liners – and travelling via Montreal meant a significant delay. So why this company suffered such indignities is unclear. Marriot records that they had missed their intended ship, the Lusitania (which sailed from Liverpool on 17 September), and had to take any crossing they could get.[49] With a large company, and associated scenery and baggage, their options may have been limited but there were half a dozen better alternatives sailing direct to New York that week (including White Star's Oceanic, just one day later), so unless every boat was full the reason the Karnos had to make do with Cairnrona remains a mystery. I can't resist speculating that Karno sent them on a converted cattle boat because the major shipping companies wouldn't sell him a ticket after he lampooned them in *Wontdetania*, but a more likely explanation is that after the accident Cairnrona tickets were cheap.

20.5 Chaplin suffering a rough crossing on Cairnrona (courtesy Roy Export/Chaplin Archive).

According to his autobiography, Chaplin already saw his future stateside, where he would be free of the British class system and could make his fortune regardless of his limited education and impoverished upbringing. As Quebec loomed on the horizon, Stan recalled Chaplin racing to the railing, waving his hat and shouting: "America, I am coming to conquer you! Every man, woman and child shall have my name on their lips – Charles Spencer Chaplin!"[50] His fellow comedians booed him, and he bowed politely. One wonders whether any of these jokers pointed out that he was shouting at Canada. Karno's advertising seemed to share his conviction: 'Presenting that clever English comedian Charles Chaplin … Oh! You'll Remember Me.'[51]

21.

Astoria

"Do you remember when we were in the Sudan?
Three days and nights without water."
"What did you do?"
"Drank it neat."
(Skating, 1909)

FROM MONTREAL they endured the long train ride to New York and had no time to catch their breath before opening with *The Wow Wows* (subtitled *A Night in a London Secret Society*) at Percy Williams' Colonial Theatre on 3 October.[1] Chaplin recalled that his first impression of New York was a disappointment: 'It was something of a let-down ... Broadway looked seedy ... however, this was New York, adventurous, bewildering, a little frightening.'[2] To their dismay, but perhaps not to their surprise, New York didn't think much of them either: 'Charles Chaplin is the ... chief comedian. Chaplin is typically English ... his manner is quiet and easy and he goes about his work in a devil-may-care manner ... Chaplin will do all right for America, but it is too bad that he didn't first appear in New York with something more in it than this piece.'[3]

Back home, *The Stage* reported their opening night rather differently: 'At The Colonial Fred Karno's Night In A London Secret Society made an enormous hit.'[4] *The Stage* was in a minority of one: American reviews were universally poor – one described them as 'a lot of blithering, blathering Englishmen.'[5] The audience, expecting typical Karno pantomime, did not respond well to the verbal comedy, much of which relied on an understanding of the British class system.

21. ASTORIA

Chaplin was mortified – with the tour in jeopardy, his big break looked like being broken before it had begun. Stan recalled that they had been due to move on to Hammerstein's Theatre, but that first performance prompted Hammerstein's to cancel. Fortunately, Alf Reeves managed to persuade Percy Williams to give them a run at his other theatres over the following weeks. Williams' gamble paid off: *The Wow Wows* quickly found its feet. Perceived wisdom is that the show was saved by Chaplin's performance and his gradual inclusion of additional gags, but given that it improved so rapidly, and that Williams evidently saw its potential from the start, I suspect the problem was primarily a lack of rehearsal. Despite these tribulations, Chaplin must have held some affection for the sketch – a few years later he named his character Mr Wow-wow in his film *Gentlemen of Nerve* (1914).

21.1 After a disappointing opening perhaps looking at situations vacant. 1911 U.S. tour; left to right: Albert Austin, Charlie Chaplin, Muriel Palmer, Fred Palmer (courtesy Roy Export/Chaplin Archive).

Their reputation partially restored, the troupe were offered a chance to appear on the opening night of Marcus Loew's new National Theatre in New York, subject to a successful try-out at one of his smaller theatres at Fall River, Massachusetts.[6] Despite the improved reviews for *Wow Wows*, Alf Reeves played safe and switched to *A Night in an English Music Hall* – it met with the usual rapturous applause, and secured them the engagement at the National. After that, Reeves had little difficulty negotiating further bookings for any sketch they cared to perform.[7] The company had redeemed itself, and Chaplin's comics held their heads high as they commenced what became a long and successful tour.

Life on the road was no bed of roses, however. While Chaplin noted that the cost of living in America was cheap, lower-paid Stan recalled it as being significantly more expensive than at home – twenty dollars per week didn't go far given that the cast had to pay for their own board and lodgings. Stan often bunked with Chaplin, and they did their best to make the digs a home from home. He recalled that one landlady banned them from cooking in their room after they exploded a tin of beans over a gas ring. The ban was ignored, but from then on Chaplin played his violin to mask the sound of illicit bacon frying, while

Stan stood ready to throw the pan out of the window should they be discovered. The late Chuck McCann told me a story recounted to him by Stan: he and Charlie were sharing a room and, as was the custom in England, they put their shoes outside to be cleaned overnight. The following morning their shoes had been stolen, and they were forced to traipse around New York in their slippers.[8]

21.2 Never before published photograph of Karno company on 1911 tour. Far left Stan Laurel, third from left Fred Karno Jr., centre Arthur Dandoe (courtesy June Fisher).

21.3 Karno company at Denver Colorado – furthest left Fred Karno Jr., second left Albert Austin, fourth left Stan Laurel (courtesy Keith Ripley/Bill Asher).

Living at such close quarters, the two comics got to know one another well. Stan described Chaplin as eccentric and unpredictable, with a tendency for mood swings. One can only imagine how the insular Chaplin fitted into a tight-knit comedy group, with the pressures of performance amplified by the constraints of living together on the road. While his colleagues played cards or swapped stories over a beer, Chaplin studied Greek and yoga. He took up the cello and

21.4 Laurel and Hardy in Berth Marks, *with surely a nod to Chaplin.*

21.5 Chaplin with Cello, Sacramento, 5 June 1911 (courtesy Roy Export/ Chaplin Archive).

embraced the bohemian lifestyle of the musician, dressing like one and growing his hair longer. He was immensely proud of an ankle-length overcoat he bought from a musician in San Francisco, which he wore throughout the tour – until someone said it made him look like a circus ringmaster. Such pretentions must surely have inspired Laurel and Hardy's *Berth Marks* (1929), in which Stan waits at a station in a full-length overcoat – carrying a cello.

As the tour continued, they reintroduced *Wow Wows*, *A Night in a London Club*[9] and *A Night in a London Slum* to their repertoire. They also staged something new – a piece they called *A Harlequinade in Black and White*:[10]

> An old-style Christmas pantomime was played at the American last week, with the performers silhouetted against a screen … it brought forth our old friends, the Clown, Pantaloon, Harlequin and Columbine … there was plenty of action … and much pleasure derived by the audience … First the characters indulged in a little general knockabout fooling, then they had fun with a stolen bottle, after which the policeman was relieved of his clothes, and another "cop" was knocked out and laid upon a table to be dissected, his internal organs being brought forth one by one. The baby was stolen from the carriage of the nursemaid, and all the characters had a "rough-house" experience while seeking lodgings. A droll duel brought forth two characters who grew and diminished in size rapidly as they fought, the phantom army appeared and paraded, and all the characters leaped "up to the moon" … it was quite a happy little idea for the holiday season, occupying about eleven minutes.[11]

The Harlequinade, first staged on Boxing Day 1910, only remained in their repertoire for a couple of weeks, but the audience certainly enjoyed the nostalgia: 'The children laughed with glee, the middle-aged folk applauded with delight and the old folk gave vent to a burst of reminiscent merriment.'[12] It may not have been the usual Karno material, but that didn't stop rivals stealing the idea: 'Gus Hill's "Vanity Fair" … one discovers that the shadowgraph idea that the Karno company put on at the American several weeks ago has already found its way to burlesque … with Ritchie and McAllister doing the comedy.'[13] Hill and Ritchie were clearly still happy to rip off Karno's material, but there were bigger vultures circling. Mack Sennett, then an actor at Biograph in New York, recalled seeing the Karno troupe there, and Chaplin's performance made a lasting impression.[14]

On 4 January 1911, Alf Reeves and Amy Minister were married at New York City Hall (Billy Reeves was a witness). There was no time for a honeymoon as Alf continued to secure new dates, which took the company from the bright lights of New York to remote theatres in rural backwaters. These small-time circuits were collectively known as the 'Death Trail' and were a challenge for any act, never mind a group of blathering Englishmen. Audiences in remote farming or mining towns like Butte, Montana (which straddles America's Continental Divide) could be tough on travelling vaudevillians, but the Karnos were good enough to impress even there, as one local newspaper reported: 'The art of pantomime is recognized in theatredom as one of the most difficult known to the profession ... Not only are various members of the cast excellent pantomime artists, but they are high class athletes and acrobats as well, for they have to take many falls and go through various stunts that only well qualified athletes could hope to successfully attempt.'[15]

This review emphasises the physicality of Karno routines. Unlike the future silent film comedians, they couldn't enhance their comedy with camera trickery, they had to be able to deliver this high-energy, acrobatic slapstick day after day, theatre after theatre, sketch after sketch, live – and at a pace that got laughs first time, every time. One begins to realise just how good they were.

21.6 Karno company at the Continental Divide, Butte, April 1911; left to right: Mike Asher, Stan Laurel, Chaplin, Arthur Dandoe, Fred Karno Jr. (seated) (courtesy Roy Export/ Chaplin Archive).

They worked their way across the country and arrived in San Francisco, where *Billboard* recorded: 'Without doubt the week of 4 June was the record week at the Empress Theatre ... The big draw was Fred Karno's London Pantomime Company, in "A Night in an English Music Hall" ... one continuous scream of laughter.'[16] Chaplin was smitten with the city, marvelling at its reconstruction after the devastating earthquake of five years earlier. California began to cast its spell over our heroes – it was a place many of them would later call home.[17]

21. ASTORIA

21.7 Karno company at Sacramento. Back row (left to right): Arthur Dandoe, Stan Laurel, George Seaman, Alf Reeves, Charlie Chaplin, Fred Karno Jr., Albert Austin. Seated: Emily Seaman, Amy Minister, Muriel Palmer, Mike Asher, Fred Palmer (courtesy Keith Ripley/Bill Asher).

We have jumped forward by following Chaplin across America. Back in Blighty, 1910 had already been a busy year for new Karno material, and it wasn't over yet. He and Herbert Sidney (now a regular collaborator) advertised a sketch in preparation entitled *The Twisters,* but we know nothing about this, and it appears never to have been staged. Meanwhile there had been some changes in the crew of the *Wontdetania,* with Shaun Glenville now supported by Harold Wellesley and Eric Campbell (stepping into Charles East's gigantic shoes as Captain). At the end of September, Glenville's company changed tack and were pressganged into a new small-scale farce, *The New Slavey,*[18] which opened at the Canterbury. *The Stage* provides a first night review:

> Mr and Mrs O'Toole … are being awfully harassed by the weird incompetence and eccentricities of an impossible domestic named Liza, who soon gets the 'sack', and threatens her master with a visit from her brother, who is a brewer's drayman. When at last Mr O'Toole gets 'suited' it is with a dainty and rather 'fetching' young damsel, who by no means wins her mistress's approval, and who is eventually caught by that lady sitting upon her husband's knee … the scene between husband and wife is speedily cut short by the appearance of Liza and

her burly brother, who drops Mr O'Toole into a convenient cucumber frame ... Shaun Glenville as Mr O'Toole and Harold Wellesley as Liza are responsible for much laughter.[19]

Apart from Eric Campbell lifting Glenville up by the ankles and depositing him in a cucumber frame, there was a notable absence of slapstick. Glenville's company went on to perform *Wontdetania*, *The New Slavey* and *The Yap Yaps* around the provinces, with Glenville as Charlie Chinn in the latter (Gus Le Clerq had moved on to pastures new).[20] Campbell left the company at the end of the year,[21] never to return to Karno. He performed in various plays and pantomimes before making his own way to America in 1914.[22] As his future movie appearances demonstrate, Campbell was a first-class 'heavy' and one wonders why Karno let this gentle giant slip through his fingers.

New year, new ideas: Karno and Herbert Sidney announced they were working on a piece entitled *Archibald's Cricket Match*. Unsurprisingly, this never materialised: exhibiting some football skills on stage is one thing, whacking a cricket ball for six over the upper circle is something else.[23] It was one of many sketches advertised as 'in preparation' which never appeared, and there were other signs that things were slowing down a little. In April Karno cut his losses and sold the Peterborough Hippodrome, having already disposed of his theatre in Maidstone (which he described as the worst show town in England). His dalliance with legitimate theatre was on the wane. Those he retained were hosting music hall acts, despite most of the industry moving in the opposite direction – as one reporter noted: 'In these days when London Music Halls are becoming largely dramatic houses, it is more interesting to chronicle a reverse state of affairs. Commencing on Monday, Mr Fred Karno will run a summer variety season at the Marlborough.'[24]

The older sketches continued and there were plenty of other diversions. A notice in *The Stage* suggested that *His Majesty's Guests* was set to tour Australia in the autumn[25] – though if it did, I've found no evidence of it – and there were the usual charitable events. April saw the next decennial census, which records Karno as the only person in residence at the Fun Factory (other than a housemaid), while Marie is listed as single and living at her parents' house in Battersea – presumably to avoid recording their scandalous co-habitation. In reality the couple were spending most of their time at Molesey, and that summer they helped organise the Thames Flower Show at Tagg's Island. Karno no doubt felt he could afford to enjoy the fruits of his labour: he was at the peak of his wealth and fame, the impending clouds of war

21. ASTORIA

were too distant to see, and he appeared oblivious to the growing impact of cinema and the failure of his theatre ventures. He began spending lavishly. Prompted by a desire for more comfortable accommodation (he described the Highland Lassie as glorified camping), and keen to demonstrate his wealth to his society friends, he decided to build himself the most opulent houseboat on the Thames.

Karno turned to Bill Day, master carpenter and Fun Factory scenery chief, to design his dreamboat. Day began by creating a perfect mahogany model for the Guv'nor's approval, then commissioned a company in Brentford to build the hull while all the resources of the Fun Factory were given over to crafting the superstructure. Karno recalled that the project cost £7,500 – about one hundred times the average annual wage at the time. It was an exercise in extravagance: a teak superstructure lined with solid mahogany; large windows glazed with lead crystal; Italian marble for the bathroom walls and floor; and a solid marble bath with gold taps. There were two sitting rooms, a galley and three bedrooms, all lavishly furnished by Maple & Co. of Tottenham Court Road. To top it off there was a sun deck, fifteen feet wide and eighty-seven feet long, shaded by an ornate wrought-iron canopy and festooned with fairylights. He called the boat Astoria and she quickly became the talk of the river, as this article demonstrates:

21.8 Astoria under construction, 1911.

> Next to the palace itself, the most interesting object to visitors to Hampton Court ... is the ... palatial houseboat built by Mr Fred Karno ... The saloon is a handsomely fitted up apartment and by a unique arrangement of partitions can be lengthened out for dances or concerts ... The sleeping quarters are handsomely appointed bedrooms, not bunks ... The dining room is a gorgeous apartment ... with seating accommodation for forty, and there will be a billiard table on deck.[26]

The article goes on to note an interesting feature for a man who claimed rarely to gamble: 'Mr Karno is fitting up a captain's bridge, with telephone attached, so that he can see the races at Hurst Park without going ashore and have a bet on through the telephone.'

In July Karno hosted a boat-warming party, where a hundred guests danced to a full orchestra under the fairylights. The river was so crammed with onlookers in small craft that he said he could have walked from one bank to the other. Forty years later, when Astoria was in the ownership of Sir James Greenwood, Fred Karno Jr. paid a return visit. Noting the elegance of the boat's design, Lady Greenwood remarked that his father must have had good taste; "No," said Fred, "good advice." One suspects that if it wasn't for Bill Day, Karno might have painted Astoria bright purple and written 'Karno's Speechless Comedians' on the side.

Extraordinarily, once Astoria was completed, and after ten years' service at the Fun Factory, Day found himself out of a job. Perhaps the project had stretched their working relationship to breaking point: it was certainly a strain on Day – he died eighteen months later.

With Karno's attention diverted up-river, the day to day business of his empire soon got beyond the control of general manager Mr Reed. Karno found himself in litigation over unauthorised purchases from Bland and Philips Ltd (which had provided costumes for *Cinderella*), and the court reports make it clear that the Fun Factory had descended into chaos: 'Mr Karno, giving evidence, said he noticed that there was a lot of leakage with regard to materials and dresses, and he once observed some of his people walking about the street with some of the things on. He then ... instituted the system of written orders.'[27]

I assume the wardrobe staff were not walking down Cold Harbour Lane

21.9 Fred and Marie relax on board Astoria (© Illustrated London News Ltd/ Mary Evans Picture Library).

21.10 Astoria as she is today (author's photograph).

21. ASTORIA

dressed as Dame Trot, but anyone could order materials, so they probably costumed themselves (and half the street) each time they prepared a new show. Endeavouring to solve this problem, Karno had issued an edict that suppliers must only take instructions in writing from him or his manager, but in the rush to pull a show together, the system failed:

> Cross examined with regard to an interview witness had with Mr Reed ... over the telephone, Mr Bland complained that Mr Reed was abusive. Mr Craig [Karno's counsel]: please do yourself and Mr Reed justice. Witness: It is very difficult to do Mr Reed justice over the telephone. (laughter). Mr Karno, in the witness box, denied any knowledge at the time of orders being given to the plaintiffs without written authority ... Karno said he did give authority for the alterations to the principal boy's dress, because it was too short, and showed too much of her figure. It was not modest enough. (laughter) ... defendant said before he issued his notice, orders were given by anyone, even the office boy if he liked. They were in a hopeless muddle.[28]

Karno was evidently still having trouble with principal boys' legs. He lost the case and had to pay up – Reed was fired. Karno appointed Fred Sandy from the Exeter Hippodrome in his place, and stability was restored.

A month after Astoria was finished, Billy Reeves returned to England and Karno persuaded him back to lead a second U.S. company, under the management of Frank Major. After three seasons in *The Ziegfeld Follies,* Reeves had become a famous name – his mere arrival back in England was newsworthy – and yet their renewed association was not widely reported. Initially Reeves had hoped to run his own version of Karno's sketches under licence, but ultimately he elected to sign up with the old firm one more time.[29] His company included Dan Raynor, George Hoare, Frank O'Neill, John Doyle and Amy Forrest. In the meantime, Alf Reeves' company had been receiving excellent reviews, especially out West, where Karno was less well known than on the Eastern circuits. For instance in Seattle: 'No act ... has made the hit that has been made this week by Fred Karno's comedians ... it is the biggest comedy act that has ever come into North-western vaudeville.'[30] And Portland: 'Nothing like Karno's comedians has been seen in the west before and the novelty made a tremendous hit at the Grand yesterday, where it heads the bill.'[31]

Chaplin and his band were experiencing the last remnants of the Old West. Gun-toting cowboys, sheriffs and saloons full of prostitutes were vividly recalled in Chaplin's autobiography, and he fell in love with the wide-open spaces and the freedom that came with them. Not everyone felt the same. The tour was actually a series of mini-circuits, between which those without permanent contracts had the opportunity to return home. The gruelling schedule had worn thin for both Stan Laurel and Arthur Dandoe, so when they were refused a rise, they called it quits. Stan later gave contradictory accounts of his reasons for leaving: in some interviews he blamed the paucity of wages, in others he said he was simply homesick and tired of travelling across the country. Either way, the pair left in early August 1911, and after sightseeing in New York, returned to England on the Lusitania[32] – they passed Billy Reeves' company sailing in the opposite direction.

21.11 Never before published photograph of the Karno company playing baseball on the 1911 tour. Chaplin diving, Fred Karno Jr. crouching, Asher and Dandoe behind (courtesy Keith Ripley/Bill Asher).

Laurel and Dandoe were replaced by Tom Cardon and Ted Banks, and by November, when the company arrived for a second time in San Francisco, Chaplin was headlining on posters which no longer needed the Karno name. Sid Grauman, legendary proprietor of the Empress, offered to stage any show Chaplin might like to produce, but Charlie was under contract and not yet ready to abandon Karno's ship.

Back in England, Laurel and Dandoe initially found work with Charlie Baldwin's troupe in a sketch entitled *The Waxworks*,[33] before touring as 'the Barto Brothers' with *The Rum uns from Rome* ('Barmicus and Silicus and their famous banana eating lion'). The duo soon went their separate ways, but Stan continued the double act with a comic called Ted Leo, which led to a continental tour as part of a troupe called 'The Eight Komiks'. When this petered out in July 1912, he returned to England, his future uncertain.

Meanwhile, both Chaplin's and Billy Reeves' companies had been touring the States with *A Night in an English Music Hall,* playing different circuits many

21. ASTORIA

21.12 Photograph suggesting Mike Asher and Stan Laurel may have contemplated a double act (courtesy Keith Ripley/Bill Asher).

21.13 Karno company in costume for A Night in a London Club. *Left to right: Chaplin, Mike Asher, Muriel Palmer, George Seaman, Amy Minister, Fred Palmer, Ted Banks, Albert Austin, Emily Seaman, Bert Williams; crouching: Fred Karno Jr. (courtesy Roy Export/Chaplin Archive).*

miles apart. Reeves' company travelled home in mid-June 1912, but he elected not to renew his contract. Chaplin's troupe returned a few weeks later, so both Charlie and Stan sailed back to England in July but from different directions and in very different circumstances: Chaplin was now the rising star of Karno's company, Stan was unemployed. Happily his brother Gordon, manager of the Prince's Theatre in London, gave Stan some work and a roof over his head. Relegated to the back row of the ensemble and supplementing his income by typing scripts, Stan must have bitterly regretted walking out on Karno.

We left the Guv'nor relaxing on board his new houseboat and able once again to think about fresh material. It had been over a year since *The New Slavey* when, in October 1911, he finally staged a new sketch: *Who's Who*. Written by Karno and Frank Calvert, it was another farce – this time a story of mistaken identity. The manager of a down-at-heel hotel has the idea of engaging a con man (Mr Cholmondeley) to masquerade as a lord,

21.14 Chaplin's name on the posters, November 1911 (courtesy Roy Export/Chaplin Archive).

whose mere presence will drum up custom. In return, Cholmondeley is offered unhindered access to the bar – what could possibly go wrong? *The Stage* sets the scene:

> As is only to be expected the same rollicking fun is to be found in this as in previous sketches. Mr Karno himself was present to supervise the production, and he must have been highly gratified at the expressions of approval which greeted the final fall of the curtain. The entire action takes place in the Hotel de Luxe; three well-staged scenes depicting the Entrance Hall, Billiard Room, and Palm Court of the hotel. One never knows who is who, and the characters get into the merriest tangle; an impecunious bogus count narrowly escaping marrying his own mother![34]

The sketch opened at the Palace Theatre in Southampton before transferring to the Kilburn Empire, but London reviewers were less enthusiastic, so it returned to the provinces for the rest of the year. *Who's Who* was quickly followed by another sketch from the writing team of Albert Bruno and Herbert Sidney: *Perkins The Purser*, which opened at the Empress, Brixton, in December. Billed as 'The Second Cruise of Wontdetania',[35] this was a slimmed-down version of the original sketch. Perkins was now working his passage while embroiled in another mistaken identity story:

> The purser of the vessel, "Mr Gibbs" ... is pursued by an irate mother in law, who wishes to assert the rights of her deceived daughter against those of another wife which the purser has in America ... Gibbs ... persuades the inimitable "Perkins" to assume his name, clothes, and duties, with the result that the voyage ... is a series of side-splitting laughs.[36]

The motion of the ship once again left the audience in awe, so Karno took to demonstrating the inner workings of the set by revealing the huge hydraulic pistons as an afterpiece. This peek behind the magic curtain generated as much interest as the sketch itself.

Perkins sailed off to more success – but below decks, trouble was brewing in the shape of an old adversary who just wouldn't go away. Aided and abetted by Fred Kitchen, Herbert Darnley had now regained his former strength, and in December persuaded Herbert Sidney to defect – depriving Karno of another quality writer. In these circumstances one might assume he would do his best to keep Albert Bruno on side, so it's surprising that Bruno was not given the lead in his own sketch: instead, Karno cast Harold Wellesley as Perkins. It was fast becoming an unhappy ship.

Christmas comes around quickly when you're writing biographies. In keeping with the rest of 1911, Karno's pantomime offering was lower-key than in previous years. He staged just one small scale production: *The House That Jack Built* at the Borough Theatre, Stratford, with a cast of unknowns other than Syd Walker as the Squire. Nonetheless, it played to enthusiastic audiences and was extended by a week. After the final show the company hosted a dinner dance on stage, at which 'Mr and Mrs Fred Karno were present.'[37] This is the first reference to 'Mrs Karno' in the press since his split with Edith – presumably he felt that after six years he was able to publicly pass off Marie Moore as his wife.

With Herbert Sidney gone, Karno turned to Syd Chaplin and Frank Calvert for his next show, and *The Hydro* opened at the Preston Hippodrome in February 1912. Set in a spa hotel, it parodied the Edwardian fascination with hydrotherapy. Intensive cold and hot water treatments, such as Turkish baths, were being prescribed for everything from aches and pains to mental illness, although Karno's brand of medicine aimed strictly for the funny bone.

The show's two scenes came with potential to shock, featuring the pump room and the interior of the 'bathe de-luxe' (complete with a pool on stage). Newspapers were quick to report that the ladies' chorus would be wearing 'regulation bathing costumes', so as not to upset the censor. Syd Chaplin led from the front as detective Nick Sharp. While in pursuit of the mysterious Lord Narkington, Sharp disguises himself as a nurse and gets distracted when he finds himself masseuse to the scantily clad ladies in the baths. He eventually gets arrested

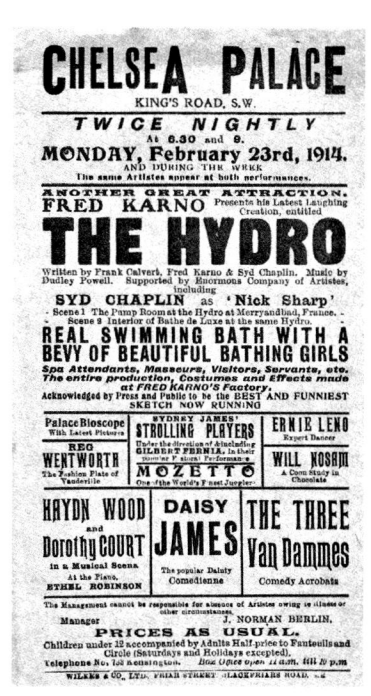

21.15 Advertising flyer for The Hydro *(author's collection).*

himself for being a 'lunatic', escapes, then makes a dramatic reappearance at the back of the auditorium and fires a pistol. For the *coup de grace*, he arrests the wrong man and falls headlong into the water tank.

Syd's appearance in the auditorium marked a new diversion – 'breaking the fourth wall' – later to become a staple of Karno comedy. Getting down among the punters for comic effect was not commonplace at the time, and even today creates excitement in the stalls. Back in 1912, Syd Chaplin popping up dressed as a nurse, firing a pistol and climbing over the orchestra to arrest his man, took the audience completely by surprise and had them in hysterics. The critic from *The Stage* wasn't keen on the idea though, advising that this device should be used only by magicians. Others noted the stamina required to deliver such a high-energy show: 'We certainly think the artistes earn the lordly salaries which Mr Karno no doubt pays them [if only they knew!], for they fall into tanks and get soaking wet in the most cheerful manner … four times a night … we begin to realise that there is a good deal of false glamour around the stage.'[38]

Many commentators suggest that Chaplin's *The Cure* (1917) borrowed heavily from *The Hydro,* but while the setting was a spa hotel and one or two gags may have been recycled – certainly plenty of people get dunked into the water – the plot bears no resemblance to Karno's sketch.

Although overlooked for *Perkins the Purser*, in March Bruno played the lead in both *Thumbs Up* (written by Karno, Bruno and Hickory Wood) and *The Big House* (by Karno, Bruno and Herbert Sidney). Both were advertised as being performed just once, 'for the statutory period', to secure copyright on the material. Since Herbert Sidney had just jumped ship, I suspect Karno felt these two titles might be stolen by Darnley. *Thumbs Up* had been identified as 'in preparation' way back in 1906,[39] and Darnley had subsequently listed it in his own advertising, so it was probably a Darnley idea. *The Big House* was perhaps a variation on *The Casuals,* since it shared the workhouse setting. Surprisingly, neither sketch appears to have been performed again. Why go to the trouble of casting them, rehearsing them and investing in props, costumes and scenery, only to do one performance? It seems Karno would go to any lengths to frustrate Darnley, even if it meant staging sketches he had no intention of producing.

While *The Big House* was probably straightforward enough, *Thumbs Up* was unlike any previous Karno sketch. In three scenes – a Roman marketplace, the exterior of a bathhouse and the Senators' meeting house and arena – it would

21. ASTORIA

have required far more work and expense to stage, and sounds like it had plenty of comic potential. The problem was not the sketch, but its writer: Albert Bruno would soon be giving Karno the thumbs down.

Not all of Karno's new output was just for show, but his next sketch didn't get off to a flying start either. *The Waltz Scream* parodied a successful musical, *The Count of Luxembourg*, and took its title from Oscar Straus' *The Waltz Dream*. Although Karno claimed it had opened at the London Palladium, this appears to be advertising licence: it actually debuted as the main Easter attraction at his own Exeter Hippodrome, where a local newspaper reported:

> At heavy expense Mr Fred Karno is bringing down his latest production, "The Waltz Scream," and when it is stated that this latest addition to a long list of sketches ... has received the seal of hearty public approval during the past fortnight at the London Palladium, patrons of the Hippodrome may rest assured that they will be thoroughly amused. The production is a travesty on modern musical comedy, invented and arranged by Mr Karno and ... Frank Calvert (who takes the part of the tale teller in the sketch) and Orlando Powell. It is ... full of mirth provoking situations from start to finish.[40]

Despite this big build-up, it died after two weeks, prompting Karno to commission a major rewrite from Leonard Durrell. *Perkins the Purser* was having more success, and by the time it arrived in Glasgow in early April, Wontdetania was firmly established as the most famous ship on the halls. The most famous ship in the country, meanwhile, was just setting sail on her fateful maiden voyage from Southampton. Five days later, in the early hours of 15 April 1912, the 'unsinkable' Titanic slipped beneath the surface of the icy North Atlantic. One imagines Harold Wellesley's Perkins struggled to get laughs on his tilting deck that week.

By May, Durrell had worked his magic (with the help of music by Dudley Powell), transforming *The Waltz Scream* into another sketch for everybody's favourite idiot: *Perkins in Paris*. It premiered at the New Cross Empire, and as the title suggests, had Perkins causing chaos on the Continent. It was in two scenes: 'The School of Art' and 'The Ballroom of the Countess of Lemonton'.

> The production is lively and brilliant ... an enterprising artist and sculptor Osmond Neversoll, gains notoriety and popularity ... With

it comes jealousy, fellow students airing their grievances that he had unfair advantage of having a living model, whilst they ... work from a dummy. They revolt, and ... Perkins ... is forthwith commissioned to procure models ... his choice creates uproarious amusement, for he introduces an absurdly varied assortment ... the Countess of Lemonton calls at the much-disordered studio and confesses her admiration and love for Osmond's art ... Osmond ... has accepted an invitation to a ball given by the Countess, but is prevented by the jealousy of his model, who claims his love. Perkins ... ludicrously impersonates Osmond at the ball. His would-be dignified entry by the elaborate stairway is somewhat hurried by a slip, owing to ... excessive refreshing. The Countess is so disappointed at his appearance that she names him as an imposter to the Count, a duellist, whose advance is humorously misunderstood by Perkins ... After combatting with pistols and rapiers, they resort to cudgels, Perkins is struck, and, announcing he is "poisoned," he ... feigns his last moments. The Countess, in attendance, implores his recovery, offering for such result to marry him.[41]

A month after the sketch launched, a press report provided an insight into its creation:

> Perkins in Paris ... has the merit of having risen on the ashes of a piece that was ... a failure. Mr Albert Bruno offered to take it in hand ... with the result that it is the success it showed at The Leeds Empire ... the run promises to be a long one, and is the cause of the postponement of "Thumbs Up" a sketch in which Mr Bruno has great faith.[42]

This report originated from Bruno himself and reveals that he still had hopes for *Thumbs Up*, but why he would take the credit for Leonard Durrell's work is a mystery. There seemed to be a lot of it about: Tom Nelson got a favourable profile piece in the press that summer in which he claimed authorship of *Perkins MP*, despite its being written by Fred Kitchen. In the same article Nelson said he was working on another sketch for Perkins entitled *Perkins the Punter*, although by then the character was wearing thin with the critics (if not the audience). This *Preston Herald* reporter had clearly seen one Karno sketch too many, and suggests that he might like to write *Perkins the Painter*, noting sarcastically:

21. ASTORIA

> Scene 1 is the detached residence ... on the ample scaffolding ... are seated 5000 practical painters. This number for the sake of economy may be reduced to five ... Perkins enters, and is immediately crowned with an inverted paint pot. A laugh may be anticipated for this novel joke, but if the audience is dense and fails to discover anything humorous, Perkins has merely to remove the pot to permit of another being dropped on his head. This process can be continued until a satisfactory atmosphere of hilarity has been established ... Scene 2 is the kitchen, and Perkins is discovered assisting Mary Jane to knead the dough. This ... will entail no expense to Mr Karno, who has a good stock of 'sticky stuff' for use in all his sketches ... he picks up the girl and hurls her head foremost into the mug of embryo bread. He then calmly opens the door and his sticky fingers adhere to the latch. Curtain please – quick![43]

Karno certainly recycled ideas, settings, characters and gags; he also staged the same sketch under different titles (with minor amendments) and combined sketches into longer shows. But to imply that he was cheap, given the investment and scale of his sketches, seems unfair. This was the man offering audiences *Wontdetania* bobbing at anchor and *The Hydro* plunge pool. Karno had written or produced over fifty shows and ten pantomimes in just twenty years – perhaps he was allowed a bit of recycling. Sandy Powell, who worked with Karno in the 1920s, said of him: 'Fred Karno was an extraordinary man. He learnt his business the hard way, working in the halls for many years before going into production ... He became a master of the art of stage presentation and was a great showman. One of his great skills was the creation of a complete show from the slender material of a sketch.'[44]

As he continued to enjoy the good life up-river, Karno didn't seem too worried by the critics. He attended Henley Regatta on his launch 'Goodbye' (perhaps named in honour of Edith), and in August joined the Water Rats for a day out at Molesey which included lunch at a run-down hotel on Tagg's Island. Perhaps it was there that an idea began to form in his mind – an idea which would ultimately lead to his downfall.

22.

Karsino's Curse

"My husband is an artist; he once painted a picture of a decayed apple."
"Was it realistic?"
"Oh yes – everyone who looked at it said it was rotten."
(Flats, 1913)

IN THE summer of 1912, music hall finally got the recognition it deserved. On the first day of July, a Royal Command Performance was staged at the appropriately named Palace Theatre, London, in the presence of King George V and Queen Mary. Competition for a place on the bill was fierce. Clarice Mayne and Harry Tate were both in the show, but other stars were notably absent – not least Marie Lloyd, who was initially considered but didn't make the final line-up. This may have been due to the risqué nature of her material, her colourful private life, or the managers exacting their revenge for her high-profile role in the Music Hall War. Whatever the reason, the decision to exclude the biggest female artiste of the day remains one of the most controversial in entertainment history. Performing at a nearby theatre, Lloyd supposedly had notices erected stating: 'Every performance by Marie Lloyd is a command performance by order of the British Public.'[1]

She wasn't the only big name overlooked, and the organising committee sought to placate disgruntled stars by staging a 'tableau' of music hall greats as a finale, billed as 'Variety's Garden Party'. Lloyd declined to take part and Karno it seems was not invited, despite several of his former apprentices being present:

22. KARSINO'S CURSE

Harry Weldon, Herbert Darnley, Fred Emney, Gus Le Clerq (now McNaughton) and Fred Kitchen. As the undisputed king of sketch comedy, Karno's exclusion is surprising, particularly given that acrobatic chaos was on the bill courtesy of 'Boganny's Lunatic Bakers'. Perhaps the presence of his rival Wal Pink on the organising committee had something to do with it.

Many saw the Royal Command Performance as the beginning of a golden age. As Naomi Jacob put it: 'Salaries were good, new halls were being built all over the country; they were attracting people who were clever, who had new ideas to sell, and knew how to sell them. The days of the "pot-house" variety were over, and the "Cinderella of the Arts" was on her way to the ball.'[2] Little did they know that music hall was about to experience a rapid decline.

Cinemas were now appearing on every street corner, and clashes were looming. One flashpoint came when cinema operators wanted to open on Sundays. Industry opinion was divided: many felt that no public entertainments should be allowed, some that Sunday performances were acceptable so long as theatres closed on another night to give staff a night off. The press was full of conflicting opinion. Karno waded in with his view, saying he would prefer theatres to stay closed on Sundays, but if cinemas were allowed to open then theatres should too. Cinema was a threat to Karno but an opportunity for others: while touring the States, Chaplin and Alf Reeves contemplated investing in a camera and persuading Karno to sell them the film rights to his sketches, but a busy tour (and the realisation that neither knew the first thing about filmmaking) prevented them taking the idea any further.

As music hall basked in the glory of the Royal Command Performance, Chaplin's troupe was finally heading home, although for some reason they did not all return on the same crossing. Chaplin travelled on the Olympic with Alf and Amy Reeves and George and Emily Seaman. Strangely, only Alf is listed as 'a theatrical' on the manifest: the two women are listed as housewives, George as a 'clerk' and Chaplin as a 'broker' – perhaps it was some sort of company in-joke. One can only imagine what it must have felt like to sail on Titanic's sister ship just three months after the disaster, but if the opulence of the White Star fleet felt tarnished, it was still a far cry from the Cairnrona – and this time they sailed second-class, arriving in Southampton on 12 July.

Chaplin had been in America for nearly two years, and in the meantime Syd had married, giving up the bachelor flat they once shared. Finding himself in what he described as a dismal lodging house, he hankered to return to the States, but had to face the reality of the Karno company's provincial touring circuit – including an engagement in the Channel Islands in August. Karno later recalled: 'It was on this visit that Charlie first appeared in front of a movie-camera; there was a carnival, and a cameraman had come from England to take it, and while the procession was in progress Charlie, to plague the cameraman, walked right up to the lens in his little straw hat … completely obliterating the carnival.'[3]

Chaplin's first appearance on film may well be an apocryphal story,[4] but Alf Reeves confirmed that while playing the Jersey Opera House, they did witness a news cameraman filming the 'Battle of the Flowers', and a pompous local dignitary constantly hogging the camera.[5] He said this amused Chaplin, and later inspired one of his first Keystone films, *Kid Auto Races at Venice* (1914). Reeves doesn't mention Chaplin being caught on camera, but we know Chaplin already had an interest in film, so it seems quite possible – if only for a moment.

Chaplin spent what was left of the summer at venues in London, and had clearly risen to the top rank of Karno comedians, since the Guv'nor invited him to drinks on Astoria. Chaplin duly marvelled at the houseboat's luxury and the two men retired to their deckchairs to soak up the tranquil surroundings. As they gazed upon the little hotel where the Water Rats had staged their summer outing, one wonders whether Karno confided in Chaplin his latest big idea. Perhaps he didn't get the chance, for Chaplin recalled that they were rudely interrupted:

> Suddenly, a falsetto, foppish voice began screaming hysterically: "Oh, look at my lovely boat, everyone! … And the lights! Ha! Ha! Ha!" … We looked to see where the effusion came from, and saw a man in a rowing-boat, dressed in white flannels, with a lady reclining in the back seat … Karno leaned over the rail and gave him a very loud raspberry, but nothing deterred his hysterical laughter. "There is only one thing to do," I said, "to be as vulgar as he thinks we are."[6]

Chaplin then proceeded to share some choice expletives, which embarrassed the young man's companion sufficiently for him to beat a hasty retreat. Chaplin later said the episode encapsulated the sort of English class snobbery he hated. He was determined to return to America – where a common man made good would be celebrated rather than reviled – but in the meantime, Karno set him a new challenge. Charles Baldwin had rewritten *Annual Sports* as *The Village Sports*, retaining the original premise in three scenes: 'Hayseed Park', 'The entrance to

22. KARSINO'S CURSE

Squire Wurzel's meadow' and 'The Sports Ground'. On 2 September it opened at the Colchester Hippodrome with Chaplin in the lead – but not for long.

Even before Chaplin's troupe had arrived back in Britain that summer, Karno was planning the next trip, and had contracted with the Sullivan and Considine circuit to send over *The Hydro* that autumn. Again the obvious thing to do was send Syd Chaplin's company, but for some reason *The Hydro* was dropped and Charlie was once again elected to lead the company. Why? *The Hydro* was a barnstormer with an international flavour – it would certainly have travelled well – and Syd, its established star, had previous experience of American tours. Perhaps accounts of Charlie's two U.S. tours have been confused (facts about them are often blended together), and it was for this second expedition that Karno decided Syd was too valuable to risk being poached by the studios, rather than the first? It's just a theory, but it would explain why they dropped *The Hydro*.

Of course, it may be that Chaplin simply persuaded Karno to let him return. Another recruit for the tour was even luckier to get a second chance. Alf Reeves had bumped into Stan Laurel in Leicester Square and asked if he'd been starring in the West End. Stan replied: "Starving in the West End more like!" Reeves offered him a place on the tour – and with the wage rise Stan had previously been refused. He jumped at it.

Despite *Variety* reporting that the company were intending to stage *Village Sports*, they stuck to the same three sketches as on the previous tour: *Wow Wows*, *A Night in a London Club* and *A Night in an English Music Hall*. Alf Reeves was in charge as usual, and they set sail on Oceanic on 2 October 1912. Alongside Charlie and Stan,[7] the troupe numbered Amy Reeves, Edgar and Ethel Hurley, Amy Forrest, George and Emily Seaman, Ted Banks and the veteran Drury Lane clown Whimsical Walker.[8] Completing the line-up was Karno's younger brother Albert, who was twenty years his junior and remains something of a mystery man – he does not appear in any Karno reviews or listings.

Karno waved them off and returned to planning the project which had now fully formed in his mind – his biggest yet. Step one was to divest himself of previous failures, selling off the last of his theatre interests: the Marlborough and his flagship Exeter Hippodrome. On a last trip to Exeter, perhaps to finalise the legal paperwork, Karno detoured via the small Somerset village of Spaxton, curious to see the headquarters of a notorious religious sect known as the Agapemone – 'Abode of Love'. The organisation had all the hallmarks of a classic cult, and the press regularly featured tales of sexual debauchery and a harem of women blindly obedient to its leader, self-professed new Messiah John Smyth-Pigott. Unfortunately Karno got a somewhat closer look than he intended when he drove head-on into a car full of Smyth-Pigott's 'soul brides'. Once the women had untangled themselves from the wreckage and it was established that no-one was hurt, the new Messiah took Karno to the Royal Clarence Hotel for lunch. He evidently failed to convert the Guv'nor, who pressed on with the sale of the Hippodrome and returned to London. Predictably, history confirms that Smyth-Pigott was not the Messiah – he was just a very naughty boy.

Abandoning his native city, Karno left behind his friend Dudley Powell, who was the Hippodrome's orchestra leader. As one newspaper put it, Karno was sighing for fresh worlds to conquer, and didn't look back. He was getting out of the theatre business and into the hotel business, and *The Pall Mall Gazette* finally revealed his masterplan: 'Mr Fred Karno, the music-hall artiste, who has for some years had a houseboat moored to Tagg's Island, East Molesey, has arranged to take over the island. He proposes to run free ferries to it from the shore and to provide entertainments and illuminations in the evening.'[9]

Tagg's Island had been a popular spot for visitors for many years. In 1850, spurred on by the arrival of the railway, the lawyer and property speculator Francis Kent bought the land, and it became known as Kent's Ait. Karno recounted that it had long been a place of ill repute – a hideout for smugglers and highwaymen, later occupied by 'gypsies' who eked out a living by weaving willow baskets there. Francis Kent wasted no time in evicting them, and legend has it that they cursed the island on their way out.

Although Kent's successors retained the freehold until 1941, the island was occupied by various tenants. At one end, a Mr Harvey built a hut-like hostelry called the Anglers' Retreat. At the other, Thomas Tagg and his four sons established a boatyard. When Harvey left in 1862 the Taggs took on the Anglers' Retreat, and ten years later they replaced it with the Thames Hotel – later the Tagg's Island Hotel.

By the time the third generation took over, in the person of George Tagg, it had inevitably become known as Tagg's Island. The boatbuilding business had been very successful but the hotel struggled after a series of wet summers (there were severe floods in 1894 and 1903) – a problem which was to haunt successive owners. In 1904 Tagg tried unsuccessfully to sell the lease, and was eventually declared bankrupt. His assets were sold but no-one would take the hotel off his hands, so he remained its reluctant proprietor and the old place continued to decline.

22. KARSINO'S CURSE

22.1 Before – The Thames Hotel, Tagg's Island (author's collection).

Karno was now practically living on the Astoria, overlooking the little hotel. He saw only opportunity – perhaps influenced by the fact that the previous summer had been a record-breaking heatwave. So when Tagg's lease expired, he decided to add this untapped goldmine to his empire. Notwithstanding his enormous wealth, fame and international success, Karno believed this would be his finest hour, recalling in his memoirs that he anticipated his scheme to be 'the crowning triumph of a lifetime.' He planned to take a twenty-one-year lease on the hotel, install a ferry and boost its entertainment offering. In October 1912 he signed on the dotted line and the project got underway – then the trouble started.

Initially modest in scale, Karno's vision quickly ballooned into a complete redevelopment of the island. He extended his lease to forty-two years and, as *The Pall Mall Gazette* reported, planned to invest as much as ten thousand pounds:

> The hotel is to be practically rebuilt, thirty new bedrooms added; croquet, tennis and other lawns are to be laid, and a new pavilion for high class entertainments is to be erected … the stage will be so built that in one direction will face an open-air auditorium, and in the other a covered-in auditorium. The scenery will be reversible, so that if the rain comes all the audience will have to do will be to … walk around to similar seats under cover … the concerts are to have the tone of Queen's Hall and the whole atmosphere is to be discreetly continental.[10]

Karno entertained millions around the country, so why on earth shouldn't he make a success of his own pleasure palace, where society could promenade by day and be entertained by dance bands in the evening. The locals were less sanguine about him taking on the place, and the lease proscribed any attempt to go downmarket, specifically prohibiting 'theatre, music hall, swing, roundabout, switchback, railway, toboggan run, cocoa nut shy, or any other such erection.'[11]

They needn't have worried: he was not about to recreate Bartholomew's fair, and the only erection he was thinking about was his own – with all those bedrooms, there would be no shortage of quiet spots for a quick bunk-up with a chorus girl. Besides, Karno shared a desire for the endeavour to be upmarket. He said the hotel would be 'a sumptuous place, with all the comforts of home and a good many more too … the finest and most luxurious river hotel in Europe … there is going to be nothing vulgar about the place … we are doing our best to keep the place refined.'[12]

One wonders how much of the project was a genuine business venture and how much was an opportunity to further his efforts at social climbing. High society had been infiltrated by a new breed of self-made, working-class industrialists who similarly aspired to be accepted among the upper classes, and while many invested their fortunes in country estates and grand houses, Karno plumped for a grand hotel instead. He remained at heart a tradesman – a supplier of services to his new-found society friends. He would never be their equal. His favourite boast – that he was comfortable in the company of dukes or dustmen – betrayed his true nature and left his social climbing horribly compromised. He would always be the bombastic music hall acrobat with a coarse turn of phrase and a regional accent, and he would always have a chorus girl as his consort. Leslie Karno believed that his father's society friends tolerated this strange cuckoo in their nest while privately considering him tasteless and crass. Karno was often the butt of their private jokes, and apparently seethed with resentment at his failure to be completely accepted. Adeler and West wrote: 'Many have tried to label Karno as an ignorant and uncultivated boor. Largely self-educated he undoubtedly is. With his sordid upbringing and the environment of his early career, any education had to be in the nature of self-improvement, which is all the more credit to him. However, such success as he enjoyed is never made without what Turner mixed his colours with – brains.'[13]

He must have left his brains at home the day he bought Tagg's Island.

Whatever his motivation, Karno embarked on his new project with relish, next turning his attention to choosing a name. He supposedly offered a prize of fifty pounds for the best idea,[14] and many suggestions came forward including Arcadia and Elysium, but a portmanteau word won the day – 'Karsino'. It seems a strange choice, given that one thing it certainly wasn't was a casino (prohibited by the gambling laws of the time), until one realises that the word casino originally meant any place of entertainment, including theatres and hotels. In his memoirs

22. KARSINO'S CURSE

Karno observed that had he been allowed a gambling casino it might have proved more successful.

With a name chosen, he needed a designer to realise his vision, and no ordinary designer would do. The legendary Frank 'Matchless' Matcham (today considered the finest theatre architect of all time) was dragged out of semi-retirement for the task – it would be one of his final commissions (he died in 1920). Karsino quickly became a nightmare project, however. Most of the island was an overgrown swamp which Karno described as a morass. The old hotel had been built on scant foundations and boasted little in the way of amenities, relying on cesspits for drainage and boreholes for drinking water (hopefully not too close to one another). Karno chose to demolish it and start again. Allen and Company of Westminster was appointed main contractor, and work got underway.

The poor ground conditions meant piled foundations were required, a procedure which called for specialist Dutch engineers.[15] Mains drainage, water and power supplies had to be laid on the riverbed by divers. Costs were stacking up before they'd even got the building out of the ground, and starting work at the onset of winter can't have helped. As Karno put it: 'There were special cables and special pipes to be laid, special gangs of workmen in special shifts and gilt-edged supervising specialists with special fees had also to be employed.'[16]

Drainage was particularly challenging, and from the mahogany toilet-seats down, the design was far from bog-standard. In fact it was so cutting-edge that when the hotel was finished, the Sanitary Inspectors' Association invited all its members to inspect Karno's 'Ventilated Hydro Dynamic Flusher and Interceptor' (presented by its inventor Isaac McShone); and after they'd had their tea, they delighted in inspecting it in operation – whatever turns you on. Karno was immensely proud of his drains – in a promotional booklet he wrote: 'The drainage ... arrangements are absolutely unique in their hygienic excellence, because they are partly on the original Shone Ejector System as applied to the drainage of the Houses of Parliament.'[17]

Once the substructures and services were dealt with, there was the small matter of the building itself. Matcham elected to use a steel frame infilled with lightweight pre-cast concrete panels, which was so innovative that it required changes to the local building bylaws before being approved by the council inspector.[18] Like all new technologies, it wasn't cheap. That cost increased further when it was decided to locate the kitchens on the top floor. The six cooking ranges weighed twelve and a half tons, and the structure wouldn't take the load.

At the eleventh hour the layouts were redesigned, the kitchens were relocated to the basement,[19] and the bills kept coming. Karno wrote to C.W. Kent: 'I am just beginning to realise the enormous magnitude of the task I have undertaken … I fear it will not be a profitable investment by any means.'[20]

That turned out to be an understatement. Despite money pouring through his fingers faster than the Thames over Molesey weir, Karno made no attempt to economise on the project. Instead he looked for ways to raise additional funds and make savings elsewhere. According to Gallagher, he reduced Edith's weekly allowance to five pounds, forcing her to take Leslie out of private school and move to a smaller house, at 258 Elm Road in Leigh-on-Sea. Then four months into the build, he took drastic action and advertised Astoria for sale: 'Astoria is undoubtedly the finest houseboat on the Thames … It belongs to Mr Fred Karno, of music-hall fame, the reason for selling being that he requires more accommodation … the owner lives on the boat all year round, and … there is every possible comfort imaginable … It will be sold as it is, fully equipped, at a low figure.'[21]

Karno's pride and joy was just eighteen months old – it must have broken his heart to offer her for sale. 'He requires more accommodation' was certainly an interesting spin on 'he needs cash to finish his hotel.' However, Astoria was not sold – he either changed his mind or found no takers – and Karno was forced to rely on a series of mortgages to finish the build.

The only saving grace was that Matcham's revolutionary design was quick to erect. The entire hotel was built within twelve weeks of the first pile being sunk – a staggering achievement. Unfortunately, it had been built on a mountain of debt that no foundation could support. Karno himself described the bill as 'colossal', and press reports suggested he had spent as much as £140,000[22] – well over ten times his budget. It may have cost the earth, but thanks to Matcham, Karsino was a beautiful building. Designed in Second Empire style, with

22.2 After – Karsino, possibly taken on opening day (author's collection).

22. KARSINO'S CURSE

mansard roofs and dormer windows, it had the appearance of a French colonial mansion. Balconies and stepped terraces gave the illusion of an intimate hotel, belying its true scale. Understated, elegant and oozing sophistication, it nestled gently into its riverside setting. As Karno put it: 'I have tried my best to bring the Continental atmosphere up-river.'[23]

Having created something so stylish Karno could hardly scrimp on the interiors, and employed a company called Ropley to oversee decoration, fittings and furniture. The dining room was in the art nouveau style with a grey and purple colour scheme, and crisp white linen tablecloths were adorned with silver cutlery fit for the first-class lounge of a White Star liner. The twenty-six bedrooms all had central heating, and beds were made up with Egyptian cotton sheets. There was electric lighting and lifts to all floors. The billiard room and lounge were lined in oak panelling, leading out onto a balcony where a sweeping staircase descended into the grandest space of all – the palm court ballroom, which could seat over six-hundred guests around its maple dancefloor. French doors along both

22.3 Karsino entrance hall (author's collection).

22.4 Karsino's Palm Court (author's collection)

303

sides opened onto the gardens, but guests could enjoy the views inside too, as the huge glazed dome was surrounded by large frescos depicting local scenes: Windsor Castle, Hampton Court, Garrick's Villa and Richmond. At one end was Matcham's innovative double-sided stage, with two prosceniums and a back wall that opened up to allow outdoor entertainment in fine weather.[24]

Outside, guests could enjoy the gardens and sports facilities, and there were also staff quarters, a laundry, greenhouses and garages. In case Karno's extravagant attention to detail is not already apparent, pets were catered for by a row of dog kennels which increased in size to suit their occupants – from lap dogs to Great Danes. Each kennel had its own little lamppost outside, graduating in scale to match its occupant. Ferries were installed for guests and their cars (even though the island had no roads and there was nowhere to drive to). Alternatively, you could arrive in your own boat or hire one of Karno's hundred-strong fleet of punts, rowing boats and launches.

As you might imagine, Karsino's grand opening was widely anticipated by the press: 'Mr Fred Karno has been devoting some of his "spare time" … to the establishment of a palace by the "fair marge of The Thames." It is a hotel and concert pavilion combined, and sounds the last note of luxury.'[25] As it neared completion Karno called on one of his discoveries to perform the topping-out ceremony: 'At Karsino … the top brick of the tallest chimney was placed on Wednesday … Mr Karno invited Miss Clarice Mayne to perform the ceremony. From a specially erected scaffolding the fair singer manipulated the trowel, and the brick was well and truly laid.'[26] Presumably the now-famous Clarice Mayne was no longer worried about people seeing her legs as she perched precariously atop the scaffold.

22.5 *Clarice Mayne performs the topping out ceremony at Karsino (© Illustrated London News Ltd/ Mary Evans Picture Library).*

As opening day approached the press could hardly contain their excitement:

> Fairyland at Hampton Court … The new hotel is first class, dainty, and charming … A chef … and a permanent staff of seventy cooks, waiters and maids will be employed … Mr G.B. Scribante, late of The Queen's Hotel, Leicester Square … has been appointed manager of the hotel.

22. KARSINO'S CURSE

> The entrance to the hotel is opposite to the boathouse, from which it is separated by a delightfully trim little Dutch garden. Tennis, croquet and badminton tournaments are being arranged ... A motor garage, with workshop and full equipment for cleaning and repairs, has been erected ... Among the military bands already engaged are the Grenadiers ... and the Coldstreams ... The hotel will also have its own staff orchestra and its own picture palace. A feature ... will be a German beer garden run on Munich lines. The summer arrangements include water carnivals, aquatic sports, a battle of flowers and a feast of lanterns. "Meet me at the Karsino tonight" should be the new "Tagg" of the profession, for no pains or money have been spared to convert the historic spot into a garden of delight.[27]

You will note that among the many attractions, Karsino had its own 'picture palace' – a nod toward the fast-growing popularity of cinema. So everything boded well, except that there were still one or two last-minute challenges to overcome, as *The Stage* reported: 'Mr Karno, who opens at Tagg's Island Sunday next, has had some trouble over his music licence for Sundays. I hope that this is not so; to have ragtime rotting our ears in every prominent hotel ... and to be deprived of the chance of hearing ... the Guards' band in the open air would be a ridiculous anomaly. Common sense I am certain will prevail.'[28] Karno had run-ins with the local authorities right up to the moment he opened (and beyond). Other battles were more worrying – there was every chance that his grand opening might be sabotaged by suffragettes.

Since their cause was clearly a just one, the violent activities of the most militant suffragettes have been somewhat whitewashed by history. As well as extensive vandalism, they were responsible for a number of arson attacks and bombings, and their campaign struck terror into many ordinary citizens. When the unpublished diary of Kitty Marion, a music hall artiste, was unearthed in 2018, it prompted a debate in the press on whether the more radical campaigners should be properly described as terrorists. Marion was among the most aggressive combatants in the movement, having been motivated by the horrors of the casting couch. Perhaps the most famous tragedy of the women's struggle was the death of Emily Davison, who was fatally injured after running in front of the king's horse at the 1913 Derby – she died in hospital a few days later. The following day, Marion and her associate Clara Giveen carried out a retaliatory arson attack which destroyed the grandstand at Hurst Park. Both were quickly arrested but released on bail. Karsino, just a suffragette stone's throw away and owned by the sort of theatrical producer Marion despised, was set to open less than two weeks later, on Royal Ascot weekend. Its potential as a target was obvious.

So Karno had a variety of reasons to be nervous when his hotel opened its doors to invited guests and press on Saturday 21 June 1913.[29] Fortunately the suffragettes left him alone – perhaps, after *Perkins M.P.*, they considered him an ally. Adeler and West later wrote: 'It is not difficult to understand the feelings of FK, the travelling tramp who had begged for work from door to door, the fairground acrobat, the self-made showman, who had become the sole owner of a glittering Palace of Delight by the banks of the silvery Thames.'

The guests arrived on Karno's ferries, which were operated by a bevy of beautiful actresses wearing dresses of white and Wedgwood blue – a display which would no doubt have infuriated any self-respecting suffragette. They were then ushered into the palm court for lunch and serenaded by the resident orchestra. Karno's friend Sir Thomas Dewar[30] presided over the civic niceties and seemed in no doubt about the potential of the place: 'Mr Karno was a bold man, a man of genius … who … had built a garden city … a place London had waited for … This establishment would, he believed, become a great feature in the social life of London, and he felt sure that this bold venture would meet with well-merited success.'[31] Had Karno not been blinded by the splendour of his achievement, the fact that Dewar and his fellow speakers all expressed how 'brave' and 'bold' they thought he was might have given him pause for thought.

The following day Karsino flung open its doors to the public. Royal Ascot weekend was already one of the busiest on the river, but Karno's marketing department had literally gone to town. Advertisements describing Karsino as 'the finest and most luxurious river hotel in Europe' were plastered all over London. They worked, and any doubts about the success of the venture must have been immediately dispelled – he had planned for two thousand visitors but over five thousand turned up. Many couldn't even get onto the island, such was the demand for the ferries, and while Karno was delighted with the numbers, it was not quite the high-society clientele he had hoped for: 'It was a motley crowd, a little too motley for Fred's liking. There were thousands there of a different class from those for whom he wished to cater but that of course could not be helped.'[32] It should have come as no surprise that London's proletariat came to see what all the fuss was about: ordinary working people were his audience, and music halls were closed on Sunday. Karno, always happy to take their shillings

22. KARSINO'S CURSE

22.6 Fred Karno greets guests on Karsino opening day, 22 June 1913 (Getty Images).

in the halls, was less enthusiastic about them coming up-river and making a mess on his lawns.

Karno had engaged his friend Sir Joe Lyons' catering company[33] to provide food for this swarm of working-class locusts, but they were quickly overwhelmed. The day was saved by calling into action an army of local suppliers. Karno's comics and several famous guests rolled up their sleeves, made sandwiches and waited on tables. Those guests who could get into the palm court were entertained by Violet Essex, Frederick Sylvester and the Society Idols. Outside on the two-storey bandstand, the Grenadier Guards' band played a specially commissioned piece by Leslie Alleyn entitled *The Karsino Valse*. Karsino lived up to the hype.

According to Gallagher, Karno and Marie Moore were walking the grounds that evening when Marie spotted a woman's lifeless body floating in the river. Karno supposedly refused to retrieve her, not wishing to drag a corpse onto his landing stage during his grand opening.[34] Drownings were not uncommon on the Thames – the weirs and locks were treacherous and there were many suicides – but these poor unfortunates were treated properly by the coroner and such discoveries (and subsequent inquests) were widely reported in the press. I can find no such report around that date. What's more, the island was absolutely packed with thousands of people – a dead body floating past would have been impossible to ignore. Shaggy dog stories aside, if it's bad omens we're looking for, Karsino was struck by lightning a few days after its launch – there was no real damage but one guest fainted in the excitement.

Dead bodies and lightning bolts notwithstanding, Karsino looked like being a great success – but building it turned out to be the easy part. Now Karno had to keep the guests coming. A huge balloon was tethered above the island and lit with the word 'Karsino' from a searchlight on the roof (although he recalled that the operator was prone to directing his spotlight onto courting couples up to no good in their punts). There were concerts twice a day and fireworks at night. He was never short of ideas for entertainment, but his lack of experience as a hotelier showed immediately.

22.7 Karsino Valse sheet music front cover (author's collection).

Most of the kitchen staff were German and Karno found them highly competent, but he had nothing but trouble with his waiters, who employed many nefarious means to earn a few extra quid. Solid silver cutlery was easily pocketed, but Karno marvelled at the more ingenious methods they used to fleece him. They would take the money for tea for four from a table then pay for tea for two at the bar (simply taking four cups to the table), or swap an expensive bottle of wine for a cheap one. Karno found himself forever placating guests who cottoned on to these scams, or who were victims of direct theft. Lord Birkenhead (the Lord Chancellor) had a rug stolen from his car, while another guest lost a cigarette case – the guilty waiter was frogmarched by Karno to the kitchen, where the stolen article was found in his pocket. The tale is included in his memoirs:

22.8 Karsino from the air (courtesy Langley Iddins).

22. KARSINO'S CURSE

> "What are you going to do about it?" grinned the man impudently. This annoyed Fred so much that he gave him a 'fourpenny one' on the point of the jaw and laid him out. When the culprit had recovered, Fred ordered him off the island. That night Fred was walking through the palm court … when the man crept from behind one of the plants and hit him over the head with a big bottle of ale. When he came to he had a bruise like a duck's egg on the back of his head and the doctor bending over him told him that if the man had hit him a little higher on the head he would have been killed … Fred remarked, "I've heard of people seeing stars, but I never believed it. On that occasion I saw a constellation with the Milky Way thrown in."[35]

This was the same waiter we encountered earlier, by the way: the man who tried to scuttle the Astoria, leaving Karno's latest conquest to abandon ship wrapped in his bedclothes.

The staff were bad but the guests caused him even greater problems. There were drunks, thieves, fighters, adulterers, ill people, dead people and every combination of the above. Keeping what he described as 'the riff-raff' off the island was a constant headache. All and sundry would lounge about in his deckchairs without spending a penny, forcing him to introduce a charge for the ferry redeemable at the hotel. When he wasn't punching waiters or ejecting riff-raff, he was hobnobbing with guests at the other end of the social scale. Karsino attracted the patronage of politicians such as Lord Curzon and Sir John Simon; socialites like Lady Diana Manners could be spotted on its terraces, and famous theatrical faces including Charles B Cochran, Alice Delysia and Gaby Deslys were regulars. Between the elite and the hoi polloi were his largest group of patrons: the young bohemians – the lower-middle-class clerks immortalised in Jerome K. Jerome's *Three Men in a Boat*. Blazers, boaters and moustaches were the order of the day for these young dandies, living life to the full before its responsibilities came upon them. It would be these young men who bore the brunt of the terrifying whirlwind that was now just a year away.

23.

Cheerio Charlie!

"With a singing voice like that.
You ought to be with Carl Rosa."
"But Carl Rosa's dead."
"I know — that's what I mean."

(Mumming Birds, 1904)

ON 11 August 1913, Karsino hosted the Grand Order of Water Rats' annual summer outing — just a year earlier they had been in the Tagg's Island Hotel as Karno dreamt up his plan. Karsino, however, was not the only significant story of the intervening twelve months.

We left Charlie Chaplin back in October 1912, sailing off to America for a second time. One of the first things the company did in New York was to go and see Billy Reeves in *A Lesson in Temperance* at Proctor's on 5th Avenue. Reeves' sketch possibly inspired *One a.m.* (1916), in which Chaplin's character, a smartly dressed man about town, returns home the worse for drink. What follows is a tour de force of solo physical comedy described by David Robinson as 'a daring display of virtuosity'[1] — Robinson says it might well be 'what happened next' to the *Mumming Birds* drunk. By this second U.S. tour, Chaplin had his drunk routine off to a tee. A contemporary photograph demonstrates how complete his transformation to the inebriate really was (judging by the costume this is probably the make-up for *A Night in a London Club*). The temperance movement was gaining momentum in America (eventually securing prohibition in 1920), and a cutting in Chaplin's archive reveals that the prohibitionists wanted to use

23. CHEERIO CHARLIE!

23.1 I saved the town: Chaplin as the drunk in A Night in a London Club (courtesy Roy Export/Chaplin Archive).

23.2 Chaplin dwarfed by Karno's advertising (courtesy Roy Export/Chaplin Archive).

this image in their propaganda. Despite not being a drinker Chaplin refused, adding: 'I consider I saved the town.'[2]

Back home Karno was up to his neck in foundations and drainage, but he didn't completely neglect the day job. Just as construction on Karsino commenced, he launched a new sketch. Statutory holiday was a relatively new idea in 1912, and most factories and mills shut down for just one week a year. For workers who had only ever known Sunday as a day off, this 'wakes week' was therefore a huge event. Karno's *Wakes Week* was the story of Joe Waddles, who spends his holiday at the racetrack and is accused of stealing the millworkers' wages to fund his gambling.[3] Waddles wins £50,000 on a bet but soon loses the lot thanks to assorted scoundrels, only to have another big win at the eleventh hour, solving all his problems. Tom Nelson took the lead, much to the delight of *The Yorkshire Evening Post*: 'Tom Nelson, the Leeds comedian ... has got a comedy part to his liking ... Joe Waddles, a North-country weaver, who, having won the Calcutta Sweep takes to the turf, an idea which should give him great scope ... the third scene ... is Tattersall's Ring on Pontefract Racecourse.'[4]

Karno recalled that although Nelson started strongly in the part, his ability to get laughs seemed to diminish – but reviews don't bear this out: 'Tom Nelson

… is astonishing and keeps the house rocking with laughter. The barest patch as far as the plot goes is sufficient ground for him … to raise a structure of hilarity.'[5] Karno disparaged Nelson in his memoirs but had no doubts about him back in 1910, when he signed him on a five-year contract – a term only ever exceeded by Fred Kitchen. Nelson stepped into Kitchen's very large shoes in *Perkins MP*, *The Bailiff* and *G.P.O.* He also co-wrote *Wakes Week*, *Spring Cleaning* and *Perkins MP*, and was described by one reviewer as Kitchen's natural successor.

While Nelson was proving himself a reliable lead, there were signs of disquiet elsewhere. In November, Fred Karno Jr. joined the Terriers[6] (the Water Rats' rivals), who had Ted Tysall at the helm. Fred Jr. had been overlooked for Chaplin's second U.S. tour – perhaps this was his way of sticking two fingers up to the old man. It prompted a response – Junior was immediately dispatched to America. Brother Leslie was similarly kept in the lower ranks of Karno's companies, and one wonders why the father didn't give his sons much chance to shine – nor his younger brother Albert, for that matter. His sons were born comics, natural storytellers and capable song-and-dance men, as we shall see, but history suggests they came into their own in later shows as light comedians; they were not strong acrobats which I think held them back. Karno was far too much of a perfectionist for nepotism, and I suspect that in their formative years both boys felt undervalued.

23.3 Tom Nelson (author's collection).

With even Fred Jr. now showing signs of disloyalty, it is perhaps no surprise that Herbert Darnley's relentless efforts to capture Karno's prize artistes threatened to bear more fruit. Albert Bruno was a superb comedian but despite co-writing *Perkins the Purser*, he was not given the lead; his sketch *Thumbs Up* was being quietly ignored; and his regular demands for more money seemed to steel Karno's determination to keep him among the jobbing ranks. Darnley seized his chance and offered to triple Bruno's wages, telling Karno that 'he was going to get Bruno away from him if he could.'[7] Unhappily for Darnley though, Karno had Bruno under contract – a 1910 agreement which gave Karno an option until 1914. Bruno tried to leave anyway and Karno took him to court.

23. CHEERIO CHARLIE!

It became apparent in evidence that their relationship had been fractious for a while: Bruno's testimony talked of regular pay disputes and arguments about the size of his billing. Karno countered that Bruno's unwillingness to play twice-nightly significantly undermined the profitability of his sketches. Newspaper reports confirm that Bruno had intended to take *Thumbs Up* to Darnley, but was prevented by Karno staging it 'for copyright purposes'. They also reveal that Bruno believed Karno had no desire to extend his contract, but had done so purely to prevent him joining Darnley.

For once Karno won the case – and perhaps by way of punishment, immediately sent Bruno's company to spend the winter touring the depths of Scotland. He must have been delivering his lines through gritted, if not chattering, teeth. Bruno's continued good reviews are testament to his professionalism, but he saw out his contract under duress, stirring up trouble whenever he could. The following spring, he wrote to *The Era* complaining that a review had failed to credit him as part-author of *Perkins in Paris* – and Karno's reply was a very public rebuke designed to keep him in line:

> Sir – in reference to Mr Albert Bruno's letter, published in your edition of May 28. I cannot allow his statement to pass unnoticed. As the proprietor of the sketch, "Perkins in Paris," and the original inventor of same, I think I know more about the matter than Mr Bruno. The facts are as follows … I produced … "A Waltz Scream," but as I found this sketch did not go well … I decided to have it rewritten … and commissioned Mr Leonard Durrell to do so … It is perfectly true that Mr Bruno has introduced many lines which were not originally in the script, and has also suggested several improvements, yet the same might equally be said of Mr George Graves and Mr Edmund Payne, who … supply their own funny business and patter, but I have never seen them billed nor have they claimed to be authors … yours faithfully, Fred Karno.[8]

The court case revealed that Bruno had approached Darnley, rather than the other way round, and for a very good reason. Bruno wrote: 'I offer you first option on my services. Knowing that Kitchen was to leave you shortly … I thought it would do you and me a bit of good.'[9] Kitchen's contract with Darnley was at an end, and he was off to set up his own company. It proved to be another bitter separation. The two men argued over whether Kitchen was committed to an optional contract extension, and it culminated in him threatening to sue Darnley for libel – they parted company. Darnley got a large dose of his own medicine, as his departing star took Harry Lappo with him – Kitchen's new company also included ex-Karno cohorts Jack Osborne, Aggie Morris and Kate Forster. *The Daily Herald* reported: 'Fred Kitchen ... is starting management on his own. He will soon produce ... a sketch "Bungle's Luck" ... Perkins and Potts were quite twin brothers, and I don't suppose we shall be able to distinguish Bungle from either of them ... But so long as he remains Fred Kitchen no one will have any cause for complaint.'[10]

Unlike the contracted comics, Karno's writers and musical directors were largely free agents. Dudley Powell had completed his contract at Exeter, and subsequently worked with both Karno's and Kitchen's companies.[11] He wasn't alone: Kitchen's co-writer on *Bungle's Luck* was Charlie Baldwin, who also worked with Herbert Landeck, another Karno alumnus to form his own company around this time. Sadly, the excitement and enthusiasm around Kitchen's new troupe was short-lived, literally – pint-sized Harry Lappo dropped dead a few months later.

Karno's victory over Bruno must have tasted all the sweeter as he watched Kitchen blow a big hole in Darnley's company. Christmas 1912 was no doubt very merry, and he found time to stage two pantomimes: *Mother Goose* at the Borough Theatre, Stratford, and *The House That Jack Built* at Olympia, Glasgow.[12] Provincial and international tours continued as the new year rolled around:[13] in March 'Karno's number 1 company' presented *Mumming Birds* at the grand opening of the Palladium Theatre, Johannesburg.[14] That same month Karno and Marie Moore (listed as Mr and Mrs Karno) adorned the top table at the Water Rats' annual ball, along with Marie Lloyd – reports confirm that a grand time was had by all.

Karno's early acrobatic sketches had required his personal supervision, but now that he was in his late forties and no longer living at the Fun Factory, this was more difficult. Perhaps it also drove his move away from knockabout slapstick toward musical comedy and farce. He no longer needed a steady flow of acrobatic comics, and gradually abandoned his policy of recruiting and training young performers. New shows would still include members of his stock company, but he increasingly cast established talent.

The next of his musical comedy sketches, *Flats*,[15] appeared five months after *Wakes Week*. Centred on an estate agent's efforts to let an apartment, the sketch was a riot of fast and furious fun, and incorporated the new musical style taking

23. CHEERIO CHARLIE!

the country by storm – ragtime. Although Karno and Charles Baldwin were credited with the sketch, a letter reveals that Syd Chaplin made a significant contribution:

> Dear Syd, I am enclosing you script of my new sketch "Flats" and shall be glad if you will … let me have your opinion, and if you think there is any little bits of business that can be put into it, please let me know. You know as well as I do, it is not the actual script that is always the thing, but the little bits of comedy, etc. that comedians like yourself can suggest. Rest assured that I shall recognize your efforts with regard to this, in the proper way.[16]

Syd added a few ideas for knockabout business and some verbal gags, as well as designing a technically complex set which included a working lift. The first scene was set in the estate agent's office, where Mr Townsend (a clerk) has to deal with a variety of clients looking for accommodation: a man about town (Billy Browning), two dodgy-looking characters (Slippy and Perks), a drunk (Mr Sardine), a wealthy Jew (Issy Rich) and Perks' battleaxe wife.

Flats

Mrs Perks is seeking a flat to rent:

>Clerk: This one has the advantage of a bathroom.
>Mrs P: What's the use of that? I'm only taking the place for a year. I suppose it has every inconvenience? Hot and cold gas? Indecent lights?
>Clerk: Everything up to date, madam.
>Mrs P: I'll take it.
>Clerk: Thank you madam. Have you any animals?
>Mrs P: Only my husband.

An attractive young femme fatale, Fluffie de Vere, enters and takes a seat to wait her turn. Oblivious to the effect she is having on every man in the office, she reads a book, and when she drops it there is a mad rush to pick it up. It is torn to shreds in the melee, and returned to her in a hundred pieces by her eager admirers. Billy enters and it becomes clear that Slippy and Perks are his criminal confederates: their swindle begins with Billy inviting all the customers to join him for drinks at his flat.

The second scene is in the lobby of Billy's apartment block: Slippy gets into an altercation with the lift attendant, they come to blows and he is thrown out. A detective appears, recognises Slippy and tells him he must spy on the party to save his own skin. Billy enters and Slippy tells him how he was beaten up by the lift attendant. When the attendant returns, Billy chastises him and (in the process of explaining what happened) Slippy suffers a repeat performance of the beating. Recovering his composure, he turns to the lift attendant and says: "See what you get for being funny?" Perks, Mrs Perks and a corpulent loudmouth named Blobbs arrive and collectively overload the lift. Blobbs is catapulted to the top of the lift shaft and the lift crashes down on the others' heads – a gag Charlie Chaplin used in *The Floorwalker* (1916). *The Stage* picks up the story:

> The last scene is the best ... Billy Browning gives a farewell party in his flat. After Fluffie de Vere has set all the guests dancing and singing "That mysterious rag," the table is turned upside down and roulette indulged in. When the excitement of the game is at its height, there is a cry of "The police!" The guests escape by a secret passage, leaving money, etc., on the table in their fright. When the police enter, they are found to be confederates of ... Billy's and they forthwith proceed to share the spoils, Billy refrains from participating, because he has fallen in love with Fluffie de Vere and means to reform.[17]

Billy and Fluffie were played by Fred Edwards and May Yates, both new to the Karno stable. Later versions starred a series of established male-female double acts (which guaranteed chemistry between the two), including Stanley Brett and Billie Sinclair. The sketch followed fashion both musically and stylistically, but while reviews suggest it was more sophisticated that Karno's previous productions, some coarse jokes remained. One reviewer singled out this gag as a candidate for removal: 'I thought she was a taxi, and wondered how far I could go for eightpence.'[18]

There was now a significant amount of snobbery among some critics towards Karno's 'low' comedy, but this reviewer enjoyed the show in spite of himself:

> There is a type of production known as the Karno sketch. It is not always produced by Mr Karno, but as he has, God help him, produced more

23. CHEERIO CHARLIE!

of it than anybody else, it may very well be known by his name. The ingredients ... are usually boisterous knockabout farce, not too well staged or acted, with a luridly melodramatic plot, usually concerning the wrongs of some incredibly innocent young lady ... The Karno sketch has been an immense financial success ... But it is not, to me at any rate, a particularly amusing form of entertainment, though here the box office is, of course, against me. I had always wondered what would happen if Mr Karno someday decided to cut his melodramatic plot, dress his productions better, and engage actors and actresses who could look and act their parts. Last week ... I saw "Flats," ... I can only say it realised my best hopes. The scenery was better than usual, the cast had some idea of how to act, and they had some lines which were quite well worth speaking ... If the excessively fat man, whose only function is to be kicked by the other characters, were cut, almost all of the blemishes of the older type of knockabout sketch would have vanished.[19]

Karno's name was now synonymous with a whole genre of comedy: performers who'd never worked with him advertised themselves as 'Karno-like' and proprietors called for companies with 'Karno-esque' material. But it was a style no longer in vogue – kicking a fat man up the arse was beginning to look old-fashioned. The huge irony, of course, is that this brand of comedy was the stock-in-trade of the silent movie comics, who at that very moment were being hailed as geniuses of originality by those same critics. Try to record how many times Chaplin and his peers kick someone's backside and you'll quickly lose count. He was fortunate to be working in an original medium, with what was often mistaken for original material.

While snootier critics had fallen out of love with Karno's slapstick, there were plenty of positive reviews for *Flats* and his older sketches too. Jimmy Russell and Edgar Cooke (the latest drunk in the box) were leading the plonks in *Mumming Birds*, which now had a new ending: the Terrible Turkey had been replaced by a playlet by 'Barry Shaw' entitled *Twixt Love and Duty* – plenty for the drunk to throw tomatoes at there. Albert Bruno was going through the motions in *Perkins in Paris,* and Tom Nelson was starring in a revival of *G.P.O.* But the standout sketch was Syd Chaplin's *The Hydro*, as this review confirms: 'Such a turn will need no recommendation, as the name Karno is known as the hallmark of theatrical brilliance.'[20]

Summer had arrived and Karno was also showing brilliance as the creator of the magnificent Karsino. Joe Lyons had helped put his catering arrangements into order, and with visitor numbers strong, Karno applied to the magistrates for permission to erect a marquee and add an extra bar. He was fast becoming the King of Tagg's Island – years later *The Stage* ran an article on the history of the place and noted: 'Karno ... did his guests extremely proud ... those were the great days, and every afternoon at three the proprietor used to make a sort of State progress down the river in a gondola so as to take a nap in a houseboat, the beauty of which was famous.'[21]

With Karsino running successfully, he turned his attention to his next production. Charlie Baldwin and Leonard Durrell did the honours with *The Steam Laundry*,[22] which opened in Southampton in September 1913. Perkins was back, this time as the good-for-nothing husband of an industrial laundry worker. Delivering his wife's lunch to the factory gate, he discovers that the girls have gone on strike in protest at mechanisation. *The Era* tells us the rest: 'The story is based upon the introduction into a laundry of a new patent washing and ironing machine ... As the work-shy Perkins, forced into the laundry as a woman by a wife who is tired of keeping him, and then put in charge of this latest invention, Mr Harold Wellesley makes the very most of the situations which naturally arise

23.4 A rare image of a Karno company on stage – The Steam Laundry (courtesy David Robinson).

23. CHEERIO CHARLIE!

for the introduction of much humour.'[23] Inevitably Perkins manages to fall into the machine and – in a scene which pre-dates Chaplin's *Modern Times* by over twenty years – finds himself thoroughly washed and ironed. The sketch may also have been an inspiration for the soapsud chaos of Stan Laurel's solo film *Collars and Cuffs* (1923).

Meanwhile, Chaplin's company was making steady progress around the States playing *A Night in an English Music Hall*, *A Night in a London Club* and *The Wow Wows*. The latter had been much improved, with Chaplin turning Archibald Binks into his well-established drunk character and adding plenty of new business, including Karno's ever-reliable punchball routine. The three sketches were now presented as 'Archie's latest adventures', as Binks became to Chaplin what Perkins had been to Fred Kitchen. It was Chaplin's first experience of playing a repeating character, and the warm audience response would not have been lost on him – perhaps encouraging him later to develop the most famous film persona of them all.

23.5 Across America by train. Left to right: Amy Minister, Emily Seaman, Muriel Palmer, Albert Austin, unknown (possibly Fred Karno Jr.), Bert Williams, Charlie Chaplin, George Seaman (standing) (courtesy Roy Export/Chaplin Archive).

Chaplin was glad to be back in America but less than enthusiastic about the tour. Back in 1910 the plonks had been a young company discovering the States for the first time, but audiences had been lacklustre (at least initially). Now it was the reverse: the reception was rapturous but the comics found it hard work. At nearly sixty, Whimsical Walker was plagued with ill-health and eventually invalided home. He recalled an arduous tour of rough towns and rougher crowds:

> We then went to Butte, 2000 feet above the sea ... we found that the theatre ... had been burnt down. Ill luck seemed bent upon pursuing us ... It was the roughest place I have ever been into. The climate, the hard travelling and the living didn't suit any of us, and the company began to feel very bad. The ladies lost their voices – the gentlemen could hardly

work, and some of them, including myself, began bleeding at the nose ... I became so bad that I thought my time had come.[24]

Chaplin found it a struggle too: 'I did absorb a great deal of tedium in the lower strata of show business. These cheap vaudeville circuits were bleak and depressing, and hopes about my future in America disappeared in the grind of doing three and sometimes four shows a day, seven days a week. Vaudeville in England was paradise by comparison.'[25]

However it wasn't all work and no play, as this report reveals:

When Alf Reeves ... was in London a short time ago, he was invited by Fred Karno to take a day's fishing at Tagg's Island ... each of them caught a pike. "Great work," said Karno, "We'll have three each by tonight." "Three each by tonight!" echoed Reeves, disgustedly. "I know where I can catch three pike a minute – and whoppers at that!" "Take me to the spot!" yelled Karno. "It's near Winnipeg, Manitoba," was the reply. "If you can give me proof of a three-a-minute catch," said Mr Karno. "I'll buy a wine supper for the entire company." ... Now for the sequel to the little story. Reeves was at Winnipeg on Aug. 6, and in fishing at Lockport with Charley [sic] Chaplin caught the required three fish in one minute. Mr Karno has since received this cable: "Karno, London, Eng. – You lose. – Reeves."[26]

Chaplin never claimed his wine supper, as we shall see. The same week that he and Reeves were catching pike in Winnipeg, an aspiring young comic called Groucho Marx witnessed *A Night in a London Club* and was amazed by Chaplin's performance: 'Chaplin sat at a small table and ate soda crackers ... A woman up front was singing ... but nobody heard a single note ... They were too intent on Chaplin's every move. A fine stream of cracker dust was coming out of his mouth. He kept that up for exactly fifteen minutes ... there will never be anyone like him. He's in a class all by himself.'[27]

Unsurprisingly, the movie studios soon had the man headlining Karno's tour in their sights, along with every gag in his repertoire – Chaplin can be found spitting crackers in both *The Pawnshop* (1916) and *The Pilgrim* (1923).[28]

Mack Sennett had been a fairly unsuccessful stage actor before joining the Biograph Company in 1908, where he learnt film-craft alongside D.W. Griffith.

23. CHEERIO CHARLIE!

23.6 U.S. advertisement for A Night in an English Music Hall (from the 'A.J.' Marriot archive).

In 1911 he was put in charge of Biograph's comedy department, and the following year established his own Keystone studios. Sennett was by no means the first to make slapstick comedies, as we've seen, but Keystone was the first studio dedicated to the art. Its output involved frantic, chaotic, non-stop physical action, personified by the famous Keystone Cops. Simon Louvish suggests Sennett stole the idea for the Cops from a 1907 Pathé film called *The Policemen's Little Run*[29] – Karno's *Jail Birds* pre-dates both.

As David Robinson notes, Sennett and Karno had a lot in common: both were from humble beginnings, rough around the edges, uneducated but intelligent, and able to manage troupes of unruly clowns. The Sennett stable included comedians who went on to be the most famous names in silent-movie history: Ford Sterling, Chester Conklin, cross-eyed Ben Turpin, Charley Chase, Mack Swain, Edgar Kennedy, Roscoe 'Fatty' Arbuckle and Mabel Normand (with whom Sennett had a long-running relationship later immortalised in the musical *Mack and Mabel*). Yet the insatiable demand for comedy shorts meant that Keystone and its rival studios continued to search for knockabout comics. In 1931 Karno wrote:

> Mack Sennett, I'm not going to say that he stole my business, but … his ideas of humour and my own were closely related … comedians I sent out from England were just the kind he wanted and he was able to offer them salaries which I could only pay by carrying on my business at a big loss. My manager sent me cable after cable for fresh men, and I began to feel the strain. At last, with many misgivings, I decided to send Charlie Chaplin over … and, as I anticipated he was a big success. As soon as he got out West, Sennett was after him … What happened afterwards the whole world knows.[30]

Karno laid the blame for the loss of not just Chaplin but all his comics on previous tours squarely on the shoulders of Sennett, but this is an error of memory – Keystone wasn't established until summer 1912. And while the whole world may know what happened next, the story of how Chaplin was stolen away varies in the telling – and all versions have two key elements for us to consider. First, when was Chaplin talent-spotted and by whom? Second, how did he escape from his Karno contract?

Let's start with the when and the whom. Mack Sennett claimed to have seen Chaplin in a Karno show at New York's American Music Hall in late 1912, and subsequently set about recruiting him. Chaplin also recalled being told that Sennett saw him at the American Music Hall, so many biographers have taken as fact that this was in 1912 on his second tour – but it is an error. A.J. Marriot's research shows that Chaplin did not play the American Music Hall that year, so either the date is right but the venue wrong, or Sennett misremembered and actually saw him on the first tour (as I suggested earlier).

Whatever the date, Sennett did not make contact with the young comic until much later. Various reports state that Chaplin was instead approached by a representative of Sennett, and there is no shortage of suspects competing to claim the credit. Some accounts say contact was made by Harry Aitken, a director of Keystone's parent company the New York Motion Picture Co. Others claim it was one of Sennett's Keystone partners: Charles Baumann or Adam Kessel Jr. However, all these claims are inconsistent with Chaplin's own account and those of his fellow plonks, which make no mention of an approach by anyone in New York – or anywhere else.

23.7 Karno's nemesis – Mack Sennett.

As usual, we can probably rely on A.J. Marriot for the most reliable version of this momentous moment in our story. At the beginning of April, in a lull between engagements, Chaplin had travelled to New York alone, spending the night at the opera and getting some much-needed rest. On 4 April he arrived back with the company in Philadelphia to find a telegram waiting: 'Is there a man named Chaffin in your company or something like that? If so will he communicate with Kessel and Baumann, 24 Longacre Building, Broadway.'[31] Chaplin turned around and headed back to New York, apparently with no inkling that he was about to be offered a contract with Keystone – instead he decided Kessel and Baumann were lawyers with news of a mystery inheritance. Once the true purpose of their message was made clear, he began negotiations enthusiastically.

He recalled that they haggled over his fee but reached an agreement in principle, and he left their office on cloud nine. The eventual agreement was $150 per week, double his Karno salary, and Chaplin felt he'd pulled off the deal of a lifetime. In reality this was by no means a massive offer: it was well below the salaries of many headline vaudeville artists, never mind movie stars.

Both Karno and his brother Albert later claimed that Keystone pestered Chaplin to death on tour until he finally gave in, but what really happened is that negotiations were ongoing after he returned to the company to see out his contract. This can't have been easy given that Chaplin was touring the country, and it was another four months before he felt able to write home to Syd:

> Dear Sid [sic] … good news … I have had an offer from a moving picture company for quite a long time but I did not want to tell you until the whole thing was confirmed … Keystone is the comedy company. I am to take Fred Mace's place … so you bet they think a lot of me … they wrote to me in Philadelphia … I went over to New York and saw them personally … a pal of mine told me that Fred Mace was getting four hundred a week well I asked then for two hundred … we haggled for quite a long time and then I had to do all my business by writing them … finally we came to an arrangement i.e. A year's contract. Salary for the first three months 150 per week and if I make good after three months 175 per week … Of course I told them I would not leave this company until we finished the SC [Sullivan and Considine] circuit, so I will join them about the beginning of Dec … I have told Alf and of course he doesn't want me to leave but he says I am certainly bettering myself … don't tell anybody about what Alf said because it may get back to the Guv'nor's ears and he will think Alf had been advising me.[32]

Despite his brother's excitement, Syd may not have been convinced he was making a good move. Back then a film career was not seen as a guaranteed route to fame and fortune, and Chaplin himself thought this spell with Keystone was merely a way to increase his currency at the theatrical box office, and that he would afterwards return to vaudeville as a major star. As he counted down the days until he could begin his new adventure, he inevitably lost some enthusiasm for Karno's sketches and this was reflected in reviews. There was one place, however, where he could not afford to put in a lacklustre performance – Los

Angeles, where he finally came face to face with his new employer. Mack Sennett watched the show and went backstage to congratulate him.

So how was it that Karno's cast-iron contract turned out to be worthless? Their contractual arrangement has been largely misrepresented thanks to confusion caused by Chaplin's autobiography. So let's unpick things. He initially told Keystone he would be able to join them in September 1913, believing this was when his commitment to Karno ended, and they drew up a contract to that effect. It was never signed though, because although he had entered into a three-year contract with Karno in September 1910, it did not commence until the following March (as we noted earlier). What's more, Chaplin's contract not only ran until March 1914, Karno had a further three-year option.

Chaplin retained the notion that when he left Karno after completing the Sullivan and Considine engagements in late November, he had worked beyond his contract end-date. Strangely, Alf Reeves was under the same impression, saying: 'Chaplin played several weeks more than his expiring contract with the company called for.'[33] However, the fact is that when Chaplin left Karno he had four months of his contract still to run. The company was committed to continue on to the Nixon Nirdlinger circuit well into the spring of 1914 and Chaplin's departure caused Karno real problems, so why did he let him go? A close look at that contract reveals Karno's critical mistake.

Chaplin's first contract had been for two years with a further year's option on pre-agreed terms; his second included a three-year option but without pre-agreeing its terms – instead Karno had written, by hand, six little words that changed history: 'At terms to be mutually arranged.'[34] In so doing he gave Chaplin an escape – he simply had to say he didn't accept the terms of the option – and that is how he slipped through Karno's fingers.

So Karno couldn't execute the option, but that doesn't explain why he let Chaplin leave four months early – not only a bad business decision, but totally out of character. Remember poor Albert Bruno, held against his will for years? Karno was furious with the studios for stealing his acts, and he would certainly have done them no favours. The only explanation I can suggest is that Chaplin had put himself in a difficult position with Keystone, and appealed to Karno's goodwill when he realised he was actually bound until March. Karno seems to have acquiesced, which (if this theory is correct) was a significant concession and perhaps explains why the two men remained on good terms. Another factor may have been Syd Chaplin, who was vitally important to Karno in England.

23. CHEERIO CHARLIE!

Syd's own contract expired in early August 1913, the same week that Chaplin wrote to say he was leaving for Keystone – coincidence? Karno's letters reveal that Syd was also being courted by someone. The details of this are unknown (we only have one side of the correspondence), but in one letter Karno wrote that he would reward Syd for his loyalty. In a subsequent one, he noted that Syd had been pleased with a gift: 'I am glad to hear that you liked the little present … I thank you for sending me the letter and wire with regard to the offer you have had. I too, do not know how they could have had the idea that you wanted a change.'[35]

Whoever was trying to tempt Syd, it occurs to me that he may have agreed to renew with Karno in return for the Guv'nor releasing his little brother early. He may even have done so on the understanding that the deal was kept strictly confidential, so that his brother remained unaware of Syd's sacrifice. If so, Charlie owed Syd a huge debt – as do a whole world of Chaplin fans.

Those six little words hurriedly scrawled on a contract allowed Chaplin to begin a career in the movies in December 1913. What if Karno had pre-agreed the terms of the option? Would Chaplin have been given the chance to join a studio three years later? Probably – Stan Laurel did – but how different would his career, and the history of comedy, be if Chaplin had not made a movie until 1917? Even more significantly, if he had stayed with Karno and returned to England he would almost certainly have been called up to fight in the First World War. Those six little words not only gave the world the Little Tramp, they may have saved his life.

Karno only felt the loss after Chaplin had gone on to fame and fortune: at the time he was just another good comic jumping ship, like many before him. It was frustrating and inconvenient but not the end of the world. Chaplin had little public profile and his departure garnered barely a mention in the theatrical press. After he found fame, of course, everyone was quick to claim they'd spotted his talent. As Charles B. Cochran recalled: 'It should be remembered that Chaplin had made no mark at all in his career before he went to America, although I have heard it said … by more people than would fill all the theatres Chaplin ever played in: "I remember picking Chaplin out by his wonderful performance as the drunken swell in Fred Karno's sketch."'[36]

Chaplin's last performance with Karno, and on any stage, was at the Empress Theatre in Kansas City on 29 November 1913. His contract with Keystone began on 16 December. Alf Reeves sent a cable to Karno in London that simply said: 'Charlie Gone.'[37]

24.

Fred Karno's Army

"I spoke to the Prime Minister today."
"What did he say to you?"
"Get out of the way."
(The Merry Book of the Moore & Burgess Minstrels, 1898)

IN HIS memoirs Karno was careful to avoid criticising Chaplin, pointing out that the star had resisted temptation for two years before being made an offer he couldn't refuse: 'The boy had his own way to make in the world, and he doubtless felt that … his future might lie in the films … The fact that he and Fred Karno are still fast friends is sufficient proof that there is no ill feeling.'[1]

Easy to say in 1939, but when it happened Karno was furious – so furious that it blinkered him to potential future opportunities in his own career. In an earlier interview he said: 'Had I not at the time of Chaplin leaving been so angry with the film pioneers, I too, might have ventured into film making.'[2]

Stan Laurel said he was sad to see Chaplin go, but he was in the minority: there was no benefit night or celebratory meal, as might be expected for a man who had led his company for three years. The fact is that Chaplin was not popular with many of his Karno colleagues. Fred Jr. couldn't stand him and Arthur Dandoe (a replacement on the tour) prepared a special leaving present – a gift-wrapped box containing old brown make-up sticks, which he described as "some shit for a shit." When Stan tried to talk Dandoe out of this joke, he replied: "It'll serve the superior bastard right."[3] In the event, he had a change of heart after Chaplin bought drinks for the company on the last night and then disappeared. Dandoe supposedly found him backstage, alone and in floods of tears. Whether this was because he was sad to leave or because (as it turned out) Fred Jr. had told him about Dandoe's gift is unclear.[4]

One person Chaplin did get on well with was Alf Reeves. As Reeves waved him off at the station Chaplin handed him a gift: a notebook with a hundred-dollar bill inside it and a note: 'A little tribute to our friendship.'[5] Stan believed his colleagues' animosity was misplaced. He felt they failed to realise that Chaplin was simply an extraordinarily shy man, and like many others who worked with him later, interpreted this as coldness – it was a problem Charlie recognised himself. Nonetheless, one wonders how Stan really felt about Chaplin's exit, given that he would be the man stepping up to lead comic – or so he thought.

The company's next engagement was that twelve-week tour of the Nixon-Nirdlinger circuit, and Alf Reeves assured them Stan would be just as good as Chaplin in the lead. I've only been able to find one contemporary account of Stan as the drunk in the box to support this assertion: Albert Whyberd, stage manager at the Queen's Theatre in Poplar (and father of the ventriloquist Ray Alan) recalled: '[Stan] was much more believable, much funnier, not so theatrical. Stan put in a few bits of business that Karno quite liked, but Chaplin couldn't do them as effectively. There was a tumble over the edge of the box and back again that Chaplin couldn't do in those days.'[6] Stan's abilities as a drunk are preserved in a number of his films, most notably *Pie Eyed* (1925) which also includes a number of *Mumming Birds* gags.

No matter how good Stan was though, he wasn't the name on the posters. Nixon-Nirdlinger rejected him, reduced Karno's fee by two hundred dollars per week and demanded he send out his lead comic from London. It was another bitter blow for Stan, who must have been disconsolate as the company sat on their hands in Philadelphia for three weeks, waiting for Dan Raynor to arrive.

Meanwhile Sennett wasted no time in getting a return on his investment – Chaplin films began being churned out at the rate of one a week. Karno's brother Albert Westcott recalled Chaplin's debut: 'Charlie wrote to Alf Reeves and told him to look out for his first picture … "Making A Living" – and no mistake, it did make him a living.'[7]

Making a Living was released on 2 February 1914, while the Karno company, now led by Raynor, was playing its seventh and final week in Philadelphia. Westcott recalled that they all went to see it and laughed when Chaplin appeared, not at the gags but at the novelty of watching their compadre on screen. They would have recognised his character too, for he was not yet the Little Tramp, instead playing a charming swindler in top hat and frock coat – a similar costume to Percy Bottlewit's in *The Football Match*. They were the only people in the cinema who had a clue who Chaplin was – everyone else was seeing him for the first time – but soon he would be the most recognisable face in the world.

In later years Chaplin hated this first film, feeling it had been thrown together and badly edited. Indeed Keystone's production methods were a huge culture shock for the young comic. Sennett's approach was largely to point the camera at his players and tell them to be funny, which generally meant lots of frenetic jumping up and down, falling into lakes, pushing people over, and chasing each other to the finale – one film historian described Keystone as 'a zoo without cages'.[8] Chaplin was the product of a more subtle school of slapstick, where sketches had plots, characterisation, pathos and meticulously choreographed acrobatic routines, perfected by weeks of daily rehearsal and months of polishing on the road. David Robinson notes that Chaplin had inherited Karno's attention to settings, scenery and blocking: 'He brought from Karno a highly developed skill in stagecraft.'[9]

24.1 Chaplin's film debut: Making a Living *(courtesy Roy Export/Chaplin Archive).*

This was not lost on Chaplin's co-star at Keystone Mabel Normand, who said: "They didn't really appreciate Charlie in those early days ... They were just so used to slapstick that imaginative comedy couldn't penetrate."[10] Chaplin found it frustrating, but it was this same creative vacuum that gave him the opportunity to shine. His talents were immediately recognised by critics, and as box-office success followed, Sennett gave him enough scope to develop his own ideas (and rehash plenty of Karno ones). At the heart of it all was pantomime. A few years later Whimsical Walker wrote: 'Much of the comic stuff which comes from America on the films is simply an exaggerated form of the old knock-about harlequinade ... The disappearances and transformations which followed a tap of the harlequinade's magic wand have been taken bodily and worked out in an outrageously burlesque form ... Even Charlie Chaplin

24. FRED KARNO'S ARMY

… at the bottom of his productions is the clown's business, and this is a sure laughter getter.'[11]

While Sennett's style was far less sophisticated than Karno's, watching these early Keystone films does demonstrate Chaplin's seemingly effortless ability to fall forwards, backwards, sideways, from great heights or down stairs – all a testament to his Karno training. Charles B. Cochran wrote:

> The Karno material and training were of immense help to Charlie … Do not the incidents of [Jimmy the Fearless] … seem a … basis for many of his … adventures on the screen? Of course, Chaplin's genius … would have eventually found an outlet, but he started in a new form of entertainment with a wonderful and unique equipment for it. A storehouse of priceless comic situations and 'business' were his, entirely through his apprenticeship to the Karno fun factory.[12]

One wonders if any of the other Karno apprentices, watching Chaplin's first film in the darkness of that Philadelphia cinema, had any inkling that they might follow in his footsteps.

Despite many biographers (and strangely Stan Laurel himself) claiming that Karno's American company broke up soon after Chaplin left, they did no such thing. They continued their tour until spring 1914, playing to consistently good reviews. Around the same time, Chaplin's first films were released in Britain,[13] and Keystone's advertising department made the most of his Karno pedigree: 'ARE YOU PREPARED FOR THE CHAPLIN BOOM? There has never been so instantaneous a hit as that of Chas Chaplin, the famous Karno comedian in Keystone Comedies.'[14] Under the headline: 'A New Comedian', one reporter anticipated that this ex-Karno plonk might be destined for great things:

> Charles Chaplin, who will be well remembered for the intensely funny work he did as the inebriated swell in Karno's "Mumming Birds," was marked out long ago as a man who could play "speechless" parts in pictures … Eight films in which he is the hero have now been finished … judging by the reports from the experts … "Chaplin" pictures are going to be as popular as "Bunny" films. He … goes through his part in the comic stories with that delightfully semi-dozed air which was so essential to the character in the "Mumming Birds."[15]

The 'Bunny films' were the Vitagraph comedies of John Bunny, a rotund star of the new medium whose Pickwickian joviality was immensely popular. Quite how big a star he might have become we'll never know – he died suddenly in 1915, aged 51. Bunny's days were numbered but Chaplin's rapid rise to superstardom was just beginning, as the British press noted: 'The one-time hero of "Mumming Birds" has leapt into the front rank of film comedians at a bound.'[16]

When Chaplin's former company ended their tour in mid-May, Fred Jr., his uncle Albert, Dan Raynor and George and Emily Seaman all sailed home together aboard the Adriatic – others chose not to return. Stan had not forgotten how tough life had been in London, and decided to stay in America and try his luck in vaudeville. With fellow plonks Edgar and Ethel (Wren) Hurley he formed the Three Comiques, and they put together a sketch called *The Nutty Burglars*. They had limited success until they reached New York, where they took the advice of booking agent Gordon Bostock and gave their skit a Chaplin twist. Renamed 'The Keystone Trio', they impersonated three of that studio's stars – Chaplin, Chester Conklin and Mabel Normand. Stan knew every nuance of Chaplin's style of course, but it's poignant that while the Tramp soared to superstardom, his old friend had to scrape a living by imitating him. A review in *The Stage* suggests Stan may also have taken inspiration from another old comrade:

> Keystone Trio ... Depending on a skit that Harry Weldon is doing in England, a Charlie Chaplin make-up and their own slapstick capabilities these two men and a woman have fixed up a desirable rough comedy sketch. It deals mostly with burglars. The main idea is the part obtained from Weldon ... The act proved a big hit.[17]

24.2 Stan with Edgar and Wren Hurley as 'The Three Comiques', 1914 (from the 'A.J.' Marriot archive).

In the months before Stan sailed off on tour, Weldon was proving hugely popular performing a solo sketch called *Jack Sheppard*, in which he played an inept burglar who fails to break into a house despite the assistance of the owner and a policeman (who kindly keeps watch). So, it is quite likely that Stan saw Weldon's act and incorporated elements into his own sketch.

Stan stood out in the Keystone Trio, much to Edgar Hurley's annoyance, and when Hurley insisted on taking the Chaplin part, Stan quit[18] and formed the Stan Jefferson Trio with a couple called Alice and Baldwin (Baldy) Cooke. They performed a similar sketch (*The Crazy Cracksman*) through to spring 1916,[19] when Stan formed a short-lived double act with Bob Martini. Along the way he met and fell in love with an Australian called Mae Dahlberg, and they paired up professionally and privately, touring as man and wife into 1918. In the meantime, Stan secured his first film role (which we'll come to later) and changed his name to Laurel. Some claim this was because Stan Jefferson had thirteen letters and he thought it unlucky; Stan said he changed it because it always appeared in small letters on posters – a shorter name literally meant bigger billing. One night in a dressing room Mae was flicking through a book and lit upon a picture of a Roman general with a laurel wreath on his head – the rest is history.

Karno had bigger things to worry about than Chaplin and Laurel. Karsino's first season had been a runaway success, but there were signs that his financial position was strained. He had already divested himself of his theatres, now he significantly reduced his press advertising. The touring companies were shrunk in size – the days of hundreds of supers were gone for good – and most telling of all, he only produced a single, small-scale pantomime for Christmas 1913, *Mother Goose* at the Marlborough. It was to be his last. Karsino was proving to be a debt-laden millstone around his neck.

Chaplin wasn't the only loss that autumn. In September J. Hickory Wood, king of pantomime writers, died – it was a blow to Karno and the industry at large. As he closed up Karsino for the winter, the impresario must have had mixed feelings about the departing year. He had realised a dream but at great financial cost; he'd launched successful new shows but was becoming yesterday's man; and the threat from the movie studios had made itself more evident than ever. Surely things could only get better in 1914?

The first sign of Karno coming out of winter hibernation was a press report in March, which shows that he had lost none of his appetite for a confrontation:

> Mr Fred Karno … was summoned before Mr Hopkins at Bow-street [magistrates court] for using threats towards Mr John Hart, proprietor of the Star Music Hall, Bermondsey … The complainant gave evidence

> that there was a dispute between him and Mr Karno about £2 ... He had twice defended county court summonses taken out by Mr Karno and beaten him on each occasion. At Hurst Park last year Mr Karno asked him for the £2, and upon the witness refusing, struck him on the back of the neck, but did not hurt him. A few days ago, the witness went to a restaurant in the Strand and saw Mr Karno there with a friend. He asked him how he was and offered to shake hands with him, but Mr Karno remarked, "I shan't shake hands until you pay me those two sovereigns." He further said that if he got him outside, he should serve him as he did at Hurst Park.[20]

It was a storm in a teacup. The magistrate decided Karno had no case to answer and awarded him costs, but the fact that he was willing to do battle over a couple of quid suggests he was either stubborn and belligerent or very hard-up indeed.

Within a few weeks Karsino opened for its second season, having established itself as the place to see and be seen. Festooned with garlands and hanging baskets by day, fairylights and lanterns by night, Astoria and the other magnificent houseboats surrounding the island were an attraction in themselves. J.M. Barrie returned to Molesey around that time, after a long absence, and found his former writer's retreat much changed:

> It was now as grand as if it were being presented nightly at Drury Lane. There remained no houseboats of our humble kind; magnificent successors encircled Tagg's Island ... there is a gorgeous hotel, and there are putting-greens and lawn-tennis courts and dancing galore ... I had thought it a gay place in my day and that I had been seeing life. Now I know that by comparison we were all humdrum folk, living prosaically round a field with a cow in it.[21]

Karno and Marie Moore began appearing like civic dignitaries at all manner of local functions, as well as running a busy programme of events on the island. Karsino was often given over to fundraisers, and the Music Hall Ladies' Guild were regular recipients of his generosity. Press reports show that relations with Edith's former entourage were exceedingly warm. Karno loved his life on the river and amassed an entire flotilla, including houseboats such as 'Bohemia' to provide additional guest accommodation, and a motor-cruiser, Lady Campbell,

24.3 Busy Karsino lawns just before the outbreak of war, 14 July 1914 (author's collection).

which he later sold to the comic Jimmy Nervo. But this watery utopia's days were numbered. Adeler and West noted: 'Karno's best customers were German and French people, who never dreamed they would be at one another's throats … The little cloud … that was to be a blight not only on Karsino but on … the whole world was practically invisible.'[22]

By May 1914 things were changing, as people became increasingly aware of rising tensions between the European powers. Karsino offered respite from such worries, as this reporter opined: 'Karsino … a panorama of exquisite beauty … putting to shame many a foreign casino of world-wide repute … In these pessimistic days it is somewhat cheering to think that the Continental open-air café providers have been beaten at their own game. A bold venture, Mr Karno. But let it be hoped that your pluck will be amply rewarded. It is richly deserved.'[23]

For its proprietor, however, there was little sign of reward, and the challenges of running the place quickly wore thin. Adeler and West noted:

> Amid all the glamour … of Karsino at the height of its popularity with money rolling in, the summer air throbbing with the music of the bands – when youth and love and laughter were supreme … FK would sometimes sigh for the comparative peace and restfulness of those former times when he used to do twenty-two shows a day for twenty-five

shillings a week ... He would have sighed still more deeply had he been able to peer into the future.[24]

The timing of his investment in Karsino couldn't have been worse. Not only was war on the way, but the music hall was undergoing significant change as 'revue' came to the fore. Unlike a music hall bill of disparate acts, a revue was a variety show performed week after week by a fixed cast, often linked by a single story and featuring sketches, songs and dance numbers. In February 1914, one such revue (at the Walthamstow Palace) included a satire on our hero and his pleasure palace:

> *Gee Whiz!* ... takes us to Karsino ... a merry little burlesque upon the life and work of Mr Fred Karno. That gentleman (impersonated by Mr Kennedy Allen, who appears very like the original) is knighted for his efforts on behalf of the English drama, and a deputation of easily recognized members of his company ... ask him to stand for Parliament. Much laughter is caused by his efforts at speech making and the introduction of familiar Karno business adds considerably to the entertainment.[25]

Sir Fred Karno! That would have raised some eyebrows at the palace. He must have been well-known enough, not just by name but by sight, for the audience to recognise the parody. Interestingly, the review suggests the skit got laughs from Karno's attempts at public speaking, and one wonders whether it was sending up parliamentary candidates in general or his particular inability to make a speech. Karno's response to the revue is not recorded, but he usually considered all publicity to be good publicity.

Given that musical comedies such as *His Majesty's Guests* were an

24.4 Cartoon from The Bystander, *July 1912 (© Illustrated London News Ltd/Mary Evans Picture Library).*

amalgamation of shorter sketches interspersed with acrobatic routines, song and dance, it was no great leap for Karno to jump on the bandwagon and simply re-label these longer shows as revue. He continued to tour the sketches though, and if they weren't yet running out of steam, some of his comics were. By April 1914 Tom Nelson had been engaged by Karno for eighty-six weeks, doing four or five shows per day, and it took its toll. As signs of ill-health began to show, Karno gave him three weeks off to rest and a new comic called Bob Selvidge took over as Perkins. On Nelson's return he placed an advert in *The Stage* to thank Karno for his holiday, and proclaimed that he was 'going strong'.[26] Nelson wasn't the only trouper putting in the hours. Two other Perkins were still doing the rounds, Harold Wellesley and the somewhat reluctant Albert Bruno, while Syd Chaplin continued in *The Hydro* and Edgar Cooke and Jimmy Russell were keeping *Mumming Birds* airborne. However this latest batch of Karno leads still stood in the shadow of Fred Kitchen, four years after he'd abandoned them, as this review reveals: 'One ... misses the inimitable Fred Kitchen from the Karno sketches of today, but in Syd Chaplin they have a detective who, if not quite a Sergeant Lightning, is calculated to reduce his victims to submission by making them laugh themselves into a state of helplessness.'[27]

24.5 *Say when, girls* – The Hydro (courtesy David Robinson).

Kitchen, Weldon, Reeves, Ritchie, Chaplin – Karno old boys littered the pages of the theatrical press, performing on stage and screen in all corners of the empire and beyond. As their individual fame increased, so their old Guv'nor's currency began to lose lustre. It was inevitable that Syd would find joining his little brother in Hollywood harder and harder to resist, assuming of course that he was allowed out of the country – the world had suddenly changed.

Rising tensions on the Continent came to a head with the assassination of Archduke Ferdinand of Austria by a Bosnian Serb on 28 June 1914. A month later Austria-Hungary declared war on Serbia; Germany supported the Austrians and Russia the Serbs – it quickly escalated into a major international conflict. On 4 August, one day after Germany invaded neutral Belgium, Britain joined forces with France and Russia against the combined might of Germany, Austria-Hungary and the Ottoman Empire (modern Turkey). The war machine mobilised immediately: in that first week of August, General Kitchener's call to arms appeared in the press. A hundred thousand volunteers were needed to supplement the regulars – and that was just the beginning.

The war was anticipated well in advance by the gossips on Karsino's lawns, and when news came through of the declaration, proceedings were unsurprisingly subdued. However, most people expected it to be no different to previous conflicts such as the Boer War: they foresaw a distant, short-lived campaign fought by the regular army – it would all be over by Christmas. There seemed no need to take dramatic action, and the government encouraged business as usual. Nonetheless, some theatres closed immediately and those that stayed open had to deal with a flurry of artistes and technicians rushing to volunteer. The number of performances and the scale of productions was cut, and urgent meetings were called by artistes, agents and proprietors to explore the implications for the industry. This initial confusion soon subsided and venues returned to a form of normality, although arguments raged between those who felt that frivolous entertainment was inappropriate in time of war and those who considered the light relief much-needed. 'Laugh and the world laughs with you, weep and you weep alone,' said the advertisements. Theatres played their part in the propaganda war, too: newsreels appeared in the music halls, alongside jingoistic singers and patriotic speakers.

Within two weeks of the declaration there were reports that Karsino was being turned over, in part, to the war effort: 'Mr Fred Karno's theatre on Karsino Island is being used by workers … making garments for the fighting forces while the orchestra plays.'[28] Despite this, Karsino continued to offer its usual services as far as possible. Karno recalled that the 'Big Five' (the heads of department at Scotland Yard) had long been regulars at the hotel, but where once they spent their evenings pointing out international crooks and conmen, they now enlisted his help in spotting fifth-columnists mingling among the guests.

Karno recalled that the country was swiftly gripped by spy mania – everyone seemed to be under suspicion and a strange accent or different skin tone was

24. FRED KARNO'S ARMY

enough to mark you out as a potential spy. Music hall speciality acts with exotic names were quick to anglicise them, but some careers still came to a premature end. One prominent example was Paul Cinquevalli, the greatest juggler of his age and a star of the 1912 Command Performance. Polish by birth but brought up in Germany, he found himself ostracised, and died in 1918 a broken man. No doubt Karno found another name for Karsino's Bavarian beer garden pretty quickly, and he recalled how his many German staff began to leave: 'They began to drift away, receiving call-up papers and so on, but they seemed to take the matter light heartedly, thinking the war would be only a matter of a few weeks … They were much liked at Karsino … and when they departed it was with many an "auf Wiedersehen" and mutual expressions of goodwill.'[29]

The threat was genuine enough, but in the age of gentlemen, spies were dealt with slightly differently. James Jupp, legendary stage-door keeper of the Gaiety Theatre, recalled suspecting that a member of the company called Count Rysbach was a spy – and being unsurprised when he borrowed a dress suit from Jupp's friend, sold a flat full of rented furniture, and disappeared. Some months later Rysbach reappeared at the Gaiety as if nothing had happened. Jupp didn't hesitate in his duty and immediately took the man out to lunch. After making clear his suspicions, Jupp instructed the spy to return his pal's suit and hand himself in to the police. Such gentlemanly conduct stood him in good stead – Rysbach received penal servitude for life, while most of his contemporaries were shot.[30]

Karno recalled how one German guest, a rich iron merchant called Oumann, would politely point out over a friendly game of billiards that his countrymen were certain to defeat the British. Such cordial fraternisation was stamped out as the war progressed and aliens from enemy nations were either interred or fled. Oumann did a midnight flit through a window just as the police arrived to detain him, later sending Karno a postcard to say he'd escaped to Holland in a fishing boat.

The war did not begin well for the Allies. Within a few months the British Expeditionary Force had been practically annihilated in France, and the need for volunteers intensified. There was significant public pressure on able-bodied men to enlist, and male performers could face a hostile audience if they looked capable of doing their duty. Programmes began to include a note saying that all men in the cast were either too old or medically unfit to enlist. *The Era* listed those artistes and theatre staff doing their duty under the heading 'The profession with the colours', and many Karno comics volunteered or were later conscripted. Harry Oxberry and Arthur Dandoe enlisted as early as October 1914, and Alf Reeves' letters record a number of others, including Jock (probably Fenton) MacKay, Dan Raynor, Jimmy Beresford, Jimmy Russell and Frank Prior. Many others signed up for war work in industries such as munitions.

Even though he was in the States, Charlie Chaplin reportedly volunteered but was declared unfit. He was nonetheless subjected to significant hostility from the British press – despite the fact that he did far more good from Hollywood than he ever might at the front. His comedies were invaluable to the propaganda machine and a tonic for those suffering the physical and mental scars of battle. He also toured the States promoting war bonds and made an accompanying propaganda film, *The Bond* (1918).

Unlike Chaplin, Stan Laurel was not a famous film star when war broke out – he was still touring in small-time vaudeville. He registered for military service but was exempted on health grounds. His registration card states 'Alien and deaf', which is something of a mystery. There is no record of Stan suffering from deafness, a fact confirmed to me by his daughter Lois, who understood that he'd been stood down because of his flat feet (although this is not on his record).[31] We'll never know whether he fooled the draft board, but it is hard to resist imagining the comic antics of Stan Laurel feigning deafness to an angry recruiting sergeant.

In late 1915 the strongarm tactics of the government's Derby Scheme generated another 300,000 volunteers, but it was still not enough – conscription came into force in January 1916. These men were the mainstay of the British army for the remainder of the war: a ragtag band of amateurs, commanded by officers increasingly struggling to find effective strategies in a conflict like none before it. Several newspapers ran pieces written by soldiers at the front, such as the anonymous volunteer who had a regular column in the *Coventry Evening Telegraph*. He recorded his experience of basic training: how the dormitory was never clean enough for his officers, and how soldiers had to beg, borrow and steal materials to scrub the place to a sparkle – their comrades christening them 'Fred Karno's Troop'. The jibe was commonplace – every shambolic unit trying to get organised in the face of material shortages, poor training and suspect leadership found itself compared to the Karnos. Here is a similar reference in a report from a member of the Motor Machine Gun Service in France:

24. FRED KARNO'S ARMY

> You cannot really imagine what the sights are out here … In a good number of streets houses were burning … our chaps were saving the furniture for the people … a couple of Tommies struggling to push a big wardrobe out of a bedroom window while the houses on each side were falling in … In the midst of all this an old chap about seventy struggled up with the 'fire engine' – an old fashioned hand pump made in the years B.C. He was got up for the job too! A big peaked cap, a tunic of a sort, and round his waist a very broad sash, all the colours of the rainbow … Talk about 'Karno's Fire Brigade!' Every soldier roared with laughter, although it was a tragic and pitiful sight.[32]

The chaos of war, and an army of men finding black humour in otherwise desperate situations, cemented Karno in the lexicon of the trenches. Sergeant Harry Fulford wrote:

> We live in caves and are garbed in an attire that is a cross between a Manchurian dandy's and a mediaeval archer's. Our legs are encased in gumboots, our bodies in goat skins, and on our heads are shrapnel helmets. When the wind is from the east, we don our gas bags which make us look like familiars of the Inquisition days. "Who are you?" inquires the driver of a passing ambulance; and the invariable report is "Fred Karno's".[33]

Another soldier wrote to the *Liverpool Echo* with match reports of his comically inept 'Karno's Korporals FC'. Makeshift theatre companies and concert parties formed within the ranks, and *The Stage* printed appeals for resources. Karno despatched costumes and props to groups including the Tykes concert party, 'the licensed fun makers of the 49th Division,' and another group at the British General Hospital in Calais.[34] One troupe was so successful it secured professional bookings after the war: 'A Message from the Rhine – Still smiling after four years on eastern and western front. Organised six concert parties, four revues, fifteen sketches, etc. Many thanks to Fred Karno … for costumes.'[35]

There were real Karno comics among the amateurs too. A report posted from the front during the Battle of the Somme describes a Kent battalion's push against German defences, telling of heroic deeds and horrific sights. But most of all it stresses the importance of humour in maintaining the men's spirits:

> Advance from Pozieres – Exploits of Men of Kent ... They have funny fellows among them ... and the amount of comedy they extract from all this grim business is astonishing. There is one of their number who was once a member of Fred Karno's troupe and has not lost his old instincts for a knock-about turn. When he took a prisoner, he caught him by the hand and danced a "pas de quatre" with him. "Offizier?" asked the astounded man. "Oui," said the comic turn, "and you? Prisonnier – savez?"[36]

In September 1916 sapper Lister Coleman wrote an account of a voyage around the Cape of Good Hope en route to East Africa: 'We have had several fine concerts on board ... A ragtime band was formed, and ... among the professionals were one or two members of Fred Karno's Mumming Birds, and they gave us a show one evening.'[37] Another example tells of an improvised theatre in France where all manner of performances were staged by the soldiers: 'A large cavalry riding school ... has been transformed ... into a fine theatre holding over 1000 and ... shows are given every week ... Many of the performers are professionals. Recent productions include Fred Karno's Mumming Birds.'[38]

Hylton Ward of a Karno revue called *Hot and Cold* was called up in June 1916, and after eighteen months in the trenches was appointed producer and organist to the 3rd Army. Karno comic Frank Douglas was awarded the Military Medal for Gallantry in November 1917. With so many Karno old boys in the thick of it, there must have been many casualties among the plonks' ranks. The most notable perhaps was a veteran of Chaplin's U.S. tours, Fred Palmer, who died of pneumonia while serving at the front in April 1917 – he was forty-one. It is hard to comprehend a war being fought by red-nose music hall comedians going 'over the top' to their deaths.

The wounded gradually returned, and where possible went back on the stage. Jimmy Russell served in East Africa, where he contracted malaria, then in France where pneumonia finally got him invalided home. He carried *Mumming Birds* through the rest of the war. One Karno cast member had a particularly dramatic tale to tell:

> Mr Albert Brouett ... this admirable French light comedian ... was appointed to the 23rd Company of Stretcher Bearers ... and he saw a great deal of bitter fighting in the Bois-le-Pêtre ... the bearers have to work in the firing trenches ... a shell burst ... and a big splinter struck

24. FRED KARNO'S ARMY

him on the chest. It did not penetrate, largely owing to the fact that a thick letter case received the impact ... he woke up to find himself in hospital at Nancy with a damaged lung ... Mr Brouett returned to England and was engaged by Mr Fred Karno for the part of the French professor in "Parlez Vous Français?" to which his smart performance is of great value.[39]

Goodness knows how Brouett must have felt walking on stage to make people chuckle after that experience. Perhaps laughter really was the best antidote to the madness. Karno certainly thought so, writing to the press: 'Fred Karno has sent a telegram to the Allies to say that he has decided to let Tagg's Island remain neutral.'[40]

24.6 The 'volunteer' – Fred Karno Jr. (from the 'A.J.' Marriot archive).

As the war continued conscription was extended: married men were included, some professions lost their exemption, and the age was gradually increased until (in 1918) it reached fifty-one. Karno himself only narrowly avoided the draft, while Leslie tried unsuccessfully to sign up in 1918, when he was fifteen.[41] So it fell to Fred Junior to carry the Karno flag into battle and do the family proud.

His war began inauspiciously. Gallagher claimed that Junior was 'more or less forced' to enlist by Karno, but neglects to mention that this followed a family scandal – Junior had got his seventeen-year-old cousin Mary pregnant. Mary Cuthbert was the daughter of Edith's youngest brother Joseph, and part of the extended family living in Green Lane, Stockport. Fred Jr. had spent most of his formative years there and clearly remained close, too close, to his cousin. Fred Jr. joined up on 23 November 1914, leaving Mary six months pregnant. The baby was born on 11 February 1915, and named Ellen Westcott Cuthbert. A month later Stockport magistrates issued an order requiring Fred Jr. to pay Mary five shillings per week until the child was sixteen, and four pence per day was accordingly stopped from his army wages. But that was the extent of his contribution, and it appears he never met his daughter.[42]

So Fred Jr. opted for the battlefields of Europe to escape his family's wrath – but if he'd hoped to flee overseas, he was disappointed. He spent the first eighteen months of his service in Britain. Like his father, Junior was able to handle horses, and he enlisted clutching a glowing reference from Fred Tandy, manager of Clegg and Co., general merchants of Coldharbour Lane: 'To whom it may concern, I have pleasure in stating that Fred Westcott, whom I have known for a number of years is a capable and efficient driver both of single and pair horses, understands grooming, feeding and general stable management.'[43] Young Fred became a wagon driver in the Horse Transport section of the Army Service Corps (ASC), the logistics heroes who performed miracles to get food, equipment and ammunition to where it was needed – the front line. Despite this, some considered the ASC to be a cushy number (its ports and supply depots were well behind the line), and those serving in combat units nicknamed it 'Ally Sloper's Cavalry' after a comic-strip character who was a lazy schemer.

The uniform didn't instil much discipline in Junior: he was reported absent without leave for two weeks in August and for three weeks in October and November 1915. The cause was another love affair, this time with the actress Jane (Queenie) Doyle, who was appearing in a revue called *Oh That Girl!* at the Margate Hippodrome. Not content with leaving his unit to woo Queenie, he added a little joyriding to his record:

24.7 Queenie Doyle in Oh That Girl!, *1914 (courtesy Ken Westcott).*

At Old Street Police Court ... Frederick Westcott ... was charged with stealing a horse and cab, and further, with being an absentee from his regiment. P.C. Rumry said that ... at 10 o'clock in Little Pearl Street, Spitalfields, he saw an overturned cab in the middle of the thoroughfare. The prisoner was holding the horse and was unable to give a satisfactory account of himself. He was taken to the police station, where he collapsed ... when charged, he said: "I do not remember taking the cab or anything that happened. If I have done anything wrong, my people are well-to-do, and they will pay for everything" ... The

24. FRED KARNO'S ARMY

witness added that the prisoner was a son of Fred Karno, who ... was prepared to recompense the owner of the cab ... it was evidently a spree ... The magistrates remarked that it was not a case of stealing, and on that charge the accused would be discharged. He and his friends must arrange with the cab proprietor as to the damage.[44]

In August 1916 the fun and games were over: he was shipped to Salonika, where he spent the next nineteen months. Salonika was one of the bloodiest but least remembered theatres of the war, where the British faced mostly Bulgarian forces in treacherous mountain terrain. It was cold, miserable and dangerous, a place where disease accounted for as many casualties as bullets. ASC troops stationed in the stores may have been relatively safe but drivers like Fred Jr. certainly were not. He would have driven horse-drawn carts through mud and snow, over mountain passes and through cratered landscapes to supply the lines.

Sitting on top of his cart – his head very literally above the parapet – one wonders how often his mind wandered to his former comrades basking in Hollywood sunshine and worldwide fame.

25.

The Millionaire Tramp

*"Don't open your mouth so wide," said the dentist.
"I intend to remain outside."*
(The Merry Book of the Moore & Burgess Minstrels, 1898)

SO MUCH for the heroes. Karno's war was rather different: in the spirit of 'business as usual' he chose the early weeks of the war to launch a new sketch, his first for almost a year. *Teeth* premiered at Chester on 17 August 1914, 'depicting the stupendous struggle of biceps and forceps against masticating molars.'[1] It was another story of industrial unrest: Bob Selvidge played Simpkins (Perkins by another name), the leader of an industrial dispute at Tuggit and Co. Dental Institute, who along with his fellow overworked dental technicians decides to set up a rival company (Simpkins, Simpkins and Simpkins) next door. The sketch had four scenes: 'the workshop', 'the rival dentists', 'interior of Simpkins', and 'the colossal American Institute'.

Initial reviews were mixed: 'Though it is not up to the standard of some of his most notable sketches, it is full of fun … Bob Selvidge … "Simpkins the toothless dentist" being really admirable … how some of the patients are treated, in a very novel dentist's chair, the administration of "gas", etc. is screamingly funny.'[2] The title was uninspiring and within a month *Teeth* became *The Dental Institute* (with scenes three and four combined into one), but still it struggled, as this review demonstrates: 'The piece hardly ranks high as a provoker of mirth … It has little in it, and Selvidge has too great a burden to carry.'[3]

It would be easy to assume that Chaplin's *Laughing Gas* (1914) was inspired by *Teeth*, some biographers even claim he appeared in the sketch, despite the fact

25. THE MILLIONAIRE TRAMP

he left Karno a year before it was staged. In fact, *Laughing Gas* pre-dates *Teeth* by two months (it was made in June 1914), so Chaplin's film couldn't be based on the sketch – or could it? A letter that Karno wrote to Syd Chaplin back in April is revealing:

> Dear Syd, just a reminder that I should like to have a … brief script of the little idea I suggested to you a little while back … to be called "Teeth". I thought of having a divided set, one the operating room, and the other the waiting room. The Dentist and his assistants are waiting for customers … some come in with bandages, and there is some comic business with regard to their waiting in agony, and the prospects of having their teeth out … You can utilize the idea with the hats which I mentioned before, and so on. Please let me have some little idea as soon as you return to town.[4]

In *Laughing Gas* Chaplin dispenses his own brand of dentistry, alternating between the surgery and the adjacent waiting room – exactly the set-up Karno asked Syd to work on a few weeks earlier. When Karno's sketch subsequently appeared it bore little resemblance to his original idea – and the Guv'nor, not Syd, was cited as the author.

Circumstantially, it looks like Syd may have leaked the idea to his brother, who quickly turned it into a film, and Karno's sketch then required a different scenario. How Syd got away with that is anybody's guess, but perhaps by then he didn't care. By the time *Teeth* was staged he was packing his bags – on 12 September he set sail for Hollywood. Chaplin had recommended Syd to Mack Sennett and he stepped into his little brother's shoes to star in several Keystone comedies, creating the character Reginald Gussle (a man not unlike Archibald Binks). Sennett had snared a second Chaplin at Karno's expense. Such was business. Sennett himself was not immune from losing artistes to better offers elsewhere – he once remarked: "Start with Sennett and get rich somewhere else."[5] Karno couldn't have said it better.

All the same, the Guv'nor had lost one of his most loyal and successful artistes. Syd was a rare personality: well-liked, business-minded, a brilliant slapstick comic and a superb writer – although he had a darker side which would later deal Karno a cruel blow. His impact on Charlie, as a person and a comic, is immeasurable. From his early paternalistic influence, through professional mentoring with Karno and later managing his brother's business interests, Syd's role in Chaplin's story cannot be overstated. It is also fair to say that he played a larger part in Karno's success than Charlie ever did.

The brothers remained on good terms with Karno in later years. Alf Reeves wrote to Syd: 'I would have certainly conveyed your remembrance to F.K. and he would have been pleased. One of his special treasures is Charlie's letter to him, he shows it to guests at the island … I don't think there is any soreness, in fact, I'm sure not. I reckon he had some of your best endeavours, and there can be no complaints coming.'[6]

The loss of Syd and the onset of war did little to dampen Karno's enthusiasm for new work. The week Syd set sail, *Home from Home* premiered at the Portsmouth Hippodrome, starring Tom Nelson. It was a farce written by Henry Chance Newton, an old hand at musical comedy:

> It deals with the trials and tribulations of a much-married but happy go lucky gentleman named Sammy Grimes, who, after many lean years, at last finds himself able to take his wife and seven children to the seaside … There are the feverish activities of packing-up … followed by several … unsuccessful interviews with various types of seaside landladies, who are either "full up" or otherwise unable to take the trippers into their care. Finally, the whole family are side-tracked into decidedly unsuitable quarters in one of those nursing homes for highly respectable persons who make a hobby of their "complaints", and, after some extravagant experiences, wisely decide to finish their vacation at home.[7]

Within a month the sketch reached London, by which time Nelson had left to set up his own company[8] – start with Karno, get rich somewhere else.

The first Christmas of the war was approaching, the Christmas when unofficial truces sprang up along the lines and British and German troops played football in no-man's land. At home the mood was increasingly sombre as it became apparent that the war would be a long haul. For the first time in ten years Karno did not produce a pantomime: perhaps such Christmas frivolity seemed inappropriate, or perhaps they were just too expensive to stage. Instead he turned his attention to revue.

Revue was not a new phenomenon – Marie Lloyd had appeared in *Under the Clock* (considered one of the first) as far back as 1893 – but it came to be the dominant form of entertainment during the war. These shows were relatively cheap to stage, relied on fewer headliners and were easier to adapt if cast members enlisted or were called up. They had other advantages too: their female chorus lines and juveniles meant the shortage of men was not a problem, and they could be adapted week by week to include topical sketches or changing trends in music and dance (helping American imports such as ragtime to come to the fore). By comparison, music hall variety programmes felt slow and old-fashioned – the rot had set in. This is not to say that revue was necessarily better than music hall. Its reliance on larger casts at a time when male performers were scarce meant that mediocre artistes often made up the numbers – and combined with a highly formulaic style, this meant the quality was often poor. Many revues relied too heavily on scenery and costumes to create a spectacle, rather than strong material. Those that did well benefitted from a genuinely outstanding performer and a strong comedy element. Karno was well placed to sprinkle his own touch of magic onto the new genre, and had already rebranded some old shows as revues – now he set about creating a totally original show.

The halls were awash with exiled French and Belgian artistes and the auditoriums were filling up with refugees and soldiers on leave. A French theme was inevitable, but finding one proved to be a challenge. Karno bought a basic script for £150 from an author he'd been introduced to via one of his comics. He then employed a second writer to work it up into a presentable format, which cost him another £100. Syd Walker was engaged to star, but the first read-through was a disaster and the script barely raised a titter – Walker dismissed it as "piffle!" Karno and Walker started again,[9] cooking up the premise of a theatre company trying to learn French before embarking on a continental tour – a twist on the experience of the thousands who found themselves in France for very different reasons. They called it *Parlez Vous Français?*, and Karno engaged the French actress Liane D'Eve as the teacher and a dance troupe 'direct from Paris'. *The Era* tells us more:

> In the first scene we are introduced to a night school, where boys and girls are being taught the French language. A somewhat coarse pupil, named James Mustard … instead of endeavouring to acquire a knowledge of French shows a disposition to make love to the girl pupils … In the second scene, we find all the people on board a steamer … bound for Nice … a visit is made to the costumier's for garments … and at the carnival at Nice a rollicking time is spent.[10]

The show opened on 7 December at the Olympia, Liverpool. It was not only Karno's first original revue but also a return to larger-scale productions – it ran for ninety minutes and had a cast of fifty. Critics were complimentary: 'Fred Karno's rollicking revue ... comes as a most interesting entertainment. The awkwardness which our "Tommies" experience while endeavouring to converse in French can readily be understood after one has witnessed this high-class entertainment, in which the language difficulty proves one of the many sources of humour.'[11]

Parlez Vous Français? toured into the new year and through the spring, arriving in the West End (at the Oxford) in May 1915. In the meantime, Karno capitalised on this success by restaging *Saturday to Monday,* a revue by any other name, and the cast included an eighteen-year-old circus-trained acrobat and juggler, billed as 'Nervo'. Jimmy Nervo would go on to a glittering career, and Karno would play another part in his fame in years to come.

Despite his earlier theatre management failures, in early 1915 Karno took over the lease of the Colchester Hippodrome. It was a venue he'd been using for try-outs, and in March he launched his next revue there, *Hot and Cold*,[12] which was described as a 'revue of beauty culture.' Its premise certainly owed something to *The Hydro,* as this review reveals: 'Karno is now making things hum in Revue-land ... "Hot and Cold," ... is a rollicking parody of hydropathy and other 20th century cures and cultures.'[13]

25.1 Parlez Vous Français? *Syd Walker and dancers 'direct from Paris' (author's collection).*

The sketch's three scenes were 'the parlour', 'a cinema' and a Turkish bath renamed patriotically as an 'Allies bath', all of which gave ample opportunity for the inclusion of an attractive chorus line. Karno engaged dancers from the various nations fighting the war, billing them 'a bevy of Allied Beauties'. The laughs were in the hands of experienced musical comedy actors A.W. Baskcomb and Eric Thorne, who impressed the critics: 'Hot and Cold is scoring a success this week ... Mr A.W. Baskcomb ... as Hunt, the doorman ... was irresistible ...

25. THE MILLIONAIRE TRAMP

Eric Thorne also stood out prominently. Miss Dorothy Frostick, as a lady journalist, and Miss Gladys Goy, as Miss Powder Puff, were distinct acquisitions to the cast.'[14]

25.2 Hunt the doorman, A.W. Baskcomb in Hot and Cold *(Burnley News © JPI media Ltd).*

Bathing scenes were a staple of revues (and the precursor to Sennett's famous bathing beauties), and this review of *Hot and Cold* shows how things had changed since the days when a flash of ankle was enough to make grown men faint: 'The dresses are wonderful, and the undresses more wonderful still. We fancy that most people would like to see a return to the vogue of approximately adequate clothing on the stage.'[15] It wasn't just the girls' costumes that were more revealing – jokes were becoming coarser and language cruder. The press bemoaned this trend, but war-weary civilians and Tommies on leave were not in the mood for Victorian morality: they wanted laughs and they didn't care how they got them. The trend would continue over coming years, as standards relaxed in an increasingly desperate attempt to attract an audience. It was a race to the bottom – literally – and the next generation saw variety degenerate into the nude revues of Phyllis Dixey.

There was now little left of the old Karno sketches. His last big name, Albert Bruno, had finally left to join Darnley, and it fell to a few old-stagers to fly the flag for knockabout comedy. Cooke and Russell's *Mumming Birds* continued to run, sometimes coupled with other sketches, and Jack Melville, Bob Selvidge and Harold Wellesley (the last Perkins) carried on gamely in *The Hydro*, *The Dental Institute* and *The Steam Laundry* respectively. But it was beginning to feel like the last hurrah of the once mighty Karno plonks – it was adapt or die. According to Adeler and West, Karno was at the forefront of these changes: 'Revue became the rage. Of course, Karno's earlier shows had practically been revues ... He was the forerunner, forefather and inventor of the English Revue.'[16]

As with all fashions, the provinces began to catch up with trends being set in London, and according to one report, Karno had an influential ear:

> New Standard of Revues for the Provinces. Many people who have been to the Leeds Empire this week must have wondered whether what they were seeing was, in truth, a Karno production. Vanished were all those "features" which the Karno productions had before, and, although

349

> remembering the long list of comedians, cradled and reared under the Karno managership, and who have brought pleasure to many, I don't think anybody missed them seriously. Indeed, the public has had a little bit too much of the comedian with the red nose, the exaggerated feet, and the "s's". Behind this change in the nature of the production lies a conference, which, I understand, was held at the Lord Chamberlain's Office, between that dignitary and Mr Karno. No doubt it was the fact that Mr Karno is the biggest producer of sketches and revues in the music-hall world, that led the Lord Chamberlain to invite him to an interview, and to explain his wishes for a raising of the standard of this branch of music-hall entertainment … The annihilation of tradition meant something to Mr Karno, but he had courage, and the great reception which has been accorded the piece [*Hot and Cold*] everywhere, must be supremely gratifying.[17]

With Karno no longer needing his training stable and demand for his theatrical supplies business curtailed by the war, the Fun Factory began to wind down. Sometime in 1914 or 1915 he moved his offices to 42 Cranbourn Street, in the very heart of the West End. He and Marie found themselves a new love nest too, apartment G3 at the Albany in Piccadilly. It was (and still is) one of the most exclusive addresses in London, a hidden gem in the centre of the great metropolis where super-rich residents are assured of privacy and discretion – no doubt the rough circus acrobat fitted right in.[18]

Karno had once been a pioneer – pushing the boundaries, developing new styles and stretching technical capabilities – but in revue he was a follower not a leader. This was not lost on critics, many of whom saw it for what it was – old material reconstituted into the new format:

> Parlez Vous Français? … is very bright and lively, and I never thought to see again a chorus dressed in tights and wearing top hats. I thought they went out with dress-improvers. I never thought to hear either the old joke about the game of making faces and the winner of the ugliest one who was not playing at all. But I did. The past, including the old Apache Dance, … returned once more, and we all applauded as if we had never seen it … this is an era of revivals.[19]

25. THE MILLIONAIRE TRAMP

As the war dragged on, staging any sort of show became more difficult, and revues were shortened until many were little more than the sketches they had replaced. Managers struggled to entice audiences into cold, dark theatres with little to offer in terms of spectacle. Paper shortages meant that even the programmes were miniaturised or scrapped completely. I suspect the grand old Wontdetania was melted down for munitions. On a more positive note, many artistes staged shows for injured servicemen in hospitals and convalescent homes, and there was a constant stream of charity performances. In May 1915, *The Dental Institute* company entertained injured troupes in Belfast with a sketch that press reports suggest was put together for the occasion: 'An enjoyable entertainment for the wounded soldiers was given in the Ulster Volunteer Force Hospital … By permission of Mr Fred Karno a sketch entitled "Jane Shore", was presented by Mr Bob Selvidge, Mr Bobby Lewis, and Albert Boisset … the production caused roars of laughter.'[20]

On 7 May 1915 the Lusitania was sunk by a German U-boat with the loss of nearly twelve-hundred souls. Many were American, which had a predictable impact on the public mood in the States – although it would be another two years before America joined the war. In the meantime, a whole battalion of British comics in Hollywood must have been watching events in Europe with trepidation. Billy Reeves was churning out one-reel comedies for Lubin Films in Philadelphia as 'the Scream of the Screen' – other Lubin comics included ex-Karnos Charlie Griffiths and Johnny Doyle. Jimmy Aubrey was making films for Mittenthal (and later worked at Vitagraph, where he made over twenty-five shorts with Oliver Hardy), and Billie Ritchie was with Henry Lehrman's L-KO. To have trained in the Karno school, the school that gave the world Charlie Chaplin, was a golden ticket to a film career.

25.3 Billy Reeves visits Chaplin at his studio (courtesy Roy Export/Chaplin Archive).

Being in Chaplin's shadow had its downside, though. Many comics battled to prove that their comedy style was their own and not merely a copy of Charlie's – they weren't helped by the literally hundreds of Chaplin impersonators (like Stan Laurel) springing up all over vaudeville. In April 1916 *The Yorkshire Evening Post* interviewed a comic called George French, appearing in a local revue, and noted that he'd had a 'Chaplin moustache' for over twelve years yet was now seen as copying the movie star. French noted that the public assumed everything followed Chaplin, when the opposite was often true: 'Mr French ... remembered Chaplin ... and he thinks there is a good deal more of Fred Kitchen about Chaplin's much copied gestures than seems to have occurred to some of the film comedian's admirers.'[21] Fellow artistes may have known the truth, but there was no competing with the assumption that everyone else's comedy was derivative.

25.4 Billy Reeves on screen – The Moving Picture World, *26 June 1915 (author's collection).*

Individual claims to Chaplin's costume, gags and even roles became a source of antagonism. Reeves and Ritchie both took to the press claiming to have originated the character of the drunk in the box. Jimmy Aubrey (the first Terrible Turkey) waded into the argument, correctly pointing out that Reeves debuted the part in England but Ritchie was first to play it in the States.[22] Reeves went so far as to place an advertisement in *The Era* offering to pay $1000 to anyone who could prove he was not the original drunk. *The Era* added: 'Reeves is best known ... as the original creator of the inebriated swell character in ... "Mumming Birds" ... The piece has been a great success in U.S.A. ... It can be safely said it was the big record of this act over there that started the furore for the comedy pictures that are now in vogue and which have employed so many former Karno comedians at large salaries.'[23]

25. THE MILLIONAIRE TRAMP

The Era credits Karno's *Mumming Birds* with the proliferation of knockabout comedies, which by then were the mainstay of the movie industry. Pause for a moment and think about that. Without Karno's material, and the comics he trained, the early development of silent movies would have been very different. His contribution and influence may be under-acknowledged today, but Laurel and Chaplin both gave credit where it was due – here is an extract from a typical interview:

25.5 Billie Ritchie as the Mumming Birds *drunk. The usher looks suspiciously like Edith Karno, but this is unconfirmed (courtesy Tony Barker).*

> Chaplin is high in his praise of Karno, whom he calls "the greatest mime in show business at the turn of the century." Karno was Chaplin's master and the little picture comedian recognizes his debt. "Karno streamlined the traditional, conventional pantomime, like that of the Drury Lane Theatre, and made it intelligible to the world audience … He was the first to synchronize pantomime with music." Chaplin says … "All of the pieces we did, as I remember them, were cruel and boisterous, filled with acrobatic humor and low, knockabout comedy. Each man working for Karno had to have perfect timing and had to know the peculiarities of everyone else in the cast so that we could, collectively, achieve a cast tempo" … Chaplin gives great credit to Karno for schooling him in the technique of pantomime … his early success in films is largely due to his long association with the first big time mastery of mimicry.[24]

Chaplin's most enduring legacy is his Little Tramp, the origins of which were (and still are) the subject of much argument. Billie Ritchie kicked up a stink when he laid claim to the character, accusing Chaplin of stealing the bowler hat, cane and moustache from him, and he may have had a point. In an unrelated legal case (between Chaplin and a blatant plagiarist called Charles Amador), it was proven that Ritchie wore a costume very similar to the Tramp five years before Chaplin did so on film.[25] Many, not least Chaplin's own PR man Rob Wagner, suggested that the Tramp costume was somehow meticulously crafted, with Charlie carefully considering each element's inherent symbolism, but the star himself always maintained it was put together spontaneously. Other claims included the idea that the outfit came from the rag-and-bone-man in *London Suburbia*. But all this theorising aside, when he first dressed himself as the Little Tramp, Chaplin undoubtedly combined elements embedded in his memory from other comics he had seen or worked with. As well as colleagues like Kitchen and Ritchie, some of the greatest comedians of his youth – Dan Leno, George Formby Senior and George Robey – had costumes which shared elements of the Tramp's attire. The character was a ubiquitous music hall type.

25.6 Billie Ritchie in his tramp costume – but who copied whom? (J. Willis Sayre collection).

It wasn't just the costume that was shaped by this melting pot of great comics. Chaplin said he'd taken the Tramp's characteristic walk from an old London character called Rummy Binks, who supposedly looked after horses at his Uncle Spencer's pub.[26] Anything is possible, but Chaplin provides a clue that this might be a tall story with his choice of name – Binks was his most famous Karno character. His story was also far from consistent – in another interview he said: 'I got my walk ... from an old London cab driver ... but part of the character was inspired by Fred Kitchen, an old fellow trouper of mine in vaudeville.'[27] Karno was in no doubt where Chaplin took his inspiration: 'Charlie's peculiar walk is not original. It started with one of my comedians, a clever fellow named Walter Groves, and I first introduced it in a character called "Perkins P.C" [actually Sergeant Lightning]. Fred Kitchen ... then elaborated this walk and when Chaplin stepped into Fred Kitchen's shoes and took his part over he also secured the legacy of the flat footed walk.'[28]

It is worth noting that Chaplin's iconic character is rarely a literal tramp. Charlie called him 'the Little Fellow', and in his movies he assumes all manner of guises – more often employed than not. Frequently, and especially in the early films, Chaplin plays the well-dressed (usually drunken) gentlemen he'd perfected in the Karno sketches.

Whatever his origins, by the time Chaplin's one-year contract with Keystone came to an end in late 1914, the Little Fellow was a global phenomenon. Sennett

25. THE MILLIONAIRE TRAMP

sought to renew, but the star had other ideas. Seeking greater control over his work, and with Syd taking his place at Keystone, he headed for Chicago to join G.K. Spoor and 'Bronco Billy' Anderson's Essanay company. He was given a golden hello of $10,000, a salary of $1,250 a week, and much more input into all aspects of the production. After making his first film in a chilly Chicago, Chaplin persuaded Essanay to move production to the west coast, where he set about recruiting more Karno old boys including Billy Armstrong,[29] who had appeared in *The New Slavey*. Armstrong became a regular co-star, notably in *By the Sea* (1915). Chaplin's filmmaking began to mature, and as the quality improved, his fame grew to an unprecedented level.

By now he had made Karno's physical slapstick his own, and the lack of any language barrier made him the first truly global superstar – all the more remarkable given that a large swathe of Europe was at war. One newspaper calculated that Chaplin was being watched by around twelve million people every day, and a new phenomenon appeared – merchandising. His image appeared everywhere: there were Chaplin ties, clocks, dolls, cocktails, songs and dances. There had never been anything like it before – and given the scale of this fame it seems almost laughable that in August 1915, Karno wrote to Chaplin to say how pleased he was to see his old protégé doing well, and suggested he take a little holiday in the old country. While he was here, Karno added, he might consider returning to the fold for a provincial tour (generously offering him a percentage)[30] – Chaplin's response can be guessed. All comedians were now judged by Charlie's standard, and one wonders if Karno ever looked at the enormous hat on his office wall and considered whether his former comic might now fit it.

Of course, the Americans weren't the only ones making movies. Before the war, European companies like Pathé were far more creatively and technologically advanced than their American counterparts, but the industry was devastated by the conflict. Studios closed and their talent pool was in combat. Before the war Max Linder had been the best-paid entertainer in the world, but when he put his career on hold to enlist, Chaplin stole his crown. Jesse Lasky wrote:

> America's domination of the international film market can be traced to … the First World War … Europe really had the jump on us … Our industry was slower starting but expanded by leaps and bounds … by the end of the war we were so far ahead technically and had such a grip on foreign audiences that our gross revenues put us in an

impregnable, commanding position. We were able to outbid any other country for their own geniuses. And by concentrating so much of the top acting, directing and writing talent of the world in Hollywood we could continue to make pictures that the whole world clamoured to see.[31]

America has dominated the world in movie production ever since, but back in pre-war Britain there were many small film companies competing with their U.S. and European rivals.

One such outfit was Folly Films, based at Eel Pie Island just down-river from Karsino. Folly was founded by brothers Fred and Joe Evans, who came from a family of performers.[32] Their grandfather Fred had been a famous Drury Lane clown, while their father (also Fred) had appeared with Karno around 1903 and then left to join Reed Pinaud.[33] The third-generation Fred Evans was the star of the Folly comedies, playing a clown called Pimple, and during the war the character was second only to the Little Tramp in the affections of British cinemagoers. But although Evans made approximately two hundred films, only a handful survive. In May 1915, *The Era* reported that Evans made one with Karno's help: 'Visitors to The Karsino ... were much amused at the antics of Syd Walker and Pimple, who were taking part in a cinema comedy on the island ... The members of the "Parlez Vous Français?" revue company also took part in the film, which will shortly be showing at all the leading cinema theatres. The party were afterwards entertained to lunch by Mr Karno.'[34]

This was probably the lost film *Pimple's Holiday*, described by the BFI as: 'Two men meet their wives on holiday at the Karsino.' It was Karno's first experience of filmmaking, and as the company were all contracted to him, one assumes he received payment. A few weeks later, reviews of *Mumming Birds* note that the sketch was accompanied by a film showing a carnival at Karsino – presumably this Pimple flick, and perhaps depicting the carnival scene from *Parlez Vous Français?*

Karno should have seized this opportunity to branch into film: by now the contrast between the growth and success of the movie industry and the struggling music hall could hardly have been more marked. That said, he was still better off than most. In a letter to Chaplin, Alf Reeves noted that his companies were bucking the downward trend: 'Things are really better than ever here ... I know because we take over so many bills, and I know the weekly

25. THE MILLIONAIRE TRAMP

receipts. Still it does not stop the dear proprietors from making the war an excuse for decreasing expenses.'[35]

In spring 1916 Chaplin's contract at Essanay ended and his older brother was released from Keystone. Syd became Charlie's manager and began in style, negotiating the biggest movie contract the world had ever seen. The Mutual Film Corporation agreed to pay Chaplin $10,000 a week and a $150,000 signing fee (which he shared with Syd – a token of thanks for a lifetime of support). From their humble workhouse beginnings, the two brothers had become the apogees of Hollywood's Golden Era: fast cars, faster women and lavish (if scandal-ridden) lifestyles.[36]

New studio, same approach. Chaplin continued to recruit ex-Karno comics, including Albert Austin who appeared in all twelve Mutual films. In *The Pawnshop* (1916) he plays the owner of a clock that Chaplin systematically destroys. Another ex-Karno co-star was Eric Campbell, signed up after Charlie saw him in a play called *Pom Pom*, in New York. Campbell was to become Chaplin's most famous 'heavy', and like Austin he made his debut in the first of the Mutual films, *The Floorwalker* (1916). With its department store full of shoplifters, this one may have swiped an idea or two from *His Majesty's Guests,* and as we noted earlier, it finishes with the crashing-lift gag from *Flats*.

25.7 Living the dream – the Chaplin brothers in Hollywood (courtesy Roy Export/Chaplin Archive).

While Chaplin was living the high life in L.A., Karno was trying to keep Karsino afloat. The war brought all manner of rules and regulations, including a legal obligation to change his name from Westcott to Karno by deed poll.[37] It also placed significant constraints on running the hotel: strict lighting regulations put paid to his fairylights. An article from September 1915 about how to drive in the blackout included a photograph of Karno in his enormous Sizaire-Berwick car, despite there being no reference to the car or Karno in the story – he was famous enough to be instantly recognisable to readers. Ironically, he was fined one pound the following year for failing to comply with lighting regulations on his houseboat, and another five shillings a few months later for driving along

Drury Lane without a light. Perhaps he wasn't the best poster boy for the lighting regulations after all – not least because his name had now become synonymous with all things chaotic.

Karno was more successful at supporting charitable events. In August 1915 he organised a river sports gala in aid of the Red Cross, with injured troops brought up from nearby hospitals for the day. And a newsreel from June 1916,

25.8 Karno in his Sizaire-Berwick (© Illustrated London News Ltd/Mary Evans Picture Library).

entitled *The Eccentric Club entertain wounded soldiers*,[38] records how six hundred wounded soldiers were invited to enjoy the delights of Karsino. A few weeks later Karno played host to over a thousand soldiers at an event attended by the Lord Mayor of London. In May 1917 he gave his palm court over to a concert for the Molesey War Hospital, and soon afterwards *The Era* named him as the largest single contributor to a Variety Artistes' Benevolent Fund charity sports event. He also continued to put Karsino at the disposal of the Music Hall Ladies' Guild, *The Era* recording one such occasion: 'The … Guild are … to take the children for their annual day's outing to the Karsino … Mr Karno has generously promised to provide the children with dinner and tea.'[39]

None of Karno's many and varied charitable efforts throughout his career are mentioned in his memoirs – perhaps at a time when everyone was doing their bit, he felt his contribution unremarkable. Besides, his support for the troops wasn't entirely altruistic – servicemen were now the bulk of his clientele.

*25.9 The Lord Mayor of London, Sir Charles Wakefield, helps to entertain wounded troops at Karsino, 12 August 1916 (*Illustrated War News, 14 August 1916*).*

The war was changing society beyond all recognition: the Bertie Wooster brigade in their blazers and boaters were consigned to history, and with them

25. THE MILLIONAIRE TRAMP

Karno's dream of an upmarket pleasure palace. He could no longer afford to be choosy about his customers, as Adeler and West noted: 'Karsino might soon have altered its name to Khaki-sino. There were military encampments both at Hurst and Kingston parks and the boys ... made the hotel their playground. As Karno gave them the run of the place, including free use of the bathrooms and a special tariff for food and drinks, he soon became personally very popular with them all.'[40] However, the behaviour of troops on leave was somewhat less refined than the residents of Upper Molesey were accustomed to, causing Karno to slip a few rungs back down the social ladder he'd worked so hard to climb. According to Gallagher, he was refused membership of the Hampton Court tennis club as a result of the 'anything goes' atmosphere at Karsino – so he bought the land, evicted the club and set sheep to graze on the courts, claiming it was part of the war effort.

The Royal Flying Corps used Hurst Park as a training airfield, and a new type of dashing hero, the flying ace, made a beeline for the island. Showing off was the order of the day, sometimes with unexpected consequences like in this incident in June 1917:

> Holiday Crowds Witness Thrilling Accident ... as the people were listening to the band at the Karsino, their attention was attracted by the brilliant evolutions of an airman ... who cleverly looped the loop, and performed most graceful spirals ... He flew rather low over the Thames, and as he did so, his machine ... struck the telephone wires ... The smash brought down some large branches ... while the biplane remained fixed among the larger limbs of the tree ... P.C. Walter Baker ... was able to throw the end of a rope to the aviator ... He was taken to the Karsino where he received numerous congratulations upon his lucky escape.[41]

Adeler and West added: 'When Fred and his assistants went to help him, they found that he was sitting upside down in his machine, calmly smoking a cigarette. They ... took him over to the island, where they adjourned to the bar.'[42]

Karno must have racked his brains as to how he might replicate this whole episode in a music hall sketch, but without success – even he couldn't crash a plane on stage.

26.

All Women

"Will you marry me?"
"No."
"Go on, just this once."
(Fred Karno personal joke archive, 15 August 1932)

EVEN IF Karno had wanted to run the risk of further defections, the war prevented him from sending further troupes to the States – Chaplin's second tour proved to be the last. With the Fun Factory winding down and his empire dwindling, he increasingly sought alliances with other producers and theatre syndicates in order to keep the Karno brand alive. One collaborator was a surprising choice, as *The Daily Mirror* reported: 'This is an age when all sorts of ridiculous rumours are flashing about. The latest absurdity is a rumour that Mr Horatio Bottomley is writing a music-hall sketch for Mr Fred Karno. The suggestion is untrue and silly.'[1] A few days later the reporter had to eat his words: 'Mr Karno corrects me. He says that negotiations are pending between himself and Mr Bottomley.'[2]

Bottomley was an extraordinary Walter Mitty character. A con-man on a grand scale, he encouraged investors to support assorted companies and ventures, most of them built on sand. His chequered career included owning or publishing several newspapers, including *John Bull*, a jingoistic weekly magazine which was a mouthpiece for his money-making schemes and political ambitions. In 1906 he became a Liberal MP, but was despised by most of his parliamentary colleagues, who saw him for what he was – a swindler. His financial ineptitude hounded him until he resigned as an MP in 1912, after being declared bankrupt. The First World

26. ALL WOMEN

War brought him back to public attention, though: he was a fierce orator, and through the pages of his magazine became a powerful force for war propaganda and recruitment. He addressed hundreds of meetings and his firebrand speeches attracted huge crowds – it was even said that his fanatical following made him the second most influential man in England, after Kitchener.

Karno and Bottomley had some shared interests. Bottomley was a keen supporter of the theatre and invested in many (mostly failed) productions – he kept plenty of chorus girls in fur coats too. But he hit the jackpot as a major investor in Leslie Stuart's *Floradora*. Another mutual friend was Charles B. Cochran, who promoted Bottomley as an orator on the halls, and all of these men shared a love of the racetrack. Bottomley was a regular at Karsino, where he would occasionally jump on a table in the palm court to deliver one of his speeches. Karno noted that Karsino was the only place where Bottomley would speak without demanding a chunky fee – although Bottomley's biographer Julian Symons recorded that he was once paid a hundred pounds to speak at Karsino, by whom is unclear. Bottomley worked hard to keep these payments quiet so as not to undermine his seemingly patriotic motives, but the length and passion of his speeches was always directly proportionate to his fee.[3]

One night at Karsino Bottomley was espousing the virtues of 'John Bull's Daughters' – the women contributing to the war effort – which prompted Karno to suggest he might like to write a sketch on the subject. Bottomley readily agreed but demanded a fee of £1000, with £500 in advance. Karno laughed him out of the palm court but Bottomley still promised to deliver a scenario a week later. They subsequently lunched at the Savoy, where their combined presence was the cause of some excitement, but no manuscript materialised and their collaboration melted away.

Despite his noisy patriotism, Bottomley remained a political outsider after the war. He used his ill-gotten gains to pay off his debts and with his bankruptcy discharged, contrived to re-enter parliament as an independent in 1918. Soon afterwards he set to work on a huge fraud, eliciting nearly a million pounds from *John Bull* readers for none-existent 'Victory Bonds'– he was eventually convicted and sentenced to seven years' imprisonment. The press ran this story about his time in clink:

> A man who has seen Bottomley in prison told me ... if it weren't so tragic his appearance would be comical. "He looks the funniest Fred Karno

convict you could imagine," he said. "You nearly cry when you see his tiny forage cap, and his trousers, which, six or eight inches too long, have been worn out at the seat and the knees by some former prisoner. I have seen him so often dressed immaculately, as was his boast, and the contrast is terrible."[4]

A Karno-Bottomley collaboration would undoubtedly have been entertaining, for if the scoundrel had anything, it was wit. The story goes that a visitor chanced upon him working on mailbags in prison: "Sewing, Mr Bottomley?" said the visitor. "No, reaping," he replied.[5]

With Bottomley out of the picture, Karno engaged a new writing team (Clifford Marquand, Harold Simpson and Willie Redstone), and the result was a show with a completely female cast: *All Ladies*. It opened on 27 September 1915 at the Colchester Hippodrome, but soon changed its title to *All Women*. Karno had explored female emancipation as far back as 1898 in *The New Women's Club,* and later in *Perkins MP* – and as we've seen, the Music Hall Ladies' Guild staged a show with an entirely female cast and crew ten years earlier. Yet Karno's revue was still considered groundbreaking. His forty-strong cast included established names like the sister act Beatie and Babs, Sybil Arundale, Frankie Carlos, Sybil Hook and Grace Vicat, and the support team were women too:

26.1 An unlikely partner – Horatio Bottomley.

> At a time when women are taking possession of workroom and munition factory it is, perhaps, not surprising that Mr Karno should give them their chance to make good in the amusement world. The "All Women" revue is managed and played by women, and no man assists in any way.
>
> Miss Emmie [sic] Thomas is the musical directress, Miss Irene Marston, stage manageress; and Miss Jackie Melville, acting manageress. Mr Karno carries his originality to the point of employing a lady advance agent, Miss Evelyn Shannon-Clyndes, who performs her duties remarkably well.[6]

26. ALL WOMEN

The five scenes (described as 'All Eves in Five Temperaments') were listed as 'the dormitory of the Finishem Academy (will she do?)'; 'the recruiting office of the Women's War Work Committee (what can she do?)'; 'the School of Instruction (doing her bit)'; 'the Shell Factory (what has she done?)'; and 'the Ladies Club (she's done it!)':

> There are no men in the cast of Fred Karno's latest production, and, let it be said at once, Mr Karno has scored all along the line with his experiment ... it might appear improbable that a revue – a form of entertainment that depends so much for its success upon humour – could be complete without the inclusion of a male comedian. That there are feminine equivalents Mr Karno has proved, and the lady he has chosen as his principal fun-provider is Miss Babs, of Beatie and Babs ... The opening ... shows us the dormitory of the Finishem Academy. It is breaking-up morning, and the girls are exchanging noisy confidences regarding future plans ... Thereafter we find the girls forming a War Work Committee, and munition workers, policemen, dustmen, etc. are found doing the common tasks in an Adamless world. Recruiting Office, School of Instruction, and Shell Factory, are all shown, and, finally, we leave the merry throng at a Ladies' Club, enjoying the pleasures of a smoking concert ... the revue is topical in character, and this should make its appeal the more successful to audiences.[7]

All Women was consistently received with surprise and incredulity, but most critics were soon won over: 'One went to the Sheffield Empire last night with slight misgivings, for it had not previously been proved that a revue composed entirely of women may be a complete success ... those misgivings were dispelled ... the humorous element was as abundant as could be desired, and nothing else was lacking ... An "All men" revue would not have been nearly as attractive.'[8]

With notable exceptions such as Lucille Ball – a trailblazer in the fifties who was supported in her early career by Buster Keaton – it would be another

26.2 Sisters doing it for themselves – Beatie and Babs (courtesy Alan Khan).

seventy years before comediennes really competed on equal terms with male comics. The late Victoria Wood would have smiled at the fact that the star of *All Women*, the first all-female comedy show, was 'Miss Babs' – the lead character in Wood's *Acorn Antiques*.

The show wasn't all chorus lines and comics, either: Karno stunned the audience by introducing some real-life working women too, as Adeler and West recorded: 'He had a ... scene showing women doing men's work ... a genuine female chainmaker from Cradley Heath, female carpenters, milkmen, butchers, bakers and candlestick makers. The theatre was packed every night with soldiers, and this scene showing the lasses ... "keeping the home fires burning" worked them up to a great pitch of excitement.'[9] Karno genuinely recognised the women's ability, saying: 'I found that I could get girls to do everything that the men had done. I got for that show one of the best stage carpenters I have ever had – the daughter of a blacksmith, who could wield a hammer with any man.'[10]

The comics' attempts at such war work were at the heart of the comedy, and one of the more surreal moments saw them try their hand at farming, including bathing a pig – which proved to be the cause of some trouble. The RSPCA alleged Karno kept the pig in too small a crate, and he found himself up before the magistrates: 'The pig had ... been brought to the Court. It had a green ribbon round its neck ... Mr Karno ... said it was fed and coddled by the ladies of the revue, given chocolates, etc. and once it had been treated to a bottle of beer. The summons was dismissed.'[11]

The pig was spoilt rotten, and was even made an honorary member of the 'Hambones', a new society formed by Fred Kitchen and Joe Elvin to raise money for Brinsworth House. Karno was a member and it sounds like great fun, but Kitchen and Elvin had set up this rival group after a bitter dispute within the ranks of the Variety Artistes' Benevolent Fund. Elvin had accused the fund of failing to offer enough financial support to its members, while its committee held that he and Kitchen had acted unilaterally in such matters. What the pig made of it is not recorded.

The press was fascinated by the all-female show, and this interview with Karno's musical director is illuminating:

> A different orchestra has to be coached in the music every week ... Knowing the innate dislike many men have to being controlled and supervised by the "weaker sex", I was rather curious to hear what Miss

26. ALL WOMEN

> Effie Thomas ... had to say on the subject. "When I make my first appearance at rehearsal on a Monday," she told me, "I am received with general suspicion, and when I tell the gentlemen how I want things done I am not met with the most genial of looks ... On Tuesday there are signs of an early thaw, and on Wednesday, well, they all seem distinctly friendly!" So evidently susceptible man has once more submitted to the irresistible charm of the opposite sex![12]

As usual the sketch developed as it ran. The 'Sisters Sprightly' occasionally deputised in the leads[13] (their bill matter was 'Bright, British and bang up-to-date'), and Karno added a practical demonstration by a real platoon of the Women's War Work Emergency Corps – although how the war effort could spare them is unclear. The following summer the show had new leading ladies: Betty Balfour in her first touring production (she went on to become the best-known British film actress of the twenties), and Lily Long, famed for being six feet tall[14] – by then *All Women* had become a firm favourite with the public.

With three revues running, things on stage were positive, but Karno had challenges elsewhere. Karsino continued to be a financial burden and he also had to deal with Fred Jr.'s drunken AWOL antics. In November 1915 a fire on the houseboat Bohemia spread to the hotel, severely damaging two rooms. That month he advertised the sale of his pantomime costume and scenery stock, with 'no reasonable offer refused'.[15] At the same time a shop opened at 72 Grove Lane selling nearly-new evening dresses 'suitable for revue', its proprietor was a 'Mrs Marie Karno'. This wasn't Marie disposing of the Karno wardrobe, however, it was actually Mary Tysall.

26.3 Betty Balfour, star of All Women *and future silent screen pin up.*

The rival Ted Karno Trio had disappeared from show listings at the start of the war (perhaps Ted's younger colleagues had enlisted), and the Tysalls were now running a boarding house at 34 De Crespigny Park, Camberwell – their new dress shop was literally around the corner. Notwithstanding this red herring, Karno was certainly in the process of divesting his assets when the task was unexpectedly done for him – on 31 March 1916 the Fun Factory went up in smoke:[16]

> Fred Karno's 'Fun Factory' on fire. Premises Destroyed and Damage Estimated at £25,000. The huge range of buildings in Vaughan Road, Cold Harbour Lane, Camberwell, London ... where sketches ... have been evolved which have provided amusement for hundreds of thousands of music-hall visitors, was practically destroyed by fire this morning. A great quantity of scenery, dresses, etc. was consumed, and the damage ... is ... estimated ... at £25,000.[17]

The account was an exaggeration: the factory was up and running again within six weeks. But given Karno's financial troubles, one can't help wondering whether fires at both Karsino and the Fun Factory within the space of six months were a co-incidence – no doubt he was well insured.

Karno seems to have chosen this moment to move on. The mighty Fun Factory's days were numbered, though exactly when he sold the place is unclear.[18] It seems likely to have been towards the end of the war, and the proceeds were presumably sucked into his Tagg's Island money pit.

Meanwhile, the war continued to make running theatres increasingly difficult. Restrictions were placed on the sale of goods such as chocolate and tobacco (they were later banned completely in theatres), and a new Entertainments Tax added enormous financial pressure. Later, performance times were restricted to save electricity. On top of all this it became harder to find talent. Karno used to have comedians literally falling over themselves to audition for him – now he had to advertise for them. The war was the making of some artistes and the final bow for others, but historian Vivyan Ellacott singles out Karno as one of the few names that could still be relied upon to fill a hall.[19] This, combined with his financial situation, explains why in January 1916 he signed a contract with Moss Empires to produce a series of new revues.

The first appeared at the Preston Empire later that month, entitled *Mustard and Cress*. Although listed as 'Presented by Fred Karno', it was produced by J.W. Jackson,[20] the man behind the Eight Lancashire Lads. The show was based on three scenes from J.M. Barrie's revue *Rosy Rapture, Pride of the Beauty Chorus,* and George Hestor was back in the Karno fold leading the cast of forty. The easiest way to get new revues on the boards was to cut and

26. ALL WOMEN

carve old ones, and *Mustard and Cress* owed much to *His Majesty's Guests*, as this review reveals:

> One has only to imagine good revue plus the … unique Karno touch, to understand that "Mustard and Cress" … ought by no means to be missed. The … show is … the story of a huge fashionable costumiere's emporium, with a plot which includes thefts, accusation of an innocent heroine by a jealous rival, the inevitable comic detective … and the usual happy ending. Rather more of a story than is usual in revue but sketched so lightly as to be never obtrusive. The scenes include the showroom of Mustard and Cress Ltd., the corridor of the Mustard and Cress Hotel, and the Mustard and Cress Nightclub … Fun, fast and furious, reigns and rages throughout the piece, led by George Hestor, as Sergeant Bloomer.[21]

Karno was no longer the king of his own empire. Hamstrung by the financial burden of Karsino and the disappearance of most of his plonks, he had become subservient to Moss and its nominated co-producers. Perhaps he was also running out of ideas. While hunting around for his next revue, Karno renamed *Mustard and Cress* as *Knick Knacks* and incorporated even more elements from *His Majesty's Guests*, including naming the shop Miffin's Emporium. He soon found himself under pressure to deliver for his new masters, as this interview makes clear:

> Mr Fred Karno … is under contract with the Moss circuit to produce no fewer than eighteen new revues between now and 1919! And Mr Karno's part is by no means nominal. The plot in skeleton is first of all worked out by himself; and then, the libretto having been written by an outsider, he sets to work again, and produces every revue that goes out under his name. … He thinks that … revue has got to the stage when it is a matter of the survival of the fittest. The 'tripe' will have to go … "Karno's Knick Knacks" … is not a mere hotchpotch, but more on extravaganza lines, and is reminiscent of "The Dandy Thieves" of many years ago.[22]

The demands of Moss were clearly undeliverable, and run ragged by this big corporation, the Guv'nor must have regretted surrendering his independence.

Moss made the most of their new arrangement and was probably responsible for Karno and Charles Cochran writing jointly to Chaplin with an offer of £1000 a week to appear in a show in London – if anyone could persuade him to return, Karno could. Chaplin replied: 'Dear Guv'nor – the figure mentioned for a London contract would have given me heart failure in the old days. But I am tied up here for some years to come, and I see no chance of appearing in London. Should I find myself able to do so, I will of course let you know before anyone else. Wishing you all the best of luck, Guv'nor – yours sincerely Charles Chaplin.'[23]

Jack Melville recalled that Karno craved the halcyon days of Chaplin and his fellow plonks: "He missed him. He never found any wonderful comedians after that … He had lots pass through his hands, but his original comedians were, I think, 'Karno' comedians. As he got on, they became a little bit too – well, not plonks."[24]

Karno must have yearned for the days of developing meticulously timed pantomime routines. Quantity rather than quality was now the order of the day, but the press was beginning to tire of formulaic revue – thanks to Karno's comedy element, his shows still stood out. He made the most of his huge back catalogue, and just as he'd always had an eye for great comics, he was adept at recruiting the best revue performers, as this *Knick Knacks* review reflects:

> Fred Karno has recruited … George Hestor and Harry Ray … best known for their success in … "The Arcadians" … of particular interest is the inclusion in the cast of Ouida Macdermott … a young lady whose numerous successes to date will lead to infinitely bigger things. Bright as is the entire revue, it is worth a visit, if solely for the beautiful and yet screamingly amusing "statue" scene between Miss Macdermott as the Goddess of Love, alive, and George Hestor as a policeman wilting rapidly under her charms. "Knick Knacks" … is one of the brightest and best cast revues to be found on tour.[25]

By early 1916 Karno's knockabout plonks were almost extinct: only the *Mumming Birds* company remained on the halls, sometimes playing a double bill with *The New Slavey*. With its music and dance elements, the sketch just about passed for revue and could be adapted to meet current trends. Edgar Cooke, Jimmy Russell and their troupe were the last of Karno's Speechless Comedians, the laughter

26. ALL WOMEN

26.4 Amy and Alf Reeves and (thought to be) Jimmy Russell (left) (courtesy Roy Export/ Chaplin Archive).

they generated now just echoes in the brickwork of every crumbling music hall around the country.

Ironically, *Mumming Birds* addicts could now get their fix at the cinema: Chaplin's *A Night in the Show* (1915) was an homage to the sketch that made his name. The film revives the drunk in the box and shares the premise of a show within a show – but there are significant differences. The first ten minutes see Chaplin causing chaos in the foyer, at the box office, and in the audience before curtain-up. There is no Terrible Turkey wrestling match finale, and the Eton Boy (now a hugely fat character) is not in an opposite box but sitting behind the drunk, removing the key component of cross-stage banter. The other protagonist is Mr Rowdy – who spills drinks and throws missiles from the gallery – also played by an almost unrecognizable Chaplin.

We have already touched on other Chaplin films which share DNA with Karno's sketches, such as *The Rink* and *Laughing Gas*, and biographers have been quick to make connections whether they exist or not. Some have suggested that *Early Birds*, for instance, may have been an inspiration for *Easy Street* (1917), but the film's plot and characters bear no resemblance to Karno's sketch. A much closer representation can be found in *Triple Trouble* (1918), where Chaplin spends the night in a doss house (run by a Jew), and a villain steals from the inmates and attempts to stab our hero in the process. The doss house scene is an extended version of that in *Police* (1916), a film that sees an inept policeman assist Chaplin in breaking into a house, passing him a mallet with which Charlie promptly knocks him out – shades of Sergeant Lightning perhaps. The subsequent burglary, where Chaplin and his accomplice manage to make as much noise as possible, may well have used business from the first scene of *His Majesty's Guests* too. Karno said: 'I have, of course, seen most of Chaplin's films. Often I have been struck with the manner in which he has introduced ... little episodes and pieces of business that he either acquired or invented during his ... days with me.'[26]

'Little episodes and pieces of business' is not wholesale larceny. While Chaplin deployed Karno gags and ideas, his plots were rarely purloined from the sketches, and I'm sure this is why Karno chose not to challenge him on infringement of copyright. Besides, by this time the Guv'nor had more to gain by capitalising on his Chaplin connection – *Mumming Birds* was now advertised with the strapline: 'The sketch that brought Charlie Chaplin to fame ... The present Company still includes his fellow artistes.'[27]

It was to *Mumming Birds* that Karno turned for his next revue: a parody of his famous legal battle with Pathé. *Oh, Law!* was written by Ronald Jeans and told the story of rival theatrical producers arguing over a disputed show called *Have a Banana!* (really *Mumming Birds*) – it even included a visit to the music hall by the judge. Karno plonks Cooke and Russell provided the knockabout elements, and he engaged impressionists Marie Dainton and Vernon Watson to portray a gallery of well-known stars in the 'show within a show'. Although disrupted by the Fun Factory fire, *Oh, Law!* was ready by the end of April 1916 – or so Karno thought. The cast was well-rehearsed; elaborate staging, costumes and props were in place; and the grand opening of the revue version of Karno's greatest ever sketch was imminent. But on the Friday before opening night, the leading lady mysteriously vanished.

The press was full of speculation about the mystery:

> Search for Famous Actress ... Mrs Dainton [Dainton's mother] ... received a telegram from her daughter ... "Don't worry; am with friends." Later information led to the belief that Miss Dainton had gone to Brighton. She had been rehearsing all this week for ... Mr Fred Karno's revue, "Oh, Law!" ... If Miss Dainton is not found promptly it will be impossible to produce the revue next Monday.[28]

Some suspected the whole episode was an elaborate publicity stunt but Karno was clearly in the dark, telling reporters: 'She attended ... final rehearsals but ... seemed dissatisfied with her part, with the result that she left the rehearsal theatre without any clear explanation. Since then he had seen nothing of her.'[29] The show must go on, and it opened with Beatrice Read in Dainton's part.[30] A few weeks later Dainton reappeared to perform in a charity concert at the Palladium, with no explanation about where she'd been, and it was another four months before she returned to playing normal engagements. So what had happened?

26. ALL WOMEN

Dainton was an experienced performer who'd appeared on the halls for over twenty years – she was a key figure in the Music Hall War, and her skill for mimicry had made her a headline act. So while it's possible that she felt the responsibility of leading a large revue was too much for her, it seems more likely that Karno was critical of her performance and she walked out. Whatever the cause, she needed a long break before she could face an audience again.

26.5 The lady vanishes – Marie Dainton.

Back to the show. *Oh, Law!* did not seem to suffer for the loss of Dainton, as this *Era* review confirms:

> We witness a famous music-hall star suing the owner of a modern revue, "Have a Banana" ... for infringement of copyright. This scene is most faithfully and excellently depicted, but instead of the witnesses giving evidence in the approved and solemn form they render it in song or dance ... The jury consists of women, and quite one of the funniest incidents is when they are asked to decide upon their verdict. Of course they disagree, and the judge decides to see the revue in question ... The scene that follows is quite "Karnovian" ... A stage is presented upon a stage, and most elaborately it is done ... everyone enjoys the fun at the Palaseum Theatre ... Over eighty artistes appear in the production, which is splendidly mounted ... Vernon Watson was excellent. He is called upon to represent such stars as Wilkie Bard, George Lashwood, Fred Emney, and Harry Weldon, and does so with remarkable sincerity and skill ... "Oh, Law!" will enjoy a long run.[31]

The idea of a courtroom farce based on his own legal battle, with the added twist of impersonations of Karno old boys such as Weldon and Emney, is a joy. Another review suggests Karno was still very much hands-on, and reveals that the show included ideas from another of his classics:

> Patrons of the Leeds Empire this week may have noted a sturdy, clean shaven man ... who watched the performance of "Oh, Law!" ... from the side of the circle or stalls, and who now and again jotted down a hasty

note. They were watching ... Fred Karno at work. I do not imagine that anybody who has seen "Oh, Law!" this week has gone away dissatisfied; but Mr Karno ... saw places where it could be improved and ... last night a reconstructed version of the last scene ... was introduced, which strengthens the whole concern ... I had a few words with Mr Vernon Watson ... He confirmed ... that it is very difficult to work from a stage upon a stage ... a mimic who is set far back from the footlights must shout, more or less, to make himself heard ... Talking of that uproarious scene ... outside the Palaseum Theatre, where ... the queue and the street entertainers have a lively ten minutes ... it is a development of a notion that was used in ... "Casuals". There, a couple of itinerant cornet blowers played to the evening queue outside a workhouse ... then passed round the hat![32]

The 'show within a show' forced the action upstage, to the obvious detriment of the verbal material. Luckily Karno still had Alf Reeves as production manager, who no doubt ensured that the knockabout business, at least, was up to scratch.

Oh Law! ran through the summer, but lost its drunk in the box when Edgar Cooke jumped ship to join a Harry Day revue. This may have prompted Karno to reduce the physical comedy, and he also changed the title to *Have a Banana!* Jimmy Russell was elevated to lead knockabout and got his name in the billing – which given his many years' service, seems long overdue. At the end of August Karno veterans Frank Prior and Bobby Lewis joined the cast and the show reverted to its original format and title.[33]

The success of this reinvented *Mumming Birds* led Karno and Reeves to secure a fourteen-week U.S. tour that September, but the realities of crossing the U-boat riddled Atlantic perhaps gave them second thoughts, and it was cancelled. In late October, *Oh Law!* was rewritten again and given its third title, *On and Off*,[34]

26.6 Advertising for On and Off
(© The Michael Diamond Collection/ Mary Evans Picture Library).

26. ALL WOMEN

with Archie Glen and Beatrice Allen joining the cast – the revamped script was by John Gerant and music was by Joe Cleve.

Tracking Karno's shows, establishing new from old and identifying revivals, can be challenging and there are occasional inexplicable discoveries. In October 1916 the Wigan Hippodrome billed a unique Karno turn: 'Fred Karno and Co. contribute an attractive electrical novelty act … *The Giant Electric Chicken*.'[35] I initially thought this must be a listing error, since it bears no resemblance to a Karno show and never appears again – however some detective work reveals that an 'electric chicken' was used that Christmas in *Red Riding Hood*, at Edinburgh's Theatre Royal. I suspect Karno manufactured the effect for the pantomime and decided to give it a try-out before despatching it to Scotland.

Chicken or no chicken, as the end of 1916 loomed even his popular revues were generating paltry profits, and some reviews were really poor:

> "Hot and Cold" may be regarded as a tolerable specimen of its class; but it is really hard to understand the frame of mind that can deliberately invent such stuff, or willingly sit it out. Mr A.W. Baskcomb, as Alfred 'Enry Hunt, the handy man, a part he played last night for the thousandth time, is too good a comedian for his surroundings … the rest is sheer inanity. A dance of chorus ladies, seemingly attired in bathing towels only, has long lost the savour of daring novelty which was once its sole defence … it fails altogether to relieve the general impression … of boredom.[36]

The Moss contract production line churned out shows with a short shelflife, so Karno needed new ones waiting in the wings. Syd Walker transferred from *Parlez Vous Français?* to take the lead in the next offering, *Pounds Shillings and Pence* (usually listed as £.S.D. or L.S.D.),[37] which opened at the King's Theatre, Portsmouth, on 20 November. Written by Karno, Walker and Percival Langley, the show satirised the government's efforts to minimise waste in support of the war effort. Walker played Horatio Higgins, the mayor of Little Middle, who becomes obsessed with economising. This review tells us more:

> Higgins … is the shining example of economy to his fellow townsmen. "Economy" becomes a rage with him … He refuses to reinsure his house against fire in order to save the trifling premium, and the next day

premises and furniture ... are burnt to a cinder. He goes into business ... and saddles himself with ... a load of weird provisions which nobody ... wants to buy ... He opens an international economy exhibition and is persuaded to sink a lot of good money in ... labour saving devices which are ... white elephants. He is the embodiment of fun ... and is admirably supported ... by a quaint collection from the Town Council Chamber and a stream of eccentric customers.[38]

Performers in these revues changed frequently, not least due to wartime circumstances. The cast of *L.S.D.*, for instance, included Harry Daniels, Kitty Collinson, Fred Terris and a superb comic character actor called Moore Marriott. (Looking like the dwarf that Snow White forgot, Marriott went on to star in films with Will Hay throughout the 1930s.) Daniels and Marriott were both called up during the run of the show.

Karno, meanwhile, was working harder than ever, trying to fulfil his Moss contract and ride out the wartime storm, but November 1916 delivered the biggest blow imaginable – the press reported that Fred Jr. had been killed in France.

26.7 Moore Marriott as his familiar alter-ego Harbottle, Will Hay's sidekick (author's collection).

27.

Making Hay

"Are we alone?"
"No."
"Who's here?"
"Me."

(Nosey Knows, 1917)

ACCORDING TO Gallagher, Marie Moore practically choked on her kippers when she read the newspaper report, while Karno seemed unperturbed. The reason became apparent when he confessed that he had put Fred Jr.'s obituary in the newspaper himself, believing it would be good publicity to have the Karno name among the heroes. When she recovered her composure, Marie suggested it might be a good idea to telegraph Edith to let her know it was a hoax. Good story – not true. It's time to unpick another Karno myth.

This family story was a favourite of Fred Junior's, but the reality was less dramatic. No obituary was ever published (at least not one I can find), but in November 1916 Karno did write to the press with news of his son, prompting this to appear in *The Era*: 'I am sorry to hear from Mr Fred Karno that his son has been badly wounded in France. He has been hit by shrapnel. Here's hoping the brave laddie will make a good recovery!'[1] Fred Jr. was actually alive and well in Salonika, and there is no shrapnel injury on his war record. So there are two possible explanations for Karno's letter: either he was seeking publicity with a fabricated story, or he'd received inaccurate news from the War Office. The former seems more likely since it would explain the exaggerated family anecdote – and if it had been a mistake, surely Karno would have sent a correction once he found out Fred Jr. was not injured. I think we can conclude it was a somewhat callous publicity stunt, but even Karno didn't go as far as pretending his son had been killed.

The great impresario was doing everything he could to keep his shows on the road, and for the first time he appointed an agent, Murray and Dawe, to try to ensure they had no free weeks. But the availability of venues was increasingly unpredictable, and he also had to deal with performers being called up or leaving of their own accord. Syd Walker took off with his own sketch, *Stolen Fruit*, stealing Karno players Kitty Collinson and Jessie Ewart away with him. Fortunately fresh blood was found: Will Hindson replaced Walker in *L.S.D.* and Karno took a large advertisement in *The Era* proclaiming that he'd unearthed a major talent in *On and Off* star Archie Glen. In December, *On and Off* went on ice while Glen honoured a previous pantomime commitment, which enabled Jimmy Russell's plonks to resurrect *Mumming Birds* until the revue recommenced after the panto season. Enthused by the reception *Mumming Birds* received over the winter, Karno decided to establish a second troupe in May 1917, with Billy Devoy as the drunk and Ernest Selig as the boy in the box – but he needn't have bothered. A month later Archie Glen was conscripted and sent to France – *On and Off* was off for good.

Fortunately Karno had another show ready and waiting – *Three Bites*. Written with John Gerant and James Willard, the plot (which Karno recalled as one of his best) was inspired by a George Lashwood song called *Three Women to Every Man*. As a result of the war eligible men are in short supply, so the government decrees bachelorhood to be a capital offence and insists that every man be allocated three wives – one of his own choosing and two foisted upon him. The first scene was set in 'The Glad Optic', a stuffy gentlemen's club, where the somnambulant members are roused to an uncharacteristic fervour by the decree. The second scene finds our hero Willy Waddle,[2] played by Jack Gallagher, ready and waiting to be allocated his new brides – *The Era* takes up the story:

> The tribunal court, at which the applicants have to show why they should not take the wives the military representative (a lady) wishes to force on them, is a most hilarious scene. Waddle insists on entering the court before he is called and says, "he has come to take a dozen." Lottie Evergreen, a middle-aged barmaid, and Sarah Brown are not,

perhaps, everything that Waddle desires, but he has his compensation in the Lady Betty Entwistle ... who later dominates his household as his favourite wife. The other two he treats as menials, until one day the committee of inspection calls and complains of their treatment and gives them the advice to make Waddle sit up ... Finally, the three wives edict is annulled, and Waddle and Lady Betty agree to share life together.[3]

The fashion for revue was fading so Karno advertised *Three Bites* as 'A Roaring Farcical Comedy – Not a Revue', and *The Stage* saw it as a return to former glories: 'Three Bites would appear to denote a revival of those wildly diverting farcical sketches which Mr Karno provided so liberally and successfully before revue became the vogue.'[4]

The summer of 1917 was an important one in the careers of Charlie Chaplin and Stan Laurel. Chaplin's happy and creative period at Mutual came to an end and he signed a one-million-dollar contract with First National – Syd negotiated $125,000 for each two-reeler plus fifty percent of the profits. As part of the deal he was able to begin construction of his own studio on Hollywood's LaBrea Avenue. Alf Reeves had remained in regular correspondence with the Chaplins and made no secret of his desire to return to the States – California was far more attractive than war-torn London, with its Zeppelin raids and shortages. That summer the Chaplin brothers invited Reeves to join them but it took some months for him to get a permit to travel, so it was late August before he handed Karno his notice. He had been a loyal manager and friend for over ten years so his departure must have been disappointing, but Karno wrote wishing him the best of luck.[5] Alf sailed for America on 15 December but his wife did not join him until a year later[6] – it must have been difficult to leave Amy behind in wartime London, and the reason he did so is unclear. After four months in Hollywood Reeves was promoted to become Chaplin's studio manager, a position he held for the next twenty-eight years.[7]

27.1 Alf Reeves and Chaplin at Chaplin's studio (courtesy Roy Export/Chaplin Archive).

Chaplin was no doubt glad to see an old friend, because as Reeves crossed the Atlantic, he lost one of his closest. Gentle giant Eric Campbell had become one of the most famous and best-liked ex-Karno clowns in Hollywood. In July Campbell's wife had died of a heart attack, and soon afterwards he and his sixteen-year-old daughter were injured in a car accident.[8] While his daughter was recuperating, Campbell met and (just five days later) married a notorious gold-digger named Pearl Gilman, who filed for divorce within weeks, forcing him out of his house. On 20 December Campbell got drunk at a cast party and drove home, straight into a head-on collision – he was killed instantly.

Stan Laurel had been touring vaudeville with Mae, but finally made his film debut that same summer. While they were appearing at the Los Angeles Hippodrome, its owner Adolph Ramish told Stan he was funnier than Chaplin and asked if he'd like to make some movies – the result was *Nuts in May*. Legend has it that Chaplin attended the preview with Carl Laemmle, the head of Universal Studios, and over dinner regaled his former Karno understudy with plans for his studio and a stock company, which he suggested might include Stan. However he failed to make a firm offer, and the men never worked together. If Chaplin had taken him on Stan would almost certainly have spent his career as a support player,[9] and there would have been no Laurel and Hardy. Instead it was Laemmle who offered Stan a contract, and a handful of films followed. Perhaps the best known is *Hickory Hiram,* in which Stan played a country bumpkin, but the movies failed to make an impact – not helped by Mae, who insisted on being Stan's co-star – and the couple found themselves back in vaudeville.[10]

We have seen that Chaplin gave work to many Karno old boys, so it's extraordinary that he did nothing to help Stan. Despite their youthful friendship one can't help thinking there was an unspoken animus between them. Stan greatly respected Chaplin and in public was consistently magnanimous, praising him as the greatest comic of his generation. Chaplin did not return the favour – Laurel does not even get a mention in his autobiography. Simon Louvish claimed that privately Chaplin's rise to fame 'drove his junior Karno partner … to paroxysms of irritation,'[11] but the most Laurel would say against him in public was that he was a very complex man. It seems likely that *Jimmy the Fearless* left an indelible mark on their relationship, sowing resentment for Laurel, guilt for Chaplin. Recently a letter came to light, written by Stan to a friend in 1957, a few years after Chaplin's exile from America as part of the McCarthy witch hunts. It reveals Stan's damning private opinion:

27. MAKING HAY

> I have to agree with you re: Chaplin being mean and cheap, he never to my knowledge had any consideration to anybody – financially or otherwise, he never had any time for any of his friends who worked with him in the early days … so you can imagine his feelings & actions towards utter strangers … he was a very eccentric character, composed of many moods at times signs of insanity which I think developed further when he gained fame and fortune … I really think he is to be pitied rather than censored – to my mind he is still the greatest artist in his field but unfortunately his ideals have run amuk [sic] & he has lost all sense of propriety … who cares or gives a damn about him – am sure I don't, whatever he thinks says or does is water on a ducks back to me. With all his millions we are happier than he is I'll guarantee and one thing for sure, he go [sic] out the same way he came in, with nothing and without friends too, there'll be no tears shed.[12]

Of course, we know that Chaplin did help many ex-Karno comrades, so Stan must have been speaking of his own experience. This uncharacteristic letter finally gives a glimpse of the hurt he felt back in those Karno days, ill-feeling which prevented them from working together as they forged Hollywood careers. Karno's decision to force Stan aside all those years before perhaps deprived us of movies starring Chaplin and Laurel, but indirectly it gave us Laurel and Hardy.

It was a busy summer for Karno too; Karsino was bustling with politicians, policemen, soldiers and spies, but wartime regulations were playing havoc with running the place. In August he was in court charged with serving alcohol after nine-thirty: Karno's defence was that the wine had been ordered during dinner and guests were allowed to consume it until 10pm. Common sense prevailed and this charge was thrown out, but he was found guilty of supplying ice cream after nine o'clock, under a regulation which made it illegal to consume more than two courses for lunch and three for dinner. One wonders whether the great impresario, in the dock for serving ice cream after hours, might have concluded that things weren't turning out quite as he'd expected, while simultaneously filing the incident away for some future sketch.

Autumn saw the cast of *Knick Knacks* take on Karno's next production, *Nosey Knows*,[13] which was promoted as a farcical sketch rather than a revue. *The Stage* tells us more:

> The central figure ... is a nondescript character known as Nosey Parker, who has an unhappy knack of spreading evil reports concerning everyone he comes in contact with. We find him first in Josiah Flitterwick's Governmental Stores, where he causes trouble ... of which circumstance a German spy, Smart, endeavours to take fullest advantage. Then, later, Nosey Parker's lying propensity is centred upon a Government Employment Bureau, whither come Flitterwick's former workpeople to enlist for National Service. Finally, having married his late employer's moneyed charwoman, Martha, Nosey Parker's curiosity finds ample scope in a suburban residential district. In this scene he secures, by the aid of the newly enlisted Flitterwick, the arrest of the spy.[14]

At the Liverpool Empire in mid-December (and two months later in Leeds) Karno's sketch shared the bill with a comic called Will Hay, who was just developing his officious, incompetent schoolmaster act. Hay had been on the halls since 1910 but with limited success, and had been forced to work as a cinema handyman to make ends meet. Soon he would find himself in Karno's schoolroom.

Accounts of Hay's time with Karno vary, but listings suggest that having shared the same circuit that winter, he was recruited to take over the lead in *Nosey Knows* from George Hestor in Birmingham in mid-February 1918.[15] Hay's wife Gladys and his sidekick schoolboy character, played by Tommy Prior, also joined the cast.[16] A later legal case between Hay and agents Murray and Dawe reveals he was initially contracted to appear in *Three Bites*, but joined the *Nosey Knows* company instead. Hay's solo slot on the tour was taken by another future Karno collaborator, Robb Wilton.[17]

27.2 Will Hay in Karno days – almost certainly in character as Nosey Knows (courtesy Trevor Buckingham).

27. MAKING HAY

Nosey Knows

Scene two: Nosey is applying for a job at a Government Employment Office:

> Rolo: What brought you here?
> Nosey: My feet.
> Rolo: What do you want?
> Nosey: I'm looking for a Government situation.
> Rolo: Have you ever worked for the Government before?
> Nosey: Very nearly. There was sufficient evidence.
> Rolo: What kind of work do you want?
> Nosey: I don't want to work. I want a Government job.
> Rolo: Are you good at book-keeping?
> Nosey: Yes, I borrowed a book from a pal of mine seven years ago, and I've still got it.

Hay quickly made the part his own and Karno allowed him to include some of his own signature material by way of a schoolroom scene, with gags like:

> Boy: Who was Noah's wife?
> Nosey: Why, er, Joan of Arc.

In late 1917 Karno had secured a revised contract with Moss Empires. Adeler and West noted: 'The value of the contract … worked out at between £60,000 and £70,000 which is sufficient proof that Karno was still a force to be reckoned with … Everything was left to the judgement of the producer a rare thing indeed in theatrical agreements.'[18] So while Karno was recruiting Will Hay to join *Nosey Knows,* he also launched a new revue for Moss called *Phew!,* written with John Gerant.

It was the story of a money-grabbing family's efforts to secure their inheritance before their dying patriarch can marry his young nurse. When it opened at the Nottingham Empire in late January 1918, local critics praised the leads (double act George Goodfellow and Jennie Gregson) but *The Stage* was scathing:

> Nottingham has afforded a congenial starting ground for many new ventures, but … there seems little to warrant a repetition of that … unless some drastic … improvements of an indifferently constructed

> work may be found ... Capable artistes ... were handicapped from start to finish by the material. Such plot as there is turned upon the avariciousness of an ill-assorted crowd of family sharks to share the potential bequests of Robin Rudd ... an inmate ... in a nursing home. The gently stimulating nursing of Lettice Hope proves more efficacious than the resources of the British Pharmacopeia and for all practical purposes the story ... might well have been allowed to close here ... But after a very unconvincing simulaerum [sic] of the front at Brighton, the audience was invited to accompany the party to a cottage on Dartmoor to which the convalescent Robin had been transported, followed by the family crowd but protected by the ever-vigilant Lettice. Of the family coterie's subsequent peregrinations, it is sufficient to add that there is represented a hasty return to London, followed by the marriage of Lettice and Rudd.[19]

He didn't like it. Undaunted, *Phew!* began a six-month tour of the provinces and reviews soon improved, this one being typical: 'The farce goes with a swing from start to finish ... the dialogue and gags being smart and well put.'[20]

The cast were responsible for organising their own accommodation, and in November tragedy struck when James Leslie was unable to find lodgings at Ashton-Under-Lyne. *The Manchester Evening News* ran the story: 'Deceased, who was 54 years of age ... arrived on Sunday with other members of Mr Karno's company at Ashton but was unable to find lodgings and spent the night rambling about. On Monday ... he failed to attend at the theatre in the evening, and yesterday morning his dead body was found in a ditch ... death ... was due to exposure.'[21] To have lived through the war only to die in a ditch in Manchester a week before the Armistice seems particularly cruel; one wonders why another member of the company couldn't have afforded the poor chap some shelter.

Early 1918 saw a huge German offensive on the Western Front: every available man was thrown into the British line and leave was curtailed. This, coupled with a new curfew order, made life even harder for the theatre industry, as *The Stage* noted: 'The ... "Curfew" order on the London theatres has been ... a blow ... Several houses ... experienced a sudden drop ... unfortunately, it synchronised with the serious war news and the consequent and conspicuous absence of khaki. People will soon adapt themselves to the 10.30 closing, but ... London must ...

27. MAKING HAY

do without ... that large element of soldier life which has so greatly helped the theatres.'[22] The men doing their duty, and those that bore the scars of it, needed Karno comedy more than ever.

In February Karno sent the *Three Bites* company (and a full orchestra) to perform at the Stoke War Hospital, and his name would have been familiar to every soldier. A few weeks earlier the press reported an appeal from Lieutenant F.T. Nettlingham, who was busy collating the songs and rhymes written by those on active service under the title *Tommie's Tunes*. Nettlingham noted: 'Some of them are ... lewd and obscene, but it would be a monstrous shame if any of them were lost ... one of the most widespread is:

> We are Fred Karno's Army, A jolly fine lot are we.
> Fred Karno is our Captain, Charlie Chaplin our O.C.
> And when we get to Berlin, the Kaiser he will say:
> Hoch! Hoch! Mein Gott! What a jolly fine lot, are the 2 _ 4th R. E. T.'[23]

This is the earliest reported account of the song I have found, and the words are almost exactly as recorded by Karno in his memoirs. It was sung to the tune of the hymn *The Church's One Foundation*. Another press report noted: 'The refrain ... appears to be highly popular, for we find it sung, with local application in the last line, by almost every regiment.'[24] The Army Service Corps had its own version, and it must have been surreal for Fred Jr. to hear his comrades singing it in the trenches of Salonika. The lyric that seems to have been most enduring was included in *The Daily Express* publication *Songs That Won the War*:[25]

> We are Fred Karno's Army, the Ragtime Infantry,
> We cannot fight, we cannot shoot, no earthly use are we?
> And when we get to Berlin, The Kaiser he will say.
> Hoch, Hoch! Mein Gott! What a bloody fine lot, are the ragtime infantry.

It became an army standard, and a few years later was reportedly taken up as the unofficial song of the Eton College Officer Training Corps. It was sung for the first time on film in MGM's *Reunion* (1933), and thirty years later it was included in the musical *Oh What A Lovely War*. 'Fred Karno's Army' passed into the British language – and it wasn't the only Karno reference that endured, as this report reveals: '"We're in Meredith!" … During the war when a German trench had been taken over it was a common thing for the victorious Tommies to rush in … with the triumphant expression on their lips.'[26] The Tank Corps supposedly named their new-fangled contraptions after Karno's sketches, going into battle with *Jail Bird*, *Early Bird* and *Mumming Bird* scrawled on the side of their machines.

Fred Jr. had a short respite from the carnage, returning to Britain on leave in May 1918. His tour of duty had not improved his discipline, and Queenie remained an irresistible temptation. He was reported absent without leave numerous times over the next few weeks, before eventually being apprehended by the civilian police on 7 June. Three weeks later he and Queenie were married at Fulham Road register office.[27] After the wedding he went absent again, but later handed himself in and was returned to his unit. The war disrupted more than Fred Jr.'s love life – in April *The Era* reported that his father had been forced to relocate at very short notice:

> Fred Karno's offices … at Ancaster House, Cranbourn Street, have been "commandeered" for Governmental war purposes. So Frederick & Co. have flitted to Lyric Chambers, 27 Shaftsbury-avenue – next door to the Lyric Theatre. Just before we went to press Karno and staff might have been observed struggling with the official safe and other necessary goods and chattels, in order to hurry up the Government's "removers" in dumping them down into the new Karnories![28]

The war had increasingly impacted people's daily lives – German submarines were now going all out to blockade Britain into starvation, leading to food shortages and rationing. For many a restricted diet was nothing new, as Alf Reeves pointed out in a letter to Syd Chaplin: 'Our rulers tell the people to eat less, a great many of these same people never had enough to eat in their lives. The Daily Mail advocates two meatless days a week. I know people … who had meat only once a week, on Sunday … and then it was only a piece of fat.'[29] Such domestic troubles were meat and drink to Karno's comedy imagination.

27.3 Comedy on rations – Robb Wilton (author's collection).

27. MAKING HAY

Karno's next sketch, *Rations*, was written by Bert Lee and R.P. Weston, a partnership best known for some classic songs of the period, including Florrie Forde's *Good-bye-ee*. Robb Wilton was hired to lead, and like Will Hay before him, Wilton was gaining his first big break in revue thanks to Karno.[30] It opened on 1 April 1918 at Colchester, and *The Stage* gives us a flavour of what it called a 'revuette':

> The first scene … opens with a public park, in which there is a depot for issuing ration cards for kissing. There are many applicants, and the work of interrogation falls upon Robb Wilton … scene two shows a queue … outside the shop of a meatless butcher … Scene [three] is suggestive of food hoarding. It is called Lady Hoardly's secret and is very funny … Scene four … hits off happily the injunction to wear less clothes … The humour comes mainly from Mr Wilton and Jack Mann as Corporation road men, whose business is to erect various structures in the thoroughfare … "snap time" comes before anything tangible has been done. During the luncheon interval the pair become sentimental; their heart-to-heart causes great merriment.[31]

With Wilton and Hay, Karno had superb leads in two of his shows, both of whom went on to become goliaths of British comedy. Hay ultimately became the bigger star, but Wilton was perhaps a more typical Karno comic. His lugubrious Lancastrian drawl was reminiscent of Fred Kitchen or Harry Weldon, a similarity not lost on the press: 'Since Fred Kitchen's day Karno has not struck a comedian like Robb Wilton, and it is doubtful whether Fred or Robb will regard this as the greater compliment.'[32]

Phew!, *Nosey Knows*, *Three Bites* and *Rations* all ran through summer 1918, as did *Mumming Birds*, and it was September before anything new appeared. Meanwhile several other producers staged revivals or new versions of Karno's shows. *All Women* was staged by producer Fred J. Grace; *Knick Knacks* was licensed to Enterprising Productions, who ran it under the title *Wit and Wisdom*; and *The New Slavey* was put on by Byron and Stanley. It is impossible to establish whether Karno was licensing his back catalogue because he could not fund productions himself, or whether Moss Empires was now in control of the rights. But one deal certainly of Karno's making was a new partnership with Leon Vint, a hypnotist turned impresario with a chain of cinemas, several stage productions

385

and four theatres of his own. Karno presumably needed Vint's financial support to produce shows outside the Moss contract, and together they began planning a joint production. Meanwhile, challenges kept mounting.

1918 heralded an outbreak of highly infectious and deadly influenza. It was one of the most significant pandemics in human history. The crisis was largely overshadowed by events in war-torn Europe, but in neutral Spain it was widely reported – it therefore became known as 'Spanish Flu'. The First World War killed around eighteen million people, Spanish Flu reportedly killed fifty million, a quarter of a million of them in Britain. Many theatres were ordered to close to help contain the outbreak, others advertised themselves as safe because they were well ventilated or because they sprayed the auditorium with 'germ-killers'. It was another good reason for punters to stay at home, and as they banged the nails into the coffin lids, Spanish Flu hammered another into music hall itself.

Against this backdrop Karno found himself the leaseholder of a West End theatre, when he and Vint took over the Kingsway.[33] Vint seems to have been the senior partner in their endeavour, but they worked together to produce their new revue *A Week-End* – written by Walter W. Ellis and launched at the Theatre Royal, York, on 26 August. After a further week in Margate it moved to the Kingsway on 12 September. *The Globe* provides some details: 'The farce concerns a country station-master with a penchant for "high-life", some visitors from London, one from Paris, and an amusing development of the spy menace. There is a certain amount of drama blended with sheer farce. Miss Yvonne Arnaud returns to the London stage in this piece … Mr Ernest Thesiger plays the station-master.'[34]

It was a quality cast: Arnaud was an accomplished French actress who went on to have an illustrious fifty-year career, while Thesiger[35] was a contemporary of Noel Coward – he is now best remembered for his later roles in Gothic horror films. As Laurel and Hardy fans will spot, the plot had shades of Arthur Jefferson's *Home from the Honeymoon*, which was the basis for both *Duck Soup* (1927) and *Another Fine Mess* (1930):

> Placed in … the country house of an absent minded professor of music … its plot centres upon … two young men friends, pretending to be in the secret service, choosing the particular week-end of the professor's expected absence at a musical festival to invite themselves and two ladies (not their wives) to the house … A railway smash brings the professor

27. MAKING HAY

back, and with the assistance of the village stationmaster, there is a general redistribution of the forces for the night. Next morning the wives arrive and add to the perplexities of the situation; and then a genuine secret service agent to confound the liars. Roars of laughter rewarded the inventor of these humours and their enactors.[36]

27.4 Leon Vint (courtesy Peter Lee, Nuneaton Local History Group).

Against the odds the show was an unqualified success, and ran at the Kingsway for six months. To add to their good fortune, just as Karno and Vint decided to close the show they were approached by producers Grossmith and Laurillard, who were desperate to find a West End home for a new show called *Oh Joy*. With as much feigned reluctance as they could muster, Karno and Vint agreed to forego the lease on the Kingsway for the princely sum of £1200 – a huge premium. What's more, Karno persuaded Moss Empires to take on *A Week-End* and it joined his revues on the provincial circuit, where the lead was taken over by A.W. Baskcomb. Despite this success, there were no further collaborations with Vint – junior partner wasn't really Karno's style.

A month after *A Week-End* appeared at the Kingsway, Karno's next Moss revue, *Kill or Kure*, opened at the Liverpool Empire. It was again written by Karno and John Gerant, with music by Joe Cleve, and saw the return of Dan Rolyat, who had starred in *His Majesty's Guests* a decade earlier. He was popular with the critics: 'Dan Rolyat ... as a funny professor whose line is flesh reducing. One of the professor's obese patients is Johnny Trundley ... the fat boy of Peckham. Rolyat ... is richly funny ... there is a grotesque semblance of plot on which hinges scores of jokes.'[37]

As ever, Karno was on trend: fashion was moving away from the Victorian hourglass figure toward the waif-like, boyish style of the twenties, so dieting was all the rage. Johnny Trundley's only claim to fame was being hugely overweight – he'd been over seventy kilograms by the age of five. He had appeared on the halls as a curiosity, amazing the audience by his mere presence, but Karno was no freak-show purveyor. He gave Trundley the only legitimate performance credit of his career: the part of an obese character in a show about losing weight.

387

27.5 Dan Rolyat (author's collection).

A month after *Kill or Kure* began its tour, the war came to an end. The Armistice, on 11 November 1918, was marked by huge celebrations and there was an immediate surge in attendance at theatres and halls (Spanish Flu be damned). Karno comics who had survived the carnage gradually returned, no doubt changed forever by the experience. Harry Oxberry survived, despite being an early volunteer, and joined the cast of *Three Bites*, while Archie Glen reappeared in *Kill or Kure* and maintained the show's good reviews:

> Fred Karno's company in Kill or Kure … achieve a laughing success … The character of Bertram Boodle, who takes a doctor's place for a short time with such hilarious effect, except to the unhappy patients, is gleefully interpreted by Archie Glen.[38]

Not all returning veterans were able to pick up where they left off, some had been fatally wounded by war – and so had music hall.

28.

Money to Burn

"What steps did you take when the trouble started?"
"Very long ones."
(Fred Karno personal joke archive, 15 August 1932)

MUMMING BIRDS had been running for over fourteen years yet was still getting rave reviews, and in September 1918 at the Borough Theatre, North Shields, the sketch welcomed a new cast member: fifteen-year-old Leslie Karno. How much time Karno had spent with his son as he grew up is unclear. Although Leslie recalled Karsino being a childhood playground, one of the letters in his archive reveals his father did not know his birthday, suggesting they spent very little quality time together.

Given that he was abandoned by Karno at a very early age, it seems surprising that Leslie should join his father's company at all, but he went further and took the stage name Leslie Karno – one imagines Edith was horrified. Perhaps he was just a typical teenager, keen to untie himself from his mother's apron strings and follow his calling as a performer. As he forged his own career with Karno, Edith worried that the apple of her eye might find life on the road too much of a temptation, writing to him: 'Be a brave little man and don't be led into temptation by some of the horrible women you … meet. If … there should be a weak moment … just stop and think to yourself, no, it is through such as these pests that my mother's life had been wrecked.'[1]

A few months after Leslie joined Karno, his older brother returned from the army.[2] Fred Jr. received a disability pension due to 'the effects of kick by mule', although quite what these were is unclear. He was fit enough to work and start a family – Queenie soon gave birth to their first son, Fred Karno Westcott.[3]

The two boys were joining a Karno empire that was a shadow of its former self. Despite his Moss contract, Karno had struggled financially since investing so much money in Karsino. Adeler and West wrote: 'The good ship Karno was not riding the war-troubled waters quite so easily as of yore. He had lost Charlie Chaplin, Kitchen had left ... and his comedians' ranks had been sadly thinned by the Great War. But was the indomitable little man downhearted? The answer is distinctly in the negative.'[4]

One wonders what steps he took to try to make Karsino pay, and this court report from December 1918 perhaps provides a clue: 'At Feltham yesterday Frederick John Karno ... was summoned for selling spirits over the maximum price. An inspector of Ministry of Food said he was charged a shilling for a "drop" of whisky ... a fine of £30 and £5 5s costs was imposed.'[5]

His operational challenges had obviously not gone away, and this brush with the authorities perhaps prompted Karno to decide that if he couldn't beat them, he'd join them. A few weeks later he stood for election to Middlesex County Council, much to the amusement of the press. As one newspaper put it: 'He will add to the gaiety of that sombre body if he succeeds.'[6] The election on 8 March 1919 was notable for a vigorous campaign by the Cinematograph Exhibitors Association, which supported sixteen candidates campaigning on a platform of Sunday opening for cinemas – presumably Karno was keen to thwart them. He was not elected and that was the end of his political career.

Keen to maintain appearances, Karno had bought himself a second-hand Rolls Royce in 1917, and with peace now bringing fresh optimism, he sold it to the former prime minister Lord Rosebery and ordered a brand-new six-litre Alpine Eagle. This was a souped-up Silver Ghost, lauded as the best car in the world and with a price-tag to match – £3,000.[7] Rolls provided the factory-built chassis and each car was then individually designed and built by one of several coachbuilding companies to the client's personal specification. Karno saw an opportunity for some publicity and launched a competition, offering a prize of fifty pounds for the best design. Avonmore Motor and Carriage Co. were the published winners, although the car was eventually built by Fountains Auto-Carriage Works of Horsham. They took their time – Karno had to wait over two years for it to be delivered. He chose an eye-catching colour scheme of 'cobaltine violet' with a black roof – you can take the man out of the circus, but you can't take the circus out of the man.

A MUSIC-HALL CELEBRITY'S LUXURIOUS COUPE.

AFTER having waited two years for the chassis and five months for the completion of the coachwork, Mr. Fred Karno, the music-hall celebrity, has just taken delivery of a Rolls-Royce, the body of which is constructed on exceptionally luxurious lines, the work being carried out by Fountain's Auto-Carriage Works, Ltd., of Horsham.

The roof and upper portion is finished in black, while the scuttle and lower parts of the body are finished in cobaltine violet. An interesting feature in the scuttle is

Below: This three-quarter front view shows the luxurious lines. Note also the "bumpers," which are fitted front and rear, and the roof extension.

the method adopted for ventilation in hot weather. A single lever acting through the agency of the Bowden wire control opens a portion of the lower part of the scuttle, which is pivoted at its centre and when closed is scarcely noticeable. The discs on the wheels, the bonnet, radiator and fittings of the car are finished in dull ozidized silver. This scheme is extended to the facia board also, which is three-sided, and has dull black fittings.

While some critics might suggest that the exterior finish of the car has been over-elaborated, the interior is the very epitome of good taste combined with luxurious comfort. The upholstery is carried out in a plain fawn cloth in which a slight mauve tint is just

Above: In the boot is a commodious double dickey, while further auxiliary seating is provided inside.

visible. It is in saddle bag style, with a perfectly plain finish. Two sliding seats are fitted which, when brought into line with one another, form one continuous seat, providing room for three people, including the driver. A fourth emergency seat is provided which, when the near side main seat is pushed right back, can be placed near the door, facing either backwards, forwards or towards the centre of the car. This small seat is kept in a locker behind the driver's seat, and can be taken out of the car and used by the roadside.

The doors are fitted with frameless plate-glass windows, which are raised by turning a small handle on the inside. Inside the doors are finished with polished wood panels in Kingswood veneer, which is quartered so that the grain forms a diamond in the centre of each panel.

28.1 Karno's Rolls, The Motor, *7 September 1921 (courtesy Graham Robinson).*

Such extravagances wouldn't pay for themselves, so in the meantime Karno had launched a new show. *Nosey Knows* had been doing good business for over a year, with Will Hay proving very popular, so he was given a new vehicle called *Moonstruck*, which opened at Newport on 30 December 1918.[8] Once again written by Karno, John Gerant and W.H. Briggs, it was described as 'an entomological, astronomical absurdity.'[9]

Hay, who was a highly accomplished amateur astronomer, played Peter Pim, an astronomical student tutored by two professors hell-bent on discovering a rare beetle. As the thing scuttled about the stage on invisible wires, they resorted to mallets and traps which did more harm to them than their quarry. The sketch ended with Hay prostrate as the others hurried off-stage with a stretcher which (they neglect to realise) does not contain him. Given Hay's established schoolmaster character it seems strange that he was not cast as one of the professors from the outset, but Karno was happy to let him develop the role into that of trainee professor, and he soon introduced material from his solo act. His co-stars were Frank Harmer and Ennis Parkes (Mrs Jack Hylton), and between them they ensured the sketch garnered excellent reviews: 'A butterfly hunt in midwinter is something of a novelty, and those who witness it ... will doubtless enter into the hilarity of the hunt with great gusto ... Will Hay ... indulges in so many quaint facial expressions and initiates ... so many laughable events, that the audience were hearty in their appreciation of his smart business.'[10]

The peace and stability of 1919 must have seemed a world away from the previous four years, as *Moonstruck* joined *Kill or Kure*, *A Week-End* and *Three Bites* on provincial circuits. The next show was a revue, and opened at the Colchester Hippodrome on 22 September. *Hustle* was written by Karno and Briggs, with music by Philip Braham and lyrics by Ronald Jeans, although later advertising credited the lyrics to Helen Dircks – the first female writer on a Karno production.[11] The show starred A.W. Baskcomb and told the story of how a chaotic stockbroker saved his struggling business by applying a miraculous system of mind and memory training. This was lampooning a craze for 'Pelmanism', a system created by the 'Pelman Institute', which claimed that the mind could be improved with training in the same way physical exercise enhances the body. *The Stage* provides us with the details:

> The action opens in the office of Simon Slack, a stockbroker ... Slack is blind to his failings, and believes he can effectively rectify his insolvency by hoodwinking his rich sister Sophie, who is about to return from abroad, and has signified her intention of settling money upon supposed children of Alan Slack, Simon's son. Alan, however, has no children, neither is he married, and a hurried quest for a subterfuge only succeeds in revealing the truth to Sophie. These facts are known to Pullman B. Swift, inventor of Pullman's Memory Magic ... Who undertakes ... to "Pullmanise" the entire business. Simon and his staff ... emerge from the treatment very successfully except Vivian Sharp, Slack's right hand man, who shows no aptitude for mind development; while Alan, being quite the reverse, becomes so obsessed by the training that he delegates Vivian to make love to Sylvia Smart on his behalf until the day fixed for the wedding. The next scene shows the resuscitated business, wherein progress and success have displaced chaos and ruin. But there is a flaw in the new order of things, and this is ultimately traced to Vivian who ... has succeeded in winning the heart ... of Sylvia. One is sorry when the whole laughable and attractive proceedings come to an end.[12]

28. MONEY TO BURN

One wonders if Karno's mind was preoccupied by his continuing money worries, since shows about hustlers and swindlers seemed to have become the order of the day. In December *Money to Burn* opened at Edmonton, this time a tale of get-rich-quick wartime profiteers. It starred Syd Howard as Mr Johons, whose 'malapropisms and misplaced aspirates' were at the heart of the comedy. Howard would go on to a successful film career, but he didn't cut the mustard with Karno and was quickly replaced by George Hestor. The show ran for almost a year to good reviews – though frustratingly, none of them tell us anything about the plot.

On the eve of a new decade, his fourth in the business, Karno placed a large advertisement in *The Era* to promote his productions, which claimed he had contracts for the next six years. No doubt frustrated at the long wait for his new Rolls, he spent £1,600 on a new Italian Isotta Fraschini – among the most luxurious cars of its day[13] – but later took the dealer to court to get his money back, complaining it was so uncomfortable that his passengers were thrown around 'like corks in a bottle'. The court report went on to say: 'Mr Karno ... drove a party ... to Henley. When they got there, they looked as though they'd been prize fighting, rather than motoring.'[14] He received little sympathy from the judge, who threw out the case and made Karno pick up the costs. He put it down to experience and invested in a new Cadillac.

The spring of 1920 marked his third new show in five months: *Isle of Troy*, starring Mark Daly. It had nothing to do with Homer's *Iliad*, and was instead the tale of a man named Troy who runs an island as a bolthole for those suffering relationship trouble.[15] Any story on that theme still had the potential to scandalise the audience, so the programme declared "For Adults Only!" – but any promise of excitement turned out to be illusory:

> There is a wild touch of travesty in "The Isle of Troy" ... The idea might, perhaps, have been used to better advantage. Apart from a tendency to allow matters to run outside of the subject, a defect is the rather sudden and unsatisfactory ending. As an excuse to introduce some rollicking fun making, the piece deserves well, and there certainly is an abundance of diverting burlesque in which matters relating to sex problems are humorously satirized ... however, the piece does not fulfil the promise of its first scene ... Mr Daly cuts a distinctly amusing figure as an itinerant bookseller, who unwittingly becomes inveigled into a matrimonial plot. Woolmer Young ... does exceptionally well as the ambitious secretary of

Troy, an idealist, who has founded an island, whither those disappointed with the relationship of the sexes can repair for solace.[16]

It would have been better named *The Isle of Atlantis,* since it sank without trace. Karno wasn't the only one having an artistic crisis: Charlie Chaplin was by now being labelled yesterday's man. He made only two films in 1919, *Sunnyside* and *A Day's Pleasure,* both of them badly received. *The Stage* noted: 'The horrid rumour gains ground that ... Charlie Chaplin, is "going off"! His last film "Sunnyside", was decidedly not up to the average ... Now the depressing news ... that his latest effort is equally deficient ... Charles, my friend, take a rest! ... Your old guv'nor Fred Karno, would be pleased to have you back – even at a slight increase in salary!'[17]

Chaplin had good reason to be off-form: he was trapped in a loveless marriage (soon to end in messy divorce) and was grieving the death of his infant son Norman. But his next film, his first feature as director, would make his critics eat their words. *The Kid* (1921) is widely recognised as a masterpiece, with Chaplin combining tragedy and slapstick in a way that took film comedy and pathos to an entirely new level. As noted earlier, some believe Chaplin used Karno's glazier business in *The Kid* – but I think not. The doss house scenes may have borrowed from *Early Birds* or *The Casuals* but an undoubted influence, was Chaplin's own experience of the Lambeth workhouse. The opening title card sums up his style: 'A picture with a smile – and perhaps, a tear', and the film prompted *The New Statesman* to call him 'A man of Dickensian genius.'[18]

We have jumped ahead. Back in spring 1920, *Moonstruck* ended its run and Will Hay licensed the sketch from Karno at a cost of one pound per week, renaming it *Entomology* (or *Find The Beetle*).[19] He went on to perform it for many years, including at the 1930 Royal Variety Performance. Hay's time with Karno greatly influenced his subsequent work: he gained experience of more physical comedy, and while he was never an acrobatic mime, his talent for facial expressions, trips and general bumbling chaos was a key component of his later comedy. Hay recalled that Karno's mantra was simply "If in doubt, fall on your arse",[20] and said: "I was one of his army of comedians and that's where I learned the discipline you need in comic acting. Most of what I know I owe to Fred Karno."[21]

Although Hay had sometimes performed his schoolmaster sketch assisted by a small boy, working with Karno encouraged him to include a wider cast.[22] As biographers Seaton and Martin noted: 'Experience with Karno had taught him

28. MONEY TO BURN

the importance of having a side character to play off, a "feed" whose contribution emphasised the comedy of the main character.'²³ Thereafter the schoolboy became a permanent feature and he added an old man to the act – Harbottle, a man deemed too stupid ever to graduate. It was a formula that made him a star both on stage and screen, most notably as the head of a memorable trio with Graham Moffatt (as young Albert) and Karno old-boy Moore Marriott (as Harbottle). With huge film successes such as *Oh, Mr Porter!* (1937) and *Convict 99* (1938), Hay probably ranks third behind Chaplin and Laurel among Karno apprentices who made good, and is considered one of the greatest British comics of all time. He was a uniquely talented reaction comic who could get big laughs simply from an expertly timed double-take, sniff or raised eyebrow. Ronnie Barker called him: 'The best straight man that ever was.' His schoolmaster character was a tour de force of officious pomposity, and went on to influence the next generation of comedians and writers – not least Jimmy Perry, who cited Hay's comedy trio as his inspiration for Captain Mainwaring, Pike and Corporal Jones in *Dad's Army*.

28.2 Will Hay in familiar guise as a schoolmaster (courtesy David Absalom, Britishpictures.com).

As another Karno discovery headed off toward a bright solo career, Karsino re-opened for the season. In July *The Era* reported that he again hosted the Music Hall Ladies' Guild's children's day out, and with a very special guest: 'The children's outing ... will rank as a red letter day in the memory of all present ... the youngsters were received as the welcome guests of ... Mr Fred Karno who provided a splendid lunch and tea ... there were games and when, later in the afternoon, Miss Marie Lloyd appeared amongst the children and sang to them before presenting the prizes, the happiness of the little ones was complete.'²⁴

A few weeks later *The Era* reported on a grand fancy dress ball:

> A very enjoyable fancy dress ball took place ... at Karsino ... Mrs Freeman secured 1st prize for ladies (an ivory mounted umbrella) as a "Coster girl with donkey barrow of fruit" (the donkey objected to enter

the ballroom) ... Premier honours (a gold bound wallet) fell to Mr Freeman as an "Oriental Slave Driver," with three small boys chained together as his slaves ... a number of other dresses were of considerable merit, especially ... Mr and Mrs Fred Karno as a Boy and a Girl, attended by Mrs F. Sandy as the Nurse.[25]

The mind boggles. That summer another British film company used Karsino as a location: 'Thespian Films ... are to specialize in films having variety or theatrical stars in leading parts ... their first venture is ... "Forty Winks", in which Rebla, the well-known comedy juggler, appears as a dreamer who dreams strange dreams at Fred Karno's Karsino.'[26] Beyond hiring out his hotel as a location, however, Karno continued to shun any involvement in the film industry. Presumably he was still scarred by years of piracy and poaching, but it was a mutual loss. Forever at the forefront of new ideas, his inventiveness would have been an interesting influence on early film development, and movies may have saved him financially.

Following the demise of the Fun Factory, Karno took on premises at 6 Church Street, Brixton, which served as storage for what was left of his theatrical stock. Meanwhile, autumn heralded a flurry of new shows. The first was *What's What*, a revamped *Isle of Troy*, which played the Moss circuit to good reviews like this: 'A screamingly funny travesty of the sex question. Full of wholesome fun, it gives ample opportunity for the abilities of Ernest Sefton (the man who tells the tale) and Christine Cooper (the girl who mustn't be told).'[27]

Karno's sons continued to forge their own careers: Fred Jr. appeared in *Hustle,* while Leslie (still a teenager) elected to plough his own furrow, spending the year in a touring production called *Any Lady* followed by a part in a festive pantomime. Christmas saw another new Karno revue, *Red Hot*, which starred another comic who would go on to achieve huge popularity – Billy Bennett. Despite having a knockabout music-hall comedian as a father,[28] Bennett didn't start performing until the age of thirty-two, after a distinguished army career. Karno recruited him just a year later and was instrumental in nurturing his talent.[29] *The Stage* gives us a flavour of the show:

28.3 Billy Bennett (author's collection).

28. MONEY TO BURN

> The adventures of a wayward and obstinate village flapper are dealt with. For the reason that her father insists on marrying her to a certain Count, she vows to marry the very first man who asks her, and, as "the girl in red", becomes a conspicuous object of admiration. As a bevy of her friends are also dressed in red, much confusion ensues. All the girls are eventually married, and the Count, in order to win the flapper's love, becomes a shop assistant in the village store, and all ends happily.[30]

Bennett played the newly appointed store manager, and made his entrance in a packing case having posted himself to save the train fare. This review fills in the rest of the story:

> The business opens in Simpson's Emporium, where there are many amusing incidents, and the second scene shows the back of number 9, to where the mysterious young lady is thought to have retreated, and where many suitors await her. The wrong girl, of course, always turns up, but, in the last scene the real lady makes her appearance and reveals her identity after all but one of her would be suitors had fallen victim to the flappers! … the setting of the final scene, giving a mansion on one side, and a "five and a tanner" house, on the other, with the amusing skirmishes that occur between the higher and the lower bred families, is very smartly done.[31]

The show had echoes of both *His Majesty's Guests* and *London Suburbia*, featuring shoplifters, burglars, policemen and even a character named Meredith to add to the nostalgia. There was a topical theme too: the new housing schemes that were springing up in close proximity to large houses, with inevitable consequences for their wealthy occupants.

With his revue production line in full swing, Karno announced that a new show entitled *Sixes and Sevens* was on the way. It appeared in February 1921, but under a different name: *Yes Papa*.[32] *The Era* sets out the story:

> A … prologue gives us the gist of story of Lord William Marsden, a pseudo chauffeur, making love to Phyllis, the eldest of nine charming daughters of Sir Bodley Bulk. His hope also centres in "Bluebottle" running in the Derby, whose ensuing victory brings success in both

ventures ... The scene opens in ... the Nursery Wing of the Bodley Bulk mansion, the eight winsome daughters engaged in music lessons. The new governess is expected, but turns out to be a man, "Evelyn" Bunthorpe ... The girls determine to keep the "governess", and the disguise is soon forthcoming. Mr Ernest Sefton is a scream ... The dialogue sparkles with witticism, his lessons to the girls on "screams" is tremendous ... When a little later the "governess" has been imbibing somewhat freely, "she" tells the butler what she thinks of him, the audience is in a roar. Baby's bath-time is also a scream, "Baby" being "cousin to Fatty Arbuckle". Miss Olive Grant, a charming lady of ample proportions, is most amusing as Baby ... A capital finale presents the "tape" giving the progress of the great race across the stage, with the victory of Bluebottle and the union of the lovers.[33]

Sefton was an experienced revue performer and a safe pair of hands, but the lead was originally intended for an actor called Donald Calthrop, who was completing production of *Will You Kiss Me?* at the Comedy Theatre. Calthrop reneged on the arrangement but seems to have compensated Karno by offering him his play – hence Karno took over *Will You Kiss Me?*[34] as his next venture.

Adapted from a novel called *Too Much Efficiency*, this piece tackled another topical subject, time-and-motion studies, as this review explains:

American methods in efficiency are at times a source of amusement not only to the sociologist but to the American people themselves ... The story is built upon a millionaire merchant who saves in his business some 200,000 dollars per annum by calling in an expert efficiency engineer. He is induced to try the methods in his fifth avenue residence, and whilst he is away on holiday the efficiency expert is installed with all the paternal powers.[35]

By the time the efficiency expert has the butler, the maids and the millionaire's children punching into a timeclock, the play had reached the limit of farcical absurdity. In the final act a love story develops between the efficiency expert and Constance, the oldest daughter, but this change in pace spoilt the piece – or perhaps it was the terribly named leading characters, Alexander Hedge and Constance Bush. The show ran to mixed reviews.

28. MONEY TO BURN

The show also caused Karno some legal trouble. He cast a comic called Billy Leonard in the lead, but Moss Empires did not rate him and insisted he be replaced – Leonard subsequently sued for breach of contract. The matter was settled amicably out of court, but the story serves to demonstrate that Karno had now lost authority over his productions. Moss was happy to overrule him, even on matters such as casting, where Karno had a proven track record.

Happily Karno had a home-grown show ready to launch that spring. Mark Daly took on *French Beans*, which opened at the Jubilee Hall, Weymouth, on 25 April 1921. It was written by Austin Melford, Eric Blore and Fenton MacKay with music by Leslie Alleyn, and ran throughout the summer to steady reviews like this:

> Caesar Montague – an elderly "kill-joy" … turns up on pleasure bent at a fashionable hotel in a French watering place. Montague's arrival brings consternation to his nephew, who has secretly married an actress … Subterfuge is adopted to conceal the fact of the marriage, and the amusing complications that ensue show the "straight-laced" uncle in a fresh light … he proceeds to have a good time, and the nephew's wife … helps him along the road to reconciliation and pardon … Mark Daly … provokes constant laughter.[36]

As new shows appeared thick and fast, Karno no longer took any writing credit – one senses he was just churning them out from a Moss-funded sausage machine to comply with his contractual obligations. On *French Beans* he wasn't even credited as producer – instead it was listed as produced by Harry Hall 'under the personal supervision of Fred Karno.'[37] Unsurprisingly these productions lacked the old Karno magic (his name above the door only went so far), and nor did they generate the returns Moss had hoped for. It was only a matter of time before something would have to be done.

Perhaps frustrated at the way he saw the industry developing, in summer 1921 Karno took a leading role in a new industry group, the Association of Touring Managers. He was one of many producers who put their name to an open letter to the theatre owners, crying foul at the growing practice of using booking agents rather than dealing with touring company managers directly. They argued that the agents added unnecessary cost to a process that had worked perfectly well without them, although why Karno felt that way is hard to fathom, given that he'd employed agents such as Murray and Dawe himself.

Karno still had one show he could rely on, and *Mumming Birds* played on through the summer of 1921.[38] One of its former stars had thrown his last custard pie, however: on 6 July Billie Ritchie died following surgery for an injury he'd received two years earlier at the Fox film studios. Ritchie reportedly died as he had lived, in slapstick absurdity, after being kicked in the stomach by an escaped ostrich, although this injury probably just accelerated the stomach cancer which was the official cause of death. Despite their public spat over the origins of the Little Tramp, Chaplin attended his funeral and subsequently employed his wife Winnie (the original *Mumming Birds* saucy soubrette) as a wardrobe mistress. Whatever Stan Laurel thought of Chaplin, for some the bonds forged in Karno days still remained. Perhaps news of Ritchie's demise prompted his old Guv'nor to think about past glories in America, since a few days after the funeral *The Stage* reported that Karno had secured a tour on the Shubert vaudeville circuit. Once again this never materialised: presumably he was unable to muster either the cast or the funds.

Chaplin, meanwhile, was planning a return to England to promote *The Kid*, and the news was met with near hysteria in the press:

> The little great man is the most popular figure in the world … Never since the world began has the name of one mere man been a household word in every … corner of the world … We older folks are a little startled perhaps by our first observing how small children accept Charlie as a natural and integral part of the world they have lately entered. As well imagine a sky without aeroplanes, or a meadow without buttercups, as a world without Charlie. It is not easy to penetrate to the heart of his secret – to explain the power he wields amongst men, women and children … but Charlie is sincere, and that is why we love him. Underlying all the nonsense we discern, perhaps unconsciously, something that answers to our own perplexities.[39]

Chaplin arrived back in the old country on 10 September 1921 aboard Olympic, the same liner that he and his fellow plonks had travelled home aboard nine years earlier. Then they had been in second class, now he had a first-class suite, but the change in accommodation was as nothing compared with the change in his circumstances. He had left England a relative unknown, he returned the biggest film star the world had ever seen. He was greeted by civic dignitaries and huge crowds in Southampton, then whisked off by train to London, where he was met by an even larger throng at Waterloo. Chaplin was bundled into a car which turned Poverty Corner and drove up York Road, flanked by police fighting back the masses. At the Ritz Hotel he appeared on a first-floor balcony, thanked his adoring public for their welcome and threw roses into the crowd.

Charles Gulliver, the over-optimistic proprietor of the London Palladium, announced his intention to make Chaplin a huge offer to appear there in one of his old Karno sketches, but Charlie was now a commodity money couldn't buy. Besides, the press noted, he had come for a holiday and would resist all calls to perform in any way. Of course, a holiday wasn't easy with crowds following his every move, but it seems that Karno may have come to his rescue. Almost lost among the pages of press coverage are a handful of reports that Chaplin would be spending his first weekend up-river: 'Charlie Chaplin duly arrived in London on Saturday, and, as expected, was terribly mobbed by enormous crowds. One of his first visits was to his old "guv'nor", Fred Karno at Karsino.'[40]

28.4 Huge crowds greet Chaplin in London, 1921 (courtesy Roy Export/Chaplin Archive).

29.

Prodigal Sons

Trainer: Remember Stiffy, whiskey is a slow poison.
Stiffy: I'm in no hurry.
(The Football Match, 1906)

IF CHAPLIN did spend his first weekend at Karsino it wasn't reported further in the press, but Karno's memoirs mention his visit so we might assume he did escape to Tagg's Island, at least for a few hours. Chaplin also attended a party at the Albany hosted by the playwright Edward Knoblock, a friend who had travelled back to England with him,[1] so Karno probably had a chance to show off his city pad too. The icing on the cake was that his Alpine Eagle was finally delivered just a week before Chaplin arrived. The Rolls meant the world to Karno: as his fortunes began to fade it increasingly came to stand for something – for a time when he could order the best car in the world without blinking, a time when the colour of its bodywork would still have pedestrians asking who on earth it belonged to. The car was as much a showman as Karno himself, and it had arrived just in time to impress Chaplin.

The superstar's return reinforced Karno's name in the public consciousness too, thanks to press reports like this:

> Chaplin's art was not invented by him. He has succeeded in … transferring to the screen the Karno tradition of dumb-show humour … Charlie is a great mimic, with a long memory and an original point of view. His work stands out because it has a more constructive dramatic quality than the rest … Chaplin antics are derived mainly from the

29. PRODIGAL SONS

> Karno school. The Karno school derives from the old clowns and ballets. The ballets are linked with the mystery plays and carnivals of the Middle Ages ... It would be possible to trace Chaplin's professional ancestry back through Roman saturnalia and ... to the earliest religious ceremonies, when living victims were sacrificed at rude altars to the accompaniment of grotesque gibberings and horrid humours.[2]

Even Karno didn't go as far as human sacrifice (*The Wow Wows* came close), but this article reinforces the idea that while his physical comedy was as old as the hills, he reinvented it for the music hall audience in an original and engaging way. Chaplin repeated the feat when he interpreted those same comic tropes on film.

Chaplin's arrival didn't slow down Karno's output. Billy Bennett's *Red Hot* had cooled down, ending its run earlier in the year, but the Guv'nor relaunched it in the autumn as *Scarlet Runners*. It opened on 10 October at the Cheltenham Hippodrome, and provided Fred Jr. with his first leading role as the oft-recurring character Meredith. Junior was well received by the critics:

> Mr Doddy Hurl and Mr Fred Westcott make a veritable riot of fun. There is a ... rehearsal of a Grecian play at a ladies' school and after an equally amusing scene on the dormitory floor at midnight, we are switched on to the interior of a stores, which is full of mirth making incidents. The fourth scene is a nice little skit of the housing scheme, and the interest of a whole street in a lovers' quarrel, a fight between two pals fresh out from the public house, and a "Bubbles" duet, are all excruciatingly funny, while the masked ball at the end ... is a fine finish.[3]

Despite reasonable reviews the sketch struggled to get consistent engagements. By November Hurl had been replaced by Gus Oxley, but not without a fight – he sued Karno for breach of contract. The court reports make for interesting reading:

> The manager said that, as they were losing money, expenses would have to come down, and that he was disappointed with the plaintiff's playing. The manager proposed to reduce plaintiff's salary one half, and was told in a letter that such reduction could not be accepted ... On the Tuesday ... plaintiff received a letter to the effect that he must take three months

holiday. He went on that evening at the second house, when he ... fell and broke his right collar bone ... There was a clause in the contract that if plaintiff was unable to perform "from any cause whatever" ... the manager could determine the contract.[4]

Since he was looking for a reason to sack Hurl, you might say Karno got a lucky break. His contract left the actor without a leg to stand on, but it brought Karno some unwanted attention:

> The Variety Artistes' Federation had a dispute with Mr Karno regarding a certain clause in his contract, whereby if an artiste was absent from three consecutive performances he or she could be summarily dismissed ... the judge said that, although he must find for Mr Karno, the contract was so unfair that he would deprive him of his costs if possible. The VAF then approached the AA [The Actors' Association] for its help in securing a more equitable contract ... Karno agreed to use the AA Standard Touring Contract, but then sent his manager to Leeds with his own contract in one hand and dismissal notices in the other.[5]

Karno did not take kindly to being told the terms on which he could employ his performers, and those unwilling to sign his contract were out. The circumstances were harsh but Karno had been right about Hurl's performance, and recasting the show greatly improved its reviews:

> Karno's comedy ... hits at the housing scheme as only Karno's can ... All he does ... is to put the smallest houses opposite the best and let the tenants meet. That is sufficient ... to produce a succession of roars ... the individuals responsible for the humour ... have such different styles and mannerisms that each is a host by himself. Oxley is bright and breezy ... Stewart is grotesque, whilst Westcott is quaint and reminiscent of H.O. Wills. What more could be wanted so far as comedy is concerned?[6]

This is the first review to reveal Fred Junior's style, comparing it to that of H.O. Wills, who was billed as 'the Curious Comedian'. Light comics were suave, sophisticated and well-dressed, interspersing their gags with patter, song and dance. There were two other 'types': character comedians like Will Hay, who took on a persona, often a figure of authority; and eccentric (or grotesque) comedians like Kitchen and Weldon, who had exaggerated mannerisms or physical characteristics – a funny walk, big boots or a speech impediment. Fred Jr.'s style made him better suited to revue than slapstick, and he was finally making a mark.

Irrespective of its positive reviews, *Scarlet Runners* was losing money within a month of being launched – and Karno's other shows were gradually slipping down the billing. The 'mini-revue', played as half of a general variety programme, had had its day, as this review reveals: 'French Beans depends solely for its success, or otherwise, on the business of Mark Daly ... The fact that he provokes considerable laughter in this role shows that music-hall fun merchants can obtain a measure of success with well-worn situations and quips, provided they are given with the requisite stage bluster ... otherwise, French Beans, would be unforgivable.'[7]

Audiences now wanted something more substantial: musical spectaculars like those being produced by Albert de Courville, Harry Day, and Wylie and Tate. Moss Empires' director H.M. Tennent realised that things had to change, and as Adeler and West wrote: 'Tennent sent for Karno ... the firm was feeling some anxiety about the big contract turning out a loss ... "Can you do a revue Mr Karno?" ... Fred felt a little hurt. He had been showing managers how to do revue for the best part of twenty years ... In a few moments he consented to ... substitute full length revues for the shorter sketches ... "Can I?" repeated Fred to himself as he emerged from the office. "Can I do a revue? I'll show 'em." And he did!'[8]

Karno immediately began work on a spectacular full-scale revue with no expense spared, unimaginatively titled *1922*. He set about finding a top-notch cast, which meant identifying a lead comic up to the task – it proved an inspired choice. Time is a healer and much water had passed under the bridge in the eleven years since Fred Kitchen betrayed his old friend and joined arch-rival Herbert Darnley. Who better to help Karno regain his former glory than his most popular comic? It was time for one last hurrah.

Kitchen had already made the transition to revue and remained firmly in the public's affections. One critic called him 'the greatest farcical comedian of our time.'[9] Now, after years ploughing his own furrow, he was delighted to be back with the old firm: he took a quarter page advertisement in *The Stage* wishing everyone festive greetings and proclaiming his return to Karno's company.[10]

29.1 Advertisement for 1922 (courtesy Simon Kitchen-Dunn).

With Kitchen and Harry Grattan, Karno pulled together a show of fourteen scenes. Willie Redstone supplied the music, J.W. Jackson the choreography, and *1922* opened at the Nottingham Empire on 16 January. The show began with Alec Regan as a lonely Pierrot, singing a wistful melody taken from *Scarlet Runners* called *Bubbles of Happiness* (which you may remember had a stage effect that landed Karno in court). Next came a scene at a railway station which introduced a female chorus supposedly on their way to the theatre. Played by Marie Blanche, the female lead leaves her vanity bag on the train, only for it to be returned by Kitchen, playing a faded old music-hall trouper. She takes pity on the old man and arranges for him to join her company.

Kitchen's involvement encouraged a return to pathos. The old comic and the young starlet share a duet, *A Glimpse of Past and Present*, before Kitchen reveals that his son is lying seriously ill. He clutches a telegram, which he dare not open as it reveals the child's fate. Blanche reads it for him and there is jubilation at the news the boy has recovered. Another scene was a Kitchen comedy masterclass, in which he attempts to assist a young couple trying to purchase some furniture on 'the hire system'. Things then descend into Karno farce, with a tenement scene called 'Classes and Masses' which was another variation on previous sketches. *The Stage* picks up the story: 'A quaintly topsy-turvy idea of a nobleman who builds tenements in his beautiful garden … and is not very pleased with the result, for his new neighbours are distinctly democratic in their habits … he gets to loggerheads with somebody, when his son saves the situation by recognizing the offender as a man who saved his life in the trenches.'[11]

29. PRODIGAL SONS

This denouement, focusing on a shared experience in the trenches, gave the scene's familiar clash of cultures an added dimension. The war had gone some way to breaking down class barriers, and the audience would have empathised with such bonhomie. *The Stage* review suggests the show was an eclectic mix of song, dance and drama:

> On the spectacular side there is the weird "Devil Dance" performed by ... Wal Norman and Mabel Holmes ... and there are several good songs ... There is a Grand Guignol burlesque which affords Fred Kitchen opportunity to display his powers as an actor. He plays the thing straight all through and gives a masterly representation of a fear-distraught, terrified man, haunted by the dread of, the audience knows not what, until ... there is a delicious anti-climax ... he is a happy father! ... A highly realistic Garage scene is quite a novelty ... with realistic looking cars. Suddenly the mascots on the cars come to life, and indulge in wild and whirling dances ... The finale to the revue is a very big feature ... "Twelve Months in Three Minutes", ... introduces the Months who, as they enter, are heralded in appropriate fashion by Alec Regan.[12]

Despite this ringing endorsement for Kitchen's straight acting, the 'Grand Guignol' playlet was discarded after the initial try-out week – Karno perhaps felt the audience would not appreciate their favourite comic in a straight role. He made other changes too, later adding a scene where the ladies' chorus appeared in negligees then invited men in the audience up on stage to 'help them dress' – how things had changed in ten years! The show was an immediate hit and quickly moved to London, where it broke records at both the Finsbury Park and New Cross Empires. Karno made the most of his new money-earner and took a month's holiday in Algiers.

The success of *1922* gave a short-term boost to Karno's smaller revues, but these all came to an end for the summer. The exception was *Mumming*

29.2 Fred Kitchen (left), Marie Blanche and Alec Regan in 1922 (courtesy Simon Kitchen-Dunn).

407

Birds, although Jimmy Russell finally hung up his schoolboy cap and retired. *1922* completed its six-month provincial tour with a week at Blackpool Opera House in late July, and although a fresh tour was planned for October, Kitchen decided it was time to move on. He and Marie Blanche joined Wal Pink for his show *If the Cap Fits.*

1922 and the short-lived but triumphant reunion with Kitchen had revitalised Karno's career, but this merely enabled him to continue throwing good money after bad at Karsino. That summer he installed an enormous 'Crystal Fairy Fountain', with five hundred jets throwing water forty feet into the air. Among the press reports of summer parties and charity functions there were occasional dramatic incidents: Karno had replaced his old hand-pulled ferry with a mechanical version, and in August a car almost fell off. It teetered precariously with its nose underwater, as its occupant Margaret Bannerman sat screaming hysterically on the back seat. Karno oversaw the rescue mission, with volunteers diving into the murky Thames, fastening cables and ropes and dragging the car to safety. Sadly this near-miss did not prompt the fitting of safety devices – a failure which was to have fatal consequences later.

Around the same time, the talk of the hotel was a mysterious face that had begun appearing at bedroom windows in the dead of night. One evening it spooked Karno's sister-in-law, and her screams alerted the Guv'nor who gave chase across the grounds (it's surprising how

29.3 Karsino car ferry (author's collection).

often Karno's real-life exploits sound like the plot of a Keystone movie). The culprit turned out to be a Belgian refugee whom Karno described as being affected by 'sex-mania' – he was eventually caught and returned to Belgium forthwith. Karno promptly surrounded his private apartment with blackberry bushes to keep future intruders at bay – a technique he also employed at the Albany, much to the astonishment of his upper-class neighbours.

1922 re-opened in the autumn with George Carney taking Kitchen's part and Beatrice Allen in the female lead. Carney had once befriended Chaplin in the ensemble of *The Football Match,* and later spent time working with the star

29. PRODIGAL SONS

in Hollywood as a gag-writer. Much of the original cast remained however, including Alec Regan and Elsie Carlisle, and Kitchen stepped in to cover for Carney at least once later in the year. There was new material too: Karno took over a Jackson Owen show called *Knight of The Garter*, staging it under the title *Oh Yes!* at Birmingham's Alexandra Theatre in late August. Owen played the lead, but further down the cast list one name stands out – Jimmy James. Whether this is the same Jimmy James who went on to become a star comic of the thirties and forties is unclear, but it's possible. Karno's memoirs don't list James among his 'discoveries' and I have never found a reference to *Oh Yes!* in any account of James's career, but Karno was certainly familiar with his work – years later he tried to persuade Hollywood studio bosses to bring the comedian to the States. What Hollywood would have made of James's famous 'Lion in the Box' routine is anyone's guess.

Oh Yes! opened to promising reviews:

> "Oh Yes!" had a capital reception … and deserved it. There is plenty of comedy and a consistent plot, which has reference to the theft of a diamond garter from Col. Chutney, whose daughter Dolly elopes … the whole company follow on the yacht "Na-poo" to Holland, and after a scene at "Bad"-wood races we come to an old English Garden where all ends merrily enough … Jackson Owen … is very funny throughout.[13]

There was always room for improvement though, as one reporter noted: 'Mr Karno was a critical member of the audience on Monday, so doubtless "Oh Yes!" will go on its way still further brightened.'[14]

Karno continued to have a role in the Association of Touring Managers, and in October took part in negotiations for new contractual arrangements between the managers and artistes. That same week the music-hall world was shocked by the death of the biggest female artiste of them all, Marie Lloyd – she was just fifty-two. One hundred thousand people lined the streets for her funeral, and they queued to visit her grave for days afterwards. Karno sent one of the four hundred floral tributes. A fortnight later his friendly rival Wal Pink also died – two deaths that must have brought Karno's own mortality into sharp focus. He wasn't getting any younger.

The next generation were going strong though, and when *Scarlet Runners* re-opened for the autumn season, Fred Jr. continued in the lead. His wife Queenie, meanwhile, made her first appearance for the family firm in *Mumming Birds*. With two small children (Fred, born 1919, and Kenneth, born 1921), they now experienced the challenges of family life as touring performers. One wonders whether Karno and Marie helped with babysitting duties that Christmas – it would be the last one they all spent together. Over the turkey Karno may have looked back with pride on a year where he stepped up to full-scale revue and was reconciled with Fred Kitchen. Both of his boys were doing well in their own right and he had two grandsons on his knee – even Karsino had enjoyed a busy summer season. If so, any optimism was misplaced: the seeds of failure were already sown, and Karno would later cite 1922 as the year that began the decline that ultimately led to his ruin.

There is a common perception of the Roaring Twenties as a period when bright young things in white tie and tails danced the Charleston in jazz clubs, but this belies the economic troubles that befell the country. Post-war Britain experienced a significant economic downturn, leaving many war veterans on the scrapheap. As Naomi Jacob put it: 'England was to be a land fit for heroes ... we let so many of the returned soldiers find out for themselves ... that it took a hero to live in it at all.'[15]

29.4 Mrs Fred Karno Jr. – Queenie Doyle (courtesy Louise Murchison).

The early part of the decade was particularly difficult, with mass unemployment and industrial stagnation eventually culminating in the General Strike of 1926. As the country spiralled into deep recession, Karno's finances continued to deteriorate.[16] *1922* was rechristened *1923*, but by then the show was losing two hundred pounds a week. The mood in the camp was further dampened by the sudden death of George Carney's wife, Vesta Pine, early in the new year.[17] Karno was now 56, and in January he wrote to Leslie saying he was winding down his productions and the boys would have to support themselves:

> I am tired of running a philanthropic institution ... sooner or later one comes to the end of one's resources ... I have impoverished myself keeping the shows running ... and I cannot do it any longer. I am getting older,

29. PRODIGAL SONS

and instead of my sons being the workers, and being able to depend on them to carry on the business, here am I slaving away to keep them ... It has got to stop now, and just see what you can do for yourself.[18]

Inevitably Karno became obsessed with saving money as he tried to keep the wolf from the door, and despite his previous philanthropy, he now developed a reputation for meanness. Leslie recalled that his father would not stretch to bus fares home for the women in his company, so Leslie found himself dipping into his own pocket. More significantly, he once again fell foul of the Actors' Association (AA) by paying his chorus girls less than the union minimum of three pounds per week. He could no longer excuse this by claiming to offer continuous employment, but with *Scarlet Runners* losing money and many actors out of work, he adopted a 'take it or leave it' attitude.

Four years earlier the VAF, the AA, the Musicians' Union (MU) and the National Association of Theatrical Employees (NATE) had formed a joint committee in order to unionise every place of entertainment and create a closed shop. This dispute was a chance to flex their muscles. It wasn't a completely united front, though: the VAF refused to agree to a walk-out unless its member George Carney continued to receive his one hundred pounds per week salary, and the other unions unsurprisingly felt it was sacrificing the lowly paid chorus girls for the sake of their highly paid star.[19] With or without the VAF, the AA had a score to settle. When the dispute made it to the press Karno's losses became public knowledge, with an inevitable impact on his ability to negotiate future production deals. He had little choice but to capitulate, and the union minimum was restored. Karno didn't like losing, and true to form he immediately closed *Scarlet Runners* and no-one got paid – so there!

The bad blood between Karno and the AA continued: it next accused him of blacklisting its members, and was only placated when he publicly advertised the names of those who had been employed since the dispute.[20]

With his theatrical enterprises now bringing nothing but losses and squabbles, Karno finally decided to seek opportunities in film. Although the circumstances are unclear, Karno entered into an agreement with Albert Brouett (who'd appeared in *Parlez Vous Français?*) to set up a film company called Brouett-Egrot. Its sole intention was to adapt Karno's sketches for the screen, and according to the British Film Institute they made *Jail Birds*, *Early Birds* and *Mumming Birds* – all written by P.L. Mannock and directed by Brouett. Amazingly, Karno

411

decided that his involvement would not be as director or producer – instead he decided to return to performing. The press reported: 'Mr Fred Karno, the music hall comedian, has followed the example of his old companion, Charlie Chaplin, and has gone "on the pictures".'[21]

> [In Early Birds] Mr Fred Karno himself appears as an old Jew, and his repulsive appearance constitutes a veritable triumph of make-up. The plot of the story is of minor importance. Those familiar with these sketches of the halls – and who is not? – are aware that they rely chiefly on their irresponsible knock about business for their humour, and it was a little surprising to find how well this brand of humour could be adapted for film purposes. Most of the scenes are laid in slum-land, and the different types of the inhabitants have been carefully and successfully chosen. Altogether, a genuinely funny film, well photographed and admirably produced.[22]

Despite complimentary reviews – 'Fred Karno ... proves himself an excellent screen comedian'[23] – the man himself does not mention his movie debut in his memoirs, even though this was the first official film of a Karno sketch. He only appeared in *Early Birds* – film acting was not for him. He later said: "I have acted for the films, but I dislike it. I found I simply couldn't be funny in front of a camera with only the hissing of an arc lamp at my ear to recompense me for the response of an audience."[24] This is a reminder that first and foremost Karno considered himself a comedian, and one who fed off the response of his public. When Brouett subsequently cast *Mumming Birds*, one of his choices was equally surprising – Karno veteran (and Darnley turncoat) Charlie Bell appeared as the boy in the box.

The Brouett-Egrot films were all twenty-minute 'two-reelers' and are now lost, but they were screened throughout the following year, so we have some reviews to call upon: 'The famous Karno sketches ... translated from stage to screen, have lost nothing in the process, and are as hilariously funny as ever ... Harry Wright ... as the drunken swell in "Mumming Birds" is deliciously droll. For genuine fun ... these comedies will be hard to beat.'[25]

In fact Harry Wright sustained a nasty injury during the filming of *Mumming Birds*, falling thirty feet, which led to a severe attack of nerves. As a consolation, he became the poster boy for 'Dr Cassell's Nervous Breakdown Tablets' – being a Karno plonk was still a risky business.

29. PRODIGAL SONS

In the summer of 1923 Fred Jr. joined the cast of *Oh Yes!* and at around the same time his cousin Freddie Westcott, the son of Karno's brother John, began appearing on the halls. Thereafter it becomes difficult to be sure whether a listing for Fred Westcott refers to Karno's son or his nephew, and critics often mixed them up.[26] However that August Fred Jr. took his father's advice to fend for himself and decided to return to America, taking Queenie and their two young sons with him. There is no evidence to suggest this was part of a Karno tour, and strangely the ship's manifest lists the couple as a chauffeur and housewife. The family sailed third class on RMS Montclare, landing at Quebec before crossing the border into the States on 9 September 1923 – three of them were never to return.

Fred Jr.'s departure prompted Leslie to return to the family fold,[27] taking over his brother's part in *Oh Yes!* Karno welcomed him with a letter full of encouragement and best wishes.[28] Thereafter, Leslie alternated between Karno shows and his own engagements. Meanwhile, his older brother arrived in Hollywood and quickly looked up his old pal Stan Laurel.

We left Stan alternating between early film work and vaudeville, but he was keen to focus on movies in order to (as he put it): 'get out of showbusiness … and live like a human.'[29] He worked with various filmmakers before, in January 1923, signing a twelve-week contract with Hal Roach Studios in Culver City, Los Angeles,[30] where he was engaged as lead comic in one of four stock companies. Stan's contract was extended to the end of the year, and by the time Fred Jr. arrived he was sufficiently influential to get him work as an extra.[31] The Karno name was a door-opener in Hollywood, so even without this patronage Fred Jr. had every chance of success. But Laurel went further: he let Fred, Queenie and the two toddlers share his house, and with Stan and Mae notorious for their tempestuous relationship, it must have been an interesting stay!

Stan introduced Fred Jr. to Charlie Hall, a Birmingham-born carpenter who had set out to seek his fortune in America and worked his way into the studios as a set-builder and then an extra. Fred Jr. and Hall both made their first appearances with Roach that September,[32] and they became firm friends.

Fred Jr.'s first film was *Near Dublin*, in which both he and Hall appear as villagers. James Finlayson played the villainous owner of a brickworks, offering ample opportunity for a staple element of silent comedy – brick-throwing. The film includes a glimpse of Fred Jr. in action: at a village fair, Stan plays a game where he is blindfolded and must bite an apple hanging from a string. Fred swaps

29.5 Fred Jr. (left) with Stan Laurel and George Rowe in Near Dublin *(courtesy Ken Westcott).*

the apple for a brick and the pair get into a tussle – two Karno old-boys and two bricks, what could be funnier?

Fred Jr. is thought to have appeared in *Smithy, Zeb vs Paprika, Postage Due, Brothers Under the Chin* and finally *Wide Open Spaces*. The studio payroll notes three leading actors in Stan's company, Mae Dahlberg (listed as Mae Laurel), Ena Gregory and Jimmy Finlayson, as well as a handful of bit-part players who were paid either forty or forty-five dollars per week. The exception is Fred Jr., who for some reason was paid fifty. One wonders why? Was Laurel giving his old pal a helping hand? Or did the Karno name enable him to negotiate a little extra? Either way, Fred Jr. always went uncredited and didn't impress enough to get a bigger break. He wasn't the only one struggling: Stan himself was failing to make an impression with the public, and his private life was problematic. He was living in sin with Mae at a time when Hollywood was making efforts to clean up its scandal-ridden act – the situation was an embarrassment to Roach, who had introduced a 'morality code' at the studio and publicised it as the most wholesome in town.

29. PRODIGAL SONS

After twelve months and over two dozen films, Stan's contract was cancelled. He found himself broke and practically unemployable, but was offered a chance by Joe Rock (who also made a series of films starring Jimmy Aubrey) on the proviso that Mae accepted a one-way ticket to Australia. Fred Jr. had beaten Stan out of the door at Roach's, drawing his last pay cheque the week before Christmas,[33] but he seems to have been thrown a lifeline by another old friend. According to David Robinson, he became the very first actor engaged by Chaplin for his epic *The Gold Rush,* which began filming on 8 February 1924. Charlie Hall also claimed to have appeared in Chaplin's masterpiece, but both are uncredited (and so far unidentified) in the film.

Chaplin clearly still had fondness for Karno. In July 1924 the British comic Georgie Wood visited Hollywood as a guest of Alf Reeves, and wrote an article in *The Era* telling of his exploits, which included reminiscing about 'the old country' with Chaplin. He said: 'I was privileged to meet them all, and especially … Charlie Chaplin. He gives great credit to Fred Karno. The world has many laughs to thank Fred Karno for!'[34]

Chaplin may still have been an advocate for Karno Senior, but the association was not enough to help Junior. One can only imagine how frustrated he must have felt working as an extra in Hollywood, supporting stars with whom he had crossed the Atlantic on the Cairnrona fourteen years earlier, and who had his father to thank for their training. Bitterness may have led to bad behaviour, diminishing his chances of success, but with his father's reputation preceding him, perhaps Fred Jr. could only fail.[35] By now convinced that there was no point pursuing a film career, Junior persuaded Charlie Hall that they should join forces and try their luck in vaudeville. Queenie went with them, leaving their two children in the care of her mother and sister, who had joined them in Hollywood. Charlie Hall recalled what happened next:

> We went off to San Francisco, and our conveyance was one of those very old types of Ford … Steam came hissing out of the radiator … we had to … call at a petrol station … and … noticed the leaking radiator … We could not get it fixed … Fred suddenly hit on a brain wave. He … got three packets of breakfast food. This he put in the radiator. After a couple of minutes the leak stopped, and off we went. After going several miles we saw what we thought was snow passing by the windows … It was so thick it covered our windscreen … the snow was Fred's breakfast

food ... pouring out of the radiator. We lifted the bonnet and saw a huge pudding. The engine was covered in it and in an instant so were we, for we had forgotten to turn off the engine. Stan later used this in one of his comedies. We eventually plodded on in that car to San Francisco and had the magnificent reward when we arrived there of finding that our contracts had been cancelled. I came back to Hollywood and joined Hal Roach again. Fred went on, I think, to Canada. I haven't seen or heard anything of him since.[36]

Laurel wrote this bit of business into *The Hoose-Gow* (1929), which we shall return to later. Fred Jr. and Queenie persevered as a double act until she could stand the life of a travelling vaudevillian no longer – in spring 1926 she followed Hall back to Hollywood.[37] Fred Jr. struggled along as a solo comic, crossing the border into Canada without realising that his American visa had expired – without regular work he could not renew it. Unable to re-enter the country, he repeatedly wrote to Queenie asking her to join him in Canada, but she was unwilling to uproot her extended family, now settled in L.A. They were estranged from that day forward, and Fred Jr. simply disappeared.

Queenie's account of all this was slightly different – and much more colourful. Perhaps not wishing to reveal to her boys that she was the instigator of the split, she told a story that passed into family legend. She omitted their time in vaudeville and suggested that her husband had abandoned the family while still in L.A. One morning, she said, Fred Jr. had assembled his wife and sons on the porch of their house to see a new car he had bought. Junior came round the corner, pulled up, waved at the three of them and drove away – they never saw him again.

30.

Stormy Weather

What are the best seats in the house?
The receipts.
(The Merry Book of the Moore & Burgess Minstrels, 1898)

THANKS TO that story Karno's grandsons grew up believing that their father had abandoned them. The truth was that Fred Jr. had great affection for his children, and losing them must have affected him greatly. Tucked away in the bottom of a dusty box in the family archive is his own version of an Irving Berlin song[1] about the joy of becoming a father, which Junior called *Little Stranger*:

A bundle of joy's come to our house, a baby has now come to stay.
Father feels so happy he's jumping with joy, all he keeps saying is "I'm glad it's a boy."
A welcome has greeted the stranger who's come to brighten their lives.
You can hear mother croon "he'll be a champion soon."
Now their cute little stranger, their cute little stranger, their cute little stranger's arrived.[2]

30.1 Queenie with Karno's grandsons, Kenneth and Fred. Was this the car Fred Jr. didn't disappear in? *(courtesy Ken Westcott).*

Years later Fred Jr. remarried and gained two stepchildren: they recall a man who lavished them with affection.

Junior's attempt to make it in movies had been a personal and professional disaster. If only he had returned to Hollywood with Queenie his marriage might have survived and he may have secured a place working with the greatest comedy double act of all time. Stan Laurel had returned to Hal Roach Studios by then, and in September 1926 Roach director Leo McCarey cast him against Oliver Hardy in what most consider to be their first true double act movie – *Duck Soup*.[3] The rest is history. Roach stayed very loyal to Laurel and Hardy's stock company, so there is every reason to believe that Fred Jr. would have had the same opportunity given to Charlie Hall, an uncredited extra in *Duck Soup* but later a regular Laurel and Hardy stooge.

So much for Junior. We left Karno Senior back in 1923, flirting with his own film projects, although after the three Brouett shorts this venture fizzled out. His theatrical fortunes took a turn for the better though, when he hitched his wagon to one of the biggest producers in the business – his friend, Charles B. Cochran. Cochran had experienced a rare flop with a revue called *Mayfair and Montmartre*, and Karno seized the opportunity to take on the show at a bargain price. One of the biggest hits of the day had been a Wylie and Tate revue entitled *The Passing Show*, which prompted Karno to rename his new revue *The Surpassing Show*. It opened at the Stratford Empire on 2 April 1923 then set off on the Moss circuit. Cochran's original was rewritten by Cyril Hemmington and W.H. Briggs, and produced by Philip Hawley, so Karno's involvement may have been nominal (he was not even mentioned in opening night reviews) but subsequent reports list it as a Karno & Cochran production.

> A succession of really funny comic scenes interspersed with some … songs for Miss Alice Lloyd cause a genial atmosphere throughout. The two best items … "The Morning after the Night Before" and "Roof Gardens" … give ample scope to Gene Gerrard for the display of much drollery. "The Oldest Tale of All" staged in medieval surroundings, also deserves mention … it is difficult to find fault … and the only point we could wish to see amended would be a repression of the frequent use of the word "blimey", which may amuse the groundlings, but is certainly objectionable to others.[4]

30. STORMY WEATHER

Karno picked a strong cast: Gerrard was an established theatre (and later film) actor and Alice Lloyd was the most accomplished of Marie's sisters. Unusually, given contemporary fashions, the show had no jazz or ragtime, which seems to have endeared it to critics who were beginning to tire of repetitive themes. Karno's production had scenes in South America, Hawaii and Paris, while a dramatic sequence about international cocaine smuggling added further exotic flavour. The highlight was a Russian ballet described by one critic as: 'The triumph of the whole revue ... "The Golden Bough", picturing a Pagan harvest festival ... a riot of colour and scenic splendour, Lilian Grace, the Golden Goddess of Corn, standing motionless as a statue, has a most difficult part to play, whilst the drama of the story is introduced by Dorothy Neville, the Spirit of Corn, and Alexis Dolinov, the keeper of the Temple, whose dancing ends in tragedy.'[5] Horace Collins, the show's business manager, later recalled that the Goddess of Corn proved problematic as her golden make-up had a high copper content, causing Lilian Grace's entire body to break out in sores – Karno had to pay her off.

A new generation of theatregoers was now discovering Karno, enabling him to dig deep into his back catalogue for the next show, which combined two of his best sketches: *The Smoking Concert* and *The Football Match* (under the title of the latter).[6] Sandy Powell was the star, and he later recalled how it came about. He was a twenty-three-year-old comic playing first turn – a three-minute spot with a few gags and a song – to almost empty houses when Karno stopped by to watch his show.[7] Powell recalled: 'I got a message round from Fred Karno – now he couldn't have judged if I was any good or not, from three minutes ... he said would I like to play the lead in The Football Match?'[8] The offer was a dream come true. Powell had started on the halls at the age of five, and as a juvenile performer his hero was Harry Weldon – now he would be playing his idol's signature part. Alongside this rising young star, *The Football Match* saw a return to the Karno fold for Will Poluski, who donned Ratty's jersey one last time.[9]

The sketch was somewhat changed from the original, with Stiffy now playing for the Hotspuds in a match against Bolton Wanderers. Additional scenes included Stiffy at home with his wife and the annual meeting of the Hotspuds Social Club (picking up the *Smoking Concert* premise). Despite the show being anticipated with enthusiasm in the press, opening night received lacklustre reviews:

"The Football Match" … should prove a profitable adventure when further cohesion is reached than was the case on Monday. Of course, much must be forgiven on the first night … but the first scene required considerable strengthening … and there were other episodes which might have been … omitted altogether. On the other hand, there are many comic moments … and some capital singing and dancing … there is the semblance of a plot … and the culminating struggle between two rival football teams brings the whole to a bustling conclusion … At the head of the cast is Sandy Powell in Harry Weldon's old part … Powell is bound to challenge comparison with his predecessor, as his method and voice are somewhat similar, but he manages to convey much of his own comic individuality into his work, and his quaint by-play helps him enormously.[10]

Powell was mortified at the poor showing on his first night, and recalled that Karno didn't pull any punches:[11]

Karno was a very peculiar man. He was a nice man, but he could be very sarcastic and very very cruel, and I was unhappy after the first house. The show didn't go well, I didn't get many laughs and I was sitting in my dressing room and Fred Karno just opened my dressing room door … and said: "To think I paid Charlie Chaplin three pounds ten a week," and walked out. Well that was just about the end of the world for me. But that was Fred Karno, he could be really vicious and sarcastic but of course he was a genius, a genius at comedy.[12]

The late Roy Hudd, who knew Powell well, told me that the young comic had found Karno a tough man to work for. Hudd included a slightly different version of Powell's story in his own book of music hall anecdotes: 'Sandy understudied the principal comic in a Karno revue and one night, as a raw beginner, he was thrown into the deep end and shoved on. After the show Sandy, thinking he hadn't done too badly, sat in the dressing-room waiting for a few kind words from the 'Guv'. Karno flung the door open, sniffed and said, "Had your chance – missed it!" and strode off.'[13]

Of course we know that Powell was not an understudy (he was the lead comic), nor was he a raw beginner (he had been performing for eighteen years), and by his own admission he had done badly in the show. Karno would have won no prizes as a motivational speaker but he was justifiably furious at Powell's poor performance. A less confident judge of talent might have sacked him on the spot, but to his credit Karno persevered with the young comic and the show developed into a great success.[14] Powell recalled that this didn't prevent more Karno 'encouragement' at subsequent performances: 'I wasn't very confident ... and I think Karno knew this. He used to stand in the wings, shouting at me, when I was on. I think he thought he was encouraging me! "Faster," he'd yell ... "They're falling asleep!" He'd get so mad he'd start booing, blowing raspberries – I was frightened to come off!'[15]

30.2 Sandy Powell and Jean Allison in The Football Match *revue (author's collection).*

Reviews improved but the show did little to help Karno's now perilous finances and this must have affected his demeanour – certainly he was no longer the inspirational mentor. Powell recalled:

> Off-stage activities were great fun ... they were a happy crowd, except when Karno was around. He wasn't a very good morale-booster ... One Monday night ... the audience was taking it out of one of the young second comics and ... standing in the wings awaiting the cue for his next entrance, his nerves were shot to pieces and he looked quite ill ... he said faintly, "Mr Karno, I do feel funny." ... Karno snapped back, "Then for goodness sake get out there, quick!"[16]

Powell never forgot the thrill of following in Weldon's footsteps, and went on to have a long and distinguished career on stage, film, radio and television. His catchphrase "Can you hear me Mother?" found its way into the British vocabulary.

With his attention focused on these revues, Karno had disbanded the *Mumming Birds* company in early 1923, but that autumn he licensed the sketch to Bert Bernard for a provincial tour. Bernard pulled off something of a coup by reuniting Billy Reeves and Charlie Bell as the drunk and the Eton boy[17] – what Karno thought of that is lost to history.

New year, new show, and a move away from revue back to musical comedy. In early March 1924 Karno launched *The Love Match*,[18] with Jean Allison (transferring from *The Football Match*) and Billy Danvers in the leads. Ironically, given his own track record, Karno again championed the cause of women in industry and their struggle for fair terms and conditions: this time the action centred on a strike at a match factory. As usual Karno had an eye on the detail – *The Stage* reported that he had been visiting match factories in search of inspiration.

The show's heroine Elaine works on the production line, where she hides a photograph in a matchbox with a message appealing for its finder to save her from drudgery and marry her. This comes to the attention of the factory manager, who decides to seduce her himself. Meanwhile the girls have gone on strike, and when Elaine spurns his advances, the manager blames her for the dispute and she is dismissed. We then find her living in poverty with alcoholic parents who, it transpires, adopted her as an infant. Without any income her evil guardians announce that she will have to turn to prostitution to pay her way. Unsurprisingly, she runs away. Finding work as a caterer she attends a hunt ball at Farnley Hall, the home of Sir Robert Ellerby. There follows a spectacular hunting scene during which it is revealed that Ellerby's son, Bobby, was the finder of her matchbox photograph, and he and Elaine finally meet. This romantic moment is spoilt by the factory owner (a guest at the ball) recognising Elaine and telling the host that she is a thief, causing her to be thrown out.

As if this plot wasn't complicated enough, it then transpires that Sir Robert's fortune is dependent on an inheritance from a late friend, Sir Jasper Merrivale. Merrivale's wife died in childbirth and, in his grief, he pushed the baby onto a villainous couple who lived nearby. The couple are implicated in the murder of a gamekeeper (there is another spectacular scene with poachers, ferrets and terriers), and through a series of incidents (which I defy anyone in the audience to have followed), Elaine is revealed as the Merrivale heiress and Ellerby has to give over his fortune to her. Bobby is now penniless and feels unable to wed Elaine, until it is revealed that she has bought the match factory – she instals Bobby as its manager. The evil boss is fired, the factory girls are reinstated and all ends happily with a spectacular wedding.

Powerful stuff, and despite all this melodrama Billy Danvers had to play the whole thing for laughs. In his memoirs Karno recalled that Danvers was ably

30. STORMY WEATHER

assisted by a performing horse, which brought the house down with a topical gag aimed at those who had avoided the draft in the war:

> This animal was a wonder … He carried out a long and animated conversation with Billy Danvers … "You don't look very well" … The horse shook his head. "Would you like a drink?" The horse nodded. "Would you like to hear a funny story?" He nodded again. "Come over here." The horse followed Danvers up stage. "There was a young lady of Gloucester – here I'll whisper the rest," … and then the horse laughed … "Did you fight in the great war?" continued Danvers. Again the horse shook his head. "Good gracious how did … you manage to swing the lead?" And the wonderful horse started to limp round the stage and down came the house … In the final wedding scene when Danvers said someone wanted to kiss the bride the young husband replied: "No one kisses my dear wife without my consent," the bride … adding: "It depends on who it is." This was the cue for the entrance of the wonder horse. The horse kissed the bride and the applause was tremendous as the curtain came down.[19]

The show was on an epic scale: as well as its equine comedian, a pack of twenty-four hounds and four horses cantered across the stage. The plot was complex too, with well-drawn characters embroiled in drama, love and comedy. *The Love Match* had a level of sophistication beyond anything Karno had tackled before – you might say it was striking.

The Surpassing Show and *The Love Match* were ambitious and successful, but any profits continued to be invested up-river, as this press report reveals: 'The season … opened under the happiest of auspices … Almost every brand of sport is catered for … Mr Karno has now even laid out a putting course … An added attraction this year is the presence of Mr Jack Hylton's Karsino Band … Altogether, with its manifold charms … Karsino is distinctly the place … for a visit.'[20]

30.3 Upstaged by a horse – Billy Danvers (author's collection).

How Jack Hylton came to take on a Karsino residency is unclear, but you will remember that he may have appeared in *Dandy Thieves* back in 1906 and

Hylton's wife Ennis Parkes had later starred in *Moonstruck*. Like many famous names in this book, Hylton's Karno connections are not widely known, but it's notable that it was after his run at Karsino that he decided to put his dance band into variety theatres, unheard of at that time – perhaps Karno suggested the idea. The huge success of this experiment, coupled with Hylton's radio performances, catapulted him to fame and fortune the following year.

30.4 Jack Hylton's Orchestra at Karsino.

Karsino now had parking for two hundred cars, illuminated grounds and a Japanese garden to explore – the brochure stated: 'Abandon mope, all ye who enter here.' Karno had done his best to ensure a successful season, but the excitement of opening week was marred by tragedy. At midnight on 21 May, Mr Alexander Small, his wife Dorothy and three friends (including a well-known racing driver called Tommy Hann) left the hotel and drove onto the ferry. On reaching the opposite bank, their car inexplicably leapt into reverse and plunged into the inky blackness of the river. The occupants scrambled for the bank but there was no sign of Dorothy. In the darkness the men's attempts to dive down to the car were futile, and it was only when it was dragged from the water that her body was discovered trapped inside. The coroner found that she had been suffering from tuberculosis and probably died from shock rather than drowning, but that was no doubt little comfort to her husband. Karno and his staff were found to have done all they could – the coroner placed the blame squarely on the malfunctioning car – but dead guests are not the best advertisement for a hotel.

30. STORMY WEATHER

Karsino's days were numbered. The growing affordability of the motor car enabled people to escape to the coast rather than holiday up-river, but Karno's biggest enemy was the British weather. He insured himself against the elements to the tune of five hundred pounds (at a huge premium of fifty pounds per day), but failed to read the small print – his policy only paid out if at least one fifth of an inch of rain was recorded on a Saturday or Sunday. Damp days of constant drizzle kept his visitors away but didn't meet the target, so he decided to go double or quits and staked £100 per day for a £1000 return – it paid out only once. Staff, food and entertainment had to be paid for whether there were guests or not, and Karno recalled that his staff were regularly twiddling their thumbs in the empty palm court, feasting (sometimes grudgingly) on fine cuisine that would otherwise have gone to waste.

Those who did brave the weather often ended up wet, cold and irritable.[21] Fishermen and day trippers were regularly dragged out of the river after their boats overturned, and despite most not being customers, were given hot baths, towels and dry clothes (often, he remembered, with little thanks). In a desperate attempt to keep the wolf from the door Karno extended the season, playing host to a 'winter club' whose members could partake of the indoor facilities. He also staged dances twice a week, collecting the meagre pickings with grateful relief.

30.5 All hands on deck – Fred Karno maintaining his boats at Karsino (Getty Images).

As Karsino's fortunes declined, Karno became reliant on the unreliable – his box office receipts. Given his battles with increasingly unionised professionals, it is perhaps no surprise that he came up with his next masterstroke – employing amateurs, a ploy that has saved many a struggling impresario. He decided to stage a countrywide search for new talent, with the lucky winner bagging a £1000 contract. He parcelled the competition up into a show and called it *Karnoisms,* and its first outing appears to have been in Bootle on 13

October 1924. The amateur competition formed part of the bill alongside a wider Karno variety company, and as this report reveals, it proved that the cruelty of the modern talent-show audition process is nothing new: 'The inclusion of local talent … contributes somewhat to the general hilarity that prevails, although the competitors do not always appreciate the merriment that greets their efforts.'[22] Any wannabes that passed muster during the week took part in a final on Saturday evening, the first winners being the Gillow Sisters, who were ceremoniously presented with their signed Karno contract by the Mayor of Bootle and then joined the variety company for the rest of the tour.

The show was a novelty which played to packed houses, and Karno quickly realised he could afford to reduce the rewards. He changed the format, offering a selection of smaller prizes in each town – which were displayed in a shop window close to the theatre. Regional winners then competed for the £1000 contract. It was retitled *Fred Karno's Follies – Karno's Quest*, but this changed town by town: *The Preston Follies*, *The Stockport Follies* and so on. Sometimes Karno would put in a personal appearance and help elect the winner, much to the excitement of the crowd. While he claimed that box-office records were regularly smashed, this was not difficult as the show was playing small halls in provincial towns. His advertising reveals that filling even these halls wasn't always easy: 'The Comedy Brainwave of the Century; The Audience – Part of the Show … The Funniest Comedy Show on the Halls … KARNO'S FOLLIES – Big audiences every evening rolling in oceans of joy. GO AND SEE IT – That is all that is wanted.'[23] The phrasing smacks of desperation, and the accompanying list of available dates demonstrates that the tour was hand to mouth. Nonetheless, press reports suggest that when Karno could find somewhere to take it, receipts were good.

Although amateur shows and competitions were commonplace, Karno seems to have hit upon an original idea by including one as part of a professional variety bill. The press certainly thought so: 'The name of Fred Karno has become almost a household simile for things original; and in … "Follies" at the Theatre Royal this week he has cast convention to the winds.'[24] The idea was cheap, popular and put the audience centre-stage to be laughed at by their peers. This report reveals that he even included the mentoring element common in today's TV talent extravaganzas: 'It is recognized by Mr Karno that many amateurs have latent talent which only needs encouragement to set such lucky possessors on the high road to success … Mr Karno's advice and assistance will be given … freely … Such advice … is of course, of the utmost value, and may conceivably supply the

30. STORMY WEATHER

golden key which will open the door to a career of glittering success.'[25] Perhaps it was this opportunity to secure a Karno contract, with the man himself as mentor, that made the show stand out, although no press report exists suggesting that the £1000 national prize was ever awarded!

As 1924 drew to a close, Karno commissioned Cyril Hemmington to write a revue which included elements of his greatest hits. *Miss 1925* was subsequently advertised with the strapline 'Sublimely Ridiculous', and opened at the King's Theatre in Portsmouth on 26 January, with Harry Herbert as lead comic.

> Miss 1925 … made a very promising debut … The revels open on New Year's Eve with a cabaret scene, in which Father Time is spurned by the merrymakers, and 1924 arrives, with only a few minutes to live. Before expiring, 1924 tells a sorry tale of a misspent life, but the Clerk of the Weather promises unlimited sunshine and general prosperity in the New Year and introduces three charming young ladies as the seasons – Spring, Autumn and Winter. There enters Harry Herbert with oilskins and umbrella as Summer, preferring a resolute disbelief in "It Ain't Gonna Rain No Mo'" … "Beautiful surprises" for everyone are promised by Miss 1925, whose arrival in a giant cracker is the prelude to an effective carnival scene … a scene in a dentist's surgery, in which Mr Herbert temporarily forsakes paper hanging to attend to the patients, is also full of fun, and he is equally amusing as William Wurzel in "The Flat". The title role is in the hands of Doris Ashton, whose expressive singing is a delightful feature of the production.[26]

The fact summer was depicted by a soaking wet comic in oilskins no doubt reflected Karno's bitter experience at Karsino. Scenes included the gambling routine from *Flats*, a healthy slice of *The New Slavey* and a paperhanger (turned dentist) routine which must have constituted elements from *Spring Cleaning* and *Teeth*.

The summer of 1925 saw the end of *The Love Match* followed by several failed attempts to find a successor. A new agent, Joseph Laurillard, was appointed to seek dates for Karno's productions and new shows were advertised as being in the pipeline, including a Christmas pantomime. But apart from a short run of his *Follies*, which included *Mumming Birds* as part of the variety bill, Karno staged nothing until the autumn. He then formed a new company, Fred Karno

Productions Ltd, to produce his next revue *Tittle Tattle*, which opened at the Coventry Hippodrome in October. In what sounds like a departure from the norm, it was described as 'a novelty dance show', but with a script by Herbert C. Sargent and Con West,[27] there was still some comedy:

> A first-class entertainment, in which clever and effective dancing is skilfully blended with talking songs, comedy sketches ... and good music ... [In] the first comedy sketch "There's Many A Slip" ... George Hirst appears as a workless down and outer, whose wife (Katy Kay) ... proceeds to raise £100 by means of a newspaper insurance "wangle" ... Terry Wilson contributes ... many favourite songs concluding with ... "Lily of Laguna" ... Another good comedy sketch is "Bet Your Boots", in which Matt Leamore displays his powers of deduction as an amateur detective ... A roller skating rink features a clever skating speciality ... The Big Brass Twelve make an imposing appearance in plumed brass helmets ... [followed by] a comedy sketch "Scared Stiff", which deals with a haunted room at an inn ... Another skilful dancing display ... leads on to ... a change of scene to the deck of a battleship ... sailors dance, while "Land of Hope and Glory" forms a spirited and patriotic finale.[28]

Dancing troupes, marching bands, old-time music hall songs, comedy sketches and a finale on a battleship with huge guns stretching out into the auditorium – this was pure revue, in a style Karno had previously shied away from. In November it was retitled *On With The Show*, a decision that brought trouble. Lawrence Wright, a producer who already had a revue by that name, slapped an injunction on Karno and the judge was highly critical, suggesting he had deliberately sought to capitalise on the established show: 'Mr Karno was doing something calculated to deceive ... he could easily go on with his entertainment under the name in which it was originally brought out.'[29]

Karno recalled that Lawrence Wright had dispatched a man to watch his show, who then asked a few locals to give their opinion. Anticipating payment for their involvement, the punters were happy to sign affidavits averring that they had bought tickets expecting Wright's production, and felt cheated. Karno could ill-afford a legal battle but felt that something was amiss, so invested in a private detective who tracked down the accusers. It turned out that they had not

30. STORMY WEATHER

received their expected reward from Wright and felt mightily aggrieved – they were quick to confess they had not even seen the show. Clutching these new affidavits, Karno confronted Wright, who denied all knowledge of his agent's subterfuge and agreed to a compromise. He paid the solicitor's fees and Karno changed the name of his revue to *The Show*, recalling: 'It is a pity all theatrical disputes could not be settled in such friendly fashion.'[30]

The Show toured to good reviews, but Karno's planned Christmas pantomime never materialised and Hart Scenic Studios in Leeds sold off the newly painted set they had made for it. Presumably he failed to find the financial backing he needed, which reveals how far the great impresario had fallen.

Despite his financial troubles, Karno had consistently paid Edith's allowance over the twenty years since they separated, but as his creditors began circling, even this proved impossible. In a poignant letter dated Christmas Eve 1925, he wrote:

> Dear Edith, I am enclosing you a cheque for £6 … I need not tell you how things have been with me. When you do not get yours you know I have not got it. The new show is too expensive to run to get anything out of it. I shall have to cut it down, am now simply working … for the benefit of Moss Empires. I hope you will have a happy Xmas, mine will not be very merry and bright. We have got the Bailiffs in the office now and one of them is sitting opposite me while I am writing this. I wish you all a prosperous New Year, yours sincerely – Fred.[31]

Suddenly the bailiffs didn't seem so funny. As winter turned to spring *The Show* was Karno's only production, and as it developed, more emphasis was given to its nostalgic elements, with Betty Warren impersonating bygone stars. One critic wrote: 'It radiates originality; intersperses rollicking farce with polished artistry … the reverberations of applause last night were reminiscent of old-time music hall enthusiasm … the production … has a singular charm in its contrasts of the old and the new music-hall fare.'[32]

It was a quality show but nonetheless a throwback, and could not maintain an audience. It closed in late spring, and for the first time in nearly forty years no Karno production graced the stage. He now wrote a long, meandering letter to Leslie suggesting it was time to hand over the family firm to the next generation:

If you want to help me find someone to take the show out … somebody's got to do it and why not you? … They whisper that I'm getting old and out of date, old fashioned … sometimes I think they are right. I do feel a bit duff at times and wonder what's the end going to be … I am afraid I'm not marketable … Fred Karno seems to be a thing of the past and I'm just telling you how I feel about it all, no prospects, no hopes, no nothing. Some of them must have forgotten that I still exist … That's why they pinch my stuff with impunity and won't give the old man a chance to live … just think all this over … you're younger and abler than I am … I think I have bored you long enough so will shut up. I have only been passing the time away and have nothing else to do. Best love from Dad.[33]

Music hall's greatest showman clearly felt his career was drawing to an end – could Leslie now restore the fortunes of the Karno empire?

31.

Riches to Rags

*"I have failed in business and I am going to arrange
matters so my creditors won't trouble me."*
"Are you going to get out of debt?"
"No. I am going to get out of town."
(The Merry Book of the Moore & Burgess Minstrels, 1898)

AS SO often, Karno's timing was bad. Leslie was in no position to help: he was busy nursing Edith, who had been diagnosed with diabetes. It was time for his father to cut his losses: he put Karsino up for sale and wrote to Leslie:

> Dear Leslie, Herewith cheque for the two weeks money for your Mother … I am very sorry to hear about her illness, and also sorry that I could not send along the money before, but things have not been too good. We have not sold the Karsino, but I expect … to let it for the summer to the Prince's Restaurant people, so that will take a lot of worry off our shoulders … Am so glad to hear little Pat [Karno's granddaughter] is going strong, she's a beautiful child. Best wishes to all. Your affectionate father, Fred Karno.[1]

On 8 May 1926, Karsino reopened under the management of Beaumont Alexander of the New Princes in Piccadilly. Alexander renamed it Palm Beach and had visions of Tagg's Island as a Floridian paradise: 'Thousands of tons of sand are to be placed on the island and hundreds of palms will be planted. There

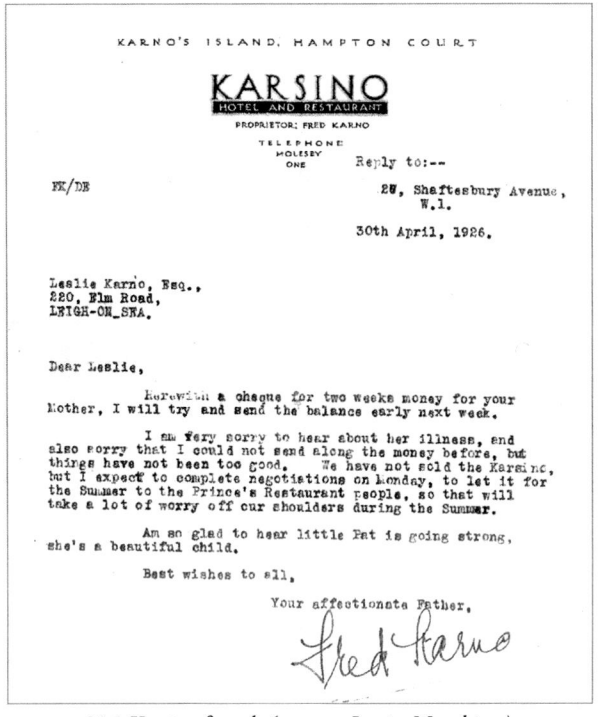

31.1 Karsino for sale (courtesy Louise Murchison).

will be large sunshades, beach chairs, provision for the enjoyment of mixed bathing and other items of amusement.'[2]

Subletting the island seemed to give Karno fresh hope, and he advertised for knockabout comics to take a tour to America. This never got off the ground, but he did succeed in mounting a small provincial tour of *Moses and Son* starring Jack Barty – it went almost unrecorded by the press.

In July, Karno and his old pal Leon Vint formed a new company called Universal Productions Ltd,[3] the second he had set up in less than a year. This appears to have been a strategy to avoid creditors, but he was merely rearranging deckchairs on his Titanic – and the iceberg was looming up out of the darkness. Meanwhile Beaumont Alexander was literally rearranging deckchairs on the newly created beaches of Tagg's Island, but his ambitious plans had overlooked the main difference between Florida and England – sunshine. Alexander's timing was as unfortunate as Karno's: his first season coincided with the 1926 General Strike. Later he breached the terms of his licence by presenting cabaret on a Sunday evening, and as joint licensee, Karno had to pay half of the twenty-pound fine. Karno terminated their agreement and in a triumph of hope over

31. RICHES TO RAGS

experience, decided to have one last punt at making his dream palace a success. There were still opportunities in the theatre too, and although *Moses and Son* ran out of steam in the autumn, he managed to license some sketches to other producers. Percy Broadhead staged a new version of *Dandy Thieves*, and this was followed by a Charles Ferrier production called *Sergeant Lightning*, which ran for over a year with George Bass in the lead. Tragically, forty-year-old Bass collapsed and died during a performance in Burnley – Sergeant Lightning finally died with him.

A second run of *The Show* that autumn received decent reviews and good houses, and when it reached Derby at Christmas, Karno described his approach to producing a revue to a local reporter: 'Building a revue is like cooking a pudding. One must take the right ingredients, mix them well, and make it taste nice.' He went on to say that although he was no longer 'hands on', he still oversaw his productions: 'I put up the scaffolding ... and then the builders come in and do the rest.'[4] By then he was scaffolding a new show, *Jumbles*, which opened in Hull on 3 January 1927.[5] It was a re-hash of a revue called *The Charlot Show of 1926*, which Karno had licensed from Andre Charlot, and he retained Dick Francis as its leading man.

> The opening is a delightful bathing scene ... Several capital sketches are included, of which "The Last Cabby" and "Atmospherics" are probably the best. In the former, Dick Francis presents a clever character study and scores with the number "When the Hansom Cabs were Lined up on the Ranks" ... One of the brightest items is "The Whimsical Pedlar" ... assisted by members of the chorus cleverly dressed to represent various toys ... a fitting finale is "Journeys End" ... in which a pleasing spectacular effect is produced by the entire company ascending the heights in single file.[6]

With a large dollop of Karno pathos, the revue's stand-out scene featured the cabbie, lamenting the change from horsepower to motor power. One critic wrote: 'Dick Francis gives a brilliant little study of an old Hansom cabman ... reflecting upon what the future may hold for himself and his faithful friend and servant between the shafts.'[7] It might have been a metaphor for Karno's own reflections on the changes in the entertainment industry. Once again the revue was well received and played to full houses – one wonders why Karno couldn't make it pay. As *Jumbles* toured Scotland, he gave another interview and radiated renewed enthusiasm – he certainly didn't sound like a man ready to retire:

> Laughter must be the foundation of your popular theatrical entertainment ... Though you never hear of a revue that has failed because scenery and dresses were not good enough ... you do often hear of failure because of the weak comedy scenes ... the comic element is therefore my most serious concern ... in the old days we used to recruit all our knockabouts from the circuses, which have now for the most part vanished ... Now for 'discoveries' I rely largely on ... seaside Pierrot companies. Every summer I make a tour of the most popular resorts on the lookout for talent ... having secured the ... turns, the job is to weld them all into an agreeable whole. There is seldom any story linking together the scenes in a revue, consequently we run the scenes together as quickly after one another as possible, linking them together with music and dancing. Pace is all important ... I travel with the company ... We rearrange the turns, we substitute new material for any that may have 'misfired', and all the time we are speeding up the production in every imaginable way.[8]

He ended by noting that it was time for things to change: 'There is something new due now in the revue world ... We can't go back to variety, for we don't have the artistes. What then, are we to do? I wish I could foresee.'

Karno was lost: for the first time in his career, he could not come up with the next big thing. Instead he concentrated on what he knew and ensured it was the best it could be. One reporter found himself sitting next to Karno at a production of *Jumbles*, in Leeds: 'Mr Karno ... was taking stock of the production ... he told me, he has only two companies on the road. With other commitments, he prefers to keep within a limit that lends itself to personal supervision.'[9]

This close attention paid dividends: reviews were extremely positive and *Jumbles* continued to develop with the introduction of an extract from *Moses and Son*. *The Show* was similarly refreshed, and in February 1927 a new young comic joined the cast – Max Miller. Miller would go on to become the biggest comedian of his generation: his stand up was edgy for its day and his near-the-knuckle gags 'painted the stage as blue as his eyes.'[10] He carried two jokebooks,

31. RICHES TO RAGS

one white, the other blue, and would ask the audience which they wanted him to use – you can guess the one they chose.

Biographer John East recounted Miller's recollection of negotiating his contract with Karno:

> Karno had a big reputation, but by the time I worked for him he was on the skids. He'd lost a fortune at that fun palace of his, Karsino ... I didn't like his manner. He treated me as if he was hiring me to be his gardener, not to star in a show for him ...
>
> "You might do I suppose" said Karno ...
>
> "Talbot O'Farrell told me you'd seen me work in 'Piccadilly' and you thought I'd be great for your revue."
>
> "What I did say, Miller, was that I could use you. Don't you start telling me how good you were in Piccadilly either. Remember, it's today what counts in this business, not what you did last week."
>
> "I got some bloody fine notices."
>
> "If you're thinking of collecting notices to dazzle people with, forget that too. There's only one thing an old review is good for, Miller – and that's to wipe your arse with. Now, down to brass tacks, what's your money?"
>
> "Twenty quid a week."
>
> "You are a comedian – but not a very funny one. You can halve that."
>
> "You can mate, but I'm not going to."
>
> "Bit of an auctioneer, eh, Miller?"
>
> "You said it, Karno. Eighteen quid."
>
> "I've said it, twelve ..." snapped Karno.
>
> "Split the difference – fifteen."[11]

It was the sparring of a young gun with an old war horse, and both were happy with the result.

Despite Miller's account, he was not the star comic in Karno's revue. Terry Wilson was the leading man, but Miller soon stood out, especially in a sketch where he played a new police recruit. He was a brilliant and powerful stand-up comic but hated working to a script or as part of an ensemble: the actress Florence Desmond (who played opposite him in another show) said: "I cannot say he was a nice man ... he was selfish. It was almost impossible to play a scene with him. He was out to exploit the comedy for himself ... playing outwards instead of to me."¹² By his own admission Miller was never a comfortable actor: 'I'm a solo turn, first, foremost and forever. I don't want production, thank you. Nobody, not God Almighty, can tell me how to perform. I'm no good acting in a scripted show.'¹³ No wonder he didn't get on with Karno, a man committed to rehearsing a production to within an inch of its life.

Miller's performances in revue were sometimes brilliant but inconsistently so, and Karno could see it. The comic admitted that he struggled, and after witnessing one dismal performance Karno came backstage to deliver a familiar verdict – although the

31.2 The Cheeky Chappie – Max Miller (author's collection).

challenges of the four years since Sandy Powell suffered his wrath had somewhat coarsened his language: 'And to think I paid Charlie Chaplin three f**king pounds a week.'¹⁴

The Guv'nor won the clash of egos but remained impossible to please. Miller recalled that one night, after a much better performance, Karno did not want to admit he was pleased: '"Didn't I get some great laughs, Mr Karno?" "Yes, you weren't too bad – but the rest of the show – it's falling apart. I want my artistes to give everything they've got; to sweat blood for me".'¹⁵ As we recounted earlier, Karno then supposedly suggested his star sleep with the chorus girls to add some energy to their performance. Unsurprisingly Miller's run as a Karno comic was short: he saw out *The Show* to the end of its tour in May, at which point Karno put the whole thing up for sale. It wasn't the only thing he said goodbye to.

It had been twenty-two years since Karno and Edith separated. Friends claimed that she continued to carry a torch for her husband, never looked at another man, and kept two pillows embroidered with their names as a reminder of the love she'd lost. In early 1927 her health rapidly declined, and she died on 27 May with Leslie by her side – she was just fifty-six. Karno supposedly visited Edith before her death but we will never know what passed between them – their conversation was in the privacy of her room. That visit and his letters confirm that they remained on reasonable terms to the end.

With Edith's death, the inaccuracies in Gallagher's Karno biography once again come thick and fast. It claimed that he refused to announce her passing in the newspapers and that her theatrical friends were furious they had not been informed, but this is untrue. *The Stage* published a death notice including details of the funeral. Thereafter, Leslie and Edith's friends Madge Proctor and Rose Powell placed memorial notices every year well into the 1930s.[16]

Friends maintained that Edith died of a broken heart, never getting over the break-up of her marriage, but this can't have been helped by looking at life through the bottom of a glass. Naomi Jacob wrote of her (along with another unnamed friend, probably Marguerite Broadfoote): 'Edie Karno is dead … brilliant women, good women, and women who were so unreasonable that nothing ever made them "fall out of love with their husbands." That was their tragedy. "Too nice, too good", Marie Lloyd once said to me of them, "They'll both die of the same complaint … a broken heart."'[17]

Edith may have been heartbroken but she remained reasonably well-off, living comfortably in Leigh-on-Sea and leaving many items to friends and family in her will. In October her remaining possessions were sold at auction and her estate was valued at just over £353, more than twice the average annual income. One wonders why no one stumped up for a headstone – she was interred in an unmarked plot.[18]

Edith's will provides an insight into her relationships: she was close to her sisters, Florrie and Polly, and they received many of her personal possessions, while the money was split between Leslie, Florrie and her grandchildren, Pat, Fred and Kenneth. Queenie received her jewellery, but for reasons known only to herself, Edith left nothing to Fred Jr. They seem to have been estranged, and he remained out of contact in Canada, unaware of his mother's death. Madge Thompson (née Proctor), her friend and faithful companion, had married just before Edith died. She received a turquoise brooch with two lovers' knots and two hearts, a Turkish rug, some pictures and china. Another interesting item in the will is the bequest of 'all photographs of Marguerite Broadfoote' to Robert Bell – Broadfoote was clearly close to her heart too. The final item is the most telling of all: 'To my husband Fred Karno, my wedding ring.'[19]

Madge Proctor told Gallagher that Edith said it was 'to prove no one could take his place in my heart.' She went on to claim that Karno promptly gave it to one of his mistresses, who threw it the fire. In truth he gave the ring to Leslie's wife Louisa, who cherished it. The story has some basis in fact though: Louisa once had a blazing row with Leslie and in temper threw it into the fire, prompting a frantic scrabble as the whole family searched for it in the grate – another family anecdote twisted by false memory. Gallagher made a great deal of the fact that Karno married 'his mistress' within days of Edith's death, her body barely cold in the ground, but consider the reality: Karno and Edith had been apart for twenty-two years, and like most separated couples, had become relative strangers. He had shared his life with Marie for many more years than he spent with Edith, but they were unable to wed while his wife was alive. When she died they didn't hesitate to legalise their relationship, and who can blame them?

Edith's death isn't the only thing that might have encouraged the couple to tidy up their affairs – Karno's health was also deteriorating. He had been suffering for some years with 'dropsy' (oedema), which causes an uncomfortable accumulation of fluid around the body, often in the feet and legs. Karno and Marie were married in a small private ceremony on 16 June 1927 at St Peter's Church, Parkstone, Dorset. There were very few guests, perhaps because all their friends and acquaintances thought they were already married.[20] Their marriage certificate shows Karno living at the Albany, but gives Marie's address as 'Bostonville', Parkstone, Dorset – almost certainly her father's address at 89 Penn Hill Avenue. Karno was sixty-one, Marie was forty-six.

In the week Edith died Karno reopened the Karsino with high hopes for a bumper season, given that the American boxer Mickey Walker had set up his training camp at the hotel. Charles Cochran was promoting Walker's first defence of his world middleweight title against the British champion, Tommy Milligan. (Coincidentally, Walker had spent time on his Atlantic voyage sparring with Will Hay, who was a keen amateur boxer and returning from his first U.S. tour.) Karno had a ring set up in the grounds and must have been delighted to see visitors flocking to watch Walker train. Meanwhile he'd also extended his putting green into an eighteen-hole miniature golf course. He was not giving up the dream easily, but desperately needed to find a way to improve his finances.

Thoughts turned to old friends. Karno wrote to Queenie, then working at the Cecil B. DeMille Studios, and asked her to pass on a letter to Charlie Chaplin – which suggests that more direct communications had been ignored. Although we don't know what the letter to Chaplin said, one assumes that it

31. RICHES TO RAGS

either asked him to find Karno an opportunity in Hollywood or invited him to return to work in Britain – either way, Karno was wasting his time. He told Queenie Karsino had struggled due to bad weather, but said 1927 was forecast to be a good summer – it turned out to be the wettest yet.[21] As his debts mounted, a creditors' petition was filed against him on 9 June – it was the first step toward total ruin unless he could come up with something very quickly indeed.

Two days earlier Syd Chaplin had arrived in England, having agreed to make a film with British International Pictures (BIP) called *A Little Bit of Fluff*[22] – his co-star would be the ex-Karno starlet Betty Balfour. Syd's film career was a roller-coaster affair: he made some good pictures and some turkeys, but could never quite escape comparison with his younger brother. He had a reputation for being difficult to work with: constantly battling with studios, accountants and the tax man in the boardroom, while securing a string of

31.3 Karno (left) with Syd Chaplin (centre) and Syd's co-star Clifford McLaglen on the set of A Little Bit of Fluff *(courtesy Roy Export/Chaplin Archive).*

conquests in the bedroom. Syd's biographer Lisa Stein concludes that he came to England in 1927 having burnt one bridge too many in Hollywood.

Syd immediately headed off on a continental holiday, and when he returned to begin filming in September, Karno wrote hoping to renew their association. There was no banter, no reminiscing, no mention of their mutual triumphs – the once-mighty Karno, Syd's old Guv'nor, was just days away from bankruptcy, and sounds almost pathetic: 'I should like to see you one day, if you can spare the time, and are not too busy with the new picture.'[23] So imagine his delight when Syd invited him to visit the set. Karno wasted no time before pushing the idea of making films of his sketches, but soon realised he would have to be patient. Syd only had a one-picture deal, and at a sky-high salary that stretched BIP to the limit – negotiating a further option was proving difficult.

Syd Chaplin wasn't the only ex-Karno star to return that year. In July Stan Laurel made a brief visit to Britain for a holiday, and although we don't know when or where Karno met him, they certainly did catch up. Their conversation seems to have encouraged Karno to think about opportunities in Hollywood. He wrote to Queenie: 'I had a long chat with Stan ... and I was pleased to hear of his success. I would very much like to come over and will certainly do so at the first opportunity. Things are very quiet over here ... and it does not look as if there is going to be any improvement.'[24]

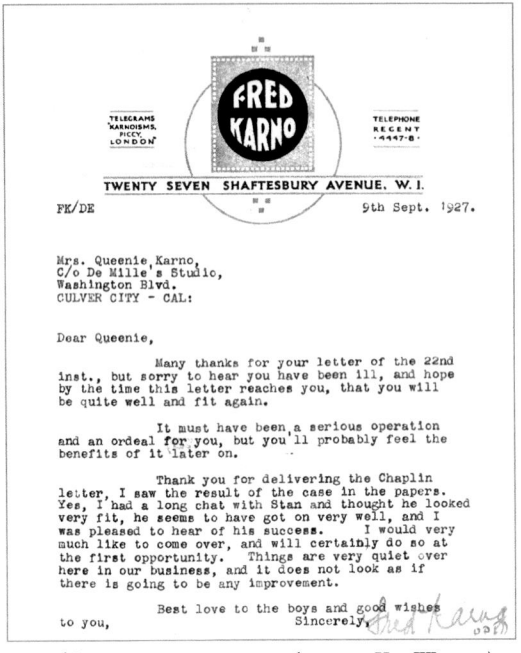

31.4 Renewing acquaintances (courtesy Ken Westcott).

No Karno show ran in the summer of 1927, but there were signs that he had projects in the pipeline. In July he placed a press notice seeking a large theatrical storage space (including room for a full-size paint frame), so he clearly had a production to put together. He also considered other money-making schemes, and set about promoting a portable dog-racing business. In partnership with a Mr H. Stanley he registered two companies: one for theatrical productions (Karno's Trust Ltd), one for the dog-racing venture. The press reported that he had big plans: 'Mr Karno says the new enterprise will be based on the idea of the travelling circus ... He said: "We shall take all our equipment with us, including an electricity generating plant ... stands for spectators, and all the

31. RICHES TO RAGS

other paraphernalia necessary for dog racing. A group of bookmakers will follow us ... We intend to run the show all the year round.'"[25]

Karno was once again on trend: the oval track and mechanical hare had been introduced to Britain the previous year, and at least two other greyhound-racing enterprises were established that same week. But it was a pipe dream: he lacked the working capital to launch his new venture.

He was asset-rich but cash-poor: he had a luxurious houseboat, a long lease on Karsino, his back catalogue and other business interests – put simply, he was a wealthy man who ran out of money. Karno had assumed that if things ever turned really sour he would be able to sell his luxury hotel – but failed to anticipate that when the axe fell, he wouldn't have time to do so. The legal documents show that his assets outstripped his liabilities, but his creditors ran out of patience and on 25 October 1927 he was declared bankrupt.

Leslie drove his father to the bankruptcy court, and would later tell his grandchildren that on the way Karno realised he was wearing a very expensive wristwatch. He thought this might be noticed by the judge and count against him, so they stopped off at a jewellery shop and bought a cheap watch. Much to Karno's disgust it stopped working almost immediately, and he spent the entire court proceedings unaware of the events unfolding around him as he tutted and messed with it. After the hearing he promptly returned to the shop and stood in the street declaring: "The man is a charlatan, he sells watches that are rubbish!" As we noted earlier, Karno could not stand 'thieves and robbers' – ironic then, that it was just such thieves and robbers that precipitated his bankruptcy.

The circumstances were bizarre: the action was brought by moneylenders R.E. Bennison and F. Andrews, to whom Karno was indebted for just £164. Not a small amount in those days, but in the scheme of things peanuts: his net assets were valued at £15,000.[26] Karno had displayed an extraordinary lack of financial judgement by borrowing money in order to lend it to someone else, and later told Adeler and West:

> My financial downfall happened over a mere trifle ... A manager ... was in dire need ... and came to me with a pitiful tale promising fervently to repay in a few days. I was willing to help him, although I ... was heavily overdrawn myself ... I borrowed £250 ... lending £200 to the friend and keeping £50 for myself. Need it be said that the other manager failed to keep his obligations? ... On top of that was pressure

> from the Income Tax authorities ... supertax for 1916 – ten years old. So, I said "I give up – I've had sufficient. I'll let the whole damn thing go," and I did.[27]

Karno even managed to get ripped off on the steps of the courthouse. He met a man claiming to be a solicitor's clerk, who recommended a lawyer who was 'the best in the business.' Karno readily agreed to appoint this expert, and gave the clerk the ten guineas he requested as an advanced payment. He arranged to meet his new legal team at court the following day – they never appeared. For someone so well versed in business, the gullibility he displayed in those dark days is truly staggering – he was a drowning man clutching at straws.

His downfall made headlines: 'Losses in connection with ... the Karsino, were stated to be the cause of the appearance at the London Bankruptcy Court today of Mr Fred Karno ... For some years past losses had been sustained owing to bad weather.'[28] Once proceedings began, forty or so creditors came forward, most of whom were owed for normal day-to-day transactions, but there was one very significant debt: the mortgage on Karsino, which was immediately called in. Already bitter and disillusioned, the behaviour of his business associates and creditors left Karno with little faith in his fellow man. Adeler and West noted: 'When the ship was sinking the vultures commenced to hover around – they fed on Fred while he was still alive and bled him dry.'[29]

Karno's assets were cast to the wind. His shares in Moss Empires and the London Coliseum were sold at a poor price; his beloved Rolls Royce (which had cost him £3,000) sold for £750. Most painful of all, his houseboat Astoria, which he described as the apple of his eye, was bought by the music hall singer Vesta Victoria. Surprisingly the fate of Karsino itself was barely reported in the press, but there must have been a sell-off. Selena Dixey, mother of Phyllis, recalled buying up some of the contents and setting up a second-hand furniture shop with the stock.

Gallagher propounded the theory that Karno had become a heavy gambler, adding that he once lost £150,000 in a single year at the track, but I have found no evidence for this and the theory is not supported by the family's oral history. Adeler and West said: 'Fred got many an alleged good tip ... but he was never much of a gambler ... He seldom had more than a modest fiver on.'[30] Gambling was not cited in Edith's long list of Karno's bad behaviour in their separation papers, nor were gambling debts recorded in the bankruptcy court reports.

31. RICHES TO RAGS

Whatever the combination of reasons for his downfall, Karno recalled that his friends and associates generally felt he had been a victim of 'cruel circumstances', exacerbated by swindlers. It mattered not – the damage was done, and although there would be new adventures and some future success, he carried the scars of this failure for the rest of his life.

It would be easy to blame Karsino's troubles on a lack of experience in the hotel trade, but one of Karno's great strengths had always been his ability to assemble a great team, and he'd employed professional managers on whom he thought he could rely. He was wrong. He understood grandeur, he understood entertainment and he created a resort that was delightful, with great facilities, a well-stocked bar, excellent entertainment and good food. But he didn't understand the day-to-day operation of a hotel, and neglected to get someone who did. Karsino's failure was the result of a perfect storm of dishonest staff, the First World War, changing tastes, the motorcar and the British weather, but Karno's biggest mistake was the excessive amount he lavished on building it in the first place, a cost which saddled him with unsustainable debt.

It is ironic that as Karno went bankrupt, the stars he'd discovered were flying high. On stage, Will Hay and Sandy Powell were top of the bill, while Jack Hylton was the biggest thing in radio. On the silver screen Chaplin was making *The Circus,* which would win him an honorary Oscar at the first Academy Awards ceremony in 1929, and Stan Laurel was just embarking on his extraordinary partnership with Oliver Hardy.

Meanwhile, their old Guv'nor was facing a harsh new reality. Karsino, the Fun Factory and Astoria were all gone, and with no source of income his Albany flat soon followed. Karno recalled waking up one morning with the realisation that after forty years in showbusiness, he had nothing. He was at rock bottom. There was only one way to go.

32.

Hooray for Hollywood

Magistrate: Are you in work?
Bill: No, I can't get a job in my trade.
Magistrate: And what is your trade?
Bill: I'm a coronation programme seller.
(Jail Birds, film version, 1940)

KARNO MAKES no mention of any member of his family in his memoirs – until now, for at this moment Marie came to his rescue. In a surprisingly candid admission, he told Adeler and West how she saved them from destitution: 'Fred told her, with tears is his eyes, that they were homeless; she replied "I think I can find a little place that will suit." Without explaining further, she took him round to a cosy furnished flat in Charing Cross Road … the flat was hers, every stick of furniture in it having been bought out of her own private savings.'[1]

Had she put this insurance policy in place because she anticipated her husband's demise? Or was the flat a bolthole – somewhere to fall back on if he left her for one of his chorus girls? Either way, a wife keeping a secret flat might raise some questions. According to Gallagher, Marie also bought back Karno's beloved Rolls, but in truth the car was sold to his solicitor, Norman Hedderwick.[2] Hedderwick may have purchased it on his client's behalf but this seems unlikely – Karno could hardly drive it around London while being pursued by his creditors. Besides, Marie had the flat but she can't have had any cash, otherwise she would have paid off her husband's modest debt and avoided the bankruptcy entirely. The family archive also reveals that over the coming

32. HOORAY FOR HOLLYWOOD

years they had to borrow money from Marie's father, so while they had a roof over their heads, they had little else. Karno was glad to have that much, and whatever the truth of his philandering, his relationship with Marie was a strong one – they were together for nearly forty years. Adeler and West wrote:

> Fred once said … "I believe I have the reputation of possessing the gift for finding stars. I discovered the ace of them all when I found my affinity." Mrs Karno has ever been guiding star, philosopher, and friend to her husband … During his happy moments she has been there to laugh with him; in his sad moments, when troubles and misfortunes heaped their spite upon him, she was always by his side to sympathize and comfort him … In later life when the battle seemed a losing one, and each hill became steeper to climb, it was Mrs Karno's philosophy and cheery optimism that helped Fred along many a weary mile.[3]

Karno needed every ounce of that cheery optimism as he now looked for ways to salvage something from the wreckage. As a bankrupt he could no longer legally run the business, and since no one had heard sight nor sound of Fred Jr. since he disappeared in Canada, he turned to Leslie to pick up the reins.

The challenge of resuscitating the empire must have been daunting, but there was no time to worry about it: Leslie had immediate matters to address. Just before Karno's bankruptcy, Alfred T. Reeve and Frederick W. Russell had agreed to finance a new production, and they stood by their

32.1 Leslie Karno – in charge of the empire (courtesy Louise Murchison).

agreement. *Hullo There!* opened at the Tivoli, New Brighton, in mid-November 1927. It was written by Arthur (Arty) Le Clerq,[4] brother of Gus Le Clerq, a prolific writer of music hall songs including *Don't Have Any More Mrs Moore, Nobody Loves a Fairy When She's Forty* and the wonderfully titled *What Can You Buy a Nudist for His Birthday?* As this review reveals, Le Clerq reworked the *Classes and Masses* sketch from *Red Hot,* which had already been reprised in both *Scarlet Runners* and *1922*:

> Anything like dullness is unknown in connection with any show which bears the name of Fred Karno, and this new production is no exception … it is vivacious and humorous … "Capital and Labour" … is one of the best things in the production … a funny picture of the discomfiture of a landlord upon whose estate cottage homes for the proletariat have been built … but the gem of the sketch is when Lord Fenutty's son … settles his love affairs all unconscious of an audience gaping from the doors and windows opposite.[5]

Jack Gallagher carried the comedy in the sketches, including playing a familiar looking drunk who interrupts the other artistes. No one seems to have noticed the rehashing of old material, and the show met with unanimous approval and plenty of advance bookings, providing some comfort for Karno holed up in his little flat, licking his wounds.

Hullo There! was followed by an abortive attempt to revive *The Yap Yaps*, but it would be a different old favourite that resurfaced next. Reeve and Russell resurrected *Mumming Birds*, with an updated script from Arty Le Clerq, and Karno personally oversaw the production. It opened at the Palace Theatre, Plymouth, in February 1928,[6] with Edgar Cooke returning to lead a company billed as 'A Variety Company of Worst-End Artistes direct from the Remand Performance.'[7] By updating the acts, Le Clerq and Karno were able to keep the sketch fresh: they even managed to write in the drunk and the Eton boy taking a screen test.

By the summer, Karno's spirits had significantly improved. In June he wrote to Queenie: 'I am pleased to tell you I have had a little change for the better. I have got rid of all my trouble at the island and have just started the old Mumming Birds again … it is going very well … Young Leslie and his wife are in it … Things are terrible here they are turning all the halls into picture palaces … Hoping you are all keeping well with best love your affectionate Grandad Fred Karno.'[8]

Leslie and Louisa were paid five pounds per week, a third of what Karno had paid his comics twenty years earlier, and for that Leslie also took on the day-to-day management of the company. Underpaid or not, he now became the face of the family firm. Karno remained in charge, of course – literally behind the scenes. Leslie's archive is full of little notes sent by his father to remind him about things to do, or suggested improvements and gags to include. Karno's

32. HOORAY FOR HOLLYWOOD

letters contain obvious affection but he could also be scathing: no doubt he was frustrated at being unable to take an active part in the business while watching Leslie learn (and make mistakes) on the job. Nonetheless he guided his son in how to manage his cast, theatre managers and agents. One note says: 'You have an opportunity now of showing what you can do as a producer – detail means everything and timing essential.'[9] In another he says of *Mumming Birds*: 'I hope you will stick at the show until you get it right … it wants presenting as a play. The show requires character and rhyme and reason, cause and effect, and timing … tighten up the laughs, cut the cackle and get to business.'[10]

When the *Mumming Birds* tour reached London it was not the only throwback on the bill, as *The Stage* noted: 'It is highly significant that the loudest laughter and applause … is caused by J.W. Jackson's Eight Lancashire Lads … and Fred Karno's revival of "Mumming Birds". It … not only proves the lasting appeal … of variety as variety but seems to indicate that a revival … of the older type of music hall entertainment would not be unwelcome.'[11] The same bill also included new comedy in the form of double act Naughton and Gold, who would later play a part in Karno's story. In May, Jack Gallagher licensed *Hullo There!* and ran it with his own company; meanwhile Reeve and Russell put together a new variety bill (including another version of *Mumming Birds*), which they toured under the title *The Reeve and Russell Roadshow*.

That summer Karno faced his public examination – and humiliation – in the London bankruptcy court; a few months later his bankruptcy was formally discharged and he was free to run the business again.[12] He established a new office at 5 Green Street, Leicester Square, and advertised that *Mumming Birds* was set to tour Europe and America. Earlier in the year he had written to Queenie (who was herself struggling to find work): 'I have been in correspondence with several American agents and I am expecting to fix something for the autumn. I think you had better stop where you are and if I come over to produce anything you shall go in it.'[13]

There were continued press reports of a planned international tour (to be led by comic Walter Niblo), but for some reason it never happened. Fortunately the *Mumming Birds* provincial tour continued into 1929, and things were going well enough that the company was split into two, with Edgar Cooke leading one and Leslie the other. Then things began to go downhill again.

Cooke was no stranger to the bottle, and this sometimes prevented him performing. When he wasn't drunk, he was arguing with Karno over the receipts.

Tempers finally boiled over in May, when Cooke began pawning the props to supplement his wages. His unpredictability forced Leslie to engage stand-ins at short notice. In January Billy Bennett took on the lead, and the rest of the cast seemed to be whoever was on the bill that night. In May, Dan Raynor was roped in as another temporary replacement. Leslie's archive reveals poor houses and falling receipts – it was an industry in its death throes. The rise of cinema had caused theatre audiences to dwindle, but the real competition came from radio. Since the advent of the BBC in 1922 people didn't even have to leave the comfort of their fireside to be entertained.

The whole tour became hand-to-mouth: dates were sometimes cancelled at the last minute, and receipts failed to cover costs. Leslie could only engage artistes for two weeks at a time, and they had to accept the possibility of being dismissed without notice. Unsurprisingly, he found himself trying to hold together an unreliable, often mutinous troupe of performers. Karno wrote to Leslie about one comic, Arthur Godfrey, whose whereabouts were a mystery to his wife:

> Mrs Godfrey has just phoned up asking where the show is, she has not heard anything from him … she has got two kiddies to keep and he has left them to starve. He is another rotter … Be sure you have it understood with the boys that they are only continuing from week to week. They are such a treacherous lot and can't be trusted. I don't want to give any of them a loophole to go the VAF demanding money in lieu of notice.[14]

Karno became desperate to find reliable talent, and gave a chance to a one-time superstar of the music halls, now down on his luck. Fred Barnes' career had been destroyed thanks to drink, drugs and wanton spending. He proved to be a disaster and was soon out of the show. Then, just when it looked like all was lost, a glimmer of hope came from an old friend.

We left Syd Chaplin in 1927, completing *A Little Bit of Fluff*. At the end of the following year he finally signed a further two-picture contract with BIP which brought him back to London in January 1929. The Chaplin archive reveals that Syd received regular updates from Alf Reeves in Hollywood, including progress reports on his brother's new film *City Lights*. Reeves reported that Karno had written to Chaplin again, seeking advice on how to get into movies: 'Karno … asked me to get Charlie's opinion as to some of his sketches

32. HOORAY FOR HOLLYWOOD

for the pictures, but Charlie has not expressed himself much so far on this, and I could not really give Fred any encouragement – so I just stalled it along.'[15] Syd stepped in where his brother feared to tread, deciding that the first of his BIP pictures would be a version of *Mumming Birds*, which he would direct himself. Syd was to pick up $100,000 for each film. How much Karno received is unrecorded, but whatever the amount, it must have promised financial salvation. Syd approached George Carney to help with the script and they all set to work in March.

They decided to incorporate elements of *Early Birds* in the film, with Syd playing the old Jewish pedlar. His character would find a lost wallet containing a ticket for *Mumming Birds* – then once in the theatre, get excited, rush the stage and take part in the sketch. This prompted another trip to the East End for inspiration, and Karno recalled them returning with plenty of photographs on which to base their characters.

32.2 Seeking inspiration in the East End – Karno and Syd Chaplin spring 1929.

Cut off from Hollywood, Syd seemed to welcome rediscovering a friend from the old days, and with wives in tow the pair went to the Derby and shared trips to Ostend and Bournemouth. Word of Karno's association with the project quickly spread, and he soon had others chasing a piece of the action. He wrote to Leslie: 'I am inundated with offers from various film companies to produce my sketches for the Talkies.'[16] He should have taken them – his *Mumming Birds* movie was suddenly cancelled. Syd Chaplin had become embroiled in a scandal that put an end both to the film and his career.

Syd led a hedonistic lifestyle and his friend, the Hollywood mogul Darryl Zanuck, suggested his behaviour was perhaps darker than mere promiscuity: '[Syd] was a predator, a hunter of vulnerable females, and his appetite was practically insatiable.'[17] Disaster struck Karno's project when a twenty-two-year-old actress named Molly Wright, who'd had a small part in *A Little Bit of Fluff*, went public on an affair she'd had with Syd. She claimed he engaged in violent sex acts and had bitten off one of her nipples. Though he denied it, rumours swept the Elstree studio. Syd did his best to keep the scandal out of the newspapers and fled to Europe. As details leaked out, he tried to discredit Wright, engaging a private detective to dig up dirt on her family. The following year she sued Syd for assault, libel and slander – his subsequent court appearance would be his final visit to Britain. BIP then sued him for the £60,000 advance on his salary, and he was later declared bankrupt.[18] His reputation destroyed, he retired to live in self-imposed exile in Nice. Karno remained silent on the scandal in his memoirs, and explained the film's cancellation by simply citing 'the vagaries of the picture world.' Carney didn't give up so easily, successfully suing BIP for the cancellation of his contract.

BIP attempted to recommence production of *Mumming Birds* the following year with a new production team, but this too was abandoned – perhaps they twigged that someone else had beaten them to it. Lupino Lane, who was making silents in Hollywood for Educational Pictures, had released *Only Me* (1929), a carbon copy of *Mumming Birds* in which Lane played all the parts. His version remains the most authentic recreation of the sketch on film, yet this copyright infringement seems to have passed Karno by.

While all this unfolded Leslie stoically kept *Mumming Birds* touring, albeit at a loss. His experience bore a remarkable similarity to the early careers of his parents – second-rate theatres and third-rate digs. When touring in Ireland the company found themselves in the middle of an anti-English riot, and had to tap-dance in the street to calm the angry mob. Leslie cabled Karno saying they were in fear of their lives: "How do we get out?" he begged. Karno replied: "How did you get in?"[19]

Dodging bullets and rioters, Leslie kept the show running, securing an engagement in Paris in early 1929. This went well, but hopes of further dates were dashed when he discovered Billy Devoy had been touring a pirated version of the sketch.[20] Karno had neither the energy nor the funds to mount a legal challenge. Leslie's troupe, which also now included Karno's nineteen-year-old niece Ray Westcott, returned to Britain and the misery of half-empty houses. In the first week of July, at the Playhouse in Colchester, the company coupled *Mumming Birds* with a piece called *Tainted*, but there is nothing to tell us what this sketch entailed and there were no further performances. Karno was by now happy to take all offers. In July he licensed *Mumming Birds* to Billy Bennett as a gap-filler after a cancellation, but it was yet more meagre pickings. Perhaps he

32. HOORAY FOR HOLLYWOOD

might have given up and retired, save for one last glimmer of hope – Hollywood finally came calling.

Karno had a love-hate relationship with America – his touring success there had been at the cost of his greatest comics. He could not forgive the studios for their larceny, but at the same time he basked in the reflected glory of Chaplin, Laurel and the others, and his name still carried some kudos. Eventually an offer arrived from William Morris, the man who had helped organise his U.S. tours twenty years before, and who now ran the biggest agency in America.[21] If Karno could get to New York there was a job waiting for him at Paramount Studios as a scenario writer and gag man for the Marx Brothers. The Guv'nor had no reason to doubt that the offer was serious – he packed a bag and borrowed the money for a one-way ticket across the Atlantic.

Before setting sail, Karno received a letter from Morris saying that the brothers' next project would be a comic love story – and tasking him with working up a storyline. This was hardly Karno's usual material so he asked Leslie for help,[22] but neither of them came up with any ideas, which didn't bode well for his new engagement. Undeterred, Karno took a short holiday in Belgium with Marie then waved her goodbye and headed for New York, full of enthusiasm and with the press following his every move: 'Fred Karno has been engaged by the William Morris Agency to supply the comedy for a Paramount Production … he will sail on Saturday [10 August] on the Aquitania.'[23] Marie wrote to Leslie telling him that Karno expected to be sending for all of them before long, and that as well as his film work, he would be trying to secure engagements for *Mumming Birds* in vaudeville, adding: 'Always know Leslie, your father will do his best for you. He has some funny little ways (we all have) but he doesn't mean it.'[24]

Karno was a legendary name in the States, and when he arrived in New York he was besieged by journalists.[25] Morris had booked Karno into the prestigious Astor Hotel in Times Square and he must have thought he'd hit the jackpot – he was to be bitterly disappointed. He found himself kicking his heels for days on end, with no welcoming committee from his supposed new employers and no word about the contract. Enquiring at Paramount's Astoria Studio (the name's irony wouldn't have been lost on him) he was told to sit tight – meetings were in the process of being arranged. Karno began to realise he was on a wild goose chase.

The William Morris Agency certainly acted for the Marx Brothers at that time, so should have known full well that they had no need of a new gag man. *The Cocoanuts* had just been released and they were about to start on their second film, *Animal Crackers* – both were based on their successful vaudeville shows penned by George S. Kaufman and Morrie Ryskind. I am left to speculate that perhaps Paramount thought they might benefit from some fresh ideas, especially for Harpo's sight gags, but the Brothers weren't interested – they had well-established routines and were already a law unto themselves.[26]

The fact that Karno had sailed across the Atlantic without a contract says a lot about his state of desperation, and now he was up a creek without a paddle. He had one card left to play: he knew the boss.

Back in 1913, Jesse Lasky had suffered a huge financial loss when his New York Folies Bergère theatre folded after just six months. His best friend, a struggling playwright called Cecil B. DeMille, declared that theatre was a waste of time, and announced he was running away to fight in the Mexican revolution.[27] To stop him, Lasky reluctantly agreed to throw his hat in with DeMille and try their hand at making movies. Lasky organised things in New York while DeMille travelled west looking for somewhere to set up a studio. He eventually settled on a barn on a dusty backroad called Vine Street in the middle of rural Los Angeles. Lasky's brother-in-law Sam Goldfish (soon to be Goldwyn) was roped in and found himself selling Lasky and DeMille's first picture to New York distributors before they'd even made it – the rest is history. By the time Karno showed up fifteen years later, Lasky was head of Paramount Famous Lasky Corporation, and one of the biggest names in the industry.

Twenty years earlier Karno had worked with Lasky to bring U.S. acts to Britain, and knew him well, which makes it surprising that he went to America without corresponding with Lasky about the true nature of the offer. He certainly wanted to now. He kept banging on Lasky's door until someone told him the boss had gone to Los Angeles.[28] With nothing keeping him in New York, Karno decided he would head west and pin down Lasky in LA. On the morning he was to set off, the studio called and asked him to come over immediately; tired of being messed around, he told them that if they wanted him, he would be in California.

32.3 Cornet player turned movie mogul – Jesse Lasky.

32. HOORAY FOR HOLLYWOOD

Karno broke his cross-country train journey with a brief stop in Tulsa to visit Marie's sister, whose family had emigrated there and supposedly struck oil. Despite this reunion, his letters to Marie reveal that once the initial excitement of New York wore off, he felt alone and a long way from home. He still had hopes that Tinseltown would be his salvation, but had been warned to expect a 'Hollywood welcome': a warm reception, kind words and promises, and all of it totally insincere. Of course, Karno was no ordinary wannabe – he must have anticipated finding a town full of his old-boys, ready to welcome him with open arms. In his mind they were still the young hopefuls he'd plucked from obscurity – they'd be only too pleased to repay him for that opportunity. In reality his discoveries were now middle-aged, highly successful comics who were about to get an unexpected reunion with their uninvited former employer. He finally arrived in the movie capital of the world on 13 September 1929, and settled himself into the Roosevelt Hotel. Having spent the journey working out his plan of attack, he decided that Lasky was a lost cause; instead, his first port of call would be the biggest star in Hollywood.

If you need convincing of Karno's influence on the studios of the late 1920s, consider the Chaplin lot on the day he arrived. Production was well underway on *City Lights*, which included Albert Austin in the cast; Alf Reeves was responsible for the operation of the studio;[29] Reeves' wife Amy, an ex-Karno plonk, was there too; and Winnie Ritchie worked in wardrobe. Many more alumni were dotted around other studios, including Stan Laurel, Charley Rogers and Jimmy Aubrey. He may have been among old friends, but Karno must have felt some trepidation when he turned up unannounced.[30]

As you might imagine, getting through the gates of Chaplin's studio was not easy. Carlyle Robinson, Chaplin's publicist, recalled his first day at Mutual back in 1917: 'Chaplin was a very difficult person to meet … it was absolutely forbidden for strangers to penetrate into the studio … the star … did not at all wish to be bothered by old friends, even those who had known Charlie Chaplin when he played in the English music halls.'[31] Karno screwed his courage to the sticking place, knocked on the door and announced his desire to see the man himself. He might not have made it further but for the fact that Alf Reeves happened by. Karno recalled: 'His eyes goggled as if he had seen a ghost, and he spluttered "What the hell are you doing here?"'[32] Not perhaps the welcome he was hoping for!

Karno put on his most nonchalant expression and said he'd come over to see what Hollywood was all about, and thought he'd stop by to say hello. Given his very public fall from grace, it must have taken some guts for him to turn up in America and seek out his former protégés – and now he was here, he had to play it very carefully. He still had his pride: he wanted to be given a chance on merit, not because he was a sad old comic in need of a break. Affecting a mix of humility, confidence and interest, he explained that he was open to opportunities – if the offer was right.

Karno sensed that Reeves saw through this front: Alf had known him too long, and immediately pressed to find out how long he intended to stay. Desperate to make Reeves believe he wasn't looking for charity, he told him he was staying at the Roosevelt, flashed his small diamond ring and asked where he might buy a car – at which point his old sidekick seemed to relax. After the inevitable small talk, Karno picked his moment to enquire after Chaplin, and they set off in search of the Little Fellow.

32.4 Alf Reeves around the time of Karno's arrival in Hollywood (courtesy Roy Export/Chaplin Archive).

Adeler and West's version of Karno's reunion with Chaplin might be taken with a pinch of salt, but it is worth repeating: this was, after all, the meeting of the greatest comedy impresario of the music hall age and his former protégé – now the biggest star in the world. They had not seen each other for eight years:

> Fred ... saw Charlie Chaplin approaching from the distance ... in his working clothes, a sweater open at the neck, disgraceful old flannel trousers, India rubber soled plimsolls and tousled hair. When he spotted Karno he stopped and looked puzzled ... stared as if uncertain until at last it seemed to dawn upon him ... "Gee" he said, "It's my old Guv'nor." He rushed over to him, put his arms round him ... "Why you haven't altered a bit," he exclaimed. He took him into a small office ... sat down and had a comfortable 'shoppy' jaw about old times ... During a momentary lull in the conversation Charlie ... said: "listen! I've got an inspiration for a song." He sat down at the piano and played by ear quite a charming melody ... when he asked Fred's opinion, the latter

was able to say with truth that it was very beautiful … "What are you doing today?" Asked Charlie. Fred replied that he was free. Chaplin then asked Reeves what his appointments were, and a portentous list was read out. "Cancel or postpone them all," ordered the star, "I'm spending the day with The Guv'nor." Then with a quaint sweet smile … he added: "D'you know I feel almost as overawed by you as ever I was!"[33]

Chaplin could easily have dismissed Karno. His friend Alexander Pollock Moore (the American ambassador to Peru) was staying with him, so he had every opportunity to make excuses and hide behind a busy schedule. Instead he embraced his old boss as a long-lost friend and honoured guest.

Chaplin whisked Karno off for a tour of his house in Beverley Hills, the scale of which was awe-inspiring even to Karno.[34] He was shown every room, the extensive grounds and the floodlit tennis courts. He joined Chaplin for a Turkish bath in the authentic hammam and was amazed to be served iced tea by a Japanese servant. As they whiled away the hours reminiscing, Chaplin sat at the piano, obsessing over his new melody. The contrast with Karno's own circumstances must have been overwhelming, and not just in terms of their personal situations: Karno had left behind a Britain struggling through difficult economic times, with rampant unemployment, deflation, rising national debt and high taxation. America boomed, and even with Prohibition dampening the mood, Hollywood was awash with wealth and success.

The day turned to evening but still Chaplin was in no mood to ditch his uninvited guest. He had a dinner engagement at the summer home of actress Marion Davies, and insisted Karno join them. Remembering the famously scruffy young lad he'd known, Karno was amazed to see Chaplin dressed for dinner – here was a sophisticated, well-groomed gentleman at the very centre of Hollywood's glitterati. The former workhouse urchin and the uneducated circus acrobat were to be guests of honour at one of the most opulent homes in Tinseltown.

Davies was the mistress of media mogul William Randolph Hearst, but it was rumoured she also had an on-off love affair with Chaplin. Hearst had built her a mansion in Santa Monica, which Karno compared to the Palace of Versailles. Even Chaplin was impressed enough to point out, in a whisper, that the doorhandles were solid gold. In his autobiography he added his own description: 'The beach house … was … a seventy-roomed Georgian structure,

32.5 Marion Davies and her extraordinary beach house.

three hundred feet wide and three storeys high, with a gold-leaf gilded ball room and dining room.'[35]

At the time Chaplin was working on an original score for *City Lights*, a first experiment in creating his own synchronised musical soundtrack. Perhaps this led him to seek reassurance as to his ability, for that night he drove the other guests mad playing his new tune. According to Karno it was an intimate gathering of five, but he didn't name the other guests – one might assume they were Alexander Pollock Moore and perhaps Hearst himself. Karno doubtless had the uncharacteristic feeling of being the least successful person in the room, and must have called on every ounce of his experience at those up-river society dinners to avoid making a fool of himself.

After dinner the party adjourned to the drawing room, where Karno was amazed to find that a full-size cinema screen appeared from the floor, the lights dimmed and a projector burst into life, all at the push of a button. Davies treated them to the rushes of her latest film, inevitably accompanied by much professional comment and observation. Karno noted that his hosts paid no heed to Prohibition, ending the evening with drinks. Davies was filming early the next day, so the two old colleagues retired to the Roosevelt, where despite Karno's protestations of tiredness, Chaplin insisted they gatecrash a gala evening. There they were joined by a friend of his, who was genuinely starstruck to meet the famous Fred Karno – which is saying something when the bloke next to you is Charlie Chaplin. Their new companion waxed lyrical about the old sketches, while Chaplin was more interested in discussing the potential of his new melody. He no doubt valued this friend's opinion – his name was Irving Berlin.

In the early hours Karno made his excuses and headed for bed; his first day in Hollywood had been memorable. That night he must have dreamed of a glorious future working with Chaplin and accompanying him to society parties – they were never to meet again.

Karno was not invited back to the Chaplin studio.[36] Alf Reeves wrote to Syd, now exiled in France, telling him of the Guv'nor's arrival, but said that Chaplin remained completely focused on *City Lights* and was keen to avoid distractions.[37] It had been the Hollywood welcome Karno feared, and it went further than just Chaplin's studio. Karno had brought with him a trunk full of material, and later said the newspapers ran pictures of him surrounded by piles of scripts, under the headline: 'Arrival of the Comedy King'.[38] The news coverage wasn't limited to Hollywood, or even the U.S.: in Australia *The Sydney Sun* ran the headline 'Hail Karno!' followed by: 'Fred Karno, who discovered Charles Spencer Chaplin … is in Hollywood.'[39]

However if Karno thought such publicity would open doors, he was mistaken – it had the opposite effect. He was perceived to be an arrogant British pensioner who claimed to have seen it all and invented most of it – he was soon aware of people bad-mouthing him around town. If he was going to get a break it could only come from the good will of old acquaintances: time for plan B.

33.

Crashing Out

"That man's a has been!"
"A has been? He's a never was."
(Nosey Knows, 1917)

THE RELATIONSHIP between Charlie Chaplin and Stan Laurel has been the subject of much debate among film historians. Despite their friendship in Karno days, they barely saw one another in America. Richard Bann suggests they simply moved in different circles: Chaplin beat Laurel to the big-time by over ten years, and Stan supposedly felt uncomfortable mixing with him socially until he had achieved significant success himself[1] – by then, they were relative strangers.

In many ways they shared a common approach to filmmaking – both were perfectionists who involved themselves in every aspect of the process behind the camera – but as people they were very different. Chaplin was the more creative artist, introverted and self-absorbed, always seeking to challenge and develop his art; Laurel just wanted to make people laugh. Chaplin was shy, and insecure about his height, his background and his talent; Laurel had only one insecurity – comparisons with Chaplin. Hal Roach felt that Laurel had an unhealthy obsession with Chaplin, and felt burdened by the need to achieve the same standard. When Roach finally added 'A Stan Laurel Production' to the credits for *Our Relations* (1936), Stan told his wife he was 'finally catching up with Charlie.'[2]

By the time Karno's memoirs were written, Laurel and Hardy were competing with Chaplin as the most popular comics of their era, yet while he talks extensively and warmly about Charlie, Karno barely mentions Stan.

33. CRASHING OUT

Chaplin is hailed as a genius, a master of pathos, whereas we are told Laurel is a slapstick comedian whose speciality is broad laughs: 'None of your highbrow stuff … They [Roach's studio] make no pretence to appeal to aesthetic appetites, there is no doubt that they achieve great popularity.'[3]

Karno dismissed Laurel and Hardy as low-brow knockabouts and there are three possible explanations for this. First, his perception was a valid one at the time. The duo's reputation has grown over the years, and they are now recognised as much more important comics than contemporary critics appreciated. Stan was one half of a comedy double act, albeit a successful one, whereas Chaplin was a global star and the head of his own studio. Laurel and Hardy were not even the biggest names on the Hal Roach lot when Karno arrived in LA: Stan was earning $1000 a week, Charley Chase $1350 and Harry Langdon $2000.[4] Second, perhaps Karno couldn't bring himself to recognise Stan's success, given his treatment of the young comic in *Jimmy the Fearless* and the fact that he overlooked him again when Chaplin left the company in 1913. However, the third reason is perhaps most compelling: Karno's experience working with Laurel in Hollywood was to prove disastrous (as we shall see) – was it simply an episode he wanted to brush under the carpet?

Stan had returned to Roach in 1925, working primarily as a writer. He was a student of comedy, always looking for new ideas and reading widely. He became an indispensable asset, with an encyclopaedic knowledge of gags and comedy business. Roach said: 'Except for Chaplin, there was no better gagman in the business than Stan Laurel. He could always get the most out of every single gag.'[5] Fellow Roach star Charley Chase suggested that the public's memory for material spanned about seven years, which explains how Laurel and Chaplin were able to make use of their Karno archive – and for that matter how Karno had managed to recycle material so frequently. Perhaps Chase had Stan in mind when he added: 'The really valuable gag man is the one who has lots of experience and can dig into his memory for what is funny to the last generation and vary it so that it's funny to this one.'[6]

Stan was persuaded to return to acting to cover for Hardy after he suffered a minor injury, and the rest is history – by the time Karno looked up his second former employee, Laurel and Hardy had made over thirty films together. And while 'Babe' Hardy was a brilliant comic actor, he had little interest in other aspects of the process: Stan was the driving force behind their films, directing, editing and writing – input for which he received little credit at the time. Karno comics had been taught the importance of such attention to detail: Will Hay once said, 'I put everything under my in-built microscope … Every line has to be scrutinized because in a sketch everything is concentrated, and you can't afford to have a word or a laugh out of place.'[7]

Given their history, Karno must have found approaching Stan for a job even more difficult, but his memoirs fail to elaborate on the details. He devotes almost an entire chapter to meeting Chaplin; by contrast, Stan gets: 'Laurel drove Fred Karno over to Culver City, eight miles from Hollywood and took him to Roach's office.'[8]

Stan deserved more credit. Charlie Hall recalled that it was he who had given Fred Karno Jr. a job with Roach in 1923, and then added: 'Later still, Stan found an interesting position for Fred Karno Senior at Roach Studios and he was mighty happy to be in a position to do it.'[9]

33.1 Stan Laurel, Fred Karno and Hal Roach getting acquainted at the Roach Studios (courtesy Ken Westcott).

It is strange that when Karno turned up at Roach's studio, no one seems to have acknowledged that Fred Jr. had worked there six years earlier. Perhaps Karno simply omitted this from his memoirs – or perhaps, given Junior's failure, it was discreetly ignored. Either way, Stan had gone out on a limb to give Junior a chance and it had backfired, now he was doing it again. Karno should have been doubly grateful, especially when you consider that Laurel did not have the sort of power Chaplin wielded at his studio – he was taking a risk with his own reputation.

Fortunately Roach had come to trust Laurel's comedy instincts, and besides, he must have felt as though he already knew Karno. Simon Louvish uses the acronym ECFK (everything comes from Karno): his alumni were all over Hollywood and Roach was constantly reminded of his influence – it's not hard to find examples if you know what to look for. When *The Second Hundred Years* was released in 1927, distributor MGM wrote to cinema managers advising them

33. CRASHING OUT

to dress Laurel and Hardy lookalikes as convicts and get them to run around the town, ending at the theatre: 'Imagine the attention this stunt will get!'[10] Imagine indeed.

Chaplin himself would occasionally appear at Roach's studio to ask Stan about some bit of business they'd done in Karno sketches.[11] So while Chaplin had whisked Karno off the lot and kept him occupied (probably while Alf Reeves changed all the locks), Laurel and Roach embraced the Guv'nor immediately. As far as Roach could see, here was the man who taught Stan Laurel and Charlie Chaplin everything they knew — what could possibly go wrong?

Roach began by asking Karno whether he knew anything about movies: he feigned complete ignorance, which is strange given that he'd made three films with Brouett-Egrot. Perhaps he realised that a little knowledge might be a dangerous thing, or perhaps he appreciated that the American studio system would be a completely different animal. Roach invited Karno to spend a few weeks learning about filmmaking, and he was only too happy to accept — he quickly immersed himself in life on 'The Lot of Fun'.

A few days before Karno arrived, Laurel and Hardy had finished filming *The Hoose-Gow*, which has the wonderful opening title: 'Neither Mr Laurel nor Mr Hardy had any thoughts of doing wrong. As a matter of fact, they had no thoughts of any kind.' This is the film that includes the business with the rice in the car radiator inspired by Charlie Hall's story (the same gag was filmed for *Bacon Grabbers* but didn't make the final edit).

33.2 Laurel and Hardy recreate the porridge in the radiator story as Charlie Hall looks on. Deleted scene from Bacon Grabbers *(1929).*

This is as good a time as any to pause for a moment and explode the much-quoted myth that Charlie Hall had been a Karno comic. Hall was born in Birmingham in 1899 and travelled to America in January 1920. His first biographer, Ray Andrew, recorded that he had been a Karno comic in England and worked with both Laurel and Chaplin before going to America, where he then connected with the U.S. Karno company and ultimately followed Stan to Hollywood. This is not correct. There is no record of him appearing in any Karno company and he was too young to have been a contemporary of Laurel and Chaplin. In fact there is no sign of Hall ever being a performer before he emigrated to America, which may explain why his vaudeville career with Fred Jr. was so short-lived. Hall himself recorded that he met Stan for the first time after arriving in Hollywood: "Stan, Babe and I got very friendly and told each other our history."[12] So where does the story come from? John Ullah points out that since Hall toured with Fred Jr. in vaudeville, 'working with Karno' may simply have been assumed by others to mean Karno Senior. However, Karno's memoirs perhaps give us the answer – Hall may have perpetuated the myth himself.

Karno recalled that his name was such a door-opener in Hollywood that it had been taken in vain. He was approached by an unnamed comic who flung himself on Karno's mercy, confessing that when struggling to find work, he had lied to the studios by telling them he was an ex-Karno man. Now he was terrified that Karno would reveal his deception and end his career. This must have been an English actor on the Roach lot, and the obvious candidate is Hall. It's just a theory, but there is another reason to suspect Hall. Karno was not the kind of person to let anyone get away with such a deceit, yet he agreed to protect the culprit – why? Well, Hall was a good friend of Fred Jr., Queenie and his new patron Stan Laurel, who must have been in on the secret. Karno wasn't so stupid as to bite the hand that fed him, and so agreed to protect the guilty party – in so doing he made at least one friend on the lot.

Laurel and Hall weren't his only supporters: Karno wrote to Leslie telling him that Charley Rogers was helping him learn the mechanics of the studio process. Rogers was another Birmingham born comic, but he really had been with Karno before emigrating to the States. Now he was acting, writing and directing with both Laurel and Hardy, and Harry Langdon.

33.3 Charlie Hall with Queenie Karno in Hollywood (courtesy Ken Westcott).

Roach historian Richard Lewis Ward wrote that Karno was taken on to fill a vacuum at the studio caused by the departure of supervising director Leo McCarey,[13] but this seems unlikely. The way Karno was treated does not suggest

33. CRASHING OUT

Roach had him in mind for the biggest creative job on the lot – and besides, Karno turned up with no experience and no advance warning, nearly a year after McCarey left. He was simply in the right place at the right time – but given his background, it can't have been easy to start from scratch in such an alien environment. Karno was a sixty-three-year-old apprentice fighting to keep a massive ego in check.

It didn't take long for Roach to make Karno a formal offer: the bankrupt impresario whose best days were behind him was offered $50,000 a year to join the team – that's £10,000, at a time when the average annual salary in Britain was around two hundred.[14] With much bravado (and the benefit of fifty years as a negotiator) Karno asked for time to think about it – but he immediately wired Marie with the good news and told her to jump on the next boat.[15] While he waited for her, he considered his options: he had only just arrived in Hollywood and might get a better offer from another studio, maybe even from Chaplin. In the meantime Laurel and Hardy had left Roach for a few weeks to make a cameo appearance in MGM's first colour talkie, *The Rogue Song* (1930), giving Karno ample time to consider whether he could lower himself to work for a former minion like Stan, the boy he'd passed over.

As he settled in, he made some friendly contacts among the Tinseltown ex-pats, including Yorkshire comedian Dick Henderson and Lupino Lane (who presumably didn't mention ripping off *Mumming Birds* less than a year earlier). Henderson introduced him to Jack Warner, who revealed that he and many other movie moguls had often frequented Karsino when they were in London – this was news to Karno. Despite all the networking, no further offers were forthcoming. It is interesting to note that Karno gave an honest appraisal of his situation, admitting he was not welcomed with open arms. For all his brashness and bluster, Karsino's failure had changed him: his memoirs reflect a humbler character, a man not afraid to tell the world he went through difficult times.

Unsurprisingly, and with a huge sigh of relief, he accepted Roach's offer and was given an office on the lot and a secretary. His comeback had begun, or so he hoped. The British press reported that he had been appointed on a five-year contract as an associate producer, although his contract actually states 'director and writer'.[16] Whatever his role, it was to commence on the 21 October 1929.[17]

In the meantime, Marie arrived and Karno recalled that they rented an apartment at El Palacio, a grand Spanish-style building in West Hollywood. The complex survives and remains an exclusive address, but it was never Karno's – El

Palacio was not built until 1931. They actually lived in Hallsworth Apartments, 1720 Taft Avenue, a few blocks from Sunset Boulevard. At the end of the street the Hollywood sign looms large on the side of Mount Lee (although back then it said 'Hollywoodland'). Taft Avenue was still a step up from what they were used to. Karno was hugely impressed by the fact that every apartment had its own bathroom with a shower, unheard of at home, and a refrigerator, noting: 'There is neither dust, dirt or smell'[18] (which tells us more about the Fun Factory than Taft Avenue). He fell in love with American customer service, delighting in the corner barbershop where he could get a haircut, a shave, a manicure and his boots re-soled all at the same time. He was equally impressed by the high standard of living, marvelling that practically everyone owned a car.

Marie was less happy and terribly homesick, so Karno invested in a modest Ford sedan[19] so they could make the most of their free time. He was surprised that the entire studio shut down at the weekend, but Marie was delighted as it enabled them to see the sights, visiting San Francisco and San Diego (both of which Karno described in glowing terms). He was less enthusiastic about the decadent party scene. Hollywood's drink and drug fuelled scandals are well-recorded elsewhere, so let's just say it was hedonistic. Karno was in his sixties, had never been a big drinker, and his parties were of the polite Edwardian tea variety; he was a fish out of water and although he enjoyed socialising with his ex-pat friends, he was shocked at the widespread flouting of Prohibition.

One legal way to crack open a bottle was to cross the Mexican border and visit Tijuana. Prohibition had made it a boom town where every conceivable vice could be enjoyed, and a base for liquor-smuggling gangsters who mixed openly with the film stars. Here's how Karno described it to Adeler and West:

> Tia Juana offers every inducement that bad liquor can devise. It consists almost entirely of one long street lined with dozens of drinking dens, dance halls and other places of even worse repute. Touts invite you to come in and see the bolero, the tango, the fandango, and the hootchi-kootchi danced by faded, jaded houris … Sordid commercialised vice in its cheapest and most horrible form … Visitors … are advised … to re-cross the border by six pm, at which time the gates are closed … Many a young man, not heeding this warning … finds himself drunk and in jail … described as being more like a cage for wild animals.[20]

33. CRASHING OUT

More to Karno's taste was the newly opened Tijuana Agua Caliente Touristic Complex, run by a syndicate of Hollywood movie bosses. In its Spanish-style gardens it had a racecourse, tennis courts, a casino and its own aerodrome so that the very wealthy could fly home and avoid the queues (and checks for contraband) at the border.

As well as friends old and new, Hollywood was the home of Karno's daughter-in-law Queenie and his two grandsons, Kenneth and Fred. Despite her separation from Fred Jr., Karno had kept in touch with her. In a typical letter (from May 1927) he wrote: 'With the two boys to look after you've got a pretty stiff proposition on your own. Glad they are well and fit, I expect by the time I see them, they will be quite grown up. It seems only yesterday that you were a small girl, now you've grown-up boys of your own.'[21] Karno always signed off letters to her with 'Dad' and 'love to the boys.'[22] He clearly had real affection for Queenie and his grandsons, who were now ten and seven, yet he and Marie did not take the opportunity to get to know them better when they came to Hollywood. The boys only vaguely recall meeting their grandfather, remembering him as standoffish. Of course, Karno was a stranger to them, and a man from the Victorian age: outward shows of affection were not his style. He gave them a photograph of himself with 'Pete the pup' (the famous dog from the Hal Roach 'Our Gang' movies) on the back of which he wrote: 'To our grandchildren with love from dad, Fred Karno 19 December 1929' – in Karno's world a photograph of himself passed as a Christmas present.

33.4 Karno's Christmas gift – a portrait with Our Gang's *'Pete the pup' (courtesy Ken Westcott).*

This detachment may have been a result of Queenie's relationship with a Roach extra named William 'Curly' Morrisey. They were married bigamously the following July, after Queenie persuaded the authorities that Fred Jr. was missing presumed dead. Having Fred Sr. around might have been awkward to say the least.

Meanwhile, Karno began work at Roach's studio. It was the first time he'd danced to someone else's tune for forty-two years – his last employer had been Bob Aubrey in 1887. The result was horribly predictable. Karno found himself

465

frustrated and dismayed by the way the studio operated. He was used to working with at most one or two writers, but in America there were whole teams of people: scenario writers, title writers, directors and producers. He had always been open to ideas from his boys, so we know he could work collaboratively, but he was used to being listened to – this was very different.

Most people would have made an effort to make friends and become accepted by the group – Karno was not most people. He took no time in telling them that the material they were using had gone out of fashion thirty years before. He deplored the reliance on custard pies and people falling into muddy pools, but his observations were not well received. Karno had failed to appreciate the truth that Mack Sennett lived by: 'We Americans like our humor laid on thick. There is considerable of the child left in every normal American … we want our jokes to be jokes of action and motion.'[23]

Paradoxically, Hal Roach had worked hard to distinguish his comedy from that broad, Sennett-style slapstick, giving Laurel and Hardy the opportunity to slow their pace and develop a unique chemistry between their characters. While Karno was right that purely physical slapstick was old hat, he failed to realise that in the hands of geniuses like Chaplin and Laurel, new life was being breathed into ancient gags. Audiences either didn't know or didn't care that much of the material was reformulated music-hall slapstick – and besides, the argument had been overtaken by a much bigger change in style. A year earlier Roach had said: 'The art of pantomime is as old as amusement itself and there isn't the slightest chance that dialogue ever will entirely displace pantomime on the screen.'[24] Well we all know how that worked out – by the end of 1929, silent film was all but dead and the industry was getting used to the new reality – talkies.

Twenty years earlier Karno's comics had made the transition from silent mime to verbal comedy on stage, then silent film gave them an easy way to pursue their true calling as pure pantomimists. In contrast, the medium of film had been a challenge for legitimate stage actors, who had to transition from the theatre and learn to mime. Now things were reversed: silent film actors, many of whom had never set foot on a stage, had to learn to talk on screen – it was the end of many a career. Laurel and Hardy were lucky: they made a successful transition to 'talkies' because their voices suited their characters – they were just as funny with sound as without.[25]

As usual Karno's timing was terrible – the man who could have helped take Roach's slapstick to a more subtle level arrived just as everyone wanted dialogue.

33. CRASHING OUT

What's more, Roach's team were grappling with a completely new way of working. Sound required scripts and tight production planning – the days of freestyle gag-making on the hoof were over. Karno might have been able to help with this: he was after all a disciplined planner who had moved his stage shows from physical to verbal comedy. But a new, disruptive influence was the last thing they needed – he was an annoying distraction at a time of great structural change.

Having his comedy ideas ignored wasn't Karno's only frustration. He tried to get Roach interested in some new names, recommending he bring over Jimmy James (then just breaking into the big time at the London Palladium) from England, but such suggestions fell on deaf ears. The whole atmosphere at the studio infuriated him. He couldn't understand the 'yes men' whose only role, it seemed, was to agree with the director. Time was wasted on ideas that clearly wouldn't work because people were scared to speak up. His unwillingness to acquiesce caused friction, and his suggestions at production meetings were met with stony silence.

In the first two weeks of November Roach made *Night Owls*, the first film to be shot while Karno was on set. Laurel and Hardy play vagrants encountered by policeman Edgar Kennedy, who persuades them to become burglars and break into the chief of police's house in order to improve Kennedy's arrest

33.5 On set of Night Owls: *If in doubt, fall on your arse.*

33.6 Karno demonstrating an idea on the set of Night Owls – *much to James Parrot's disgust.*

record. Karno suggested some comedy business that he knew would work, but as usual he was ignored. His memoirs include a photograph (fig 33.6) taken as he was demonstrating the idea, and he describes the look on director James Parrot's face as being so clearly murderous it could have been used as evidence in a court of law – this is not a happy team.

Their next film, shot in December, was *Blotto,* in which Stan and Babe visit a nightclub after first swiping Stan's wife's bottle of illicit booze. She has replaced the contents with cold tea, but oblivious to this switch, the boys spike their sodas and soon believe themselves drunk.

33.7 The finished scene from Night Owls.

33. CRASHING OUT

The result is a wonderful uncontrollable giggling fit which ranks as one of the most joyous Laurel and Hardy film sequences.

In the third week of January work began on *Brats*, in which our heroes are left babysitting the kids (also played by Stan and Babe), with hilarious consequences. Their miniaturisation was achieved by building oversized sets and props. By coincidence Karno had bumped into a scenic artist he knew called Ernest Glover, who showed him a detailed set model he was working on for another studio. Karno showed the model to Roach's technicians and asked whether they were taking the same approach for *Brats*. Much to his surprise, they said Roach sets were assembled 'ad-lib'. Karno, the meticulous planner and experienced provider of sets and props, thought this a risky approach and was proved right. The set took two weeks to build, and the early rushes demonstrated that its scale was completely wrong. It had to be remade from scratch and the scenes re-shot, costing Roach thousands of dollars and two weeks of lost time. Karno was quick to say "I told you so."

While the Guv'nor was making himself generally unwelcome, Stan Laurel was not averse to his contribution – Stan had, after all, been advocating Karno material on the set for the previous two years. So it seems strange that he was unable or unwilling to do more to help Karno become accepted. Perhaps this was because Roach was happy for Karno to stoke conflict. He apparently told Stan: "Don't worry about old Fred – I know he gets the boys' backs up, but … a few prods in the ass don't do any man harm! And we don't have to pay any attention to what he says anyway!"[26]

Some of Karno's new colleagues agreed that his ideas were strong, but there always seemed to be some reason they wouldn't work – insufficient time or an unobtainable prop. Karno said the final straw came the day he proposed a sure-fire winner that no one could find an argument against. It involved a small lapdog that was being minded by a smartly dressed man. Karno suggested the man's hat was knocked to the floor, and he inadvertently picked up the dog to brush it down.[27] Much to Karno's surprise the director agreed to use the gag, and he was delighted to be presented with a choice of dogs for the scene, picking out the perfect little black pooch. The following day he arrived on set full of enthusiasm, determined to show them how good he was. He set up the gag, directed the actors in the business of dropping the hat, and explained the pay-off. At the last moment he was told the dog had been run over and killed on the way to the studio. "This is a plot!" screamed Karno and stormed off the set. Although a replacement dog was apparently found and the gag used,[28] he'd had enough – he threw in the towel.

So much for Karno's short-lived career as a Hollywood film director – or at least for his account of it. But his personal archive reveals that there was much more to the story. The first unanswered question is why did Roach give Karno a job at all? If he thought the old stager could bring his unique skills to the lot, why wasn't he asked to write or direct anything for Laurel and Hardy, or anyone else? Karno offered Roach all his sketches, but they were rejected out of hand. *The Bailiff* would have made a fantastic Laurel and Hardy film – although historian Frank Scheide notes that Laurel had already used it as the basis for *Bacon Grabbers*[29] – and although most of the other skits were written around one lead comic rather than a double act, they would have worked for Charley Chase or Harry Langdon. Why would Roach ignore this ready-made goldmine of material?

Roach's engagement with Karno was clearly half hearted. Perhaps he'd been persuaded to give the Guv'nor a job by Laurel, acting out of sympathy for his former boss – nothing more than a charity case. But if so, it wasn't the only reason he chose to bide his time before embracing Karno's back catalogue, as we shall see.

Whatever Roach's motivation for hiring him, the idea that Karno subsequently quit seems unlikely. He had nothing to go home to: before leaving England he'd done his best to ensure Leslie could keep *Mumming Birds* running, but their correspondence paints a bleak picture of events back home. In December Karno had written suggesting that if the show was losing money Leslie should close it down, promising he would find work for his son in LA as soon as he could. Now the whole family's future was riding on things working out in Hollywood. What's more, Karno loved the place: in Britain he was a has-been – America called him the king of comedy. He had a nice apartment, plenty of friends, his wife to look after him, his grandsons down the road and a five-year contract with a big fat salary – there is no way on earth that he would have quit. In which case Roach must have fired him, but how? He had a rock-solid contract – didn't he?

Once again all was not what it seemed. Karno's letters reveal he was actually serving a six-month probationary period, during which he was purely meant to be observing. This tallies with the fact he only had a six-month visa, and he was worried it might not be extended. He subsequently wrote that his probation had been reduced to ten weeks, which must have been verbally agreed since his contract simply states that Roach was able to terminate his employment at any time by giving thirty days' notice[30] – Karno's five-year deal wasn't worth the paper it was written on.

33. CRASHING OUT

Now it becomes clear why he was ignored by Roach's team – he was only supposed to be an observer. It also explains why Roach seemed uninterested in Karno's sketches: he wouldn't want to commit to a long-term contractual relationship before the man had proved his worth.

Let's see if we can solve another puzzle. Once his contract began (on 21 October) Karno started getting paid, so why do his letters reveal he was desperately short of cash? He chased Leslie for his share of the income from the *Mumming Birds* tour, even though there was precious little to give, and his cables and letters became increasingly desperate. In one he wrote: 'I have had practically nothing since I left you … although I have almost got used to it.'[31] So how did he keep afloat in the weeks between arriving and starting his contract?[32] His correspondence reveals all. He had met his initial living expenses on credit, so even when he began to be paid, his wages were already spent. His car was purchased on the 'hire system' and his first few weeks' income had gone on repaying the cost of his passage. He wrote to Leslie: 'I had to borrow the money from Mrs K's father and … have been sending him instalments and am pleased to say I have paid him back in full.'[33]

Karno might have struggled to manage even this, since despite the press reports, he was not being paid $50,000 a year. His contract with Roach was incremental. The first three months were at just $250 per week; the next nine months at $500; then six months at $600 and so on. The third year would have earned him $1000 per week, year four $1250, and year five $1500. Over the life of the five-year contract, this averages around $50,000 per year, but in those first few months he was being paid just a fifth of that. There is more bad news: his contract allowed Roach to suspend work for up to twelve weeks with no pay, and just a few weeks after he started, the lot closed for a month. Karno wrote to Leslie: 'Have just heard that Hal Roach studio closes for a month vacation commencing Jan 1st so don't forget me and send me some money as soon as you can, love Dad.'[34]

So Karno was scraping along with very little money – and he wasn't the only one at Roach worried about the future. While having a haircut, Karno got some gossip from his barber: "They're mixing it for you. They're all afraid of losing their jobs. We hear everything here, and I know what I'm talking about."[35] Karno may have been a pain in the backside of Roach's creative team, but he wasn't a direct threat – the truth was they knew cuts were coming and wanted to make sure the old man was top of the hit list. Indeed there was a much bigger story behind Karno's demise: on 29 October, just a week after his formal contract with Roach began, the America dream fell spectacularly to earth.

'Wall Street Lays an Egg' ran the *Variety* headline, as America's economic bubble burst. The Wall Street Crash was the most devastating stock market collapse in U.S. history, and lit the touchpaper on the Great Depression. The market lost thirty billion dollars in two days. Personal fortunes disappeared overnight, entire companies and banks failed, and the Roaring Twenties came to a sudden and distressing end.

Reflecting that winter's malaise, Laurel and Hardy began work on their next short *Below Zero*, in which they play two vagrant musicians busking in the freezing cold. It is a great film with a heavy dose of pathos, which Simon Louvish describes as 'perhaps the most melancholy and dark of all the boys' duo films.'[36] It is tempting to suggest that Karno's presence encouraged Stan to look for more pathos and a deeper emotional connection between the two characters than in previous films, but the truth is that directors needed only to look out of the studio window for inspiration. Vagrants and hobos were swiftly replacing cop chases and custard pies.

The film industry was not immune to the crisis:[37] some reports suggest that box-office receipts plummeted by more than thirty percent, and one in five cinemas had closed by 1932. The studio bosses had to make swift decisions against a backdrop of disastrous economic predictions. Those who relied on New York bankers suffered most, and a flurry of company failures followed. Fox Film Corporation went into receivership in 1929, and William G Fox ended up in jail for trying to bribe the judge at his bankruptcy hearing. Paramount got into difficulties and Lasky was ousted in 1932 – the company went bankrupt in 1935. Charlie Chaplin was out of the country on a world tour when things really began to bite, so it was left to Alf Reeves to mothball his studio and lay off most of the staff. He wrote to Chaplin in April 1931: 'General conditions are bad here. The picture business is going down generally.'[38]

Over the next few years there was something of a backlash against Hollywood in general, and Hal Roach noted at the time: 'Things in America ... are not so good ... There is so much unemployment, and the down-and-outs are sick and tired of hearing about the film stars' inflated salaries ... resentment is setting in. People are refusing to patronise American films ... six thousand cinemas are closed in America.'[39]

Despite all this, most accounts suggest that Roach rode out the financial crash, protected by a distribution deal with the era's most resilient operator MGM, but Richard Lewis Ward's history of Roach's studio tells a different story. His deal with MGM, which ran from 1927 until 1938, did provide some protection – demonstrated by the fact that he was the only independent producer of shorts to survive the 1930s. But the Depression, the rise of double features, and the cost of sound all created commercial pressures. Roach reported profits of nearly $90,000 in 1930, but the following six months showed a loss of over $40,000 and the banks forced him to appoint Henry Ginsberg, a tough new general manager who set about making drastic savings. Back in late 1929 Roach must have been extremely nervous about the economic climate, and would have been looking to make any easy cuts he could – Karno didn't stand a chance.

In the first week of January 1930 he sent an urgent cable to Leslie: 'Studio closing down next month may have to return, wire immediately all cash in hand … shall need every penny. Love Dad.'[40] The following day he penned a lengthy letter confirming that Roach was laying people off:

> The firm that I am with is a bit rocky … and if nothing turns up, I shall have to come home … There is a big slump set in here with all the picture firms. Fox's has gone broke and many others have been hit very badly through a stock market scare. The firm that I am with have not the money to carry on and they have been reducing their staff for some weeks past. I shall try of course and get a job with some of the other firms, but the prospects look very bad.[41]

By the end of January Karno knew his fate:

> I am finishing with this firm on Feb 3rd … they have no money to carry on … my arrangement with them was to come in for ten weeks to get to know the tricks of the trade and then to start on my big contract to produce my shows, and they told me that they are not in a position to take up the option on my contract and also they had no money. Mr Roach I understand has been hit very hard on the stock market and has lost about a million dollars … they only produce comedies for the Metro Goldwyn and receive a lump sum for each one … They have also had a lot of flops with a comedian called Harry Langdon … The Gang pictures [Our Gang] are also getting stale and not getting run. Their only chance now to keep going is the Stan Laurel and Hardy pictures. They have been going very well but the people are beginning to get

sick of them as they repeat themselves in every picture. I have not had a chance to show them what I can do ... the other producers ... don't like me to interfere or to make any suggestions. They are afraid of losing their jobs and they stick to the old slapstick comedy of throwing pies at each other ... I wanted to put on Hot and Cold, the Bailiff, the New Slavey, etc. but could not get them interested.[42]

It becomes abundantly clear that he didn't quit. Like so many others, he was just collateral damage in a worldwide financial disaster. As the strains of Auld Lang Syne echoed around the sound stages, Roach cancelled Karno's contract.[43] His total earnings there amounted to just $1500.

Hal Roach had great respect for Karno – his influence and impact on the silent film comics was undeniable. But many years later he told Richard Bann that Karno had failed to impress in person, that he was a businessman not a comic. Perhaps Roach was unwilling to front up about his financial problems, even many years later, and his description of Karno is ironic given that it more accurately describes himself: a businessman not a performer, whose creative contribution usually involved dreaming up a basic idea and then instructing his director and gag men to "work it out."[44] Roach's recollections are evidently unreliable: in one account he even took credit for paying Karno's fare to America: 'I hired him after working with Chaplin and Laurel and always hearing them talk about Karno, Karno, Karno. I thought, hell, this guy must know a lot of gags. His business had gone to pot ... so I told him how much I'd pay him ... and paid his way over.'[45]

It seems to me that even without the Wall Street Crash, Karno would have failed. He had arrived in Hollywood ten years too late. He was a sixty-three-year-old Victorian in a young, dynamic, fast-moving industry. A silent-comedy expert who turned up just as the movies began to talk. The greatest comics in the business had spoken of the Guv'nor in such hallowed terms that his name had become legend around the studios, but he couldn't possibly live up to the hype – the real Fred Karno was bound to be a disappointment.

Karno once again faced destitution – and the chance of finding another opportunity was slim. Every studio was making lay-offs, and word had probably got around that he was difficult to work with. Then salvation appeared to come from the most unlikely quarter: in March 1930 Karno reportedly signed a contract to work for his nemesis – Mack Sennett.[46]

34.

We're All Crazy Now

He's so tight he takes his wife's teeth out between meals.
(Laffs, 1930)

SENNETT'S STUDIO needed new blood: perhaps he saw genuine potential in Karno, or maybe he just thought he owed the old man a chance. Oh, to have been a fly on the wall in their meeting, if it even happened – it may simply have been an inaccurate press story, since neither mentioned it in his memoirs and no deal materialised. It wouldn't have saved Karno anyway. Sennett was a spent force, lagging behind Roach, overshadowed by Chaplin and dwarfed by the major studios. If Roach's ideas were old hat, Sennett's were positively prehistoric, and his fortunes were tied to struggling Paramount – he was declared bankrupt in 1933.

Karno swallowed his pride and contacted William Morris in New York to see if his original offer might still be open. He wrote to Leslie:

> Morris ... replied saying he is coming down here with Mr Lasky and that he will probably fix me something when he gets here. So I am waiting until he arrives. It is no use seeing Charlie Chaplin because he has been on his picture nearly two years and they have no idea when it will be finished, besides I felt a draught when I went over to his studios. I don't mean from Charlie but from Alf Reeves who started raking up some old sores about me not paying him for three weeks when the show was not working when in England. They are a lot of ... creepers over here. I never saw such a lot of two-faced people in my life.[1]

During Karno's last few weeks in LA, Laurel and Hardy made *Hog Wild*, in which they attempt to erect a radio aerial on a roof. Stan's old boss was getting an equally bad reception – it was time to go. Although Karno finished with Roach in early February, he didn't leave Hollywood until the end of April; what happened in the interim is unknown.[2] Perhaps he just sat tight waiting to be rescued by Morris and Lasky: if so, he waited in vain – the New York cavalry never came.

In his memoirs Karno claimed he had good reason to return to England: Marie's father was seriously ill and 'things at home were being mismanaged.'[3] But these excuses are belied by the fact that he didn't head straight back, electing instead to take a leisurely road trip across America. He and Marie left at dawn on 27 April 1930, and as he swung his sedan out of Taft Avenue onto Hollywood Boulevard, he left his best (but not his last) chance of movie success behind.

They were embarking on a 4000-mile journey along Route 66, connecting California to Chicago via eight states. On the first day they drove three hundred miles across the Mojave Desert (a death trap for a stranded motorist), and barely saw a soul before reaching Needles. As they journeyed on, they passed through shanty towns built around goldmines that were not yet completely worked out. At Oatman, Arizona, Karno was surprised to find that many of the prospectors were young English fortune-seekers. They journeyed on to the Grand Canyon, then paid a return visit to Marie's relatives in Tulsa. En route they watched a tornado rip through a landscape which would soon become the Dustbowl of Steinbeck's *Grapes of Wrath*. Eventually they crossed the Mississippi in St Louis and headed north to Chicago, a city in the grip of gangland violence led by public enemy number one, Al Capone. It was just fifteen months after the St Valentine's Day Massacre, and 'Scarface' was at the height of his powers. Capone was the first celebrity criminal and Karno hoped to catch a glimpse of him, but was disappointed. They travelled on to Niagara Falls, which Karno felt was already too commercialised, and then made a short detour into Canada, where his name was recognised at customs and he was greeted warmly. They re-crossed the border on 14 May, drove over the Catskill Mountains and on to New York. This odyssey must have been quite a challenge: Karno recalled driving on roads that were little more than ploughed fields, along rocky paths, over precipices, and through 'oceans of mud'[4] and floods that lapped the running boards of his Model A. Amazingly they had no car trouble and only one puncture. In his memoirs Karno was gushing about the performance of his little car and the network of service stations on route – Ford should have used him in their advertising.

They had travelled from the glamour of Chaplin's Hollywood via the gangsters of Capone's Chicago to arrive in New York a few months after the Wall Street Crash, just as the Chrysler Building opened and the Empire State Building was being constructed. It was a road trip through a remarkable period in American cultural and social history.

34.1 Karno and Marie, around the time of their journey across America, looking every bit the Chicago gangster (courtesy Heritage Collection, Bournemouth Library).

In New York Karno secured a meeting with an unnamed production company (perhaps this sparked the Sennett news story), and was delighted when they seemed enthusiastic about producing films of his sketches. He stayed to broker a deal, while Marie continued on to England alone.[5] It soon became clear however that the studio bosses expected Karno to meet the entire cost of a production before they'd back him – estimated at $200,000. Under the headline 'Fred Karno Insulted', *Variety* noted that they had told him: "It may be all right but we don't know you … produce a short yourself over here … so we can get a line on what you can do." Karno headed for the next boat. *Variety* added: 'If the "Tuscania" doesn't blow up before it reaches Southampton, Karno will.'[6]

With his pride wounded, a disappointed and disillusioned Karno arrived back in England on 24 June 1930. On the same day, Laurel and Hardy began filming *Pardon Us*, their first feature-length talkie – ironically, it was released in Britain under the title *Jailbirds*.

On his return, Karno gave a long interview to *The Era*:

> Most travellers come back from Hollywood impressed and excited … Imagine my surprise, therefore, when I asked Mr Fred Karno … for his impressions of the place, and he replied … "I was very disappointed in it … With the exception of Charlie Chaplin, no one knows anything at all about comedy … none of the film producers has any knowledge

of stagecraft at all … Their 'gags' are … pudding throwing, siphon-squirting and tearing the other fellow's clothes off his back. It is all so elementary and years out of date … I found so many of the people there to be so artificial. The whole atmosphere of the place is false … you are expected to say 'yes'… Make any real suggestion, point out any glaring error … and you will have the whole place round your ears" … "Hasn't the influence of Chaplin done anything for the other producers of comedies?" I asked Mr Karno. "Chaplin works on his own. He is reserved and doesn't mix much … he has no rivals at all … He is, of course, a genius … Charlie … is very averse to the 'talkies' … Personally, I think he has nothing to fear. When he was with me, he was at his best in speaking parts." "What did you find to admire in Hollywood?" I asked. "Camera technique there is miles in advance of ours. Also, they are not afraid of spending money … Here people seem afraid to launch out and take the initiative … On the way home I motored from Hollywood to New York … at every town … I made it my business to go around to the theatre and … I was told everywhere that the … principal demand was for comedy … My advice to them is to import more English comedians and comic writers, and to the film producers here I say: Make better use of the enormous amount of material at your very doors … and we could conquer the whole world, for English humour is the kindliest and the most universal in its scope."[7]

Though he had failed in his ambition to take Hollywood by storm, Karno had learnt a lot from the experience. He came home refreshed, relaxed and determined to reclaim his rightful place in the British theatre industry. Sadly, there wasn't much of it left.

In Karno's ten-month absence, Leslie had kept *Mumming Birds* going while waiting for the cable telling him to jump on a ship to America. With the old man back, his dreams were in tatters. Leslie's archive provides a fascinating insight into his battle to keep the business going on a shoestring. Louisa would later tell her granddaughter how she and Leslie played to practically empty houses, while fending off angry creditors, disgruntled artistes and moribund theatre managers.

By now no Karno review or listing failed to mention Chaplin, and *Mumming Birds* (which had run almost continuously for twenty-six years) was forever billed as 'the show that made Charlie Chaplin famous.' Even Leslie couldn't resist

34. WE'RE ALL CRAZY NOW

giving a Chaplin story to the press in May 1930: "In those days … Charlie was just one of the boys … nobody thought he was anything extraordinary. His chief title to fame lay in his eccentricities which sometimes proved embarrassing … he would get out of a train with his shoes tied with white ribbons or walk through Woolworths throwing yards of streamers about."[8] The fact that Leslie was only nine years old when Chaplin last set sail for America didn't get in the way of a good story – he needed all the help he could muster to promote a failing show.

On the way down, Leslie met some future stars coming up. His variety company included a teenaged Tessie O'Shea, but such talent was the exception among a group of performers past their prime. Many were unreliable – or inebriated – so Leslie had to play multiple parts. His skinny frame was perfect for the comedy wrestler, and at the end of the sketch, someone would come on and play his ribs like a xylophone. Later he took on the drunk in the box, to consistently positive reviews. Good reviews didn't pay the bills though, and working on a fifty-fifty box office split with the venue, Leslie's receipts typically amounted to around £115 – the artistes' salaries alone cost him £140. Such losses were unsustainable, and yet the troupe soldiered on. Leslie's file is full of correspondence from agents chasing their commission or bemoaning the receipts, such as this from Harry Leat: 'I am very sorry that business is so terrible this week at Dudley; we look like losing a packet.'[9] There were exceptions: Henry Buckland, the manager of the Crystal Palace, saw *Mumming Birds* in Paris in early 1929 and booked the show for Christmas as part of his *Grand Continental Circus* – Leslie incorporated *Love in a Tub* for old time's sake.

As if keeping the company going wasn't hard enough, Karno had left Leslie with a headache. In April 1929 his father had signed a contract[10] with a writer, Arrar Jackson, to pen his life story. By Christmas it was largely written, and Jackson entered into an agreement with *The People* to publish some extracts. Having done so, the magazine received a writ from a lawyer in Dundee stating that Karno had already given the rights to his story to another party. Jackson had to withdraw the material and repay his fee. He also had to renege on a publishing deal for the book in America. Leslie was left to placate Jackson, who was rightly aggrieved – a year's work went on the fire. No alternative Karno biography appeared, and his subsequent letters suggest that he instructed the injunction because Jackson failed to let him approve the manuscript before publication.

On his return, Karno's view of how badly Leslie had been handling things must have been tempered by the realisation that the industry was on its knees. His solution was to throw money at the problem. He set about signing up some bigger names to the variety company, including xylophone virtuoso Teddy Brown, a big star in every sense of the word. Karno paid Brown sixty-five pounds per week, but he was throwing good money after bad – the 'talkies' had accelerated the popularity of cinema and music hall had practically disappeared. Comics found the only regular work available was performing in cinemas, filling the gaps in the film where the projectionist had to change the reel or allow the projector to cool down – these remaining stalwarts became known as 'lantern coolers'.

According to his memoirs Karno quickly decided that it would be suicide to embark on any further stage productions, claiming he did not launch another show until 1932 – but his memory let him down. In reality he wasted no time before embarking on a project that he believed would reverse music hall's fortunes – and amazingly, he was right.[11] His brainwave revolutionised stage comedy and set the tone for the remaining twenty years of British variety.

Karno had already played with the concept of breaking the fourth wall and involving the audience in the show: first with a fake crowd in *Mumming Birds*, then by putting actors among the punters in *The Hydro,* and finally by inviting the audience on stage in *Karno's Follies* – each had been an innovation. Now he and co-writer Arty Le Clerq made theatregoers an integral part of the show. His comics were given *carte blanche* to run riot in the auditorium, and to mercilessly interrupt and play tricks on the other artistes as they tried to perform. *Karno's Krazy Komics* opened at the Birmingham Empire on 4 August 1930, just two months after he returned from America; the following week it changed its title to *Laffs*. The critics were divided. One wrote: 'Members of the company mingle with the audience and have amusing arguments with artistes on the stage. The fun is boisterous and well sustained.'[12] Another said: 'Karno's Krazy Komics, with much flourish of trumpets, offer comedy cameos, amusing enough, but not all in good taste.'[13] Love it or hate it, Karno had launched a completely new comedy style on the unsuspecting British public. It was anarchic, it was surreal, it was 'Krazy', and as *The Stage* noted, audiences lapped it up:

> Karno's Krazy Komics, cause a great deal of laughter by broadly burlesque methods which are not always confined to the correct side of the footlights. Perhaps the real spirit of this irresponsible offering is apparent in the fact that its cast of performers is printed upside down in

34. WE'RE ALL CRAZY NOW

the programme. It has all been planned in a spirit of happy topsy-turvey-dom, and audiences appear to enter whole-heartedly into the fun.[14]

This small-scale revue was incredibly fast-paced, combining physical, verbal and visual gags in a constant stream of comedy. The apparent anarchy was sprinkled with running gags: a plant in the audience would shout "Oi! Which of you is Karno?" throughout the show until, at the end, one of the comics would announce that he was Karno and the plant would shoot him on the spot. The show set off on tour, played to full houses everywhere and gradually refilled Karno's bank account.

Karno hadn't given up on film, though. A.C. Astor wrote a column for *The Stage* called *Just Jottings*, and that November he recounted a chat with Billy Bennett and Karno in the bar of Liverpool's Adelphi Hotel. Bennett was appearing on the same bill as *Laffs* at the Hippodrome, and together they contemplated the death of variety. *Just Jottings* subsequently announced: '[Karno] has just signed a five-year contract with the Gainsborough Film Company to supply and produce the ever-essential comedy.'[15] As *Laffs* came to the end of its initial run, he was finally ready to make his mark in movies.

Karno passionately believed that the British film industry had an opportunity to do things better, or at least funnier, than the Americans, if only they would approach filmmaking with the same enthusiasm and properly invest in the product. In early January 1931 Gainsborough placed a full-page advertisement in *The Era* listing their forthcoming film projects, including 'a long list of Karno subjects with Bobby Howes as star.'[16] Howes had supposedly appeared in *Red Hot* (although I've yet to find him in any listing), and years later he shared his memories of working with Karno: 'He would simply take a blank book, hand it to me and say: "Go on and be funny."'[17]

Gainsborough's advertisement proved to be premature: Karno had to wait another eighteen months before filming got underway. In the meantime, his meeting with A.C. Astor sparked another project, as *Just Jottings* revealed:

> When Billy Bennett and I sat up with Fred Karno ... a month or so back ... I suggested what excellent material a "Life of Karno" would provide. I met Edwin Adeler the other day, who told me that he was now engaged on the task of writing it. Mr Adeler was enthusiastic, "He has given me such a wealth of copy that my only difficulty is to know what to cut

out." [I know the feeling] ... "We could make two or three volumes ... it would practically embrace the entire history of the modern music hall."[18]

Within a few months of his return from the States, Karno had staged *Laffs*, Adeler was writing his memoirs and he finally had a decent film contract. It must have been frustrating to then spend months clicking his heels waiting for Gainsborough to get things moving. His son Leslie, meanwhile, had returned to ploughing his own furrow, and in January 1931 Karno allowed him to include *Mumming Birds* in a touring variety show called *Alice in Funderland*.[19] Leslie's company benefitted from a fresh wave of interest in the sketch generated by Charlie Chaplin's return to England as part of a world tour promoting *City Lights*, and he was once again in demand for interviews:

> Leslie still throws custard pies ... Charlie's old associations have put the present-day "Mumming Birds" in an awkward position. As soon as the London theatrical head learned that the famous comedian was coming home, they ... offered the proprietors a nice sum to arrange for it to appear in London in the hope that Charlie would come along and provide a great draw ... but "Mumming Birds" is booked for Bradford next week ... they are hoping that Charlie will be able to accept an invitation to call on them.[20]

Chaplin fever once again gripped the press, and Karno wrote an article under the headline 'Charlie Chaplin's Karno Days', which has been much quoted elsewhere in this book. It ended as follows: 'I saw Charlie for the first time for many years in Hollywood last year ... to me he was just the same simple, dreaming comic-pathetic Charlie Chaplin of the old Fred Karno days ... Visionary and dreamer as he was then, so he is today.'[21]

On 27 February, Karno was in the invited audience for the London premiere of *City Lights* (no doubt quite a long way back). Chaplin sat next to George Bernard Shaw, made a short speech of thanks, and was greeted with the sort of hysterical response from the crowd not seen again until the heyday of the Beatles. Thousands crowded the streets in the pouring rain, hoping for a glimpse of their hero. The press was full of reports of Chaplin being asked to see or appear in *Mumming Birds* for old time's sake, but his itinerary was on a slightly different intellectual plane. His engagements included lunch with the Prime Minister

34. WE'RE ALL CRAZY NOW

Ramsay MacDonald at Chequers, and on the return leg of his world tour that autumn he met both Winston Churchill and Mahatma Gandhi. Chaplin hadn't completely forgotten his fellow artistes though: he found time to be inducted into the Grand Order of Water Rats by its King Rat, Will Hay.

Chaplin wasn't the only former employee Karno must have marvelled at. Stan Laurel was now reported as being the best paid-comic in talkies, and perhaps their success, and his experience with *Laffs*, prompted Karno to tell *The Stage*: 'I think sketches are coming back.'[22] Karno was also reported to be in discussions with Fred Kitchen and Archie Glen about a revival of *The Bailiff* and *The Football Match*. Sure enough, Archie Parnell, Alfred Zeitlin and Paul Murray produced *The Football Match* at the Wolverhampton Hippodrome in September,[23] with Archie Glen as Stiffy leading a company of fifty, which included Charlie Baldwin. The show appears to have run for just a week, the reason for its failure now lost in the mists of time.

Although 1931 had proved to be a year of false starts and frustrations, there was an interesting diversion in December when Karno was approached by Walter Mycroft of BIP to act as slapstick adviser on a film called *Bad Companions*, scripted by Con West and directed by John Orton. The story was that of a jam-maker battling to win back the love of his girl from the factory foreman. Karno didn't hesitate: his experience in Hollywood may have been bitter, but it convinced him that filmmaking was child's play. He wrote to Leslie: 'I have had all the experience of picture business and know all the tricks of the trade now.'[24] Karno suggested all sorts of gags and bits of business and was credited as co-writer. Con West described the experience as just the sort of open, collaborative environment that Karno had found so lacking in Hollywood.[25]

After a turbulent few years, the Guv'nor was gradually rebuilding his reputation and his own confidence. The following spring he managed to get himself a piece of the biggest show in town.

The London Palladium had been converted to a cinema after the war, but in 1928 General Theatres Corporation tasked George Black with turning it back into a variety theatre. Black and his deputy Val Parnell became two of the most powerful men in the industry, and over the next twenty years practically saved variety from extinction. They gave Max Miller and Jimmy James their big breaks, but their most significant influence on comedy was bringing together a ragtag group of performers who crystallized into a powerhouse of anarchic comedy, known as 'The Crazy Gang'. As Palladium historian Ian Bevan put it:

'In the history of the music-hall there has never been another single attraction which has brought people to one theatre, in such large numbers, over such a long period.'[26]

There are varied accounts of how the Gang came about, so let's start with Bevan's version:

> The idea … was almost an accident … Parnell … was trying to keep a firm hold on all the good comedians, and he had a barring clause in the contracts … Towards the end of 1931, a last-minute change in pantomime plans left Naughton and Gold free to accept a West End engagement outside the barring period … The need to keep them away from Stoll [the rival circuit] was urgent, although it meant booking them for a week when Nervo and Knox and Caryll and Mundy had already been engaged. Parnell recalled a touring revue called 'Young Bloods of Variety', in which Nervo and Knox had given a new twist to their own act by intruding on other turns, and he thought he might avoid the monotony of three double acts … by mingling all three.[27]

Nervo and Knox were comedy gymnasts with a delightful turn in slow-motion wrestling, and in the tradition of Karno alumni, Jimmy Nervo would become the creative force behind the Gang. Naughton and Gold were 'The Napoleons of Fun', a pair of diminutive comics whose knockabout antics had made them a favourite on the halls for twenty years, while Caryll and Mundy were a real-life married couple whose act consisted of them bickering at each other for laughs. These three double acts were supplemented by the most anarchic of them all – the red-nosed comedy juggler 'Monsewer' Eddie Gray, who claimed to be descended from a long line of bachelors.

The Gang nearly didn't happen though: Naughton and Gold and Nervo and Knox had previously had a professional fall-out, so it took some diplomacy from Parnell to get them to work together. The first programme opened on 30 November 1931, and was so chaotic it was dubbed 'Crazy Week'. *The Daily Herald* wrote: 'It has been the maddest, the most riotous, the noisiest week ever known in a London music hall. The closing scenes were like the last night of a record-breaking pantomime in the old days. If there were a few more artistes like Naughton and Gold, Nervo and Knox, Billy Caryll and Hilda Mundy, and Eddie Gray, and they could join up as these did all last week, Variety would be saved.'[28] *The Era* was equally gushing: 'Last week's Palladium show ... will be talked about for years. I went in three nights and laughed as I have never laughed before. The house was packed for every performance and I have never known so many "pros" pay for their seats!'[29]

Young Bloods of Variety had first appeared in March 1928, a traditional variety show which included Nervo and Knox's wrestling routine,[30] but it gradually developed into a more chaotic format. In May 1928 *The Stage* reported: 'A singularly entertaining bill ... the principals do not confine their appearances to their own particular turns but assist each other to the great benefit of the programme.'[31] A month later reviews were even closer to what the Crazy Gang became: 'Nervo and Knox burlesque wrestling ... and a very funny conjuring episode in which Arthur Pond does capital work as the magician who is harassed by the irrepressible twins from the audience.'[32] Anybody else reminded of *Mumming Birds*? *Young Bloods of Variety* ran until spring 1930, closing a few months before Karno staged his anarchic *Laffs*.

34.2 The Napoleons of Fun – Naughton and Gold, 1911 (author's collection).

So *Young Bloods* may have been an inspiration for Parnell, but Crazy Week was not a show as such – it was a concept. Black began to stage a Crazy Week whenever he felt he had a bill of artistes able and willing to blend their acts together and make it work – any number of resident lunatics were given *carte blanche* to create havoc. A few weeks after the first attempt *The Stage* noted:

> Another Crazy Week is promised at the Palladium on Monday. It should prove to be highly successful seeing that Nervo and Knox, Robb Wilton ... Eddie Gray ... and Tommy Handley are in the bill. That Mr George Black's idea of occasional Crazy Weeks whenever the make-up of the bill allows is a good one ... was amply proved by the recent experiment, when ... record audiences were drawn to the Palladium.[33]

The Era critic subsequently told how the gang started causing havoc even before the curtain went up:

> They made a mad-dog rush at the stage as soon as the overture began. Half-way through the act of Will Power, the unicyclist, they circled casually past, picked the eggs out of the egg cups his page had placed in line, and went away breakfasting. As soon as Robb Wilton had settled down at his desk in "The Charge Officer", they rushed on, one by one, to lay bets with him on races that had already been run ... Eddie Gray comes before the curtain to proclaim his "acrobatic tripe", he is struck over the top hat ... the tabs part to disclose Nervo and Knox, their company ... grouped in the grand Romano manner before their ringmaster ... sends them all flying. They are in such a hurry to escape, Eddie Gray is left hanging from the trapeze ... down at last ... Gray takes off his coat, flings it into the wings and is immediately buried under an avalanche of coats.[34]

You get the idea. That same review ends with a clue that such comedy was actually as old as the hills: 'Nothing like it has been seen since the palmiest days of the harlequinade.'

So this wasn't a consistent group of the same comics, and nor did it happen just at the Palladium. The first week of January 1932 saw Nervo and Knox creating mayhem at the Victoria Palace, while Caryll and Mundy were doing the same at the Holborn Empire. The following week Nervo and Knox and Eddie Gray were at the Metropolitan, and the week after that Caryll staged a Crazy Week at the Portsmouth Hippodrome. Halls all over the country were jumping on the bandwagon. Artistes on every variety bill in Britain found themselves being interrupted, lampooned, lassoed, covered in paint or subjected to similar slapstick pranks by their counterparts – and to packed houses. By March the trend had spread to Europe, with similar shows being staged in Holland.[35] In April 1932 the Palladium put on two Crazy Weeks back to back, with Naughton and Gold in charge of proceedings for the first and Caryll and Mundy for the second. Flanagan and Allen, who had risen to prominence performing as part of Florrie Ford's stock company, were a stand-alone double act on that bill who bore their share of the chaos so well that Black was keen to repeat their success.

The following month the Palladium played host to the Royal Variety Performance, and it was a given that it would include this new theatrical sensation. Black looked to the acts who originated the idea, with the addition of Flanagan and Allen. *The Era* noted:

> Whatever the final form of the programme ... a marked preference will be shown for comedians who have specialised in "crazy weeks" ... Their greatest effort will probably be as "the finest troupe of acrobats in captivity". With Eddie Gray as the showman who is left on the trapeze until discovered still hanging there several turns later ... one of the funniest achievements of knockabout humour witnessed in our lifetime. The company who appear before their Majesties ... are likely to have Bud Flanagan as their new recruit. As the comedian who has made the most progress during the past year ... in crazy antics he now, of course, ranks among the best.[36]

Flanagan recalled that he and Allen were not welcomed with open arms by the other comics: 'Who could blame them? After all, they had pioneered this new entertainment and naturally didn't want a couple of jumped-up comics in the act.'[37] In the event, the Royal Variety Performance pitched together Naughton and Gold, Nervo and Knox and Flanagan and Allen (Gray, Caryll and Mundy did not appear). A few weeks later Black united the whole team at the Palladium for a 'Crazy Month', commencing 6 June 1932. *The Era* reported: 'The next Crazy season at the Palladium will ... so Mr Black told me, last for four weeks ... "There was a marvellous spirit amongst the artistes in our first venture of this kind ... I have never seen anything like it ... everyone working for the programme as a whole and not for himself."'[38] This was the first time all nine comics came together, and only then did the press christen them the Crazy Gang. Black was hailed as 'Variety's Presiding Genius',[39] packing the Palladium to capacity despite it being a hot and sunny June – 200,000 people saw the show in four weeks.

The Gang created mayhem off stage as well as on. Roy Hudd recalled appearing in a show with Eddie Gray and Charlie Naughton at the end of their careers, when they were in their eighties: their digs were opposite the theatre and every evening the veteran comics would cross the road putting on terribly crippled walks, stopping the traffic as they made painfully slow progress. Halfway across they would jump up in the air and dance away, to much effing and blinding from the waiting drivers. One of Eddie Gray's legendary gags was to approach a pillar box and shout into the slot: "Well how did you get in there?" He would continue the conversation until he'd collected a crowd, then simply walk away.[40]

By giving free rein to these practical jokers, Black had unwittingly created a monster. The whole idea was that professional discipline, courtesy and etiquette went out of the window in a mad comedic free-for-all, and this could easily get out of hand. Black was hamstrung: the shows were so successful that he could do little to control the performers, but that didn't stop him trying. One day he gave them all a dressing down: "You're all bloody lucky to be here. As acts outside the Crazy Gang, you'd be hard pushed to make a living. Take Max Miller – he's got more talent in his little finger then any of you have got in your whole body – remember that!"[41]

Miller might have been a better gag teller, but the Gang had a superhuman ability to perform as a team, with chaotic slapstick and verbal humour flowing effortlessly between them. Making anarchic comedy look natural and unrehearsed when you are working with five other people, improvising with other artistes and involving the audience is about as hard as it gets. The Crazy Gang won the respect and love not just of their audiences, but of their fellow performers too.

The comedy writer Denis Norden had a lasting memory of seeing the Gang when he was aged eleven.[42] On arrival at the theatre he recalled an incompetent usher misdirecting his family on a circuitous route around every corner and back corridor of the theatre before they eventually reached their seats, much to his father's frustration. It was only later they realised it was Bud Flanagan – a joke that would have been witnessed by no one other than Bud himself. The Gang's performance extended to the foyer, the bar and beyond.

What has all this got to do with Karno, I hear you ask? So far there has been no sign of the Guv'nor anywhere in the Crazy Gang's story, although one reporter spotted a similarity in the very first Crazy Week in 1931: 'The outstanding event of the … year … at the London Palladium – "Crazy Week" … when Nervo and Knox, Naughton and Gold and Billy Caryll clowned in the way that Charlie Chaplin used to do in Mumming Birds.'[43] Later writers would also notice connections: John Fisher wrote: 'Young Bloods of Variety … allowed [Nervo and Knox] to get hilariously involved in the other acts on the bill, a seemingly spontaneous style no doubt influenced by Fred Karno's Krazy Komics, the original of all the comedy groups … whose speciality was well ordered chaos.'[44]

34. WE'RE ALL CRAZY NOW

Despite the evident similarity in style, I have yet to find a mention of Karno's involvement in the Crazy Gang story in the contemporary press, any history of the Palladium or any of the Gang's biographies. So it seems extraordinary that Adeler and West described him as 'the father of all Crazy Shows'. They added: 'Krazy Komics was the forerunner of the crazy shows, and crazy weeks that have since become popular all over the country.'[45] So was Karno just an influence, or was he actively involved?

Sorting out the origins of the Gang turns out to be a minefield of misinformation and misdirection.[46] Let's summarise what we know: Nervo and Knox introduce some anarchy into their otherwise mainstream revue *Young Bloods*; soon afterwards Karno stages *Laffs*, with significant audience participation – it is hailed by the critics as an innovation. A year later Parnell and Black create Crazy Week, partly by accident and partly off the back of *Young Bloods*, and the idea sweeps the country. Black includes it in the Royal Variety Performance and decides to run a show for a full month – at which point the regular team members become firmly established and 'The Gang' is born.

It seems likely that the success of *Crazy Month* in June 1932 prompted Black to consider how to turn the anarchy into something more manageable. With such an unpredictable team, maintaining the idea over a longer run would require a degree of scripted control. And of course, Karno had already developed a scripted show with a similar feel, *Laffs*, which fitted the bill exactly. On 12 July Black wrote: 'Dear Mr Karno, the purpose of this letter is to confirm [our] arrangement ... whereby it is agreed that we will use your script licensed as "Laffs" for the Crazy Comedians at the London Palladium, we to pay you

34.3 The Crazy Gang (minus Chesney Allen). Centre, Bud Flanagan, clockwise from bottom left: Jimmy Nervo, Teddy Knox, Eddie Gray, Charlie Naughton and Jimmy Gold (© Illustrated London News Ltd/ Mary Evans Picture Library).

a fee of £10 for each week that the script is used.'[47] Black then continued to call on Karno for advice on gags, props and scenery, in another letter writing: 'Would you look in at the Holborn Empire … as I shall be rehearsing there, and should very much like to have the benefit of your advice relative to the Krazy Komics.'[48]

So while Karno wasn't directly involved in the first Crazy Weeks, when Black needed a more structured Gang show he turned to the old stager. At least that's how it appears, but there are one or two things that don't add up. Why isn't his input recorded anywhere? And why did Black, king of the Palladium with unlimited resources at his disposal, need Karno's script when he could have commissioned his own? My theory is that he didn't involve Karno by choice.

Consider this: Karno's *Laffs* had run out of steam by December 1930; a year later Black stages a show at the Palladium using similar techniques. It is hailed as a sensation, and within weeks it's the biggest thing in theatreland. Is Karno, a man in need of income and with a litigious streak, likely just to sit there and ignore the fact he'd coined the same idea twelve months earlier? No chance: he would have contacted Black and threatened to sue. So what does Black do? He's got the biggest show in the country and it's about to have an injunction slapped on it – I think he bought Karno off and they dressed it up as him purchasing the rights to *Laffs*.[49]

So far so good, but that doesn't explain why Karno received no public credit for the show. You would expect him to be shouting from the rooftops: his name in lights at the Palladium would have catapulted him back to the top. I think Black insisted on his involvement being confidential, and he agreed – but why? We shall consider Karno's acquiescence in the next chapter, but it's easy to imagine why Black was keen to keep Karno's name out of it. Some digging reveals a surprising turn of events which puts Karno squarely in the frame as inspiration for the Gang. Three years earlier, while his attention was focused on making his film with Syd Chaplin and Leslie was touring *Mumming Birds* around the provinces, George Black brazenly ripped him off.

On 4 March 1929, the Palladium bill included Naughton and Gold, Will Hay and Charlie Austin. After their own solo turns, the entire ensemble worked together in a sketch finale they called *A Night in an Old-time Music Hall*. It was *Mumming Birds*: Austin played the drunk, Hay played the old uncle. Reviews were lacklustre and it seems to have appeared for just one week, but the press noted that it was a chaotic free-for-all between the artistes. It was a precursor to the Crazy Shows, and I believe it was this, as much as *Young Bloods of Variety*,

34. WE'RE ALL CRAZY NOW

that sprang to Parnell's mind two years later. Amazingly, given that back then Karno was struggling to find theatres to take his sketches, he seems to have been totally unaware that Black was staging a version of *Mumming Birds* at the London Palladium! What's more, reviews reveal that a similar sketch had previously played at the Holborn Empire, and the instigators of that pirated version were Naughton and Gold. Alongside an ex-Karno comic called Ernie Gerrard, they were still performing it in July – and were back at the Holborn Empire when Karno finally caught up with them. He wrote to Leslie:

> I went to the Holborn and saw Gerrard and Naughton and Gold doing the conjuror exactly as we do it. Gerrard came on with the introduction and Naughton and Gold were in the house box. They ... did everything as we did it. I could not stand it so ... went on the stage and stopped the show ... There was a terrible scene ... Gerrard and Naughton and Gold were paralysed when they saw me walk on, they were speechless and dumbfounded. What a dog Gerrard is.[50]

So now we know that Karno was no fan of Naughton and Gold, and it seems likely that he eventually got wind of what had gone on at the Palladium. All these threads lead back to *Mumming Birds* as the original inspiration for Crazy Week, and support the idea that he may have threatened Black with legal action.

There is another reason Black may have wanted to keep Karno's name off his new show. Crazy Weeks were being marketed as the latest thing, an innovation – the saviour of variety. A Karno association would immediately suggest the comedy of a previous age, old-fashioned – dare we say it – music hall. Black couldn't risk an Emperor's new clothes moment, when his punters suddenly realised they'd seen it all before.

So Karno's involvement was known to very few people – but when you know what to look for, there is plenty to suggest he was hovering in the background. The running gag of "Oi, are you Karno?" from *Laffs* manifested itself in the cry of "Oi!" that followed every Crazy Gang comic set-up, and on the eve of the opening night of the Palladium's 1932 Crazy Month, Bud Flanagan recalled: 'Someone had the idea of driving us ... in a huge cage, from the Holborn Empire to the Palladium ... you can imagine the crowds. It was a good stunt and kept the box office busy.'[51]

I can't image who came up with that!

491

35.

Reel to Real

"My name's Mackintosh and I'm drowning!"
"With a name like that you ought to be waterproof."
(Real Life, 1932)

THE CRAZY Gang was the future of comedy, Karno was the past, but he remained a well-known figure in the industry. In April 1932 he was a witness at a Commons committee considering legislation that would prevent children from training in acrobatics until the age of twelve. When called to give his opinion, Karno was unable to resist a touch of showmanship – as one reporter put it: 'The star turn was Mr Fred Karno, who danced down from his seat and shuffled his feet before he talked of his early days, acting in dumb ballet.'[1]

1932 was turning into a good year. Gainsborough, a subsidiary of Gaumont British Picture Corporation, finally began production of its Karno series. A studio press release stated: 'It is hoped to build up a British Comedy School, and the Karno plays, sketches, etc. will be used as the nucleus.'[2] The first film was directed by Frank Cadman and produced by Christopher Clayon Hutton, who years later collaborated with Gallagher on his Karno biography.[3]

Clayton Hutton was a huge fan of music hall, and of Karno in particular. In 1909, aged sixteen, he had cycled through the streets of Birmingham to see Karno's comedians every night they played his local hall. After one show he managed to get the showman's autograph at the stage door – and when he explained that he'd been to see the show every night, Karno bought him supper in appreciation. Clayton Hutton never forgot his kindness. However, his real passion was magic. In the Second World War he put his love of gadgets

35. REEL TO REAL

and tricks to good use as a member of MI9, the division of the British Secret Service dedicated to helping prisoners of war to escape. Clayton Hutton's job was to design ways to smuggle essential equipment into the German camps. His compass-concealing buttons, murderous fountain pens and silk maps hidden in chess pieces were the stuff of 'Q' in the James Bond novels. He also worked with the games manufacturer Waddingtons to conceal maps on the back of playing cards and in monopoly sets, and since Karno had once been a director and major shareholder of the company, one wonders if he may have helped to set that up.

All that was to come. Back in 1932 there were films to be made, but first we have a little unpicking of our story to deal with. Gallagher's account suggests that Karno's original agreement back in November 1930 had been with Ideal Films, one of three divisions of Gaumont, and that this had stalled because Ideal found Karno difficult to deal with. Then in May 1932, Clayton Hutton was working as head of publicity at the company, and was supposedly unaware of the Karno contract (despite the fact his own department had advertised it in the national press) when he decided to push for Gaumont to make some Karno films because, in his words: 'Karno's stuff was packing the Palladium.'

This begs the question: how did Hutton know that Karno was involved with the Crazy Gang? Well, George Black's General Theatres Corporation was itself a subsidiary of Gaumont, so as head of publicity, perhaps Clayton Hutton was aware of the connection. Gallagher went on to suggest that at that moment, and quite coincidentally, Karno approached Clayton Hutton bemoaning the fact Ideal had not made any progress with his film contract. The stars aligned and Clayton Hutton was authorised to produce a series of Karno shorts (even though he was not a producer), on the strict understanding that the budget would be limited to £850.[4]

Although there are some obvious holes in this story, it would explain the eighteen-month delay in Karno's sketches making it into production.

Clayton Hutton now found himself in charge as he and Karno turned their attention to the first film: *The Bailiffs*. Bobby Howes had been dropped (or was unavailable), and Clayton Hutton was keen to cast Flanagan and Allen. However, George Black was understandably reluctant to release his stars from their Palladium contract, so Clayton Hutton supposedly went above Black's head to Isidore Ostrer, the president of Gaumont, who forced Black to play ball.

This story gets less plausible by the minute: Black was king of the Palladium and head of Gaumont's entire theatre division, Clayton Hutton was a publicity man who was about to make his first film – a low-budget short with a troublesome music-hall has-been. He was hardly in a position to go to the president and demand that Black release the stars of the biggest comedy show in London. Isn't it more likely that Black was persuaded to release Flanagan and Allen by Karno, as part of their negotiations for *Laffs*? By the way, *The Bailiffs* was made in June 1932, at the same time as that first *Crazy Month* at the Palladium,[5] which supports my theory that Black and Karno were working together, or at least in negotiations, before the month-long show which really founded the Gang, and at least six weeks before they did the deal to formally license *Laffs*.

Back to Gaumont, and we are left with the big unanswered question in the last chapter. Why did Karno agree to keep his name off the Crazy Gang show? He gave Black the rights for *Laffs* and, it seems, the whole Crazy concept, for the princely sum of ten pounds per week. There must have been something else to sweeten the deal, which leads me to believe that the Crazy Gang story and the Gaumont film contract story are one and the same. Let's go back to the beginning of this complicated saga. I believe Karno approached Black and threatened to slap an injunction on the Crazy shows just as his month-long extravaganza was due to open at the Palladium. Meanwhile he was frustrated that he had a contract with Gaumont but after eighteen months still no sign of any film. What if, as part of the Crazy Gang deal, Karno demanded that Black persuade his bosses at Gaumont to film the sketches and release the Gang to appear in them? Black is now able to buy him off cheaply, because he gives Karno the one thing his heart desires – to finally film his sketches. Gaumont complies reluctantly, but insists on a limited budget and hands the task to the only person in the studio who is a Karno fan – the head of publicity who has never made a film before.

That's my theory – make of it what you will.

Flanagan and Allen filmed during the day and then returned to the studio after the Palladium show, working into the early hours. The arrangement was hardly conducive to great performances. The mood on set was further dampened by the death of Bud Flanagan's father on the first day of filming. Karno and Clayton Hutton supposedly had to try and remember the script as best they could, and although Karno was allowed to take control and direct the action, much of his work ended up on the cutting-room floor.

In July the second title in the Karno series was announced as *Painless*, presumably based on *Teeth* – but this seems to have been dropped, and work stalled through the summer. Things got moving again in September, when

35. REEL TO REAL

Flanagan and Allen were reported to be embarking on *Wontdetania* while Naughton and Gold were to tackle *G.P.O.* A week later reports suggested *G.P.O.* would now star Joey Porter and Jack Williams, under a new title – *Post Haste*. Meanwhile, *The Bailiffs* had been completed and was eagerly anticipated in the press: 'Fred Karno and Flanagan and Allen – a truly irresistible combination … Few stars of the variety stage enjoy so wide – and so vociferous! – a following … Their entry into talking films has long been anticipated, and it is certain that their screen following will … create a persistent demand for more.'[6] Sadly it turned out to be far from the triumph Karno had hoped for.

The Bailiffs begins with Fred Karno himself, walking briskly down a suburban street and smoking a fat cigar, closely followed by Flanagan and Allen. Karno flings his cigar butt into the gutter and the bailiffs pounce on it – a gag stolen from Chaplin.[7] Imagining he's out of shot as he exits, Karno breaks into a broad grin, clearly enjoying himself. Perkins and Meredith next select a house at random, flicking through a calendar to decide on a number, then taking the first house they come to regardless. This was their first comedic mistake. The whole set-up for the original sketch is that they get the wrong house in error, they don't just choose one at random – the premise is ruined before they start. Flanagan (as Perkins) and Allen (as Meredith) are also cast the wrong way around – Meredith should be the idiot, Perkins the 'brains'. Dressed in silk top hat and frock coat, Allen couldn't have looked less like a bailiff's idiot assistant if he'd tried. Then there are gags which must surely have been lost in the edit. In the original sketch Perkins tears the warrant in two, giving one half to Meredith "in case you're in first" – nonsensical but funny. In the film this line becomes: "The number's on the warrant," to which

35.1 Flanagan and Allen in The Bailiffs.

Perkins replies: "Well the warrant's all torn up" – it makes no sense (we don't even see the warrant). Various attempts to enter the house follow, until they confess to being bailiffs and are admitted, but this is the sum total of the film: the set-up scene at Moses and Son's office and the subsequent scene where the house's contents are auctioned off, are both gone – the story has no beginning or end.

Even allowing for the passage of ninety years, the film barely raises a titter. The best gag in it is: "Madame, we've come to demonstrate our vacuum cleaner," to which the maid replies: "But our vacuums aren't dirty." Karno's film lacked pace, gags and slapstick, and Flanagan and Allen were lost without a live audience. Watching it makes me think how Laurel and Hardy would have made the same material sublime – what an opportunity missed.

Karno hated the film, complaining that his best work had been edited out and jokes were added which didn't land. With the bitter experience of Hollywood fresh in his mind, he had stepped back and let Gainsborough do it their way – Adeler and West noted that it was a decision he regretted: 'It had to be admitted ... that Karno had been right ... One of the heads of the company made the declaration that in future Karno's word was to be 'law'. However, the damage was done. The exhibitors ... were not anxious to have any more from the same stable.'[8]

This statement in his memoirs was an attempt to bury a whole series of lacklustre movies: in reality *The Bailiffs* was far from a one-off. John Rawlins directed Flannagan and Allen again in *They're Off*, which was reported to be based on the 'Fred Karno Racing Sketch'[9] – although which one is unclear. We know nothing about this film, but Gallagher claimed that Karno was so frustrated on set that he punched Rawlins on the jaw. This might explain why *Post Haste* and a second Porter and Williams film, *Tooth Will Out* (presumably a re-titled *Painless*), were directed by Frank Cadman – Karno was credited as writer. Another, *Sign Please*, starred Naughton and Gold and was reportedly based on a non-existent Karno sketch called *The Salesman*. Any record of these films is largely lost, but they were certainly part of the same series. According to Gallagher, Naughton and Gold also made another with Karno called *Handy Men*, but I can find no trace of it. These films were comedy shorts – here today, gone tomorrow – and got relatively little attention in the press, although Clayton Hutton recalled them as being 'a great success.'[10]

As Karno was trying to get his film career off the ground, Laurel and Hardy came to England for a holiday – which turned into a publicity tour. They had become as popular as Chaplin with British audiences, and much to their surprise, they received a similar reception. After docking at Southampton on 23 July 1932, they caught a train to Waterloo where they were mobbed by a thousand people. Such scenes were repeated in every provincial destination. The press was full of stories of Laurel's British roots and his days as a plonk,

35. REEL TO REAL

but the contrast between Karno's response to Stan's arrival and that of Chaplin the previous year is notable. There was no dashing down to meet him at the port, no interview giving his version of the Stan Laurel story, not even a meeting to share old times – Karno's experience in America must have left him very bruised indeed.

That experience didn't prevent Karno persevering with British film projects though. The following year he collaborated with Con West and Walter Mycroft again and is credited as co-writer on *Oh What a Duchess!* (sometimes called *My Old Duchess*), directed by Lupino Lane.[11] It's been suggested that this film was based on *Mumming Birds*, but it bears absolutely no resemblance to the sketch. The plot revolves around a troupe of actors, one of whom (George Lacy) inadvertently creates chaos during a play. Leaving the theatre, they are caught in a storm and forced to take shelter in an empty country house. Here they are mistaken for the owners by visiting Americans, forcing Lacy to impersonate the titular duchess. A clumsy script and dreadful acting prompted Karno to rename it 'Oh What a Disappointment'.[12]

His much healthier bank balance must have been some consolation. Income from *Laffs*, the Crazy Gang contract and his Gainsborough deal had put him back on a sound financial footing. Feeling positive about the future, he and Marie moved lock stock and barrel to Parkstone, in Dorset, where they set about building a new house – 101X, Penn Hill Avenue. It was a large detached property just a few doors away from Marie's father, and they called it Karmore.[13] Karno might have been forgiven for putting his feet up, but Karmore was to be no retirement bolthole. Disaffected by his film efforts, Karno decided that the novelty of 'talkies' had worn off and people were crying out for live performance again. Many others shared his view – this article was written by film director Sinclair Hill:

> Every week I attend a variety show … I invariably find the same thing – packed houses … variety is definitely in demand … The English music hall provides much of the finest picture talent in this country … particularly … comedians … the biggest names in motion pictures … were music-hall trained … take the supreme example Charlie Chaplin, whose comic genius is the product of the old Karno school – and what a school that was! … Variety is the hardest school of training in the world … Any man or woman who can … face a music hall audience

... is capable of holding any screen audience ... The "pictures" owe a debt of inestimable value to the music-hall.[14]

In December 1932 Karno took the bull by the horns and announced his intentions in the press: 'Fred Karno is to produce a show ... entitled "Real Life", with Jenny Howard and Joey Porter ... The book is by Fred Karno and Con West.'[15] *Laffs* had been his only stage production in the previous five years, so he must have approached the venture with some trepidation, but the press were supportive: 'Revues labelled "Book by Con West", or "Constructed by Fred Karno", are always to be relied upon for really sound entertainment, so that when the pair combine efforts ... the result is doubly pleasing.'[16]

35.2 Leslie Karno (far left) in Real Life *(courtesy Louise Murchison).*

Karno had always placed great importance on the first day of rehearsals for a new show, so it was a great surprise when he failed to appear. As time went on the cast, which included both Leslie and his nephew Freddie Westcott, became increasingly worried, and they were right to be – he'd been involved in a serious road accident. Speeding up to London from Dorset, Karno had no doubt been preoccupied with the new show: his long overdue comeback, the restoration of his reputation and the inevitable flood of offers that would come his way – you might say he careered off the road.

Press reports reveal that he had a lucky escape: 'Mr Fred Karno ... had to be dragged from his motor car when it overturned following a collision ... He was given first aid and was then driven to London.'[17] He eventually appeared at the theatre covered in cuts and bruises, his head bandaged and his arm in a sling. Despite being pulled from an overturned car just that morning, this sixty-six-year-old impresario was determined to run his rehearsal, which says a lot for his fitness, his tenacity and how much the show meant to him. The drama wasn't over yet: three days before opening night his leading lady, Jenny Howard, was rushed to hospital with appendicitis. Understudy Lena Laughton stepped in and the show opened at the Theatre Royal, Leicester, on Boxing Day.

Reviews were positive: 'This revusical comedy … will give much satisfaction … Joey Porter is a comedian of the front rank and keeps the house in a good mood throughout.'[18] While he no doubt welcomed the response, Karno must have thought the show was jinxed when Porter had an accident three weeks into its run: 'Joey Porter … was … knocked out during the … performance … During the garage scene, a … petrol pump overbalanced and struck Mr Porter on the head. The comedian was unable to resume for several minutes … His re-appearance was greeted with sympathetic applause.'[19]

After these initial challenges, *Real Life* settled into a long and successful provincial run. One manager wrote to Karno to say: 'The comedy is extra vintage – just what we might expect from a past-master in the manufacture of mirth.'[20] So, what was it all about? This review tells us more:

> "Real Life" at The Empire marks the return … of Fred Karno … it is mainly composed of comic sketches … varied by a touch of revue. There is a Hyde Park Lido scene with a big tank of real water, in which several of the characters … disport themselves with mirthful results … A Gown Emporium complete with mannequins, a Surrey beauty spot invaded by a merry band of the hiking brother and sisterhood, and a Tote club are among the scenes, and the end is reached with a panoramic representation of the T. T. motor cycling race in the Isle of Man, some of the actual machines used in the event being introduced on the stage.[21]

With an 11,000-gallon water tank and a real motorcycle race, the show was reminiscent of Karno's glory days. For the T.T. scene he even enlisted well-known motorbike racers, who met with cheers from the crowd.

With a success on his hands, Karno once again found himself at the mercy of pilferers. One scene involved a city gent walking along reading a newspaper and then falling head-first into a lake. The comics drag him out (eventually) with cries of "Quick give him artificial perspiration!", at which point a jet of water sprays up from the hapless victim's mouth (thanks to a complicated arrangement of pipes and pumps). A few months later Karno saw this exact gag play out in a movie, and wrote to the film's director to complain – he responded that he had assumed the gag was 'originated by Noah'. Karno replied: 'Like many others who have used my material and have quoted Noah as the originator … I think it is because I have produced so many comedy shows during the last fifty years that I am the Noah they refer to!'[22]

Some pirates were even more blatant. Karno submitted a new sketch, *You Can't Come In*, to a producer (who rejected it), only to find it being staged a few weeks later under a different title. He wrote to Leslie: 'I am a kind of universal provider, when in doubt pinch Karno's stuff.'[23] Such experiences prompted him to write to *The Stage*:

> Wholesale piracy now exists in our business. It seems to be a common practice for certain alleged performers and unprincipled producers to purloin with impunity anybody's business and gags … some of these plagiarists … whisk out their notebooks and take down verbatim every line that got a laugh … I have frequently been requested by the local management (after the first house) to cut out this or that because it has been done there so many times lately. So, I have been compelled to cut out my own property … A producer or author who racks his brains to invent … original ideas is not allowed to retain them, as … with lightning rapidity they are introduced into all the dud revues in the country … to enter into costly litigation is a waste of time and money, as I know from bitter experience … So, what is one to do?[24]

This prompted a lively debate in the press. Con West chipped in, blaming the nature of cheap revue. Many shows used the same hit songs (under licence) set to standard choreography, around which producers threw some second-hand scenery and then left the cast to find a few gags to fill the gaps. Inevitably the comics would throw in material they'd used or heard before. No wonder revue was unable to stop the industry's decline.

Plagiarists aside, the *Real Life* tour was a great success, and the highlight for Karno came in April 1933 at the Hackney Empire.[25] He received a message that someone wanted to see him at the box office, went front-of-house and was pleased to find 'house full' signs and people being turned away. Imagine his feelings when he pushed through the throng and discovered that his visitor was Hal Roach. The theatre manager squeezed Roach into a box and Karno was able to revel in the satisfaction of knowing the Hollywood mogul was watching his show among an enthusiastic crowd. Roach had arrived in Britain ten days earlier, and straight off the boat had namechecked his former employee:

> Mr Hal Roach, Hollywood's most notable director of comedies, arrived in London yesterday to make a talking film with the best British comedians he can find. "More than half the best comedians in the world are British … The Fred Karno tradition was the most valuable groundwork for the early silent films, and Charlie Chaplin its greatest exponent" … for a fortnight he will search every music-hall, theatre and cabaret possible for comedians for "International Revue" which he will direct here this spring.[26]

Roach's presence at *Real Life* wasn't a social call – he was talent-spotting. He was part of an influx of Americans to British film studios at the time, prompted by the downturn in the U.S. industry. Roach envisioned *International Revue* showcasing the best British talent, and hoped to sign up Jack Buchanan and Gracie Fields.[27] He scrapped his plans after just a few days, realising that good variety artistes were few and far between, and all were tied to long contracts. Nonetheless he returned to America a few weeks later having bagged a handful of lesser British artistes for his studio, including double act Billy Nelson and Dougie Wakefield, who was Gracie Fields' brother-in-law.[28] Another recruit was Jack Barty, who had appeared in Karno's revival of *Moses and Son* in 1926 and later in Crazy Gang shows at the Palladium. Barty was signed to work as an assistant director and bring 'English comedy angles' to Roach's films.[29] His appointment suggests Roach thought he'd missed an opportunity with Karno – one wonders whether the Guv'nor had any words of advice before Barty set off.[30]

Roach was seeking a successful formula for his 'All Star' film series, and Wakefield and Nelson ultimately numbered among a string of failed attempts. They made eight movies (in which Queenie Karno appeared as an extra), but they failed to take off and their contract was cancelled in 1935.

Real Life embarked on a second tour in autumn 1933, with Frank Randle and Violet Victoria taking over the lead roles. Randle went on to have a successful film career and become hugely popular, especially in his native Lancashire, but back then he was just another jobbing comic. Karno's show was his first break in revue and the beginning of his rise to fame, as this critic notes: 'Frank Randle, remembered for some clever individual efforts on the variety stage, blossoms forth as a fully-fledged comedian in Real Life.'[31] Other reviews were even more gushing: 'His mimicry of a man sewing on a button, with imaginary needle and thread, is a triumph of burlesque ... but the most hilarious scene of all is that in which he appears as a reveller on the "morning after the night before" ... by his tomfoolery the comedian renders the audience well-nigh helpless with laughter.'[32] Randle was to be Karno's last great discovery.

35.3 Frank Randle – Karno's last discovery (author's collection).

With *Real Life* beginning a profitable second season, Karno managed to pull together a troupe to stage *Mumming Birds* from time to time. Leslie had by then joined a Wallace Parnell revue called *You'll Be Surprised*, and without his support Karno found it difficult to organise the company, so he elected to license the sketch to W.B. Crabtree, who staged it throughout 1934. A final piece of bad luck brought *Real Life* to an end in May, when it was 'unexpectedly vacant' after a fire at the Palace Theatre, Halifax – it was never staged again. Karno recalled that the show had been as successful as the best of his old sketches, which was a fitting way to end – it turned out to be his last stage production.

Karno was settled in his new house in Dorset and able to look back on a life well lived, one with fame and fortune, excitement and adventure, and plenty of ups and downs. Now sixty-eight, his health was declining and he had to follow a strict diet after being diagnosed with what he described as 'a touch of diabetes'.[33] Treatment for the illness had not moved on greatly since it killed Edith in 1927, because many people (including Karno) refused to take insulin, believing it to be a dangerous drug. He should have settled into a comfortable retirement, but found himself with money in his pocket and nothing to do – a dangerous combination. He decided to have one last roll of the dice.

Karno had concluded that the reason for his film failures was obvious – he hadn't been in complete control. He didn't need BIP, Syd Chaplin, Roach,

35. REEL TO REAL

Gainsborough or Christopher Clayton Hutton, he would do it all himself. In August 1934 the press trumpeted his ambitious (and delusional) plan to make Dorset the Hollywood of the South Coast: 'Fred Karno will be the producer for a new syndicate who propose to open a film studio in the Bournemouth area.'[34] He toiled on his grand scheme for the next six months, writing to Leslie in January that he had found financial backers and was working on a script. In his memoirs he recalled that his only real glitch was finding a distributor – it was a problem that would cost him dear.

The Fred Karno Film Company was born. Its motto, 'Asbestos Gelos' (literally 'Fireproof Laughter'), was a phrase used by Homer to describe the laughter of the gods – defiant, unquenchable laughter; laughter in the face of fear and adversity. It was highly appropriate: a year of hard work delivered nothing other than his company's headed notepaper. He suffered months of abortive ideas, blind alleys and wrong turns, sometimes literally – the next time he appeared in the press was in spring 1935, when he was prosecuted for driving the wrong way down a one-way street.

By July 1935 there were signs he was finally making progress. He had abandoned the Bournemouth studio idea and instead secured a production slot at the Hammersmith Studios, and gave a typically bullish interview to the press:

> Fred Karno – now 65 years old [actually 69] who started more comedians on the road to fame than anyone in history has formed a British film company ... "We begin work next month ... to make six feature comedies a year ... I shall use as many of my former stars as possible, with some new ones. My aim is to found a 'school' of British broad fun ... I intend to make a 'Karno Cavalcade' with a lot of the boys who started with me. One of them, Stan Laurel has promised to make some special scenes for me in Hollywood and send them over."[35]

Karno's belief in the potential of the British film industry was unshakeable. He envisaged a new Fun Factory for film comics, able to beat anything Hollywood could offer. His first project would be an homage to his old material and the comics that made it, and you will have noticed his nod to Stan Laurel – once again the only old-boy to support him.

By this time Karno had secured a distributor for his output, but he soon found himself arguing with them at every turn. *Karno Cavalcade* went on the back-burner, and he turned his attention to the film script he had begun earlier in the year. He was keen to engage Con West to work on it, but the distributors insisted on a more experienced screenwriter, Michael Barringer. Karno dug his heels in until common sense prevailed – they agreed to all work together.

Karno's script had started out as an adaption of *Hot and Cold,* but by the time Barringer and West had finished it bore no resemblance to the original show, and had the working title *When We Are Married.* Nonetheless, Karno wrote to Leslie saying he was pleased with the script and had managed to persuade them to use a few of his gags. Filming began in the autumn with Robb Wilton in the lead role, supported by two well-established double acts: Haver and Lee and Revnel and West. Karno also gave small parts to his nephew Freddie Westcott and Mike Asher,[36] a veteran of the Chaplin American tours. Leslie had by now given up performing.

The film had two intertwining plots. First, two bookmakers design a dog-racing betting scam, running into all sorts of trouble involving detectives and a relative who's a member of a puritan anti-gambling league. Meanwhile Sam

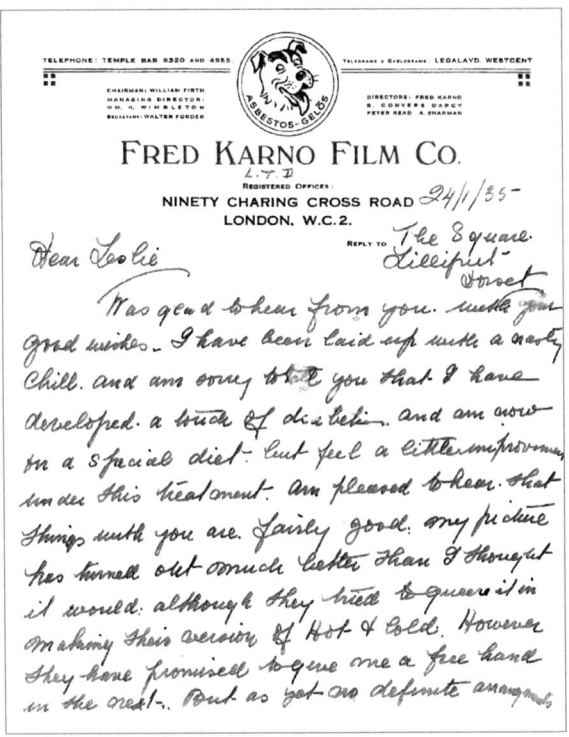

35.4 Karno had high hopes for Don't Rush Me, *24 January 1935 (courtesy Louise Murchison).*

35. REEL TO REAL

(chairman of the puritans) has been engaged to Amy for thirty years – and convinced that he will never propose, she runs away to London where she falls into the hands of some unsavoury characters.

One press report gives us a glimpse of Karno on set: 'I had a long talk with genial Fred Karno at the new studios by Hammersmith Bridge this week ... watching Norman Lee making scenes for "When We Are Married" ... I found Karno full of anecdotes ... but rather bewildered at the need for free adaptations of slapstick comedy.'[37] In truth, the old man was bewildered by the whole process: film production and distribution proved very different from writing or directing, and he was completely out of his depth. Finding himself working into the early hours to meet the film's gruelling schedule, he began to feel his age, telling Leslie: 'I now begin to feel a bit old in the tooth'.[38]

Once completed the film was retitled *Don't Rush Me*,[39] and Karno declared himself delighted with it. This time he had the right script, the right star, the right director and he'd kept control of every aspect of the production – nothing could go wrong. He spent a relaxing Christmas and saw in the New Year eagerly awaiting its release.

36.

Finale

*"You should go to the Isle of Man for your holidays
– and take the wife."*
"I thought you said it was a holiday"
(The Football Match, 1906)

DON'T RUSH Me had its trade premiere at the Prince Edward Theatre, London, in the first week of January 1936. Karno was overwhelmed by messages of support from friends in the business. The Crazy Gang and several old-boys sent congratulatory telegrams, including one from Stan Laurel and Babe Hardy which said: 'One touch of Karno makes the whole world grin. Keep up the good work and make the whole world happy.'[1] Will Hay wrote: 'Best of luck from one of your old apprentices.'[2] But the one he cherished most was the 'heartiest congratulations and best wishes'[3] from Charlie Chaplin.

The house was packed and Karno found it hard to contain his excitement until, just before the film began, someone told him he'd be expected to make a speech afterwards. Given the importance of the occasion he felt he had little choice but to say a few words, so he beat a hasty retreat from the auditorium and found a quiet room to prepare something. Nervous and rushed, he spent so long writing his speech that when he returned the credits were rolling. He was disappointed to have missed the film and seen the audience's reaction, but worse still he wasn't called upon to make a speech after all. Perhaps this was because they didn't think much of it. *The Era* critic was unusually supercilious and scathing:

36. FINALE

> Rambling story of provincial who gets mixed up in his modern nephew's greyhound activities … humour and dialogue couched in obvious form … for the docile popular audience. Fred Karno produced this typical effort in farce … We do not profess to know as much as he does of what is demanded of the successful music-hall sketch, but we do submit that in the matter of screen comedy his methods require radical changes. Unless of course, he wishes no other world to conquer than the provincial … The characters are extremely foolish, even for farce, and their antics bring forth a type of comedy which is aptly summed up as broad. There is any amount of earnestness put into this production, so it is possible the hard work will bring results with those audiences who appreciate downright exuberance alone.[4]

He didn't like it – but he was right to predict that it would go down well in the provinces. Karno recalled that the public reaction was consistently positive, and provincial critics were enthusiastic: 'It is an uproarious farce, produced with sparkle and polish.'[5] Another noted: 'With this infectious and high-spirited comedy, Fred Karno makes his entry into the ranks of film production; the result is a film of which few old-timers would not be proud.'[6]

Despite these reviews, the film had relatively few showings – the one part of the process Karno couldn't control let him down, distribution. It was in the hands of the Producers Distributing Corporation (P.D.C.), and why they made so little effort to keep up their part of the bargain is a mystery – perhaps they saw the press night critics' assessment and lost confidence in it. *Don't Rush Me* was a good film badly distributed, and what should have been a triumph turned into disaster. Karno had put everything he had into the film. Midway through production, with costs spiralling, he had sold Karmore and borrowed further from a variety of backers. Now it became clear that the film would not cover its production costs.[7] It had taken Karno nearly ten years to get back on his feet: now he was only able to avoid a second bankruptcy by entering into a repayment agreement with his creditors.

Fortunately, Karno had an insurance policy. While working on *Don't Rush Me* he had embarked on a sideline that gave him a small but secure income. He'd become the proprietor of Lilliput Wine Stores, at 296 Sandbanks Road, Lilliput, Parkstone.[8] Having sold Karmore, Karno and Marie moved into a flat next to the shop.

Gallagher said that after the failure of *Don't Rush Me* Karno was once again penniless, and set up his wine store in April 1937 thanks to a handout from the Music Hall Benevolent Fund. Other sources claim that Chaplin gave him £1000 to fund the new venture. Both stories appear to be nonsense.[9] The Music Hall Benevolent Fund ceased to exist in 1907, to be replaced by the Variety Artistes' Benevolent Fund, and no record of any such financial support appears to exist – nor is there any evidence of Chaplin's act of charity in the archives.[10] £1000 was ten times the average annual wage at the time, enough to buy the off-licence and the row of shops next door – such an act of generosity is unlikely to have gone unremarked in Karno's letters to Leslie. Furthermore, these theories are dispelled by the irrefutable fact that Karno went into the wine store business *before* the failure of his film. He is recorded as the owner of the store in 1935,[11] months before *Don't Rush Me* was completed and long before it became apparent that he would not recoup his costs. His personal correspondence confirms that his financial problems began after he took on the shop, and also that he had a business partner, Mr M. Stacey (who invested fifty percent) – it was far from a charity case. This doesn't mean to say that everything in Karno's garden was rosy at the time: making *Don't Rush Me* was a challenge, and he had been forced to sell his home. The man who sold him the shop remembered Karno as "the most miserable little so-and-so I ever came across."[12]

36.1 The giant's rest – Lilliput Wine Stores.

36.2 Down amongst the wines and spirits – Karno behind the counter.

Having done enough to keep his creditors happy for a while, Karno focused on building up his new business and Marie found work at a nursing home.

36. FINALE

Writing to Leslie in July 1937, Karno seemed to have found contentment in his semi-retirement. He enjoyed chatting with his customers about the old days and was always eager to tell a joke or hear a good story while making his deliveries – he certainly had plenty to tell. There was trouble brewing though: a residual debt came back to bite him eighteen months after the film was released.

One of the companies that had financed *Don't Rush Me* went broke before it was finished, forcing Karno to take out a loan with Lloyds Bank to complete it. Although still playing at some cinemas the film was clearly never going to recoup its costs, and Lloyds called in the loan. Karno was jointly liable with his production partners, and unable to pay his share, he found himself summoned to court on 11 August 1937. He wrote to Leslie: 'They may sell up this little business and make me bankrupt. I shall lose everything. However, I am hoping for the best, it's no use worrying about it. I have had so many knocks that I have got used to them. But all the same it does not tend to make you very happy … I passed my 70th birthday last March, so am getting near the end of the game.'[13]

What happened next is unclear but he must have reached an arrangement with Lloyds, because by November the danger seems to have passed and his letters were full of the success of his little shop – surely nothing now could interrupt his peace and quiet? Then, in late October, Fred Jr. knocked at Karno's door – he had not seen or heard from his son for over ten years.

A.J. Marriot's research reveals that Fred Jr. had appeared in Canadian vaudeville between October 1925 and January 1927,[14] but after that his whereabouts are unclear. Family legend has it that he struggled on in Canada, including spending time as a department store Santa, although an intriguing and mysterious report from New Britain, Connecticut, published in *Variety* in September 1928, reads: 'Polychrome Romance – Sadie Anderson, 33, billed … as the "Woman of Many Colors," and Fred Karno, 33, vaudeville performer … have filed marriage intentions in this city. She is in the records as "colored." Her skin is of three colors. He is white. She speaks 27 languages.'[15] If this is our man the relationship must have fizzled out, for it was a single Fred Jr. who found his way to Karno's door in 1937, en route to London. Karno wrote to Leslie and told him to expect a visit, then returned to his shop counter.

Despite his forced exile from showbusiness, Karno made occasional public appearances. On 15 February 1938 he took part in a local radio programme called *Fred Karno's Army, Old Comrades* – presumably a selection of recordings from comics he'd worked with in his career. On 10 May he contributed to a broadcast about Charles B. Cochran, entitled *Showmen of England*. That same week he wrote to Leslie that the heavy lifting of deliveries was becoming too much for him and he was intending to sell his share of the shop. He and Stacey had built up a roaring trade and he expected to do well out of the sale. In the meantime, they had a windfall: Marie's father died in May 1938, leaving her well over £5000 in his will. It seems likely that this was kept in Marie's name to avoid Karno's creditors – it would need to last them the rest of their retirement. And another boost came that summer when *Don't Rush Me* reappeared in cinemas, after P.D.C. sold the rights to a new distributor, Wardour Films.

It was around this time that work was completed on Karno's memoirs. He remained optimistic about the future and retained his boundless energy, confidence and self-belief. Signing off their final chapter, Adeler and West left him still planning a comeback: 'Karno's retirement is doubtless but a lull before the storm of applause that will greet some new comedy offering at present discreetly concealed up the maestro's sleeve.'[16]

They were right: it wasn't long before the glamour of shopkeeping began to wear off. The bright lights of showbusiness once again beckoned as Karno contemplated the latent value of his back catalogue. On 16 July he registered a new company, Karno Kine Plays Ltd, 'to carry on the business of producers of kinematograph plays and films.'[17] *The Era* reported that he hoped to resurrect his *Karno's Cavalcade* idea, and had lined up a particularly exciting leading man:

> Charlie Chaplin has promised Fred Karno that he will appear in "Karno Cavalcade", a full length film, which the veteran producer and actor is planning to make … Chaplin has written to Mr Karno that he will either appear in the film in this country or will make some of it in his own Hollywood studios … Other former Karno artistes who have promised to appear … are Stan Laurel, Max Miller, Naughton and Gold and Will Hay … the company is to film all the Karno stage successes … at M.P. Studios, Elstree … Mr Karno is conducting a search … to find artistes who appeared in the sketches originally … to play their old parts. A distribution company will be formed by Mr Karno and his colleagues.[18]

Nostalgia seems to have been the name of the game here, but Karno had learnt one lesson from *Don't Rush Me* – this time he would handle the distribution himself. His plans, as always, were ambitious:

36. FINALE

> Fred Karno is searching for "an aristocratic looking woman with a very definite comedy face" to play in certain of his comedies, the first three of which are scheduled to go into production ... during the next few weeks. "The Bailiffs", "Hydro", and "Mumming Birds" will be the first films, and these will be followed by "Fred Karno's Air Force", "Fred Karno's Waxworks", new subjects, and "Perkins in Paris". Twelve are to be made in quick succession.[19]

Predictably, the films never materialised. Karno spent a few more months behind the shop counter before hanging up his apron for good. He sold his share in the store for £2500 but the bank seized the lot, leaving him with no demonstrable source of income. Lloyds called time on his repayment arrangement and he was declared bankrupt for a second time in November 1938.

The pressure of all this turmoil took its toll, and Karno's health went into serious decline. He had to spend long periods of time in bed, dutifully nursed by Marie. After Christmas they moved to a first-floor flat at 24 Dorrich Court, Wharfdale Road.[20] Karno wrote to Leslie: 'We have taken a smaller new flat ... it is a cheap block of flats in rather a poor working-class neighbourhood. But we can't help ourselves and must economise as we have only a little bit to live on – no occupation and no prospects ... I am thinking of applying for the old age pension. My love to all, from your affectionate Dad.'[21]

Despite once again hitting rock bottom, he told Leslie he had been to London to pitch a film of *The Love Match* to 'these unreliable picture people'.[22] At seventy-three, bankrupt, living in a small bedsit in Dorset and in failing health, Karno still refused to give up. Remarkably, the studio in question apparently agreed to his proposal, subject to him securing Dougie Wakefield as the lead comic. Karno quickly established that Wakefield was committed to a long contract with Paramount, so the project was scrapped. It is possible that the film company was humouring him for old times' sake and stipulated conditions they knew he could not meet, but Con West continued to lobby various production companies on Karno's behalf.

Karno and Marie settled in at Wharfdale Road, and despite its humbleness found that it was cosy, modern and provided for all their needs. He still had a car (Marie's father had paid for that), a garage and a small garden to look after. Shortly after they moved in a Mrs Watkinson and her baby son Peter moved in below them. Peter shared with me a recording of an interview his mother gave to the BBC in 1986, in which she remembered Mr and Mrs Karno as very kind, nice people – the Guv'nor had obviously mellowed with old age.[23]

With Karno now effectively retired, it was finally time for the next generation to pick up the mantle. Leslie returned to the stage as part of a double act (Karno sent him a selection of gags he might find useful), while Fred Jr. attempted to stage his own version of *Mumming Birds*.[24] Karno confessed to Leslie that he didn't expect too much of the production, but gave Fred Jr. his blessing to put on the show – it doesn't appear to have made it to the stage.

Meanwhile, against the odds, Con West managed to get a bite from those unreliable picture people and was commissioned to write the screenplay for a film version of *Jail Birds*. It was directed by Oswald Mitchell, produced by Butchers Film Service, and released in early 1940. It starred Albert Burdon as Bill Smith; Charles Hawtrey of *Carry-On* film fame; and Shaun Glenville, last encountered leaping aboard the *Wontdetania* thirty years earlier: 'Based on Fred Karno's well known stage production ... The mirth-provoking adventures of the convicts at this prison (where men are released for being too dangerous!) make excellent material for this first-rate comedy.'[25]

36.3 French poster for Jail Birds *(author's collection).*

The plot involved stolen jewels hidden in a loaf of bread which ends up at Bill Smith's house and is discovered by a detective, who happens to be courting Smith's daughter. Although it bore little resemblance to the Karno original, the film was a knockabout comedy with plenty of slapstick, including an anarchic scene in a bakery. It was well-received by the critics: 'Funny as the original stage comedy was, this version is funnier than description. It is one long series of delicious nonsense and well repays a visit.'[26] *Jail Birds*' success came too late for Karno: other than allowing West to use the script, for which he received a writing credit, he was not involved in the film. He tried unsuccessfully to get Leslie a part, and received only a minor financial reward.

On 31 May 1939 Karno's memoirs were finally published, prompting renewed press interest. Most of this focused on Chaplin, whose fiftieth birthday was hogging the papers, and Stan Laurel, who was also in the news for his third

36. FINALE

divorce and recent reunion with Babe Hardy (after settling a contractual dispute with Hal Roach). Karno was now little more than a footnote in their stories. The title of the biography, *Remember Fred Karno*, summed up the swiftness of his disappearance from the public consciousness. It brought back memories for a few critics though: 'It was so interesting … I read it through twice … and I have relived the enjoyable times I had watching every one of Fred Karno's sketches. My lasting memory is of the production night at the Paragon of his sketch "Wontdetania", with Harry Lauder on the same bill. The house was so full that you might say that the audience stood on one another's heads.'[27] While noting that the biography gave very little information on Karno's personal life, reviewers were reminded of his impact on the development of comedy:

> He looks back upon a career which, despite its ups and downs, he has every right to be proud of, for, of all living showmen, he surely has caused the greatest amount of hearty laughter to ring through theatre and music-hall in this country. To make people laugh! That was always Fred Karno's aim, and he succeeded-partly through knowing the sort of humour which pleased the average democratic audience and partly through genius in the matter of finding and developing comic talent. Everyone knows by now that Charlie Chaplin was a Karno discovery, but so was almost every other British comedian of note.[28]

With his book hot off the press, Karno and Marie took a motoring holiday around the north west of England. In Blackpool they went to see a variety show, where he was spotted in the audience. The comic (almost certainly Frank Randle)[29] dragged him onto the stage to a rousing reception – the people of Lancashire had not forgotten him. It was the last time Karno set foot on a stage, and he wrote to Leslie saying that the applause had meant the world to him. Unfortunately the holiday did him more harm than good, as sticking to his strict diet was impossible – by the time they returned he was seriously ill. Karno was now living on borrowed time, and so were millions of other people – on the first day of September, the country once again found itself at war.

Operation Pied Piper, the evacuation of children from major cities, was put into effect on the very first day. Bournemouth was a reception area and because Karno had a car, he was signed up for national service. His job was to ferry bewildered evacuees arriving at Poole station to their new homes. He was delighted to be 'doing his bit', and told Leslie the children all seemed in good spirits. This wasn't his only good deed: his neighbour Mrs Watkinson recalled Karno and Marie taking her and her son on day trips in his car – a treat they relished. Karno even built an air-raid shelter in the garden of Wharfdale Road specifically because young Peter lived downstairs. As they huddled together in the darkness of the shelter, listening to bombers droning overhead, Karno kept them entertained with stories of his career – stories Mrs Watkinson must have found hard to believe. She also recounted how he built a reinforced table to protect the cot, declaring: "We must look after the young ones"[30] – I wonder if she realised his speciality was collapsible props.

Although they wrote to one another occasionally, Karno and Leslie drifted apart as the business ebbed away, and he seems to have lost touch with Fred Jr. completely. He wrote to Leslie: 'I have not heard from Fred for months, perhaps he has joined up. I hope so as it would do him a bit of good.'[31] Fred Jr., now aged fifty-two, was actually serving as a volunteer policeman while trying to maintain a career on the stage. In February 1940 he advertised his show *Making More Stars,* promising seven big acts and 'The Eight Karnoettes', but I can find no evidence of it being staged. Neither son visited Karno in those final years. Mrs Watkinson had no idea that he even had children of his own – in fact in the two years she lived below the Karnos, she didn't remember them receiving a single visitor.

The Karno name may have disappeared from theatrical listings, but it was writ large elsewhere throughout the war. After the previous conflict, the Treaty of Versailles required that Germany was 'forbidden to maintain or construct any fortification … on the Left bank of the Rhine,'[32] an agreement ratified in the Locarno Treaty. When the Germans remilitarised in 1936, one newspaper noted: 'When Germany marched into the Rhineland … somebody suggested that the Locarno room in the Foreign Office … should be renamed the Fred Karno room.'[33] In respect of Chamberlain's appeasement of Hitler at Munich, another report noted: 'The Fred Karno method would not see them through the next struggle.'[34] The organisation of air-raid precautions was often cited as being 'Karno-esque', even in the House of Commons: 'Air raid wardens would like to have some form of contract of service. It would make them feel they had some status and were not "a sort of Fred Karno's Army".'[35]

The Home Guard carried the label from day one, but by the end of the war had proved their worth. Home Secretary Herbert Morrison had this to say of

36. FINALE

those much-maligned heroes: 'There were many who thought of the motley collection of Civil Defence workers as a ragtime army ... the men and women ... provided the answer to the doubts and criticism. How ... magnificently the Fred Karno's Army stood up to the test is now history.'[36] For the next generation, the Home Guard will always be the characters in *Dad's Army*.[37] Its theme tune, *Who Do You Think You Are Kidding Mr Hitler?*, was the last recording made by Bud Flanagan – he died shortly afterwards. When the series was launched, *The Daily Mirror* said: 'The Home Guard had their funny side as viewers will see in the new comedy series "Dad's Army" ... the C.O. ... is Arthur Lowe ... a bank manager, named Mainwaring ... backed up by a regular Fred Karno troupe.'[38]

Karno was surprised that Con West's *Jail Birds* got made given the outbreak of war, but its release prompted him to think about other opportunities. In spring 1940 he and West approached the BBC suggesting that his sketches would be perfect for entertaining the troops, but to no avail. Karno even tried to enlist the help of some of his old boys, writing to Will Hay: 'Dear Will ... Perhaps you could get someone interested in myself and comedies for the troops abroad. They want laughs and you know I have got them. I have the material and scripts of 'Mumming Birds', 'The Smoking Concert', 'Rations' and 'All Women'. Most suitable and easily played with a few props. A suggestion from you to the right quarter would be much appreciated ... We are Fred Karno's army.'[39]

Hay could have helped: he was doing his bit as the head of the Variety Section of the Entertainments National Service Association (ENSA) – sometimes known as Every Night Something Awful. But Karno's appeal fell on deaf ears. Still the old man didn't give up: he and West discussed a possible radio series, and West began work on a stage show called *Fred Karno's Army*. Karno never stopped talent-spotting either. In April 1940 he saw a virtually unknown comedian and wrote to West telling him he was the finest he had seen in years, predicting he would become a sensation. It was another three years before that comic hit the big time – his name was Sid Field.

A year went by with no interest in his material, so Karno placed a large advertisement in *The Stage*: 'What this country now needs is more laughs – FRED KARNO is prepared to let or sell for screen or stage, any of his FAMOUS COMEDIES.'[40] The advertisement went on to list fifty-nine shows, some of which had never been produced. Amazingly, he got a bite: a month later Karno licensed *Mumming Birds* to producer Cecil Buckingham – there was life in the old girl yet.

There was precious little life left in the man himself, however. On 16 September Marie wrote to Leslie to say that his father had 'sprained his heart ... but was not feeling too bad.'[41] By the time he received the letter, Karno was dead.

He passed away in his sleep on 17 September 1941. Marie was at his side while Mrs Watkinson sprinted pointlessly to the phonebox to call a doctor. The funeral was held three days later: Chaplin was one of many who sent floral tributes. Mrs Watkinson remembered Chaplin's wreath being huge – impossible to miss outside her flat, propped up against the bins.

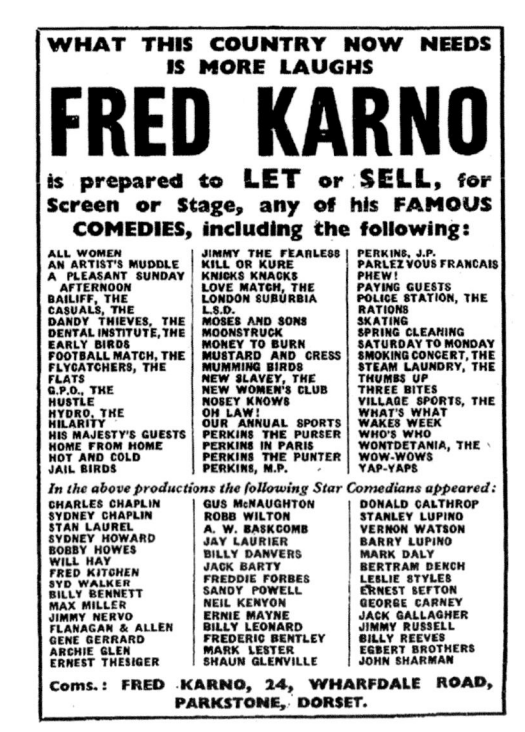

36.4 One last try, The Stage, 3 April 1941.

It was a small service at Bournemouth crematorium, where Karno's ashes were then scattered – there was no marker or memorial. Fred Jr. recalled that the funeral was commemorated by an undesired fly-past of German bombers, and he, Marie and Leslie had to spend the night in the air-raid shelter.

Karno had run away with the circus before making his London music hall debut in 1888; he was still in the game when he died, just a few weeks before Japan attacked Pearl Harbour. It was an extraordinary period of history and an extraordinary life, during which he created a comic legacy unequalled before or since.

Quite how impoverished he and Marie were at the end is unclear. In 2008 an unidentified member of an online film forum posted this story:

> I actually met Fred Karno about 6 weeks before he died. I had been evacuated from Portsmouth to stay with an aunt ... I had been down to Alder Road Park ... and ... a man beckoned me from across the road, "come here Sonny." I could see that he wasn't well and had difficulty

36. FINALE

in standing. "Could you get me my rations from the shop?" he handed me his ration book and half-a-crown … and pointed back to the house behind. "I live on the top floor, I'll be there." I watched him walk with difficulty to the door to the stairs, then went to the shop for him. I noticed the name on the ration book was Fred Karno, but it meant nothing to me then. When I took his rations back, I walked up the stairs, which were bare boards … There was no furniture, only a couple of tea chests, and Fred was sitting upon one. Apart from that there were only a couple of threadbare offcuts of carpet on the floor … I noticed … posters on the walls … Charlie Chaplin on one and Stan Laurel on the other. "Did you know them?" I said. "Know them – I made them!" he replied. He then began to tell me how he had trained them to be the great artistes they had become. He praised Stan Laurel as a gentleman and told how he always sent a Christmas card and some money each year, but was very bitter about Charlie Chaplin who he denounced as mean and ungrateful, using terms that cannot be written here. I listened fascinated as he told tales of triumphs and travelling to Hollywood to make films, then realised I would be late home and my mother would be worried. When I explained where I had been, she was upset and forbade me to enter Fred's flat again but said I could go to the shop for him if he met me at the gate … I am not sure that she believed it was really him. So, for the next few weeks I got his rations, then … I read … that Mr Karno had died … the headline was something like: Great Impresario Dies in Poverty.[42]

Much was made in the press of the fact that Karno left only forty-two pounds in his will (Edith left ten times as much), but this doesn't mean they were penniless: the average annual wage was only two hundred pounds. What's more, Marie still had her own nest-egg – she left a sizeable legacy of her own when she died a few years later. So the account of the boy fetching Karno's rations back to his empty flat seems at odds with the facts. There is no mention of Marie in the story, even though she was working as a nurse and she and Karno were living there happily together. Why did Karno need a boy to fetch his rations? What's more, Marie had plenty of money tucked away – why would they be reduced to tea chests? Curiouser and curiouser.

That anonymous testimony is interesting in another respect too. It suggests Karno felt Chaplin abandoned him in his hour of need, whereas Laurel sent him a regular Christmas gift. Perhaps at the end, the Guv'nor accepted the truth about Chaplin and Laurel: he knew which of them had offered help when he needed it, and he knew how he'd treated them in return. Perhaps, unable to forgive himself, his embittered old age was tortured by the realisation that he had fêted the wrong protégé.

A flurry of obituaries cited Karno's influence on comedy, emphasising the scale of his once-mighty empire and contrasting this with his death in impecunious obscurity. One said: 'In a world expertly conducted there would be a professorship of practical laughter, and it would be held by Mr Frederick Westcott.'[43] *The Yorkshire Post* contributed:

> With good fortune and the major virtues of the Industrious Apprentice, a man may make his mark in life, may even after death be remembered … But how many of us can hope to give our native tongue a new and enduring phrase? … How many times did our warriors of the last war sing … "We are Fred Karno's Army"? How often have we ourselves condemned something to the limits of makeshiftness by describing it as a "Fred Karno sort of affair"? … We may remember Fred Karno … as the discoverer of Charlie Chaplin and Stan Laurel; as a lord of laughter. But will he ever be forgotten as the maker of a phrase?[44]

At the end of Karno's memoirs, Adeler and West had wondered whether that phrase would endure: 'No doubt it will eventually become a national phrase, handed down to posterity, like "Shank's pony" and "Hobson's choice". Probably our great-great-grandchildren will fly over to Australia for the weekend to see the Test Match, and on returning declare that it was "a proper Fred Karno affair".'[45] After Karno's death West contributed his own touching tribute for *The Stage*:

> I would like to pay my tribute to the memory of the late Fred Karno, who was undoubtedly one of the greatest personalities of the theatre. When he was at the height of his fame and fortune, I obtained an appointment to see him, and as a mere stripling I nervously read my first script. Fred Karno was just as courteous and considerate to me then as he was in recent years when he asked me to collaborate in the writing of his biography. Karno's life was devoted to comedy, and for that he will always be remembered. The Grand Parade goes on. New faces, new

36. FINALE

jokes, new business. But for a moment let us pause to salute the passing of "The Guv'nor". A great man; a good friend; a grand loser.[46]

In the same issue of *The Stage,* Marie Karno placed a notice thanking all those who sent messages of sympathy, 'too numerous to answer individually'. Many must have come from people who owed him their careers, none of whom had helped him when he needed it.

Karno may not have left much in his will, but his legacy was a mountain of comedy material and a legion of famous comics. He had been at the leading edge of comedy development; he challenged the licensing restrictions and pioneered verbal sketches; he helped to secure copyright protection for performers and writers; he stretched the boundaries of what could be done physically on the stage; he added musical accompaniment before anyone else thought of it; he pioneered breaking the fourth wall; and he developed the talent show. His discipline and approach created a genre of comedy that became synonymous with his name, and the comics of the Karno school were the best in the world. For all this, perhaps his greatest attribute was his ability to spot talent. He once said:

> It takes two people to make a star – the performer himself, and the man who can spot him … I've been fortunate in being able to spot them. Where other managers and producers have just seen a small-time comedian … I've seen a potential world-beater; and sometimes I've been wrong … but not often … What … made me back their chances? … there aren't any rules of thumb. I can't say "to be a successful comedian it is necessary to have absolute confidence, bow legs, quick answers, a red nose, a sense of rhythm" … some of these things can be acquired, others aren't necessary. All I can tell you about qualifications is that a man … must have something – and it must be different. The something needn't be fully developed; but it must be there, latent … Sometimes it's pathos – Charlie Chaplin. Sometimes it's an innocent, imbecile grin – Stan Laurel … in every case it provides a keynote for a personality that can be worked up, evolved, perfected …

Karno went on to tell the story of his discovery of Chaplin, before returning to his thoughts on the making of comedians:

It's got to be developed of course ... hour after hour I'd work at them, coaxing it out, helping them develop their special line ... fanning the spark of genius that was burning so feebly sometimes you could hardly see it. But if you were lucky, you could feel its warmth – and I was lucky. Stan Laurel was one of these. Very raw material was Stan – very raw indeed. I paid him thirty-five shillings a week, and often wondered why; and then I'd remind myself that I'd seen a glimmer, once or twice, and where there's a spark there can be a blaze. If you were to ask me the most essential quality in the making of a star ... I'd give you two. First, he must have an instinct for the dividing line between comedy and parody ... once he overdoes the comedy, he's lost. And he must be memorable ... he's got to come with you out of the theatre or cinema, his face must get between you and your work, his gags and his tricks of voice and gestures make you smile to yourself every now and then, set you humming or whistling snatches of his songs, repeating bits of patter to your friends. He's got to mean something in your life, so that you want to see him again ... he has got to make the same people laugh over and over again – and louder each time ... We producers can back our fancy – but the box-office is the sole judge of a winner.[47]

Karno was a circus acrobat who became the most significant exponent of sketch comedy and physical slapstick the stage has ever seen. Over the course of his half-century-long career he reinvented himself as a prolific producer of farce, musical comedy and revue. He employed well over 2000 performers over the years, and many that came through his school went on to become the best in the business. Some made their names on the halls: Fred Kitchen, Charlie Baldwin, Walter Groves, Harry Roxbury, George Hestor, Harry Weldon. The next generation kept variety alive and dominated British film long after Karno was forgotten: Will Hay, Robb Wilton, Sandy Powell, Frank Randle, Syd Walker, Billy Bennett, Max Miller and the Crazy Gang. Most significantly of all, Karno comics were the beating heart of early Hollywood film comedy: Syd Chaplin, Billy Reeves, Albert Austin, Jimmy Aubrey, Charley Rogers, Billy Armstrong, Billie Ritchie, Eric Campbell and most of all Stan Laurel and Charles Spencer Chaplin. The impact and subsequent influence of these comedians is hard to overstate – there can be no doubt that Karno DNA continues to course through the veins of comedians today.

36. FINALE

In a 1957 interview Stan Laurel was asked whether his Karno colleagues learnt anything from Chaplin, or vice versa. He replied that everything came not from Chaplin but from Karno, that they had all been graduates of the school of 'Karnoisms'.[48] He remembered Karno fondly: 'He had no equal. His name was box-office. He was a great boss, kindly and considerate – and I hate to remember how he turned out eventually. He made a lot of money, and he deserved it … Karsino … eventually ruined him … It was a real tragedy. But when I knew him … he was on top of the world.'[49]

Chaplin, Laurel and some of the others were young men with little or no experience when they came under Karno's wing, but even comics who had already known success credited him with helping to develop their style. Not all of them liked him, some felt the sharp end of his tongue, but all respected him and recognised his genius.

If Karno wished to be remembered, I think it would not be as the greatest comedy impresario of his time, or even as the discoverer and mentor of the world's greatest comics, but as a great comedian himself – a spreader of fun, laughter and surreal mischief. When the BBC aired *Review*, the 1971 documentary about Karno, *The Daily Mirror* said: 'The BBC pays a special tribute tonight to a man acknowledged to be one of the funniest comedians of his day – Fred Karno … it is a most fantastic story even by show-business standards.'[50] I couldn't agree more, and it's about time his remarkable story was once again revealed to a new generation. I hope you've found it interesting and entertaining but if not, as Karno used to say: "Never mind – might go better second house."

37.

Encore

"He's got plenty of go, hasn't he?"
"Yes — he's gone."
(Fred Karno personal joke archive, 15 August 1932)

AFTER KARNO'S death his family found themselves battling to protect his legacy and reputation, while being consistently sidelined by those purporting to have an interest in his story.

On 3 March 1942, the BBC Home Service broadcast a programme entitled *Good Old Timers – Fred Karno*, with contributions from Mark Daly, Syd Walker, Dick Francis and Dolly Elliott (who was Karno's secretary for eleven years). They told his life story and shared anecdotes about their time with the Guv'nor. The Karno family were not invited to participate. Marie wrote to Leslie to express her dismay. She particularly hated Daly's portrayal of Karno as a Cockney, rather than what she described as his 'quiet muttering kind of voice with a hint of a Devonshire accent.'[1] Naomi Jacob had similar feelings: 'I hated and loathed the whole broadcast.'[2] It was the first of many similar experiences, always resulting in a flurry of angry letters from the family to the offender.

Marie died just three years after Karno, aged sixty-three.[3] Her estate was valued at a very substantial £4485,[4] presumably the residual value of her inheritance. Mrs Watkinson recalled that after Marie's death the family descended on the flat and stripped the place "like locusts",[5] but quite who this was is a mystery. Neither Leslie nor Fred Jr. received anything from Marie's estate.

Karno's sons had a love-hate relationship. They spent the next twenty years trying to make something of their father's legacy but there was more squabbling

37. ENCORE

than collaborating, so it did neither of them any real good and both scraped along in poverty. Perhaps tension between the brothers was inevitable: they were relative strangers who grew up apart and with a twelve-year age gap between them. On the face of it they were very different: Fred Jr. was a feisty comic with his father's temperament and an unreliable nature; Leslie described his older brother as a loose cannon, as did Junior's friend Stan Laurel. He was nonetheless a solid comic, who could hold his own among the Karno plonks. Leslie was a debonair light comedian and a well-organised and reliable manager, but never quite good enough for the old man.

Of the two, Fred Jr. had the greater opportunities: playing with Karno when he was at the height of his fame, going to America with Chaplin and Laurel, and making films with Hal Roach. Yet he lacked either the talent, the drive or the temperament to make the most of them. Leslie's chances were more limited: he had to try to forge a career in the lean years after the First World War. Leslie enjoyed telling stories about his brother, the black sheep of the family, recalling that at times when he was out of work, Fred Jr. would harass his father in the street, shouting to the world that Marie was not really Mrs Karno. There was even a tale that he once set up a barrel organ outside the Fun Factory, complete with monkey, and hung a sign around his neck that simply read 'Fred Karno's Son'. These stunts continued until Karno found him a position in one of his companies. How much truth these stories bear we'll never know, but we must take them with a pinch of salt. The listings show that Fred was rarely out of work with Karno, from when he was a teenager up to the First World War and again on his return. Perhaps he occasionally did something to upset the apple cart and was kicked out, only to be readmitted once he'd learnt his lesson.

In a letter to a friend in 1957, Stan Laurel wrote: 'Am not surprised to hear re Fred Karno Jr. being in trouble – he always has been! Through all the years I've known him, he sure threw away some wonderful opportunities … If he had behaved himself, he would have acquired all those shows, but he was too fond of the four-ale bar dept.'[6]

37.1 Fred Karno Jr. (right) – front cloth comic, circa 1950 (courtesy Ken Westcott).

523

There were, however, many similarities between the two sons. Leslie's daily routine also revolved around the opening hours of the local pub, and although both boys had attended private school, it was mild-mannered Leslie who supposedly got expelled.

Fred Jr.'s stage career continued to be patchy at best. Two years after his father's death, he re-staged *Mumming Birds* and *The Stage* reported that it remained very popular. The following year it appeared at Collins' Music Hall in Islington Green, where it was billed as 'The show that made Charlie Chaplin and Laurel and Hardy.'[7] Two years later Fred and some fellow old-boys (including Arthur Dandoe) toured a show he called *Fred Karno's Flashbacks*, featuring selections from classic Karno sketches. However, there is one final myth to correct: Junior did not appear in Chaplin's *Monsieur Verdoux* (1947). This common misconception came about because Chaplin named a very minor character 'Mr Karno' as a nod to his former Guv'nor, but Fred Jr. does not play the part. The actor in question is uncredited and to date unidentified, but my money is on it being the Chaplin veteran Leo White.

Leslie worked at the OXO factory before rediscovering his theatrical abilities and joining ENSA during the Second World War. He travelled widely entertaining the troops, and became an area manager for his unit. His daughter Pat, meanwhile, worked at Bletchley Park helping to crack the Enigma code, while keeping the family legacy alive organising concert parties. Leslie was discharged in December 1945, but took a position as a cinema manager for the Navy Army and Air Force Institute in Italy. With his wife Louisa he also found work from time to time as an extra in British films, supposedly appearing in crowd scenes in, amongst others, *The 39 Steps* (1935) and *The Silk Noose* (1948). Cast in a biblical epic Leslie found himself half-naked and strung up on a cross – when the crew broke for lunch they forgot he was there. When they eventually got him down he collapsed, subsequently contracting pneumonia. He had a long spell in hospital and had to have half a lung removed. A press report in June 1948 confirms that with Leslie unable to work, his family had fallen on very hard times indeed: 'When Fred Karno died, he left to his son ... only £42 and the legal control of his scripts ... Leslie Karno has had a rough time in recent years. Forced to give up acting for a while because of ill health, he was at one time sleeping in the crypt of St. Martin-in-the-Fields.'[8]

Fred Jr. had found himself in similar circumstances, although quite when is unclear: another article from around the same time describes how he too had lived among the vagrants on the Embankment. He recalled once being a guest at a show in honour of his father, and being given a lift 'home' by Herbert Morrison MP. Morrison thought Fred was joking when he said home was the shelter at St Martin-in-the-Fields. The article noted that he was not working, and had been ill for some time following a fever he caught while playing the rear end of a pantomime cow.

In a letter to his son Kenneth in February 1948, Fred Jr. confirmed how bad things were for him, and although Queenie was by then in a bigamous marriage with Curly Morrissey, he told his son he would always love her and the two boys he hadn't seen since 1924. He never got to see them again. By April 1948 he was back in *Mumming Birds* as part of a variety show called *Palace of Varieties,* and the press reported that he'd written to try to persuade Chaplin to make a film of Karno's life story. He said: 'It was my father's last wish that Chaplin should have the chance to make the film.'[9]

The Karno plonks made their fortunes on the ability to tumble down staircases, out of theatre boxes and into trapdoors. But despite this training, Fred's career came to an abrupt halt on Halloween night 1948 when he fell down the stairs at Margate's Theatre Royal and fractured his thigh. He always said he had been pushed by the theatre ghost. His injury was serious enough to keep him in hospital for nearly a year. While recuperating at his digs in Cliftonville, he fell in love with his landlady, Olive Bridge. It was two years before he was fit enough to perform again, announcing his potential comeback in *The Stage* in 1950, but his performing days were largely behind him. Smitten with Olive, he had to deal with the small obstacle of still being married to Queenie, so got back in contact with his family in America. When they were finally divorced in April 1952, the judge cited desertion by Queenie. Eighteen months later Fred and Olive were married,[10] and with a new wife and two young stepchildren, he settled into the only stable family environment he had ever known.

Queenie died in 1994 at the age of ninety-four, the matriarch of a large family of children, grandchildren and great-grandchildren. Her sons both worked in the business: Kenneth was a props master with Hal Roach and subsequently for Lucille Ball's production company Desilu, while Fred Westcott III (who was always known as Sonny) became a musician playing double bass around Hollywood.[11]

In June 1950 Con West wrote a radio series for the BBC called *The Fred Karno Story* – this is how one newspaper listed it: 'The life-story of Fred Karno, the great showman who climbed to the pinnacle of success in his profession and then, in the words of his friend and biographer, Con West, "came spinning down the hill with his human brakes out of control and crashed at the bottom."'[12] West recommended Leslie to the producers and he played his father in the show. His cousin Freddie Westcott also had a small part, and Robb Wilton played himself. Fred Jr. was overlooked, much to his annoyance. Following on from that series, Leslie was reported to be involved in making a film version of his father's life, but this never materialised. After the radio show he hoped for further engagements, but his archive is full of polite 'don't call us, we'll call you' letters.

In 1951 West staged his revue *Fred Karno's Army*, a collection of sketches and songs loosely based around a First World War storyline. It appears to have borrowed nothing from Karno other than the name of the lead character – Perkins. It was extremely successful and ran for three years, which upset the Karno brothers. Junior wrote to *The Stage* to advise that the show was nothing to do with him. West wanted Leslie to have a part in the revue but producer Percy Manchester refused, prompting more angry correspondence. Manchester wrote to Leslie: 'I am not trying to avoid you! … If you had asked me when the Karno show was coming out again I would have told you … I note your brother is on the warpath – has he ever been off it, I wonder?'[13] It caused a bitter falling-out between them all, and Con West placed a notice in the press stating that Karno had given him the rights to use the title.[14] A sequel set in the Second World War appeared in 1954 – *Sons of Karno's Army* starring Albert Burdon, but whether West was involved is unclear.

Shared resentment at their father's name being used by others was the catalyst to finally bring the brothers together, and in March 1952 they attempted to re-stage *Mumming Birds* yet again. It was one of the few times Fred and Leslie got together professionally or socially. While they agreed to share the spoils, they recognised that they were unable to work in tandem. A legal document in the archive shows that they were co-producers in name only: 'There will be no interference by the aforementioned Frederick Arthur Westcott in any entertainment productions whatsoever and all will be under the sole personal authority of Leslie Karno.'[15] Leslie placed press advertisements seeking investors, but to no avail and the plan was scrapped. The curtain had finally come down on the longest-running music hall show in history. Leslie's final professional engagement was playing to seaside day trippers in a black-faced minstrel troupe. His performing career was over at fifty-one – he went on to scrape a living valeting cars.

37. ENCORE

Fred Jr. attempted to establish a double act on the cabaret circuit, but he rarely trod the boards again. He never left Margate, spending his final years as the proprietor of a 'guess your weight' booth at Dreamland amusement park. It may seem a sad end for a war veteran who'd stood shoulder to shoulder with Stan Laurel and Charlie Chaplin, but the last ten years of his life were perhaps the most contented: he had a happy marriage, two stepchildren he adored, and daily fun at the fairground entertaining punters with his gags and stories. When he died on 3 February 1961, the local newspaper described him as 'Dreamland's greatest personality'.[16]

By then music hall had vanished. Variety fought off the challenge of cinema and radio for a while, limping on thanks to a handful of big-name stars who still had real drawing power: Gracie Fields, Max Miller, Will Hay and the Crazy Gang – three out of four were Karno alumni. But the writing was on the wall. Denis Norden wrote: 'Variety was an inter-war phenomenon ... After the war, it died of television, nude shows and the indifference of the young.'[17]

Karno's old-boys crossed paths regularly in the 1940s and '50s, before time took its inevitable toll on them too. Billy Reeves died aged 79 in December 1943; his brother Alf, tireless manager to Chaplin until the end, followed in April 1946. Fred Kitchen passed away aged 77 in 1951. By then, their names meant nothing to the post-war generation. Jack Hylton became a theatre impresario, and in 1946 staged a Con West revue called *For Crying Out Loud*, which starred Nervo and Knox and Will Hay. It was Hay's last engagement before being debilitated by a stroke – he died aged 60 in 1949. Hylton was responsible for reforming the Crazy Gang after the Second World War: they starred in a series of revues at the Victoria Palace Theatre, and became a fixture of Royal Variety Performances before finally retiring in May 1962.

In 1958 the man Karno blamed for the demise of his cherished school of comedians gave a rare interview. Mack Sennett was by then all but forgotten, and the parallels with Karno's demise are striking: 'Mack Sennett, one-time king of the movies ... lives today in a small apartment overlooking a gasoline station ... in near poverty ... "Someday they're going to make a picture of my life ... It will be a story about comedy and laughs. I always trusted myself on picking talent."'[18] He died two years later.

Laurel and Hardy continued to make films until 1951, as well as performing a sketch routine on the variety stage. Their final tour of Britain in 1954 was cut short by Hardy's ill health.[19] Stan hung up his black derby when Babe died in 1957. He spent his retirement answering thousands of letters from friends and fans, before following his partner in February 1965.[20] Syd Chaplin died in Nice two months later. His younger brother, branded a communist by Joseph McCarthy, left America to see out his days in exile in Switzerland. Charlie Chaplin's last film, *A Countess from Hong Kong*, was released in 1967. He was welcomed back to Hollywood like royalty when awarded an honorary Oscar in 1972, and welcomed *by* royalty when he received a knighthood in 1975. The Little Fellow had come a very long way indeed. He died on Christmas Day 1977.

And what of the ill-fated Karsino? It went from one doomed owner to the next. In June 1928 Herbert Cyril took on a forty-two-year lease and christened the place the Thames Riviera. Cyril built indoor tennis courts and a skating rink, but lost more money in the first ten weeks than Karno had in ten years. The receivers were called in by late August, but kept it running. In April 1929 they offloaded it to A.E. Bundy, head of British Instructional Films. Karno must have known Bundy, since in a letter to Syd Chaplin he says he stayed at Karsino that summer. Perhaps he was engaged in a consultancy role in those first few months – if so, it didn't help. Bundy spent the next three years trying to sell it. *The Daily Herald* eventually reported: 'The Thames Riviera on Tagg's Island near Hampton Court ... is to be abandoned at the end of this month by Mr A.E. Bundy ... who has lost £33,000 on the venture.'[21]

Five months later it reopened as 'Tagg's Island Casino' under the ownership of Charles Clore. Clore was just starting out on a career that would make him a world-famous property magnate and philanthropist. Even he couldn't make a go of the place, and the receivers were called in again. Finally, a company called Tagg's Island Properties Ltd managed to shake off the gypsy's curse, running it as a going concern until the Second World War. In 1940 William Hurlock of AC Cars bought the lease (and later the freehold) of the island and it was given over to war work. The Ministry of Supply installed a bridge and 5000 people made munitions inside what had once been the skating rink. After the war AC Cars produced invalid carriages on the island while 'The Casino' was refurbished and reopened. It was the venue for the first post-war Water Rats' outing – no doubt the memory of its Karno heyday remained fresh in the minds of many.

The hotel remained a challenge for subsequent owners, before being closed for good in 1970 and falling into dereliction. The tattered palm court was used as a location for Stanley Kubrick's 1971 cult classic *A Clockwork Orange*. The Billy Boys fight takes place inside, with nine actors performing acrobatic tumbles, falls

37. ENCORE

and tricks that Karno would have been proud of – although in Karno's routines no-one was brutally beaten to death at the end.

In February 1971, an American called Leon Bronesky was granted planning permission to replace Karsino with a 244-bedroom leisure complex. After taking possession of the island, he swiftly imported some 'gypsies' to exorcise the curse.[22] On the day of demolition a dinner was held in the palm court, attended by well-known comedians of the day and Karno veterans like Sandy Powell, Jimmy Russell and Jack Melville. The occasion was filmed for the BBC documentary *Review*.[23] After dinner, Melville raised a glass to Karno: 'God bless Fred Karno! The man who put more laughter into the world in his day than anybody else.' Then they broke up the stage and took pieces home for souvenirs. As he watched the bulldozers move in, Melville shared his thoughts: 'I'm sure his old spirit is lurking around here somewhere. I bet he's looking on and thinking, there's old Fred Karno's Army. Poor old Fred, I feel sorry for him really because he was so big in his day.'[24] The camera cut to Sandy Powell walking over the bridge into the sunset, then Karsino was seen in soft focus as a pile of smouldering rubble – the literal ashes of Karno's hopes and dreams. Having razed the place, Leon Bronesky disappeared and his new hotel never materialised – probably for the best.

Remarkably the BBC did not invite Leslie to take part in the documentary or attend that final dinner – the first he knew of it was when it popped up on his TV screen. He was understandably hurt and angry at this extraordinary oversight, and wrote to the BBC to express his dismay and refute the film's claims of Karno's womanizing: 'Great pity the research dept. did not … reach me … I lived for many years on the island and the houseboat you mention, though I do not recall any of my father's many leading ladies making use of the marble bath. Still a laugh's a laugh no matter how one gets it.'[25]

Tagg's island is now a very somnolent place. Little remains of either the hotel or the land it occupied – the centre of the island has been dredged to create a sleepy lagoon, full of houseboats. There is something ethereal about it, a doughnut-shaped island with just a gravel track overhung with a canopy of trees – it is quiet, private and slightly foreboding. The last vestige of the once-great hotel is a flight of overgrown steps leading to the water's edge, where the cream of London society and entertainment's greatest names once stepped ashore. If you listen carefully you might still hear convalescing troops singing 'Fred Karno's Army', the echoes of laughter and the clinking of champagne glasses.

37.2 All that remains of Karsino, Tagg's Island (author's photograph).

37.3 The Fun Factory today (author's photograph).

I am glad to say that two great relics of Karno's empire survive. His Fun Factory still stands much as it did a century ago, although its address is now 38-42 Southwell Road. Part of the Factory has been restored as a private house, while the rest is a collection of artists' workshops known as the Clockwork Studios. In 2012 I was lucky enough to be involved in helping the Music Hall Guild of Great Britain and America place a blue plaque on the building to record its role in Karno's story.

An even more spectacular survivor is Karno's palatial houseboat Astoria, beautifully preserved almost as he left her by its current owner David Gilmour, of the rock band Pink Floyd. Gilmour bought it in 1986 and uses one of the two sitting rooms as a recording studio.[26] She retains every ounce of the grandeur Karno and Day designed into her, and has been fortunate to find subsequent owners who lovingly maintained her.[27]

In Autumn 1971, six months after Karsino's demolition, J.P. Gallagher's biography *Master of Mirth and Tears* was published. Prior to this Karno had been universally spoken of as a genius, a legend to whom the world of comedy owed a debt.

37.4 Astoria – as beautiful as the day she was built (author's photograph).

37. ENCORE

He was exalted as deserving his place in the history of music hall, theatre and film, and I have yet to come across a single negative article or report about him professionally or personally – then Gallagher published his book. Karno's reputation was destroyed overnight as the press seized on his salacious stories. One report said: 'He was one of the greatest showmen this country has ever known. He was also a thoroughly unpleasant little man, brutal, sadistic, lecherous, perverted, vindictive and mean, as J.P. Gallagher makes clear.'[28]

That depiction of Karno has been compounded by every subsequent biographer of Chaplin and Laurel. Some have even projected this narrative onto his earlier career, suggesting that 'revelations' about his depravity were a factor in his downfall and bankruptcy in 1927 – despite there being no evidence of this nor any negative publicity about him until 1971. We now know that many (if not all) of Gallagher's stories were fiction, exaggeration or errors of memory. As I noted at the start of this book, Leslie was devastated by the biographer's portrayal of his father and spent the last ten years of his life trying to clear Karno's name. Appeals to the publishers fell on deaf ears and he could not afford to take legal action – besides, the damage was done. Karno was condemned to infamy. Leslie kept fighting for his family's reputation until the day he died, aged eighty, in 1983.

The Guv'nor wasn't quite done yet, however. In May 1984 Tony Staveacre, the producer of the 1971 documentary, staged a play based on Karno's life at the Bristol Theatre Royal – also called *Fred Karno's Army*. Later that year the BBC were reported to be filming a series entitled *The Fred Karno Story*, but this never appeared. Then in 2010 this author took up the mantle, writing and producing a Karno musical, *Khaotic!*

Sixty years earlier, when his life story was broadcast on radio, one newspaper had written:

> The BBC had better be on their toes ... when the red light is seen in the studios, I am sure an imp will ... muddle the script sheets, cross the wires, and unscrew the microphones. For Fred Karno, alive, could never abide pompous solemnity. His fun was crazy, gimcrack, absurd. The temptation I feel, for his ghost to leave the immortals and take a hand in the production will be strong.[29]

They may have been on to something, for when we staged *Khaotic!* we suffered a series of mishaps, including our lead comic being rushed to hospital with a suspected heart attack (fortunately a false alarm) – we all felt Karno was looking down on us giggling.

Through that project I was fortunate to meet fellow researchers and biographers, as well as Karno family members and relatives of many of his comics – this biography is the result. It has taken ten years to write. I have looked at every newspaper reference for Karno I could find (well over 40,000 entries); I have trawled archives in London, Los Angeles and Paris; I have read well over a hundred biographies, autobiographies and scholarly works by other researchers in the field; I have received contributions from as far afield as New Zealand and Brazil; I have spent hours with Karno's family in Britain and America, delving into letters, newspaper articles, contracts and all manner of ephemera. And while I will have made my own mistakes, I can say with certainty that Gallagher did Karno a great disservice.

37.5 The author with Karno's grandsons, Kenneth (left) and Fred (right), Palm Springs, 2010 (author's photograph).

He was not a saint, but in the context of a life which arced all the way from the seedy music halls of Jack the Ripper's London through scandal-ridden 1930s Hollywood and into the Second World War, Karno's infidelities seem no more dramatic than his contemporaries – most had chequered private lives. Syd Chaplin's career was ended by a violent sex scandal; Stan Laurel and Babe Hardy struggled through numerous bitter divorces; and Charlie Chaplin saw three marriages end that way, including one to sixteen-year-old Lita Grey, who accused him of abnormal sexual deviancy and abuse. The allegations against these comic geniuses are arguably more serious than any against Karno, but their work is so beloved that few fans worry about their character failings. The lurid stories are taken with a healthy pinch of salt and a tacit acceptance that these men were products of their time – Karno has not been served so charitably. I hope this biography will help him step back into the light and resume his rightful place among comic pioneers, as perhaps the single greatest influence on comedy of the last one hundred and fifty years.

Is there a future for Karnoisms? Slapstick? Physical comedy? The power of the visual over the verbal? Well, styles certainly come and go. In May 1930, *The*

37. ENCORE

People bemoaned the fact that the talkies were lacking good comedians: 'The real trouble is that the nurseries of nonsense are empty, the cradles of comedy stilled ... Fred Karno shows ... were the real nurseries of nonsense. They attracted and bred comedy in its most hilarious form.'[30] In 1936, *The Era* similarly lamented the dying art of stand-up: 'Where are the coming single-act comedians? ... practically every one is a double male team ... it is very difficult for newcomers ... There is no Fred Karno to train comedians.'[31]

The saviour of the solo comedian turned out to be the northern working men's clubs, which filled the void left by the disappearance of variety theatres. These clubs were (and still are) more akin to the earliest music halls than the theatre. Singers, comics and variety acts entertain an audience coming and going as they please, eating and drinking at tables, and with a bar in the same room. My grandfather George Garbett was the entertainments manager at a large club in Birmingham, and I fell in love with live performance there long before I ever stepped into a theatre.

Through the second half of the twentieth century comedy developed in multiple directions, with each decade bringing new fashions. There were radio comics (solo artistes and troupes), anarchic comics, 'alternative' comics, sketch teams and double acts – all were popular, albeit perhaps with different audiences or in different media. Today solo stand-ups are the prevalent force, prompting the legendary comedy writer Barry Cryer to pen an article lamenting the disappearance of the double act.[32] The market, he said, is saturated with solo comics doing observational comedy – pure gags are considered old hat.

Fashions change.

Today's comedy might seem a million miles away from Karno, until you consider the slapstick comedians of the last thirty years. There is plenty of Karno in *Mr Bean*, *The Young Ones*, *Vic and Bob* and their successors, and budding students in the art of physical comedy and performance can still find Fun Factories if they know where to look.[33] So perhaps Karno's mantra will endure: "If in doubt fall on your arse" – I hope so.

Endnotes

1. Preface
1   John McCabe, *Charlie Chaplin*, (Robson Books, London, 1978) p.27.
2   api.parliament.uk/historic-hansard/commons/2002/mar/25/railtrack.
3   api.parliament.uk/historic-hansard/lords/2005/mar/01/prevention-of-terrorism-bill-1.
4   Charles Chaplin, *My Autobiography* (Penguin Modern Classic version, 2003) p.98.
5   Andrew Horrall, *Popular Culture, London 1890-1918 – the transformation of entertainment* (Manchester University Press, 2011) p.42.
6   Adeler is credited with being one of the first performers to utilise the character of the Pierrot to supplant the black-faced minstrel acts at the end of the nineteenth century (Martin Banham, *The Cambridge Guide to Theatre* [Cambridge University Press 1998] p.857) and ran various 'Adeler and Sutton's Pierrots' seaside troupes well into the twentieth century.
7   Letters to Con West from Fred Karno, 6 October 1934 & 14 November 1937 (courtesy of David Robinson).
8   Paul Bailey, *Three Queer Lives* (Penguin, 2001) p.183.
9   J.P. Gallagher, *Fred Karno, Master of Mirth and Tears* (Robert Hale, London, 1971) Author's Preface.
10   Ibid.
11   *The Stage*, 5 July 1962, p.4.
12   Letter to Robert Hale & Co. from Leslie Karno, undated, Leslie Karno archive.
13   J.P. Gallagher, 'Fun, Sex and Ruin with Fred Karno', *Mayfair*, Volume 11 No 1 (January 1976) p.36.
14   Ray Seaton & Roy Martin, *Good Morning Boys – Will Hay, Master of Comedy* (Barrie and Jenkins, London, 1978) p.32.

2. Running Away with the Circus
1   Naomi Jacob, *Me Again* (Hutchinson and Co. London, 1939) p.12.
2   Fred Karno's birth certificate records his father as a cabinet maker, whereas the 1881 and 1891 censuses lists him as a French polisher.
3   Careys Place was between 38 & 40 Coalpit Lane (1871 and 1881 censuses).
4   Adeler and West, p.23. Since this must have been between 1871 and 1875, their stay in Birmingham was brief.
5   This was the main Nottingham gaol at that time, in St John's Street, a stone's throw from his house. The prison was demolished in 1925, and is now the site of a nightclub called Pryzm.
6   Adeler and West, p.30. The Alhambra had previously been the original Nottingham Theatre Royal built in 1760, it was renamed in 1865.
7   In Karno's memoirs and all reviews Olvene is spelt this way but Gallagher spelt it Alvene; the error is perhaps due to the misspelling in an article in *Pearson's Weekly* (25 June 1908, p.2).
8   1881 census. There are other Thomas Hillerys in the census but none of them have a child of the right age called Charles W.
9   Con West was certainly in touch with Olvene's family as late as 1950 (Letter to Leslie Karno from Con West, 10 July 1950, Leslie Karno archive).
10   The Crown and Cushion was the oldest music hall in Nottingham and had many names during its lifetime including, Star Palace, Walker's Varieties, Metheringham's Varieties, Varney's Varieties, and Coleno's Varieties (John Beckett & Ken Brand, *Nottingham an illustrated history* [Manchester University Press, 1997] p.69).
11   Originally British circuses were housed in permanent buildings (often wooden structures) many as grand as any theatre, but in America touring circus had developed with the innovation of the 'big-top' in 1825. The idea of travelling from town to town took off in Britain only after a big-top was imported from America in 1836 but many retained bases to overwinter.
12   *Cardiff Times*, 12 November 1870, p.4.
13   Adeler and West, p.35.
14   Ibid. p.36. Charles Dickens wrote of a trip to Astley's in *Sketches by Boz* (Penguin Classics Edition,

Penguin London, 1995 [first published 1839]) p.132.

15   Online article, 'Looking Back: Thrills and Spills at the old wooden circus theatre', 12 August 2010. walesonline.co.uk/lifestyle/showbiz/looking-back-thrills-spills-old-1902701.

16   Adeler and West, p.20. John McCabe states that Karno was the first to use an actual custard pie routine in the music hall in 1897, followed a year later by the first U.S. appearance of a similar routine in *The Corn Curers* in New York, but does not note a source for this theory (McCabe, *Charlie Chaplin*, p.57).

17   *Woolwich Gazette*, 27 November 1908, p.4.

3. The Long Road to London

1   A few years later Karno placed an advert in *The Era* seeking 'James Alexander, gymnast, late of Proctor's circus,' hence my assumption that Proctor's was his new employer.

2   *The Stage*, 28 March 1884, p.6.

3   Adeler and West, p.44. The same edition of *The Stage* which lists Leonaro, confirms Travers announced a big company under the patronage of Archer for the following week.

4   Bud Flanagan, *My Crazy Life* (Frederick Muller Ltd, London, 1961) p.98.

5   Simon Louvish, *Chaplin The Tramp's Odyssey* (Faber and Faber, London, 2009) p.29.

6   In press articles (e.g. *Pearson's Weekly*, 25 June 1908, p.2) Karno claimed to have performed with Fred Ginnett and Lord George Sanger's circuses, but there is no contemporary record of this, and he does not mention it in his memoirs.

7   *The Era*, 3 October 1885, p.22. Presumably Platoff Row, Gedling Street.

8   Ibid., 10 July 1886, p.20.

9   Ibid., 24 July 1886, p.17.

10   Ibid., 11 July 1885, p.16.

11   No hall seems to have existed with the name MacDonald's Music Hall, so this was almost certainly the Royal Music Hall, in Dunlop Street, run by the great Scottish comedian J.C. MacDonald.

12   The Scotia was where the Aubreys had been when they asked Karno to contact them to arrange an audition which may explain Karno's confusion.

13   Fred Kitchen, *Meredith We're In, the life story of Fred Kitchen told by himself* (Frederick Simon Kitchen Dunn, 2012) p.141.

14   *The Era*, 20 November 1886, p.20.

15   Ibid., 30 April 1887, p.17.

16   Ibid., 25 June 1887, p.23.

17   Midge Gillies, *Marie Lloyd – The One and Only* (Orion, 2001) p.23 and Hansard records online – api.parliament.uk/historic-hansard/lords/1888/jun/11/observations.

18   Daniel Farson, *Marie Lloyd & Music Hall* (Tom Stacey Publishing, 1972) p.29.

19   *The Era*, 1 March 1902, p.21.

4. The Three Karnos

1   The junction of Stamford Street and York Road is ironically now the site of London's BFI Imax cinema with the largest cinema screen in Britain, the address is 1 Charlie Chaplin Walk.

2   1901 UK Census.

3   De Frece was a veteran agent and music hall manager. The De Frece family were well-known in the industry for many years. Maurice married music hall actress Peggy Pryde. His nephew, Walter married Vesta Tilley.

4   Adeler and West, p.53.

5   Ibid., p.56.

6   Ibid., p.55. Their contract was extended until the 16 June 1888.

7   *The Era*, 20 February 1886, p.23.

8   *Nottingham Evening Post*, 22 February 1888, p.1. A diorama was a popular music hall exhibit, where a huge vertical scroll with painted scenes was gradually unwound to present panoramic views.

9   *Motherwell Times*, 25 August 1888, p.2.

10   *The Era*, 16 October 1886, p.23.

11   Eugene Stratton married the daughter of George 'Pony' Moore.

12   *Floradora* was a huge hit, running for over 450 performances in London and even more in New York.

13   *Morning Post*, 17 December 1888, p.1.

14   *The Graphic*, 22 December 1888, p.5.

15   Trav S.D. (Donald Travis Stewart), *No Applause – Just Throw Money – The book that made vaudeville famous* (Farrar, Strauss & Giroux, New York, 2006) p.37.

16   Moore and Burgess Minstrels, *Jokelets* (Saxon & Co, London, 1898) p.45.

17   *The Graphic*, 29 December 1888, p.9.

18   *The Era*, 22 December 1888, p.15.

19 John M. East, 'Karno's Folly, or How to Lose a Show-Business fortune', *Theatre Quarterly*, No. 1 (July-September 1971) p.60.
20 *The Era*, 25 June 1887, p.23.
21 The street remains but renumbering makes it difficult to be certain which was the original number three. Research by the late David Broadhurst suggests that Edith's home is now number 271 Green Lane (David Broadhurst, 'Fred Karno at Green Lane', *Stockport Heritage Magazine*, Volume 5 No. 8 [Winter 03/04] p.36 and Carolyn Broadhurst interview with the author).
22 Children could leave school at age ten (although education was provided until 13). The age of sexual consent in Britain was 13 until 1885 when it was raised to 16, so it was not unusual for a girl of Edith's age to leave home and marry.
23 *London and Provincial Entr'acte*, 3 September 1887, p.3.
24 *The Era*, 28 April 1888, p.22.
25 The Aubreys played two venues, the Metropolitan and the Middlesex, every night for three weeks.
26 Naomi Jacob, *Me – A Chronicle About Other People*, (Hutchinson, London, 1933) p.79.
27 Flanagan, p.7.
28 *The Era*, 27 July 1889, p.15.
29 Rowland G.M. Baker & Gwendoline F. Baker, *Thameside Molesey – A towpath ramble from Hampton Court to Hampton Reach* (Barracuda Books Ltd, Buckingham, 1989) p.38.
30 Jerome K. Jerome, *Three Men in a Boat* (Penguin Books, 2004 edition) p.50.

5. How About a Sketch?
1 *Glasgow Herald*, 4 June 1888, p.10.
2 *The Era*, 2 March 1889, p.12.
3 'Leg-mania' may be hard to imagine these days. Tony Staveacre points out that the basis of physical comedy is in the legs (Tony Staveacre, *Slapstick, the Illustrated Story of Knockabout Comedy* [Angus & Robertson, London, 1987] p.64). From the leaping Georgian Harlequin, through Little Tich, Chaplin, Groucho Marx, Max Wall right through to Python's Ministry of Silly Walks, many a physical visual comic has relied on the intrinsic comedy of bandy legs and big feet.
4 I am assuming that Edith was with them on the tour, she certainly had the same break in her listings.
5 Adeler and West, p.67.
6 Jem and Pooley Mace were actually cousins.
7 There are no other dates when these three acts convened on the Amphitheatre around the same time, and a year later (Christmas Day 1890) the Amphitheatre burnt to the ground.
8 *The Era*, 22 March 1890, p.22.
9 Ibid., 5 April 1890, p.22.
10 Karno noted the boxing ball routine only as an encore to *Hilarity*.
11 *The Stage*, 7 May 1891, p.15.
12 *The Era*, 16 August 1890, p.7.
13 The 1891 census lists Karno as 'professional gymnast' in London but also shows Karno's parents living at 2 Olive Row, Nottingham where Karno is listed again as a 'plumber'. Perhaps the Westcotts were unsure how to complete the census and listed their children whether they were present or not.
14 *The Glasgow Evening Post*, 3 March 1891, p.7.
15 For instance, they appear at the Birmingham Gaiety for two weeks in June (*The Era*, 30 May 1891, p.15) then back up to Dundee, then Liverpool.
16 *The Era*, 27 June 1891, p.16.
17 *London Evening Standard*, 4 September 1891, p.1.
18 Adeler and West, p.71.
19 Ibid., p.72.
20 *The Era*, 26 September 1891, p.16.
21 David Robinson, *Chaplin His Life and Art* (Grafton, London, 1985) p.75
22 *Hull Daily Mail*, 21 November 1899, p.5.
23 *The Era*, 20 February 1897, p.20.
24 Ibid., 22 January 1898, p.18.
25 *Hartlepool Northern Daily Mail*, 29 November 1892, p.3.
26 *Music Hall and Theatre Review*, 23 September 1892, p.18.
27 Rick Klaie first appears in listings in 1885 with 'The Klaie Troupe of Laughter Makers'. 'Klaie and Karnes' appear in spring 1889; described variously as 'eccentric niggers', 'premier chair vaulters', and 'song and dance artists'. Some have therefore assumed that this is Rick Klaie and Fred Karno but this is not the case. The Three Karnos appear in different cities from Klaie and Karnes in the same weeks.

ENDNOTES

28 *The Era*, 31 December 1892, p.31.
29 Ibid., 25 February 1893, p.21.
30 Ibid., p.27.
31 Edward Moss and Richard Thornton owned a number of halls, later merging with Oswald Stoll's company to form the largest syndicate in the country, the mighty Moss Empires.
32 Adeler and West, p.72.
33 *The Era*, 20 May 1893, p.26. The notice gives Karno's address as 2 Wincott Street, Kennington Road, London.
34 Ibid., 25 March 1893, p.12. This birth notice is the only written evidence I've found which confirms that Edith and Winnie Warren were one and the same.
35 The Karno Trio were sometimes listed as Ted Karno's Company or The Karno Four. In broad terms any reference to the Three Karnos from 1887 to 1893 is likely to be Karno, Sewell and Tysall; thereafter Karno, Sewell and others (such as Rick Klaie). Any reference to 'the Karno Trio' from spring 1893 onwards is likely to refer to the Ted Tysall trio.

6. The Show Must Go On.
1 *London Evening Standard*, 8 August 1893, p.6.
2 *London and Provincial Entr'acte*, 12 August 1893, p.5.
3 *Brighton Gazette*, 5 October 1893, p.8.
4 *The Era*, 7 October 1893, p.12.
5 Ibid., 22 September 1894, p.12.
6 Ibid., 17 November 1894, p.17.
7 Ibid., 10 November 1894, p.22.
8 Ibid., 5 October 1895, p.12.
9 Incorrectly stating this as being in Naples rather than Dresden.
10 *Music Hall and Theatre Review*, 8 November 1895, p.10.
11 Andrew McConnell Stott, *The Pantomime Life of Joseph Grimaldi – laughter madness and the story of Britain's greatest comedian* (Canongate Books, 2009) p.14.
12 1814 saw the first principal boy, i.e. a woman playing a man (known as a 'breeches role') and in 1826 Thomas Dibden first staged a pantomime at Christmas rather than the traditional Easter.
13 McConnell Stott, p.321.
14 *The Era*, 1 February 1896, p.18.
15 Elaborate effects like this were not completely unknown in melodrama but were unusual in the music hall.
16 Simon Louvish, *Stan and Ollie – The Roots of Comedy* (Faber and Faber Ltd, London, 2001) p.54.
17 S. Theodore Felstead, *Stars Who Made the Halls* (T. Werner Laurie Ltd, London, 1946) p.123.
18 The phonograph, invented by Thomas Edison in 1877, had been marketed as an office dictating machine by J.H. Lippincott who had acquired the rights. It was 1894 before Edison re-secured the rights to his own invention and started to market it for general sale.
19 The national average annual wage at the time was around £65 so £15 sounds like a huge amount of money, but in 1891 the phonograph initially sold in America at $150 (the equivalent of £30) and prices were falling rapidly.
20 Adeler and West, p.61.
21 Karno wasn't the only one embellishing the truth. In 1897, in Ramsgate, a man called Steve Cook claimed to be presenting the phonograph for the first time outside of London (Kitchen, p.118).
22 *The Era*, 10 October 1896, p.21 & p.30.
23 The theatrical press carried advertisements for 'exhibition' phonographs for hire (interestingly charging £15 per annum) in spring 1895 (*The Era*, 11 May 1895, p.24).
24 This may have been when they both appeared at the Tivoli at Easter 1896 (*Music Hall and Theatre Review*, 10 April 1896, p.22).
25 Naomi Jacob, *Our Marie – A Biography* (Hutchinson & Co Ltd, London, 1936) p.84.
26 Whilst Karno had nothing to do with the phonograph, his name was attached to it for posterity: in the 1920s, three models of 'Decca Portable Gramophone' were advertised: 'the Minster', 'the Beltona' and, wait for it, 'the Karno' – coincidence? Probably, but perhaps someone in Decca's marketing department associated Karno's name with the instrument.
27 *The Era*, 5 December 1896, p.18.
28 *Daily Telegraph and Courier (London)*, 28 October 1896, p.1.
29 Attributed.
30 *Music Hall and Theatre Review*, 15 April 1897, p.9.
31 *Dundee Evening Telegraph*, 8 March 1932, p.10.
32 *The Era*, 24 April 1897, p.19.
33 The Chatham Palace of Varieties was run by another Barnard, Samuel, who is

credited with originating the 'twice nightly' performance, prompted by troops stationed in the town who had an early or a late pass (Harry Stanley, *Can You Hear Me Mother? Sandy Powell's Lifetime of Music Hall* [Jupiter Books, 1975] p.102.). Others claim to have originated the idea, including the De Frece family, but whatever its origins, a twice nightly show was the norm throughout the music hall industry.
34 *Music Hall and Theatre Review*, 20 March 1897, p.10.
35 *Sheffield Daily Telegraph*, 25 September 1897, p.3.
36 *The Era*, 9 October 1897, p.19.

7. The Showman
1 Online article: Percy G. Court, *Memories of Show Business* (1953). www.arthurlloyd.co.uk/MemoriesOfShowbusiness (courtesy of Matthew Lloyd).
2 *London Evening Standard*, 10 August 1897, p.6.
3 *The Era*, 9 January 1909, p.22.
4 Ibid., 22. January 1898, p.25.
5 *The Stage*, 12 December 1907, p.14.
6 Original music was provided by Hughes and Perry.
7 The phrase came from an 1877 book entitled *A Woman Hater* by Charles Reade, which made the case for female emancipation.
8 John Major, *My Old Man – A Personal History of Music Hall* (Harper Press, London, 2012) p.266.
9 *The Era*, 27 August 1898, p.18.
10 Online article, Bella Bathurst, *Bicycles: The chains that set women free, Daily Telegraph*, 31 March 2011. telegraph.co.uk/lifestyle/wellbeing/diet/8419028/Bicycles-The-chains-that-set-women-free.
11 *The Era*, 24 September 1898, p.18.
12 *Morning Post*, 31 May 1898, p.6.
13 *The Era*, 22 April 1899, p.27.
14 Ibid., 10 June 1899, p.16. Although advertised, I have found no listing for this first *Dossers* performance.
15 *The Stage*, 7 December 1899, p.27.
16 *The Era*, 30 December 1899, p.18. After *Her Majesty's Guests* was launched, *The Burglary* still occasionally appeared as a stand-alone sketch (with just six in the cast) at smaller venues.
17 Ibid., 6 January 1900, p.14.
18 Whittaker was married to the sister of Amy Minister (later Amy Reeves).
19 *The Era*, 14 April 1900, p.3.
20 *London Evening Standard*, 27 March 1900, p.3.
21 *The Era*, 31 March 1900, p.11.
22 *The Stage*, 29 March 1900, p.15.
23 Ibid., 5 July 1900, p.21.
24 *The Era*, 8 December 1900, p.7.
25 The lead part of Jack Tatters was initially played by Bernard Mervyn, but France stepped into the part when Karno moved Mervyn to replace Walter Groves in *Her Majesty's Guests*.
26 *The Era*, 1 December 1900, p.24.
27 *The Stage*, 25 October 1900, p.20.
28 Karno recorded the sequence of events wrongly in his memoirs. He thought that it was *Marked for Life* that inspired him to produce shows with dialogue and subsequently *Her Majesty's Guests*. It was actually the reverse.
29 Adeler and West, p.89.
30 Jerome, p.x.
31 *The Era*, 12 January 1901, p.22.

8. Slumming It
1 *The Stage*, 24 January 1901, p.10.
2 *Leamington Spa Courier*, 1 February 1901, p.4.
3 Herbert Westcott's death certificate gives the address as 18 Bath Row, Birmingham. *Jail Birds* had just played the Empire Palace.
4 Fred Jr. recalled that Edith may have lost as many as five children (Fred Karno Jr., *Fred Karno as I Knew Him* [handwritten memoir], Jo Sexton archive) but census records suggest five babies were born alive, three of which later died.
5 *The Showman*, 10 May 1901, p.18.
6 *The Era*, 14 September 1901, p.10.
7 Ibid., 14 December 1901, p.23.
8 Kitchen, p.144.
9 Karno incorrectly recalled this as being eight weeks.
10 *The Era*, 14 June 1902, p.10.
11 Rowan Gibbs kindly provided this information and suggested that Tom may have been a cousin of George 'Pony' Moore, but notes that when Tom attended Pony's funeral in 1907, he was listed amongst the Moore and Burgess old boys not the family. When Moore and Burgess broke up, Tom set up his own company 'Tom Birchmore's London Entertainers'.

12 Marie Moore's sister performed on the halls as Winnie Moore. She married Humphrey Brammall, manager of the Crystal Palace.
13 Two companies toured *His Majesty's Guests* from then on, Kitchen playing Lightning in one group and Walter Purvis in the other.
14 *Sunderland Daily Echo and Shipping Gazette*, 24 January 1902, p.3.
15 *The Era*, 7 June 1902, p.9.
16 *Hull Daily Mail*, 3 June 1902, p.4.
17 Joe Cleve started out as a clog dancer, and had known Karno since at least 1889 when they shared a bill at Barnard's Amphitheatre Portsmouth, the week that the Three Karnos first staged *Love In a Tub*. He appears as both Cleve and Cleeve in the listings.
18 Adeler and West, p.76.
19 Radio broadcast, *Forty Years of Films*, BBC Light Programme, broadcast 15 October 1952.
20 Adeler and West, p.77.
21 *Irish Independent*, 11 January 1904, p.4.
22 Karno and Arthur Jefferson knew each other well and their careers had much in common. They shared a flair for publicity, owned their own theatrical supplies company, embraced new technology (Jefferson formed his own short-lived film company in 1901), owned and managed theatres, had alcoholic wives, and eventually overstretched themselves in business to the point of bankruptcy.
23 *The Era*, 15 November 1902, p.8.
24 Pink was a stalwart of the GOWR, and the original secretary (Scribe Rat). The show was staged on the 24 November 1902.
25 *The Era*, 29 November 1902, p.22.
26 Charles Chaplin, *My Life in Pictures* (Bodley Head, London, 1974) p.57.
27 *Coventry Evening Telegraph*, 10 February 1930, p.6.
28 Fields first appeared in London in February 1901 and toured Britain many times (Simon Louvish, *Man on the Flying Trapeze – the Life and Times of W.C. Fields*, [W.W. Norton & Company, New York, 1997], p.86).
29 Naomi Jacob, *Me Looking Back* (Hutchinson & Co, London, 1950) p.82. I have been unable to find any baptism record to prove that Stuart was Leslie's godfather.
30 Gallagher, *Fun, Sex and Ruin with Fred Karno*, p.42.

9. Saturday to Monday
1 *The Era*, 21 February 1903, p.38.
2 Ibid., 28 February 1903, p.27.
3 Fisher, p.26.
4 Adeler and West, p.18.
5 *Manchester Courier and Lancashire General Advertiser*, 7 March 1903, p.20. The speed limit at the time was 14 mph.
6 *Yorkshire Evening Post*, 4 June 1903, p.3.
7 *Sussex Agricultural Express*, 22 August 1903, p.12.
8 *The Era*, 7 May 1904, p.25.
9 *Edinburgh Evening News*, 8 March 1904, p.2.
10 *Hull Daily Mail*, 12 April 1904, p.4.
11 Ibid., 14 February 1905, p.4.
12 Adeler and West, p.91.
13 Ibid., p.92.
14 Exactly when he bought the Highland Lassie is unknown, but 1903 seems likely.
15 *The Surrey Comet*, 10 August 1907, p.8.
16 Charlie and Clara Bell's daughter Edith was Edith Karno's goddaughter and probably named after her.
17 Her address at that time was 102 Hillside Road, Streatham.
18 Chaplin, *My Autobiography*, p.98.
19 *The Era*, 29 November 1902, p.22.
20 The boy in the box is sometimes incorrectly described as 'fat' but this was not the case. The misconception comes from Chaplin's subsequent film version *A Night in The Show* (1915).
21 This may have had its roots in real life experience since early music halls had boxes literally on the stage itself and the male occupants sometimes had to be locked in to prevent them getting onto the stage to tickle the dancers' legs (G.J. Mellor, *The Northern Music Hall* [Frank Graham, Newcastle Upon Tyne, 1970] p.142).
22 *The Stage*, 28 April 1904, p.18.
23 A.J. Marriot, *Chaplin Stage by Stage* (Marriot Publishing, Hitchen, 2005) p.158.
24 John McCabe, *Mr Laurel and Mr Hardy – An Affectionate Biography* (Robson Books, London, 2003 Ed.) p.28.
25 Charles B. Cochran, *Showman Looks On* (J. M. Dent & Sons Ltd., London, 1945) p.273.
26 Many lay claim to have originated 'the hook'. Harry Lauder recalled its enthusiastic use when he first appeared as

an amateur in Glasgow (Harry Lauder, *Roamin' in the Gloamin'* [J.B. Lippincott Company, Philadelphia & London, 1928] p.80). Americans credit its invention to Henry Clay Miner, proprietor of Miner's Bowery Theatre in 1903 (Louvish, *Man on the Flying Trapeze – the Life and Times of W.C. Fields*, p.63).

27 Henry Chance Newton, *Idols of the 'Halls' – Being My Music Hall Memories* (Heath Cranton Ltd, London, 1928; 1975 Ed. [EP Publishing Ltd]) p.231.

28 *Music Hall and Theatre Review*, 24 June 1904, p.7. It did still occasionally appear as *Twice Nightly* for a while.

29 Jacob, *Me – A Chronicle About Other People*, p.26.

30 Chance Newton, p.232. A later version of the script, dated April 1915, in the British Library archive, cites Baldwin as Karno's co-author.

31 Kenneth S. Lynn, *Charlie Chaplin and his Times*, (Simon and Shuster, New York, 1997) p.86.

32 Karno was probably himself inspired by either 'Professor Burko' (who's bill matter read 'The laughter making magician ... Screams of laughter over every trick') or by magician, turned theatre manager, Leotard Bosco. David Robinson puts forward the theory that in the week Chaplin was born his father was performing at Bosco's theatre in Hull, and the name may have somehow filtered down into Chaplin's consciousness as a result (Robinson, p.12).

33 McCabe, *Charlie Chaplin*, p.32.

34 *The Era*, 2 July 1904, p.20.

10. From Here to Paternity

1 Gallagher, *Fred Karno, Master of Mirth and Tears*, p.60.

2 Westcott vs Westcott in the High Courts of Justice Probate and Divorce and Admiralty Division, 1904.

3 Louvish, *Stan and Ollie: The Roots of Comedy*, p.137.

4 Gallagher, *Fred Karno, Master of Mirth and Tears*, p.16.

5 Westcott vs Westcott, answer of respondent 20 July 1904.

6 Ibid., 23 July 1904.

7 Husbands would sometimes retain custody of the children to punish their ex-wives. Jacob noted that Marie Lloyd's ex-husband similarly developed a sudden interest in his child which he'd hitherto ignored: (Jacob, *Our Marie – A Biography*, p.76).

8 Edith responded on 10 August denying that she had ever been drunk or exhibited any violent behaviour toward him. She stated that she had not condoned the adultery and added that even if she had, his subsequent cruelty had revived her claim.

9 Strangely, and frustratingly, the testimony of Edith's witness is not included in the court record.

10 Karno was ordered to pay just over £60 in further costs (Westcott vs Westcott, 25 May 1905).

11 Note that tax records show that Karno was renting Vaughan Road, he did not own it at that point (London England Tax Records 1692-1932).

12 Jacob, *Our Marie – A Biography*, p.231.

13 *Exeter and Plymouth Gazette*, 24 August 1912, p.2.

14 Broadfoote's husband, agent Ernest Edelsten, decided enough was enough and gave Jacob her marching orders just before the First World War. Jacob believed Marguerite died of a broken heart in 1915 (Bailey, p.114).

15 Online article, Simon Watney, 'A treasure, a trouper and a tartar', *Evening Standard*, 15 October 2001. standard.co.uk/showbiz/a-treasure-a-trouper-and-a-tartar-6308537.

16 Jacob, *Our Marie – A Biography*, p.66.

17 Naomi Jacob, *More About Me* (Hutchinson & Co., London, 1939) p.124.

18 James Norbury, *Naomi Jacob: The Seven Ages of Me* (William Kimber & Co., London, 1965) p.176.

19 Bailey, p.101.

20 Jacob, *Me – Looking Back*, p.82.

21 Professor Catherine Lavender wrote: 'These women often turned to other women for consolation ... loving other women became a way to escape ... male domination inherent in a heterosexual relationship.' (Catherine J. Lavender, 'Notes on New Womanhood, Women in the City', The College of Staten Island/CUNY, [1998] p.4.)

22 A Christmas event for the Music Hall Ladies' Guild in 1910 (*The Stage*, 29 December 1910, p.14).

23 Edith Westcott's last will and testament, 10 December 1926, Leslie Karno archive.

24 Wilkie Warren was certainly a friend (he is a contributor to her biography of Marie Lloyd), so Jacob could have replaced one with the other in her story with Wilkie's blessing (Jacob, *Our Marie – A Biography*, p.134).

25 Gallagher, *Fred Karno, Master of Mirth and Tears*, p.67.

26 Letter to Leslie Karno from Naomi Jacob, undated but the text suggests Spring 1929, Leslie Karno archive.
27 Gallagher, *Fred Karno, Master of Mirth and Tears*, p.68. If this was the last time Jacob saw Karno, one wonders what 'her famous interview with Karno' was (which Gallagher referred to but I have never unearthed).
28 Gallagher, *Fred Karno, Master of Mirth and Tears*, p.120. We have no date for the story, but Leslie was supposedly working with a Karno company in Paris which places it after the First World War. Whilst we can't prove Leslie and Karno argued, it might explain why, having made his debut with his father's company in September 1918, Leslie left the Karno company and ploughed his own furrow, he returned to the family firm some years later.
29 Leslie Stuart (edited and annotated by Andrew Lamb), *My Bohemian Life* (Fullers Wood Press, Croydon, 2003) p.100.
30 At the same time Stuart was declared bankrupt as a result of what the registrar called 'reckless extravagance'. (Stuart and Lamb, p.79). He died a penniless alcoholic in 1928.
31 Jacob, *Me – Looking Back*, p.82.

11. Princes and Principles
1 Jacob, *Me – A Chronical About Other People*, p.74.
2 Jacob, *Me Looking Back*, p.82. Jacob confirmed elsewhere that she never saw Edith perform on stage (letter to Leslie Karno from Naomi Jacob, 9 June [year unknown but during WW2], Leslie Karno archive).
3 Roxbury placed a notice in *The Stage* noting that he had been re-signed by Karno for the season: 'Retained at big increase' (*The Stage*, 15 December 1904, p.4).
4 *Music Hall and Theatre Review*, 15 September 1905, p.9, provides a full review.
5 *The Thanet Advertiser*, 10 May 1924, p.8.
6 Karno remembered this as 1902 but it was in fact Christmas 1904 (Adeler and West, p.105).
7 *The Stage*, 19 January 1905, p.14.
8 Adeler and West, p.106.
9 *The Era*, 11 March 1905, p.11.
10 Lasky was a young entrepreneur who had tried various jobs to support his mother and sister, after his father died at a young age, including trying his luck in the Alaskan gold fields – an experience that mirrored Chaplin's in *The Gold Rush*.
11 Jesse L. Lasky, *I Blow My Own Horn* (Victor Gollancz Ltd, London, 1957) p.62.
12 *Motherwell Times*, 14 December 1906, p.2.
13 James W. Tate also found great success with partner Julian Wylie, with revues and pantomimes of their own, before his sudden death in 1922, aged 46.
14 Purser and Wilkes, p.39.
15 Gallagher, *Fred Karno, Master of Mirth and Tears*, p.152.
16 *The Pall Mall Gazette*, 10 July 1885, p.4.
17 Denis Norden, *Clips From A Life* (Harper Perennial, London, 2008) p.79.
18 Purser and Wilkes's biography confirms that Dixey was continuously engaged in Parnell shows through 1931-1934.
19 Purser and Wilkes, p.11.
20 Ibid., p.7.
21 Ibid., p.147.
22 None of these stories appear in Fred Jr.'s own Karno biographical notes so I can only assume that they were passed on to Gallagher by Olive Karno in person.
23 Gallagher, *Fred Karno, Master of Mirth and Tears*, p.117.
24 John M East, *Max Miller the Cheeky Chappie* (Robson Books, London, 1977) p.69.

12. Thieves and Tricksters
1 Fred Karno Jr, *Fred Karno as I Knew Him* (unpublished memoir, 1960), Fred Karno Junior archive.
2 Adeler and West, p.165.
3 The auction was held on 19 October 1904.
4 *Sheffield Daily Telegraph*, 20 October 1904, p.6.
5 He sold them in June 1906 (*Music Hall and Theatre Review*, 8 June 1906, p.12).
6 The Acton College note is from Gallagher but the family can't verify it.
7 Adeler and West, p.174.
8 *Yorkshire Evening Post*, 28 March 1925, p.5.
9 Adeler and West, p.175.
10 Ibid., p.18.
11 Robinson, p.334.
12 McCabe, *Charlie Chaplin*, p.29.
13 Louvish, *Stan and Ollie – The Roots of Comedy*, p.50.
14 Adeler and West, p.101.
15 Ibid., p.28.
16 *The New York Clipper*, 2 September 1905, p.695 and *The Era*, 12 August 1905, p.32.
17 *The Era*, 19 August 1905, p.31.
18 *The Era*, 31 March 1906, p.36.
19 Gallagher claimed Karno avoided using his real name in his legal battles but press

reports indicate that Karno did not shy away from having his name in the court records – he was keen to be seen to stand his ground to dissuade others from taking him on.
20 This is one of the few I've come across where his name is listed as Westcott (although the court notes state that he was also known as Karno), and the first where a theatre accuses him of direct breach of contract. He certainly would not have wanted other venues to believe him to be unscrupulous, but hiding behind his real name was futile, he was one of the best-known characters in the industry.
21 *The Stage*, 23 March 1905, p.19.
22 Years later (when an established film star) Chaplin once sent Linder a photograph inscribed: 'To Max, the Professor, from his disciple.' (McCabe, *Charlie Chaplin*, p.117).
23 Paul Merton, Silent Comedy (Arrow Books, London, 2009) p.41.
24 The Court of Appeal had previously deemed that only publishable 'dramatic pieces' could constitute a play for the purposes of copyright protection.
25 *The Stage*, 30 April 1908, p.16.

13. I Want to be in America
1 The sketch was listed as being written by A.W. 'Needle'-ero, and was a parody of a popular play called *A Wife Without a Smile*, staged by A.W. Pinero.
2 *Nottingham Evening Post*, 20 March 1905, p.5.
3 *The Era*, 17 June 1905, p.31.
4 Ibid., 5 August 1905, p.3.
5 Ibid., 12 August 1905, p.22.
6 In 1922 the company expanded into game production.
7 Reeves opened on the 4 October 1905.
8 *The Era*, 16 September 1905, p.3.
9 Undated unreferenced cutting in Chaplin Archive.
10 They opened with *A Night in the Slums of London* at the Alhambra, New York (*New York Daily Tribune*, 16 September 1906, p.4).
11 *The Era*, 28 October 1905, p.31.
12 Ibid., 30 September 1905, p.29.
13 Ibid., 23 June 1906, p.23. Marinelli was a former contortionist whose bill matter was 'The Boneless Wonder'.
14 *Variety*, 23 April 1910, p.10.
15 Seaton and Martin, p.126.
16 The Paragon had a large Jewish audience, perhaps that is why he didn't launch the sketch there.
17 Kitchen, p 158.
18 Adeler and West, p.112.
19 *The Era*, 23 December 1905, p.22.
20 Barry Lupino recalled that there was a bit of business in *Early Birds* where the Jewish peddler dropped a coin on the stage. The cast would hide these coins under their boots and steal them away. With losses mounting up, Karno had hundreds of fake coins made to use on stage. Karno coins come up for sale regularly at auction but all are inscribed 'Fred Karno Grand New Production 1905-6 – Moses and Son', so whilst it's possible that these were some sort of entrance token for *Moses and Son* it seems likely that these were the fake *Early Birds* coins but distributed to the audience to promote the latest show (the same idea was used twenty years later to market Chaplin's *The Gold Rush* [1925]).
21 *The Era*, 3 February 1906, p.24.
22 *The Stage* incorrectly named him as Tipple and others reported him as Kipple.
23 *The Era*, 20 January 1906, p.38.
24 Ibid., 12 August 1905, p.22.

14. Stabbed in the Back
1 *The Era*, 3 February 1906, p.31.
2 Ibid., 17 February 1906, p.27.
3 Ibid., 7 April 1906, p.44.
4 Darnley was presumably the original writer, but the eventual sketch was by Karno and Harold Gatty.
5 *The Era*, 17 February 1906, p.27.
6 *Falkirk Herald*, 14 February 1906, p.7.
7 *The Era*, 7 April 1906, p.44.
8 Ibid., 2 February 1907, p.31.
9 Writing about Arthur Jefferson's *Home From The Honeymoon* (Danny Lawrence, *Arthur Jefferson Man of the Theatre and Father of Stan Laurel* [Brewin Books, Studley, Warwickshire, 2017] p.205).
10 In the same month Bruno joined Karno, Fred Jr. obtained his first confirmed listing in *Moses and Son* (*The Era*, 14 April 1906, p.34).
11 Later versions of the sketch had the protagonists as 'the Bumblers' Angling Society', and the social as a 'ladies evening'.

12 *The Era*, 21 April 1906, p.23.
13 Ibid., p.9.
14 *The Era*, 20 October 1906, p.39. Crabtree had a longstanding writing partnership with Harry Royston.
15 *The Stage*, 29 March 1906, p.3. The New King's Theatre opened on Christmas Eve 1906 but Karno's name doesn't appear in connection with it again so his involvement here was presumably short lived.
16 *The Era*, 21 July 1906, p.31.
17 Ibid., 6 October 1906, p.24.
18 I can find no evidence of this tour in the Australian press.
19 There was another comedian called Jack Hylton at that time so there's plenty of room for error here, but while J. Hylton is with *Dandy Thieves* in London, comic Jack Hylton is on a bill in St Helens, so they are not one and the same. Faint notes that our Jack was born Hilton, and changed the spelling after being incorrectly billed as the other Jack Hylton: a curious example of someone changing their name to be the same as the person they were being confused with (Pete Faint, *Jack Hylton* [Pete Faint, 2014] p.13).
20 *Edinburgh Evening News*, 15 August 1906, p.6.
21 Weightman, p.17.
22 *The Era*, 22 December 1906, p.23.
23 *Music Hall and Theatre Review*, 21 December 1906, p.32.
24 Ibid., 16 November 1906, p.5.
25 *The Era*, 10 November 1906, p.39.
26 Dickens, p.141.
27 *The Sportsman*, 25 December 1906, p.4.
28 *The Sketch*, 11 March 1925, p.20.
29 *The Era*, 22 December 1906, p.23.
30 Whimsical Walker, *From Sawdust to Windsor Castle* (Stanley Paul & Co, London, 1922) p.189.
31 Cochran, p.42.
32 Reports stated that he had successfully restrained Charles Frohman of the Vaudeville Syndicate, from producing a version of *Mumming Birds*, possibly Pinaud's troupe. After an illustrious career as a producer Frohman went down with the Lusitania in 1915.
33 *The San Francisco Call*, 5 June 1906, p.9.
34 *Variety*, 20 October 1906, p.19; see also Kerry Segrave, *Piracy in the Motion Picture Industry* (McFarland & Company Inc., London, 2003) p.7.
35 *London and Provincial Entr'acte*, 7 September 1906, p.7.
36 *Nottingham Journal*, 29 October 1906, p.8. He also signed papers to enable Alf Reeves to act on his behalf in all legal matters in the States (*Variety*, 13 October 1906, p.4).
37 *Music Hall and Theatre Review*, 28 September 1906, p.10. This and *Variety*, 15 September 1906, p.4, confirms it was his first visit to the U.S.
38 *Variety*, includes a review of the show in Philadelphia that week, noting it as a rip-off of *Mumming Birds*, and describing it as 'trashy … the piece is impossible.' (*Variety*, 22 September 1906, p.6).
39 Karno had to take Hill to court a second time to actually get his money. Ironically, Hill later sued another operator (the Empire Circuit Company) for producing another pirated version of the sketch in Chicago, which infringed on the exclusive rights he'd purchased.
40 Article in Arthur Gallimore's archive, source unknown, dated January 1907 (courtesy Marianne Morgan collection).
41 *West London Observer*, 16 August 1912, p.6.
42 *The Stage*, 6 February 1908, p.14.
43 Initially 'Charlie Chaplin' is listed as being in the American company (*The Era*, 28 July 1906, p.35), but this is an error – he hadn't joined Karno at that point. It was perhaps confusion between Syd and his father, at that point the only famous Chaplin; the following week Syd is properly recorded.
44 Charlie Chaplin's birth certificate is lost. A birth notice stated that he had been born on 15 April, but he celebrated his birthday on the 16th. Alternative dates and locations for his birth include one theory that he was born in a Romany Gypsy encampment in Smethwick, Birmingham, known as 'Black Patch'.
45 There is some confusion over which company staged *Repairs*. Chaplin's autobiography omits the show completely but recalls that Syd had been with 'Charlie Manon's troupe'. Robinson concludes that Syd had joined the Manons but then switched to a new company run by Fred Regina to produce the Pink sketch. Syd's biographer Lisa Stein concludes that the sketch was

written by Pink, performed by the Manons under the management of Regina. However, whilst there was a Manon Troupe performing in the mid-1890s, they seem to have disappeared completely by Chaplin's time and I can find no record of Syd being with them. Advertising consistently describes it as a Wal Pink sketch with Regina as company manager. The only connection to Manon I can verify is the note in Chaplin's autobiography, perhaps Pink recruited some former Manons to appear in the sketch.

46 This hugely simplified account of the Chaplins' early life is an attempt to capture a common thread from conflicting Chaplin biographies, but for a comprehensive account of Chaplin's stage career, A.J. Marriot's *Chaplin Stage by Stage* is hard to beat (see bibliography).

47 Robinson, p.400.

48 Syd Chaplin's Karno contract dated 24 June 1907, Chaplin archive, Paris.

15. Strikers

1 *The Era*, 3 November 1906, p.23. An Australian newspaper reported that Fred Karno was present, but this appears to be an error – it was actually Mrs Fred Karno (*Sydney Evening News*, 8 December 1906, p.3).

2 Jacob, *Our Marie – A Biography*, p.85.

3 *The Era*, 6 October 1906, p.22.

4 Ibid., 29 December 1906, p.20.

5 Weldon had appeared on the same bill as *Mumming Birds* in mid-March. Two weeks later Weldon announced in the press that he was engaged by Karno for his Christmas production (*Music Hall and Theatre Review*, 30 March 1906, p.3).

6 Seaton and Martin, p.94.

7 *The Era*, 29 December 1906, p.21.

8 Television programme, *Review*, BBC2 (producer Tony Staveacre), broadcast 19 March 1971.

9 *Music Hall and Theatre Review*, 28 December 1906, p.15.

10 Stan Laurel used the same arm folding gag in *Pardon Us* (1931).

11 Stanley, p.15.

12 Some players toured for months with the sketch, others came and went. One ex-footballer, J.A. Fitchett, found a new career treading the boards in his own right until 1909 when he became assistant manager at Karno's Exeter Hippodrome.

13 Spiksley and Karno may have met at the racecourse, Spiksley never missed the Derby and would certainly have witnessed the famous Karno company trip in 1898 (Ralph Nicholson interview with the author).

14 Seaton and Martin, p.32.

15 Adeler and West, p.129.

16 Gallagher, *Fred Karno, Master of Mirth and Tears*, p.15. Gallagher may have picked up on a report in *The Daily Herald* in 1950 whereby a Bert Johnson, claimed to have rescued a table from the bombed out Enterprise, and that this was the very table where Karno used to pay Chaplin his wages. The Enterprise, at 171 Coldharbour Lane, is still standing (today it is a café).

17 No apparent connection to Tagg's Island.

18 John Harding, *Football Wizard – The Billy Meredith Story* (Robson Books, London, 1998) p.153.

19 Undated press cutting, but probably May 1908 – author's collection.

20 *The Era*, 20 February 1909, p.22.

21 *Manchester Courier and Lancashire General Advertiser*, 30 January 1907, p.2.

22 A formidable Irish actress who appears regularly in Naomi Jacob's autobiographies.

23 *The Era*, 4 May 1907, p.13.

24 The MHARA annual dinner on 10 February 1907 (at the height of the strike) was one occasion where Edith Karno is listed as being in attendance with 'Miss Karno', her mystery companion.

25 Gillies, p.176.

26 Flanagan, pp.13-14.

27 *Music Hall and Theatre Review*, 1 February 1907, p.9.

28 This (along with several later events) puts paid to Gallagher's claim that Lloyd refused to appear on stage with Karno after he abandoned Edith. He also claimed that Lloyd stormed out of a VAF meeting when Marie turned up purporting to be 'Mrs Karno', but Karno is not recorded as attending any VAF meetings.

29 Ted Karno (Tysall) is also on the list, as is 'Mrs Fred Karno' but it is not clear whether this was Edith or Marie Moore.

30 *The Era*, 2 February 1907, p.23.

31 Leeson, p.47.

32 Television programme, *Review*, BBC2 (producer Tony Staveacre), broadcast 19 March 1971.

33 Staveacre's *Slapstick the Illustrated Story of Knockabout Comedy*, confirms my

conclusion that it was an isolated Karno dispute in 1912 (Staveacre, p.75).

16. Bodies and Bailiffs
1   *The Era*, 12 October 1907, p.25.
2   Ibid.
3   Edith and Leslie moved to 93 Oakleigh Park Drive, Leigh-on-Sea.
4   It's hard to establish when Edith stepped down as treasurer but certainly Elmore is listed in the post by September 1908.
5   Farson, p.84. (Every Lloyd biography tells this story slightly differently).
6   Elmore and her husband are listed at a GOWR fundraiser in March 1909, as is Karno (*Music Hall and Theatre Review*, 12 March 1909, p.10).
7   Jacob, *Our Marie – A Biography*, p.143.
8   *The Era*, 19 January 1907, p.8.
9   Ibid., 9 November 1907, p.42.
10 Karno's was not suggesting his artistes were cargo, but rather that his buses were used solely for business purposes. Although he lost, the judge noted that the law on licensing commercial vehicles was unclear as to whether employee transport was commercial or private, so Karno had a legitimate point.
11 *The Stage*, 7 November 1907, p.14.
12 *London Evening Standard*, 26 April 1907, p.10.
13 *Swindon Advertiser and North Wilts Chronicle*, 26 April 1907, p.7. Not surprisingly, Karno had to pay £10 damages and costs.
14 *The Stage*, 11 June 1908, p.12.
15 Unreferenced article, *Fooling for the Film*, (part 1 undated, part 2 dated 2 October 1915), Chaplin archive, Paris.
16 Stan Laurel used this gag in a script for a 1938 radio pilot called: *The Wedding Party*.
17 *Music Hall and Theatre Review*, 30 April 1909, p.7.
18 *The Era*, 27 April 1907, p.21.
19 Adeler and West, p.126.
20 McCabe, *Charlie Chaplin*, p.27.
21 Kitchen, p.305.
22 McCabe, *Charlie Chaplin*, p.115.
23 Source unknown but widely attributed.
24 *Hull Daily Mail*, 11 February 1921, p.4.
25 Attributed.
26 Letter to Chaplin from Winston Churchill, 29 November 1952, Chaplin Archive, Paris.
27 *The Stage*, 30 May 1907, p.13. A 'felo-de-se' is literally a 'felon of himself', i.e. one who has committed suicide.
28 *The Era*, 13 July 1907, p.23.
29 Ibid., 23 May 1908, p.23.
30 *West London Observer*, 1 November 1907, p.6.
31 Felstead, p.123.
32 Adeler and West, p.20.
33 East, *Max Miller the Cheeky Chappie*, p.68.
34 John M. East, *Karno's Folly, or How to Lose a Show-Business fortune*, Theatre Quarterly, No. 1 (July-September 1971), p.61.
35 Felstead, p.130.
36 Fred Karno Junior, *Fred Karno as I Knew Him* (unpublished memoir, 1960), Fred Karno Jr. archive.
37 *Derby Daily Telegraph*, 14 January 1925, p.4.
38 Adeler and West, p.116.
39 McCabe, *Charlie Chaplin*, p.117.
40 Ibid., p.210.
41 Robinson, p.385
42 *Derby Daily Telegraph*, 14 January 1925, p.4.

17. The Little Fellow
1   *South Bucks Standard*, 25 June 1909, p.5.
2   The Fourteen Black Hussars appeared with the variety company (*The Era*, 18 May 1907, p.35).
3   *The Era*, 30 November 1907, p.29.
4   *Music Hall and Theatre Review*, 29 November 1907, p.10.
5   workhouses.org.uk/Poplar.
6   He took the post in July 1908. Established in 1867, as the Music Hall Provident Sick Fund, this was a 'Friendly' or 'Provident' society where artistes could put away a small amount of money each month and then be supported by the fund should they fall on hard times.
7   *The Stage*, 20 June 1907, p.12.
8   *The Era*, 30 November 1907, p.35.
9   Ibid., 8 February 1908, p.39.
10 Comic Billy Danvers said that the corner move was common in Karno companies as a way of working a chase around a small stage (Robinson, p.70 & 120).
11 *The Era*, 16 May 1925, p.9.
12 Adeler and West, p.134.
13 McCabe, *Charlie Chaplin*, p.26.
14 *The Gleaner*, 19 October 1929, p.36.
15 McCabe, *Charlie Chaplin*, p.29.
16 Fred Karno, *I Saw Stars*, The Picturegoer, 7 December 1935, p 26.
17 *Dundee Evening Telegraph*, 23 February 1931, p.3.

18 A.J. Marriot notes that it was during this time (autumn 1907), while his work with Karno was insecure, that, for one night only, Chaplin tried his hand in a music hall as a solo comic, portraying a Jewish comic calling himself 'Sam Cohen'. He died on his feet. This failure coincided with Syd returning to London and, seeing how badly this failure affected his brother, Syd determined to persuade Karno to engage his brother (Marriot, *Chaplin Stage by Stage*, p.86).

19 Adeler and West, p.128.

20 Syd learnt the basics in the workhouse exercise yard, and as part of his naval training. Charlie's interest sparked by meeting two trainee acrobats whilst he was with the Lancashire Lads and, impressed by the fact they were earning much more than he was, he apparently taught himself some basic skills. (Chaplin, *My Autobiography*, p.49).

21 Lisa K. Stein, *Syd Chaplin, A Biography* (McFarland and Co. Inc., London, 2011) p.33.

22 *Dundee Evening Telegraph*, 12 January 1927, p.2.

23 Chaplin, *My Autobiography*, p.98.

24 *Dundee Evening Telegraph*, 23 February 1931, p.3.

25 To get an idea of Chaplin as a villain watch Keystone's *Mabel at the Wheel* (1914).

26 Chaplin, *My Autobiography*, p.99.

27 Staveacre, p.70.

28 Adeler and West, p.134.

29 Television programme, *Review*, BBC2 (producer Tony Staveacre), broadcast 19 March 1971.

30 *Daily Herald*, 15 April 1939, p.8.

31 *The Gleaner*, 19 October 1929, p.36.

32 Adeler and West, p.134.

33 *The Stage*, 2 April 1908, p.13.

34 *The Northern Whig*, 13 April 1908, p.7.

35 Adeler and West, p.181.

36 Will Letters was starring in *Saturday to Monday*.

37 *Manchester Courier and Lancashire General Advertiser*, 26 September 1908, p.10.

38 *The Era*, 7 March 1908, p.32.

39 The American titles varied from time to time so *A Night in the Slums of London* might sometimes be *A Night in the London Slums* etc.

40 Known as 'The Ritchie-Hearn London Pantomime Company', but often mis-listed as a Karno company. *Variety*, 20 July 1907, p.8.

41 *The Stage*, 14 May 1908, p.20.

42 *Variety*, 8 August 1908, p.8.

43 The music hall, originally on the back of the Montpelier pub at 18 Montpelier Street, went through various incarnations and rebuilds before being renamed the Montpelier Palace in 1908. In April that year it was advertised as available to rent for rehearsal although by June it was also operating as a cinema.

44 Marriot, *Chaplin Stage by Stage*, p.105. Marriot notes that there was no such theatre. The Streatham Empire was a cinema which opened in 1910.

18. Postmen, Pugilists, Politicians and Pratfalls

1 *The Era*, 31 October 1908, p.26.

2 The fact these were legitimate theatres didn't stop Karno staging his own shows. *Saturday to Monday* was staged shortly after he took over at Exeter and the following year he began staging his knockabout sketches.

3 *Kilburn Times*, 2 October 1908, p.4.

4 *The Era*, 31 October 1908, p.29.

5 Adeler and West, p.147.

6 *The Stage*, 10 December 1908, pp.13-14.

7 *Sporting Life*, 26 December 1908, p.7.

8 Le Clerq (who later changed his stage name to Gus McNaughton) went on to have a long career on stage and screen, appearing in many films perhaps most notably, Hitchcock's *The 39 Steps* (1935) where he makes a memorable appearance as a lingerie salesman in the train carriage scene.

9 McCabe, *Charlie Chaplin*, p.28.

10 *Triple Trouble* was cobbled together by Essanay from unused Chaplin material.

11 This South American tour was from late spring 1909 to February 1910.

12 Fred Emney Junior was also a successful comic actor, best remembered today for cameos in *Oliver!* (1968), and *The Italian Job* (1969).

13 *Islington Gazette*, 11 February 1909, p.4.

14 Press reports suggested he was also considering theatre developments in Folkestone and Slough, although these came to nothing.

15 *The Era*, 3 April 1909, p.26. He established rinks in places such as Hull, Exeter and Peterborough (the latter two being close to his theatres).

ENDNOTES

16 Karno consistently gave opportunities for his lead comics to write their own material and Syd proved to be more than capable, although he was fortunate to have an experienced co-writer to learn from.

17 *The Era*, 8 May 1909, p.23. This review is from the sketch's second week at the Holborn Empire.

18 In his youth (around 1907), Charlie Chaplin wrote a sketch entitled *The Twelve Just Men*, which, despite his best efforts, never saw the light of day. However, the 'dude' character was called Archibald and it seems likely that Syd was instrumental in incorporating the name into Karno sketches.

19 Letter to Fred Karno Jr. from Stan Laurel 3 July 1959, Leslie Karno archive.

20 This anonymity was a regular complaint by reviewers who were unable to single anyone out. Karno was happy to name the artistes in his musical comedies (such as Bruno, Kitchen and Weldon) so the plonks weren't kept anonymous to avoid creating egos.

21 *The Melbourne Herald*, 27 September 1924, p.15 and an article in *Pearson's Magazine Weekly* undated but reproduced in Marriot, *Chaplin Stage by Stage*, p.109.

22 Tony Staveacre's book includes a script of a sketch from Jack Melville's archive called *The Means Test Committee* with Melville and Weldon noted as the leads, but this doesn't appear in any Karno archive or listing (Staveacre, p.109).

23 Seaton and Martin, p.108.

24 Stiffy the warder was probably an inspiration for Hay's character in *Convict 99* (1938).

25 *The Gleaner*, 19 October 1929, p.36.

26 *Irish Independent*, 26 June 1909, p.4.

27 Louvish, *Man on the Flying Trapeze – the Life and Times of W.C. Fields*, p.63 and 492.

28 Kitchen, p.165.

29 This was the sketch Francis Cox claimed was plagiarised from his sketch *Timothy MP*.

30 *The Stage*, 5 August 1909, p.13.

31 *Woolwich Gazette*, 9 August 1910, p.1.

32 *The Era*, 21 August 1909, p.23.

19. All at Sea

1 John McCabe states that Chaplin was given the lead in *Mumming Birds* immediately following his initial success in *The Football Match* (McCabe, *Charlie Chaplin*, p.35) but as we know it was in fact nearly two years later. David Robinson said that Chaplin 'seems to have been performing the role' in Paris, confirming that it is not clear when he first played the lead (Robinson, p.85).

2 Chaplin, *My Autobiography*, p.114.

3 *The Era*, 25 December 1909, p.18 and Chelsea Palace flyer for same week – author's collection.

4 Marriot, *Chaplin Stage by Stage*, p.119.

5 After breaking box office records at the Broadway he transferred it to the Marlborough.

6 John M. East, *'Neath The Mask* (George Allen & Unwin Ltd, London, 1967) p.252.

7 One of these was entitled *Home from the Honeymoon* which was made into a film by Laurel and Hardy twice: *Duck Soup* (1927) and *Another Fine Mess* (1930).

8 The date of Stan's Panopticon debut is unknown. Arthur Jefferson's biographer Danny Lawrence believes it may have been early 1907 rather than the accepted wisdom which states it as June 1906. (Lawrence, p.210) and A.J. Marriot believes it to have been summer 1907 (A.J. Marriot, *Laurel Stage by Stage* [A.J. Marriot, Blackpool, 2017] p.16.

9 *Todmorden Herald* (undated), reproduced in A.J. Marriot, *Laurel and Hardy the British Tours* (A.J. Marriot, Blackpool, 1993) p.26.

10 *Tit-Bits*, 14 November 1936 (reproduced in Marriot, *Chaplin Stage by Stage*, p.120).

11 Letter to Fred Jr. from Stan Laurel, 21 March 1959 (courtesy lettersfromstan.com).

12 In the meantime Stan may have remained with Frank O'Neill's company or transferred to Syd Chaplin's *Skating* company which was at the Palace Manchester.

13 *The Stage*, 13 January 1910, p.12.

14 *Tit-Bits*, 14 November 1936 (reproduced in Marriot, *Chaplin Stage by Stage*, p.121).

15 *South Bucks Standard*, 25 June 1909, p.4.

16 *The Stage*, 13 January 1910, p.13.

17 *Sheffield Daily Telegraph*, 21 December 1909, p.11.

18 *The Referee*, 30 January 1910, p.6.

19 *Music Hall and Theatre Review*, 27 January 1910, p.9.

20 *The Era*, 29 January 1910, p.22.

21 Review from a performance at the

Nottingham Empire (*The Era*, 5 February 1910, p.8).
22 *The Era*, 12 February 1910, p.9.
23 *Wigan Observer and District Advertiser*, 1 February 1910, p.3.
24 *The Stage*, 10 March 1910, p.15.
25 Chaplin, *My Autobiography*, p.117.
26 *The Stage*, 31 March 1910, p.13. It opened on 28 February (*The New York Sun*, 27 February 1910, p.3).
27 Karno recalled that he was inspired to write the sketch after the launch of the Lusitania, although that had been four years earlier.
28 In October 1910 Karno successfully sued Walter Gibbons, claiming he had short changed Karno in payment for *Wontdetania*. Reports reveal that Karno charged £200 per week for the sketch, his costs were £135 and he had over forty performers in the company.
29 Online article, Percy G. Court, *Memories of Show Business* (1953). www.arthurlloyd.co.uk/MemoriesOfShowBusiness (courtesy of Matthew Lloyd).
30 *Music Hall and Theatre Review*, 14 April 1910, p.10.
31 *The Era*, 16 April 1910, p.23.
32 *Music Hall and Theatre Review*, 14 April 1910, p.10.
33 Felstead, p.126.

20. Mr Fearless
1 *Dundee Evening Telegraph*, 23 February 1931, p.3.
2 Staveacre, p.72. Melville's theory can be quickly dismissed since Chaplin would not have succeeded in legitimate theatre alongside the likes of William Gillette if he couldn't project beyond the footlights, besides, the sketch barely had a line in it.
3 *Tit-Bits*, 14 November 1936, reproduced in Marriot, *Chaplin Stage by Stage*, p.124.
4 Radio broadcast, *Turning Point*, broadcast 14 August 1957.
5 McCabe, *The Comedy World of Stan Laurel*, p.14.
6 Marriot, *Chaplin Stage by Stage*, p.124.
7 McCabe, *Charlie Chaplin*, p.36.
8 Adeler and West, p.131.
9 Marriot, *Chaplin Stage by Stage*, p.126.
10 Chaplin, *My Autobiography*, p.116.
11 McCabe, *Charlie Chaplin*, p.36.
12 Radio broadcast, *Turning Point*, interview of Stan Laurel by Arthur Friedman, recorded 14 August 1957.
13 *The Stage*, 28 April 1910, p.12.
14 There were four main scenes: '1. A hearty supper and its after effects – the nightmare, 2. The Dog's Nose drinking saloon – Deadman's Gulch, 3. The Rocky Mountains – the attack – the hand to hand fight – saving the girl – the rescue – Jimmy triumphs, 4. Then he awoke.'
15 *The Era*, 30 April 1910, p.22.
16 *The Stage*, 28 April 1910, p.12.
17 *Dundee Evening Telegraph*, 23 February 1931, p.3.
18 Perhaps music hall comic singer G.H. Chirgwin (known as the White-eyed Kaffir) was the inspiration. He did a routine with two clay pipes 'dancing' on a tray in the same way. David Robinson also notes that Fatty Arbuckle performed the dance of the rolls in a film in 1918 (Robinson, p.375).
19 Adeler and West, p.132.
20 McCabe, *Charlie Chaplin*, p.36.
21 Ibid., p.128.
22 Ibid., p.36.
23 Marriot, *Laurel and Hardy the British Tours*, p.111.
24 Adeler and West, p.131.
25 Louvish, *Stan and Ollie: The Roots of Comedy*, p.152.
26 Lawrence, p.271.
27 *The Stage*, 26 May 1910, p.10.
28 *Mr Justice Perkins* (later called *Perkins JP*) was another three-scene sketch: 'The Village Green – Spoddleton', 'Corridor of Spoddleton Police Court', and 'Interior of the Court House'.
29 *The Stage*, 21 July 1910, p.10.
30 *The Wow Wows* was written by Karno and Herbert Sidney with music by Joe Cleve. The strange title was occasionally mis-listed, for instance *Wallah Wallah* (*Music Hall and Theatre Review*, 4 August 1910, p.8).
31 Marriot notes that it was probably based on a Charles Baldwin sketch entitled *A Night in a Chamber of Horrors* (Marriot, *Chaplin Stage by Stage*, p.136).
32 *The Stage*, 11 August 1910, p.11.
33 *The Stage*, 22 September 1910, p.13.
34 Adeler and West, p.133.
35 Ibid., p.132.
36 For example, Bill Fern toured vaudeville in a copycat version of *Early Birds* called *A Night in the Slums of Paris* and Bert Weston formed a double act with a girl called Nellie Lynch (*Variety*, 1 April 1911, p.18).
37 Gallagher, *Fred Karno, Master of Mirth and Tears*, p.80.

ENDNOTES

38 Adeler and West, p.16.
39 Ibid., p.133.
40 *The Gleaner*, 19 October 1929, p.36.
41 *Variety*, 10 September 1910, p.4.
42 Marriot, *Chaplin Stage by Stage*, p.132. *Jimmy the Fearless* at the Liverpool Empire in mid-August was cancelled at short notice (*The Era*, 13 August 1910, p.8), which supports Marriot's theory.
43 1959 interview of Stan Laurel by Tony Thomas for his series *Voices from the Hollywood Past*.
44 *The Gleaner*, 19 October 1929, p.36.
45 Cochran, p.43.
46 *The Stage*, 22 September 1910, p.4. Other accounts record that she sailed on the 22nd but it was certainly late on the 20th as confirmed by the passenger manifest in the National Archives (UK Outward Passenger Lists, 1890-1960), and she is noted as passing the Lizard (Cornwall) on the twenty-first (*Lloyds List*, 21 September 1910, p.4).
47 Aberdeen Press and Journal, 19 April 1910, p.3.
48 The journey was delayed by three days due to a damaged rudder (or propeller) (Chaplin, *My Autobiography*, p.119 and *The Adelaide News*, 23 December 1933, p.6).
49 Marriot, *Laurel and Hardy the British Tours*, p.31. I've been unable to confirm whether they were booked on the Lusitania.
50 McCabe, *Charlie Chaplin*, p.39.
51 Chaplin, *My Life in Pictures*, p.26.

21. Astoria

1 *Variety*, 8 October 1910. Stan incorrectly recalled in a 1959 interview that they had opened at the Alhambra Theatre, but this was actually their second week (Marriot, *Chaplin Stage by Stage*, p.236).
2 Chaplin, *My Autobiography*, p.119.
3 McCabe, *Charlie Chaplin*, p.40.
4 *The Stage*, 20 October 1910, p.24.
5 A.J. Marriot tracked down this review to the *The New York Clipper* week commencing 10 October 1910.
6 Stan recalled that the National Theatre was initially called Loew's Million Dollar Theatre. A.J. Marriot's research records that the Percy Williams shows were all badly received and the week at Fall River was the last of their Williams dates but my research suggests that reviews had improved and the Fall River date wasn't on the same circuit. Stan's recollection was that they played five weeks with Williams then Reeves secured a chance with Loew but they had to change the sketch (to *Mumming Birds*) and prove they could do it at a small out of town hall before he'd let them play it at his big launch night.
7 Stan recalled that their next engagement, at Morris's American Music Hall, allowed them to play a different sketch every week for six weeks although Marriot's research shows that that they first played the Nixon theatre Pennsylvania, then the American Music Hall for five weeks, with *Night in an English Music Hall* being played twice. The other sketches being: *Night in a London Club*, *Wow Wows* and *Night in a London Slum* (Marriot, *Chaplin Stage by Stage*, p.236).
8 Chuck McCann interview with the author. This story appears in several other books.
9 David Robinson suggests that *A Night in a London Club* was a new sketch improvised by the company (Robinson, p.94), but reviews indicate it was heavily based on *The Smoking Concert*.
10 Karno had used shadow play in both *The Thirsty First* and *London Suburbia*.
11 Undated and unreferenced cutting Chaplin archive, Paris.
12 Undated and unreferenced cutting in Chaplin Archive, Paris.
13 Unreferenced and undated cutting in Chaplin archive, Paris.
14 Various biographers give different dates and venues for Sennett's first sighting of Chaplin, but Marriot's research puts it between 3 October 1910 and 7 January 1911 (Marriot, *Chaplin Stage by Stage*, p.146).
15 *The Butte Inter Mountain*, 18 April 1911 (reproduced in Marriot, *Laurel Stage by Stage*, p.73).
16 *Billboard*, 24 June 1911.
17 A blow by blow account of Chaplin's Karno tours is detailed in A.J. Marriot's superlative book *Chaplin Stage by Stage* (see bibliography) which corrects many inaccuracies in other Chaplin biographies and adds greatly to our understanding of his early career.
18 *The New Slavey* was written by Karno and Herbert Sidney.
19 *The Stage*, 29 September 1910, p.13.

20 The double act of brothers Tom and Fred McNaughton had broken up when Tom went to America, Le Clerq joined up with Fred and thereafter called himself Gus McNaughton.
21 He left to appear in a production of *Aladdin* in Birmingham.
22 Some biographers incorrectly claim that Campbell travelled to America with Karno but he is recorded on the passenger list of the Minnehaha as part of another company in July 1914. None of his colleagues were Karno comics and there was no U.S. tour that year (UK Outward Passenger Lists 1890-1960).
23 In 1908 Oswald Stoll staged a match between Middlesex and Surrey professionals on the Coliseum stage – a safety net was strung across the proscenium.
24 *The Stage*, 23 May 1912, p.14. He staged a summer variety season at both the Marlborough and the Borough Theatre, Stratford.
25 Ibid., 15 June 1911, p.16. See note on Australian tours in appendices.
26 *Music Hall and Theatre Review*, 15 June 1911, p.11.
27 *The Stage*, 9 November 1911, p.16.
28 *Yorkshire Evening Post*, 2 November 1911, p.5.
29 *Variety*, 24 June 1911, p.6 and 19 August 1911, p.15. See also *The Stage*, 17 August 1911, p.11.
30 *Seattle Post Intelligencer*, 6 May 1911, reproduced in Marriot, *Chaplin Stage by Stage*, p.155.
31 *The Daily News*, 23 May 1911, cutting in Chaplin archive, Paris.
32 The Lusitania left New York on the 15 August 1911.

Strangely they are both listed on the manifest as 'clerks' (UK Incoming passenger lists 1878 – 1960).
33 Marriot, *Laurel Stage by Stage*, p.248. Accounts of Stan's career at this stage vary but Marriot's research provides the most comprehensive and reliable account.
34 *The Stage*, 26 October 1911, p.15.
35 Ibid., 14 December 1911, p.14. The sketch was originally intended to be called *Perkins in Port*.
36 *Falkirk Herald*, 17 January 1912, p.5.
37 *The Stage*, 15 February 1912, p.19.
38 *Daily Herald*, 21 May 1912, p.2.
39 It was originally listed in 1906 as *Thumbs Down*.
40 *Exeter and Plymouth Gazette*, 5 April 1912, p.3.
41 *The Stage*, 16 May 1912, p.13.
42 *Yorkshire Evening Post*, 29 June 1912, p.3.
43 *Preston Herald*, 25 May 1912, p.11.
44 Stanley, p.107.

22. Karsino's Curse

1 Jacob, *Me – A Chronicle About Other People*, p.112. This may be a much quoted but apocryphal story, there appears to be no contemporary evidence that this happened.
2 Ibid., p.26.
3 Fred Karno, *I Saw Stars*, *The Picturegoer*, 7 December 1935, p.26.
4 A.J. Marriot points out that it appeared years after the event and in various rehashed forms: one article attributed the tale to Fred Kitchen, who wasn't even with Karno at the time (Marriot, *Chaplin Stage by Stage*, p.174).

5 Article dated 16 August 1924, source unknown, Chaplin Archive, Paris and *Photoplay*, April 1919, p.71.
6 Chaplin, *My Autobiography*, p.133.
7 Curiously, Stan is recorded twice on the passenger list: as Stan Jefferson, aged 30, and then as Arthur S Jefferson, aged 25 (UK outward passenger lists 1890-1960).
8 Walker was a last-minute replacement, but this was his ninth trip to America in a distinguished career as a clown in circuses and pantomime (Walker, p.159).
9 *Pall Mall Gazette*, 7 October 1912, p.7.
10 Ibid., 8 October 1912, p.7.
11 Baker and Baker, p.83.
12 Ibid., p.84.
13 Adeler and West, p.94.
14 Ibid., p.161 (although I have found no evidence of the competition in the press).
15 The extant building specifications in the public record show that the structural engineers were in fact Shone and Ault.
16 Adeler and West, p.153.
17 Karsino Valse sheet music and promotional material – author's collection.
18 The licence for the hotel passed to Karno from Tagg on 12 January 1913, the council granted full permission on 11 March 1913.
19 Shone and Ault Engineers letter dated 3 March 1913 and Frank Matcham letter dated 26 April 1913 (Tagg's Island planning application, PLA/09667, 14/1/1913, Richmond upon Thames Local Studies Library and Archive).
20 Baker and Baker, p.83.
21 *The Pall Mall Gazette*, 22 January 1913, p.11.

22   *The Era*, 14 June 1913, p.22. Although, in his memoirs he also claimed it was variously £70,000 and over £100,000.
23   Baker and Baker, p.85.
24   Some accounts suggest that the palm court was a later addition to the hotel, but this is not the case, it is described in detail in the advertising and reports of the grand opening.
25   *The Era*, 10 May 1913, p.20.
26   Ibid., 14 June 1913, p.18.
27   Ibid., p.22.
28   *The Stage*, 19 June 1913, p.21.
29   In his memoirs Karno incorrectly stated that Karsino opened on 20 May.
30   Dewar was a well-travelled and highly successful whiskey magnate who Harry Lauder described as the finest after dinner speaker in the world (Lauder, p.179).
31   *The Stage*, 26 June 1913, p.16.
32   Adeler and West, p.154.
33   Of the famous 'Lyons Corner Houses'. Lyons was from humble stock and had a close connection with the music hall; his wife was the daughter of the manager of the Pavilion Theatre, Whitechapel Road.
34   J.P. Gallagher, *Fun, Sex and Ruin with Fred Karno*, Mayfair, Volume 11 No 1 (January 1976) p.37.
35   Adeler and West, p.157.

23. Cheerio Charlie!

1   Marriot, *Chaplin Stage by Stage*, p.181 and Robinson, p.180.
2   Cutting in Chaplin archive, undated and unknown newspaper but during a performance at the L.A. Empress (they performed there numerous times on both tours).
3   This was almost certainly the final version of *Perkins the Punter*
4   *Yorkshire Evening Post*, 26 October 1912, p.3.
5   *Burnley News*, 26 February 1913, p.8.
6   Neither of Karno's two sons joined the Water Rats.
7   *The Stage*, 12 December 1912, p.26.
8   *The Era*, 14 June 1913, p.19.
9   *Yorkshire Evening Post*, 5 December 1912, p.7.
10   *Daily Herald*, 11 January 1913, p.6.
11   The press reported that in Dudley Powell's farewell speech from the Exeter Hippodrome, he said: 'The only thing that pleased him at leaving was that he was going back to his old friends, Mr Fred Karno and Mr Kitchen.' (*Exeter and Plymouth Gazette*, 9 December 1912, p.5).
12   Followed by a move to the Palace Theatre, Aberdeen, after one week.
13   *Mumming Birds* continued to do good business. Constantly updated, the line-up was now Hally Hampion (otherwise Harry Champion) the red nosed comet, Flossie Flood (otherwise Florrie Ford) the ballad monger, and Lizzie Dripping the saucy serio (*Hartlepool Northern Daily Mail*, 4 January 1913, p.1).
14   The company was led by Mr Westbury. *The Era*, 29 March 1913, p.20. I have been unable to establish whether this was a Karno tour or a licensed company.
15   *Flats* premiered at the Royal Theatre, Worcester, before moving to the Euston.
16   Letter to Syd Chaplin from Karno, dated 13 February 1913, Chaplin archive, Paris.
17   *The Stage*, 13 March 1913, p.15.
18   Ibid., 23 October 1913, p.25. This gag also appeared in *The Football Match*.
19   *Daily Herald*, 31 March 1913, p.11.
20   *Derbyshire Advertiser and Journal*, 2 May 1913, p.6.
21   *The Stage*, 25 April 1929, p.14.
22   It was in three scenes: 'The gates of White's laundry at dinner time', 'The receiving office of the laundry', and 'The washing and ironing department'.
23   *The Era*, 3 September 1913, p.22.
24   Walker, p.160.
25   Chaplin, *My Autobiography*, p.135.
26   *The Era*, 27 August 1913, p.20.
27   *Photoplay Magazine*, 1936, reproduced in Merton, p.31.
28   Stan Laurel used the same gag in *The Driver's Licence*, a sketch which he and Oliver Hardy played on a tour of Britain in 1947.
29   Simon Louvish, *Keystone the Life and Clowns of Mack Sennett* (Faber and Faber, London, 2003) p.30.
30   *Dundee Evening Telegraph*, 23 February 1931, p.3.
31   Chaplin biographies have various wordings, so I have quoted from Chaplin (Chaplin, *My Autobiography*, p.138).
32   Letter to Syd Chaplin from Charlie Chaplin dated the week of 4 August 1913, Chaplin archive, Paris.
33   Article dated 16 August 1924, source unknown, Chaplin archive, Paris.
34   Chaplin's Karno contract dated 19 September 1910 (which commenced

6 March 1911), Chaplin archive, Paris.
35 Letter to Syd Chaplin from Karno, dated 23 January 1914, Chaplin archive, Paris.
36 Cochran, p.41.
37 *The Gleaner*, 19 October 1929, p.36.

24. Fred Karno's Army
1 Adeler and West, p.133.
2 *Dundee Evening Telegraph*, 12 January 1927, p.2.
3 McCabe, *Charlie Chaplin*, p.47.
4 Chaplin, *My Autobiography*, p.140. The next time Dandoe and Chaplin met was when Chaplin returned to London in 1931, and he supposedly tripped over his old comrade in the street. Dandoe had by then resorted to busking as a pavement artist (*The Western Mail*, 26 November 1931, p.8 and *The Adelaide News*, 30 December 1933, p.6).
5 Robinson, p.113 and Chaplin, *My Life in Pictures*, pp.103-104.
6 Bruce Crowther, *Laurel and Hardy Clown Princes of Comedy* (Columbus Books, London, 1987) p.12.
7 Adeler and West, p.158.
8 Travis Stewart, *Chain of Fools – Silent Comedy and Its Legacies from Nickelodeons to YouTube*, p.78.
9 Robinson, p.113 and Chaplin, *My Life in Pictures*, p.127.
10 McCabe, *Charlie Chaplin*, p.51.
11 Walker, p.220.
12 Cochran, p.45.
13 The first British Chaplin releases were in June 1914, six months after their release in America.
14 Robinson, *Chaplin His Life and Art*, p.136.
15 *Manchester Evening News*, 6 June 1914, p.6.
16 Robinson, p.136.
17 *The Stage*, 10 June 1915, p.10 – quoting a report from *Variety*, 12 February 1915.
18 Stan was replaced by another Karno comic Ted Banks.
19 When Stan left the trio, his part was taken over by Will Crackles, another ex-Karno comic Stan recommended to Baldy Cooke.
20 *Pall Mall Gazette*, 17 March 1914, p.5.
21 Baker and Baker, p.70.
22 Adeler and West, p.157.
23 *The Globe*, 30 May 1914, p.11.
24 Adeler and West, p.157.
25 *The Stage*, 26 February 1914, p.18.
26 Ibid., 7 May 1914, p.12.
27 *Manchester Courier and Lancashire General Advertiser*, 23 May 1914, p.11.
28 *Dundee Evening Telegraph*, 18 August 1914, p.3.
29 Adeler and West, p.160.
30 James Jupp, *The Gaiety Stage Door* (Jonathan Cape, London, 1923) p.330.
31 Email to the author from Lois Laurel, 4 February 2010 (with thanks to Richard Bann).
32 Ibid., 26 August 1915, p.2.
33 *Yorkshire Evening Post*, 7 January 1916, p.5.
34 *The Stage*, 2 December 1915, p.16. Karno also supplied footballs and boxing gloves for another battalion's makeshift gymnasium (*The Era*, 19 April 1916, p.14).
35 *The Era*, 1 January 1919, p.35.
36 *The Liverpool Daily Post*, 9 August 1916, p.7.
37 *Hendon and Finchley Times*, 29 September 1916, p.6.
38 *Western Daily Press*, 9 January 1917, p.5.
39 *Nottingham Evening Post*, 22 January 1916, p.3.
40 *Sporting Times*, 2 September 1916, p.1.
41 Leslie wrote to the RAF, via Naomi Jacob, to see if they would take him (letter to Jacob from RAF night training squadron [signature unreadable], 7 April 1918, Leslie Karno archive).
42 Mary never married and Ellen was passed off in the family as Mary's sister. Ellen became known as Nellie, married John Lodge in 1941, and ran the Strawberry Gardens pub in Stockport. She died in 1988 (thanks to Melanie Carr for this information).
43 Fred Karno Jr. Army Service Record.
44 *Hull Daily Mail*, 10 November 1915, p.4.

25. The Millionaire Tramp
1 *Cheshire Observer*, 15 August 1914, p.1.
2 Ibid., 22 August 1914, p.9.
3 *Yorkshire Evening Post*, 15 September 1914, p.3.
4 Letter to Syd Chaplin from Karno, 7 April 1914, Chaplin archive, Paris.
5 Louvish, *Keystone the Life and Clowns of Mack Sennett*, p.85.
6 Letter to Syd Chaplin from Alf Reeves, undated but late 1916 or early 1917, Chaplin archive, Paris.
7 *The Stage*, 1 October 1914, p.12.
8 *Yorkshire Evening Post*, 26 January 1915, p.4. Nelson went on to have some success but was struck down with the illness which appears to have been bubbling beneath the surface for some years and died in June 1918.

9 Karno and F. Firth Shepherd actually took the writing credits, with music by Joe Cox.
10 *The Era*, 9 December 1914, p.12.
11 *Dundee Evening Telegraph*, 17 August 1915, p.5.
12 John Gerant and Percival Langley were credited as Karno's co-writers in the press, although the licensed script credits F. Frith Shepherd. Music was by Joe Cleve.
13 *Birmingham Daily Gazette*, 30 March 1915, p.3.
14 *The Stage*, 4 March 1915, p.6.
15 *Sheffield Evening Telegraph*, 23 March 1915, p.3.
16 Adeler and West, p.169.
17 *Yorkshire Evening Post*, 19 June 1915, p.3.
18 Karno later moved to a ground floor flat (H1).
19 *The Tatler*, 26 May 1915, p.10.
20 *Belfast Newsletter*, 29 May 1915, p.10.
21 *Yorkshire Evening Post*, 22 April 1916, p.3.
22 *The Ogden Standard*, 26 June 1915.
23 *The Era*, 26 May 1915, p.16.
24 Undated and unreferenced article from late 1941 or early 1942, Chaplin archive, Paris.
25 McCabe, *Charlie Chaplin*, p.90. Billie Ritchie is not to be confused with W.E. Ritchie who billed himself as 'the Original Tramp Cyclist' (*Music Hall and Theatre Review*, 11 June 1897, p.1).
26 Ibid. p.54.
27 Ibid.
28 *The Gleaner*, 19 October 1929, p.36.
29 Armstrong later worked at several studios as a solid ensemble comic but died of tuberculosis in 1924 at just thirty-three.
30 Letter to Charlie Chaplin from Karno, 17 August 1915, Chaplin archive, Paris.
31 Lasky, p.110.
32 Their uncle, Will Evans, was the most well-known comic in the family.
33 I have not been able to prove conclusively that Karno's Fred Evans was the father of Pimple, but it seems highly likely. Karno's Fred Evans' brother Harry was also a Karno comic, who died in September 1905 whilst with a Karno troupe in Glasgow.
34 *The Era*, 26 May 1915, p.12.
35 Letter to Charlie Chaplin from Alf Reeves, 19 January 1916, Chaplin archive, Paris.
36 Syd founded the first scheduled passenger airline, Chaplin Airlines, in 1919.
37 Karno's name change was noted on his subsequent marriage certificate and in his obituary (*Evening Despatch*, 18 September 1941, p.1), but I have not been able to find any official record of the legal change.
38 The Eccentric Club was one of many charities established to take on the challenge of supporting the wounded (*The Era*, 8 August 1917, p.11). The film can be viewed online at www.londonsscreenarchives.org.uk/title/19841.
39 *The Era*, 27 June 1917, p.12.
40 Adeler and West, p.161.
41 *Surrey Advertiser*, 2 June 1917, p.7.
42 Adeler and West, p.161.

26. All Women
1 *Daily Mirror*, 10 August 1915, p.10.
2 Ibid., 21 August 1915, p.10.
3 Julian Symons, *Horatio Bottomley* (House of Stratus, Kelly Bray, Cornwall, 2001 Edition) p.156.
4 *Yorkshire Evening Post*, 8 July 1922, p.6.
5 Symons, p.221.
6 *Western Mail*, 27 May 1916, p.7.
7 *The Stage*, 7 October 1915, p.15.
8 *Sheffield Daily Telegraph*, 28 November 1916, p.5.
9 Adeler and West, p.163.
10 *Dundee Evening Telegraph*, 12 January 1927, p.2.
11 *Portsmouth Evening News*, 5 May 1916, p.6.
12 *Yorkshire Evening Post*, 29 January 1916, p.3.
13 *All Women* seems to have occasionally run under the title *All Eves*, although this causes some confusion with Fred Kitchen's sketch *All Eyes*.
14 Although Beatie and Babs had ended their contract, Karno's posters had their names on for the next few weeks of the run and they successfully sued him for damages.
15 *The Stage*, 18 November 1915, p.29.
16 One of the interesting things about the reports of the fire, was the consistent use of 'the Fun Factory', as the name by which his premises were known. Karno never used that name in his advertising or listings – it was always 'Karno's Theatrical Factory'.
17 *Yorkshire Evening Post*, 31 March 1916, p.8.
18 It was probably in late 1918 or early 1919. It appears in British Phone Book records until 1918.
19 Vivyan Ellacott, *Oh What A (Not so) Lovely War! The Music Hall During the*

Great War, The Call Boy, Volume 54 No 2 (summer 2017) p.28.
20 Jackson continued to work closely with Karno including on a revised version of *Parlez Vous Français?* Its schoolroom scene was replaced with 'the Garden of the Ladies Seminary,' but it still starred Syd Walker, with the addition of Jackson's 'Continental Dancers'.
21 *Lancashire Evening Post*, 25 January 1916, p.4.
22 *Yorkshire Evening Post*, 29 January 1916, p.3.
23 *The Gleaner*, 19 October 1929, p.36.
24 Television programme, *Review*, BBC2 (producer Tony Staveacre), broadcast 19 March 1971.
25 *Sunday Post*, 12 March 1916, p.5.
26 *Dundee Evening Telegraph*, 12 January 1927, p.2.
27 *Dundee Courier*, 23 March 1916, p.1.
28 *Sunday Post*, 7 May 1916, p.2.
29 *The People*, 7 May 1916, p.9.
30 Karno eventually found a permanent replacement for Dainton in Melilsande D'Egville.
31 *The Era*, 10 May 1916, p.7.
32 *Yorkshire Evening Post*, 10 June 1916, p.3.
33 *The Era*, 23 August 1916, p.7. Through September it was listed under both titles, one assumes slightly different versions perhaps depending on the size of the venue.
34 Confusingly, reviews confirm that they were different versions of the same show, yet *Oh, Law!* and *On and Off* sometimes appeared concurrently in the listings.
35 *Wigan Observer and District Advertiser*, 31 October 1916, p.3.
36 *Yorkshire Evening Post*, 5 September 1916, p.3.
37 'L.S.D.' is from the Latin 'librae, solidi, denarii', and is not to be confused with the hallucinogenic drug LSD which was not created until 1938.
38 *Western Morning News*, 13 February 1917, p.5.

27. Making Hay

1 *The Era*, 22 November 1916, p.14.
2 The licensed script dated 16 June 1917, names the lead character as Mr Bright.
3 *The Era*, 27 June 1917, p.10.
4 *The Stage*, 13 December 1917, p.13.
5 Letter to Syd Chaplin from Alf Reeves, 25 September 1917, Chaplin archive, Paris.
6 He sailed on the St Paul on 15 December 1917. Amy (actually Clara Amy) sailed on the Adriatic a year later (1 December 1918).
7 Reeves was made studio manager on the 15 April 1918 (Robinson, p.730).
8 Ibid., p.214. Some accounts report his daughter was hit by a car whilst shopping for a mourning dress, but this seems to be dramatic licence.
9 McCabe, *Mr Laurel and Mr Hardy – An Affectionate Biography*, p.50. A.J. Marriot thinks it unlikely that Chaplin would have considered Laurel for his stock company, since he would never have risked competition from someone as good as Stan (Marriot, *Laurel Stage by Stage*, p.184), but the meeting and dinner were Stan's recollections so I've included it.
10 Stan's tortuous route into film, and his vaudeville career is well documented in Marriot, *Laurel Stage by Stage* (see bibliography).
11 Louvish, *Keystone the Life and Clowns of Mack Sennett*, p.152.
12 Letter to Ed Patterson from Stan Laurel, 14 October 1957. Online article, Dalya Alberge, 'Stan Laurel's Secret Jibes at "mean, cheap", Charlie Chaplin.' *Daily Mail Online*, 1 December 2017. Dailymail.co.uk/news/article-5137711/Letter-shows-Stan-Laurel-thought-Charlie-Chaplin-mean.
13 Karno had wanted to call the sketch *Nosey Parker* but Charlie Austin persuaded him to change the title to avoid confusion with his own act, *Parker P.C.*
14 *The Stage*, 11 October 1917, p.9.
15 *Birmingham Daily Gazette*, 19 February 1918, p.4.
16 Seaton and Martin, p.32 and Graham Rinaldi, *Will Hay* (Tomahawk Press, Sheffield, 2009) p.39.
17 Karno recalled that Jimmy Nervo also appeared in *Nosey Knows* but I've yet to find him in any listing.
18 Adeler and West, p.169.
19 *The Stage*, 31 January 1918, p.11.
20 *Aberdeen Evening Express*, 26 February 1918, p.4.
21 *Manchester Evening News*, 6 November 1918, p.3.
22 *The Stage*, 11 April 1918, p.12.
23 *Chester Chronicle*, 10 November 1917, p.8.
24 *Liverpool Daily Post*, 27 December 1917, p.3.
25 Louis S. Giraud, *Songs That Won the War Daily Express Community Song Book No. 3* (Lane Publications, London, 1930) p.91.

26 *Derby Daily Telegraph*, 13 January 1926, p.6.
27 On 29 June 1918.
28 *The Era*, 24 April 1918, p.12.
29 Letter to Syd Chaplin from Alf Reeves, undated but probably late 1916 or early 1917, Chaplin archive, Paris.
30 Later reports certainly suggest that it was *Rations* which set Wilton on the path to fame (*The Sydney Daily Telegraph*, 1 March 1924, p.16).
31 *The Stage*, 11 April 1918, p.13.
32 *The Era*, 8 May 1918, p.6.
33 The Kingsway was originally called the Novelty Theatre and was in Great Queen Street, Holborn.
34 *The Globe*, 6 September 1918, p.4.
35 Thesiger was reported as having been in Karno's revue companies as early as January 1916, but he does not appear in any other Karno listing.
36 *Western Morning News*, 4 March 1919, p.5.
37 *Evening Despatch*, 15 October 1918, p.2.
38 *The Stage*, 20 February 1919, p.12.

28. Money to Burn
1 Letter to Leslie Karno from Edith Karno, 15 January 1921, Leslie Karno archive.
2 Fred Jr. was demobbed on the 24 April 1919 but doesn't reappear in listings until August.
3 Fred Karno Westcott was born 3 November 1919.
4 Adeler and West, p.167.
5 His fine was reduced to ten pounds on appeal after he contested that the waitress in question had used the wrong measure.
6 *Hull Daily Mail*, 24 February 1919, p.1.

7 Karno's new Rolls had registration number XF9584 chassis number 63YE (with thanks to Graham Robinson).
8 *Western Mail*, 31 December 1918, p.4. The Lord Chamberlain's licensed script in the British Library states that it was to open at the Colchester Hippodrome on the 23 December, but there is no evidence of this (with thanks to Graham Rinaldi for this information).
9 *Nottingham Journal*, 18 January 1919, p.4.
10 *Western Daily Press*, 3 February 1920, p.3.
11 It is unclear if this is the same Helen Dircks who is known for her First World War poetry, but it seems likely.
12 *The Stage*, 25 September 1919, p.21.
13 Karno paid £500 and part exchanged his Daimler. Court reports reveal that Karno had a new car every year, previously buying the Daimler and a Belgian Metallurgiue, from the same dealer.
14 *Yorkshire Evening Post*, 4 May 1920, p.6.
15 The show's three scenes were: 'Winkle's House', 'Exterior of the Marriage Mart' and 'The Isle of Troy – the simple life'.
16 *The Stage*, 11 March 1920, p.14.
17 Ibid., 8 January 1920, p.19.
18 McCabe, *Charlie Chaplin*, p.115.
19 Seaton and Martin claim that Hay wrote the original sketch for Karno, but Karno's archive and newspaper listings confirm that Hay used *Moonstruck* as the basis of his subsequent solo sketch and paid Karno a royalty accordingly (Letter to Leslie

Karno from Fred Karno, 6 January 1930, Leslie Karno archive).
20 Seaton and Martin, p.32.
21 Ibid., p.94.
22 Seaton and Martin suggest that the boy wasn't added to the act until the 1920s but in fact he was included from 1915. Harbottle was added after Hay left Karno (Rinaldi, p.35 and p.48).
23 Seaton and Martin, p.36.
24 *The Era*, 14 July 1920, p.12
25 Ibid., 1 September 1920, p.14.
26 *The Stage*, 5 August 1920, p.11.
27 *Sheffield Independent*, 2 November 1920, p.6.
28 Jock Bennett was half of the double act Bennett and Martell, billed as: 'Those murderous knockabouts'.
29 He would go on to become a well-loved comedian, appearing on stage, radio and film, up until his death in 1942.
30 *The Stage*, 2 December 1920, p.13.
31 *Gloucestershire Echo*, 7 December 1920, p.5.
32 Written by Eric Blore and Austin Melford.
33 *The Era*, 23 February 1921, p.5.
34 Calthrop continued in the lead for the first few weeks (Finsbury Park Empire programme, 14 February 1921, author's collection).
35 *Sheffield Daily Telegraph*, 17 November 1920, p.6.
36 *The Scotsman*, 21 June 1921, p.7.
37 *The Stage*, 21 April 1921, p.11.
38 Jimmy Russell was the Eton boy, by now its longest running exponent. At the

end of August, Edgar Cooke stepped back into the drunk role.
39 *The Stage.*, 25 August 1921, p.13.
40 Ibid., 15 September 1921, p.13.

29. Prodigal Sons
1 Knoblock had been working on scenarios with Chaplin in Hollywood (Robinson, p.286).
2 *Dundee Evening Telegraph*, 20 September 1921, p.10.
3 *Gloucester Citizen*, 11 October 1921, p.3.
4 *The Stage*, 18 May 1922, p.2.
5 Ibid., 8 March 1923, p.20.
6 *Burnley News*, 8 March 1922, p.6.
7 *The Stage*, 23 February 1922, p.10.
8 Adeler and West, p.170.
9 *The Umpire*, 23 July 1916.
10 *The Stage*, 29 December 1921, p.11.
11 Ibid., 19 January 1922, p.17.
12 Ibid.
13 *The Era*, 13 September 1922, p.13.
14 *The Stage*, 14 September 1922, p.12.
15 Jacob, *More About Me*, p.35.
16 As Karno hunted around for a way to reverse his fortunes there were plenty of false starts. For instance, the press announced that he would produce a tour of *Polly*, a rehashed version of *The Beggar's Opera* which had opened at the Kingsway on 30 December 1922, but Robert Courtneidge subsequently secured the rights.
17 Carney subsequently married Vesta's sister Minnie.
18 Letter to Leslie Karno from Fred Karno, 2 January 1923, Leslie Karno archive.
19 The dispute revealed a split between the unions and, as a result, the AA, MU and NATE formed the Entertainments Federal Council, which took an aggressive stance for artistes' rights, while the VAF argued against collaborative action (siding with Karno's Association of Touring Managers).
20 *The Stage*, 21 June 1923, p.17. Karno's advertisements prove that he was subsequently offering three pounds per week to chorus girls (*The Stage*, 19 July 1923, p.21).
21 *Daily Herald*, 8 February 1923, p.5.
22 *The Era*, 28 March 1923, p.10.
23 *Leeds Mercury*, 24 May 1924, p.11.
24 *Dundee Evening Telegraph*, 12 January 1927, p.2.
25 *The Era*, 19 December 1923, p.8.
26 Helpfully, Fred Jr. was generally listed as Fred Westcott whereas his cousin was usually Freddie.
27 Prior to his return Leslie had most recently been playing, as Leslie West, in a seaside concert party called *The Vagrants*.
28 Letter to Leslie Karno from Fred Karno, 23 November 1923, Leslie Karno archive. He joined *Oh Yes!* in October 1923.
29 Radio broadcast, *Turning Point*, interview of Stan Laurel by Arthur Friedman, recorded 14 August 1957.
30 Five years earlier Stan had spent a short and unsuccessful spell at Roach's Rolin Studios, their star comedian at the time was Harold Lloyd.
31 Fred Junior first appears on the Hal Roach payroll, listed as part of Stan Laurel's company, week commencing 24 September 1923.
32 Hall's first Roach film is disputed by his biographers but was probably *Mother's Joy*, made in September 1923 (John Ullah, *This is More Than I Can Stand* [Brewin Books, Studley, Warwickshire, 2012], p.14).
33 His last week at the Hal Roach studio was week commencing 17 December 1923.
34 *The Era*, 30 July 1924, p.9.
35 As noted by Richard Bann, interview with the author.
36 *London Weekly News*, 3 September 1938, reproduced in, Ray Andrew, *On the Trail of Charlie Hall* (self-published, 1988) p.70.
37 Queenie found small parts in films and did extra work.

30. Stormy Weather
1 Berlin's original is called *Somebody's Coming to my House*. Oliver Hardy sings it in *Chickens Come Home* (1931). With thanks to A.J. Marriot for directing me to the original.
2 Fred Karno Jr. archive.
3 They had appeared together in several other movies, but most consider this their first intentional pairing as a double act.
4 *The Stage*, 5 April 1923, p.14.
5 *Leeds Mercury*, 8 May 1923, p.3.
6 Cyril Hemmington was credited as the writer.

7 As a solo comic Powell had shared the bill with Karno companies several times.
8 Television programme, *Review*, BBC2 (producer Tony Staveacre), broadcast 19 March 1971.
9 *The Stage*, 20 September 1923, p.12. The sketch also starred Leslie Crowther; thought to be the father of the presenter of 1980's TV show *The Price Is Right*. Crowther Sr. changed his professional name to Leslie Sargent in 1950 to avoid confusion with his son.
10 *The Stage*, 27 September 1923, p.12.
11 Despite this account, Powell wrote in his autobiography that the first week at Stoke Newington had gone well, and it was in fact a subsequent week at the Shepherds Bush Empire when Karno had left him under no illusions as to his abilities.
12 Television programme, *Review*, BBC2 (producer Tony Staveacre), broadcast 19 March 1971.
13 Roy Hudd, *Roy Hudd's Book of Music-Hall, Variety and Showbiz Anecdotes* (Robson Books, London, 1993) p.105.
14 A few weeks after his tour with Karno, Powell shared a bill with Max Miller, who later worked with Karno and recounted an almost identical experience – one wonders whether Miller was re-hashing Powell's anecdote.
15 Staveacre, p.78.
16 Stanley, p.108.
17 *The Stage*, 8 November 1923, p.14. Billie Reeves only performed in the sketch for a week or two, before returning to his own sketch company; George Hunter took over the lead.

18 Not to be confused with the 1955 Arthur Askey film of the same name.
19 Adeler and West, p.172.
20 *The Era*, 21 May 1924, p.12.
21 He was once sued by two women whose dresses were ruined when they were drenched by rainwater which had collected on the roof of the bandstand. Quite how this was Karno's fault is unclear, but he had to pay up four pounds and twenty shillings (*Surrey Advertiser*, 18 November 1916, p.6).
22 *The Stage*, 5 March 1925, p.13.
23 Ibid., 4 December 1924, p.27.
24 *Sheffield Daily Telegraph*, 20 October 1925, p.10.
25 *Exeter and Plymouth Gazette*, 7 March 1925, p.5.
26 *The Stage*, 29 January 1925, p.23.
27 Another advertised show, *Tally Ho* (which may have been born of *The Love Match* hunting scene), never made it off the drawing board.
28 *The Stage*, 15 October 1925, p.8.
29 *Yorkshire Post and Leeds Intelligencer*, 25 November 1925, p.3.
30 Adeler and West, p.177.
31 Letter to Edith Karno from Fred Karno, 24 December 1925, Leslie Karno archive.
32 *Hull Daily Mail*, 2 March 1926, p.9.
33 Letter to Leslie Karno from Fred Karno, undated but a reference to a revue called *Paris Nights*, dates it to late 1925 or early 1926, Leslie Karno archive.

31. Riches to Rags
1 Letter to Leslie Karno from Fred Karno, 30 April 1926, Leslie Karno archive.

2 Baker and Baker, p.87.
3 Karno's address was given as 27 Shaftesbury Avenue (*The Stage*, 5 August 1926, p.2).
4 Derby Daily Telegraph 29 December 1926, p.4.
5 Although it is not mentioned in the listings, this revue may have been in conjunction with Leon Vint and their new company.
6 *The Stage*, 6 January 1927, p.8.
7 *Nottingham Evening Post*, 15 March 1927, p.7
8 *Dundee Evening Telegraph*, 12 January 1927, p.2.
9 *Yorkshire Evening Post*, 19 February 1927, p.5.
10 East, *Max Miller the Cheeky Chappie*, p.15.
11 Ibid., p.67.
12 Ibid.
13 Ibid., p.18.
14 Ibid., p.68.
15 Ibid., p.69.
16 For instance: 'In loving memory of Edie Westcott Karno – "Sleep on dear Pal, thy sweet memory lives forever in the heart of one who loved thee." – Madge Thompson' (*The Stage*, 31 May 1928, p.4).
17 Jacob, *Me – A Chronicle About Other People*, p.74.
18 She was interred on 2 June 1927 at Sutton Road Cemetery, Prittlewell, in plot number 6737 (with thanks to Roger Robinson for this information).
19 Edith Karno last will and testament, 10 December 1926, Leslie Karno archive.
20 Karno created the impression that he and Marie were married throughout this period. However, archive records are confusing, for example the 1918 electoral roll records Karno and Marie living at the Albany, the next

few years records Fred and Edith Blanche Karno living there. This suggests that Marie was masquerading as Edith in respect of the legal status of her relationship with Karno (source London Electoral Registers 1832-1965).
21 Letter to Queenie Karno from Fred Karno, 27 May 1927, Ken Westcott archive.
22 Based on the Walter W. Ellis play of the same name.
23 Letter to Syd Chaplin from Fred Karno, 19 September 1927, Chaplin archive, Paris.
24 Letter to Queenie Karno from Fred Karno, 9 September 1927, Ken Westcott archive.
25 *Northampton Chronicle and Echo*, 13 September 1927, p.4.
26 The court records show that he had liabilities of £10,118 but assets of £25,454.
27 Adeler and West, p.186. There is no mention of the supertax demand in the bankruptcy filings.
28 *Yorkshire Evening Post*, 2 November 1927, p.9.
29 Adeler and West, p.182.
30 Ibid., p.186.

32. Hooray for Hollywood
1 Adeler and West, p.191. The flat was number 9 Charing Cross Mansions at 26 Charing Cross Road, next door to Wyndham's Theatre – the building remains unchanged today.
2 Extraordinary detective work by Graham Robinson, living in Brazil, managed to trace the Rolls through various ownerships ending with Christopher Southall in Redditch in the 1950s. Robinson tracked down a relative of Southall's living in Peru, who put him in touch with a nephew, back in Britain, who had a significant archive of Southall's photographs. In an extraordinary co-incidence, that nephew turned out to be this author's next-door neighbour! You couldn't make it up. Sadly, the Rolls itself has remained elusive.
3 Adeler and West, p.192.
4 With music by Henley Peters and Dorothy Elliot (*The Stage*, 10 November 1927, p.14). It is unclear whether this is the same Dorothy Elliot who was Karno's secretary for many years.
5 *The Stage*, 17 November 1927, p.6.
6 *The Stage*, 23 February 1928, p.8. There were reports suggesting that they had secured a four-week run in Paris, but this doesn't seem to have happened (*The Stage*, 13 October 1927, p.14).
7 Ibid. *The Stage*, 12 April 1928, p.11.
8 Letter to Queenie Karno from Fred Karno, 12 June 1928, Ken Westcott archive.
9 Letter to Leslie Karno from Fred Karno, 26 June 1929, Leslie Karno archive.
10 Letter to Leslie Karno from Fred Karno, 29 May 1929, Leslie Karno archive.
11 *The Stage*, 19 April 1928, p.11.
12 Karno's public examination was on 6 July 1928. His bankruptcy was discharged on 30 November.
13 Letter to Queenie Karno from Fred Karno, 12 June 1928, Ken Westcott archive.
14 Letter to Leslie Karno from Fred Karno, 16 May 1929, Leslie Karno archive.
15 Letter to Syd Chaplin from Alf Reeves, 21 January 1929, Chaplin archive, Paris.
16 Letter to Leslie Karno from Fred Karno, 7 April 1929, Leslie Karno archive.
17 Stein, p.135.
18 Syd later claimed that it was a set up to enable BIP to wriggle out of the contract due to their failure to gear up the film for sound (although Stein has demonstrated that this was not the case).
19 In a later letter Karno added: 'What a terrible time you must have had in Londonderry. We must bar that town forever of course.' Louise Murchison – interview with the author and letter to Leslie Karno from Fred Karno, 3 December 1928, Leslie Karno archive.
20 Devoy had played in Karno's *Mumming Birds* in 1917.
21 The William Morris Agency, at 1560 Broadway, was one of the biggest in the States. They represented Chaplin, the Marx Brothers, Mae West and Al Jolson to name a few. Their office building, built in 1924, still stands – a rare survivor in the skyscraper landscape of Times Square. Morris had taken over Karno's interests in America from Marinelli way back in 1907 (*Variety*, 26 January 1907, p.8).
22 Letter to Leslie Karno from Fred Karno, 31 July 1929, Leslie Karno archive.
23 *The Stage*, 8 August 1929, p.11.
24 Letter from Marie Karno to Leslie Karno, 14 August 1929, Leslie Karno archive.
25 He arrived on 16 August 1929.
26 Simon Louvish notes that it is highly unlikely that Karno was asked to work with the Marx brothers (Louvish, *Stan and Ollie: The Roots of Comedy*, p.261) but Karno's letters prove that he definitely received the offer, if not a contract, from William Morris.

ENDNOTES

27 Lasky, p.91.
28 Lasky maintained the New York operation to enable him to capitalise on Broadway talent that wouldn't or couldn't move to California, dividing his time between the two coasts.
29 Alf Reeves occasionally made fleeting appearances in Chaplin films including *A Dog's Life* (1918) and *Shoulder Arms* (1918).
30 Today it is the Jim Henson Studio, the home of *The Muppets*, so anarchic comedy continues to be created there. A huge statue of Kermit the Frog, dressed as Chaplin's Little Tramp, stands above the gates.
31 Robinson, p.209.
32 Adeler and West, p.199.
33 Ibid., p.200.
34 The house (which is now 1085 Summit Drive) had fourteen rooms and sat in six and a half acres, with tennis courts, swimming pool and a view of the ocean.
35 Chaplin, *My Autobiography*, p.306.
36 Karno confirmed in a letter to Leslie that he'd not seen Chaplin since that first meeting (letter to Leslie Karno from Fred Karno, undated but circa October 29, Leslie Karno archive).
37 Letter to Syd Chaplin from Alf Reeves, 25 September 1929, Chaplin archive, Paris.
38 Adeler and West, p.208. I've yet to find these reports. There was certainly some press attention, but as far as I can discover, only after he signed with Hal Roach and even then, it was fairly low key.
39 *The Sydney Sun*, 22 December 1929, p.9.

33. Crashing Out

1 Richard Bann interview with the author.
2 Online article, Richard Bann, *Our Relations – how and why iii*, laurel-and-hardy.com/films/features/ourrelations-h&w3.
3 Adeler and West, p.209.
4 Oliver Hardy was only paid $600 a week (reflecting Stan's additional input behind the camera). Hal Roach Studio payroll records, 26 October 1929, University of Southern California archive.
5 John McCabe, Al. Kilgore, Richard W. Bann, *Laurel and Hardy* (Ballantine Books, New York, 1975) p.20.
6 Louvish, *Stan and Ollie: The Roots of Comedy*, p.111.
7 Seaton and Martin, p.63.
8 Adeler and West, p.210.
9 Andrew, p.71.
10 Louvish, *Stan and Ollie: The Roots of Comedy*, p.216.
11 Richard Bann interview with the author.
12 Andrew, p.50.
13 Richard Lewis Ward, *A History of the Hal Roach Studios* (Southern Illinois University Press, Carbondale, 2005) p.74.
14 At the time, the exchange rate was around $5 to £1 sterling.
15 Adeler and West, p.210. Marie left England on the Aquitania on 21 September (UK outward passenger lists 1890-1960) and arrived in New York on 27 September 1929.
16 The family archive includes his official studio photo, on the back of which is written: 'Fred Karno, famous London music hall impresario, who has just signed a five-year contract with Hal Roach as associate producer.' Ken Westcott archive.
17 Hal Roach Studio records, board meeting minutes, 25 October 1929, University of Southern California archive and Karno/Roach contract dated 18 October 1929 (courtesy of David Tomlinson).
18 Adeler and West, p.211.
19 Karno described it as a 'Lizzie', which suggests a Model T. However, if he bought this new it was more likely to have been a Model A Tudor sedan which was introduced in 1928.
20 Adeler and West, p.219.
21 Letter to Queenie Karno from Fred Karno, 27 May 1927, Ken Westcott archive.
22 Letter to Queenie Karno from Fred Karno, 12 April 1932, Ken Westcott archive.
23 Louvish, *Keystone the Life and Clowns of Mack Sennett*, p.193.
24 Lewis Ward, p.73.
25 Laurel and Hardy's first 'talkie' was *Unaccustomed As We Are*, released in May 1929.
26 Gallagher, *Fred Karno, Master of Mirth and Tears*, p.147.
27 David Robinson states that this gag comes from a Karno sketch, but I've yet to establish which (Robinson, p.91).
28 I've been unable to find this gag in any film of the period. However, Karno did use it in his own 1936 film *Don't Rush Me* (*The Brisbane Telegraph*, 19 November 1935).
29 Frank Scheide, *The Influence of English Music Hall, Dan Leno, and Fred Karno on the Film Comedy of Stan Laurel*, article included in Alan Burton and Laraine Porter, *Scene-Stealing*, (Flicks Books, London, 2002), pp.58-63.
30 Karno/Roach contract dated 18 October 1929, p.6 (courtesy David Tomlinson).

31 Letter to Leslie Karno from Fred Karno, 2 December 1929, Leslie Karno archive.
32 Gallagher thought that Chaplin gave Karno £500 to set him up but Karno doesn't mention it in his letters, and his lack of cash suggests it unlikely.
33 Letter to Leslie Karno from Fred Karno, 6 January 1930, Leslie Karno archive.
34 Note to Leslie Karno from Fred Karno, 2 December 1929, Leslie Karno archive.
35 Adeler and West, p.217.
36 Louvish, *Stan and Ollie: The Roots of Comedy*, p.268.
37 Stan reportedly lost $30,000 in the Wall Street Crash (A.J. Marriot, *Laurel and Hardy the U.S. Tours* [Marriot Publishing, Hitchin, 2011] p.45).
38 Robinson, p.468.
39 *Todmorden Advertiser and Hebden Bridge Newsletter*, 21 April 1933, p.2.
40 Cable to Leslie Karno from Fred Karno, 5 January 1930, Leslie Karno archive.
41 Letter to Leslie Karno from Fred Karno, 6 January 1930, Leslie Karno archive.
42 Letter to Leslie Karno from Fred Karno, 21 January 1930, Leslie Karno archive.
43 Hal Roach Studio, board meeting minutes, 25 January 1930, University of Southern California archive.
44 McCabe, *Mr Laurel and Mr Hardy – An Affectionate Biography*, p.122.
45 Louvish, *Stan and Ollie: The Roots of Comedy*, p.260.
46 *Illustrated Sporting and Dramatic News*, 8 March 1930, p.27.

34. We're All Crazy Now
1 Letter to Leslie Karno from Fred Karno, 21 January 1930, Leslie Karno archive.
2 The Federal census, taken on 11 April 1930, states that he is not working.
3 Adeler and West, p.220.
4 Ibid., p.221.
5 She sailed on the Caronia, arriving in Southampton on 14 June 1930, Karno followed on the Tuscania (UK incoming passenger lists 1878-1960).
6 *Variety*, 18 June 1930, p.57.
7 *The Era*, 6 August 1930, p.9.
8 *Western Daily Press*, 23 May 1930, p.5.
9 Letter to Leslie Karno from Harry Leat, 27 September 1929, Leslie Karno archive.
10 Contract dated 15 April 1929, Leslie Karno archive. Karno probably met Jackson at BIP where he had been a screenwriter.
11 Karno registered under the Theatrical Employers Registration Act which confirms that his address as 26 Charing Cross Road (*The Era*, 30 July 1930, p.3).
12 *The Stage*, 7 August 1930, p.2.
13 *Yorkshire Evening Post*, 12 August 1930, p.3.
14 *The Stage*, 21 August 1930, p.4.
15 Ibid., 6 November 1930, p.8.
16 *The Era*, 1 January 1931, p.22.
17 *Daily Express*, 18 September 1941, cutting in Leslie Karno archive. Howes went on to have a successful career in musical theatre and film.
18 *The Stage*, 19 February 1931, p.5.
19 Which opened at the Capitol Theatre, Horsham in January 1931. This show had nothing to do with Karno, other than him giving Leslie permission to use the sketch in the bill, and so it is not included in our 'Karnography'.
20 *Yorkshire Evening Post*, 19 February 1931, p.12.
21 *Dundee Evening Telegraph*, 23 February 1931, p.3.
22 *The Stage*, 3 September 1931, p.9.
23 It opened on 7 September 1931 and was noted as being produced 'by arrangement with Fred Karno.'
24 Letter to Leslie Karno from Fred Karno, 6 January 1930, Leslie Karno archive.
25 Adeler and West, p.234. In contrast, Gallagher suggested that Mycroft was notoriously difficult to work with, and clashed spectacularly with Karno. Where this claim comes from is unknown, but since Con West worked with Karno on the film we might treat his account with more credibility.
26 Ian Bevan, *Top of The Bill – The Story of The London Palladium* (Frederick Muller Ltd, London, 1952) p.96.
27 Ibid., p.97.
28 *Daily Herald*, 7 December 1931, p.8.
29 *The Era*, 9 December 1931, p.15.
30 *The Stage* called it: 'A variety entertainment on orthodox lines' (*The Stage*, 19 April 1928, p.19).
31 Ibid., 3 May 1928, p.8.
32 Ibid., 8 November 1928, p.13.
33 Ibid., 17 December 1931, p.5.
34 *The Era*, 23 December 1931, p.12.
35 *The Stage*, 31 March 1932, p.4.
36 *The Era*, 4 May 1932, p.3.
37 Flanagan, p.137.

38 *The Era*, 20 January 1932, p.3.
39 Ibid., 25 May 1932, p.3.
40 Hudd, p.87.
41 East, *Max Miller the Cheeky Chappie*, p.73.
42 Norden, p.216. Twenty years later, with his writing partner Frank Muir, Norden would be engaged by producer Jack Hylton to write for the Crazy Gang's post-war revues.
43 *Daily Herald*, 31 December 1931, p.6.
44 Fisher, p.68.
45 Adeler and West, p.20.
46 For instance Flanagan's autobiography incorrectly records his first 'Crazy Week' as being March 1931 (Flanagan, p.138).
47 BBC radio script 1950 (Leslie Karno archive) and letter to Fred Karno from George Black, 12 July 1932, Con West archive (courtesy of David Robinson).
48 Letter to Fred Karno from George Black, 13 July 1932, Con West archive (courtesy of David Robinson).
49 The only problem with this theory is that Karno doesn't mention it in his letters to Leslie. Of course, we have no idea if Leslie's archive is complete.
50 Letter to Leslie Karno from Fred Karno, 19 July 1929, Leslie Karno archive.
51 Flanagan, p.138.

35. Reel to Real

1 *Sheffield Daily Telegraph*, 7 April 1932, p.7.
2 Clayton Hutton press release, 23 June 1932, Leslie Karno archive.
3 Clayton Hutton's involvement with Gallagher's biography was short lived.
4 Gallagher, *Fred Karno, Master of Mirth and Tears*, pp.153-7.
5 *Daily Herald*, 27 June 1932, p.13.
6 *Todmorden Advertiser and Hebden Bridge Newsletter*, 1 September 1933, p.5.
7 Chaplin used the gag in *The Gold Rush* (1925) and *City Lights* (1931).
8 Adeler and West, p.236.
9 *The Era*, 16 November 1932, p.17.
10 *The Stage*, 5 July 1962, p.4.
11 Released in January 1934.
12 BBC Radio script 1950, Leslie Karno archive.
13 On-line article, Tom Hill, *A house with a secret and a sensational showbiz past* (3 June 2009), poolepeople.co.uk. Marie's father lived at 89 (letter to Leslie Karno from Fred Karno, 16 May 1929, Leslie Karno archive).
14 *The Era*, 26 August 1936, p.14.
15 *The Stage*, 17 November 1932, p.9.
16 *Hull Daily Mail*, 10 April 1934, p.5.
17 *West London Observer*, 16 December 1932, p.4.
18 *The Era*, 30 December 1932, p.54.
19 *Nottingham Evening Post*, 10 January 1933, p.1.
20 Adeler and West, p.241.
21 *Nottingham Evening Post*, 10 January 1933, p.9.
22 Adeler and West, p.240.
23 Letters to Leslie Karno from Fred Karno, 31 July 1935 and 29 September 1933, Leslie Karno archive.
24 *The Stage*, 3 August 1933, p.10.
25 This was week commencing 17 April 1933, and since Karno recalled that it was Friday night, it must have been 21 April.
26 *Daily Herald*, 6 April 1933, p.3.
27 *Todmorden Advertiser and Hebden Bridge Newsletter*, 21 April 1933, p.2. A later British 1936 comedy by Buddy Harris has the title *International Revue*, so perhaps Roach sold the rights on.
28 He sailed on the Mauretania on 1 July 1933. Interestingly *Variety* reported Roach's return and noted that the abandoned film project had been entitled *A Night in an English Music Hall* (*Variety*, 16 May 1933) – with thanks to A.J. Marriot for bringing this to my attention.
29 *Shields Daily News*, 1 July 1933, p.6.
30 Barty went on to appear in films with Wakefield and Nelson, and notably as Jitters the butler, in Laurel and Hardy's *Oliver The Eighth* (1934).
31 *Hull Daily Mail*, 10 April 1934, p.5.
32 *Burnley Express*, 18 April 1934, p.3.
33 Letter to Leslie Karno from Fred Karno, 24 January 1935, Leslie Karno archive.
34 *The Stage*, 23 August 1934, p.6.
35 *Daily Herald*, 4 July 1935, p.9.
36 Mike Asher appeared under his stage name Hal Walters. He went on to make several films including a sizeable part in *Where There's A Will*, with Will Hay, in 1936. He can also be seen playing a barman opposite George Robey in *A Girl Must Live* (1939). Tragically, Asher was killed (along with his wife and daughter) during an air raid in 1940. (Note that internet listings often confuse him with actor Henry Paul Walters, but Hal Walters was definitely Mike Asher.)

37 *Daily Herald*, 20 September 1935, p.15.
38 Letter to Leslie Karno from Fred Karno, 24 January 1935, Leslie Karno archive.
39 The film is often listed as *Mother, Don't Rush Me*.

36. Finale

1 Adeler and West, p.245.
2 BBC radio script, 1950, Leslie Karno archive and Adeler and West, p.245.
3 Ibid.
4 *The Era*, 8 January 1936, p.10.
5 *Burnley Express*, 7 November 1936, p.5.
6 Adeler and West, p.246.
7 Letter to Leslie Karno from Fred Karno, 22 October 1935, Leslie Karno archive.
8 This building still survives – at the time of writing it is an estate agency.
9 Gallagher probably got the story from Felstead's book, which is full of Karno inaccuracies (Felstead, p.123).
10 David Robinson told me he felt it was the sort of thing Chaplin might do but, like the Chaplin archive in Paris, he had no evidence that it happened, and if they don't – no-one does.
11 British Phone Book 1880-84.
12 Television programme, *Magical History Tour*, BBC2, broadcast 7 February 1986.
13 Letter to Leslie Karno from Fred Karno, 21 July 1937, Leslie Karno archive.
14 Fred Karno Jr. is listed a handful of times in the mid-1920s. He appears in a show called *Sons of the Sea* (*The Lethbridge Daily Herald*, 31 October 1925, p.8) and two years later in *Captain Plunckett's Revue of 1926* (*The Lethbridge Daily Herald*, 18 January 1927, p.10). (With thanks to A.J. Marriot for bringing these listings to my attention.)
15 *Variety*, 5 September 1928, p.58.
16 Adeler and West, p.249.
17 *The Stage*, 28 July 1938, p.14. The directors were stated as Fred Karno of The Square, Lilliput, Dorset, Charles H. Reynolds and Frederick T. Reynolds.
18 *The Era*, 4 August 1938, p.1.
19 Ibid., 11 August 1938, p.7.
20 Some sources suggest that this property was subsequently demolished, but Peter Glanville confirmed to me that the existing house is the same one Karno lived in.
21 Letter to Leslie Karno from Fred Karno, 23 January 1939, Leslie Karno archive. At that time there was no universal old age pension, however those over seventy on low income could apply for one.
22 Ibid. *The Love Match* staring Arthur Askey was unrelated to Karno's show, and was based on a different play.
23 Television programme, *Magical History Tour*, BBC2, broadcast 7 February 1986. Mrs Watkinson (by then Mrs Kisielewski) was interviewed for the documentary (with thanks to Peter Glanville for sharing it with me).
24 It was advertised as part of a variety roadshow, produced by Ethel Whitty (*The Stage*, 30 March 1939).
25 *Exeter and Plymouth Gazette*, 2 February 1940, p.6.
26 *Wiltshire Times and Trowbridge Advertiser*, 8 June 1940, p.7.
27 *The Era*, 1 June 1939, p.7.
28 *Daily Mirror*, 2 June 1939, p.9.
29 Randle, who was by then an institution in Blackpool, was appearing on the North Pier in *On With The Show*.
30 Television programme, *Magical History Tour*, BBC2, broadcast 7 February 1986.
31 Letter to Leslie Karno from Fred Karno, date unknown, Leslie Karno archive.
32 The Treaty of Versailles (1919), Article 42.
33 *The Evening News*, 27 October 1936 (reproduced in Adeler and West, p.181), see also *The Sphere*, 27 March 1926, p.48.
34 *The Scotsman*, 2 November 1938, p.7.
35 *Yorkshire Post and Leeds Intelligencer*, 2 March 1939, p.6.
36 *Gloucestershire Echo*, 15 November 1944, p.4.
37 In one episode (series 3, episode 6, *Room at the Bottom*) an over-zealous drill sergeant calls the Dad's Army platoon a Fred Karno outfit.
38 *Daily Mirror*, 16 March 1968, p.11.
39 Seaton and Martin, p.124.
40 *The Stage*, 3 April 1941, p.5.
41 Letter to Leslie Karno from Marie Karno, 16 September 1941, Leslie Karno archive.
42 britmovie.co.uk. I tried in vain to track down the writer of this account. I include it here with thanks and the hope that he would have been happy to have his story preserved in print.
43 *Birmingham Mail*, 18 September 1941, p.3.
44 *Yorkshire Post and Leeds Intelligencer*, 19 September 1941, p.2.
45 Adeler and West, p.181.
46 *The Stage*, 25 September 1941, p.3.

47 Fred Karno, *I Saw Stars, The Picturegoer*, 7 December 1935, p.26.
48 Radio broadcast, *Turning Point*, interview of Stan Laurel by Arthur Friedman, recorded 14 August 1957.
49 McCabe, *Mr Laurel and Mr Hardy – An Affectionate Biography*, p.26.
50 *Daily Mirror*, 19 March 1971, p.19.

37. Encore
1 Letter to Leslie Karno from Marie Karno, unknown date in March 1942, Leslie Karno archive.
2 Letter to Leslie Karno from Naomi Jacob, 17 March 1942, Leslie Karno archive.
3 Marie's death certificate, 15 November 1944.
4 England and Wales National Probate Calendar (index of wills and administrations, 1858-1966).
5 Peter Glanville interview with the author.
6 Letter to Ed Patterson from Stan Laurel, 14 October 1957. Online article, Dalya Alberge, *Stan Laurel's Secret Jibes at 'mean, cheap', Charlie Chaplin. Daily Mail Online*, 1 December 2017. Dailymail.co.uk/news/article-5137711/Letter-shows-Stan-Laurel-thought-Charlie-Chaplin-mean.
7 *Mumming Birds* poster, A.J. Marriot collection.
8 *Daily Herald*, 8 June 1948, p.2.
9 *Sunday Empire News*, 22 February 1948 (cutting in Fred Karno Jr. archive).
10 They married on 24 October 1953.
11 Fred Karno Westcott III can be seen playing double bass as Ann Miller sings *Too Darn Hot* in MGM's *Kiss Me Kate* (1953).
12 *Nelson Leader*, 9 June 1950, p.4.
13 Letter to Leslie Karno from Percy Manchester, 2 March 1952, Leslie Karno archive.
14 *The Stage*, 8 May 1952, p.3. A letter to Con West from Fred Karno, dated 25 February 1941, confirms his agreement to West going ahead with *Fred Karno's Army*, Con West archive (courtesy of David Robinson).
15 Legal agreement, 19 January 1952, Leslie Karno archive.
16 *The Thanet Times*, 7 February 1961, p.1.
17 Norden, p.72.
18 Louvish, *Keystone the Life and Clowns of Mack Sennett*, p.291.
19 Laurel and Hardy's stage tours are well documented in a series of books by A.J. Marriot (see bibliography).
20 Famously Stan's number was listed in the phone book, and he was always happy to chat with fans who called him up.
21 *The Daily Herald*, 22 January 1935, p.10.
22 *The Times*, 16 March 1971, p.4.
23 Television programme, *Review*, BBC2 (producer Tony Staveacre), broadcast 19 March 1971. With huge thanks to Tony Staveacre for sharing it with me.
24 Ibid.
25 Letter to the BBC from Leslie Karno, 21 April 1971, Leslie Karno archive.
26 Pink Floyd apparently played a gig in the palm court before it was demolished (article by Jeff Touzeau, 2005, Tapeor.com).
27 I am immensely grateful to David Gilmour and Astoria's custodian, Langley Iddins, for allowing me to visit her, and to A.J. Marriot for arranging it.
28 *Coventry Evening Telegraph*, 16 September 1971, p.6.
29 Newspaper cutting, Leslie Karno archive – unknown source, 1950.
30 *The People*, 11 May 1930, p.12.
31 *The Era*, 17 June 1936, p.5.
32 Online article, BBC.co.uk/news, 17 August 2017.
33 For example, L'École Internationale de Théâtre Jacques Lecoq, Paris. I have David Pugh and Jos Houben to thank for bringing this modern-day Fun Factory to my attention.

Karnography

I. Index of Karno Productions

The following is a list of Karno productions in order of appearance. Inevitably some sketches may have been performed earlier without being listed, while others were advertised as being 'in preparation' but have not been found in listings. Some of these were never produced, others appeared with different titles. Still more are sometimes confused with Ted Karno's troupe.

Some try-out performances were under different titles, in these cases I have listed productions under their most common name, with alternatives noted. The date of the first production refers to its first identified listing under any title.

The key to the Karnography is as follows:
Title: date of first performance – venue of first performance – (source) – alternative title(s) (U.S. = American title) – further comments.

1. **Summer Boarders:** 26 December 1888 – St James's Hall, London – (*The Graphic*, 22 December 1888, p.3) – originally a Moore and Burgess sketch, later played by the Three Karnos on tour.
2. **Love in a Tub:** 4 November 1889 – Barnard's Amphitheatre Portsmouth – (*The Era*, 9 November 1889, p.20) – the sketch is not listed but other evidence suggests this as the week in question.
3. **The American Boxing Ball:** 14 July 1890 – Follies Variety Theatre Manchester – (*The Era*, 19 July 1890, p.17) – the routine was also later performed by Ted Tysall's Karno Trio.
4. **Hilarity:** 22 June 1891 – Gaiety Concert Hall, Birmingham – (*The Era*, 27 June 1891, p.16) – first performance was as **He Knocked Them**, after this try-out, it appears as **Hilarity** on the 31 August 1891 at the Royal Aquarium, Westminster (*London Evening Standard*, 4 September 1891, p.1) – also played under the title **The Lover's Serenade** for two weeks in September 1893 at The Star, Dublin. Once incorrectly recorded as **Frivolity** by a critic in the *Music Hall and Theatre Review*.
5. **Jail Birds:** 23 December 1895 – The Paragon, London – (*The Stage*, 26 December 1895, p.11).
6. **The Karnophone:** 22 September 1896 – The Empire, Portsmouth – (*The Era*, 26 September 1896, p.22 & 31) – also listed as **Karnograph**, Karno's memoirs suggest possibly much earlier, around 1892, at the People's Palace Bristol.
7. **A Day Out:** 16 March 1897 – Barnard's Palace of Varieties, Chatham – (*Music Hall and Theatre Review*, 20 March 1897, p.10) – possibly a try-out or shorter version of **New Woman's Club**.
8. **New Woman's Club:** 30 May 1898 – The Oxford Music Hall, London – (*The Era*, 4 June 1898, p.31).
9. **Early Birds:** 12 June 1899 – Royal Albert Music Hall, London – (*The Era*, 10 June 1899, p.16) – first performance was as **The Dossers** (this was advertised at the Royal Albert, but no listing or review exists). Also: **A Night in a London Slum** (U.S.) or **A Night in the Slums of London** (U.S.) – First appearance as **Early Birds** is 24 September 1900 at Collin's Music Hall, Islington (*The Era*, 22 September 1900, p.16).
10. **The Burglary:** 26 December 1899 – The London Music Hall, London – (*The Era*, 30 December 1899, p.18) – sometimes listed as **The Burglars** – probably a stand-alone version of the first scene from **Jail Birds**, subsequently used in **Her Majesty's Guests**.
11. **Her Majesty's Guests:** 26 March 1900 – Princess of Wales Theatre, Kennington – (*The Era*, 3 March 1900, p.4) – **His Majesty's Guests** from 4 February 1901 (*The Stage*, 7 February 1901, p.2) – the title was changed after Queen Victoria's death.

12. **Marked for Life:** 29 October 1900 – Victoria Theatre, Walthamstow – (*The Era*, 3 November 1900, p.13).
13. **The Dandy Thieves:** 20 January 1902 – Empire Palace, Edinburgh – (*Edinburgh Evening News*, 21 January 1902) – shorter version of **His Majesty's Guests**.
14. **My Japanese Cherry Blossom:** 23 February 1903 – Circus of Varieties, Rochdale – (*The Era*, 28 February 1903, p.27).
15. **Saturday to Monday:** 4 November 1903 – Prince of Wales Theatre, Grimsby – (*The Stage*, 19 November 1903, p.12) – sometimes **The New Mama**.
16. **Mumming Birds:** 25 April 1904 – Chelsea Palace, London – (*The Stage*, 28 April 1904, p.18) – first performed as **Twice Nightly**, also known as **A Stage Upon a Stage** and **A Night in an English Music Hall** (U.S.) – first listing is as **Twice Nightly** on 25 April but a later legal case suggests that it was staged on the 14 April at The Star, Bermondsey (*The Stage*, 30 April 1908, p.14); if so it went unrecorded. First confirmed appearance as **Mumming Birds** is 6 June 1904 at the Canterbury Music Hall (*Music Hall and Theatre Review*, 3 June 1904, p.5).
17. **The Thirsty First:** 14 November 1904 – The Paragon, London – (*East London Observer*, 19 November 1904, p.7) – not staged again until relaunched on 29 January 1906 at The Star, Bermondsey.
18. **Pot Pourri:** 7 January 1905 – The Paragon, London – (*East London Observer*, 7 January 1905) – probably a 'greatest hits' of the early knockabout sketches, cited as being played at a benefit concert for one time only.
19. **Diving Birds:** 15 June 1905 – The Metropole, Camberwell – (*The Era*, 17 June 1905, p.31) – advertised as being performed; 'for copyright purposes', but there is no record of this or any subsequent performance.
20. **Moses and Son:** 18 December 1905 – Bordesley Palace, Birmingham – (*The Era*, 23 December 1905, p.22).
21. **The Smoking Concert:** 16 April 1906 – The Oxford Music Hall, London – (*The Era*, 14 April 1906, p.34) – **A Night in a London Club** (U.S.) or **The Amateur Entertainers** – possibly also played as **Our Annual Social** by Lee Simpson's Company at the Glasgow Palace, 16 April 1906.
22. **Fred Karno's Old Time Richardson's Show:** 24 December 1906 – Olympia, London – (*London Daily News*, 17 December 1906, p.1) – part of C.B. Cochran's 'Fun City'.
23. **The Football Match:** 24 December 1906 – Palace Theatre Manchester – (*Manchester Courier and Lancashire General Advertiser*, 21 December 1906, p.1) – a later revue version was staged in 1923 (see below).
24. **What Uncle Lost:** 24 January 1907 – The Empress, Brixton, London – (*Music Hall and Theatre Review*, 1 February 1907, p.9) – staged for three nights only during the Music Hall War. This may have been rewritten as **A Trip to Whitby** the following year (see below).
25. **Dame Trot:** 11 March 1907 – Ardwick Empire, Manchester – (*Manchester Courier and Lancashire General Advertiser*, 7 March 1907, p.1) – this was a sketch version of Karno's pantomime *The House That Jack Built*.
26. **Grand Mammoth Easter Fete and Gala:** 29 March 1907 – Balmoral Show Ground, Belfast – (*The Era*, 30 March 1907, p.34).
27. **The Bailiff:** 15 April 1907 – Wigan Hippodrome – (*Wigan Observer and District Advertiser*, 18 April 1907, p.1) – it was locally advertised as being performed initially under the title **The Hire System** although Karno's own advertising has it as **The Bailiffs** (note the 's'), it occasionally is listed as **The Hire System** and later **Perkins in Possession**, but **The Bailiff**, is the most common title.
28. **London Suburbia:** 17 June 1907 – Canterbury Music Hall, London – (*The Era*, 15 June 1907, p.18).
29. **A Tragedy of Errors:** 8 July 1907 – Manchester Hippodrome – (*The Era*, 6 July 1907, p.30) – also **Up the Pole**, a slang term meaning insane.
30. **The Casuals:** 9 March 1908 – The Opera House, Tunbridge Wells – (*The Era*, 7 March 1908, p.44) – first performed as **The Outcasts**. First appears as **The Casuals** at the Palace, Stoke Newington, 30 March 1908 (*The Era*, 4 April 1908, p.20).

31. **A Trip to Whitby:** 8 June 1908 – The Palace Theatre, Maidstone – (*The Stage*, 28 May 1908, p.14) – the sketch is advertised in advance for this week, but no record or listing has been found to support this. Possibly a version of **What Uncle Lost** as it had the same writer.
32. **The G.P.O.:** 19 October 1908 – Sheffield Empire – (*Sheffield Independent*, 16 October 1908, p.8).
33. **The Yap Yaps:** 30 November 1908 – Margate Hippodrome – (*The Music Hall and Theatre Review*, 27 November 1908, p.5).
34. **Skating:** 3 May 1909 – Queen's Palace of Varieties, Poplar – (*The Era*, 1 May 1909, p.20).
35. **Perkins MP:** 12 July 1909 – Palace Theatre, Leicester – (*Melton Mowbray Mercury and Oakham and Uppingham News*, 15 July 1909, p.1).
36. **Spring Cleaning:** 16 August 1909 – Empire Theatre, Newport – (*The Era*, 21 August 1909, p.23).
37. **The Wontdetania:** 11 April 1910 – The Paragon, London – (*The Era*, 9 April 1910, p.20) – advanced advertising shows that it was originally intended to open at the Ilford Hippodrome but for some reason the venue was changed.
38. **Jimmy the Fearless:** 18 April 1910 – Willesden Hippodrome and Ealing Hippodrome (unconfirmed) – (*The Stage*, 28 April 1910, p.12) – also **The Boy 'Ero** – First performance is unconfirmed, advanced press reports suggest that it was intended to open on the 11 April at Holloway Empire, but that did not transpire. A.J. Marriot's research indicates that it opened on 18 April, playing both Willesden and Ealing (Marriot, *Laurel Stage by Stage*, p.244). First verifiable listing is the following week 25 April 1910, at the Stratford Empire, London.
39. **The Annual Sports:** 9 May 1910 – Islington Empire, London – (*The Stage*, 12 May 1910, p.12) – later rewritten and produced in 1912 as **The Village Sports** (see below).
40. **Mr Justice Perkins:** 11 July 1910 – Palace Theatre, Bristol – (*The Music Hall and Theatre Review*, 7 July 1910, p.5) – also **Perkins JP**.
41. **The Wow Wows:** 8 August 1910 – Tottenham Palace, London – (*The Stage*, 11 August 1910) – **A Night in a London Secret Society** (U.S.), at least one listing in its first week has it as **Wallah Wallah**.
42. **The New Slavey:** 26 September 1910 – The Canterbury, London – (*The Stage*, 29 September 1910).
43. **A Harlequinade in Black and White:** 26 December 1910 – The American Music Hall, New York, NY – (A.J. Marriot, *Chaplin Stage by Stage* [Marriot Publishing, Hitchin, 2005] p.236).
44. **Who's Who:** 23 October 1911 – Palace Theatre, Southampton – (*The Stage*, 26 October 1911).
45. **Perkins The Purser:** 11 December 1911 – Empress, Brixton, London – (*The Stage*, 14 December 1911) – originally advertised as **Perkins in Port**, it was a follow up to **Wontdetania**.
46. **The Hydro:** 26 February 1912 – Preston Hippodrome – (*Preston Herald*, 24 February 1912).
47. **Thumbs Up:** 1 March 1912 – Aston Hippodrome, Birmingham – (*The Stage*, 14 March 1912) – listed in advance (whilst a work in progress), as **Thumbs Down** – played just one performance for copyright purposes.
48. **The Big House:** 1 March 1912 – Aston Hippodrome, Birmingham – (*The Stage*, 14 March 1912) – played just one performance for copyright purposes.
49. **The Waltz Scream:** 8 April 1912 – Exeter Hippodrome – (*Exeter and Plymouth Gazette*, 5 April 1912) – advertising suggests that its appearance at Exeter was after two weeks at the London Palladium but there is no evidence for this.
50. **Perkins in Paris:** 13 May 1912 – New Cross Empire, London – (*The Stage*, 9 May 1912) – rewritten version of **The Waltz Scream**.
51. **The Village Sports:** 2 September 1912 – Colchester Hippodrome – (*The Stage*, 29 August 1912) – rewritten version of **Annual Sports**.
52. **Wakes Week:** 14 October 1912 – Birmingham Hippodrome – (*Birmingham Daily Gazette*, 16 October 1912, p.1) – may have started life as **Perkins the Punter** – Karno's memoirs and a *Stage* listing suggest that it may have opened on the 30 September 1912 at the Palace, Blackburn (*The Stage*, 26 September 1912, p.10), but 14 October is the first confirmed listing.

53. **Flats:** 10 March 1913 – Royal Theatre, Worcester – (*The Stage*, 13 March 1913).
54. **The Steam Laundry:** 1 September 1913 – Southampton Hippodrome – (*The Stage*, 11 September 1913).
55. **Teeth:** 17 August 1914 – Royalty Theatre, Chester – (*Cheshire Observer*, 15 August 1914) – also **The Dental Institute**.
56. **Home from Home:** 7 September 1914 – Portsmouth Hippodrome – (*Portsmouth Evening News*, 7 September 1914).
57. **Parlez Vous Français?:** 7 December 1914 – Liverpool Olympia – (*The Era*, 9 December 1914, p.12).
58. **Hot and Cold:** 1 March 1915 – Colchester Hippodrome – (*The Stage*, 4 March 1915, p.6) – the first listing in *The Stage* suggests that it may have appeared elsewhere before this first confirmed listing.
59. **Jane Shore:** 28 May 1915 – Ulster Volunteer Force Hospital – (*Belfast Newsletter*, 29 May 1915, p.10) – one-off performance for injured troops (*Jane Shore* was an historical drama, so this was presumably a parody of that).
60. **All Women:** 27 September 1915 – Colchester Hippodrome – (*The Stage*, 30 September 1915, p.6) – also **All Ladies** or **All Eves** – From time to time this is incorrectly listed as *All Eyes* (instead of *All Eves*) and appears to be confused with a Fred Kitchen sketch of that title.
61. **Mustard and Cress:** 24 January 1916 – Preston Empire – (*Lancashire Evening Post*, 22 January 1916, p.4) – renamed **Knick Knacks** from 7 February 1916 at the Liverpool Empire (*Liverpool Echo*, 4 February 1916, p.6).
62. **Oh, Law!:** 8 May 1916 – The King's Theatre, Southsea, Portsmouth – (*Sunday Post*, 7 May 1916, p.2) – also appeared as **Have a Banana**.
63. **On and Off:** 16 October 1916 – The Empire Theatre, Sunderland – (*Sunderland Daily Echo and Shipping Gazette*, 17 October 1916, p.5) – revised version of **Oh, Law!**
64. **L.S.D.:** 20 November 1916 – King's Theatre, Southsea, Portsmouth – (*Hampshire Telegraph*, 17 November 1916, p.6) – also **Pounds, Shillings and Pence** or **£.S.D.**
65. **Three Bites:** 18 June 1917 – Boscombe Hippodrome – (*The Bournemouth Graphic*, 15 June 1917, p.4).
66. **Nosey Knows:** 8 October 1917 – The Bedford, London – (*The Stage*, 11 October 1917, p.9).
67. **Phew!:** 28 January 1918 – Nottingham Empire – (*Nottingham Evening Post*, 29 January 1918, p.3).
68. **Rations:** 1 April 1918 – Colchester Hippodrome – (*The Stage*, 11 April 1918, p.13).
69. **A Week-End:** 26 August 1918 – Theatre Royal, York – (*The Era*, 28 August 1918, p.11).
70. **Kill or Kure:** 7 October 1918 – Liverpool Empire – (*Liverpool Echo*, 7 October 1918, p.1).
71. **Moonstruck:** 30 December 1918 – Newport Empire – (*Western Mail*, 31 December 1918, p.4) – the script deposited at the British Library suggests it may have played the Colchester Hippodrome a week earlier.
72. **Hustle:** 22 September 1919 – Colchester Hippodrome – (*The Stage*, 18 September 1919, p.14).
73. **Money to Burn:** 15 December 1919 – Edmonton Empire (*The Stage*, 18 December 1919, p.14).
74. **Isle of Troy:** 8 March 1920 – Stratford Empire, London – (*The Stage*, 4 March 1920, p.12).
75. **What's What:** 13 September 1920 – Salisbury Palace – (*The Stage*, 9 September 1920, p.10) – a revised version of **Isle of Troy**.
76. **Red Hot:** 6 December 1920 – The Coliseum, Cheltenham – (*The Stage*, 2 December 1920, p.13).
77. **Will You Kiss Me?:** 14 February 1921 – Finsbury Park Empire, London – (*The Stage*, 17 February 1921, p.12) – this first listing suggests that it may have been staged at the New Cross Empire, London, two weeks earlier.
78. **Yes Papa!:** 21 February 1921 – The Coliseum, Cheltenham – (*The Stage*, 17 February 1921, p.12) – originally intended to be called **Sixes and Sevens** but never produced under that title.

79. **French Beans:** 25 April 1921 – Jubilee Hall, Weymouth – (*The Era*, 20 April 1921, p.23).
80. **Scarlet Runners:** 10 October 1921 – Cheltenham Hippodrome – (*Gloucester Citizen*, 8 October 1921, p.8) – possibly initially called **Tit for Tat**, but no record of it being played under this title – revised version of **Red Hot**.
81. **1922:** 16 January 1922 – Nottingham Empire – (*The Stage*, 29 December 1921, p.10) – renamed **1923** in January 1923.
82. **Oh Yes!:** 21 August 1922 – Alexandra Theatre, Birmingham – (*The Stage*, 24 August 1922, p.2) – revamped and retitled production of Jackson Owen's *Knight of the Garter* – the first listing suggests it may have played elsewhere before this date but no evidence of this has been found.
83. **The Surpassing Show:** 2 April 1923 – Stratford Empire, London – (*The Era*, 28 March 1923, p.17) – re-titled C.B. Cochran review *Mayfair and Montmartre*.
84. **The Football Match** (revue version): 24 September 1923 – Alexandra Theatre, Stoke Newington – (*The Stage*, 20 September 1923, p.12) – a revue which incorporated new versions of **The Football Match** and **The Smoking Concert** sketches.
85. **The Love Match:** 3 March 1924 – The King's Theatre, Southsea, Portsmouth – (*Portsmouth Evening News*, 28 February 1924, p.1).
86. **Karno's Follies:** 13 October 1924 – The Metropole, Bootle – (*The Stage*, 16 October 1924, p.6) – also **Karnoisms**, **Karno's Quest**, **Fred Karno's Quest of Stage Talent**, or individually titled for each location it played; e.g. **The Preston Follies** etc.
87. **Miss 1925:** 26 January 1925 – The King's Theatre, Southsea, Portsmouth – (*Hampshire Telegraph*, 23 January 1925, p.12).
88. **Tittle Tattle:** 12 October 1925 – Coventry Hippodrome – (*The Stage*, 15 October 1925, p.8) – retitled **On with The Show** (November 1925) and subsequently **The Show**.
89. **Jumbles:** 3 January 1927 – The Palace Theatre, Hull – (*The Era*, 29 December 1926, p.29).
90. **Hullo There!:** 14 November 1927 – The Tivoli Theatre, New Brighton – (*The Stage*, 10 November 1927, p.14).
91. **Tainted:** 1 July 1929 – The Playhouse, Colchester – (*The Stage*, 11 July 1929, p.12) – described as a burlesque "talkie", but whether this was a sketch or a short film is unclear, it was played for one week only along with a revived version of **Mumming Birds**.
92. **Laffs:** 4 August 1930 – Birmingham Empire – (*The Stage*, 31 July 1930, p.8) – also **Karno's Krazy Komics** – subsequently licensed to George Black for use by the Crazy Gang at The London Palladium but not under this title.
93. **Real Life:** 26 December 1932 – Theatre Royal, Leicester – (*The Era*, 30 December 1932, p.54).

Note: the above list of Karno productions does not include *Over the Garden Wall* which was a Rick Klaie company sketch in which the Three Karnos appeared for one week only. However, for completeness the details are: **Over the Garden Wall:** 17 April 1893 – The Middlesex, Drury Lane, London – (*Music Hall and Theatre Review*, 21 April 1893, p.22). The Three Karnos also appeared, performing both *Hilarity* and the harlequinade, in *Bluebeard* at the Shakespeare Theatre, Liverpool, in December 1892. This is not included above as it was not a Karno production.

II. Karno Pantomimes

The following are Karno produced Christmas pantomimes. In Karno's day some pantomimes played in one venue initially and then toured to other cities, for instance Cinderella in 1905 started in Dublin then was played in Manchester, Sheffield and Hull. Only the first place of performance is listed below.

1. 1904: **Cinderella:** 29 December 1904 – The Alexandra Theatre, Stoke Newington (*The People*, 1 January 1905, p.4).
2. 1905: **Cinderella:** 26 December 1905 – The Gaiety Theatre, Dublin (*The Irish Times*, 5 December 1905, p.6).
3. 1906: **The House That Jack Built:** 5 December 1906 – The Grand Theatre, Glasgow (*The Scottish Referee*, 7 December 1906, p.6).
4. 1907: **Humpty Dumpty:** 4 December 1907 – The Grand Theatre, Glasgow (*The Scottish Referee*, 2 December 1907, p.6).
5. 1907: **The House That Jack Built:** 24 December 1907 – The New King's Theatre, Sunderland (*Newcastle Daily Chronicle*, 23 December 1907, p.5).
6. 1908: **The House That Jack Built:** 26 December 1908 – The Marlborough Theatre, Islington, London (*The Referee*, 27 December 1908, p.4).
7. 1909: **Mother Goose:** 8 December 1909 – The Grand Theatre, Glasgow (*Music Hall and Theatre Review*, 2 December 1909, p.4).
8. 1909: **The House That Jack Built:** 26 December 1909 – The Broadway Theatre, New Cross, London (*Kentish Mercury*, 24 December 1909, p.4).
9. 1910: **Dick Whittington:** 7 December 1910 – The Grand Theatre, Glasgow (*The Stage*, 1 December 1910, p.21).
10. 1910: **Cinderella:** 24 December 1910 – The Broadway Theatre, New Cross, London (*The Era*, 31 December 1910, p.16).
11. 1911: **The House That Jack Built:** 26 December 1911 – The Borough Theatre, Stratford, London (*East London Observer*, 16 December 1911, p.4).
12. 1912: **The House That Jack Built:** 2 December 1912 – Olympia, Glasgow for just one week, then The Palace Theatre, Aberdeen (*The Stage*, 5 December 1912, p.24 & *Aberdeen Press and Journal*, 9 December 1912, p.1).
13. 1912: **Mother Goose:** 26 December 1912 – The Borough Theatre, Stratford, London (*The Sporting Times*, 28 December 1912, p.5).
14. 1913: **Mother Goose:** 26 December 1913 – The Marlborough Theatre, Holloway, London (*Shoreditch Observer*, 3 January 1914, p.8).

III. Karno Filmography

Apart from **The Bailiffs** (1932), **Oh What a Duchess** (1934) and **Jailbirds** (1940), all of these films appear to be lost and release dates are unknown. Karno's own memoirs fail to mention most of them. Further research on these would be a welcome addition to the Karno story:

1. **Early Birds:** 1923 (released 1924) – first recorded film made by Brouett-Egrot starring Karno himself as the Jewish pedlar.
2. **Jail Birds:** 1923 – Brouett-Egrot Film Company.
3. **Mumming Birds:** 1923 – Brouett-Egrot Film Company.
4. **Bad Companions:** 1932 – BIP. Karno acted as advisor to Con West and John Orton on the physical comedy in the film and received a writing credit.
5. **The Bailiffs:** 1932 – Gainsborough/Gaumont British Pictures Corporation Ltd. Flanagan and Allen's first film, with a cameo appearance by Karno.
6. **Post Haste:** 1933 – Gainsborough/Gaumont British Pictures Corporation Ltd. Starred Joey Porter and Jack Williams. Based on *G.P.O.*

7. **Tooth Will Out:** 1933 – Gainsborough/Gaumont British Pictures Corporation Ltd. Starred Joey Porter and Jack Williams. Based on *Teeth*.
8. **Oh What a Duchess** (or **My Old Duchess**): 1934 – BIP. Supposedly based on *Mumming Birds* but bears no resemblance to it. Karno is credited as one of the writers.
9. **Don't Rush Me** (sometimes recorded as **Mother Don't Rush Me**): 1936 – Fred Karno Film Company. First and only production by Karno's own film company.
10. **Jailbirds:** 1940 – Butchers Film Service. Starred Charles Hawtrey, Albert Burdon, and Shaun Glenville.

Other films to note, although their existence (and Karno's involvement) is uncertain:

11. **They're Off** – 1933, Gainsborough/Gaumont British Pictures Corporation Ltd. Starred Flannagan and Allen. Press reports suggest this was based on a Karno sketch, so it may have been another in the Gaumont series of 1932/1933.
12. **Sign Please** – 1933, Gainsborough/Gaumont British Pictures Corporation Ltd. Starred Naughton and Gold. Part of the same series but unclear if Karno was involved. The Internet Movie Database (IMDb) credits Karno as writer and states that the film was based on the Karno sketch *The Salesman* – but no such sketch exists.
13. **Handy Men** – Unknown but assumed to be 1933 – Gallagher records this as another in the Gainsborough series with Naughton and Gold, based on a Karno sketch (which probably would have been *Spring Cleaning*). But no other record of this film exists.

The following are films known or thought to have been based on Karno sketches but made by others:

1. **A Raid on a Club:** 1905 – Based on a Karno sketch (probably *New Woman's Club*) by the Walturdaw Film Company. It is not known if Karno was involved in this film or was even aware of it.
2. **Au Music Hall:** 1905 – Pathé Frères film version of *Mumming Birds* which led to a prolonged legal battle with Karno.
3. **Only Me:** 1929 – Lupino Lane film version of *Mumming Birds* in which he plays all the parts; and the film which is closest to Karno's original sketch.

IV. Unproduced Sketch Titles

These titles appeared in Karno's advanced advertising, usually as being 'in preparation', but do not seem to have been staged (the year stated is the year they first appear in an advertisement):

The Gladiators (1906); **The Yellow Birds** (1906); **The Fire Brigade** (1906); **Sea-view Hotel** (1906); **English Sports** (1906) [probably became **The Smoking Concert** combined with **The Village Fair** or possibly later reincarnated as **The Annual Sports**]; **The Cab Rank** (1906); **The Village Fair** (1906); **The Washerwoman** (1906); **The Baby Farm** (1906); **The Nursery** (1906); **The Wedding Party** (1906); **The Explorers** (1906); **Daisy's Downfall** (1906); **The Colliers** (1906); **The Book Worms** (1906); **Willie's Birthday** (1906); **Flanagan's Restaurant** (1906); **The Painter and Decorators** (1906) [probably became **Spring Cleaning**]; **Our Neighbours** (1906); **Skylarks** (1906); **The Cowboys** (1906); **The Chimney Sweeps** (1906); **The Marines** (1906); **The Hop-pickers** (1906); **The Three Brass Balls** (1906); **The Auction Mart** (1906); **The Waxworks** (1906); **The Crooked House** (1906); **The Haymakers** (1906); **The Twisters** (1910); **Archibald's Cricket Match** (1911); **An Artist's Muddle** (1941); **A Pleasant Sunday Afternoon** (1941); **The Flycatchers** (1941); **Paying Guests** (1941); **The Police Station** (1941) (a script of this exists in Con West's archive but I can find no record of it being produced).

V. Fred Karno Junior Archive – Additional Titles

The following sketch titles are listed amongst Fred Karno Jr.'s papers in an index of sketches, but no scripts for these exist in the various archives I have searched, and they do not appear in any review, listing or advertisement in the British Newspaper Archive. They may have been alternative titles, additional sketches which never got beyond a title, or Fred Jr.'s own sketches as a solo comic after his days with Karno:

Account Rendered; **After Closing Time**; **Houses for All** (possibly an alternative title for any of the shows which included the 'class and masses' routine); **Holidays**; **Night and Morning**; **Our Lodge**; **Our Nollie**; **Soapsuds** (this could be an alternative title for **The Steam Laundry**); **Tatters and Sells**.

VI. Ted Tysall (Ted Karno) Sketches, as 'The Karno Trio'

The following sketches are known to be by the Karno Trio, i.e. Ted Karno (Tysall) and <u>not</u> Fred Karno:

1. **The Boxing Ball** (1893).
2. **Blunders** (1893).
3. **Copped** (1896).
4. **Pot Pourri*** (1899).
5. **A Quick Supper** (1900).
6. **The Traveller's Rest** (1902).
7. **The Merry Carpenters** (1905).
8. **The Dinner Hour** (1906).
9. **A Weekend at Hotel de Quick** (1909).

*Not to be confused with Karno sketch of the same name (see Karno productions 18).

VII. Miscellaneous Oddities

I have come across the following oddities which are included in this index for completeness and to clarify their status to other researchers.

1. **Ticket-of-Leave Man.** This is included in some music hall books as a Karno show (e.g. Felstead, p.43) but I have never seen it listed as such or found any reference to it in Karno's archive. It was a long-running Victorian melodrama well before Karno's time.
2. **The Popular Workhouse.** Wal Pink's sketch for a Water Rats' charity matinee in November 1907, which Karno helped write but there is no evidence that he appeared in it.
3. **Fancies.** A single listing notes this as a Karno show in June 1926, but it was not. It appears to either be an error, or the reporter meant that it was in the style of Karno (*The Stage*, 24 June 1926, p.4).
4. **Alice in Funderland.** A 1931 revue staring Leslie Karno. Karno let Leslie include *Mumming Birds* in the revue, but it was not a Karno production.
5. **Keeping the Patient Alive.** In Sydney in July 1933, Scott Alexander staged this show, reportedly a Karno sketch (*The Sydney Morning Herald*, 22 July 1933, p.8) – it may have been a version of *Kill or Kure*.
6. **Let's Go Somewhere.** Karno writes about this sketch in his correspondence with Con West in late 1940, but I have found no other record of it. It may have been a new idea he was trying to pitch to the BBC or ENSA.

VIII. A Note on International Tours

Tracking Karno productions around the world is generally beyond the scope of this book; although Karno companies toured the U.S. and Continental Europe many times and I have referred to these where it is relevant to the wider text, especially in telling Chaplin and Laurel's stories. I would recommend A.J. Marriot's *Chaplin Stage by Stage* and *Laurel Stage by Stage* for more detail of those tours they appeared in.

I have mentioned productions as far afield as Russia, Australia, South Africa and South America, but many of these were licensed productions by others such as Bert Bernard, rather than Karno himself. Tracing international tours is complicated by the existence of locally licensed or copycat companies in many countries, and these are often mis-listed as Karno shows.

A review of online resources reveals that evidence of Karno shows appearing in Australia is scant. However, advanced advertising suggests a troupe toured in August 1908 (*Sydney Sportsman*, 27 May 1908, p.8) and Bernard's company intended to tour with *His Majesty's Guests* in spring 1910 (*The West Australian*, 22 October 1909, p.2), but I can find no confirmed listings for either in subsequent press reports. Humphrey Bishop certainly staged *The Bailiff* in Perth in 1921 in conjunction with ex-Karno writer Leonard Durrell (*Weekly Judge*, 21 January 1921, p.5). A 1924 production of *Mumming Birds* in Perth was reported as being staged 'for the first time' by Ed Warrington's company; it is unclear whether this was a Karno licensed production (*The Daily News*, 28 November 1924, p.1 and 5). A version of *Mumming Birds* was also staged as *An Old Time Music Hall*, in Perth in 1936, probably a copycat production (*The West Australian*, 10 February 1936, p.2).

I leave it to other Karno enthusiasts to make their own journeys of discovery accordingly.

International tours: Karno's man in America – Alf Reeves on the St Lawrence Ferry, Montreal, September 1907. As well as being tour manager Reeves also played 'Uncle Charlie', the old man in the Mumming Birds *box opposite the drunk (courtesy David Robinson).*

Bibliography

Adeler, Edwin and West, Con, *Remember Fred Karno – The Life of a Great Showman*, John Long, London, 1939.
Andrew, Ray, *On the Trail of Charlie Hall*, self-published, 1988.
Anthony, Barry, *Chaplin's Music Hall – The Chaplins and their Circle in the Limelight*, I.B. Taurus, London, 2012.
Assael, Brenda, *The Circus and Victorian Society*, University of Virginia Press, Charlottesville, 2005.
Baker, Richard Anthony, *British Music Hall an Illustrated History*, Sutton Publishing Ltd, Stroud, 2005.
Baker, Roland G.M. & Baker, Gwendoline F., *Thameside Molesey, A Towpath Ramble from Hampton Court to Hampton Reach*, Barracuda Books Ltd, Buckingham, 1989.
Bailey, Paul, *Three Queer Lives – an Alternative Biography of Fred Barnes, Naomi Jacob and Arthur Marshall*, Hamish Hamilton, London, 2001.
Banham, Martin, *The Cambridge Guide to Theatre*, Cambridge University Press, Cambridge, 1998.
Beckett, Ian, *The Home Front 1914-1918: How Britain Survived the Great War*, The National Archives, Richmond, 2006.
Beckett, John with Brand, Ken, *Nottingham an Illustrated History*, Manchester University Press, Manchester, 1997.
Bevan, Ian, *Top of the Bill – The Story of the London Palladium*, Frederick Muller Ltd, London 1952.
Bowers, Judith, *Stan Laurel and Other Stars of the Panopticon – the Story of the Britannia Music Hall*, Birlinn Ltd, Edinburgh, 2007.
Brough, Lawrence and Kemble, John R., *Jokelets – Being the Merry Book of the Moore & Burgess Minstrels*, Saxon & Co. London, 1898.
Chance Newton, Henry, *Idols of the 'Halls' – Being my Music Hall Memories*, Heath Cranton Ltd, London, 1928; 1975 Edition (EP Publishing Ltd, Wakefield).
Chaplin, Charles, *My Autobiography*, Bodley Head, London, 1964 (Penguin Modern Classic version, 2003).
Chaplin, Charles, *My Life in Pictures*, Bodley Head, London, 1974.
Cochran, Charles B., *Showman Looks On*, J.M. Dent & Sons Ltd., London, 1945.
Crowther, Bruce, *Laurel and Hardy: Clown Princes of Comedy*, Columbus Books, London, 1987.
Cullen, Frank, with Hackman, Florence and McNeilly, Donald, *Vaudeville Old & New – an Encyclopaedia of Variety Performers in America Volume 1*, Routledge Taylor & Francis Group, New York, 2007.
Dickens, Charles, *Sketches by Boz* (Penguin Classics Edition), Penguin London, 1995 (first published 1839).
Earl, John, *British Theatres and Music Halls*, Shire Publications Ltd, Princes Risborough, 2005.
East, John M., *'Neath the Mask*, George Allen & Unwin Ltd, London, 1967.
East, John M., *Max Miller the Cheeky Chappie*, Robson Books, London, 1977.
Faint, Pete, *Jack Hylton*, Pete Faint, 2014.
Farson, Daniel, *Marie Lloyd & Music Hall*, Tom Stacey Ltd, London, 1972.
Felstead, S. Theodore, *Stars Who Made the Halls*, T. Werner Laurie Ltd, London, 1946.
Fisher, John, *Funny Way to be a Hero*, 2nd Edition, Preface Ltd, London, 2013.
Flanagan, Bud, *My Crazy Life*, Frederick Muller Ltd, London, 1961.
Gallagher, J.P., *Fred Karno Master of Mirth and Tears*, Robert Hale, London, 1971.
Gillies, Midge, *Marie Lloyd The One and Only*, Orion, London, 2001.
Giraud, S. Louis, *Songs That Won the War – Daily Express Community Songbook No. 3*, Lane Publications, London, 1930.

Harding, James, *George Robey and the Music Hall*, Hodder & Stoughton, London, 1990.
Harding, John, *Football Wizard – The Billy Meredith Story*, Robson Books, London, 1998.
Honri, Peter, *Music Hall Warriors, A History of the Variety Artistes Federation 1906-1967*, Greenwich Exchange, London, 1997.
Horrall, Andrew, *Popular Culture, London 1890-1918 – the transformation of entertainment*, Manchester University Press, 2011.
Hudd, Roy, *Roy Hudd's Book of Music-Hall, Variety and Showbiz Anecdotes*, Robson Books, London, 1993.
Jacob, Naomi, *Me A Chronicle About Other People*, Hutchinson & Co Ltd, London, 1954.
Jacob, Naomi, *Me Again*, Hutchinson & Co Ltd, London, 1939.
Jacob, Naomi, *Me and Mine*, Hutchinson & Co Ltd, London, 1949.
Jacob, Naomi, *Me Looking Back*, Hutchinson & Co Ltd, London, 1950.
Jacob, Naomi, *More About Me*, Hutchinson & Co Ltd, London, 1939.
Jacob, Naomi, *Our Marie a Biography*, Hutchinson & Co Ltd, London, 1936.
Jerome, Jerome K., *Three Men in a Boat*, Penguin Books, London, 2004 edition (originally published 1889).
Jupp, James, *The Gaiety Stage Door – Thirty Years Reminiscences of the Theatre*, Jonathan Cape, London, 1923.
Kilgarriff, Michael, *Grace, Beauty and Banjos – Peculiar Lives and Strange Times of Music Hall and Variety Artistes*, Oberon Books Ltd, London 2nd edition, 1999.
Kilgarriff, Michael, *Sing Us One of the Old Songs – A Guide to Popular Song 1860-1920*, Oxford University Press, Oxford, 1998.
Kitchen, Fred, *Meredith We're In! – The Life Story of Fred Kitchen Told by Himself*, Frederick Simon Kitchen-Dunn, 2012.
Lasky, Jesse, *I Blow My Own Horn*, Victor Gollancz, London, 1957.
Lauder, Harry. *Roamin' in the Gloamin'*, J.B. Lippincott Company, Philadelphia & London, 1928.
Lawrence, Danny, *Arthur Jefferson Man of the Theatre and Father of Stan Laurel*, Brewin Books, Studley, Warwickshire, 2017.
Le Roy, George, *Music Hall Stars of the Nineties*, British Technical and General Press, London, 1952.
Leeson, R.A., *Strike – A Live History 1887-1971*, George Allen & Unwin Ltd, London, 1973.
Lewis Ward, Richard, *A History of the Hal Roach Studios*, Southern Illinois University Press, 2005.
Louvish, Simon, *Chaplin the Tramp's Odyssey*, Faber and Faber, London, 2009.
Louvish, Simon, *Keystone the Life and Clowns of Mack Sennett*, Faber and Faber, London, 2003.
Louvish, Simon, *Man on the Flying Trapeze – the Life and Times of W.C. Fields*, W.W. Norton & Company, New York, 1997
Louvish, Simon, *Monkey Business – The Lives and Legends of the Marx Brothers*, Faber and Faber, London, 1999.
Louvish, Simon, *Stan and Ollie: the Roots of Comedy*, Faber and Faber, London, 2001.
Lynn, Kenneth S., *Charlie Chaplin and His Times*, Simon and Shuster, New York, 1997.
Major, John, *My Old Man – A Personal History of Music Hall*, Harper Press, London, 2012.
Marriot, A.J., *Chaplin Stage by Stage*, Marriot Publishing, Hitchin, 2005.
Marriot, A.J., *Laurel and Hardy the British Tours*, A.J. Marriot, Blackpool, 1993.
Marriot, A.J., *Laurel and Hardy the U.S. Tours*, Marriot Publishing, Hitchin, 2011.
Marriot, A.J., *Laurel Stage by Stage*, A.J. Marriot, Blackpool, 2017.
McCabe, John, *Charlie Chaplin*, Robson Books Ltd, London, 1978.
McCabe, John, *Mr Laurel and Mr Hardy – an Affectionate Biography*, Robson Books, London, 2003 edition (originally published by Chrysalis, London, 1976).
McCabe, John, *The Comedy World of Stan Laurel*, Doubleday & Company Inc., New York, 1974.
McCabe, John and Kilgore, Al and Bann, Richard W., *Laurel and Hardy*, Ballantine Books, New York, 1975.
McConnell Stott, Andrew, *The Pantomime Life of Joseph Grimaldi*, Canongate Books Ltd, Edinburgh, 2009.
Mellor, G.J., *The Northern Music Hall*, Frank Graham, Newcastle Upon Tyne, 1970.

BIBLIOGRAPHY

Merton, Paul, *Silent Comedy*, Arrow Books, London, 2009.
Norbury, James, *Naomi Jacob the Seven Ages of Me*, William Kimber, London 1965.
Norden, Denis, *Clips from a Life*, Harper Perennial, London, 2008.
Owen, Maureen, *The Crazy Gang a Personal Reminiscence*, Weidenfeld & Nicolson, London, 1986.
Purser, Philip and Wilkes, Jenny, *The One and Only Phyllis Dixey*, Futura Publications Ltd, London, 1978.
Rinaldi, Graham, *Will Hay*, Tomahawk Press, Sheffield, 2009.
Robinson, David, *Chaplin His Life and Art*, Grafton, London, 1985.
Scagnetti, Jack, *The Laurel and Hardy Scrapbook*, Jonathan David Publishers, New York, 1976.
Seaton, Ray & Martin, Roy, *Good Morning Boys – Will Hay, Master of Comedy*, Barrie and Jenkins, London, 1978.
Segrave, Kerry, *Piracy in the Motion Picture Industry*, McFarland & Company Inc., London, 2003.
Stanley, Harry, *Can You Hear Me Mother? Sandy Powell's Lifetime of Music Hall*, Jupiter Books, London, 1975.
Staveacre, Tony, *Slapstick, The Illustrated Story of Knockabout Comedy*, Angus & Robertson, London, 1987.
Stein, Lisa K., *Syd Chaplin, A Biography*, McFarland and Co. Inc. London, 2011.
Stevenson, David, *1914-1918 The History of the First World War*, Penguin Books, London, 2004.
Stone, Rob, *Laurel or Hardy, The Solo Films of Stan Laurel and Oliver "Babe" Hardy*, Split Reel Books, Temecula, California, 1996.
Stuart, Leslie (edited by Andrew Lamb), *My Bohemian Life*, Fullers Wood Press, Croydon, 2003.
Symons, Julian, *Horatio Bottomley*, House of Stratus, Kelly Bray, Cornwall, 2001 Edition (Originally published by Cressett Press 1955).
Trav S.D. (Travis Stewart, D.), *Chain of Fools – Silent Comedy and its Legacies from Nickelodeons to YouTube,* Bear Manor Media, Duncan, 2013.
Trav S.D. (Travis Stewart, D.), *No Applause – Just Throw Money: The Book That Made Vaudeville Famous,* Farrar, Strauss & Giroux, New York, 2006.
Ullah, John, *This is More Than I Can Stand*, Brewin Books, Studley, Warwickshire, 2012.
Walker, Whimsical, *From Sawdust to Windsor Castle*, Stanley Paul & Co., London, 1922.
Weightman, Gavin, *Bright Lights Big City – London Entertained 1830-1950*, Collins and Brown, London, 1992.
Wood, Georgie, *Royalty, Religion and Rats*, Central Printing Co. (Chas. Sowden) Ltd., Burnley, 1963.

For a thoroughly entertaining fictionalised version of Karno's story, I would highly recommend Chris England's Arthur Dandoe Trilogy: *The Fun Factory*, *Box Car of Fun*, and *Chaplinoia*.

Index

Notes on index:

Initials/acronyms:
FK = Fred Karno, EK = Edith Karno, FKJ = Fred Karno Jr., LK = Leslie Karno, CC = Charlie Chaplin, SL = Stan Laurel, L&H = Laurel and Hardy, GOWR = Grand Order of Water Rats.

Image references:
References in *italics* relate to images. References in [*italics*] means both a reference and an image on the same page.

Subheadings:
For ease of reference four approaches are taken depending on circumstances:
1. Alphabetical: the majority of listings with simple subheadings.
2. Chronological: where this is more logical, e.g. First World War, Karsino development, etc. These are prefixed {Chr}.
3. Mixed approach:
   a. Individuals with significant subheadings have been separated into those which relate to a person's life and career, prefixed {L+C}, which are listed chronologically; and then general themes, prefixed {GT}, which are listed alphabetically.
   b. Significant productions with subheadings are split into two sections: basic sketch information, prefixed {SI}, listed broadly chronologically, then general themes prefixed {GT}, listed alphabetically.

In all circumstances miscellaneous and passing references are always listed last as 'also'.

End notes are indexed where additional information is provided which would not otherwise be located via other index references. 'Karnography' sections are not indexed – see pages 564-72.

39 Steps, The, (1935), 524, 546
1922 later *1923*, (FK revue), 405, [*406-7*], 408, 410, 445

Acorn Antiques, 364
Actors' Association, 404, 411, 556
Adams, Robert, 164
Adeler and West, *also* 'Karno's memoirs' *see also* Adeler, Edwin *and* West, Con (for references to FK *see* FK subheadings, included here are other references):
  errors or notable omissions in, 12, 23, 34, 36, 39, 46, 52, 103, 150, 218, 312, 358, 409, 412, 450, 475, 480, 496, 538, 541, 551
  general references, 2, 5, 15-16, 90, 225, 262, 272, 349, 441, 489, 518
Adeler, Edwin, *see also* Adeler and West, 2-3, 173, 199, 481-2
Adney Payne, George, 62, 64, 66, 146, 195
Agate, James, 208
Aitken, Harry, 322
Alan, Ray, 327
Albany, Piccadilly, The, 350, 402, 408, 438, 443
Alexander, Beaumont, 431-2
Alexandra Palace, 121
Alexandra Theatre, Birmingham, 409
Alexandra Theatre, Stoke Newington, 128
Alexandra, Nottingham, The, [*10*]
Alhambra, Brighton, 99
Alhambra, Nottingham, also Royal Alhambra, [*11*]
Alhambra Theatre, Bradford, 157, 265,
Alhambra Theatre, New York, 542, 549
Alice in Funderland, 482
All Women also *All Eves* also *All Ladies*, 362-5, 385, 515, 553

Allen, Beatrice, 373, 408
Allen, Chesney, *see also* Flanagan and Allen *and* The Crazy Gang, 487, [*495*]
Allen, Frank, 108
Allen, Kennedy, 334
Alleyn, Leslie, 307, 399
Allison, Jean, *421*, 422
Alone in the World, 248
Amador, Charles, 353
Amateur Entertainers, The, see *Smoking Concert, The*
American Boxing Ball, The, 46-7, 185
American Music Hall, New York, (Morris's), 322, 549
Anderson, 'Bronco' Billy, 355
Andrew, Ray, 461
Animal Crackers, (1930), 452
Annual Sports, The, see also *Village Sports, The*, 268, 296
Another Fine Mess, (1930), 386, 547
Anstell, William, 156
Anthony, Susan B., 73
Any Lady, 396
Aquarium, Brighton, 34, 65
Aquarium, Westminster, Royal, 34, 48, [*49*], 51, 53
Arbuckle, Roscoe 'Fatty', 235, 321, 398, 548
Arcadians, The, 252, 368
Archer, Fred, 18-19
Archibald's Cricket Match, 282
Armstrong, Billy, 355, 520
Army Service Corps (ASC), 342-3, 383
Arnaud, Yvonne, 386
Around the Clock, 177
Arthur, Robert, 78
Arundale, Sybil, 362
As the Church Bell Chimes, 55
Asher, Mike, *real name* Mike Sipple, *aka* Hal Walters, 265, [*274*], 280-1, *286-7*, 504
Ashton, Doris, 427
Askey, Arthur, 557, 562
Askwith, George, 195
Association of Touring Managers, The, 399, 409, 556
Astley, Philip, 13, 15, 59, 534
Astor, A.C., 481
Astoria (houseboat), [*283-4*], 296, 299, 302, 309, 332, 442-3, [*530*]

576

INDEX

Astoria Studios, 451
Athersmith, W.C., 185, 187, 192
Attenborough, Richard, 106
Au Music Hall, (1905), 148-9
Aubrey, Alto, *see also* Four Aubreys, The, 21, 23
Aubrey, Bob, *see also* Four Aubreys, The, 21-3, 31, 38-40, 99, 176, 200, 465
Aubrey, Charles, 21-3
Aubrey, Jimmy, 176, 226, 351-2, 415, 453, 520
Aubrey, Sarah, 21
Auction Mart, The, 166,
Austin, Albert, 159, *254*, 265, [*274*], *277-8*, *281*, *287*, *319*, 357, 453, 520
Austin, Charlie, 126-7, 490, 554
Avenue Theatre, Sunderland, 89

Baby Farm, The, 166
Bacon Grabbers, (1929), [*461*], 470
Bad Companions, (1932), 483
Bailey, Paul, 3, 119
Bailey, William, 32-3, 39-40
Bailiffs, The, (film, 1932), 493-4, [*495*], 496
Bailiff(s), The, (FK sketch), 198, 202, 204, 208, 214, 245, 251-3, 268, 312, 470, 474, 483, 511
Bailum and Barmey's – The Thickest Show on Earth, 168
Baldwin, Charles:
 FK comic, 80, 100, 483, 520
 FK writer, 80, 99, 109, 152, 253, 256-7, 260, 268, 296, 315, 318
 also, 286, 314, 548
Baldwin's Bank Clerks, 253
Bale Troupe, The, 30
Balfour, Betty, [*365*], 439
Ball, Lucille, 363, 525
Bank, The, (1915), 233, 266
Banks, Ted, 286, *287*, 297, 552
Bann, Richard, 458, 474
Barker, Ronnie, 395
Barnard, Charles, 44, 46
Barnard, David, 43-4
Barnard Palace of Varieties, Chatham, The, 68, 537-8
Barnard's Amphitheatre, Portsmouth, 43-4, 46, 536, 539
Barnes, Fred, 448
Barnstormers, The, 251
Barnum, P.T., 49, 66
Barrie, James M., (Sir), 42, 332, 366
Barringer, Michael, 504

Barto Brothers, The, *see also* Laurel, Stan *and* Dandoe, Arthur, 286
Barty, Jack, 432, 501, 561
Baskcomb, A.W., 348, *349*, 373, 387, 392
Bass, George, 433
Bean, Mr, 533
Beatie and Babs, 362, [*363*], 553
Bedini, Jean, 177-8
Bell, Charlie, [*85*], 97, 102, 108, 158, 165, 168, 251-2, 412, 422
Bell, Clara, 102, 158
Below Zero, (1930), 472
Bennett, Billy, 41, [*396*], 397, 403, 448, 450, 481, 520
Bennett, Jock, *396*, 555
Beresford, Jimmy, 254, 338
Berlin, Irving, 417, 457
Bernard, Bert, 235, 237, 421
Berth Marks, (1929), *278*, 279
Bevan, Ian, 483-4
Big House, The, 290
Biograph Company, The, 279, 320-1
Bioscope, 253
Birchmore, Tom, *see* Moore, Tom
Birkenhead, Lord (F.E. Smith, 1st Earl of Birkenhead), 308
Birrell, F., 158
Black, George, 135, 483, 485-91, 493-4
Blanche, Marie, [*406*], *407*, 408
Blore, Eric, 399, 555
Blotto, (1930), 468
Bluebeard, 52
Blunders, 53
Bodie, Dr Walford, 181
Boer War, 80, 336
Boganny, Joe *also* Boganny's Lunatic Bakers, 64, 295
Boisset Family, The *also* Albert Boisset, 50, 351
Bond, The, (1918), 338
Bonson, Agnes, 158
Book Worms, The, 166
Bootblack, The, 66
Booth, General Bramwell, 230
Booth, William, 8
Bordesley Palace, Birmingham, 161,
Borough Theatre, North Shields, 91, 389
Borough Theatre, Stratford, 289, 314, 550
Bosco, Leotard, 540
Bostock, Gordon, 330
Boston Boys, The, *see* Moore, Tom
Bottomley, Horatio, 360-1, [*362*]
Boy 'Ero, The, see *Jimmy the Fearless*

Bradbourne, John, 210-11
Braham, Philip, 392
Brammall, Humphrey, 539
Brats, (1930), 469
Brett, Stanley, 316
Brigands of Tarragona, The, 251
Briggs, W.H., 391-2, 418
Brinsworth House, 195-6, 364
Britannia Panopticon, Glasgow, 27, 47, 247
British International Pictures Ltd (BIP), 439, 448-50, 483, 502, 558, 560
Britt, Jimmy, 234
Broadfoote, Marguerite, 89, 117, 119-23, 437
Broadfoote, Robert, 123
Broadhead, Percy, 433
Broadway Theatre, New Cross, 246
Bronesky, Leon, 529
Brothers Luck, The (Six), 64, 75
Brothers Under the Chin, (1924), 414
Brouett, Albert, 340-1, 411-12
Brouett-Egrot Film Company, 411-12, 418, 461
Brown, Teddy, 480
Bruno, Albert:
 disputes and defection to Darnley, 141, 268, 312-14, 324, 349
 FK comic and writer, 169, 184, 202, *203*, 230, 253, 268-9, 288-92, 317, 335, 547
Bubbles of Happiness, 148, 403, 406
Buchanan, Jack, 501
Buchanan, R.C., 171-2
Buckingham, Cecil, 515
Buckland, Henry, 479
Bundy, A.E., 528
Bungles Luck, 314
Bunny, John, 329-30
Burdon, Albert, [*512*], 526
Burgess, Frederick *see* Moore and Burgess
Burglary, The, also *Burglars, The*, 77, 538
Burley and Burley, 248-9
Burnett, B.T., 175
Busch's Plunging Elephants, 257
By the Sea, (1915), 355
Byron and Stanley, 385

Cab Rank, The, 166
Cadman, Frank, 492, 496
Cairnrona, SS, [*274-5*], 295, 415
Calthrop, Donald, 398, 555
Calvert, Frank, 230, 287, 289, 291

577

Camille Quartet, The, 78, 87, 100
Campbell, Eric, *254*, 255, 281-2, 357, 378, 520
Campbell, Herbert, 72, 85, 87
Canterbury Music Hall, 89, 108-9, 112, 182, 215, 269, 281
Capitol Theatre, Horsham, 560
Capone, Al, 476-7
Cardon, Charles, 156, 158
Cardon, Tom, 286
Carkeek, Jack, 104
Carlisle, Elsie, 409
Carlos, Frankie, 362
Carney, George, 221, 408-11, 449-50
Carnot, Marie François Sadi, 34
Carré's Circus, Oscar, Cologne, 22-3
Caryll and Mundy, *also* Caryll, Billy *see also* Mundy, Hilda *and* The Crazy Gang: 484, 486-8
Casey's Circus, and *Casey's Court*, 181, 217
Casino, Paris, The, 72
Casuals, The, also *Outcasts, The*, 224, 250, 290, 372, 394
Cave, Joseph, 147, 174-5
Chamberlain, Neville, 514
Champion, The, (1915), 235
Chance Newton, Henry, 108, 346
Chaplin, Charles Spencer, (Sir):
{L+C}:
  early life and pre-Karno career, 40, 160, [*180*], 181, 204, 217-8, 544, 546
  joins FK, 173, 213-14, 217, [*218*], 219-20, 546
  Fun Factory training and rehearsal, 1, 173, 219, 241, 329, 353, 497, 521
  villain in *The Football Match*, 185, 220-2, 245-6, 546-7
  miscellaneous roles and tours, 222, 224, 240-2, 272
  first lead as Stiffy, 240-1, 245, [*246*], 263
  Mumming Birds, as the drunk, 245-6, 250, 547
  lead comic in UK tours, [*250*], [*254*], 296-7
  Jimmy the Fearless and rejection of lead, 261-7, 548
  recruited for U.S. tour and sails on Cairnrona, 272-3, [*274-5*]
  1st U.S. tour (1910-1912), *170*, 227-8, [*273*], 276, [*277-8*], 279, [*280-1*], [*286-7*], 295, 543, 549
  visits Astoria, 296

2nd U.S. tour (1912-1913), 297, 310, [*311*], 312, [*319*], 320-7, 329-30, 360
recruited by Keystone, 279, 321-6
impact of CC loss on FK, 324-5, 331, 368, 390
First World War period, 325, 338, 356, 383
dealings with FK after leaving, 355, 368, 401-2, 438, 448-9, 482
entertains FK in Hollywood, 453-7, 460-1, 463, 475
returns to England (1921 and '31), 400, [*401*], 402, 482-3, 497
support for FK in later life, 506, 508, 510, 516-8, 562
later career, exile and death, 528
{GT}:
CC on FK, 2, 90, 102, 353, 415
character traits, 142, 209, 213, 222, [*223*], 267, 278-9, 327, 379
consistency of character in comedy, 61, 159, 319
contractual negotiations with FK, 255, 273, 324-5
contribution to FK shows, 277, 319, 547
fame, extent of, 355, 395, 459, 483
fame, subsequent impact on FK and his company, 110, 370, 451, 461, 474, 478-9, 482, 518, 524
film career, 149, 325, 327, [*328*], 329-30, 354-5, 357, 377, 394, 443, 472
FK material, in CC films, 19-*20*, 23, 82, 110, 185, 225, 233, 235, 243, [*254*], 266-7, 275, 277, 290, 296, 316, 319-20, 328, 344-5, 357, 369, 394
FK era influence on CC's training, comedy, style and approach, 1, 90, 101, 142, 162, 170, 176, 208, 212, 217-9, 222, 266-7, 317, 328-9, 352-4, 369-70, 402-3, 461, 497, 501, 521
FK on CC, 217-9, 222, 224, 241, 261, 266, 321, 326, 354, 369, 458-9, 477-8, 482, 519
friendship with Max Linder, *148*, 225, 542
impersonators (inc. SL), 142, 330-1, 352-3

musician and composer, 90, 224, [*278*], 454-7
opinion of film before joining Keystone, 273, 323
pathos in CC's work, 82, 208-9, 235, 267-8, 394, 459, 519
performers claims of friendship or working with CC, 12, 128, 217, 325, 461-2, 479
personal life, 228, 357, 394, 512, 532
recruiting Alf Reeves and FK comics, 255, 355, 357, [*377*], 378, 415
relationship with colleagues in FK troupes, 221-2, 250, [*265*], 278, 326-7, 353
relationship with Syd Chaplin and impact on CC's career, 224, 295, 323-5, 345-6, [*357*], 377
relationships with former music hall colleagues once famous, *131*, *351*, 353, 378-9, 400, 408-9, 415, 453, 525, 552
SL, comparisons to CC, 267-68, 327, 459
SL on CC and relationship with, 250, 262-5, 267, 277-8, 326-7, 378-9, 400, 458, 459, 521, 554
also, 3, 6, 92, 104, 126-7, 327, 335, 340, 351, 412, 420, 436, 466, 477, 488, 495-6, 504, 520, 523, 527, 531, 536, 541-2, 544, 558-62
Chaplin, Charles, Snr., 6, 55, 179-80, 540, 543
Chaplin, (1992), 106
Chaplin, Hannah, *aka* Lily Harley, 40, 179-80, 209
Chaplin, Minnie, *née* Gilbert, *also* Mrs Syd Chaplin, [*239*]
Chaplin, Norman (CC's son, died in infancy), 394
Chaplin, Sydney:
{L+C}:
  early life and pre-FK career, 179, [*180*], 181, 543-4, 546
  early days with FK, [*176*], 179, 181, 184, 200, 215, *216*, 219, 543-4
  persuades FK to recruit CC, 218-20, 546
  as lead FK comedian, 224, [*225*], [*238-9*], 240, 242, 270, *271*, 272-3, 289-90, 297, 317, *334*, 335, 547

INDEX

writer for FK, 238, 289, 315, 345, 547
role in CC being released from FK contract, 324-25
leaving FK and film career, 335, 345-46, 355, 520
Films at BIP and with FK, [*439*], 440, 448, [*449*], 490, 502
Scandal and exile, 449-50, 457, 528, 532, 558
{GT}:
relationship with CC, 224, 295, 323-5, [*357*], 377
also, 6, 126, *131*, 384, 553
Charlot Show of 1926, The, also Charlot, Andre, 433
Chase, Charley, 321, 459, 470
Chelsea Palace, London, *110*, 238, [*246*], *256*, 289
Chickens Come Home, (1931), 556
Childs, Gilbert, 245
Chimney Sweeps, The, 166
Chippendale, William, 173
Chirgwin, G.H., 548
Church's One Foundation, The, 383
Churchill, Winston, (Sir), (MP), 209, 483
Cinderella, 128-9, 140, 156, 284
Cinematograph Exhibitors Association, 390
Cinquevalli, Paul, 337
circus life, history and dramatic pantomime ballets, 13-18, 43-4, 59, 403, 534
Circus of Varieties, Rochdale, 97
Circus, The, (1928), 23, 110, 243, 443
City Lights, (1931), 82, 448, 453, 456-7, 482, 561
Clayton Hutton, Christopher, 4, 492-4, 496, 503
Cleve, Joe, 90, 165, 210, 373, 387, 553
Clips From A Life, 133
Clockwork Orange, A, (1971), 528
Clore, Charles, (Sir), 528
Coborn, Charles, 32
Cochran, Charles B., (Sir), 106, 173-5, 273, 309, 325, 329, 361, 368, 418, 438, 510
Cochran's Fun City, 173-4, *175*
Cocoanuts, The, (1929), 451
Colchester Playhouse, 450
Coliseum, Dalston, 44
Coliseum, Glasgow, 187, 217
Coliseum, London, 90, 192, 220, 224, 236, 442, 550
Collier's Dying Child, The, 170

Colliers, The, 166
Collin's Music Hall, 67, 524
Collins, Horace, 419
Collins, Lottie, 132
Collins, Monty, see Boston Boys, The
Collinson, Kitty, 374, 376
Colonial Theatre, New York, 276
Come Birdie Come and Live with Me, 105
Comedy Theatre, The, 398
Comical Boxing Ball, The, (Ted Tysall's Trio), 53, *54*
Confessions of a Fan Dancer, 133
Conklin, Chester, 321, 330
Convict 99, (1938), 395, 547
Coogan, Jackie, 19
Cook, Maisie, 156
Cook, Peter, 271
Cooke, Alice *also* Baldwin, see Stan Jefferson Trio, The
Cooke, Edgar, 317, 335, 349, 368, 370, 372, 446-8, 556
Cooke's Circus, Greenock, 22
Cooper, Christine, 396
Cooper, Tommy, 61, 105, 271
Count of Luxembourg, The, 291
Countess from Hong Kong, A, (1967), 528
Court, Percy, 70, 257
Courtenay, Percy, 116-7, 540
Courtneidge, Robert, 252, 556
Courville, Albert de, 405
Covent Garden Theatre, 59-60
Coward, Noel, (Sir), 386
Cow Boys, The, 166
Cox, Francis, 147, 547
Cox, Joe, 553
Crabtree, J.W. 185, 187, 192
Crabtree, W.B., 171, 502
Crackles, Will, 226, 552
Craig Troupe, The, 103
Craig, George, 79, *89*, 108, 156, 215
Crantons, The, 171
Crazy Cracksman, The, 331
Crazy Gang, The, also *Crazy Month*, 135 483-8, [*489*], 490-4, 497, 501, 506, 520, 527, 561
Crewe, Bertie, 230
Crippen, Dr Hawley, 199-200, 545
Crooked House, The, 166
Crown and Cushion, Nottingham, The, 12, *13*
Crowther, Leslie, Snr., *aka* Leslie Sargent, *also* Crowther, Leslie, Jnr., 557
Cruel Cruel Love, (1914), 266
Crump, Stanley, 215-16

Cryer, Barry, 533
Crystal Palace, The, 214, 479, 539
Culeen's Circus, Accrington, 23
Cure, The, (1917), 290
Curzon, Lord, (George Nathaniel Curzon), 309
Cuthbert, Edith Blanche, see Karno, Edith (EK)
Cuthbert, Ellen (EK's mother) *also* John (EK's father), 38
Cuthbert, Ellen Westcott, *aka* Nellie (EK's granddaughter) *also* Cuthbert, Mary, (EK's niece), 341, 552
Cuthbert, Joseph, (EK's brother), 341
Cyril, Herbert, 528

D'Alberg, Rose, 158
Dad's Army, 395, 515
Daddy Wouldn't Buy Me a Bow-Wow, 34
Dahlberg, Mae, 331, 378, 413-15
Dainton, Marie, 370, [*371*]
Daisy's Downfall, 166
Dale and Karno, 58
Dalston Coliseum, 44
Daly, Mark, 393, 399, 405, 522
Dame Trot, *131*, 202, 214
Dandoe, Arthur:
{L+C}:
as FK comic, 158, 176, 254, [*265*]
U.S. tour with CC, [*274*], *278*, 280-1, [*286*], 326
double act with SL, [*286*]
dislike of CC, [*265*], 326-7
military service and later career, 338, 524, 552
Dandy Thieves, The, 88, 92, 99, 156, 172, 230, 245, 253, 255, 367, 423, 433, 543
Daniels, B.A., 254
Daniels, Harry, 374
Danvers, Billy, 422, [*423*], 545
Danzer's Orpheum, Vienna, 39
Dare, Zena, 147
Darnley, Albert, 77, 158-9, 162-3, 168, 224, 243, 269
Darnley, Emily, 162, 168
Darnley, Herbert:
{L+C}:
collaborations with FK, 77-8, 80, 87, 152
FK's business manager, 77, 145, 153-4, [*164*]
rivalry and feud with FK, 165, [*166*], 167-71, 173, 176, 210, 251-3, 255, 257, 268,

579

271, 288, 290, 312-14, 349, 405, 412
also, 159, 295
Davies, Chris, 75, 89
Davies, Marion, 455, [*456*]
Davison, Emily, 305
Dawe, Tommy, 211
Day Out, A, 68, 74
Day, Bill, 283-4, 530
Day, Harry, 372, 405
Day's Pleasure, A, (1919), 394
De Frece, Maurice, 31, 34, 39, 538
De Frece, Abraham Walter, (MP), 535
D'Egville, Melilsande, 554
De Vereeniging Theatre, Amsterdam, 23, 55
Delpini, Carlo Antonio, 61
Delysia, Alice, 309
DeMille, Cecile B., 438, 452
Dental Institute, The, see also *Teeth*, 344, 349, 351
Dentists, The, 166
Deslys, Gaby, 309
Desmond, Florence, 435
D'Eve, Liane, 347
Devoy, Billy, 376, 450
Dewar, Thomas, (1st Baron Dewar), 85, 306
Dibdin, Charles, 59, 257
Dibdin, Thomas, 59-60
Dick Whittington, 78, 255
Dickens, Charles *also* Dickensian, 81, 174, 181, 208, 215, 394, 534
Dillon, Bernard, 116
Dinner Hour, 54
diorama, 168, 535
Dircks, Helen, 392
Diving Birds, 152-3, 155-6, 166-8, 257
Dix, Frank, 169
Dixey, Phyllis, 4, 132-6, 349, 442
Dixey, Selena, 134-6, 442
Dog's Life, A, (1918), 559
Dolinov, Alexis, 419
Don't Dilly Dally on the Way, 28
Don't Have Any More Mrs Moore, 445
Don't Rush Me, also *When we are Married*, also *Mother Don't Rush Me*, (1936), [*504*], 505-10, 559, 562
Donald, John, 78
Dossers, The, see also *Early Birds*, 76, 81, 89
Douglas, Frank, 340
Downey, Robert, Jnr., 106
Doyle, Jane (Queenie), *see* Karno, Queenie

Doyle, Johnny, 116, 158, 254, 285, 351
Driver's Licence, The, 551
Drury Lane Theatre, 44, 59-60, 87, 175, 183, 209, 233, 297, 332, 353, 356
Duchess of Albany, (Princess Helen of Waldeck and Pyrmont), 102
Duck Soup, (1927), 386, 418, 547
Duke of Cambridge, (Prince George, 1819-1904), 139, *140*
Dunne Bright, Mary Chavelita, 124
Dunville, T.E., 65
Durrell, Leonard, 129, 202, 210, 291-2, 313, 318

Eagle Tavern, London, 28
Earls Court, 238
Early Birds (FK sketch) see also *The Dossers*, see also *Night in a London Slum, A*:
{**SI**}:
launch, plot and reviews, 81, [*89*]
UK tours, 97, 102, 119, 152, 156, 158-9, 172, 200, 237, 245
U.S. tours, see *A Night in a London Slum*
licensed and copycat versions, 143, [*144*], *145*, 235, 548
{**GT**}:
accidents and injuries, 147, 164
CC's work, evidence of influence in, 19, 82, 369, 394
innovations: revolve, musical accompaniment, drama and pathos, 82, 90-91, 208
CC in audience as a young man, 218
also, 109, 216, 384, 449, 542
Early Birds, (film, 1924), 411-12
East, Charles A., 247, 258, 260, 281
East, John M., 137, 435
East, John M., Snr., 37
Easy Street, (1917), 369
Edelsten, Ernest, 540
Eden Theatre, Brussels, 23
Edison, Thomas, 65, 537
Edward VII, King, 260
Edwards, Fred, 316
Edwards, Alfred H., 229, 237
Eight Komiks, The, 286
Eight Karnoettes, The, 514
Eight Lancashire Lads, The, *see also* Jackson, John Willie, 180, 366, 447, 546

Eldorado Theatre, Paris, 32-3
Elen, Gus, 169, 236
Eliot, T.S., 42
Ellacott, Vivyan, 366
Elliot, Dorothy (Dolly), 522
Ellis, Walter W., 386, 558
Elmore, Belle, 198, [*199*], 200
Elstree Studios *also* M.P. studios, 450, 510
Elvin, Joe, 64, 86, 195, 236, 364
Emney, Fred, 209, [*236*], 246, 295, 371
Emney, Fred, Junior, 546
Empire Palace, Dublin, 242
Empire Palace, South Shields, 97
Empire, Ardwick, 131, 138
Empire, Birmingham, 480
Empire, Camberwell, 200
Empire, Dewsbury, 58
Empire, Dundee, 200
Empire, Edinburgh, 271
Empire, Edmonton, 393
Empire, Hackney, 500
Empire, Holborn, 160, 194, 210, 486, 490-1, 547
Empire, Holloway, 260, 264
Empire, Kilburn, 230, 243, 288
Empire, Leeds, 292, 349, 371
Empire, Liverpool, 156, 161, 380, 387, 549
Empire, New Cross, 217, 237, 260, 291, 407
Empire, Nottingham, 180, 381, 406, 548
Empire, Portsmouth, 65
Empire, Preston, 366
Empire, Sheffield, 363
Empire, Shepherd's Bush, 557
Empire, Stratford, 264-5, 418
Empire, Streatham, 228
Empire, Swansea, 53
Empress, Brixton, 195, 197, 288
Empress, Camberwell, 146
Empress, Kansas City, 325
Empress, Los Angeles, 551
Empress, San Francisco, 280, 286
English Sports, 166
Enterprising Productions Ltd., 385
Entertainments National Service Association (ENSA), 515, 524
Entomology also *Find The Beetle*, 394
Essanay Studios, 355, 357, 546
Essex, Violet, 307
Etherege, George, (Sir), 44
Euston Music Hall, 25-6, 93, 146, 551
Evans, Fred, (Drury Lane clown), 356
Evans, Fred, II, (FK comic), 85, 97, *144-5*, 356, 553

INDEX

Evans, Fred, III, *aka* Pimple, 356, 553
Evans, Harry, 553
Evans, Joe, 356
Evans, May, 65
Evans, Will. 553
Evening in an English Music Hall, An, 145
Ewart, Jessie, 376
Explorers, The, 166

Faint, Pete, 173, 543
Farini, The Great, *real name* William Leonard Hunt, 49, 55-6
Farnley, George, 240
Farson, Daniel, 25, 118
Felstead, Sidney Theodore, 64, 211, 228, 260, 562
Feminism and emancipation, *see also* suffragettes *and* the New Women's Movement, 27-8, 72-3, 362, 540
Ferdinand, Archduke Franz, 336
Fern, Bill, 106, 158, 176, 226, 548
Ferrier, Charles, 433
Ffolliott, Gladys, 193
Field, Sid, 515
Fields, Gracie, 501, 527
Fields, W.C., 93, 233, 242
Finlayson, James, 413-14
Fire Brigade, The, 166, 227
First National Pictures, 377
First World War:
  {Chr}:
  build up, events and progress, 336-8, 341, 346, 377, 382, 388
  FK comics in action, 338-41
  FK influence on troops and support of concert parties, 338-9, 383-4, 552
  impact on FK company and theatre generally, 164, 336-7, 340-1, 344, 346-7, 349-51, 361-2 366, 372, 374-6, 382-4, 388
  impact on film industry development, 355-6
  Lusitania sinking, 256, 351, 543
  also, 54, 117, 134, 361, 375, 386, 407, 443, 523, 526
Firth Shepherd, F., 553
Fisher, John, 488
Fitchett, J.A., 544
Flagen's Circus, Rotterdam, 23
Flanagan and Allen, *see also* Allen, Chesney *and* Flanagan, Bud *and* The Crazy Gang, 486-7, 493-4, [*495*], 496

Flanagan, Bud, *see also* Flanagan and Allen *and* The Crazy Gang, 19, 41, 194, 487-8, *489*, 491, 494, [*495*], 515, 561
Flanagan's Restaurant, 166
Flats, 294, 314-5, 317, 357, 427
Floorwalker, The, (1916), 316, 357
Floradora, 34, 87, 94, 102, 124, 169, 361
Folies Bergère Theatre, New York, 131, 452
Folies Bergère, Paris, 33, 39, 46, 155, 242, 245
Folly Films, 356
Football Association, The, 187, 191-2
Football Match, The:
  {SI}:
  match fixing scandal origins, 191-2
  launch, plot and reviews, 183-6
  writers, 183
  extracts, 55, 182, 188-90, 214, 245, 402, 506
  UK tours, 192, 200, 217, 224, 236, [*240*], 245, [*246*], 271
  charity matches, 192-3, 236
  revivals, 419, 483
  {GT}:
  accidents and injuries, 186
  influence on CC's career, *see* Chaplin, Charles Spencer
  innovations – football players in the cast, 185, 187
  technical complexity and scale, 186
  Weldon's performance *see* Weldon, Harry
  also, 166, 222, 233, 235, 328, 408, 547, 551
Football Match, The (revue version), 419-20, *421*, 422
For Crying Out Loud, 527
Forbes, Freddie, 141, [*212*], 213
Forde, Florrie, 385, 486, 551
Forester's Music Hall, London, 74
Formby, George, Senior, 97, 354
Forrest, Amy, 285, 297
Forrest, Arthur, 176, 228
Forster, Kate, 314
Four Aubreys, The, *see also* Aubrey, Bob *and* Morganti, William *and* Zulia, Mademoiselle *and* Aubrey, Alto *and* Aubrey, Sarah, 21-4, 37-41, 50
Four Janowskys, The, 258
Four Polos, The, 49

Fourteen Black Hussars, The, 129, 179, 545
Fox and Fox, 51
Fox Studios *also* Fox Film Corp., *also* Fox, William G., 400, 472-3
Frame's Royal Concert Hall, 22
France, George, 81
Francis, Dick, 433, 522
Fred Karno Film Company Ltd, 503, *504*
Fred Karno Story, The, (BBC, TV, 1984), 531
Fred Karno Story, The, (BBC, radio, 1950), 525
Fred Karno's Air Force, 511
Fred Karno's Army *also* Fred Karno outfit *also* Fred Karno's Circus (expression), 1-2, 202, 225, 514-15, 518, 562
Fred Karno's Army, We Are (song), 383, 529
Fred Karno's Army, (revue, 1951), 515, 526
Fred Karno's Army, (musical play, 1984), 531
Fred Karno's Army, Old Comrades (radio, 1938), 509
Fred Karno's Flashbacks, 524
Fred Karno's London Fire Brigade, (Billie Ritchie copycat company), 226
Fremton, Cissie, 158
French Beans, 399, 405,
French, George, 215, 352
Frivolity, 50
Frohman, Charles, 144, 543
Frostick, Dorothy, 349
Fun Factory, The:
  {Chr}:
  Purchase and various names, 67, [*68*], 540, 553
  family home and life with EK and MM, 83, 85, 93-5, 99, 102, 111, 155, 282, 314
  business headquarters, [*69*], 70, [*75*], [*92*], [*154-5*], *158*, *164*, 191
  creative hub, rehearsal and training base, 1, 75, 83, 186, 219, 224, 329, 503
  development and expansion, 153, [*171*]
  management challenges and disarray, 137, 196, 284
  fire, 366, 370
  decline and sale, 350, 360, 366, 396, 443
  also, 139, 143, 200, 283, 464, 523, [*530*]
Fun in a Gymnasium, 51
Funiculi Funicula, 41

581

Gaiety Concert Hall,
  Birmingham, 44-7, 58, 536
Gaiety, Dublin, 156
Gaiety, London, 337
Gaiety, Portsmouth, 46
Gainsborough Film Company,
  The, 481-2, 492, 496-7, 503
Gallagher, Jack, 376, 446-7
Gallagher, Joseph P., *see also*
  Master of Mirth and Tears:
  background to FK biography,
    sources and approach, 2-5,
    37, 117, 121, 132, 135, 492
  critical reaction to biography
    and damage to FK
    reputation, 5, 114, 116,
    530-1
  description of EK and MM,
    40, 111, 122
  glazier story as inspiration for
    The Kid, 19
  FK's Gainsborough films,
    493, 496
  FK's gambling and money
    troubles, 302, 442, 444,
    508
  FK's infidelity, 132-7
  FK's relationship with EK
    and divorce, 3-4, 48, 94-5,
    112, 115, 120, 122-3, 128,
    437-8
  notable errors, doubt or areas
    of confusion, 3-4, 37, 48,
    58-9, 84, 95, 112, 117,
    125, 134, 307, 341, 437,
    508
  also, 23, 36, 85, 126, 191,
    211, 359, 375, 532, 541,
    560
Gallimore, Arthur, 97, 107,
  [*156*], 158, 177
Gandhi, Mahatma, 483
Garrick, David, 42, 59, 304
Gatty, Harold, 160, 169, 542
Gaumont British Pictures
  Corporation Ltd, 492-4
Gee Whiz!, 334
General Strike, The, (1926),
  410, 432
General Theatres Corporation,
  483, 493
Gentlemen of Nerve, (1914), 277
George V, King, 294
Georgian theatre, clowning and
  pantomime development, *see
  also* Grimaldi, Joseph, 15, 52,
  59-62, 537
Gerant, John, 373, 376, 381,
  387, 391, 553
Gerrard, Ernie, 491
Gerrard, Gene, 418-9
Get 'Em Young, (1926), 275

Giant Electric Chicken, The, 373
Gibbons, Walter, [*146*], 194, 548
Gilbert's Circus, 230
Gillette, William, 180-1, 548
Gillow Sisters, The, 426
Gilman, Pearl, 378
Gilmer, Albert, 66
Gilmour, David, 530
Ginnett's, George, *also* Fred,
  circus, 21
Ginsberg, Henry, 473
Girl Must Live, A, (1939), 561
Giveen, Clara, 305
Gladiators, The, 159, 166
Glen, Archie, 373, 376, 388, 483
Glenville, Shaun, 258, 281-2,
  512
Glimpse of Past and Present, A,
  406
Glover, Ernest, 469
Godfrey, Arthur, 448
Gold Rush, The, (1925), 266,
  415, 541-2, 561
Gold, Jimmy, *see* Naughton and
  Gold, *see also* The Crazy Gang.
Golding Bright, Reginald, 124
Goldwyn, Sam *aka* Sam Goldfish
  see also MGM, 452
Good Old Timers – Fred Karno,
  (BBC Radio, 1942), 522
Good-bye-ee, 385
Goodfellow, George, 381
Goons, The, 36
Goy, Gladys, 349
G.P.O., The:
  {**SI**}:
  launch, plot and reviews,
    230-3
  writers, 230
  extracts, 151, 231-2
  UK tours, 237, 242, 268,
    312, 317
  film versions, see *Post Haste*
  {**GT**}:
  CC appearances, 221-2
Grace, Fred J., 385
Grace, Lilian, 419
Grand Continental Circus, 479
Grand Fete des Theatres, 214
*Grand Mammoth Easter Fete and
  Gala*, 202
Grand Order of Water Rats, The,
  (GOWR):
  {**Chr**}:
  history of, 86
  FK involvement, 85-6, 92,
    99, 104, 151, 176, 214-5,
    236, 314
  Inspiration for *Mumming
    Birds*, 92, 103-4, 106, 539
  at Tagg's island, 293, 296,
    310, 528

CC membership, 483
  also, 144, 312, 545
Grand Theatre, Birmingham, 128
Grand Theatre, Glasgow, 129,
  131, 247-8
Grand Theatre, Hanley, 158
Grand Theatre, Liverpool,
  85
Grand Theatre, Portland,
  OR, 285
Grand Varieties, Sheffield, 52
Grapes of Wrath, 476
Grattan, Harry, 406
Grauman, Sid, 286
Graves, George, 313
Gray, Eddie, *see also* The Crazy
  Gang, 484-7, *489*
Gray, George, 208
Grayson, Victor, (MP), 243
Great Depression, The, 472-3
Green, Mabel, *132*
Greene, Evie, 102
Gregory, Ena, 414
Gregson, Jennie, 381
Grey, Anna, 183
Grey, Lita, 532
Griffith, D.W., 320
Griffiths, Charles, 156, 158,
  274, 351
Grimaldi, Joseph, 16, 60-1, 63,
  74, 147, 175, 209, 211-12
Grossman, William, 177
Grossmith and Laurillard, 387
Groves, Walter, 78-80, 87, 354,
  520, 538
Gulliver, Charles, 401

Hackenschmidt, Georg(e), 106
Half a Man, (1925), 275
Hall, Charlie, 413, 415-16, 418,
  460, [*461-2*]
Hall, George, 75
Hall, Harry, 399
Hamilton's Diorama, 32
Hamlet in a Hurry, 175
Hammerstein's Victoria Theatre,
  New York, 157-8, 227, 277
Hancock, Tony, 209
Handley, Tommy, 485
Handy Men, (1933), 496
Hanlon Brothers, The, *aka*
  Hanlon-Lees, 50
Hann, Tommy, 424
Harding, Muriel *see* Petrova, Olga
Harding, John, 192
Hardy, Oliver Norvell *aka* 'Babe',
  see also Laurel and Hardy:
  {**L+C**}:
  personal life, 113, 532
  films with Jimmy Aubrey, 351
  partnering with SL, 418, 443,
    459, 513

INDEX

on his screen character, 203
with FK in Hollywood, *467*, [*468*], 469
death, 527
also, 68, 462, 506, 551, 556, 559
Harlequin Statue or the Bogie and the Fairy, 175
Harlequinade in Black and White, A, 279
Harlequinade *and* Harlequin, 52, 60, 74, 78, 87, 147, 279, 328, 486, 536
Harmer, Dolly, 78-9
Harmer, Frank, 391
Harrington, J.P., 160
Harris, Augustus, (Sir), 87, 175
Harris, Buddy, 561
Have a Banana! see also *Oh Law!*, 370-2
Haver and Lee, 504
Hawley, Philip, 418
Hawtrey, Charles, [*512*]
Hay, Gladys, 380
Hay, Will:
{**L+C**}:
appearances with FK companies, [*380*], 381, 391-2
later stage and film career, 374, 443, 520, 527, 555, 561
support for FK in later life, 506, 510, 515
{**GT**}:
comedy characterisation and style, 159-60, 241, 394, [*395*], 404
influence of FK era on career, 385, 394-5, 547
on comedy, 191, 460
also, 6, 438, 483, 490
Haymakers, The, 166
Haynes, Joey, 16, 24
Haytor, Frank, 103-4
Hearst, William Randolph, 455-6
Hemmington, Cyril, 418, 427, 556
Henderson, Dick, 463
Henderson, John, 79-80,
Henderson's, Coney Island, 177
Her Majesty's Guests, see *His Majesty's* Guests.
Herbert, Harry, 427
Hestor, George, 158, 252, 366-8, 380, 393, 520
Hickory Hiram, (1918), 378
Hicks, Seymour, 147
Highland Lassie, The, 102, 155, 283

Hilarity also *Lover's Serenade, The*, also *He Knocked Them*:
{**SI**}:
origins and background, 45-8, 51
debut details and alternative titles, 47-8, 56
launch, plot and reviews, 47-51
writers, 45, 58
UK tours, 51-2, 55-8, 62, 64, 68, 89, 156, 237, 245
{**GT**}:
accidents and injuries, 68
second FK company formed, 71-2
also, 53, 60, 536
Hill, Gus, 177-8, 279
Hill, Jenny, 32
Hill, Sinclair, 497
Hillery, Charles *aka* Nestal, [*12*]
Hillery, Tom *see* Olvene
Hilliard, Harold, 147
Hindle, Joey, 85, 227
Hindson, Will, 376
Hippodrome, Bury, 250
Hippodrome, Cambridge, New, 171
Hippodrome, Cheltenham, 403
Hippodrome, Colchester, 297, 348, 362, 385, 392, 555
Hippodrome, Coventry, 428
Hippodrome, Ealing, 264
Hippodrome, Exeter, New, *also* Royal Public Rooms:
FK purchase, rebuilding and sale, 229-30, 297, 544
management challenges, 237, 253
also, 285, 291, 546, 551
Hippodrome, Hulme, 249
Hippodrome, Liverpool, 481
Hippodrome, London, 257
Hippodrome, Los Angeles, 378
Hippodrome, Manchester, 210, 249
Hippodrome, Mansfield, 168
Hippodrome, Margate, 342
Hippodrome, Peterborough, New, 229-30, 253, 282
Hippodrome, Portsmouth, 346, 486
Hippodrome, Preston, 289
Hippodrome, Salford, Royal, 249
Hippodrome, Wigan, 202, 373
Hippodrome, Willesden, 246, 264
Hippodrome, Wolverhampton, 483
Hire System, The, see *Bailiff, The*
Hirst, George, 428

His Majesty's Guests, also *Her Majesty's* Guests:
{**SI**}:
origins and background, [*77*]
launch, plot, reviews, and writers, 77-8, 80, 88, 126-7
UK tours, 83-5, [*86*], 88-9, 91-3, 100, 151, 156, 158, 172, 200, 237, 253, 282, 539
rehashed into later FK shows, 367, 397
also, 167, 228, 251, 334, 357, 369, 387, 538
His Prehistoric Past, (1914), 266
Hitchcock, Alfred, 546
Hitler, Adolf, 35, 118, 514
Hoare, George, *104*, *239*, 285
Hog Wild, (1930), 476
Hoity Toity, 97
Holmes, Mabel, 407
Home from Home, 346
Home from the Honeymoon, 386, 542, 547
Hook, Sybil, 362
Hoose-Gow, The, (1929), 416, 461
Hop-pickers, The, 166
Horrall, Andrew, 2
Hot and Cold, 340, 348, [*349*], 350, 373, 474, 504
House That Jack Built, The, 129, *130*, 131, 146-7, 179, 236, 246, 289, 314
Howard, Jenny, 498-9
Howard, Lizzie, 65
Howard, Syd, 393
Howes, Bobby, 481, 493
Hoxton Music Hall, 27
Huda, Joe, 156, 158
Hudd, Roy, 420, 487
Hughes and Perry, 538
Hughes, Nick, 81
Hullo There!, 445-7
Humpty Dumpty, 131, [*132*], 201
Hunter, George, 557
Hurl, Doddy, 403-4
Hurley, Alec, 72, 116, 182
Hurley, Edgar *also* Hurley, Ethel, *aka* Wren, *see also* Keystone Trio, The, 297, [*330*], 331
Hurlock, William, 528
Hustle, 392, 396,
Hutchinson and Tayleur's Circus, 13, 16
Hydro, The:
{**SI**}:
launch, plot, reviews, and writers, [*289*], 290
UK tours, 317, *334*, [*335*], 349

583

aborted U.S. tour, 297
rehashed into later FK revue, 348
also, 196-7, 293, 480, 511
Hylton, Jack, (bandleader), 172-3, 391, 423 [*424*], 443, 527, 561
Hylton, Jack, (comedian), 543

I Love Rebecca, 160
Ideal Films, 493
If the Cap Fits, 408
Immigrant, The, (1917), 275
International Revue, (Buddy Harris film, 1936), 501
International Revue, also *Night in an English Music Hall, A*, (abandoned Hal Roach film project), 501, 561
Isle of Troy, see also *What's What*, 393, 396
Italian Job, The, (1969), 546

Jack Sheppard, 330
Jack the Ripper, 2, 24-5, 81, 160, 532
Jackson, Arrar, 479
Jackson, John Willie (J.W.), *see also* Eight Lancashire Lads, 180, 366, 406, 447
Jacob, Naomi *aka* Mickie, 41, 94, 109, 114, 117, [*118*], 119-124, 126-7, 183, 199, 295, 410, 437, 522, 541
Jail Birds (Brouett-Egrot film, 1923), 411
Jail Birds (FK sketch):
  {**SI**}:
  launch, plot and reviews, 10, 63, 66
  UK tours, *62*, 66, 69, 75, 83, 86, 88, 97, 156, 172, 181, 538
  U.S. tours, 176
  rehashed into later FK shows, 77-8
  {**GT**}:
  publicity ideas and gags, 67, 71
  technical complexity and scale, 63-4, 74, 152
  also, 70, 109, 173, 384
Jailbirds (L&H film, 1931), see *Pardon Us*.
Jailbirds, (Butchers Film Service film, 1940), 444, [*512*], 515
James, Jimmy, 409, 467, 483
Jane Shore, 351
Jeans, Ronald, 370, 392
Jefferson, Arthur (SL's father), 66, 91, 151, 251, 247-8, 268, 386, 539, 542

Jefferson, Gordon (SL's brother), 287
Jefferson, Margaret (Madge) (SL's mother), 247
Jefferson, Arthur Stanley, *see* Laurel, Stan.
Jelf, Richard, (Sir), 149, 225
Jerome, Jerome K., 42, 81, 309
Jim: A Romance of Cockayne, 180
Jim Henson Studio, also *The Muppets*, 559
Jimmy the Fearless, also *Boy 'Ero, The*, 260, 261, 263, [*265*], 266-8, 272-3, 321, 329, 378, 459, 548-9
Jitney Elopement, (1915), 266
John Jay, Junior, 251
John Waddington Ltd., 155, 493
Johnson, Jack, 233
Jolson, Al, 558
Joseph, Young, 233-4
Jubilee Hall, Weymouth, 399
Jumbles, 433-4
Jupp, James, 337
Justice Perkins, Mr, also *Perkins J.P.*, 268-9

Karno, Alice *also* Karno, Ethel, 121
Karno and Lester, 58
Karno Cavalcade, 503, 510
Karno, Della, James, 53
Karno, Edith Blanche (FK's first wife), née Cuthburt, *also* Edith Westcott, *aka* Winnie Warren:
  {**L+C**}:
  solo career references, 40, 45, [*46*], 48, 51, 53-4, 57-8, 127, 537
  on the road with FK company, 41, 45, 48, 55-9, 68, 83-5, 88, *353*, 536
  family life, children – pregnancies, births and deaths, 48, 52, 54-9, 77, 83-85, 93-4, 96, [*112*], 538
  brawl with Winifred Stewart, 88-9, 112
  marriage breakdown, domestic violence toward each other, and judicial separation, 3-4, 84, 89, 91, 94-6, 99, 102, 111-17, 122-6, 137, 152, 442, 539-40
  LK's legitimacy, 123-4
  writes *The Prince of Monte Carlo*, 126-8
  involvement with MHLG and charity work, 121, 182-3, 198-9, 544-5
  contact with FK after separation, 115-6, 122-3, 375, 429, 436

  life after FK, ill health and death, 3, 119, 121, 182, 198, 302, 389, 431, 436-8, 502, 517
  {**GT**}:
  alcohol use, 3, 96, 112, 114-5, 117-9, 122, 125, 437
  character and personality, 40, 48, 89, 111, 120, 122
  Marie Lloyd, friendship with, 62, 92, 116-7, 182-3
  Naomi Jacob, friendship with, 3, 117-24, 127, 541
  sexuality, 89, 120-5
  also, 136, 165, 289, 293, 332, 341, 558
Karno, Frederick Arthur, Junior, (FKJ), (FK's son), *real name* Frederick Arthur Westcott:
  {**L+C**}:
  birth and early family life, 5, [*48*], 51, *112*, 115, 140
  as FK comic, 159, 172, 183, 216, 312, 396, 403-4, 409, 413, 542
  U.S. tours, [*274*], 278, 280-1, 286-7, 312, *319*
  family scandal and military service, 136, [*341*], 342-3, 365, 374-6, 383-4, 389, 514
  marriage to Queenie Doyle and family life, 342, 416-7
  friendship with SL, 240, 413, 523
  Hollywood film career, 413, [*414*], 415, 418, 460
  vaudeville tour with Charlie Hall, 415-6
  disappearance in Canada, 416, 437, 445, 465, 509
  destitute in London, 523-25
  later career, 105, 110, 512, 514, 524-5
  marriage to Olive Bridge and later life, [*523*], 525-7
  death, 4, 527
  {**GT**}:
  character traits, 123, 342, 523, 526
  FK, stories about and opinion of, 20, 94, 136, 138-9, 211-12
  FKJ memoirs, source for Gallagher biography, 4, 19-20, 95, 541
  relationship with CC, 219, 262, 326-7, 415, 524
  relationships with his children, 416-8, 525
  also, 5-6, 231, 284, 516

INDEX

KARNO, FREDERICK JOHN (FK), *real name* Frederick John Westcott, *aka* Leonaro:
{**L+C**}:
early life and discovery of gymnastics, [*7-8*], 9-11, 226
apprenticeship with Olvene, as Leonaro, 11-16, 226
acrobat, itinerant, solo and with various partners, 17-21
Four Aubreys – tours of Europe *see* Four Aubreys, The
EK, meeting and marriage, *see* Karno, Edith
London, arrival in, 23, [*24*], 25, 29, 38
Three Karnos formation, 30-34, 39-40
with Moore and Burgess, *see* Moore and Burgess Minstrels
Three Karnos period, 34-7, 40-43, 45-7, 49-53, 97, 536-7, 539
family life with EK and on tour, *see* Karno, Edith
children's births and deaths, *see* Karno, Edith
Love in a Tub, staging of, see *Love in a Tub*
development of first original sketch, see *Hilarity*
Three Karnos break up, 53-5
Karno troupe expansion and tours (to his semi-retirement from performing), 52, 54-9, 62-4, 66-9, [*70*], 71-93, 96-97, 99-103
Karnophone routine, *see* Karnophone
Fun Factory purchase, development and expansion, *see* Fun Factory
musical comedy, development into, see also *His Majesty's Guests*, 76-77, 100-1
Darnley, Herbert, friendship and feud with FK, *see* Darnley, Herbert
drama, excursion into, see *Marked for Life*
Moore, Marie, affair and eventual marriage, *see* Moore, Marie
marriage breakdown, domestic violence toward each other, and judicial separation, *see* Karno, Edith
LK's legitimacy, *see* Karno Edith
Reed Pinaud, legal battle *see* Reed Pinaud, Theodore
Music Hall War, role in, *see* Music Hall War
Pathé Frères case, *see* Pathé Frères
contact with EK after separation, *see* Karno, Edith
relationship with MM, *see* Moore, Marie
Thames, river life and social climbing, *see also* Karsino, 2, 42, 102, 155, 214, 282-3, [*284*], 287, 293, 296, 298, 300, 306, [*307*], 318, 332-3, 359
Astoria construction and ownership, *see* Astoria (houseboat)
Tagg's island interest and purchase, *see* Karsino
First World War period, *see* First World War
revue era, 137, 148, 334-5, 340, 346-51, 356, 360-8, 370-4, 376-7, 379-83, 385-7, 392, 396-9, 403-11, 418-22, 427-9, 433-6, 500
Moss Empires revue contract, *see* Moss Empires
business decline and downfall, 293, 331, 349, 360, 365-8, 376, 390, 405, 410-11, 421, 425, 429-31, 439, [*440*]
1st bankruptcy, 439, 441-5, 447
with CC and SL in Hollywood, 409, 448, 451-7, [*460*], 461-6, [*467-8*], 469-76, [*477*], 559-60
sketch tours run by LK, 445-8, 470-1, 478-80
final stage productions, see also *Laffs* and *Real Life*, 480-1, 483, 497-502
involvement with The Crazy Gang, 483, 488-91, 494
2nd bankruptcy, 507, 509, 511, 531
Second World War, experiences, 513-515, *516*
semi-retirement, Lilliput Wine Stores ownership, ill health, poverty and death, 5, 438, 497, 502, 507, [*508*], 509-18
{**GT**}:
FAME:
establishment figure, 176, 226, 350, 492
fame, extent of, 2, 56, 58, [*70*], 80, 93, 176, 235, 265, 316-7, 426-7, 451, 456-7
in the lexicon, *see* Fred Karno's Army (expression) *and Fred Karno's Army, We Are* (song)
scale of Karno Empire, [*92*], 93, 97, 142-3, 154-5, 157-8, 172
INNOVATIONS:
all female production, 360-5
breaking the fourth wall, 104, 106-7, 290, 480, 519
circus comedy in music hall and more sophisticated pantomime, 16, 49-51, 59, 61, 353, 402-3, 535
constant development of new material, body of work, 64, 66, 164, 166, 168-9, 269, 293, 396, 399
contemporary events, use of in sketches, 72, 106, 191-2, 215, 238, 242, 289, 347-8, 373, 380, 385, 392, 398
musical accompaniment, 56, 90, 353
pathos in comedy, 24, 65, 81-2, 89-91, 161, 208-9, 235, 267-8, 406, 433
principal boy's costume, 132
promotion and advertising, 15, 18, 66-7, 71, 75-6, 139-40
revolve, first use in Britain, 90-1
scale of sketches, scenery and effects, 50-1, 63-4, 73-5, 81, 107, 131, 152, 185-6, 234, 243-4, 256-9, 288, 290-1, 293, 423, 499, 537
sportsmen in sketches, 184-5, 187, 233-4, 499
talent shows, 425-6, 519
LEGACY, IMPACT AND INFLUENCE on:
CC and FK material in his work, *see* Chaplin, Charles Spencer
popular culture and comedy, 1-2, 6, 16, 424, 443, 497, 513, 520, 527

585

silent film comedy, 10, 63, 272, 317, 351-3, 453, 501, 520
SL and FK material in his work, *see* Laurel, Stan
style, material, or approach of other comedians, 1, 142-3, 227, 233, 235, 241, 243, 254, 266-7, 290, 310, 316-7, 319, 328-30, 335, 344-5, 352-5, 357, 369-70, 394, 402-3, 415, 459, 460-1, 484-5, 488, 520-1.

PERFORMER:
acrobatic comedy, clowning, and the art of pantomime, 11-18, 24, 38, 41, 44, 47, 50, 56
animals, working with in circuses, 13-15, 17
drag, performing in, [36], 74
joke archive, 30, 360, 389, 522
musical abilities, 41, 46-7, 52, 92, 102, 176
principal comedian and actor, 49, 53, 57, 59, 68, 70, 89, 91, 93, 102-3, 211, 412, 495, 521

PERSON:
appearance, 1-2, 211, 222
character traits and personality, 1-2, 5, 9-10, 15-16, 18, 29, 59, 102, 112, 134-5, 138-9, 143, 191, 209, 211-13, 248, 255, 300, 321, 331-2, 411, 420-1, 463, 465-6, 512, 518, 531
charitable support and generosity *see also* GOWR, 47, 52, 58, 71-2, 85, 91-2, 99, 102, 143, 151-2, 176, 192-3, 195-6, 214-5, 236, 240, 282, 332, 339, 351, [358], 364, 383, 395, 545
children, relationships with, *see* Karno, Fred, Junior *and* Karno, Leslie
horse racing and gambling, 19, 71, 101, 187, 283, 361, 442
industry organisations, involvement in, *see also* GOWR *see also* charitable support, 194-7, 215, 399, 409, 545

infidelity, womaniser, *see also* Moore, Marie, 5, 102, 132-5, [136], 137, 300, 436, 438, 445
loyalty and support to fellow artistes, 49, 52
motoring, love of, and offences, 76, 98, 152, 357, [358] 390 [391], 393, 402, 442, 444
practical joker, 138-9, [140]
sex life, 5, 94, 111-12, 120, 122, 125
sharp dealing, intolerance of, 143, 441
voice, accent, use of language, literacy, and fear of public speaking, 2, 137, 162, 211-2, 236-7, 247, 260, 300, 334, 506, 522

PRODUCER, WRITER, DIRECTOR, and IMPRESARIO:
business management skills and challenges – Fun Factory, 69, [75], 137, 143, 156, 164, 173, 196, 200-1, 284-5
Christmas pantomime involvement and productions, 37, 52, 128-32, 138, 156, 201, 217, 236, 246-7, 251, 285, 289, 314, 331, 346, 373, 427, 429
comics being poached by rivals and film companies, 176-7, 227, 251-2, 271-2, 289-90, 297, 312-3, 320-326, 331, 335, 345-6, 355, 376, 396, 451
contemporary standing, relationship with competitors, *see also* Darnley, Herbert, 63-4, 165, 295
creative contribution to material as writer or director, *see also* film work, 43, 45-6, 48, 50-1, 62-3, 66, 69-70, 72, 77-8, 80, 109, 128, 130, 160-61, 169, 183, 216, 224, 230, 233, 242-3, 246, 287, 315, 345, 372-3, 391-2, 399, 406-7, 409, 434, 446-7, 469, 474, 505, 542, 548-9, 553

directing style, and rehearsal approach, 15-16, [75], 97, 108, 141-3, 161, 173, 181, 191, 212, 241, 255, 272, 288, 371-2, 421, 433-6, 447, 481, 557
disputes, retention of and negotiations with performers, 58, 127, 140-2, 156-7, 159, 164-9, 193-7, 200, 244, 251-2, 255, 262-3, 268, 273, 288, 297, 312-13, 324-5, 346, 403-4, 411, 435, 544-5, 556
film work in Britain and films of sketches, 4, 148-50, 326, 356, 396, 411-2, 418, [439], 448, [449], 450, 461, 481-3, 492-7, 502-8, 510-12
hard taskmaster, 70, 84, 141-2, 212-3, 420, 436
legal battles, litigiousness and copycat companies, 9, 70-1, 143-50, 155, 168, 177, [178], 179, 201-2, 211, 225-8, 237, 253, 279, 284, 312-13, 331, 390, 393, 399, 403-4, 428-9, 432, 450, 479, 490-1, 500, 541-3, 548, 553, 557
licensing material to others, 110, 135, 138, 143-5, 171, 235, 237, 285, 385, 394, 421, 433, 447, 450, 489, 502, 515
none-theatrical business ventures, *see also* Karsino, 238, 440-1
on comedians, 101, 141-2, 217, 519-20
talent spotter, trainer and mentor, 1, 16, 98, 129, 141-2, 169, 172-3, 184, 212-3, 217, 219, 241, 248-50, 267, 314, 329, 350, 353, 376, 380, 394-6, 409, 415, 419-21, 426-7, 434, 460, 502, 513, 515, 519-20, 547
theatre ownership and investment, 171-2, 225, 229-30, 237, 253, 282-3, 297-8, 348
theatrical supplies company, 70, 153-6, 171, 238, 350
U.S. FK personal visits, 129, 177-9, 409, 451-77, 482, 543

INDEX

U.S. FK tours, 110, 155-9, 171-2, 176-9, 181, 226-8, 237, 255-6, 272-81, 285-7, 295, 297, 310-12, 319-30, 360, 372, 400, 413, 432, [*440*], 447, 451
RELATIONSHIPS with other key protagonists, *see* individual index listings
MISCELLANEOUS:
accidents and injuries, 18, 22-3, 57, 59, 67-8, 74, 93, 147, 164, 186, 253, 258, 404, 408, 412, 419, 424, 498-9
animals in FK productions, 70, 130-1, 201, 423
impact of cinema on FK *see also* comics being poached by rivals and film companies, 227, 230, 253, 271-3, 283, 295, 326, 331, 356, 390, 448, 480
memoirs, origin of various versions, 2-5, 479, 481-2, 510, 512, 518
sketch origins and legal jeopardy, 35, 49-50, 59-62, 207-8
women's rights, interest in, *see* feminism and emancipation
ALSO: throughout.
Karno Kine Plays Ltd, *also* Kinematograph, 510
Karno, Leslie (LK) (FK's son), *real name* Leslie Karno Westcott, *aka* Leslie West:
{**L+C**}:
birth and growing up, 93-4, 96, [*112*], 114-5, 121, 140, 183, 302, 389, 545
parentage, *see also* Leslie Stuart, 123-4, *125*, 541
relationship with EK in adulthood, 116, 389, 431, 436-7
young comic, 312, 389, 396, 410-11, 413
running the FK empire, 429-30, [*445*], 446-50, 470, 478-9, 490-1, [*498*]
FK letters from Hollywood, 462, 470-1, 473, 475
relationship with FK, 116, 389, 410-1, 431, 441, 451, 505, 514
later life, career and working with FKJ, 482, 502, 512, 523-4, 526, 541

contribution and response to FK biography, 4-5, 128, 531
{**GT**}:
letters from FK and MM, miscellaneous, 483, 500, 503-4, 508-11, 513-14, 516, 561
on FK, 211-12, 300
also, 34, 120, 122, 134, 136, 143, 341, 438, 522, 529
Karno, Louisa (LK's wife), *née* Louisa Millar *also* Louisa Westcott, 134, 257, 438, 446, 478, 524
Karno, Marie (FK's second wife), *see* Marie Moore
Karno, Olive (FKJ's second wife), *née* Bridge, 4-5, 136, 525, 541
Karno, Queenie (FKJ's first wife), *née* Doyle, *also* Queenie Westcott, *real name* Jane Doyle:
{**L+C**}:
life with FKJ, [*342*], 384, 390, 409, *410*, 413, *417*
U.S. tour with Charlie Hall, 415-416, *462*
split with FKJ, 416, 418, 525
film career, 501, 556
FK visits in U.S., 462, 465
letters from FK, 438-40, 446-7
also, 437
Karno, Ted, *see* Tysall, Edwin (Ted)
Karno Trio, The, (Ted Tysall's company), 53, [*54*], 56, 91, 365, 537
Karno, William (Ted Karno Trio), 54
Karno's Follies, also *Karno's Krazy Komics, Karno's Quest, Fred Karno's Quest of Stage Talent, Karnoisms, The Preston Follies*, etc., 425-27, 480
Karno's Krazy Komics, see *Laffs*
Karno's Trust Ltd, 440
Karno's Vaudeville Road Show, 214
Karnophone, *also* Karnograph, *also* phonograph, 64-6, 253, 537
Karnoscope, The, 253
Karsino Valse, The, 307, *308*
Karsino *also* Tagg's Island *see also* FK, Thames river life:
{**Chr**}:
Three Karnos busking at Molesey Lock, [*42*]
history of Tagg's Island and Tagg's Island hotel, 298, [*299*], 310

FK ownership, 293, 298-300, 318
Design, construction and opening 301, [*302*] *303*, [*304*], 305-6, [*307-8*], 311, 551
growth, operational and financial challenges, 308-9, 331, [*333*], 336, 365-7, [*408*], 410, 423, [*424*], 438-9
events and fundraisers *see also* impact of First World War, 332, 395
CC visit, 401-2
impact of First World War, 333-4, 336-7, 341, 357, [*358*], 359, 379, 390
film location, 356, 396
causes of decline and attempts to sell, [*425*], 431, [*432*], 442-3
post-FK ownership, 528-9, *530*
also, 134, 136-7, 310, 320, 361, 389, 427, 435, 441, 463, 521
Kaufman, George S., 452
Kay, Katy, 428
Keaton, Buster, 159, 267, 363
Keith Circuit, 177
Kelly, Hetty, 228
Kennedy, Edgar, 321, 467
Kent, C.W., 302
Kent, Francis, 298
Kenyon, Neil, 128, [*131*], 247, 251
Kessel and Baumann, *also* Kessel, Adam *and* Baumann, Charles, 322
Keystone Studios *see also* Sennett, Mack,
CC and Keystone, 296, 322-5, 328-9, 354
Syd Chaplin at Keystone, 345, 355, 357
also, 68, 321, 408
Keystone Cops, 98, 321
Keystone Trio, The, *also* The Three Comiques *see also* Laurel, Stan *and* Hurley, Edgar *and* Hurley, Ethel, 330-1
Khaotic!, 531
Kid Auto Races at Venice, (1914), 296
Kid, The, (1921), 19, *20*, 82, 266, 394, 400
Kill or Kure, 387-8, 392
King in New York, A, (1957), 243
King's Theatre, Southsea, Portsmouth, 373

587

King's Theatre, Sunderland, New, 171
Kingsland, Lord, (Christopher Prout), (MP), 1
Kingsway Theatre, The, 386-7, 556
Kirby's Flying Ballet, 130, 146
Kiss Me Kate, (1953), 563
Kitchen, Fred:
{L+C}:
career pre-FK, 87
FK comic, 80, [*86*], 87-8, 91, 99-100, [*101*], 158-162, 169, 202-3, 230-1, 242-3, 539, 547
writing for FK, 99, 160, 183, 202, 230, 292, 406
pantomime dame, 129-30, 200
rise to fame and ongoing success, 87, 93, 99, 108, [*207*], 242, 295, 520
defection to Darnley and solo career, 167-8, 244, 251-3, 288, 313-4, 390
legacy on FK company ongoing association, 255, 312, 335, 385
returns to FK, 405, [*406-7*], 408-10, 483
death and epitaph, 207, 527
{GT}:
character and popularity, 101, 252
relationship with and influence on CC, 101, 162, 221-3, 266, 352, 354
pathos in his work, 208, 406
also, 22, 49, 97, 127, 140, 184, 193, 319, 364, 550-1, 553
Kitchen, Fred, Jnr., 100
Kitchen, Richard H. (Dick), 22, 99-100, 158, 200
Kitchener, General, (Horatio Herbert, 1st Earl Kitchener), 336, 361
Klaie, Rick, *also* Klaie and Karnes, 45-7, 49-50, 52, 54-5, 58, 536
Knick Knacks, also *Wit and Wisdom*, see also *Mustard and Cress*, 367-8, 379, 385
Knight of The Garter, 409
Knoblock, Edward, 402
Knockout, The, (1914), 235
Knowles, R.G., 196
Knox, Teddy, *see* Nervo and Knox *see also* The Crazy Gang
Kubrick, Stanley, 528
Kyre, Alice, 158

L'Enfant Prodigue, 150
La Scala, Antwerp, 23, 39
La Scala, Copenhagen, 144
Labour movement *also* Labour Party, 117, 193-4, 242
Lacy, George, 497
Laffs, also *Karno's Krazy Komics*, 132, 134-5, 475, 480-3, 485, 488-91, 494, 497-8
Lake, Lew, 64
Landeck, Herbert, 160, 202, 314
Lane, Lupino, 450, 463, 497
Langdon, Harry, 459, 462, 470, 473
Langley, Percival, 373, 553
Lappo, Harry, 252, 314
Lashwood, George, 371, 376
Lasky, Jesse, 129-31, 179, 355, [*452*], 453, 472, 475-6
Lauder, Harry, 260, 513, 539, 551
Laughing Gas, (1914), 344-45, 369
Laughton, Lena, 499
Laurel and Hardy, *see also* Laurel, Stan *and* Hardy, Oliver:
{L+C}:
Success, fame and transition to talkies, 418, 458-9, 466, 496
working with FK in Hollywood, 459, 461-3, [*467*], 468, 469-70, 472-3, 476
later career and tour of UK, 496, 527
{GT}:
FK comics working with L&H, 462, 561
influence of SL's time with FK and CC, 278, 279, 461, 470
style and characterisations, 61, 159, 203, 466
also, 378-9, 386, *461*, 477, 524, 547, 559, 561
Laurel, Stan, *real name* Arthur Stanley Jefferson:
{L+C}:
Family, early life and pre-FK career, 27, 66, 91, 151 [*247*], 248, 254
joining FK, early appearances and meeting CC, 248-9, [*250*], 327, 547
Jimmy the Fearless experience, 262-7, 378, 459
U.S. tours with FK company, 272, [*274*], 275, 277, [*278*], 280-1, [*287*], 297, 329, 549-550

First World War conscription, 338
friendship with FKJ, 413-14, 418, 523, 527, 556
other stage work, 286, [*330*], 331, 352, 378, 550-52
solo film career, 325, 331, 377-8, 413, [*414*], 415, 459, 554
impersonating CC, 142, 330, 352
working with FK in Hollywood, [*460*], 461-3, 466, *467*, [*468*], 469-70
support for FK in later life, 503, 506, 510, 517-18
retirement and death, 527-8, 563
{GT}:
creative force behind L&H, 459-60
FK material in SL work, 319, 327, 470, 544-5, 551
FK view of or approach to SL and SL's work, 267-8, 458-60, 497, 517-20
influence of FK era on career, 1, 186, 208, 266, 268, 275, 460-1, 470, 474, 520-21
on FK and FK period, 1, 110, 142, 208, 235, 521
pathos in his work, 267-8, 472
personal life and name change, 331, 413-15, 512, 532, 560
relationship with and opinion of CC, 250, 262-7, 277-8, 326, 378-9, 400, 458, 554
also, 2-4, 6, 101, 240, 395, 416, 440, 443, 451, 453, 483, 496-7, 531
Laurent, Jean Baptiste, 60
Lauri, Charles, 44, 50
Laurillard, Joseph, *see also* Grossmith and Laurillard, 427
Lawrence, Danny, 547
Le Clerq, Arthur (Arty), 445-46, 480
Le Clerq, Gus *later* McNaughton, 145, 234, 282, 295, 445, 546
Le Fre, James *also* Le Fre, W., *145*
Le Neve, Ethel, 199
Leake, Alex, 191
Leamore, Matt, 428
Leamore, Tom, 43-4, 46
Leat, Harry, 479
Lee, Bert, 385
Lee, Norman, 505
Leeds City Varieties, 27
Lehrman, Henry 'Pathé', *also* L-KO Kompany, 351

INDEX

Leno, Dan:
  collaborators in common with FK, 77, 233
  crossing paths with FK, 64-5, 72, 85
  influence on FK, SL and CC, 247, 268, 354
  mental health 99, 209
  also, 7, 87, 128
Leo, Ted, 286
Leonard, Billy, 399
Leopolds, The, 50
Lesson in Temperance, A, 310
Let's All Go to the Music Hall, 105
Letters, Will, 225, 546
Lewis Ward, Richard, 462, 472
Lewis, Bobby, 351, 372
Leybourne, George, 26
Lily of Laguna, 34, 428
Limelight, (1952), 209
Linder, Max, [*148*], 209, 225, 355
Little Bit of Fluff, A, [*439*], 448-9
Little Tich, 87, 99, 151, 536
Livermore Brothers circuit, 64
Lloyd George, David, 242
Lloyd, Alice, 151, 418-19
Lloyd, Arthur, 251
Lloyd, Harold, 159, 556
Lloyd, Marie:
  {**L+C**}:
  success and fame, 28, 62, 409
  friendship with EK and Naomi Jacob, 92, 116-119, 182-3, 437
  involvement with MHLG and Belle Elmore, 182-3, 198-9
  Music Hall War role, 194-5, 197
  exclusion from Royal Command Performance, 294
  death, 409
  {**GT**}:
  personal life, 116-18, 182, 540
  working and relationship with FK, 28, 62, 64, 92, 117, 195, 197, 236, 314, 395, 544
  also, 25, 65, 87, 128, 151, 184, 346, 419
Lloyd, Rosie, 184
Lockhart's Elephants, 195
Loew, Marcus, 277, 549
London Music Hall, The New, 55, 74, 77
London Suburbia, 166, 215, [*216*], 219-20, 235, 354, 397, 549
Long, Lily, 365
Lord Chamberlain *and* Lord Chamberlain's Office, 61-2, 350

Louvish, Simon, 19, 63, 113, 142, 242, 321, 378, 460, 472, 558
Love in a Tub, 18, 43-47, 97, 166, 479, 539
Love Match, The, 422-3, 427, 511, 557
Lowe, Arthur, 515
L.S.D., also *£.S.D.* and *Pounds, Shillings and Pence*, 373-4, 376
Lubin Manufacturing Co., 351, 352
Lupino, Barry, 542
Lyons, Joseph, (Sir), 307, 318
Lyric Theatre, The, 384
Lytton, Henry, (Sir), 102, 214

Mabel at the Wheel, (1914), 546
Mabel's Married Life, (1914), 235
Macdermott, Ouida, 368
MacDonald, James Ramsey, (MP), 483
MacDonald's Music Hall, Glasgow, 22
Macdonald, J.C., 535
Mace brothers, (Jem and Pooley), 43, 46
Mace, Fred, 323
Mack and Mabel, 321
MacKay, Fenton 'Jock', 338, 399
Madrali, Ahmed, 106
Major, Frank, 285
Making a Living, (1914), 327, 328
Making More Stars, 514
Manardo, Tom, 85
Manchester, Percy, 526
Manley's Chinese Circus, 18, 44
Mann, Jack, 385
Manners, Lady Diana, (Viscountess Norwich), 309
Mannock, P.L., 411
Manon, Charles, 543-4
Marinelli, H.B., 159, 558
Marines, The, 166
Marion, Kitty, 305-6
Marked for Life, 81, 538
Marlborough Theatre, The, 131, 171, 229, 236, 282, 297, 331, 547
Marquand, Clifford, 362
Marriot, A.J.:
  CC and SL with FK generally, 220-2, 242, 246, 255, 261, 263-6
  FK U.S. tours, 157, 272, 275, 322
  CC meeting Hetty Kelly, 227-8
  CC and SL stage careers pre-FK, 217, 546-7, 549, 550, 554

  FKJ in Canada, 509
  also, 563
Marriott, Moore, [*374*], 395
Marston, Irene, 362
Martinetti, Paul, 50, 151
Martini, Bob, 331
Marx Brothers, The, *also* Marx, Groucho, 320, 451, 536, 558
Mary, Queen, 294
Maskell, Lew, 79
Matcham, Frank, 301-2, 304
May, Theresa, (MP), 1
Mayfair and Montmartre, 418
Mayne, Clarice, *also* Clarice Mayne and That, [*132*], 294, [*304*]
Mayo, Sam, 193
McAllister, Dick, 156, 279
McCabe, John, 2, 90, 106, 142, 181, 213, 218-9-25, 250, 267, 547
McCann, Chuck, 278
McCarey, Leo, 418, 462-3
McCarthy, Joseph, 378, 528
McConnell Stott, Andrew, 61, 212
McLaglen, Clifford, *439*
McNaughton, Fred, 550
McNaughton, Tom, 103, 215, 550
Melford, Austin, 399, 555
Mellini's Theatre, Hanover, 59
Melroyd, Frank, 239, [*274*]
Melville, Jack:
  FK comic, 129, 158, 196-7, 349
  on CC, 222-3, 262
  also, 211-12, 368, 529, 547
Melville, Jackie, 362
Meredith, Billy, 191, [*192*], 204
Merrick, Joseph, 13
Merry Carpenters, The, 54
Mervyn, Bernard, 80, 538
Metro-Goldwyn-Mayer (MGM) Studios, 383, 460, 463, 472-3
Metropole Theatre, Camberwell, 152
Metropole Theatre, Glasgow, *see also* the Scotia, 247
Metropolitan Music Hall, *aka* The Met, Edgware Road, London, 31, [*32*], 33, 39-40, 64, 246, 269, 486, 536
Middlesex Music Hall, London, 38, 55, 62, 127, 536
Miller, Ann, 563
Miller, Fred, 108-9, 172, 230
Miller, Max:
  fame and success, 483, 488, 520, 527
  FK comic, 137, 211, 434-5, [*436*], 557
  FK film project, 510

589

Milligan, Spike, 209
Milligan, Tommy, 438
Miner, Henry Clay, *and* Miner's Bowery Theatre, 540
Minister, Amy *real name* Clara Amy Minister *also* Amy Reeves:
{L+C}:
FK comedienne, 78, 108, 129, 158, *369*
U.S. tours, 176, 226, [*274*], 280, *281*, *287*, 295, 297, *319*
also, 272, 377, 453, 538, 554
Miss 1925, 427
Miss Saigon, 257
Mitchell, Oswald, 512
Mittenthal Film Company, 351
Modern Times, (1936), 254, 266, 319
Moffatt, Graham, 395
Money to Burn, 393
Monsieur Verdoux, (1947), 524
Montpelier Palace., The, 228
Monty Python, 536
Moonstruck, 391-2, 394, 424
Moore and Burgess Minstrels:
extracts, 1, 7, 17, 70, 83, 96, 111, 126, 138, 229, 326, 344, 417, 431
minstrel troupes background, 35-6
Three Karnos engagement, [*34*], 35-7, 41, 51
also, 87-8, 94, 538
Moore, Eliza (MM's mother), 88
Moore, George Washington 'Pony', *see also* Moore and Burgess, 34, 88, 535, 538
Moore, Marie (MM), *also* Karno, Marie (FK's second wife):
{L+C}:
birth and family background, 88, 539
affair with FK, 88-9, 94, 102, 111-12, 115, 122-3, 127, 152
with FK after separation from EK, 112, 128, 137, 155, 282, *284*, 289, 314, 350, 375, 410, 557-8
at Karsino, 307, 332
marriage to FK, 438
saves FK from destitution, 444-5
Hollywood with FK, 463-5, 476, [*477*]
retirement to Dorset, 497, 507-8, 510-11, 513-4, 561
FK ill health and death, 511, 516, 519
Final years, 516-7, 522.

also, 159, 365, 451, 453, 523, 544
Moore, Tom, *aka* Tom Birchmore, 88, 445, 471, 538, 561
Moore, Winnie, (MM's sister), 539
Moran, William, *145*
Morecambe, Eric, 271
Morgan, Harry, 248-9
Morganti, William, *see also* Four Aubreys, The, 38
Morris, Aggie, 138, 160, 202, 269, 314
Morris, Lily, 247
Morris, William, *also* William Morris Agency, 451, 475-6, 558
Morrisey, William 'Curly', 465, 525
Morrison, Herbert, (Baron Morrison of Lambeth), (MP), 514, 525
Moses and Son:
{SI}:
launch, plot, reviews and writers, 155, 159-62, 167, 251, 432-3
UK tours, 156, 172, 184, 501
rehashed into later FK shows, 202, 434
also, 193, 207-8, 252, 542
Mosley, Mary (Polly), 48, 58, 437
Moss and Stoll circuit, *see also* Edward Moss *and* Oswald Stoll, 187
Moss and Thornton circuit, *see also* Edward Moss *and* Richard Thornton, 53, 194
Moss Empires:
FK revue contract, 366-7, 373-4, 381, 385, 387, 390, 396, 399, 405, 429
also, 108, 131, 260, 442
Moss, Edward, *see* Moss and Thornton circuit *and* Moss Empires
Mother Goose, (Dibden pantomime), 61
Mother Goose, (FK pantomime), 131, 246-7, 314, 331
Mother's Joy, (1923), 556
Motoring, 76
Moving In, 165-6, 168
Muir, Frank, 561
Multi-millionaire, The, 160
Mumming Birds (FK sketch), *also Twice Nightly* also *Stage Upon a Stage, A*, see also *Night in an English Music Hall, A*:

{SI}:
origins, debut details and alternative titles, 103, [*104*], [*108*], 109, [*110*]
launch, and comics' reticence, 107-8, 111-2, 137-8
reviews, 109-10
plot, gags and comedy business, *106*, [*107*], 317
writers, 109, 126-7
technical complexity and scale, 107, 152
extracts, 310
UK tours, 156, 158-9, 172, 181, 224, 236, 249-50, 317, 335, 340, 349, 368, 376, 385, 389, 400, 407-8, 410, 551
UK tours under LK management, 446-7, 450, 470-1, 478-9, 502
U.S. and international tours, see also *A Night in an English Music Hall*, 157, 179, 245, 314, *321*, 372, 451
licensed and copycat versions, 110, 138, 143-5, 157, 171, 177, 235, 421, 450, 490-1, 543
film version legal dispute, *see also* Pathé Frères, 148-50, [*225*]
role in establishing copyright legislation for stage productions, [*178*]
FKJ and LK versions, 110, 482, 512, 524-6
later tours benefitting from association with CC, 110, 370, 478, 482
rehashed into later FK shows, 170, 370, 372, 427
other film versions (some aborted), 369, 411-2, 449-50, 463, 497, 511
{GT}:
CC appearances, 224, 245-6, 250, 255, 310, 547
CC importance to career, 110, 246, 329-30
First World War connections, 340, 384
influence on CC, SL, other comics and silent film comedy generally, 310, 327, 352-3, 369
influence on The Crazy Gang, 485, 488, 491
mummers definition and history, 109, 174-5
SL appearances, 248-50

INDEX

SL opinion of show, 110
also, 155, 168, 176, [*249*], *353*, 356, 480, 515, 539, 558
Mumming Birds (film, 1923), 411-2
Mumming Birds (aborted Syd Chaplin film, 1929), 449-50
Mundy, Hilda, *see also* The Crazy Gang *and* Caryll and Mundy, 484
Murray and Dawe, 376, 380, 399
Murray, Bert, 272
Murray, Paul, 483
Murray, Will, 181, 217
Muscles, 168
Music Hall Artistes' Railway Association, The, (MHARA), 193, 544
Music Hall Guild of Great Britain and America, 530
Music Hall history, 25-28, [*29*], 30, 61-2, 172, 295, 386, 388, 448, 480, 527
Music Hall Ladies' Guild, The, 182-3, 198-9, 332, 358, 362, 395, 540
Music Hall Sick Fund, The, 215
Music Hall War, The, 194, [*195*], 197-8, 200, 225, 294, 371
Musicians' Union, The, 411, 556
Mustard and Cress, see also *Knick Knacks*, 366-7
Mutual Film Corporation, The, 357, 377, 453
My Japanese Cherry Blossom, 96-7
Mycroft, Walter, 483, 497, 560

National Association of Theatrical Employees, 411, 556
National Football Agency, 192
National Sporting Club, Covent Garden, The, 233-4
National Theatre, New York, *also* Loew's Million Dollar Theatre, 277,
National Vigilance Association *see* Vigilance Committees
Naughton and Gold, *also* Naughton, Charlie *and* Gold, Jimmy, *see also* The Crazy Gang, 447, 484, *485*, 486-8, *489*, 490-1, 495-6, 510
Naughton, Charlie, *see* Naughton and Gold, *see also* The Crazy Gang
Near Dublin, 413, *414*
Nelson, Billy, *see* Wakefield and Nelson
Nelson, Tom, 243, 292, 311, [*312*], 317, 335, 346

Nervo and Knox, *see also* Nervo, Jimmy *and* Knox, Teddy, *see also* The Crazy Gang, 484-8, [*489*], 527
Nervo, Jimmy, *see also* Nervo and Knox, *see also* The Crazy Gang, 333, 348, *489*, 554
Neville, Dorothy, 419
New Mama, The, see *Saturday to Monday*
New Slavey, The, 196-7, 281-2, 287, 355, 368, 385, 427, 474
New Star, Liverpool, The, 51
New Woman's Club, (*The*), 66, 68, 72, *73*, 74, 78, 89, 120, 150, 269, 362
New Women, (song), 72
New Women's (or Woman's) Movement, The, *see also* suffragettes *and* feminism, 72, 89, 120, 124, 540
New York Motion Picture Co., The, 322
Niblo, Walter, 447
Night in a Chamber of Horrors, A, 548
Night in a London Club, A, see also *The Smoking Concert*:
{**SL**}:
U.S. tours, *170*, 177, 208, 279, *287*, 297, 310, *311*, 319, 549
{**GT**}:
CC and SL use of material in films, 320, 551
Night in a London Secret Society, A, see also *Wow Wows, The*, 276
Night in a London Slum, A, see also *Early Birds*, 176-7, 226, 279, 542, 549
Night in an English Music Hall, A, see also *Mumming Birds*, 157, 172, 176-7, 226-7, 277, 280, 286, 297, 319, *321*, 549
Night in an Old-time Music Hall, A (copycat version of *Mumming Birds*), 490
Night in the Show, A, (1915), 369, 539
Night in the Slums of Paris, A, 548
Night Owls, (1930), [*467-8*]
Nixon Nirdlinger Circuit, 324, 327
Nixon Theatre, Pennsylvania, 549
Nobody Loves a Fairy When She's Forty, 445
Noel, Cossie, 100, 140
Norbury, James, 119
Norden, Denis, 133, 488, 527
Norman, Wal, 407

Normand, Mable, 321, 328, 330
Nosey Knows, 375, 379, [*380*], 381, 385, 391, 458, 554
Nothing To Do With Me, 160
Nursery, The, 166
Nuts in May, (1917), 378
Nutty Burglars, The, [*330*]

O'Gorman, Joe, 176
O'Malley, Syd, 195, 225
O'Neill, Frank, 159, 248, [*249*], 250, 260, 262, 285, 547
O'Shea, Tessie, 479
Oh Joy, 387
Oh, Mr Porter!, (film, 1937), 395
Oh! Mr Porter, (song), 197
Oh That Girl! [*342*]
Oh What a Duchess, also *My Old Duchess*, (1934), 497
Oh What A Lovely War, (1969), 383
Oh Yes!, 409, 413
Oh, Law!, see also *Have a Banana!* see also *On and Off*, 370-2
Old Time Richardson's Show, The, 174, [*175*]
Oliver!, (1968), 546
Oliver the Eighth, (1934), 561
Olvene, Monsieur, (*real name* Tom Hillery), 11, [*12*], 13-16, 22, 52, 226
Olympia, Glasgow, 314
Olympia, Liverpool, 348
Olympia, London, 106, 147, 173, [*175*], 202, 238
Olympia, Paris, 156, 158
Olympic Music Hall, London, 55-6
On and Off, see also *Oh, Law!* [*372*], 376
On with the Show, (Frank Randle revue), 562
On with the Show, (FK revue), see *Show, The*
One a.m., (1916), 310
Only Me, (1929), 450
Opera House, Blackpool, 408
Opera House, Bury, 158
Opera House, Jersey, 296
Opera House, Stockport, see Theatre Royal, Stockport.
Ormiston Chant, Laura, 72
Orpheum, New York, 177
Orton, John, 483
Osborne, Jack, 314
Ostrer, Isidore, 493
Our Annual Social, 171
Our Gang Series, [*465*], 473
Our Neighbours, 166
Our Relations, (1936), 458

591

Outcasts, The, see *Casuals, The*
Over the Garden Wall, 55
Owen, Jackson, 409
Oxberry, Harry, 78-9, 85, 239, 338, 388
Oxford Music Hall, The, 25, *27*, 72, 92, 96-7, 149, 169, 171, 233, 245-6, 348
Oxley, Gus, 403-4

Painful Predicament of Sherlock Holmes, The, 181
Painless, also *Tooth Will Out*, (1933), 494, 496
Painter and Decorators, The, 166
Palace of Varieties, 525
Palace of Varieties, Hammersmith *also* West London, 119, 211
Palace Theatre, Aberdeen, 551
Palace Theatre, Blackburn, New, 171
Palace Theatre, Glasgow, 171
Palace Theatre, Halifax, 502
Palace Theatre, Leicester, 20, 243
Palace Theatre, London, 294
Palace Theatre, Maidstone, 229, 282
Palace Theatre, Manchester, 86, 93, 99, 102, 128, 183, 186, 547
Palace Theatre, Plymouth, 446
Palace Theatre, Southampton, 158, 288
Palladium, Johannesburg, 314
Palladium, London, 132, 134-5, 291, 370, 401, 467, 483, 485-91, 493-4, 501
Palmer, Fred, also Palmer, Muriel, 129, 158, [*274*], 277, *281*, *287*, *319*, 340
Panorama, The, 168
Paragon, London, The:
  association with FK company, 62-3, [*64*]
  FK premieres, 151, 215
  launch of *The Wontdetania*, 256-8, 260, 513
  also, 93, 140, 233, 542
Paramount Famous Lasky Corporation *also* Paramount Studios, 451-2, 472, 475, 511
Pardon Us, also *Jailbirds* (1931), 477, 544
Paris Nights, 557
Parker P.C., 554
Parks, Ennis, 391, 424
Parlez Vous Français?, 341, 347, [*348*], 350, 356, 373, 411, 554
Parnell, Archie, 483
Parnell, Val, 135, 483-5, 489, 491

Parnell, Wallace, 133-5, 502, 541
Parrot, James, *467*, [*468*]
Passing Show, The, 418
Pathé Frères, 148-50, 225, 228, 230, 321, 355, 370
Paulo, Harry, 174
Pavilion, Liverpool, 250
Pavilion, London, 92, 99, 551
Pavilion, Swansea, 41
Pawnshop, The, (1916), 320, 357
Payne, Edmund, 313
People's Hall, Manchester, The, 38
People's Palace, Sunderland, 89
Perkins in Paris, 291-2, 313, 317, 511
Perkins in Port, see also *Perkins the Purser*, 550
Perkins MP, 242, 244, 251-3, 268, 292, 306, 312, 362
Perkins the Punter, see also *Wakes Week*, 292, 551
Perkins the Purser, see also *Perkins in Port*, 288, 290-1, 312
Perry, Jimmy, 395
Petrova, Olga *also* Muriel Harding, [*131*], 132
Pharmacist, The, (1933), 233
Phew!, 381-2, 385
Photographers, The, 252
Pickard, Albert E., 247
Piddock, J.C., Jr., 269-70
Pie Eyed, (1925), 327
Pilgrim, The, (1923), 320
Pimple, *see* Evans, Fred, III
Pimple's Holiday, (1915), 356
Pine, Vesta, 410
Pinero, A.W., 542
Pink Floyd, 530, 563
Pink, Wal:
  {L+C}:
  CC and Syd Chaplin with Pink, *180*,181
  decorator routine origins, 243, 543-4
  collaborations with FK, 92, 214-5
  rivalry with FK, 165, 295
  also, 408-9
Plaza, New York, The, 255
Poli Circuit, The, 157
Police, (1916), 369
Policemen's Little Run, The, (1907), 321
Pollock Moore, Alexander, 455-6
Polly, 556
Poluski, Will, Jr., 184, 186, 220-1, 245-6, 271, 419
Pom Pom, 357
Pond, Arthur, 485
Pong, Ping, 158
Popular Workhouse, The, 214, 224

Porter, Joey, 495-6, 498-9
Post Haste, 495-6
Postage Due, (1924), 414
Pot Pourri, (FK sketch), 152,
Pounds, Courtice, 102
Pounds, Shillings and Pence, see *L.S.D.*
Poverty Corner, 30, *31*, 37, 39, 54, 401
Powell, Dudley, 87, 99-100, 129, 160, 236, 253, 291, 298, 314
Powell, Orlando, 291
Powell, Sandy:
  {L+C}:
  debut in *The Football Match*, 419-20, [*421*]
  later success, 443, 520
  Karsino demolition party, 529
  {GT}:
  comedy style, 159
  also, 186-7, 293, 436
Power, Will, 486
Prince Edward Theatre, London, 506
Prince of Monte Carlo, The, 126-8, 156
Prince of Wales Theatre of Varieties, Northampton, 18
Prince of Wales Theatre, Birmingham, 58
Prince of Wales Theatre, Grimsby, 100
Prince's Theatre, Bradford, 91
Prince's Theatre, London, 66, 287
Princess of Wales Theatre, Kennington, 77-8
Princess Theatre, Leeds, 38
Prior, Frank, 338, 372
Prior, Jimmy, 234
Prior, Tommy, 380
Private Potts, 251, 257
Proctor, Madge (Marguerite), *also* Madge Thompson, 3, 120-1, 437
Proctor's circus, 17, 23
Proctor's Theatre, New York, 310
Producers Distributing Corporation (P.D.C.), 507, 510
Professor, The, (1919), 110
Provincial Theatre Group, 172
Pryde, Peggy, 535
Purser and Wilkes *also* Philips Purser *and* Jenny Wilkes, 133-5
Purvis Walter, 539

Queen's Palace of Varieties *also* Queen's Theatre, Poplar, 238, 327,
Quick Supper, A, 54

INDEX

Raid on a Club, A, (1905), 150
Ramish, Adolf, 378
Randle, Frank, 501, [*502*], 513, 520
Rations, 385, 515, 555
Raw Recruits, The, see *Skirmishers, The*
Rawlins, John, 496
Ray, Harry, 368
Raynor, Dan, 285, 327, 330, 338, 448
Read, Beatrice, 370
Reade, Charles, 538
Real Life, 492, [*498*], 499-502
Rebla, *real name* Albert Stevens, 396
Red Hot, see also *Scarlet Runners*, 396, 403, 445, 481
Redfern, Fred, 72
Redstone, Willie, 362, 406
Reed Pinaud, Theodore, 110, 138, 143, [*144*], 145, 155-7, 168, 234, 356
Rees, Ernest, 120
Reeve and Russell, *also* Alfred T. Reeve *and* Frederick W. Russell, 445-447
Reeves, Alf:
 {**L+C**}:
 management of FK U.S. tours, [*156*], 157-8, 176-7, 179, 226-7, 237, 255-6, 272-4, 277, 280, *281*, 285, 295, 297, 327, 543
 friendship with CC, 320, 327
 on CC leaving FK, 323-5
 management for FK after U.S. tours, 346, *369*, 372
 First World War experiences, 338, 356, 384
 CC studio manager, [*377*], 378, 415, 448, 453, 472
 FK meets Reeves in Hollywood, 453, [*454*], 455, 457, 461, 475
 film appearances with CC, 559
 also, 296, 527
Reeves, Amy, *see* Amy Minister
Reeves, Billy:
 {**L+C**}:
 FK comic, 74, 85, 97, [*99*], 107, [*108*], 155
 defection to Reed Pinaud, and then Darnley 155-6, 168
 U.S. Tours with FK, 176, 179, 226, 285-7
 Ziegfeld Follies appearances, 227, 285
 solo stage career and FK influences, 227, 310, 335
 film career, [*351-2*], 520

reunited with Charlie Bell, 422
 also, 280, 527
Regan, Alec, 406, [*407*], 409
Regina, Fred, 543-4
Registry, The, 214
Repairs, *180*, 181, 243, 543
Residenztheater, Munich, 91
Reunion, (1933), 383
Review, (BBC documentary), 521, 529
Revnel and West, 504
Rich, John, 59
Rink, The, (1916), [*254*], 369
Ritchie, Billie,
 {**L+C**}:
 FK comic, 78-80, 85, 97, 107
 U.S. FK company tours, [*156*], 158, 176
 in copycat shows, use of FK material, 177-8, 226, [*227*], 279
 film career, 335, 351, 520
 dispute over the original Drunk and claims to CC's Tramp, 352, [*353-4*]
 death by ostrich, 400
Ritchie, W.E., 553
Ritchie, Winifred, 97, 108, 156, 158, 177, 400, 453
Roach, Hal *also* Hal Roach Studios, 413-16, 418, 458-9, [*460*], 461-3, 465-7, 469-75, 501, 513, 523, 525, 559
Roberts, Arthur, 208
Robey, George, 64-5, 169, 196, 354, 561
Robinson Crusoe, 89
Robinson, Carlyle, 453
Robinson, David:
 CC and FK, 23, 255, 328, 540, 547, 562
 CC physical comedy, 310
 compares FK to Sennett, 321
 Hanlon Brothers influence on FK, 50
 also, 105-6, 415, 543, 548-9, 559
Rock City, Nottingham, [*10*]
Rock, Joe, 415
Rockingham, Madge, 208
Rogers, Charley, 453, 462, 520
Rogerson, Amy, 228
Rogue Song, The, (1930), 463
Rolin Studios, 556
Rolyat, Dan, 387, *388*
Rosebery, Lord, (Archibald Primrose), (MP), 390
Rosy Rapture, Pride of the Beauty Chorus, 366
Rowe, George, *414*
Roxbury, Harry, 100, 126-8, 156, 520

Royal Albert Music Hall, 76
Royal Command Performance *also* Royal Variety Performance, 294-5, 394, 486-7, 489, 527
Royal York Pavilion, Southampton, 46
Royal Theatre, Worcester, 551
Royston, Harry, 97, 156, 176, 179, 184, 543
Rum uns from Rome, The, 286
Russell, Jimmy:
 {**L+C**}:
 FK comic, 200, 215, 224, *238*, 239, 269, 317, 335, 349, 368, *369*, 370, 372, 376, 408
 U.S. tours, 184
 also, 338, 340, 529, 555
Ryskind, Morrie, 452

Sadler's Wells, 59-60, 257
St. James Quintet, 87-8
St. James's Hall, London, 34, 37
Saintsbury, H.A., 180
Salesman, The, 496
Sandy, Frederick, 237, 285, 396
Sanger's Circus, Lord George, 535
Sargent, Herbert C., 428
Saturday to Monday also New Mama, The:
 {**SI**}:
 launch, plot, reviews, and writers, 99, [*100*], 132, 168
 UK tours, 102, 138, 156, 158-9, 172, 348
 {**GT**}:
 influence on CC, 266
 also, *101*, 140, 167, 228, 252, 546
Savoy Opera, 102
Scarlet Runners, also *Tit for Tat*, see also *Red Hot*, 403, 405-6, 409, 411, 445
Scheide, Frank, 470
Scotia Music Hall, Glasgow, *see also* Metropole Theatre, Glasgow, 21-2, 52, 247
Seaforth, Selina, *and* Seaforth, Daltry and Higgins, 121
Seaman, George *also* Seaman, Emily, 265, [*274*], *281*, 287, 295, 297, *319*, 330
Seaton and Martin, 6, 394
Sea-view Hotel, 166
Second Hundred Years, The, (1927), 460
Second World War, 2, 118, 492, 513-5, 524, 526-8, 532
Sefton, Ernest, 396, 398
Selbini trick cyclists, 30

593

Selig, Ernest, 376
Sellers, Peter, 209
Selvidge, Bob, 335, 344, 349, 351
Sennett, Mack:
{L+C}:
CC and Keystone, 279, [*322*], 324, 327-8, 345, 354
contract with FK, 474-5, 477
bankruptcy and death, 475, 527
{GT}:
FK view of Sennett and similarities, 321
origins of Keystone, Sennett's material, style and approach, 149, 320-1, 328-9, 466
also, 68, 345, 349
Sewell, Alfred, 54
Sewell, Bob, *see also* Three Karnos, The, 30-3, 39, 41, 45, 49, 54, 59, 537
Sewell, Elizabeth, 45, 54
Shah of Persia, (Mozaffar ad-Din Shah Qajar), 103
Shakespeare Theatre, Liverpool, 52
Shanghaied, (1915), 275
Shannon-Clyndes, Evelyn, 362
Shaw, George Bernard, 482
Sheridan, Mark, 209
Sherlock Holmes, 180-1
Sherlock Junior, (1924), 267
Shoulder Arms, (1918), 266, 559
Show, The, also *On With the Show*, see also *Tittle Tattle*, 428-9, 433-4, 436,
Showmen of England, 510
Shubert Circuit, 400
Sidney, Herbert, 269, 281-2, 288-290, 548-9
Sign Please, (1933), 496
Silk Noose, The, (1948), 524
Simon, John, (Sir), 309
Simpson, Harold, 362
Simpson, Lee, 171
Sinbad The Sailor, 37
Sinclair, Billie, 316
Sipple, James (Jem), 164
Sisters Sprightly, The, 365
Six (or Ten) Little Burglars, 87, 92, 167
Sixes and Sevens, see *Yes Papa*
Skating, [*238*], *239*, 240, 250, 254, 276, 547
Skirmishers, The, 167-8
Skylarks, 166
Sleeping Beauty, 248
Smith, Edgar, 97
Smithy, (1924), 414
Smoking Concert, The, also Amateur Entertainers, The, see also *Night in a London Club,*

A, 165, 169, [*170*], 171, 177, 216, 224, 242, 269, 419, 515, 549
Smyth-Pigott, John, 298
Society Idols, The, 307
Somebody's Coming to my House, 556
Somossy's Orpheum, Budapest, 39
Songs That Won the War, 383
Sons of Karno's Army, 526
South London Music Hall, The, 66, 218
South London Palace, The, 37
Spice of Paris, 134
Spiksley, Fred, 185, 187
Spoor, G.K., 355
Spring Cleaning, 166, 243-4, 312, 427
Stacey, M., 508, 510
Stan Jefferson Trio, The, *also* Cook, Alice *and* Cook, Baldwin *see also* Laurel, Stan, 331, 552
Stanley, H., 440
Star, Bermondsey, The, 255, 331
Star, Dublin, The, 56
Staveacre, Tony, 531
Stead, W.T., 133
Steam Laundry, The, [*318*], 349
Stein, Lisa K., 219, 439, 543, 558
Sterling, Ford, 321
Stewart, Winifred, 88-9, 122
Stolen Fruit, 376
Stoll, Oswald, 90-1, 138, 193, 229, 484, 537, 550
Stratton, Eugene, 34, 41, 64-5, 72, 99, 236
Stromberg, John, 97
Stuart, Leslie, 34, 94, [*124*], 233, 361, 541
Suffragettes at St. Stephens, The, see also *Timothy MP*, 147
Suffragettes, *also* Women's Union of Suffrage Societies, *see also* female emancipation *and* the New Women's Movement, 72-3, 117, 215, 242-3, 305-6
Sullivan and Considine Circuit, 297, 323-4
Summer Boarders, 35, 37, 45-7, 51
Summers, Johnny, 233-4
Summers, Walter, 128-9
Sunnyside, (1919), 394
Surpassing Show, The, 418, 423
Swain, Mack, 321
Sylvester, Frederick, 307
Sylvester, Thomas Montague, 229-30
Symons, Julian, 361

Tabrar, Joseph, 34
Tagg, George *also* Thomas Tagg, 298-9, 550
Tagg's Island, *see* Karsino
Tainted, 450
Tally Ho, 557
Ta-ra-ra Boom-de-ay!, 132
Tate, Harry, 76, 99, 129, 140, 151, 169, 215, 236, 294
Tate, James W., *see also* Wylie and Tate, 132, 160
Teeth, see also *Dental* Institute, The, 344-5, 427, 494
Tennent, Henry M., 405
Terriers, The, 86, 312
Terris, Fred, 374
That's the Time to Go, 159
Theatre Marigny, The, 145
Theatre Royal, Bristol, 531
Theatre Royal, Edinburgh, 373
Theatre Royal, Glasgow, 248
Theatre Royal, Leicester, 499
Theatre Royal, Margate, 525
Theatre Royal, North Shields, 151
Theatre Royal, Preston, 158
Theatre Royal, Sheffield, 129, 138, 426
Theatre Royal, Stockport, *also* Stockport Opera House, 37-8
Theatre Royal, York, 386
Theatrical Managers' Association, The, 207
Thesiger, Ernest, 386
Thespian Films, 396
They're Off, (1933), 496
Thirsty First, The, 151, 153, 155-6, 162, 164, 167, 251, 549
Thomas, Effie, 362, 365
Thorne, Eric, 348-9
Thornton, Richard, *see* Moss and Thornton circuit
Thornton's Varieties, South Shields, 69
Three Bites, 376-7, 380, 383, 385, 388, 392
Three Brass Balls, The, 166
Three Carnos, The, *also* Fred, Hugh, Harry, John, *and* Henri Carno, 31-3, 36, 39-40
Three Comiques, The, *see also* Keystone Trio, The, [*330*]
Three Karnos, The, *see* Karno, Fred *and* Tysall, Ted *and* Sewell, Bob
Three Men in a Boat, 42, 309
Three Women to Every Man, 376
Thumbs Up, also *Thumbs Down*, 159, 166-7, 290, 292, 312-3
Tilley, Vesta, 32, 535
Timothy MP, see also *Suffragettes at St. Stephens, The*, 547
Tindall, Tom, 224

INDEX

Tit for Tat, see *Scarlet Runners*
Tittle Tattle, see also *Show, The*, 428
Tivoli Theatre, New Brighton, 445
Tivoli, London, The, 64, 96, 537
Tommie's Tunes, 383
Tonne, Alfred, 80
Too Darn Hot, 563
Too Much Efficiency, 398
Tottenham Palace, London, 269
Tracey, Jack, 135
Tragedy of Errors, A, also *Up the Pole*, 210, 269
Travers, Hyram, 18, 20
Travis Stewart, D., 35
Tribune, Deane, 258
Trip to Whitby, A, 225
Triple Trouble, (1918), 235, 369
Trundley, John, 387
Turpin, Ben, 321
Twelve Just Men, The, 547
Twisters, The, 281
Two Macs, The, 50
Tysall, Edwin (Ted), *aka* Ted Karno, *see also* Three Karnos, The, *and* Karno Trio, The, 30-33, 39-41, 45, 52-4, 312, 544
Tysall, Mary, *aka* Cora Carnot, 40, 45, 53, [54]

Ullah, John, 462
Unaccustomed As We Are, (1929), 559
Uncle Tom's Cabin, 37
Under the Clock, 346
Universal Productions Ltd, 432
Universal Studios, 378

Variety Artistes' (later The Music Hall), Benevolent Fund, The, 92, 176, 195, 358, 364, 508
Variety Artistes' Federation (VAF), 194-6, 214, 404, 411, 448, 544, 556
Vaudeville Club, The, 85
Vento's Varieties, Portsmouth, 40
Vic and Bob (Vic Reeves and Bob Mortimer), 533
Vicat, Grace, 362
Victoria Palace Theatre, The, 486, 527
Victoria Saloon, Dresden, 58
Victoria Theatre, Walthamstow, 81
Victoria, Queen, 25, 66, 83-5, 260
Victoria, Vesta, 442
Victoria, Violet, 501
Vigilance committees, *also* National Vigilance Association, 62, 72, 208

Village Fair, The, 166
Village Sports, The, see also *Annual Sports, The*, 296-7
Vint, Leon, 385-6, [387], 432, 557
Vitagraph Company, 330, 351
Vivian, Mona, 131-2

Wagner, Rob, 353
Wakefield and Nelson *also* Wakefield, Dougie, *and* Nelson, Billy, 501, 511, 561
Wakefield, Charles, (Sir), [358]
Wakefield, Dougie, *see* Wakefield and Nelson
Wakes Week, see also *Perkins the Punter*, 311-12, 314
Walker, Mickey, 438
Walker, Syd, 246, 268, 289, 347, *348*, 356, 373, 376, 520, 522, 554
Walker, Tom 'Whimsical', 175, 297, 319, 328
Wall, Max, 536
Wall Street Crash, 472, 474, 477, 560
Wallace, Lionel, 102
Walrus Hunt, The, 129
Walthamstow Palace, 334
Walton, H., 158
Walturdaw Film Company, 150
Waltz Scream, The, also *The Waltz Dream*, 291, 313
Ward, Hylton, 340
Wardour Films, 510
Warner, Jack, 463
Warner, Richard (Dick) *and* Warner and Co., 31, 33, 36, 39-40, 46, 228
Warren, Betty, 429
Warren, Wilkie, 119-121, 540
Warren, Winnie, *see* Karno, Edith
Washerwoman, The, 166
Washington Music Hall *also* Theatre, The, 67-8
Watkinson, Mrs (FK's neighbour), 511, 514, 516, 522
Watson, Peter, 86
Watson, Vernon, 370-2
Waxworks, The, (Charles Baldwin sketch), 286
Waxworks, The, also *Fred Karno's Waxworks*, (FK unproduced sketch) 166, 511
Weber and Fields, 50
Wedding Party, The, (SL radio script), 545
Wedding Party, The, (unproduced FK sketch), 166
Weekend at Hotel de Quick, A, 54
Week-End, A, 386-7, 392

Welch, George, 158, 176, 226
Weldon, Harry:
  {L+C}:
  FK comic, [184], 185-6, *187*, 191, 217, 220, 236, [*240*], 245, 547
  captain of the Karno first XI, [*192*], 193
  solo career, 190, 200, 241, 271
  success and fame, 335, 520
  alcohol use and premature death, 191, 241
  {GT}:
  style and delivery, 184, 186, 191, 405
  relationship with CC, 221-2, 240-1, 246
  influence on SL and other comics, 241, 330-1, 385, 419-21
  also, 194, 295, 371
Wellesley, Harold, 253, 268, 281-2, 289, 291, 318, 335, 349
West, Con, *see also* Adeler and West:
  {L+C}:
  juvenile performer, 173
  FK writer, 428, 498
  screenwriter on films with FK, 483, 497, 504, 511-12, 515, 560
  origin of FK memoirs, 2-3
  author of FK radio series, 525
  {GT}:
  on FK, 518, 526
  writer of revues and plays, 526-7
  also, 500
West, Mae, 558
Westcott, Albert, (FK's brother), 159, 297, 312, 323, 327
Westcott, Emily, (FK's mother), 7, 9, 19, 85, 96
Westcott, Fred Karno III (1920-2011), (FK's grandson), (Sonny), 4-5, 390, 410, *417*, 437, 465, 525, *532*, 563
Westcott, Freddie John (1896-1965), (FK's nephew), 5-6, 413, 498, 504, 526
Westcott, Frederick Arthur (1891-1961), *aka* Fred Karno Jnr., *see* Karno, Fred Jnr.
Westcott, Frederick John (1866-1941), *aka* Fred Karno, *see* Karno, Fred
Westcott, Herbert, (FK's son, died in infancy), 77, 84-5, 93
Westcott, Horace, (FK's son, died in infancy), 54-8, 84

595

Westcott, John, (FK's brother), 413
Westcott, John, (FK's father), 7-9, 11, 19, 85, 96, 228
Westcott, Kenneth, (FK's grandson), 4, 410, *417*, 437, 465, 525, *532*
Westcott, Leslie Karno, *see* Karno, Leslie
Westcott, Nellie, (FK's daughter, died in infancy), 57-8, 84
Westcott, Ray, (FK's niece), 450
Weston, Albert, 158, 163, 216, 227, 255, 548
Weston, R.P., 385
What Can You Buy a Nudist for His Birthday?, 445
What Uncle Lost, 195, 225
What's What, see also *Isle of Troy*, 396
When We Are Married, see *Don't Rush Me*
Where There's a Will, (1936), 561
White, Leo, 524
Whitehouse, Nick, 115-6
Whittaker, Fred, 78-9, 130, 158
Whittaker, Tommy, 20-1
Who Do You Think You Are Kidding Mr Hitler?, 515
Who's Who, 287-8
Why am I Always the Bridesmaid?, 247
Whyberd, Albert, 327
Wide Open Spaces, 414
Wife With a Smile, The, 151
Wife Without a Smile, 542
Wilkinson, Matt, 214

Will You Kiss Me?, 398
Willard, James, 376
Williams, Albert (Bert), 158, 265, [*274*], *287*, *319*
Williams, Arthur, 209-10
Williams, Bransby, 129, 177, 181
Williams, Jack, 495-6
Williams, Kenneth, 209
Williams, Percy, 276-7, 549
Williams, Robin, 209
Williams, W., 254
Willie's Birthday, 166
Wills, H.O., 404
Wilmer, Winifred, 79
Wilson, Terry, 428, 435
Wilton, Robb, 159, 241, 380, *384*, 385, 485-6, 504, 520, 526
Wilton's Music Hall, 27
Winter Gardens, Berlin, 158
Wit and Wisdom, see *Knick Knacks*
Woman Hater, A, 538
Wontdetania, The:
{**SI**}:
launch, plot, reviews and writers, [*256*], 257-60, 264, 513
UK tours, 281-2, 291
{**GT**}:
technical complexity, scale and problems, 257-8, 293, 548
also, 268, 275, 495, 512
Wood, J. (Jay) Hickory, 233, 236, 238, 247, 253, 256, 290, 331

Wood, 'Wee' Georgie, 78, 415
Wood, Victoria, 364
Woodward, Vivian, 190
Work, (1915), 243
Wow Wows, The, see also *Night in a London Secret Society, A*, 261, 269-70, *271*, 272, *273*, 275-7, 279, 297, 319, 403, 549
Wright, Harry, 412
Wright, Lawrence, 428-9
Wright, Molly, 449-50
Wylie and Tate, *also* Wylie, Julian *see also* Tate, James W., 405, 418, 541

Yap Yaps, The, 43, 166, 233-5, 255, 262, 269, 282, 446
Yates, May, 316
Yellow Birds, The, 166
Yes Papa!, also *Sixes and Sevens*, 397
Yorke, Harry, 181
You Can't Come In, 500
You Naughty Naughty Man, 105
You'll Be Surprised, 502
Young Bloods of Variety, 484-5, 488-90
Young Ones, The, 533

Zanuck, Darryl, 449
Zeb vs Paprika, 414
Zeitlin, Alfred, 483
Ziegfeld Follies, The, and Ziegfeld, Florenz, 227, 285
Zuila, Ella, 30
Zulia, Mademoiselle, *see also* Four Aubreys, The, 21-2, 38